in her place

Katharine T. Corbett

in her place

A Guide to St. Louis Women's History

MISSOURI HISTORICAL SOCIETY PRESS · ST. LOUIS

Distributed by University of Missouri Press

© 1999 by the Missouri Historical Society Press
All rights reserved
Published in the United States of America by the Missouri Historical Society Press
P.O. Box 11940, St. Louis, Missouri 63112-0040

03   02   01   00   99   5   4   3   2   1

Library of Congress Cataloging-in-Publication Data

Corbett, Katharine T.
    In her place : a guide to St. Louis women's history / Katharine T. Corbett
        p.   cm.
    Includes bibliographical references and index.
    ISBN 1-883982-26-X (pbk. : alk. paper) – ISBN 1-883982-30-8 (cloth : alk. paper).
    1. Women – Missouri – Saint Louis – History. 2. Women – Missouri – Saint Louis
Biography. 3. Women social reformers – Missouri – Saint Louis History. 4. Women in
community organization – Missouri – Saint Louis – History. 5. Women in charitable
work – Missouri – Saint Louis – History.   I. Title
    HQ1439.S87C67   1999
    305.4'09778'66 – dc21
                                                                    99-43356
                                                                    CIP

Distributed by University of Missouri Press

Design by Robyn Morgan
Photo edited by Duane Sneddeker
Printed by Walsworth Publishing Company
United States

Cover illustration by Robyn Morgan after a photograph of the Soulard neighborhood, ca. 1910, from the
Swekosky Collection at School Sisters of Notre Dame.

To the memory of Caroline Balmer Thomas, 1910–1997

Contents

Chapter 4: St. Louis Women and the Civil War 76

Chapter 5: Women in the Industrializing City 100

Chapter 6: Progressive Era Women 152

Chapter 7: Changing Places 216

Foreword

There have been numerous and varied books about the history of St. Louis. Some works are comprehensive, covering the pre-1803 period to the modern day. Many others deal with specific eras, events, or personalities. Few have so ably, personally, and fairly drawn to our attention a neglected aspect of the community's history as has this book.

The role St. Louis women played in the establishment and development of St. Louis, from the pre-1803 colonial settlements on the riverfront to the 1960s suburban relocation, has been uniquely presented by the author. She has brought to our attention individuals and groups of women whose work in building this community has hitherto been underplayed or only partially recognized. Each chapter consists of a general essay dealing with an overview of the particular period, followed by a series of essays highlighting individual or group contributions to the development of St. Louis. Thus, the book covers the span of the history of St. Louis through short studies of specialized periods.

Each chapter relies on images to enrich the story. Maps locate the sites for readers to visit if they wish to see the actual places where the contribution to the society occurred or where the contributors lived. And finally, some chapters contain excerpts from letters, diaries, and other primary source materials to give readers a flavor of the local thoughts and expressions of the time.

All varieties of women, either in groups or as individuals, get the spotlight. The author's materials cross race, class, religion, and ethnicity. The book recounts the contribution of Roman Catholic nuns throughout the community's long history, and public school teachers, women's clubs, and women workers get the attention they have so long deserved. Individual women such as Victorire, Mary Hempstead Lisa, Harriet Hosmer, Adaline Couzins, Josephine Baker, Edna Gellhorn, and Irma Rombauer are recognized for their contributions in the specialized periods in which they made their greatest contributions.

This book is a welcome addition to the many texts about the history of St. Louis. As a guide, it is the beginning of one's study of how women—from the frontier into nineteenth- and twentieth-century urban St. Louis—came out from their domestic spheres to shape society by becoming decision makers. All devotees of the region will welcome this addition.

–BLANCHE M. TOUHILL
CHANCELLOR
UNIVERSITY OF MISSOURI–ST. LOUIS

Preface

In 1764 a small band of Creole adventurers and their slaves built a fur trading post on the St. Louis riverfront. Two hundred years later other St. Louisans erected a soaring memorial to American westward expansion on that same space. In the years between, thousands of men and women lived in the metropolitan community that developed west of the Gateway Arch. Most of the written history of that community has focused on men—their activities, concerns, and effect upon the city. *In Her Place* lays a foundation for the other half of the story—women's experiences that have shaped the history and landscape of St. Louis.

Most early St. Louisans, and most Americans, believed that "women's place was in the home"—in the houses of their fathers, husbands, or masters. Her concerns were properly domestic. Over the years women pushed the boundaries of their lives into the public arena. In doing so, historian Sara Evans contends, they changed the meaning of American life itself. Women transformed their communities when they created voluntary associations located between the private space of the home and the public arenas of work and politics, when they enlarged the meaning and rights of citizenship, when they insisted on a voice in decisions about the nature and conditions of work, and when they pushed their way into areas of public life considered to be the exclusive province of men.

Many factors contributed to the specific ways this American story played out in St. Louis—a city with its own political, economic, and cultural context and unique racial and ethnic mix. But a number of themes persist through time, even as they form and re-form in response to changing circumstances. Domesticity, benevolence, work, political action, education, and creative expression have transcended race, class, and ethnicity, and have cut across gender lines as well. Everyone participated in domestic life; men and women often worked together for social and political goals.

This book focuses primarily on St. Louis women's changing domestic roles and on the public projects in which women took the lead, made decisions, and exercised power. Their activities are not always easy to determine, particularly when women were affiliated with

important male-run institutions—churches, governments, unions—or where law or custom concealed their influence. For the most part, the organizations and activities we included were clearly the work of women.

In Her Place is a guide to the changing definition of women's place in St. Louis. Women's place carries a deliberate double-meaning, referring both to social norms and to physical locations. Every occurrence has a place as well as a time. Physical settings sometimes help explain past events but almost always help give them a tangible immediacy. St. Louis abounds with historic women's places.

Each chapter explores the experiences of women during a specific time period and includes a map identifying relevant sites. Introductory essays set the national and local context for the short essays that follow. By highlighting individuals, organizations, and events, these essays trace the expansion of "women's space" over time and the growing influence of women on the city's civic, social, and economic life. As it was for almost every other aspect of American life, World War II and its aftermath marked a turning point in women's history. The civil rights movement, the modern women's movement, federal policies and spending, accelerated suburbanization, and Vietnam all made St. Louis and other American cities very different places. This book's final chapter, covering the years between World War II and 1964—the St. Louis bicentennial, is an overview by Anne Valk, a young scholar from Southern Illinois University at Edwardsville. I hope it is the starting place for a second volume, which I would enjoy reading from my retirement home in Maine.

This book is neither a comprehensive history nor an encyclopedic handbook. It is, instead, a guide to issues and themes and an invitation to further research. The short essays, which reflect the diversity of St. Louis women's experience at a particular historical time, conclude with discussions of primary materials and useful secondary sources. The largest number of these local materials are in the collections of the Missouri Historical Society and the Western Historical Manuscripts Collection at the University of Missouri–St. Louis. Many women's organizations, particularly Roman Catholic religious orders, still hold their own historical records, which they make available to researchers.

Specific individuals and organizations appear in *In Her Place* because they were particularly significant, left visible evidence of their work on the landscape or culture of the city, illustrate the variety of women's experience, or sometimes simply because historical information was more readily available about one group than about another of similar significance. White Anglo-Saxon Protestant women, for example, are overrepresented in terms of their numbers; Jewish women are underrepresented in terms of their influence. There is little discussion of specific immigrant women or their association, in part because their diaries, letters, and personal records were seldom in English and many remain in private hands, unavailable to researchers. Such documents, local German newspapers and the records of German-speaking churches and *vereins,* would reveal whole areas of women's experience in St. Louis barely hinted at here. Irish immigrant women left even fewer traditional records than German immigrants, but many descendants still wait to be interviewed. We barely touched on the experiences of female entrepreneurs and businesswomen, who would feature prominently in a subsequent volume. And, for reasons of space and time, what is properly a regional story stops, for the most part, at the city limits.

However, the book does offer a sustained, thematic interpretation of St. Louis women's history from the colonial period to the mid-twentieth century. It examines the relationship of women's domestic work in the home to the work they did for pay. It explores the local history of women's voluntarism–the least recognized area of women's activity. Through their voluntary charitable institutions, American women made social service a responsibility of citizenship by insisting that the community care for those unable to care for themselves. Nowhere was this more true than in St. Louis. *In Her Place* offers the first nonsectarian recognition of the enormous contributions of Roman Catholic women's religious orders to the social history of the city. Finally, it explains not only the historical context for discrimination based on race, class, and gender, but also the strategies and tactics women used to fight for their rights as workers, citizens, and individuals.

Women's place means both social role and social space; neither is understandable without the other. While *In Her Place* is not a tour book of women's places in the city, we have included addresses and some photographs of significant structures and public art. As you drive around St. Louis you will see evidence of women's individual and collective effort to make the city a more attractive and equitable place. History, like much of women's work, is never done. Please treat this book not as a set of final answers but as a collection of beginning questions about the other half of St. Louis history that has always been there, but that has only recently laid claim to its place in the story.

–KATHARINE THOMAS CORBETT

Acknowledgments

Traditionally, much of women's work has been communal. This book is no exception. Although only one author's name appears on the title page, *In Her Place* was a cooperative venture. Susan Beattie, Joan Cooper, Katherine Douglass, Kathleen Butterly Nigro, Mary Toothill, and Anne Valk, researched and wrote the essays attributed to them and helped to shape the overall themes and analysis by sharing their ideas during months of lively weekly discussions.

This book really had its beginning more than twenty-five years ago when, as what was then called a mature returning student, I studied history and women's studies at the University of Missouri–St. Louis. Teachers, mentors, and fellow students helped to shape the questions I have been asking ever since about the uses of the past. Special thanks to Ann Lever, Susan Hartmann, Dick Miller, Irene Cortinovis, George Lipsitz, and Alex Yard.

I owe much to supportive friends and talented colleagues from more than eighteen years at the Missouri Historical Society. Many shared their knowledge of St. Louis and of the MHS resources, but I am particularly grateful to the 1980s education department and the 1990s interpretation and exhibit staff who made doing public history at the museum productive and fun.

Research for interpretive programming and exhibits led us to the diaries, letters, and organizational records at MHS and the University of Missouri–St. Louis that became the starting point for *In Her Place*. Library and archives staff from both institutions and other St. Louis archives were helpful to all who worked on the book. Special thanks to Helen Vollmer and Sister Dionysia Brockland, S.S.N.D.

Marsha Bray, Karen Goering, and Robert Archibald made possible an initial research leave and continuing MHS support for the project. Lee Sandweiss, director of publications, enthusiastically carried it through to completion. Matt Heidenry was a generous editor and a pleasure to work with; Robyn Morgan's maps and design reinforced the sense of place that underlay the text. Katherine Douglass, Ellen Thomasson, Josh Stevens and Allecia Vermillion helped to make a lot of pieces into a book.

In addition to the authors of the signed essays, including Pamela K. Sanfilippo and Sharra Vostral, others made substantive contributions to the analysis and interpretation. Kathy Petersen and Mary Seematter made us aware of the enormous contribution of Roman Catholic nuns to the well-being of all St. Louisans. In this project, as with others, Mary was always there to solve a research problem as were Carolyn Gilman, Leslie Brown, Eric Sandweiss, and Eileen Eagan. Students in my University of Missouri–St. Louis women's history class brought fresh perspectives to the material. St. Louis historians Dick Miller and Patricia Adams read the manuscript with critical eyes. We appreciated Dick's candor and invaluable editorial advice and Pat's informed sensitivity to issues of race, class and gender in St. Louis.

in
her
place

1764–1803

1. Esther's Home
2. Cerré Home, Victorire Delile Residence
3. Marie Thérèse Bourgeois Chouteau Home
4. Jeanette Forchet Home

— St. Louis City Limits 1764–1822

(now DELMAR)

(now WASHINGTON)

Rue Quicapou (now PINE)
Rue Missouri (now CHESTNUT)
Rue de la Place (now MARKET)

Rue de la Tour (now WALNUT)

(now CLARK)

La Petite Rivière (MILL CREEK)

Rue des Granges (now THIRD)

Rue Royale or La Rue Principale or Grand Rue (now MAIN)

Rue de L'eglise (now SECOND)

Colonial Women

In 1694 Aramepinchieue Roenasa, the seventeen-year-old daughter of a Kaskaskian Indian chief, married Michel Accault, a French fur trader. Cross-cultural marriages and less formal liaisons were commonplace in the mid-Mississippi valley. In this military, economic, and social borderland, then called the Illinois Country, several different Indian and European cultures met and mingled. The result was a *métis* society that reflected the various traditions of its different people.

Aramepinchieue's people, the Kaskaskians, were one of several groups of Algonquian-speaking Indians living in villages on both sides of the Mississippi River in the late seventeenth century. They were almost as new to the area as the French, having been pushed west from the Ohio valley by the Iroquois earlier in the century. Known collectively as the Illini, they alternately fought or formed shifting alliances with each other, with generally hostile Iroquois to the east, Siouan-speaking tribes to the west, and with the British, French, and Spanish invaders.

St. Louis in 1770. Engraving by C. Heberer after Frederic Billon, 1886. From *The Annals of St. Louis in its Early Days* by Frederic Billon, St. Louis, 1886. MHS-Library

French Habitation in the Country of the Illinois. Hand-colored engraving by Tardieu l'aine from Victor Collot, *A Journey in North America,* Paris, 1826. MHS–PP

When French fur traders and Jesuit missionaries settled in the region near the end of the eighteenth century, as many as ten thousand Illini Indians lived in the Illinois Country, primarily Kaskaskia, Cahokia, and Peoria. Small bands of Siouan Indians, mainly Missouri and Osage, also occupied the area. In spite of their varied origins, these groups were hunters and farmers who built semipermanent villages where the elderly and some of the women farmed. Most able-bodied men and women lived part of the year in hunting camps, returning to the villages in the winter.

Although the status of women varied in all Indian societies, the relationship between gender and power differed significantly from European cultures. Even in nominally male-dominated groups, men actually had limited power over women. Indian culture stressed individual autonomy and relative personal freedom, independent of gender. Men could not dominate women as in a Christian society, which operated on elaborate patriarchal gender system. Indian women and men had separate but equally important economic roles in community life. Hunting and warfare gave greater prestige and power to men, but the relative lack of social domination and submission in interpersonal relations lessened the impact on women.

Power itself in Indian cultures took different forms. Authority, requiring formal political offices usually held by men, was more fluid and limited. Female influence, the ability to affect political decisions without holding formal office, had a complex and recognized role in decision-making. Indian mythology valued female deities and principles. In general, the Indians who encountered Europeans in the Illinois Country emphasized complementary gender roles and personal autonomy over hierarchy and interpersonal dominance.

Once Indians and French settlers began to live together in the Illinois Country, they found themselves continually negotiating, each trying to convince the other that what they wanted was in the other's best interest. They used each other to hold enemies at bay, shifting alliances when the situation warranted. Indians sold captive slaves and furs to the French for European trade goods and liquor. Roman Catholic missionaries actively sought converts, offering the promise of heaven to the dying victims of European diseases and their terrified survivors. French fur traders hired unmarried Indian women as domestic workers and sex partners. Some Indian women, like Aramepinchieue Roensa, married French traders for both personal and political reasons, strengthening alliances between influential Indian families and French officials.

The contact between Indians and French settlers and Christian missionaries changed both groups, but ultimately it decimated Indian people and traditional Indian culture. Tribal power more often turned on relationships outside the Indian community. Frequent warfare and the shift from informal Indian power relations to formal political power exchanges with Europeans gave Indian men more leverage over Indian women. At the same time, contact with French settlers brought more employment and marriage opportunities for women. Meanwhile, the expansive market economics of the international fur trade destroyed both men's and women's control over resources.

All of these momentous changes were well underway in the Illinois Country before Pierre Laclède and his team of fur traders arrived in 1764. No women were among the men who established the first permanent colonial outpost that winter on the west bank of the Mississippi, just south of its confluence with the Missouri River. The landing by employees of the Maxent, Laclède and Company from New Orleans, celebrated as the founding chapter of St. Louis history, was only one of many entrepreneurial forays into the Illinois Country by the late eighteenth century.

The majority of the first white women in St. Louis moved into the region from French

Canada prior to Laclède's arrival. They were living in Kaskaskia, Cahokia, and other small communities east of the Mississippi River. Their husbands and sons were farmers and fur traders. A few families of fur merchants had far-flung business interests and owned considerable land and many slaves.

After the English gained control of all French territory east of the Mississippi in 1763, they expelled French settlers from Acadia on the east coast of Canada. French families in the eastern Illinois Country, anxious to leave before British soldiers arrived, accepted Pierre Laclède's invitation to join him in building a new settlement in Spanish territory just across the river. He offered free building lots in the village and farming land on the outskirts. Margaret Blondeau Guion, who may have been the first woman to live in St. Louis, immediately moved over from Cahokia with her husband, a stonemason.

Over the next two years about fifty families moved into St. Louis, as the British gradually occupied the eastern Illinois Country. Most were Creoles, people of French or Spanish descent born in America. Some came from New Orleans and French settlements in the lower Mississippi valley: artisans, boatmen, traders, and merchants who brought their slaves with them. In 1770, 339 whites, 33 free blacks, and 274 Indian and African slaves occupied the village. By the time of the Louisiana Purchase 33 years later, 1,039 people lived there, while another 1,438, many of them Anglo-American farmers, lived nearby.

Colonial St. Louis was a cluster of buildings on a thirty-foot bluff overlooking the river. Unlike isolated homesteaders on the Anglo-American frontier, Creole families lived close together in compact communities surrounded by agricultural fields and pasture land. Laclède's men had laid out the village in a grid pattern, similar to other French and Spanish river towns, with large house lots fronting on three long streets that ran parallel to the Mississippi. Despite its orderly configuration, the village itself was haphazard in appearance, with narrow streets that dissolved into mud with every rain. Except for clerical and governmental functions, all business, community, and personal activities took place in the residents' homes.

The diversity of the population guaranteed that St. Louis culture would be richly varied and adaptive. Located in the wilderness far from the centers of political and economic power, Creole residents subscribed to a mixture of French and Spanish customs, class values, and legal traditions, modified by the peculiar circumstances of colonial

military administration and a mercantile capitalist economy. Although Catholicism was the state-supported religion, a shortage of priests and lax enforcement of anti-Protestant regulations encouraged St. Louisans to practice their faith communally and tolerantly. Lines of authority were formally clear but often informally implemented. Drawing on common values, Spanish government officials easily settled most disputes among individuals and cooperated with the merchant elite in drafting laws to maintain social order and facilitate local commerce. Fertile land and a profitable fur trade minimized desperate poverty.

In many respects, the appearance of community cooperation, relative prosperity, and rough social equality that visitors to St. Louis observed was a realistic portrait. However, elaborate imported clothing, large private libraries, and extensive slave ownership attested to the wealth and international connections of the merchant class and to an established system of human bondage.

There were far fewer women than men in colonial St. Louis, although the ratio of men to women, which had been as high as five to one in the early years, fell to two to one by 1794. Because the local economy depended on the international fur trade and not on agriculture, Creole women were more likely to be the wives and daughters of merchants, traders, and craftsmen than farmers. While in their mid-to-late teens, women usually married men many years their senior. They were pregnant most of their childbearing years, and one-third of their children died in infancy. Nearly half the female population was white, while the rest were free and enslaved Indians, Africans, and their mixed-blood descendants. With the exception of some female slaves who worked the outlying fields, women's lives centered on village life and the daily needs of its people.

Women's childbearing and domestic skills were essential to the community's survival. In this respect women of various economic means and status had much in common with each other. The wealthy had no better medical care than the poor. Frontier housekeeping required the effort of every woman in a home; the tools, skills, and chores to be done varied only slightly from household to household.

Although black slaves had the fewest legal rights, race was not the primary determinant of status in colonial St. Louis. Whiteness alone did not carry the status it would later. Many respected residents were the children of white men and Indian women; free blacks had most of the legal rights as free whites. Social class and legal status most differentiated women from each other and determined their options. Women had little control over these conditions but could use them to their advantage.

All free women in Creole St. Louis enjoyed more property rights than did women living under Anglo-American laws. Although administered more by custom than by statute, the French legal system prevailed in Spanish Louisiana throughout the eighteenth century. The goal of a society with high mortality rates was to keep property within a family and to provide some measure of security for descendants. Unlike English primogeniture laws that favored males and the first-born, under the *coutumes de Paris* (local laws based on the French legal system) sons and daughters inherited equally from their parents. Wives, therefore, often brought their own property to a marriage, or stood to inherit after they married.

More than half of all free women in upper Louisiana, regardless of economic position, further protected their property with marriage contracts. In 1773 Jeanette Forchet, a free black widow, asked officials to inventory her assets before entering into a contract for her second marriage.

When drawing up a marriage contract, both parties determined which assets, usually inherited family property, they wanted to designate as community property. Property from a first marriage did not have to be included in the community property of a second. A couple's individual contributions were their *propres*, or their own property. The system granted the surviving spouse half of the community estate upon the death of the other. The remaining half was divided equally among their children. If they had no children, the surviving spouse could use all the couple's property for life. In addition, marriage contracts stipulated a *douaire*, or dower, that the wife was entitled to when the husband died. Even without a marriage contract, widows were entitled to half the couple's community property. In contrast, Anglo-American wives normally received only one-third of the husband's estate and sometimes less.

These inheritance laws enabled a wife, if she so chose, to retain control of the property she brought to a marriage. She also had the option of renouncing the community property if the estate was burdened with debts when her husband died. In that case she received her douaire, her propres, and her personal effects before the creditors made their claims on the remainder of community property. Because there was no discrimination against women in inheritance laws and the disposition of marital property, many free St. Louis women enjoyed the independence and self-confidence that comes with having one's own economic resources.

In frontier St. Louis society, class position did not follow Old World hierarchies. Instead, wealth and high social status derived from the ability of male family members to prosper in the New World. The St. Louis merchant elite accumulated property, slaves, and credit and protected its wealth by creating a network of kinship relations through intermarriage.

It was the responsibility of young elite women to marry these homegrown aristocrats or their sons, produce children, and nurture family alliances. Although Marie Thérèse Bourgeois Chouteau never married Pierre Laclède, the father of her four youngest children, their three daughters married older men solidly within the merchant class. Marie Pelagie Chouteau was not yet sixteen when she wed Silvestre Labbadie, a successful French immigrant then in his late thirties. Joseph Marie Papin, the husband of Marie Louise Chouteau, came from a wealthy French Canadian family. Victoire Chouteau married Charles Gratiot, an urbane Swiss with connections in Montreal. Neither Papin nor Gratiot possessed the entrepreneurial talent of Silvestre Labbadie, but their connection to the first family of St. Louis insured their wealth and position. The three Chouteau daughters had a total of thirty-two children, twenty-four of whom lived to marry. Along with the wives of their brothers, Auguste and Pierre, they made possible the network of familial connections that kept wealth and influence in the family.

Elite women like the Chouteaus who owned both black and Indian slaves probably did plenty of home management and little direct domestic labor. Large family gatherings were commonplace; visitors stayed for months. Because their homes were the most spacious and best-furnished structures in town, men used them to conduct political and business affairs. Fur merchants and traders, who spent months away from home, frequently left their wives in charge of family business, and some of them became accomplished businesswomen. Women from affluent families who focused on domestic concerns during their marriages usually had the funds and experience to participate actively in the local economy after their husbands' deaths. All widows had greater freedom and fuller control of their daily lives than did married women, but wealthy widows enjoyed the most security, the highest social status, and the greatest independence.

In matters of property the law was not racially biased. Free black women like Jeanette Forchet made marriage contracts and inherited just as white women did. Free women married to artisans and craftsmen enjoyed the same legal protection for their property as did the wives of merchant capitalists. This protection was even more important for women who were not members of the Creole elite, with its close, supportive family alliances and substantial assets. All free women in the Illinois Country seem to have taken a greater interest in business and legal affairs than contemporary Anglo-American women, perhaps because the law recognized married women as economic individuals. Their participation also suggests that long-standing laws of coverture, which gave husbands control over their wives' legal activities, were rarely enforced on the Illinois Country frontier.

Women earned money—or more likely credit, services, or goods—by taking in laundry, midwifing, or providing room and board for the hundreds of unmarried boatmen and trappers who passed through the village. Few, however, engaged in home industries like spinning or weaving, which had been banned under French rule and apparently were not taken up later under the Spanish administration. There are also numerous instances of married women buying and selling land, trading goods, and entering into contracts, particularly when their husbands were away. Free black women, who were often experienced farmers, sometimes acquired land on which they grew produce to sell.

Despite the sophistication of their economic and legal transactions, most women in colonial St. Louis were illiterate, as were most men. Unless they engaged in activities recorded by someone else, they left little evidence of their daily lives or concerns. For poor women in the Illinois Country, laws that safeguarded property had little relevance. The same coutumes de Paris that protected a woman's assets did not protect her from the unquestioned authority of her husband. Article 255 specifically declared, "The Husband is Lord." A man had the legal right to physically abuse his wife as well as make all decisions affecting her and her children.

Only in extreme instances would the law step into a domestic conflict. The community was well aware of Gaspard Roubieu's drunken behavior, which had prompted the local priest to pay at least one visit to the family home. Late one night in 1778, Roubieu came home drunk and attacked his wife and one of his step-daughters when she tried to protect her mother. Madame Marie Anne Roubieu ran sobbing to Governor Fernando de Leyba's

house for help in rescuing her two teenage daughters. A soldier quickly brought the girls to safety. The next day a neighbor helped Marie Anne Roubieu prepare a petition for legal separation and the governor took testimony from all witnesses. Before he could act on the petition, however, Madame Roubieu dropped the suit against her husband but agreed to place her daughters in the care of a guardian.

Marie Anne Roubieu's reasons for remaining with her abusive husband went unrecorded. Although civil and clerical law forbade divorce, separation was possible and not uncommon. Separation, however, required assets, either one's own or community marital property. Women living in a society that made no provision for people without earning ability or private property had few options. The unequal sex ratio meant men confronted a shortage of sexual partners, stepmothers, and housekeepers. Women who wanted or needed to marry usually could.

The St. Louis women with the fewest options were black and Indian slaves. Many more black St. Louisans were enslaved than free; probably fewer than one hundred free blacks lived in eighteenth-century Missouri. French Jesuit missionaries and lead miners had brought black slave labor into the region before 1750; the Spanish permitted settlers to bring slaves to the territory and authorized the slave trade to increase agricultural production. Slaves performed the work essential for

Kitchen Utensils. Creole bowl, ca. 1820; skimmer; toasting fork; fireplace shovel; pewter plate. Photograph by David Schultz, 1998. MHS–PP

survival in a frontier community: farming, building, skilled labor, boat tending, and domestic work. The 1787 census revealed a roughly equal number of male and female slaves living in the village.

French and Spanish administrators enforced the slave system through restrictions that regulated the behavior of all residents of the community. The black codes, or French *Code Noir*, considered slaves both human beings—entitled to food, clothing, and medical care—and property. Masters could physically abuse slaves but could not kill or imprison them without due process. Laws stipulated regular hours of work and prohibited sexual exploitation or interracial cohabitation. In line with official church practice, the law honored the Roman Catholic sacraments: slave marriages were encouraged, and slave children were baptized. It was illegal to break up conjugal families or to separate mothers from young children. Owners, however, could not free a slave without government authorization.

Spanish laws were similar to the French Code Noir, with a few differences. Slaves could, under certain circumstances, own property and sue their masters for ill treatment. The law permitted slaves to purchase their freedom and prohibited Indian slavery, although this was interpreted to mean Indian slaves could not be sold. For their part, of course, slaves were to accept that they were the property of their masters and were legally required to do as they were told. Changes in the Code Noir over time reflected the tension within any slave system. Ordinances prohibiting slave gatherings and dancing indicated that St. Louis slaves maintained a culture separate from their masters' and that owners always feared resistance and rebellion.

On the face of it, the situation of an enslaved woman differed little from that of a poor, free woman whose husband was her legal master. Even the poorest free woman, however, had the right to separate from her husband and try to make it on her own or with the help of her family. In practice, slave women had no assurance that the protective provisions of the Code Noir would be enforced. The church sanctioned very few slave marriages because owners wanted to reserve the right to sell individual members of a slave family. No matter how benign the circumstances of a female slave's daily life, at any moment her master could sell her away from everything and everyone she cared about. Although there were few reported murders of slaves by owners, numerous examples of brutality appear in colonial accounts.

When St. Louis was founded, there were more Indian than African slaves in the Illinois Country.

Many were *mestizos*, mixed-blood descendants of Europeans, Indians, and Africans. In an attempt to reduce regional hostility, Spanish authorities outlawed Indian slavery in 1769, but the loosely enforced decree did not free Indians already enslaved. In St. Louis 10 percent of the white residents still owned Indians in 1772. They were regulated by the Code Noir, with some special provisions designed to control contact with other Indians. Unlike Africans, Indians had been enslaved in their own country and could easily slip back into the wilderness. Owners feared that Indian slaves would escape, form marauding bands, and retaliate against their enslavers. In 1795 eight Indian slaves fled their St. Louis owners but were discovered in a barn before they could implement any plans. Although owners may have freed Indians more frequently than they did black slaves, more often they were illegally bought, sold, and willed to heirs.

Over time, slavery became identified solely with African Americans. Indian slavery declined at the end of the eighteenth century as officials began enforcing the laws. In addition, as more Anglo-Americans moved into the region, they generally viewed people of African descent as possessing characteristics of physical endurance and docility best suited for slavery.

Forty-one of the sixty-nine Indian slaves recorded as living in St. Louis in 1772 were female. Several reasons account for this ratio of men to women. Warring Indians had often sold captured females to Europeans, female slaves were less likely than men to escape, and, like black women, they were in demand as domestic workers and sexual partners. Female Indian slaves sometimes lived with white men who freed them after the birth of a child. Many years later the descendants of Marie Scypian, a captive Indian woman sold into slavery in the 1740s, won their freedom by proving her Indian descent.

Free Indian women had been the wives and unmarried sexual partners of Creole traders, boatmen, and trappers since the French first came to the Illinois Country. Christianized Indian and mixed-blood women married easily when there were few white women in the area. Their numbers declined in the later eighteenth century, but their children knitted the mixed-blood and Creole population together in the next generation. At the turn of the century, one or both parents in 80 percent of St. Louis families were at least one-eighth Indian.

Some Indian wives stayed with their own people, while their husbands often had other wives and families in St. Louis. Both white and Indian traders tried to use marriageable women to strengthen business ties: Indians to keep the balance of power from shifting too far to the traders; traders to curry favor with powerful Indian leaders. Auguste and Pierre Chouteau, St. Louis's leading fur merchants, probably had Indian wives and families living with the Osage in the wilderness. The Osage used intermarriage and honorary kin relationships as a strategy for dealing with other Siouan-speaking groups and Europeans. Both Chouteau brothers spent long periods of time with the Osage, who had made them honorary members of influential families. These marital relationships placed women between two legal and social cultures. Although Spanish law required fathers to acknowledge free Indian children in their wills, the laws that protected wives in legally sanctioned marriages did not apply to most of these arrangements. When men considered them to be either temporary or supplementary, women and their children suffered.

The daily experiences of most St. Louis women in the colonial period centered on domesticity, but their actual work varied greatly. Elite women managed the slave women who did the housework. Slaves belonging to Susanne Dubreuil, the wife of a merchant, polished her furniture and waxed her bare walnut floors every day. The wives and widows of ordinary working men did their own housework and frequently turned their homes into workplaces by taking in laundry or boarders. Owners appropriated the domestic skills of slave women, leaving them to construct separate, private domestic lives or forgo them. All women expressed themselves through their domestic skills, creating a female culture that blended several different traditions.

The frontier Creole village was a social organism in which individual success depended on mutual obligation. Benevolence and charity toward neighbors was as much a social obligation for elite women as paternalistic political service was for elite men. Compassionate women skilled in folk medicine regularly visited the sick; families called on them in crises as they would a physician. Madame Loisel acted as a midwife. Women did not, however, interfere in the health and welfare of slaves without their owners' permission.

Not surprisingly, political activity in a remote colonial outpost of an absolute monarchy was severely limited and linked directly to class status. There was no tradition of democracy in colonial St. Louis. Women had no formal public role in the community, but the nature of the legal system and the close physical proximity between all village functions suggests that some, at least, influenced public affairs beyond their own family circle.

Most formal education that St. Louis women acquired in the colonial period was attained somewhere else. Some wives and daughters of the Creole elite attended convent schools in New Orleans or Canada, but no order of women religious came to the village in the eighteenth century. In 1794 Madame Maria Josephe Rigauche opened a school at the request of the Spanish colonial governor where some girls learned to read and write. In 1795 Madame Angelíque La Grange Pescay, a French widow and refugee from the Santo Domingo slave insurrection, opened a school for girls. Ultimately, neither woman's enterprise was successful. A few fur merchants sent their sons to school in Canada and Europe, but not their daughters. St. Louis women were, for the most part, either illiterate, like the majority of other residents, or they learned at home from other family members and an occasional tutor.

Music, dance, and other forms of artistic expression were important to Creole culture. As in other Louisiana communities, women organized social events and served the food for which mid-Mississippi French settlements were renowned: cordials, preserves, and pralines. In the early years community activities frequently crossed lines of culture, class, and race, but as elite families accumulated wealth and in-laws, they withdrew more and more into their own society. Nicolas de Finiels, a French military officer who visited the area in 1797, remarked that daily life in Upper Louisiana was a mixture of city and rural customs: "Everyone is more or less an urbanite and a peasant at the same time." He observed, however, that the community's complex social structure was fragmenting and the people of the Illinois Country, like people everywhere, exhibited "a mixture of qualities and virtues, defects and vices."

Because of its eighteenth-century location in the mid-Mississippi valley, colonial St. Louis was a métis society that blended social, legal, and cultural traditions in ways that, when compared to Anglo-American colonies, usually benefitted women. The village's marginal frontier existence made every able-bodied person essential. The unbalanced gender ratio made women more valuable, hence giving them potentially more leverage. And the French legal system more often worked in women's favor than did the British Common Law and American slave codes that were instituted after the Louisiana Purchase.

Sources: This essay draws on information from William E. Foley, *The Genesis of Missouri: From Wilderness Outpost to Statehood* (Columbia: University of Missouri Press, 1989), the best overview of this period in St. Louis history and a highly readable, well-researched narrative of Missouri in the colonial and territorial periods. Foley places the history of St. Louis in a larger historical and geographical context and addresses the history of women as well as men, particularly in the chapter about Creole culture reprinted as "Galleries, Gumbo, and 'La Guignolee'," *GH* 10, no. 1 (summer 1989): 3–17. Additional information is from James Neal Primm, *Lion of the Valley, St. Louis, Missouri*, 3d ed. (St. Louis: MHS Press, 1998). Written by a St. Louis professor of Missouri's economic history and based largely on secondary material, this volume has not been substantially revised since the original 1981 edition. It is the most comprehensive narrative of St. Louis to date, although it does not include much about women's concerns or activities.

Information on the history of Indians in the Illinois Country comes primarily from Sara J. Tucker, *Indian Villages of the Illinois Country: Atlas* (Springfield: Illinois State Museum, 1942), 11–56. Anthropologists have explained Indian culture better than most historians. The analysis of gender and power in culture draws on Daniel Maltz and JoAllyn Archambault, "Gender and Power in Native North America," in *Women and Power in Native North America*, eds., Laura F. Klein and Lillian A. Ackerman (Norman: University of Oklahoma Press, 1995).

See Richard White, *The Middle Ground: Indians, Empires, and Republics in the Great Lakes Region, 1650–1815* (Cambridge, Mass.: Cambridge University Press, 1991) for a discussion of how French settlers and Algonquian Indians found a "middle ground" on which to negotiate their interaction. See also Helen Hornbeck Tanner, ed., *Atlas of Great Lakes Indian History* (Norman: University of Oklahoma Press, 1987), and Bruce Trigger, ed., *Northeast: Volume 15, Handbook of North American Indians* (Washington, D.C.: Smithsonian Institution, 1978).

The best description of the material culture of colonial St. Louis is a reprint of a study made by the National Park Service in connection with riverfront redevelopment, Charles E. Peterson, *Colonial St. Louis: Building a Creole Capital*, 2d ed. (Tucson, Ariz.: Patrice Press, 1993). First published in 1947, it gives a detailed description of how the colonists apportioned land, constructed buildings, and used both. Some information on Creole culture comes from the richly illustrated Charles van Ravenswaay, *Saint Louis: An Informal History of the City and Its People, 1764–1865* (St. Louis: MHS Press, 1991); a better source is Frederic L. Billon, *Annals of St. Louis in Its Early Days Under the French and Spanish Domination* (St. Louis, 1886), an idiosyncratic compilation of government documents, official reports, travel accounts, and memoirs providing information about events, people, and places in the colonial community.

See also Nicolas de Finiels, *An Account of Upper Louisiana*, eds., Carl J. Ekberg and William E. Foley (Columbia: University of Missouri Press, 1989), for a snobbish but interesting account of this French military officer's visit to St. Louis in 1797. Quoted material is on pages 116–17.

The best primary sources, but the most difficult to use, are the records of the St. Louis Colonial Archives, a collection of documents consisting of public legal transactions of the community in the Spanish period. Records of land sales, inventories of estates, marriage and death records, disputes between individuals over contracts and agreements, and similar documents not only provide information about everyone involved in these transactions, but also give insight into power relationships in the community. MHS holds the original French and Spanish documents. Translations made in the 1930s by the National Park Service are sometimes inaccurate, incomplete, and insensitive to nuance, but they provide a good place to start looking. See also Carl J. Ekberg, *Colonial Ste. Genevieve: An Adventure on the Mississippi Frontier* (Gerald, Mo.: Patrice Press, 1985). Based on colonial records, this detailed, descriptive account of colonial Ste. Genevieve illustrates how research in the St. Louis sources might uncover valuable data for interpreting women's experiences.

Information and analysis on the legal status of free women is from Susan C. Boyle, "Did She Generally Decide? Women in Ste. Genevieve, 1750–1805," *William and Mary Quarterly* 44, no. 4 (October 1987): 775–89. Based on evidence from Ste. Genevieve, Boyle argues that active participation in the economy gave women with assets experience and decision-making power that men generally respected.

For an analysis that argues St. Louisans settled more disputes by custom and convention than by formal colonial law, see Stuart Banner, "Written and Unwritten Norms in Colonial St. Louis," Washington University School of Law, Working Paper Series, 1995.

For Indian slavery, see Russell M. Magnaghi, "The Role of Indian Slavery in Colonial St. Louis," *BMHS* 31, no. 4 (July 1975): 264–72. Tanis C. Thorne, *The Many Hands of My Relations: French and Indians on the Lower Missouri* (Columbia: University of Missouri Press, 1996) explains the relationship between St. Louis fur traders and Indian women. See Sylvia Van Kirk, *Many Tender Ties: Women in Fur-Trade Society, 1670–1870* (Norman: University of Oklahoma Press, 1980), and William E. Foley and C. David Rice, *The First Chouteaus: River Barons of Early St. Louis* (Urbana: University of Illinois Press, 1983), for the history of Auguste and Pierre Chouteau's relations with the Indians. See also Willard H. Rollings, *The Osage: An Ethnohistorical Study of Hegemony on the Prairie-Plains* (Columbia: University of Missouri Press, 1992).

Opportunities for further research abound in the MHS Archives. Collections of family papers from the colonial period include information about women. Because archivists indexed these collections, letters and legal documents related to women—family members, slaves, parties to business transactions—can be easily identified. However, the focus of most collections is the public and private records of men, making it more difficult to reconstruct the activities of women and interpret their domestic and economic situations, particulary since almost all the personal material for the colonial period is in French. Although contemporary descriptive accounts and even later translations reflect the biases of the educated elite, these serve as rich sources.

The Marriage of Aramepinchieue

In 1694 Fort St. Louis, located on the upper Illinois River, was the wilderness encampment of French soldiers, Jesuit missionaries, and fur traders. Kaskaskian Indians lived in a village nearby. Each party needed something from the other: military allies, Christian converts, fur pelts, trade goods, protection, or women. It therefore pleased Chief Roenasa of the Kaskaskias when fur trader Michel Accault wanted to marry his daughter, Aramepinchieue. The union would strengthen the alliance between the leading Kaskaskian family and the French at the fort. But his daughter, drawing on Illini traditions of female autonomy, refused to wed Accault. To get what she wanted from the arrangement, Aramepinchieue used her own allies to negotiate a compromise.

Traditionally, Indian women viewed marriage differently than the French. A husband was not necessarily the central relation in a Kaskaskian woman's life. Her family or even her own autonomy might hold as much importance. Although a married Indian woman was clearly subservient to her husband's wishes, she could leave him at any time without losing status. Indian women enjoyed much more sexual latitude than French women, who, if sexually active, were usually either married or considered to be prostitutes. Although Illini brothers tried to influence their sisters' sex lives, in general the only barrier to premarital sex was fear of pregnancy. Women who chose to be sexually active, but not to marry, were socially accepted.

Because few French women lived in the Illinois Country until the mid-1700s, French soldiers and traders sought out Indian women as domestic servants, sexual partners, and wives. Unmarried women who agreed to work for men freely entered into sexual relationships as well. Because they made no contract between families, these were jobs, not marriages.

Christian missionaries found these arrangements appalling and affronts to Roman Catholic doctrines of premarital chastity. Since 1690, Jesuits had baptized nearly two thousand Indians in the Illinois Country, many of them young women. Priests stressed the cult of the Virgin Mary to convince female Indian converts to change their sexual practices. By appealing to Indian values of female autonomy, priests also encouraged women to choose sexual abstinence over sexual experimentation.

Jesuits did condone marriages between Christian Indian women and Frenchmen, since intermarriage helped control Indian female sexuality. French officials, worried that intermarriage might give hunters and trappers an edge over the military in dealing with Indians, disapproved unless they saw a political advantage in a particular union. Commanders preferred that men marry Christian Indians, however, rather than unconverted women, considered to be licentious

Kaskaskian Woman. Hand-colored engraving by George Catlin, from *Illustrations of the Manners, Customs, and Condition of the North American Indians*, 10th ed., 1866. MHS–PP

heathens who would leave husbands on a whim. Indian men encouraged intermarriage because it cemented useful political alliances.

All these considerations played out in the negotiations over the marriage of Aramepinchieue and Michel Accault. When his daughter refused to marry Accault, Roenasa drove her from his house. Aramepinchieue, a devout Christian, took refuge in the mission where the priests, who disapproved of Accault, told her God did not require her to marry. She could choose to remain chaste.

At least fifty women and their children gathered at the church to support Aramepinchieue's decision to exercise her right, as an autonomous Indian women and as a pious Christian, to defy her father. Roenasa, a non-Christian, called an Indian council for support. Frenchmen were split between allies of the clergy and supporters of the military commander, who did not want to give in to Jesuits or lose the alliance with Roenasa.

Aramepinchieue forced a compromise. She agreed to marry Accault if Roenasa would publicly renounce his opposition to Christianity. In the end, Roenasa and the commander sealed their alliance, the Jesuits gained Roenasa's endorsement for Christianity, Accault got a wife, and Aramepinchieue kept her relationships to her father and the Christian community. Chief Roenasa and his wife were baptized shortly after their daughter's marriage, Accault returned to the church, and Aramepinchieue took the Christian name of Marie.

Four years later, Jesuit missionaries briefly settled on the west bank of the River des Peres, south of St. Louis. Illini Indians encamped nearby, on both sides of the Mississippi. The French abandoned Fort St. Louis, and in 1703 Chief Roenasa established a village across the river from Ste. Genevieve, a few miles east of the mouth of the Kaskaskia River, to avoid conflict with Sioux. French traders, missionaries, and Indians lived in close proximity, each dependent on the other. Most Kaskaskian Indians became Roman Catholics. Of twenty-one baptisms recorded at Kaskaskia between 1704 and 1713, eighteen listed an Indian mother and a French father.

After her marriage, Marie, her husband, and two sons lived in an Indian village near Cahokia, but in 1700 she moved to Kaskaskia. In 1704 she had the first of six children with her second husband, French trader Michel Philippe. When she died in 1725, Marie left her considerable estate to her children. One of Accault's sons had gone to live with Indians, but she insisted that he give up Indian life before receiving his inheritance.

The numbers of Illini living in the Illinois Country steadily diminished. Weakened by disease and living in small defenseless groups, the Illini were unable to cooperate with their potential allies to ward off their enemies. In 1750 about two thousand Illini lived in four villages, with Roenasa as their principle chief. After the British took over in 1765, a village of Peorias settled south of St. Louis. Small groups of Shawnee and Delaware Indians lived as squatters in the St. Louis region as well. By the end of the colonial period, most Indians had ceded their land in the immediate region of St. Louis and moved into western Missouri.

Sources: Information and analysis comes from White, *The Middle Ground*, 50–75. White uses the story of Aramepinchieue's marriage as an example of the negotiations Indians and Frenchmen used to find a "middle ground" in their dealings with each other in the eighteenth century. Information about the later life of Marie Aramepinchieue is from Judith A. Franke, ed., *French Peoria and The Illinois Country, 1673–1846* (Springfield: Illinois State Museum, 1995), 22–27.

See also Carl J. Ekberg, *French Roots in the Illinois Country: The Mississippi Frontier in Colonial Times* (Urbana: University of Illinois Press, 1998); Klein and Ackerman, eds., *Women and Power in Native North America*; Thorne, *The Many Hands of My Relations*; Tucker, *Indian Villages of the Illinois Country*; and Carol Devins, "Resistance to Christianity by the Native Women of New France," in *Major Problems in American Women's History: Documents and Essays* 2d ed., Mary Beth Norton and Ruth Alexander, eds. (Mass.: D.C. Heath and Co., 1996), 25–33.

Marie Thérèse Bourgeois Chouteau

In 1795, Marie Thérèse Chouteau demanded that her son-in-law, Joseph Papin, pay her for the loss of her slave, Baptiste. She informed Spanish Governor Francisco Cruzat in writing that Papin caused her overseer's death by ordering the black slave to detain some escaped Indian slaves "without my knowledge or permission." Baptiste was killed in the crossfire between the slaves and their masters. "I ask your authority that I be paid for my loss. His services were invaluable to me . . . no money can remunerate me," she wrote. Because the law forbade employment of a slave without permission of the owner, Madame Chouteau felt Papin should pay her one thousand *piasters*. It was small compensation for Baptiste, she argued, "considering his great value to me."

In this petition, her only surviving correspondence, Madame Chouteau presented herself as an unsentimental slave owner and businesswoman demanding her rightful due. For fifty years she lived in the center of the St. Louis community in a limestone house a few hundred feet from the riverfront. Madame Chouteau's familial relationship to the village's leading fur merchants guaranteed her social status. Opportunities created by colonial Louisiana culture and law enabled her to use that advantage to acquire her own wealth and influence in colonial St. Louis.

Born in 1733 to a New Orleans immigrant from Spain and her French husband, Marie Thérèse Bourgeois came from a family with some property and social position. Her father died before she was six years old, and the family reportedly sent her to an Ursuline convent orphanage where the nuns taught her to read and write. Although her mother quickly remarried, Marie Thérèse may have boarded at the convent until age fifteen. In 1748 the family arranged for her to marry René Chouteau, a French-born innkeeper.

About a year later, after the birth of their son Auguste, Marie Thérèse and René Chouteau separated. Evidence of abuse in their marriage suggests she may have found him intolerable. In any case, he returned to France alone about 1752. Marie Thérèse Chouteau remained in New Orleans, either an abandoned wife or one who refused to follow her husband. No evidence of a separation agreement exists, and civil and ecclesiastical law prohibited divorce.

Sometime after 1755, she met Pierre de Laclède Liguest, another French immigrant, but one with more education and better financial prospects than her husband. Marie Thérèse Chouteau and Pierre Laclède had four children in New Orleans: Jean Pierre, Pelagie, Marie Louise, and Victoire, all baptized with the name of Marie Thérèse's absent husband. In the 1763 census, the thirty-year-old mother referred to herself as *Veuve* (widow) Chouteau, a title of respectable independence.

That same year, Laclède, a partner in the firm of Maxent, Laclède and Company, decided to relocate to a trading post six hundred miles up the Mississippi. He left New Orleans on a keelboat with Auguste, now age fourteen, thirty employees, and a load of supplies. Pregnant and responsible for three children under age six, Marie Thérèse stayed behind. She joined Laclède in the village of St. Louis later in 1764, after Victoire's birth. Whether or not she wanted to live in the wilderness, Marie Thérèse had cast her lot with the ambitious fur merchant.

Laclède prospered in St. Louis, and as the acknowledged town founders, he and his family

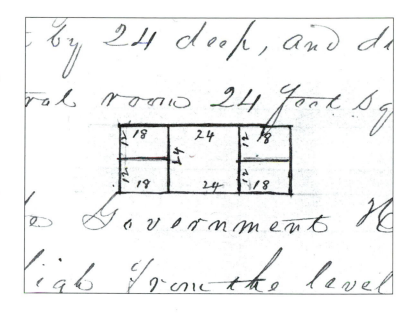

Floor Plan of Chouteau Mansion. From Frederic Billon, Notes on the Laclède House, Frederic Billon Papers, MHS Archives

enjoyed the status and power that enabled them to conduct their personal lives as they saw fit, within the social norms of their time and place. Laclède built the family a large home and gave it in trust to Veuve Chouteau "in consideration for the faithful service" of Auguste Chouteau and "the affection" he had for the other four children "of the marriage of" Marie Thérèse Bourgeois and her husband, René. He also gave her a farm lot, three black slaves, and two Indian slaves, one a fourteen-year-old girl, Thérèse. Laclède lived in the new house with the family, but Marie Thérèse bore him no more children. As was customary in a community of private homes, a number of unrelated people also boarded with the family. Louis St. Ange de Bellerive, former commandant of French Illinois, resided there with his Indian slave mistress until his death.

Because Veuve Chouteau and Laclède were not married, they had no community property. She apparently received few assets from her parents or husband. With the assistance of Laclède and her sons, she acted to establish herself as an independent woman of property. She was so successful that when her husband, René Chouteau, returned to New Orleans in 1767 and sought to reassert his marital rights, Spanish Lieutenant Governor Pedro Piernas in St. Louis acknowledged the legal point but argued that she functioned as an independent widow "established in her separate house, owning land in this post with her own slaves that work for her." Protected both by her social

Although she undoubtedly accepted advice and assistance from her family, Madame Chouteau became an accomplished businesswoman and home manager through her own perseverance and skill. She traded in land, furs, and grain; her large farm in the *Grande Prairie* common fields had a house, orchard, barn, and cabins for slaves. In 1787, her household consisted of eighteen people. Two unmarried men boarded in her home, a laborer and a carpenter. She employed three free black men and owned eight female slaves and four male slaves. In 1805, after she had sold off some of her holdings, assessors valued her real estate at three thousand piasters, which made her one of the ten or fifteen wealthiest individuals in the village.

Veuve Chouteau achieved financial and personal independence in large part because she had a staff of enslaved workers. House slaves grew and prepared food for the extended household within her large village compound. Others tended her livestock and produced wheat, tobacco, and corn on her farm property under the direction of Baptiste, until his death in 1795. She did receive compensation for the loss of her slave's services. Although Governor Cruzat took sixteen months to respond to Veuve Chouteau's petition, he ordered her son-in-law and the other owners of the runaway Indian slaves to pay her a total of six hundred piasters in compensation.

Veuve Chouteau and wealthy women like her suffered physical hardships common to women at the end of the eighteenth century, but they did not experience unrelieved drudgery or deprivation. St. Louis was less culturally isolated than its remote location might suggest. Engaged in international trade, merchant families possessed surprisingly cosmopolitan tastes and interests. Luxury goods as well as necessary dry goods and staples arrived regularly on boats that took furs away to international markets. Marie Thérèse Chouteau wore fine imported clothes and jewelry; her china came from France; and her candlesticks were silver. Like most affluent women, she wore silk dresses and satin shoes for special events, which by the end of the eighteenth century were most often gatherings of the large interconnected merchant families.

Veuve Chouteau maintained her personal independence in her old age, living in her house with her slave, Thérèse, who managed her daily affairs. She freed the Indian woman in her will and left her sixty piasters, some flour, a cow, and a calf. When Veuve Chouteau died in 1814, more than fifty grandchildren lived within a mile of her home.

position and her financial independence, Marie Thérèse Chouteau convinced Spanish officials not to comply with the Louisiana governor's order that she be returned to the authority of her husband in New Orleans.

Having successfully fought off extradition, Veuve Chouteau actually did become a widow in 1776 when René died. She did not, however, marry Pierre Laclède, who still lived in her home. By then, his fortunes had changed and he would have brought only debts to the marriage. Pierre Laclède himself died in 1778 on a business trip to New Orleans. Veuve Chouteau purchased some of his mortgaged property from Maxent, at a price so low that the business partners had probably negotiated it before Laclède's death.

Marie Thérèse Bourgeois Chouteau. Oil on canvas attributed to Francois Guyol de Gairan, ca. 1814. MHS Art Collection

The marriages of her sons and daughters into other wealthy merchant families created kinship networks whose influence extended far into the trans-Mississippi west. The names of Chouteau, Papin, Gratiot, and Labbadie would be prominent in St. Louis society and business for generations, but not the name Laclède. The family never publicly acknowledged Veuve Chouteau's relationship with Pierre Laclède.

Sources: Until recently, most of the historical interest in Veuve Chouteau focused on her relationship to Pierre Laclède, a matter of great concern to her descendants. This essay is based on Katharine T. Corbett, "Veuve Chouteau, a 250th Anniversary," *GH* 3, no. 4 (spring 1983): 42–48, but includes information not available at the time of its publication. See also William E. Foley, "The Laclède-Chouteau Puzzle: John Francis McDermott Supplies Some Missing Pieces," *GH* 4, no. 2 (fall 1983); St. Louis Manuscript Census, 1787; Frederic L. Billon, *Annals of St. Louis*; Marie Thérèse Bourgeois Chouteau, reference file, MHS; Marie Thérèse Bourgeois Chouteau, Will, Wills Envelope, MHS; Pierre Chouteau Collection and Chouteau Collections, MHS; Mary B. Cunningham and Jeanne C. Blythe, *The Founding Family of St. Louis* (St. Louis: Midwest Technical Publications, 1997); John F. McDermott, "Pierre Laclède and the Chouteaus," *BMHS* 21, no. 4 (July 1965); "Historic Sites and Building Worksheets 33-001: House of Madame Chouteau," Jefferson National Expansion Memorial, National Park Service; Glen E. Holt, "The Laclède Cycle: The Search for St. Louis' Founder," unpublished manuscript, 1982; and St. Louis Recorded Archives, WPA–NPS Transcription Project, JNEM.

See Billon, *Annals of St. Louis*, 233–48, for the full story of Baptiste's death and the subsequent suit. Other sources include Foley, *Genesis of Missouri;* Foley and Rice, *The First Chouteaus;* van Ravenswaay, *An Informal History of St. Louis;* and Peterson, *Building a Colonial Capital.* For a discussion of the twentieth-century controversy over the nature of the Chouteau-Laclède relationship, see Corbett, "Veuve Chouteau," and van Ravenswaay, *An Informal History of St. Louis.*

Jeanette Forchet

Jeanette Forchet was in her late sixties and dying in January 1803. As was customary in colonial St. Louis, she asked a literate neighbor to transcribe her last will. With the exception of a running account at the general store, Jeanette Forchet had no debts. Her house on Church Street had been mortgaged for a considerable sum, "which sum my daughter

Susana [sic] has satisfied through her work and effort." She made Susanna "absolute owner of said house and land by possession and right." Pierre Laclède had granted the town lot to Jeanette in 1765, and she had put up the twenty-five-by-twenty-foot house where she had raised a family and supported herself for more than thirty-five years. One of the few free black residents of St. Louis at the time of her death, Jeanette enjoyed the same rights of property as other free St. Louis women.

Jeanette was born about 1736, probably in the Illinois Country, and was a free woman in 1766 when she and her first husband received one of the original St. Louis town lots and a farm lot in the common fields. Jeanette's husband Gregory, a free blacksmith, died in 1770. She was left with her wooden "house of posts" on *Rue de L'eglise* (later Second Street), her farm plot, two sons, and two daughters. She and the children supported the family by growing corn and keeping cows, pigs, and chickens.

Women's Cotton Plainweave Empire Dress of Indigo Blue Calico Print, ca. 1795. Photograph by David Schultz, 1998. MHS–PP

She may also have taken in laundry and practiced folk medicine; she owned many kettles and three pairs of smoothing irons, as well as a mortar with an iron pestle.

In 1773, Veuve Forchet married a free black gunsmith, Pierre Ignace, known in the community as Valentin. Like most free people in colonial St. Louis, they prepared a marriage contract and signed their names with a mark. Before marrying Valentin, Jeanette Forchet requested the customary inventory to establish legal ownership of the property she brought to the marriage. A committee of townspeople assigned a value of 1,349 *livres* (roughly 266 piasters) to her possessions, which included her real estate, animals, household goods, and "two copper candlesticks, half used and mended." Valentin's assets totaled 1,220 livres.

In 1787, Jeanette lived in her house with Valentin, her two daughters, and two free black laborers, who were probably boarders. The family grew wheat, tobacco, and corn on their farm property. Valentin, however, worked as a trapper as well as a gunsmith and sometime farmer. The following year, he got permission from the Spanish authorities to leave the village to hunt in the territory of the Grand Osage Indians, southwest of St. Louis. Valentin never returned, and in 1790 Jeanette learned that he had been dead for a year. Finding herself a widow again at age fifty-four, Jeanette Forchet went back to the authorities to request an inventory of the community property acquired during her second marriage.

In the seventeen years they were married, Jeanette and Valentin had increased the value of their assets to 3,763 livres. She now had two walnut armoires, her copper candlesticks, and some "plate" dishes and forks in addition to the spoons and earthenware she had owned in 1773. Because Jeanette and her husband had no children together and he had agreed in 1773 to make her his sole heir, she also acquired his gunsmithing tools and thirty-seven old gun barrels. To settle a debt of 1,372 livres owed to Charles Sanguinet, the merchant whose home stood on the lot adjacent to hers, Jeanette gave him a mortgage on her house and personal effects. She repaid him in 1798.

By 1803, her sons were gone from St. Louis: Ignace had died and Augustin lived in New Orleans. One daughter, Marie-Louisa, was also dead. Francesca Sueyeuse, the teenage daughter of a Creole man and an Osage Indian woman, had lived in the house with Jeanette, but she left in 1802 to marry Michel Vallé, a native of Montreal. In her will, Jeanette asked that money from her estate be used for her funeral and burial in the Parish Cemetery and for saying four Masses for the comfort of her soul. Her debt to Gregory Sarpy, a St. Louis–based merchant, was paid from her assets. Her house, free and clear, went to her only surviving daughter, Susanna, who had helped to pay off the mortgage. Jeanette asked that her other heirs "enjoy what remains of my goods with God's blessing and my own."

Jeanette Forchet had fewer possessions in 1803 than she had in 1790, and most were very old. But she still owned one walnut armoire and one copper candlestick, and she still had land in the common fields and her house in the center of town. Over the years her descendants subdivided the town lot among themselves and eventually sold it to developers. Her daughter, Susanna, married J. B. Irbour and had a daughter, Julie, who later married Antoine Labbadie, considered one of St. Louis's wealthiest black men in 1850.

One of a small number of free blacks living in colonial St. Louis, Jeanette Forchet retained her personal freedom and many rights denied to slaves. Like all free women she was entitled to own property, have a recognized marriage, and enter into legal contracts. The economy provided opportunities for her to earn a living to supplement her husbands' incomes and retain her independence after their deaths.

Like all St. Louisans of African descent, however, Jeanette Forchet was bound by social and legal restrictions designed to maintain the slavery system. She needed permission to leave town. Manumitted slaves were re-enslaved for infractions of the law. And unlike Madame Chouteau and other Creole widows, she never enjoyed the right to be called Veuve Forchet, the honorific title for widows in colonial St. Louis.

Sources: The essay is based on information in the St. Louis Recorded Archives and the 1787 Manuscript Census, the only places containing historical records of Jeanette Forchet. In the 1930s, WPA workers catalogued the original colonial records and translated some documents from the French and Spanish. These translations are fragmentary and often misleading. This essay used new translations by William S. Maltby. See also the reconstructed map of St. Louis in 1804 by Pitzman's Company of Surveyors & Engineers, which shows ownership of property with dates of houses and types of construction.

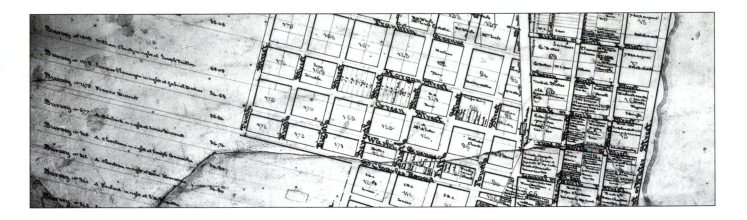

Esther

A former black slave, Esther fought in court to keep the St. Louis property she acquired through her association with Jacques Clamorgan, a ruthless speculator in land, furs, and other risky colonial enterprises. Esther litigated her claims until her death in 1833, and though she lost most of her property in the courts, she managed to keep her house at Third and Poplar and preserve a large piece of valuable land for her descendants.

Esther was born in Virginia about 1753 and came to Kaskaskia in the Illinois Country with her owner's family. About 1785 Esther's master gave her to Jacques Clamorgan to settle a debt. Clamorgan, a West Indian native of Welsh descent, was a glib, aggressive entrepreneur known for his liaisons with black women and shunned by polite Creole society.

With Esther, Clamorgan seemed willing to lead a more conventional domestic life. He purchased Esther's daughter from her master and brought her to live with them in St. Louis. Conversant in both French and English, Esther acted socially as the mistress of Clamorgan's house. She assumed many of the duties and responsibilities of a wife, but with none of the legal protection afforded free women.

Esther received her freedom so she could hold property in her own name. In 1793 Clamorgan organized the Missouri Company, an extremely risky fur-trading venture. Fearing his holdings might be vulnerable to creditors, Clamorgan freed Esther and transferred some of his property to her for safekeeping. He also signed Esther's daughter, Sally, over to her.

Clamorgan did not marry his former slave. He assumed that she understood she was but a straw party in the transactions and that he continued to control the property. Esther thought otherwise: she farmed the land, tended the orchard, and treated the property as her own. She began to resist putting her mark without question on every piece of paper he asked her to sign.

Clamorgan was an abusive man, and when his behavior became too much for Esther to bear she left him, taking her deeds with her. Although the Spanish government upheld her right to the property, Clamorgan managed to get much of it back after the American takeover in 1804. The Americans required proof of ten years' possession before they would certify Spanish land claims. Clamorgan went to the recorder's office and somehow managed to sign the deeds over to himself, backdate them to 1794, and forge Esther's signature and those of witnesses. He also threatened to take possession of Esther's daughter by altering the papers that had transferred her to her mother.

Esther, unaware of the fraud until 1808, spent the rest of her life fighting Clamorgan and his heirs in the courts. Although Esther, a free woman, was entitled to a fair and impartial judgment from the court, it is unlikely that she received it. Her property was too valuable. An illiterate black woman, even one as resourceful as Esther, could not protect herself from powerful men intent on using the legal system to further their own goals.

Sources: This essay draws on information from Judith A. Gilbert, "Esther and Her Sisters: Free Women of Color as Property Owners in Colonial St. Louis, 1765–1803," *GH* 17, no. 1 (summer 1996): 14–23, and on research by Mary Seematter. Additional information about Esther's fight for her property exists in the records of her court cases. See especially testimony from *Esther v. Carr*, filed in St. Charles County in 1832, located at the St. Charles Historical Society, St. Charles, Missouri.

City of St. Louis Surveyed According to the Resolution of the Board of Aldermen, July 10, 1823. Detail showing property of Esther Clamorgan, a free mulatto, and the common fields (far left). [Map] ink on paper by Charles DeWard, 1823. MHS Archives

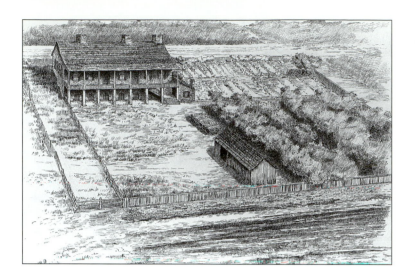

Victorire Delile

Victorire was the daughter of a black slave woman and an Indian man, Joseph Delile. She was the property of Gabriel Cerré, a fur trader from Montreal who was the principal merchant in Kaskaskia from 1755 until about 1780, when he moved his family to St. Louis. The Cerré family lived on *La Rue Royale* (later the corner of Main and Vine Streets) in an imposing stone house that dominated a compound the size of a city block. Cerré also had a large tract of farmland south of the village (near present-day Broadway and Soulard) where he built a country house. The Spanish governor also granted him several large tracks of land in the surrounding countryside.

Female slaves, like Victorire, did most of the domestic labor in the Cerré homes. They worked under the direction of Catherine Girard Cerré or one of her three daughters. The Cerré family controlled Victorire's working conditions, and local slave codes defined the boundaries of her public life outside the compound walls. Whatever private life she managed to maintain in her off hours she prudently hid from her masters, and hence from historians as well.

The Cerré household was large, although by 1787 only one of the Cerrés' four children still lived at home. Marie Ann had moved to Montreal with her merchant husband in 1781; Marie Thérèse had married Auguste Chouteau in 1786. Julia still lived with her parents, as did four Cerré nieces and nephews, aged twelve to twenty-two. Nine white

male workers, ranging in age from twenty-one to forty-eight, and twenty-eight slaves made up the rest of the household. By 1792, the Cerré household had grown to sixty-one persons, including forty-three slaves. Some of the slaves and workmen probably stayed on the outlying farm property.

Under the watchful eye of her mistress, Victorire would have done a variety of domestic chores for this large household. Creole slave-owning women, much praised for their kindness, were also known for the rigid discipline they imposed on slave women. Owners seldom trusted their slaves, whom they characterized as either indolent or thieving. Madame Cerré would have never let the keys to her storeroom leave her hand.

Whatever her other duties, Victorire probably helped prepare food. The Cerré slaves made meals for the family in the detached kitchen. Because the kitchen was far from the dining room, young cook's apprentices ran back and forth carrying hot food to the table. Cooking on an open fireplace was a long, tedious operation that required years of training; good slave cooks sold for high prices. Because French Creoles prided themselves on the variety and quality of their food, domestic slave workers probably ate fairly well in the kitchen. Masters, however, saved scarce wheat bread for themselves; slaves, like Indians, ate cornbread. Although the mistress chose the menus, the results reflected her cook's African heritage, particularly gumbos, which became a staple of Creole cuisine. Shawnee Indians sold game in the village; Indian slaves prepared it and introduced other native foods into the family's diet as well.

In addition to meal preparation, Victorire probably worked in the enclosed yard surrounding the house. Slaves planted, hoed, and harvested the vegetable garden, picked and preserved fruit from the orchard, milked cows, slopped pigs, and tended the chickens. In the house, they also waxed and polished the bare walnut floors that Creole housewives took such pride in. Owners kept their slaves busy polishing furniture, washing windows, and performing other chores that made the homes of the merchant elite sparkle.

The Cerré town home was large by local standards, but it may have had only three rooms on the first floor, with a sleeping loft above. A gallery, or porch, extended the length of the back, shading the windows in the basement which was probably used for storage. House slaves probably lived in a cabin or shed in the yard.

Gabriel Cerré Residence [Rear view]. Ink on paper by Clarence Hoblitzelle, 1898. MHS–PP

House slaves regularly left the owner's compound to fetch water from the Mississippi River. There were no wells in colonial St. Louis; most water was hauled in earthen jugs up the steep bank at the foot of Walnut Street, a climb of about fifty feet to La Rue Royale. Because the Cerré property backed on the river, slaves probably brought water directly up from the river in jugs either by cart or suspended from a yoke attached to their shoulders.

Slaves did not haul Mississippi River water for doing laundry. Instead, black women carried bundles of soiled clothes, balanced on their heads or in carts, to *La Petite Rivière* and to Chouteau's Pond on the southern end of the village. Cerré's slaves washed the family's clothes in the pond, standing on platforms built out into the water to wring the wet garments and linens. They hung the wash to dry on nearby bushes. When it rained, they did the laundry in cabins built on the banks of the pond. When the pond froze, they broke through the ice and either washed in the freezing water or carried water to the cabins.

Not all the women washing clothes in Chouteau's Pond were slaves. Free black women did the family wash there and earned money washing for others. Flor, a free black woman, supported her four children as a washerwoman. While most free women did their own domestic chores for their families, laundry was the first task women paid others to do if they could afford it. Doing laundry together became a social event for the town's black women, an opportunity to sing, bicker, gossip, nurture friendships, and have some time away from the watchful eyes of white St. Louisans.

Victorire's life changed in 1796 when her father, known as Joseph the Indian belonging to—probably working for—Madame Delile, asked Cerré to let him lift "the unfortunate yoke of bondage" from his daughter by buying her freedom. Cerré named a price of one thousand piasters. Compared to appraisals made five years later of five hundred piasters for a nineteen-year-old male slave and three hundred piasters for a ten-year-old girl, this was an exorbitant amount for a female slave, even one in the prime of life. Joseph appealed to Zenon Trudeau, lieutenant governor of the territory, who called Cerré to appear before him. Cerré expressed concern that someone who wanted to use Victorire for "debauchery" was funding her father's offer. He agreed, however, to submit the case to arbitration. He promised to accept the arbitrated price if in the end Victorire would be "given her liberty fully

without any claim against her, neither by her father or by anyone else who may be able to advance the sum."

Each of the three parties selected an appraiser. Joseph first chose Gabriel Sarpy, who declined, and then picked Jacques Clamorgan, the fur trader. Cerré chose Jean Marie Papin, a leading merchant. Trudeau chose as referee appraiser Antoine Berthe, also a merchant. Clamorgan appraised Victorire at six hundred piasters in local currency; five hundred dollars in hard cash. Papin estimated her value at eight hundred dollars hard cash. The official referee, Berthe, agreed with Papin. Trudeau set the price at eight hundred dollars and informed Joseph Delile that "upon payment of this sum we declare her to be free from slavery from that day."

Cerré left no records that indicate whether or not he sold Victorire. The appraisers may have set a price too steep for her father. Despite Cerré's professed interest in saving Victorire from debauchery, in truth slave women had no protection from sexual exploitation. Freedom would not have put her at greater risk. Slaves had the fewest options and least control over their lives of any women living in colonial St. Louis.

Sources: Most black and many Indian women who lived in colonial St. Louis were enslaved, and few had the opportunity that Victorire may have had to be freed. Little evidence remains of their individual experiences apart from their owners' records, where they appear only as property. This essay does not describe Victorire's actual work but is extrapolated from several sources. Her background and the story of her sale are from the Cerré Collection, MHS. Descriptions of domestic work in the village comes from Edward Villiere Papin, "The Village Under the Hill: A Sketch of Old St. Louis," *MHS Collections* 5 (1927), 18–37, which Papin based on the old-age recollections of Pierre Chouteau, reveal racial, cultural, and gender biases, but they also describe the work slaves did. See also Rachel Fran Vogel, "Social Life in St. Louis, 1764–1804" (master's thesis, Washington University, 1921). Additional information from Foley, *Genesis of Missouri* and the St. Louis Census of 1787 and 1792.

1804–1840

1. St. Louis Protestant Orphan Asylum
2. Marguerite McNair Home
3. City Jail, Elizabeth
4. Anne Ewing Lane Home
5. Pierre Chouteau Home,
   Celeste and Catiche Scypion Residence
6. Mary Paddock's Boardinghouse
7. Henry von Phul Home
8. The Sisters of Charity Hospital
9. Mary Hempstead Lisa Home
10. Religious of the Sacred Heart School and Convent,
    Philippine Duchesne
11. Sisters of St. Joseph of Carondelet
    School and Convent

▬ St. Louis City Limits 1822–1840
▬ Present-day Gateway Arch grounds

2

Women on the Urban Frontier

Although France sold the Louisiana Territory to the United States in 1803, control of St. Louis did not pass into American hands until the following spring. A lavish dinner and ball followed an emotional flag-raising ceremony in the town square on March 4, 1804. As the fur merchants' wives danced with officials of the new government and the black and Indian slave women prepared and served refreshments, all present must have reflected on how the day's events might affect them. Like their husbands, wealthy Creole women feared that American newcomers with their foreign ways would not only overturn traditional political and economic power, but also upset village life and challenge their place as social leaders. Slaves, on the other hand, welcomed the change in power. Americans had outlawed slavery across the river in Illinois more than a decade ago; perhaps they would liberate St. Louis as well.

Bank of St. Louis Banknote, $10, with View of St. Louis [detail]. Engraving, 1817. Collection of Eric P. Newman. The illustration highlights the architectural difference of the U.S.–influenced buildings to the right, with the Creole-style Laclède-Chouteau mansion of the upper left.

Over the next forty years, as the little village grew into a thriving commercial entrepôt, Creole culture lost its community dominance. The women of the elite families either adapted to change or retreated into private society. Their children became Americans. Black women soon discovered that American republicanism, quite capable of coexisting with American slavery, did not mean equality for all. Indians, enslaved and free, discovered they were no longer welcome in the St. Louis area.

The cultural, economic, and political transformation that followed the American takeover affected all women in St. Louis. The American legal system, based on English Common Law, replaced the old French *coutumes de Paris*, which had given them considerable control over property and protection from their husbands' creditors. New Anglo-American inheritance laws voided their traditional community property rights and obligations. Parents could now even disinherit their children.

Enslaved women also fared poorly under American justice. To appease influential Creoles and attract eastern slave owners, Americans immediately strengthened, not abolished, the institution of slavery. New codified slave laws based on those of Virginia outlawed slave marriages. Owners now had the right to break up slave families and sell children away from their mothers.

St. Louis Scene. Ink and wash on paper by Anna Maria von Phul, 1818. MHS Art Collection

Although St. Louis was a community of many cultures, Creoles, in general, had not been influenced by eighteenth-century Anglo-American settlers. Mostly outlying farming families and transient boatmen, the Yankees had made little cultural impression on the French-speaking Catholic community, which had a close-knit traditional social hierarchy and European connections. Moreover, too many of the nineteenth-century newcomers were politically active lawyers, aggressive speculators, and Protestant clergymen, all noisy promoters of individualistic republican values.

Money and influence quickly won out over tradition and taste. Ambitious Americans promptly acquired land and influence by marrying the daughters of old wealthy families, and the Creole elite were just as quick to make alliances with promising new residents by strategically arranging their daughters' marriages. English, the official language after 1804, slowly became the dominant language. And since language is the prime carrier of culture, by mid-century Creole culture had mostly retreated into the private world occupied by the few remaining French-speaking families with ties to New Orleans and France.

Although Americanization had an immediate social and political impact, noticeable change in outward appearance came slowly. Of the nearly twenty-five hundred people in the area in 1803, less than half lived in the village of St. Louis. The rest farmed their own land nearby or gathered in small communities like Carondelet. Population grew slowly until the War of 1812 eliminated the possibility of British attack. By 1821 approximately 4,000 people occupied 458 houses in town, 190 of them built after 1815. Families with large holdings in the surrounding countryside, the remnants of privately held colonial common fields, turned big profits by subdividing and selling land for development. When economic depression hit St. Louis in 1821, some profiteers snapped up bankrupt holdings at a discount. So many people suffered financial failure and left town, however, that when the electorate extended the western boundary to Seventh Street and approved the town charter in 1822, barely three thousand residents remained. William Carr Lane, an eastern physician who had moved his family to St. Louis in 1819, became the first mayor in 1823.

In the 1820s land speculators, lawyers, artisans, and other opportunists seeking their fortunes in the West came to St. Louis from all parts of the eastern United States. Many brought families; some also brought slaves. One-fourth of the population was African American in 1830, but only one in five was a free person. Although there were four white males for every three white females in St. Louis, the gender balance was closer to equal than ever before. Population figures were deceiving though, because many men were transient workers who lived briefly in boardinghouses before moving on.

By 1835 St. Louisans had become full participants in a national market economy by exploiting their locational advantage at the center of the inland river system. The engine of change was steam. Over the next five years the city's population doubled to 16,439; steamboat trade had made St. Louis a commercial center and the shipping point for a burgeoning hinterland. In 1841 voters expanded the incorporated area from less than one square mile to nearly five, and drew its western boundary at Eighteenth Street. By then new European immigrants had come up the Mississippi from the port of New Orleans or traveled overland to settle in Missouri. Lured by promises of democratic government, religious tolerance, and a natural environment similar to that of western Europe, immigrants from German states swelled an already diverse population.

By 1840 St. Louis was still a frontier town with muddy streets and open sewers, but it had begun to take on the appearance of a real American city. While always financially and socially stratified, the colonial village had been culturally diverse, with everyone living crowded together sharing their daily lives. Now the Yankee imperative to succeed– to better others in the race for wealth–accelerated divisions in the community. St. Louisans began to separate socially and economically as their city spread out spatially. When New Yorker Mrs. Eliza Steele visited St. Louis in 1841 she found a get-ahead western river town with a bustling wharf. On busy Main Street "one may obtain goods from all quarters of the world . . . and domestic wares from the country around. As you descend from the river the streets are wider and better built, and the upper end of the city is laid out in wide streets fast filling up with handsome buildings. . . . Here many eastern people dwell." In the older Creole district "the streets are narrow and present quite a foreign and antique appearance."

Specific local circumstances made life in St. Louis unique, but all women in rapidly growing American frontier communities in the early nineteenth century shared similar and potentially all-consuming concerns that focused on family health and physical welfare. They had reason to worry,

because germs traveled with the immigrant ships; the age of transatlantic migration was the age of global epidemics. Primitive medical knowledge was no match for poor sanitation in crowded living conditions. Because no one understood the relationship between germs and infection, childbirth frequently resulted in a healthy baby followed a few days later by a dead mother. Death from undiagnosed cancer and other terminal illnesses was often long and painful, unrelieved by effective treatment or drugs. Women assumed primary responsibility for everyone's health care: mothers, daughters, cousins, aunts, slaves, and servants nursed the sick and comforted the survivors.

Women relied on each other for help in isolated frontier towns. Although mail and travelers took weeks, not days, to cover distances between places like St. Louis and Cincinnati, women created supportive long-distance communities of interlocking family relationships. The specter of sudden, life-threatening illness fostered enduring bonds that stretched across the miles.

Women in St. Louis, especially those with slaves or servants to do domestic chores, often extended their domestic concerns beyond their own homes. They performed many private acts of benevolence. As the town grew larger, the numbers of needy, particularly women and children, increased. In response, a group of prominent women decided that "there were many cases of extreme wretchedness, beyond the reach of individual charity" for whom they felt a collective, civic responsibility. They created a private, voluntary organization, the Female Charitable Society, to do something about it.

Foreign visitors to the United States often noted this peculiarly American tendency to tackle all sorts of personal and public problems by creating special-purpose, private voluntary associations. White men participated in a wider range of public activities in the nineteenth century than ever before. When states abandoned property requirements for voting, vigorous political parties emerged. Business, fraternal, and civic groups proliferated in every community.

Americans thought civic activity and public life appropriate for men, but not for women. Whether or not they actually had political or economic influence, most women agreed with men that public responsibility, like domestic responsibility, was gender-bound. Men were naturally best suited to the rough-and-tumble public arena of politics and business; women's natural domain was the private, morally nurturing haven of home.

In the 1820s women in St. Louis, as in many other American communities, broadened their sphere to include organized community charity. The local Female Charitable Society, founded in 1824, was unusual only in that it crossed religious lines, although probably not class boundaries.

Religious organizations met both men's and women's spiritual needs, but for women they also provided crucial, legitimate channels for moral influence and benevolence. Protestant women organized denominational orphanages and shelters for the sick and dependent, particularly abandoned women. While Catholic lay women engaged less in organized charity work, women in religious orders made benevolence their lifework. Unlike other American cities, St. Louis had many Catholic residents, legacies of its Creole past. Early in the nineteenth century, Bishops William DuBourg and Joseph Rosati recruited women religious from Europe to organize orphanages and hospitals. Nuns, who gave their private lives to the church, were not motivated by the same republican values that led other American women to work for social welfare, but the community benefit was much the same.

When they organized for charity, American women did not propose to change their social role; they merely meant to enlarge its area of activity. But in doing so they began to redefine the meaning of public and private life. Women, in St. Louis and elsewhere, combined two culturally acceptable norms to create a new female role. As women, they embarked on a legitimate moral mission; as Americans they organized democratic voluntary associations to carry out the mission in their communities. When American cities like St. Louis grew larger and more complex in the nineteenth century, this new public role for women became a legitimate reality of urban life. In future debates over how to apportion responsibility for community welfare, women's charities would be a significant factor distinct from either the family or government.

Women's subtly self-expanded role was significant in nineteenth-century schooling. Female education had been largely an informal enterprise in colonial St. Louis and continued to be among Creole families. Some newcomers, however, brought with them a New England tradition of female schooling and sought private education for their daughters in St. Louis or at eastern boarding schools. Catholic, and some Protestant, girls attended the local convent school opened by the Religious of the Sacred Heart in 1818. The sisters held separate classes for their paying students and for the girls whose parents could not afford tuition. In the 1840s the Sisters of St. Joseph operated a free school for girls in Carondelet that was partially subsidized by town funds. Mary Sibley founded Lindenwood School for Protestant girls in St. Charles in 1832. The first public schools in St. Louis opened in 1838 with five hundred girls enrolled. Although school attendance in the frontier community probably lagged behind urban eastern norms, most white St. Louis females were literate by mid-century.

The classical education women received at private academies stressed the social skills that readied them for marriage. It also prepared them for teaching, one of the few respectable occupations for unmarried middle-class women. Widows and other unmarried or financially independent women often became dressmakers. Skilled at cutting and fitting, they might have spent several days a year helping the women of a household make new garments or alter old ones. Early St. Louis city directories listed only a few seamstresses and milliners in business for themselves. Women who worked in family-owned businesses, like stores and taverns, went unrecorded. However, most women were not employed, but they cared for their own families and sometimes found ways of adding to family income.

Most employed women did domestic work for others, often in boardinghouses. Middle-class white women who did not own slaves frequently hired them from their owners or employed free black women to cook, clean and do laundry. Though not as sharp or as visible on the urban frontier as in eastern cities, class distinction had telling indicators: whether a woman did housework for others, did her own housework, worked in her home with the help of a slave or servant, or expected someone else to do the housework altogether. Despite the boom and bust economy of early St. Louis, these roles remained remarkably stable.

During the transitional era when Creole colonial St. Louis grew into an American city, some women remained enslaved; some lost economic or cultural security; and others saw opportunity in change and began to create for themselves new and more public places in the community.

Sources: For a contemporary description of territorial St. Louis, see Henry Marie Brackenridge, *Views of Louisiana: Together with a Journal of a Voyage Up the Missouri River, in 1811* (Pittsburgh, 1814). For a discussion of tensions between Creoles and Americans in the early nineteenth century, see Jay

Gitlin, "'Avec bien du regret': The Americanization of Creole St. Louis," *GH* 9, no. 4 (spring 1989). Descriptions of St. Louis before 1840 are drawn largely from William Foley, *The Genesis of Missouri: From Wilderness Outpost to Statehood* (Columbia: University of Missouri Press, 1989) and James Neal Primm, *Lion of the Valley, St. Louis, Missouri*, 3d ed. (St. Louis: MHS Press, 1998). See also *SLAH*, Units 2, 3, and 4. Richard C. Wade, *The Urban Frontier: The Rise of Western Cities, 1790–1830* (Cambridge, Mass.: Harvard University Press, 1959) places St. Louis in the context of other frontier communities in this period. Steele's impressions of St. Louis are from Eliza R. Steele, *A Summer's Journey by Mrs. Steele* (New York: John S. Taylor, 1841), excerpted in *SLAH*, Unit 3. Quotation on St. Louis's poor is from the Constitution of the Female Charitable Society, 1824, MHS. The most quoted foreign visitor was Alexis de Tocqueville who made observations about American voluntary associations in *Democracy in America* (London: Saunders and Otley, 1836–1840). Information is also drawn from census data, St. Louis city directories, and tax roles available at MHS.

The analysis of women's changing public role relies heavily on Sara M. Evans, *Born for Liberty: A History of Women in America* (New York: The Free Press, 1989), as does much of the later interpretation of women in public life. See also Anne Firor Scott, *Natural Allies: Women's Associations in American History* (Urbana: University of Illinois Press, 1991) for more on middle-class women's reasons for organizing.

Historians have argued over the definition of the middle class and its characteristics. They agree that nineteenth-century Americans, particularly those living in cities, began to experience their lives and values as different from both the tiny upper class and the expanding, more clearly defined working class. While one's education and economic position in the community were important factors, they were not the only indicators of class status.

Philippine Duchesne

As a child in France, Rose Philippine Duchesne listened to tales of Jesuit missions in far-off Louisiana. "I envied their labors without being frightened by the dangers to which they were exposed, for I was at this time reading stories of the martyrs." Thirty years later, the now forty-eight-year-old nun, whose heart still thrilled at the words "Propagation of the Faith" and "Foreign Missions," volunteered to lead a mission to the Louisiana frontier. Mother Duchesne and four other members of her religious order, the Religious of the Sacred Heart, arrived in St. Louis in 1818. Her venture into the mission field not only brought her closer

to a life-long dream, but also to far greater economic and organizational responsibilities than most women of her class and time. Working within the structure of the Roman Catholic Church, Philippine Duchesne combined a personal life of service with a public role in the St. Louis community.

Rose Philippine Duchesne was the convent-educated daughter of a wealthy French family from Grenoble. At age eighteen she entered a Visitation Monastery but returned to her home after the French Revolutionary Assembly abolished monastic orders in 1792. In 1804 she joined the newly established Religious of the Sacred Heart, a Roman Catholic order devoted to the education of elite young women. Members of both religious orders came from wealthy families who were willing to pay large sums in the form of dowries for their daughters to join cloistered communities.

Mother Philippine Duchesne. Photograph of painting. MHS–PP

Sister Duchesne was a convent school administrator when Bishop DuBourg came to Paris seeking missionaries and funds for his remote North American diocese. He convinced Duchesne's superior that the St. Louis Catholic community, and especially the daughters of the Creole elite, desperately needed a convent school to preserve French religious and cultural traditions from the rising threat of American Protestantism.

Upon her arrival in St. Louis, Mother Duchesne discovered that the bishop did not plan to establish the school in St. Louis as he had promised, but rather in the village of St. Charles, a day's travel to the west. With characteristic energy and administrative skill, she made the best of the situation. In September 1818, she opened the first free school for girls west of the Mississippi and a day school for local residents who could pay a nominal tuition. The next month she added a boarding school, hoping that student fees would subsidize the free school. The curriculum included religious instruction, reading, writing, and counting. Duchesne admitted mulattoes and Indian students to the day school until the bishop forbade it. She did, however, persuade him to allow the sisters to teach black students in segregated classes one day a week.

DuBourg soon acknowledged that choosing the remote St. Charles location had been a mistake. In 1819 the sisters moved the school to Florissant, an old Creole village even smaller than St. Charles but closer to St. Louis. The new location attracted more boarding students and the daughters of the local elite, Protestant as well as Catholic. In 1824 the curriculum offered English, grammar, writing, arithmetic, history, and geography to the eighth-grade level, as well as sewing and embroidery, both traditional skills for well-educated young women. In 1827 John Mullanphy traded Duchesne the use of a house in St. Louis for a school and convent, in return for her promise to take in twenty orphans of his choice every year. By 1828 Mother Duchesne oversaw six female academies–three in the St. Louis area–attended by more than 350 students.

Mother Duchesne's expanding enterprises depended on her ability to raise money. Over the years she solicited help from the motherhouse and relatives in France, pressured the bishop to release funds the church owed to the nuns, and successfully negotiated with philanthropist John Mullanphy, who drove a hard bargain. She understood rates of interest, building contracts, exchange rates, and the consequences of an inflationary economy.

As a well-educated daughter of the French bourgeoisie, Duchesne was not prepared for raw-boned St. Louis. The sheer contrast between her cloistered Parisian convent and the hardships of public life in a frontier town was disturbing enough without having to deal with American republican attitudes. As an aristocratic Frenchwoman, she did not understand why St. Louisans balked at servants' work. Frustration over the problem eventually led her order to buy slaves, despite her professed aversion to slavery. Duchesne shared the French language and Catholicism with the local elite but shuddered at the careless Creole daughters in fancy dresses who used their sleeves as handkerchiefs. Although she accepted the belief that the lower status of African Americans and Indians was natural, she despised American racism. She never questioned the authority of her superiors; the mission of the church was her own. But she used the institution to further her own mission of educating all frontier women. Her concerns for their spiritual and educational welfare transcended class, race, and ethnicity.

By 1840, Mother Duchesne's advancing age, still-faltering English, and austere style made her a less effective administrator in St. Louis. The following year she finally had the opportunity to work with Indian girls in Sugar Creek, Kansas, but poor health soon forced her back to Missouri. She died in St. Charles in 1852. In 1988 the Roman Catholic Church, the institution that had enabled a cloistered French nun to exercise her talent, energy, and will on the American frontier, canonized Rose Philippine Duchesne.

Sources: This essay draws largely on two biographies: Louise Callen, *Philippine Duchesne, Frontier Missionary of the Sacred Heart, 1769–1852* (Westminster, Md.: The Newman Press, 1965), and Catherine M. Mooney, *Philippine Duchesne: A Woman with the Poor* (New York: Paulist Press, 1990), which are informed by Mother Duchesne's extensive correspondence housed in the archive of the Religious of the Sacred Heart at Maryville University, St. Louis County. See also Barbara O. Korner, "Philippine Duchesne: A Model of Action," *MHR* 86, no. 4 (July 1992); Louise Callen, "Rose Philippine Duchesne," in *NAW* 1, 524–25; Nikola Baumgarten, "Education and Democracy in Frontier St. Louis: The Society of the Sacred Heart," *History of Education Quarterly* 34, no. 2 (summer 1994); and Mary Ewens, *The Role of the Nun in Nineteenth Century America* (Salem, N.H.: Ayers, 1984). For a secondary school lesson plan that uses selections from Mother Duchesne's letters, see *SLAH*, Unit 2.

Scypion Sisters Versus Pierre Chouteau

In October 1805, Celeste and Catiche Scypion, two Indian-African women held as slaves by St. Louis families, filed writs of *habeas corpus* with the territorial court of Upper Louisiana. They claimed to be free women based on the status of their mother, Marie Jean Scypion, a Natchez Indian woman sold into slavery during the French regime. Although a slave under that government, Scypion would have been a free woman under the succeeding Spanish administration, which prohibited Indian slavery. Because slave status followed maternal lines, Judges J. B. C. Lucas and Rufus Easton freed the two women. The tangle of appeals and court cases that followed embroiled the Scypion family in a thirty-year struggle with prominent white St. Louis citizens for recognition as free persons. Missouri law both helped and hindered the petitioners, revealing the paradoxes in the system Americans devised to justify slavery in a democracy.

Marie Scypion was born about 1740 near Fort Chartres in present-day Illinois. Her mother was an Indian slave, and her father was a black slave named Scypion. Marie eventually became the property of Joseph Tayon, who brought her to St. Louis shortly after 1764. Spanish colonial administrators declared Indian slavery illegal, but they permitted slave owners like Tayon to retain their already enslaved Indians. Since most Indian slaves after the Spanish takeover were women, there were few full-blooded Indians enslaved in St. Louis.

Marie had three daughters in St. Louis. Their fathers may have been slave or free black men or white men, but each baby was enslaved from birth. Despite colonial slave codes that forbade breaking up slave families, Madame Tayon gave Marie's daughters, Celeste and Catiche, to her own two married daughters. Marie Scypion, who cooked and cleaned for the Tayon family, was known as a capable housekeeper as independent as her situation permitted. After his wife died, Tayon took Marie and her third daughter, Marguerite, with him to live in the household of Pierre Chouteau, reputedly a harsh slave master like his brother, Auguste.

In 1799 Tayon attempted to sell Marie and her three daughters, but his own daughters refused to give up Celeste and Catiche, insisting that the slaves had been gifts from Madame Tayon. The local Spanish official to whom Tayon appealed suggested that slaves descended from Indians could not legally be sold, so Tayon decided to back off.

Celeste and Catiche stayed with Tayon's daughters and Tayon's son took Marguerite and her daughters to his home.

As soon as the Americans took over the Louisiana Territory, Joseph Tayon again tried to sell the daughters and grandchildren of the now deceased Marie Scypion. His own daughters tried to stop the sale by raising the issue of the Scypion family's Indian ancestry. In October 1806, the daughters testified in court that the women were free Indians who worked for them voluntarily.

Although Tayon's daughters sought to thwart their father's plans and retain their domestic help, their testimony strengthened the Scypion sisters' case for freedom. Not only did they give evidence affirming Celeste and Catiche's free status, but they were also white women willing to speak in support of black women. Territorial law considered a black person's testimony against a white person invalid. As soon as Judges Lucas and Easton ruled in favor of the two Indian-African women, Marguerite filed for her freedom too. It is unlikely that Lucas, a slave owner himself, wanted to free the Scypions, but the 1804 territorial slave code had no clear instructions for determining who could legally be enslaved.

Once freed, Celeste, Catiche, and Marguerite lost no time getting out of St. Louis. The children ran away from their masters and joined their mothers in St. Charles County. An angry Joseph Tayon sought a warrant for their arrests, insisting that they were still his slaves. While the court would not return the sisters, he did retain custody of their children. Pierre Chouteau himself retrieved Marguerite without a warrant.

Later in 1806 Tayon brought the case before the court again. This time a jury had to decide whether or not the Scypions' partial Indian ancestry superseded Tayon's right to the women as his property. The foreman of the jury who decided that the Scypions were black slaves and the property of Joseph Tayon was Pierre Chouteau's brother-in-law. A month later Tayon sold most of the family to Pierre Chouteau for $1,142.

It seemed that the sisters had no other options but to remain slaves. However, nearly twenty years later, in 1824, new legislation brought them to court again. The Missouri Legislature passed a law allowing slaves who believed they were being held illegally to sue for their freedom. To resolve the contradiction of persons with no legal rights bringing suits into court, the legislature devised a petitioning process. If slaves produced evidence of their claim, the court could authorize them to sue as "poor persons." This carefully devised category accorded slaves the rights of free persons in the courtroom while maintaining their slave status outside its doors. As poor persons, slaves were entitled to legal counsel at state expense, and some of the community's most prominent lawyers represented the Scypion sisters.

In 1826, after several unsuccessful attempts by the Scypions to reopen their case for freedom, Judge George Thompson ordered the suit to proceed. Hamilton R. Gamble and other experienced attorneys represented the sisters and their children. Although the family had been separated for years, they planned their strategy together. Pierre Chouteau, furious that his slaves were once again taking him to court, hired two St. Louis attorneys with strong proslavery sentiment to defend his interests. He also beat Catiche until she filed a separate five hundred-dollar suit against him for assault and battery.

The Scypion sisters were probably only one-fourth Indian and their children only one-eighth. Missouri law held that persons with one grandparent of African descent were mulattoes, who could legally be enslaved. The sisters' case rested on their claim of maternal Indian ancestry and the illegality of Indian slavery under the Spanish government. Although Chouteau's witnesses took great pains to describe Marie's African appearance, the judge instructed the jury to consider the plaintiffs legal slaves if their grandmother had been a lawful Indian slave taken in war and sold as a slave in the French regime, facts not disputable. The jury decided against the Scypions, and the Missouri Supreme Court upheld the decision.

Five years later Marguerite's attorney asked the State Supreme Court to review its ruling, and in 1834 the court decided that the judge's 1827 instructions to the jury had been invalid. After a change of venue to Jefferson County, a new jury returned a unanimous verdict that finally set the Scypion family free. Although the jury ruled in favor of Catiche in her assault case against Pierre Chouteau, it fined him only one dollar, upholding the right of masters to treat slaves as they wished. Chouteau appealed his case against the sisters to the U.S. Supreme Court but was denied a hearing.

Although Marguerite and Catiche were still alive to enjoy their freedom in 1834, many of Marie Scypion's descendants had died in slavery. Their long struggle to prove themselves free, however, encouraged other individuals caught in the convoluted legal system of slavery to use the courts if they could see a legal way out. To perpetuate a racist social and labor system, white Missourians allowed themselves to hold any American with a black grandparent in slavery unless that slave could prove a legal exemption. Missourians consigned some people to perpetual slavery based solely on arbitrary racial categories and the legal status of their great-grandmothers, while offering them almost every option available to free persons, which included free access to skilled legal counsel if they could make a case within the system for their freedom. The thirty-year contest between three black women and their St. Louis oppressors was an example of this paradox of American democracy.

Sources: This essay is primarily a summary of William E. Foley, "Slave Freedom Suits Before Dred Scott: The Case of Marie Jean Scypion's Descendents" *MHR* 79, no. 1 (October 1984): 1–23. Foley explained this complicated story clearly and in much greater detail, providing references to the relevent legal records. Legal references usually cite *Marguerite v. Chouteau*. See also Russell M. Magnaghi, "The Role of Indian Slavery in Colonial St. Louis," *BMHS* 31, no. 4 (July 1975): 264–72; Anthony Trexler, *Slavery in Missouri, 1804–1865* (Baltimore: The Johns Hopkins Press, 1914); and Lorenzo Greene, Gary R. Kremer, and Antonio F. Holland, *Missouri's Black Heritage* (St. Louis: Forum Press, 1980) for legal status of Indians and African Americans in St. Louis. Testimony from some of the appeals the Scypions made to the Missouri Supreme Court is in Louis Houk, ed., *Reports of Cases Argued and Determined in the Supreme Court of the State of Missouri from 1821 to 1827* (St. Louis, 1890), located in the MHS library. Testimony from other appeals is available in subsequent volumes.

Mitain

In 1814 Mitain, the daughter of an influential Omaha Indian, married Manuel Lisa, a Creole fur merchant. The following year she gave birth to a daughter, and in 1818 she and Lisa had a son. Although Lisa lived in St. Louis with his white wife part of the year, he spent the winter with Mitain at Fort Lisa, the trading post he had built in 1812 on the Missouri River near present-day Omaha. When Mitain married Lisa, she knew of his other wife. She was not surprised when he told her in 1818 that he wanted to take her three-year-old daughter Rosalie back to St. Louis to live with the white people. She reluctantly consented but grieved for her lost child. Shortly afterward, while she worked in the fields, a Sioux war party ambushed her and her infant son. Mitain managed to save herself and her baby, although she suffered disfiguring facial wounds.

Before Manuel Lisa returned the following summer, he sent a message to his Indian wife. His St. Louis wife had died and he had married another white woman, Mary Hempstead. Since he was bringing his new wife to Fort Lisa, he ordered Mitain to take their baby and return to her village sixty miles upriver. Later, he sent for her, renounced the marriage, and demanded the boy. When Lisa offered her a generous present to go peacefully, Mitain reportedly replied that she would not sell her child like a dog to the man she had married for life. Why, she asked, did he hate her so much that he would banish her and take her two children?

Marriages between ambitious traders and the daughters of Siouan leaders did not all end this tragically, but because they were political arrangements made in an era of shifting alliances, they were precarious. Creole traders realized that the ability to operate in both the white and Indian worlds was essential to successful trade relations. Lisa, the Chouteau brothers, and other merchant families developed kinship networks with Indian families into the first quarter of the nineteenth century. Many led double lives as polygamists.

In the volatile political and economic climate of the trans-Mississippi West, Indians used intermarriage and honorary kinship–making unrelated people family members–to promote peace, cooperation, and trade with other groups of Indians. Because Indians in positions of power needed a steady supply of goods to distribute, they formed these relationships with Europeans as well. The Missouri River tribes were sophisticated traders, conscious of social and economic stature. They promoted marriages between families of equal rank and generous giving between "fathers" and "sons." Over time these long-term associations created kinship networks based on common language and culture. People of mixed blood, with feet in both worlds, filled an important function in the fur trade.

After the Louisiana Purchase, traders like Manuel Lisa who needed the support of the United States tried to break up alliances between the Missouri River tribes and British traders. Indians, however, frequently considered British guns and other trade goods to be of better quality than those offered by Americans. After the United States forced the British out of the American West

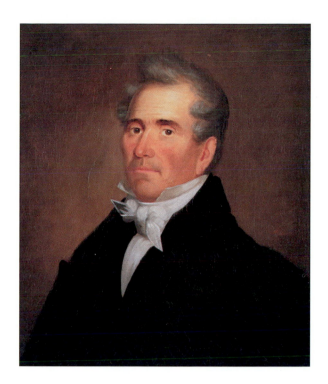

Manuel Lisa. Oil on canvas, 1818. Fur traders often had two wives, one Indian and one Creole or Anglo-American. Lisa was no exception. Though Mitain and Mary Hempstead Lisa knew of his dual marriages, the knowledge sat uneasily with both. The fur trade occasioned many such extended kinship networks that bridged two cultures. Photograph by David Schultz, 1997. MHS Art Collection

Former Lisa Residence, Second and Spruce Streets, SW Corner. Left penniless after Manuel's death, his widow Mary Hempstead Lisa's only income came from renting rooms in this house. Copy photograph of daguerreotype, ca. 1850, by H. Hazenstab, 1910. MHS–PP

in 1816, the fur trade expanded up the Missouri River. Traders and settlers poured into the Missouri Territory.

The interests of St. Louis traders shifted to the American cause once the United States took control of the Missouri River. Some second-generation Creoles, from families such as the Papins and Chouteaus, chose to marry and live in Indian Country rather than compete with Americans in St. Louis. Few Indians and whites married in St. Louis after the Louisiana Purchase, and American settlers and American culture gradually pushed the old Creole Indian bicultural population out of the area. Americans viewed a community of emigrant Indians and mixed-blood people living in Rogertown, near present-day Bridgeton, as squatters and pressured for their removal to free up the land for white settlers.

As the head of the Missouri Fur Company, Manuel Lisa sought to win Indian loyalties to the American cause, and to his own cause. Although he had opened up the Missouri River trade, he feared that his influence would decline because he now had more competitors. His proposal of marriage to Mitain was a political move designed to create an alliance with her family. He promised to treat her well and to welcome her family to his fort. He told them he would bring his and Mitain's children into the fur trade, insuring continuity between the Omahas and the American traders.

According to legend, Mitain fell deeply in love with Lisa, but she simply may have expected him to keep his end of the bargain. He might have, had he not married Mary Hempstead. She was the daughter of a Connecticut Revolutionary soldier, the sister of some of the most energetic, influential Americans in town, and a founding member of the First Presbyterian Church of St. Louis. French Creole women, like Lisa's first wife, had more tolerance for Indian "country wives" and a much higher comfort level with Indian culture, developed over years of interaction. Most Anglo-Americans wanted only to eliminate them. Timothy Flint, a Presbyterian missionary active in Missouri from 1815 to 1825, denounced racial "amalgamation." He opposed intermarriage between Americans and Indians, whom he characterized as filthy and drunken. Flint saw a "natural affinity between Catholic Creoles and Indians" but not between Indians and Protestant Americans. By 1825 Indian removal from Missouri was American policy; the last Indians left the eastern half of the state in 1833.

Mitain did not give up her son to Manuel Lisa in 1818. She had asked him to let her live near the boy in St. Louis, and when Lisa denied her request, she refused to surrender him. Only the intervention of Colonel John O'Fallon, a prominent American St. Louisan, prevented Lisa from taking him by force. Mitain and her son stayed with the Omahas. In 1833 members of Prince Maximilian's expedition going up the Missouri River glimpsed a woman with scars like hers on a riverbank.

Lisa placed Mitain's daughter Rosalie with a white family. After his death in 1820, she lived for a while with his widow, Mary Hempstead Lisa. In 1842 Rosalie married an Illinois farmer who was also a Baptist preacher. She had eight children and died at age eighty-nine in 1904.

Sources: Mitain's story comes primarily from two biographies of Manuel Lisa: Walter B. Douglas, "Manuel Lisa," *MHS Collections* 3 (1912), and Richard E. Oglesby, *Manuel Lisa and the Opening of the Missouri Fur Trade* (Norman: University of Oklahoma Press, 1963). The account of Mitain's abandonment appears in Edwin James, *Account of an Expedition from Pittsburgh to the Rocky Mountains: Under the Command of Major Stephen Long* (Barre, Mass.: Imprint Society, 1972), 393–400.

Information and analysis placing Mitain's story in the context of Indian-White relations comes from Tanis C. Thorne, *The Many Hands of My Relations: French and Indians on the Lower Mississippi* (Columbia: University of Missouri Press, 1996), 111–33. For Rogertown and Indian-White relations on the Lower Mississippi, see John Mack Faragher, "'More Motley than Mackinaw': From Ethnic Mixing to Ethnic Cleansing on the Frontier of the Lower Missouri, 1783–1833," in *Contact Points: American Frontiers from the Mohawk Valley to the Mississippi, 1750–1830*, eds., Andrew R. L. Cayton and Fredrika J. Teute (Chapel Hill: University of North Carolina Press, 1998).

Mary Hempstead Lisa

In 1810 Mary Hempstead Keeny, a thirty-three-year-old widow with a young son, lived in Connecticut with her parents. Because her husband's estate had gone to his creditors, she was financially dependent on her father, Stephen Hempstead. Her three brothers, who had moved to St. Louis, were part of the vanguard of American fortune-seekers hurrying west after the Louisiana transfer of 1804. Already prominent in business and politics, they convinced their father to buy a farm five miles north of St. Louis on the Bellefontaine Road. Mary's move to Missouri brought her a marriage to a Spanish Creole fur trader, a richly furnished St. Louis home, and the opportunity to visit Indian villages far up the Missouri River. However, frontier economic volatility and territorial inheritance laws that favored creditors over widows combined to again leave Mary Hempstead Lisa destitute and dependent on her family. Because they had so few options in territorial Missouri, women's welfare depended even more than men's on accidents of good luck and timing.

Between 1811 and 1818 Mary and her son, Christopher, lived on the Bellefontaine farm where her father and his slaves raised corn and livestock. Her daily life revolved around her extended family and St. Louis's First Presbyterian Church, of which she was a founding member.

The Hempstead brothers dealt daily with the merchant capitalists of the Creole elite. Through these business connections Mary met Manuel Lisa. One of the most flamboyant and successful of the Missouri River fur traders, Lisa kept an Omaha Indian wife, Mitain, and two children upriver. His legal wife, Polly, who lived in St. Louis, died in the winter of 1818. Six months later Lisa and Mary Hempstead married.

The union between the hot-tempered Catholic Creole fur trader and the New England Protestant widow might have surprised their contemporaries, but surviving correspondence suggests mutual affection and concern. In 1819 Mary Lisa became one of the first white women to travel in Indian Country when she accompanied her husband to Fort Lisa, his fur-trading post near present-day Omaha, Nebraska.

In St. Louis the Lisas lived in a lavishly furnished brick house on Main Street. Among their many possessions were three dozen dining room chairs, about ten dozen dinner plates, and an elaborate chandelier. In her own home, whether or not its opulence reflected her taste, Mary was no longer her family's poor relation.

Mary's world collapsed when Manuel Lisa died suddenly in 1820. The fur trade lived on credit, and Manuel had mortgaged everything he and Mary owned. When the Missouri Fur Company failed after his death, Mary lost everything to her husband's creditors. She was in part a victim of bad timing. Although the old Spanish common property laws had long been abolished, until 1817 Mary was entitled to one-third of her husband's property–her dower–ahead of any other claims on the estate. But in that year the territorial legislature changed the law to give a widow her share only after all just claims on the

estate were paid. After 1825, Missouri law protected a widow's dower, but these reforms came too late for Mary Lisa.

Mary's only income after Manuel's death was the rent from a house at Second and Spruce, an earlier bequest from her brother. She could not depend on her beloved, feckless son, Christopher, who died young and in debt. Moreover, the crushing depression of the early 1820s depleted her father's holdings. Until she died at age eighty-seven, "Aunt Manuel," as they called her, boarded with her surviving brothers' families, caring for children, nursing the sick, and serving the Presbyterian Church.

Sources: Steven Hempstead kept a daily diary in which he briefly recorded the activities of his large family, including Mary. This analysis of her financial resources draws mainly on her father's diary, the few letters she

Mary Hempstead Lisa. Oil on canvas, ca. 1818. MHS Art Collection

sent and received from family members in the Hempstead and Manual Lisa Collections at MHS, letters about her in the William Clark Papers, and the available primary and secondary sources on the business affairs of the men in her life. For information about Mary Hempstead Lisa, see *SLAH*, Unit 2; Douglas, "Manuel Lisa"; and Oglesby, *Manuel Lisa and the Opening of the Missouri Fur Trade*.

These sources describe the ruin of Manuel Lisa's fortune, but they do not analyze it from his widow's perspective. Correspondence, legal records, newspaper articles, and other manuscript material about prominent St. Louis men frequently contain evidence useful for uncovering the experiences of their wives and daughters. The class bias inherent in these archival collections is, of course, as true for women as for men. Other manuscript collections from the families of prominent St. Louisans of this period that contain information about female family members include Chouteau Collection, James Campbell Papers, Antoine Soulard Papers, Sublette Papers, DeMun Papers, William Carr Lane Papers, John B. C. Lucas Papers, among others. Like many early American residents, Mary Hempstead Lisa helped found a Protestant church. Women were also instrumental in founding Methodist, Baptist, and Episcopal congregations in St. Louis, and the records of their influence are contained in the various church archives.

Anna Maria von Phul

In the spring of 1818, Anna Maria von Phul arrived in St. Louis to visit her merchant brother and his family. At age thirty-two, she still hoped for marriage, perhaps to an interesting man of her brother's social circle. She brought some art supplies with her from Lexington, Kentucky, and during the summer filled a portfolio with watercolors of Creole fashions, buildings, and local street life. Anna Maria von Phul's romantic sketches and paintings are some of the earliest St. Louis images to survive into the twentieth century. Her impressions of a fading Creole culture are, however, more valuable for their rarity than their artistry. As art, they are similar to the drawings made by dozens of young women educated on the urban frontier, for whom painting was a personally satisfying and socially acceptable means of creative expression.

In 1800, Catherine von Phul, Anna Maria's mother, moved her family to Lexington, Kentucky. She had recently lost her husband and several children to yellow fever in Philadelphia. Known as the most cultured city in the West, Lexington was a promising place to start over. Catherine enrolled

Two Young Ladies. Watercolor on paper by Anna Maria von Phul, 1818. MHS Art Collection

Creole Woman with Bucket and Boy. Watercolor on paper by Anna Maria von Phul, 1818. MHS Art Collection

fourteen-year-old Anna Maria in Mrs. Beck's young ladies' academy, where the curriculum stressed drawing and watercolor. Painting, like needlework, was an essential domestic skill for all accomplished women of Anna Maria's social class. Her teachers considered her talented.

Catherine von Phul died in 1810. Her two sons soon left Lexington in search of careers. Henry von Phul took his chances in St. Louis, where he went into business and married Rosalie Saugrain, from one of the community's leading French families. Anna Maria remained in Lexington with her widowed sister, attending social events that might lead to marriage. Family members, and even local painters, encouraged her to continue drawing, but no one, least of all Anna Maria, considered her art to be more than a pleasant diversion. As she prepared to visit St. Louis in 1818, she doubtless had more than art on her mind. She already considered herself a spinster and a failure at her most important job—finding a suitable husband.

In St. Louis, Anna Maria was welcomed into her sister-in-law's circle of old Creole families. She enjoyed their society and her visits to Madame Saugrain's famous garden on Second Street, near Mulberry. Anna Maria's St. Louis drawings reflect a tourist's fascination with an exotic culture very different from Philadelphia or Lexington.

Anna Maria von Phul failed to find a husband during her summer in St. Louis. Back home in Lexington at least one good prospect married someone else. In 1821 she left Kentucky for good. When not visiting her remarried sister in Edwardsville, Illinois, Anna Maria lived with her brother in St. Louis. There, she tried to turn a profit from art by selling paintings on consignment from a Lexington dealer, but her attempt at business failed. In 1823 Anna Maria von Phul died in Edwardsville.

Sources: The Missouri Historical Society received the von Phul drawings in 1953 from a descendant of Anna Maria's brother, Henry. Material used to reconstruct the artist's biography came from the von Phul, Saugrain, and McCree Manuscript Collections. Articles based on the collections and papers include Charles van Ravenswaay, "Anna Maria von Phul," *BMHS* 10, no. 3 (April 1954), and Karen McCoskey Goering, "St. Louis Women Artists 1818–1945: An Exhibition," *GH* 3, no. 1 (summer 1982). Many examples of creative work made by St. Louis women in the early nineteenth century are in the MHS collections and provide a material culture link to the lives of women who are, for the most part, otherwise unknown.

Mary Paddock's Boardinghouse

Mary Paddock was a married woman who earned money working at home. From 1818 to 1831 she helped support her family by running a St. Louis boardinghouse. The boardinghouse provided income and a home for her and some of her children, and its success enabled her husband, Gaius, to buy land and build a family farm near Edwardsville, Illinois. Like many other families, the Paddocks' income depended as much on her work as his.

On September 15, 1815, Gaius and Mary Paddock took nine of their ten children and their new son-in-law and left Woodstock, Vermont, for St. Louis. It was a hazardous trip down the Ohio River to Cincinnati, where they spent the winter before settling for a while in St. Charles. By 1817 the family had moved to St. Louis, where Gaius looked for a suitable home.

Anna Maria von Phul. Photograph of painting. MHS–PP

Running a boardinghouse was an ideal business for a woman with a family; it capitalized on domestic skills and fit in with raising children. Moreover, it provided the older children with work, particularly the girls, who expected to stay in the home until they married. Apart from the demand for lodgings in the growing frontier river city, boardinghouses provided socially acceptable places for women to earn money and not upset the gender division of labor. Widows and single woman often owned or managed boardinghouses.

"Mrs. Paddock's" was well-known in the city, often serving as a directional landmark. St. Louisans considered the Paddocks a respectable family with boarders of the best class. Mary acquired a reputation for giving extra care to some of her guests; in one case she nursed a young Frenchman until he died. Reportedly, Chester Harding, who boarded at Paddock's, painted a portrait of his landlady as a dignified, bonneted woman.

However, not all her guests were so complimentary. Margaret Hunter Hall, a snobbish Englishwoman who traveled America finding fault, dismissed Mrs. Paddock's as "the worst we have yet been in." She found the Paddock daughters quite civil, but their mother "a little, blunt, niggardly Yankee" who squeezed "all she [could] out of her boarders."

Gaius died in August 1831. After his death, Mary and her five unmarried daughters, aged between twenty-four and forty-one, moved to the farm, known then as Paddock's Grove. They still needed to generate additional income. Mrs. Paddock was paid at least once for carding wool, and later received a pension for Gaius's service in the Revolutionary War. Susan raised and sold bulbs and plants. She and sister Joanna made and sold a local delicacy, "log farm cheese." Sister Mary taught school at various times in Springfield, Illinois. Susan dispatched at least one lot of twenty pairs of socks to sell in St. Louis. In addition to producing income or goods for sale or their own consumption, the women supported each other emotionally: siblings wrote often, made extended visits, and helped each other in periods of illness or financial stress. It was unusual for the time and place that none of the sisters married.

The activities of Mrs. Paddock and her daughters illustrate the importance of women's work, paid and unpaid, to family welfare on the urban frontier. The five Paddock sisters and their mother were literate, competent, energetic, and responsible individuals who actively participated in the region's market economy.

In 1818 Gaius, disgusted by city life and the presence of slavery in Missouri, retreated to the Illinois countryside. He and his son-in-law bought a large tract of farmland. Because the land needed work, time, and money, Mary agreed to remain in St. Louis with the family while he improved the farm.

Gaius was fifty-nine when he, a son, his son-in-law, and a hired man started clearing his land and building a house. By 1819 Gaius had developed the farm enough for Susan, a twenty-seven-year-old unmarried daughter, to move from St. Louis and assume the domestic duties. Mary, now fifty, remained in St. Louis and looked after the rest of the family. After Susan left in 1819, Mary Paddock probably had seven of her children with her; one married and five unmarried daughters and one son, ranging in age from fourteen to thirty-one. The boardinghouse, which may have opened earlier, appeared in the first St. Louis Directory in 1821, listed as "Paddock, Gaius. Boarding house, 24 north Main, N.W. corner A."

Mary Wood Paddock. Oil on canvas, artist unknown. MHS Art Collection

—Joan Cooper

Sources: For additional information, see the Paddock Family Papers; Frederic Billon, *Annals of St. Louis in its Territorial Days, 1804–1921* (St. Louis, 1888); John A. Paxton, *The St. Louis Directory and Register* (St. Louis, 1821); Una Pope-Hennessy, ed., *The Aristocratic Journey: Being the Outspoken Letters of Mrs. Basil Hall Written During a Fourteen Months' Sojourn in America, 1827–1828* (London, 1931); and Charles van Ravenswaay, *St. Louis: An Informal History of the City and Its People, 1764–1865* (St. Louis: MHS Press, 1991).

Female Charitable Society of St. Louis

In 1824 a group of women met in the St. Louis home of Marguerite McNair, the wife of Alexander McNair, then serving as Missouri's first governor. Some of the women, like McNair herself, were French Catholics, but others were American Protestants like her husband. Everyone in the room had two things in common: each was married to a prominent St. Louisan and each hoped in some way to "relieve distressed females and children" and "encourage industry among the poor." Several had only recently moved to St. Louis from the East.

These women founded the Female Charitable Society of St. Louis, the city's first organized benevolent association. Praised by the clergy at its inception for "producing a happy union of Catholic and Protestant, French and American ladies," the society did not survive long enough to leave any record of its accomplishments. Women's charitable associations that endured in nineteenth-century St. Louis were organized along religious, racial, and ethnic lines. The impulse to organize for benevolence rose out of domestic concerns that transcended the social divisiveness of ethnicity and faith on the urban frontier. But the society's membership may have been unable to set aside their differences long enough to agree on implementation.

The new organization's bylaws gave explicit instructions for collecting the members' annual dues of one dollar and distributing aid to the needy. A board of sixteen managers, headed by a first directress, conducted the society's affairs. Board members made recommendations and decided on a case-by-case basis who should receive the emergency financial assistance. The treasurer collected the dues, distributed money by order of the board, and reported to the membership twice a year. There were no explicit guidelines for encouraging industry to the poor. In 1824 there were 170 members.

Perhaps inspired by similar efforts in eastern cities and possibly more significant than the organization itself, the Female Charitable Society's constitution was a remarkable document. As an explicit expression of attitudes more widespread in subsequent decades, its rhetoric is as self-consciously ironic as it is genuinely heartfelt and persuasive.

Responding to claims that charities drew women from "the retired sphere of domestic duty which Providence has assigned them," the preamble to the new society's constitution asserted that organized benevolence was a proper female activity. They reminded potential critics that Christianity encouraged believers to reach out to the suffering beyond one's own family.

Since St. Louisans had already demonstrated the "superiority of social and combined effort, to individual exertion, in every other pursuit," surely women working together could do more good for the suffering than each could do alone. Although "sensitive unobtrusive delicacy, which retires from the world's broad stare, is indeed one of the most lovely traits in the female character," women should not shrink from their acknowledged duty simply because it is performed in public. Business and government were properly the concerns of men, but might not women "claim . . . the more humble field of benevolence as their appropriate sphere of action; where they may employ to advantage whatever portion of time, of wealth, and of mental energy, they may have to spare from the service of their families?" By blurring the

Governor and Mrs. Alexander McNair's Residence. Ink on paper by Clarence Hoblitzelle, 1898. MHS Art Collection

boundaries between public and private life, the constitution of the Female Charitable Society stands as an early benchmark of the shifting social geography of women's place in St. Louis.

Sources: The standard historical sources for this period briefly mention the founding of the Female Charitable Society, and none discuss the success or failure of its work. Its constitution, however, is a particularly useful document for discussing the arguments women used to justify their public activity in this period. All quotations are from a copy of the constitution and bylaws, printed in 1924 and available at MHS.

Whether or not the society persisted, the constitution shows that St. Louis women acted and thought the way middle-class women did in other urban areas. See Scott, *Natural Allies*, for an in-depth discussion of the Female Charitable Society movement.

The usefulness of the concept of "separate spheres" of activity for women and men is a contested issue in women's history, considered by some to be more of an intellectual construct than a description of how women acted at the time. See Linda Kerber, *Toward an Intellectual History of Women: Essays* (Chapel Hill: University of North Carolina Press, 1997) for a full discussion of the controversy. Since the women who wrote the Female Charitable Society constitution in 1824 used the expression to describe commonly accepted ideas about women's proper place in the community, one should take it seriously as evidence of early nineteenth-century ideology, if not reality.

Elizabeth

Elizabeth, an enslaved African American, lived in St. Louis from 1827 to 1832 when she was sold down the Mississippi River to a slave trader in New Orleans. She spent her final days in St. Louis imprisoned, probably at the City Jail at Sixth and Olive Streets. Elizabeth had seven children by seven different men. Two of her children died young; one was sold to another owner and three left no traces. One escaped from slavery, renamed himself William Wells Brown, and became an abolitionist lecturer and writer. He wrote about his and Elizabeth's experiences in the *Narrative of William Wells Brown, a Fugitive Slave, Written by Himself,* published in 1847.

Though Elizabeth bore seven children, she had little control over her domestic life. William's father was a white relative of her master, John Young. Elizabeth carried her newborn on her back while she worked the fields and was whipped for leaving her work to nurse him. In 1814 Young moved Elizabeth and her children from Lexington, Kentucky, to Missouri, where she worked as a field hand until 1827. Shortly after he arrived in St. Louis, Young sold Elizabeth and all of her children, except William, to other St. Louisans. Elizabeth and three of her five living children belonged to Isaac Mansfield. This proximity to her family did not last. Mansfield sold her daughter in 1832, and Elizabeth never saw her again.

Following his sister's sale, William persuaded his mother to flee to Canada. It was not an easy decision on Elizabeth's part, for she was reluctant to leave her other children behind in slavery. She and William escaped across the river, but 150 miles from St. Louis in the free state of Illinois, slave catchers apprehended them and returned them to the city.

In St. Louis, the slave catchers put Elizabeth in jail, and a few weeks later, Mansfield sold her to a slave trader who would sell her to a southern plantation. She may have spent time in Lynch's slave pen at the corner of Fifth and Myrtle Streets. The pen consisted of one room, plastered, with one small window high up near the ceiling. The floor was bare earth, and three backless, wooden benches stood next to the walls. Both men and women shared this space.

Because Brown could not gain access to the jail to say good-bye to her, Elizabeth did not see her son until the day she left for New Orleans. He found his mother on the levee "in company with fifty or sixty other slaves. She was chained to another woman. On seeing me, she immediately dropped her head upon her heaving bosom. She moved not, neither did she weep. Her emotions were too deep for tears." Elizabeth urged her son to escape from slavery and told him, "Do not, I pray you, weep for me. I cannot last long upon a cotton plantation." It was the last time Elizabeth saw her son.

Elizabeth's public and private lives were not as clearly divided as they were for white women. She could not keep separate her domestic life and her work. She lived near the fields that she tilled and harvested and most likely did cooking, laundry, and other household chores with other slave women. Because she was her master's property, however, she could not legally protect herself from sexual exploitation or other intrusions on her privacy.

In St. Louis, her owner hired out Elizabeth to a third party, a common practice in cities; in most cases, owners received the slave's wages. Many women worked as laundresses, seamstresses, and domestic servants. Slaves hired out by their owners faced different opportunities and constraints than those working in gangs on plantations.

The practice often meant that slaves worked both as full-time wage laborers and as part-time servants for their masters. The substitution of wage labor for domestic servitude allowed slaves a degree of privacy from their owners, but white citizens also feared slaves who walked around as if they were free. St. Louis supplied many slaves to the southern states; the threat of being "sold down the river" was not an idle one in a city situated on the Mississippi in the early 1800s.

An enslaved woman's situation regarding work and family was deeply paradoxical. Enslaved women were valued for their ability to bear children, who by law were born slaves. But masters also expected enslaved women to work whenever possible, and many did so while pregnant and nursing. Though enslaved women were encouraged and sometimes forced to bear children, they generally were not permitted to have close relationships with them. Often, mother and child were sold to different masters. Some had opportunities to forge relationships with their sons and daughters. This was easier for urban slaves, as cities held denser populations and slaves had more mobility under the hiring-out system. Thus, Elizabeth could see her son regularly, though they had different masters.

The proximity of St. Louis to the free state of Illinois gave slaves more opportunities to run away and made slaveholders less secure of their control. This produced a system of slavery less stable than that on the cotton plantations farther down the Mississippi. And while slaves escaped more easily, they were often caught, as Elizabeth and her son were. Those who remained in slavery suffered the often unpredictable violence of masters.

–*Katherine Douglass*

Sources: We do not know when or where Elizabeth was born. As with many slaves, material evidence of her life is hard to find. There are no receipts, real estate deeds, or tax papers relating to her. Slaves were prohibited from buying and selling commodities, and those who conducted business with a slave without the owner's permission were liable for four times the value of the item bought, sold, or received. Though Elizabeth was considered the property of her master, Isaac Mansfield, there are no records of her life or her sale to a slave trader in 1832. The few recorded facts about Elizabeth come from her son, William Wells Brown, who escaped from slavery and later recorded his experiences in his memoir, *Narrative of William Wells Brown*. Originally published in 1847 by the Anti-Slavery Office, an abolitionist group in Boston, Massachusetts, Brown's narrative recounts his life as a slave in Lexington, Kentucky, and in St. Louis, ending with his escape to Canada in 1834. Though

undoubtedly motivated in part by his personal experience, Brown's tale also served the larger goal of abolishing slavery within the United States. As such, the narrative must be seen as a political tract in addition to a memoir. All quoted material in this piece comes from Brown's book.

Background information on St. Louis during this time is from Katharine Corbett, "History and Memory: The St. Louis of William Wells Brown," unpublished manuscript; Lloyd A. Hunter, "Slavery in St. Louis, 1804–1860," *BMHS* 30, no. 4 (July 1974): 233–65; and Maximilian Reichard, "Black and White on the Urban Frontier: The St. Louis Community in Transition, 1800–1830," *BMHS* 33, no. 1 (October 1976): 3–17. Widely recognized as the seminal work on American women in slavery is Jacqueline Jones, *Labor of Love, Labor of Sorrow: Black Women, Work, and the Family from Slavery to the Present* (New York: Basic Books, 1985).

See also the 1830 census of St. Louis, MHS; and to learn more on slave laws, see "A Law Entitled a Law Respecting Slaves," in *Laws of a Public and General Nature, of the District of Louisiana, of the Territory of Louisiana, of the Territory of Missouri, and of the State of Missouri, Up to the Year 1824*, vol. 1 (Jefferson City, 1842), 27–33.

Sisters of Charity

On November 25, 1828, four Roman Catholic nuns, Sisters of Charity, arrived in St. Louis to open a hospital in some old frame buildings near the corner of Spruce and Third Streets. They had never been so far west. Founded in Emmetsburg, Maryland, in 1809 by Elizabeth Seton and later affiliated with the Daughters of Charity of St. Vincent de Paul of France, the American Sisters of Charity dedicated their lives to providing hospitals, orphan homes, and institutions for the insane. They helped fund their charitable institutions by operating academies for young ladies. When John Mullanphy, a local Catholic businessman, offered land and an endowment for the city's first hospital, Bishop Joseph Rosati immediately wrote to Emmetsburg: "Please, send the Sisters."

The hospital's primary mission was to serve the poor and "strangers" who had no family to care for them. Patients were, as the bishop explained in 1830, "a large number of laborers, sailors, negroes and others who are there received, gratis, and treated with kindness and solicitude," Protestant and Catholic alike. Under the supervision of Sister Frances Xaverius, Superior, the nuns made do in the old buildings until Mullanphy and other St. Louisans, both Catholic and Protestant, provided more funds.

In 1831 the sisters built a new hospital on the southeast corner of Spruce and Fourth, followed by a convent and orphanage in Carondelet. In 1836 they opened a boys' orphan asylum and school just west of the Cathedral on Second Street. Support for these institutions came not only from private donations and the church, but also from a state-sanctioned lottery that raised ten thousand dollars in 1833 and an 1834 fair staged by "prominent young ladies and matrons of the city" at the National Hotel.

During the 1832 Asiatic cholera epidemic, the city sent all cholera patients to the "Sisters' Hospital." Two of the eight nuns died nursing victims; three more arrived from Emmetsburg to take their place. By 1838 the city paid the nuns 31 cents a day to care for indigent patients because there was no public hospital or poor house.

Although most people still looked upon hospitals as places where the poor went to die, some solvent St. Louisans now chose to go to the Sisters' Mullanphy Hospital, renamed for its benefactor. Hospital fees, the city subsidy, and the unpaid work of the sisters made the institution economically viable. The hospital was a godsend to a booming frontier city still too new and raw to have social infrastructure, and still reeling from cholera. Founded by private philanthropy, managed by a female religious order, the Sisters' Mullanphy Hospital nonetheless served the whole community. In 1844–1845, 659 people received hospital care at a cost to the city of $18,000. Only twelve of these patients had been born in Missouri. German and

Hospital of the Sisters of Charity. Engraving from *Thoughts on the City of St. Louis* by John Hogan, 1854. MHS–PP

Irish immigrants accounted for 355 of the total. Although the rate charged for indigent patients did not cover the cost of their care, in the late 1840s the city built its own public hospital to save money.

In 1838, Henry Miller, an itinerant Protestant stonemason from Pennsylvania, praised the hospital in his journal: "Persons are taken care of there for $3.50 per week; this is no more than the common price of boarding in the city. . . . Last year there was a wing put up larger than the former or center building; and this summer there is another going up at the East. . . . I have been informed by some who have been there that they were treated with the greatest attention by the Sisters. This institution is a blessing to the City."

Sources: Information on the Daughters' of Charity extensive work in health care is found in John C. Crighton, *The History of Health Services in Missouri* (Omaha, Neb.: Barnhart Press, 1993), and Mother Anne Kathryn Webster, R.S.C.J., "The Impact of Catholic Hospitals in St. Louis" (Ph.D. dissertation, Saint Louis University, 1955). See also J. Thomas Scharf, *History of St. Louis City and County*, vol. 2 (Philadelphia: L. H. Everts & Co., 1883), 1549, and Thomas M. Marshall, ed., "Journal of Henry B. Miller," *MHS Collections* 6 (1931): 257. The Daughters of Charity maintain an archive at 7800 Natural Bridge Road, the former site of the order's Marillac College.

Anne Ewing Lane

Anne Ewing Lane grew up unusually bright, high-spirited, and by her father's and her own estimation, plain and opinionated. St. Louis Mayor William Carr Lane was a proud father and wanted the best for his daughters. He saw to it that Anne and her younger sister, Sarah, were well educated, both in St. Louis and Philadelphia, and trained in the social graces that would lead to good marriages. Lane worried most about Anne, whom he thought the brighter but less attractive and sweet-tempered of the girls. He hoped she would return from her eastern boarding school not only "vastly learned– scientific in every way accomplished," but also "good tempered–kind-hearted & benevolent." William Carr Lane's admonitions that his eldest daughter be both smart and sweet haunted Anne throughout her life. Her efforts to live up to his and her own expectations reveal many of the tensions between female potential and woman's place in antebellum St. Louis.

William Carr Lane was born in Pennsylvania and took medical training in Philadelphia. In 1816, while serving in the military, he met Mary Ewing, whose large family farmed near Vincennes, Indiana. They married two years later, while Lane was stationed at Fort Bellefontaine, just north of St. Louis. Anne was born in 1819 at her grandparents' Indiana farm. Soon afterward Lane left the army, settled in boom-town St. Louis, and opened a medical practice. Ambitious and energetic, he quickly broadened his St. Louis interests from medicine to land speculation, business investments, and local politics. Lane served eight terms as mayor and one term in the Missouri Legislature.

Meanwhile, Mary Ewing Lane bore eight children, but only Anne and Sarah survived to maturity. Illness, death, and melancholy consumed Mary's life. Following the death of the first of three daughters all named Julia, Mary turned to her family for consolation. "The anxiety that I suffer . . . until all life is fled is more than I can bear," responded a sister who had also buried infants. "I look at them with a certainty of seeing them a corpse in a few days." With each child's death, Mary withdrew further from society and even from her husband and surviving daughters. She retreated more and more from St. Louis, spending months at a time at her parents' Indiana home.

Like many St. Louisans in the 1820s, the Lanes moved frequently. Their household was always unsettled, their domestic privacy frequently interrupted by patients calling on Dr. Lane. Sometimes when Mary was away, the Lanes hired out their slaves and roomed in a boardinghouse. When she was in residence the family more often "went to housekeeping," living for several years in the 1820s in a two-story frame house at 127 South Main Street.

As Lane prospered, he bought property and more slaves, some of which he conveyed to his wife and daughters for their financial security—and to protect these valuable assets from creditors. When times were hard, Lane rented the family home and moved into more cramped quarters. In 1837 they lived at 24 North Fifth Street.

In the mid-1820s Anne and Sarah attended Mother Philippine Duchesne's school for girls, in spite of their father's nagging Protestant suspicions that the sisters were "meddling with my children's faith." When poor health forced Anne to leave the Academy of the Sacred Heart in 1830, Duchesne wrote regretfully to Lane that losing "a student so intelligent is truly a sacrifice." Mother Duchesne added, "The praise I give my dear Anne takes nothing from her sister, Sarah, whose excellent heart deserves a return of affection."

Between her ninth and eleventh years, Anne boarded in Lexington, Kentucky, receiving treatment at the home of a physician probably for scoliosis of the spine. Although she studied French and knitting, her letters described lonely hours kept immobile, "lying on the floor sometimes reading but very often doing nothing."

By 1834 both Anne and Sarah were in Philadelphia studying at Madame Signoigne's fashionable school for girls. Although their mother rarely wrote, William Carr Lane maintained a regular correspondence, filling his letters with fatherly advice. He cautioned Sarah against vanity and urged her to be kind and ladylike. He admonished Anne to do the same, reminding her that she was "the more fretful of the two." When he sent books to both girls he explained to Anne: "Sarah's will amuse her. . . . As for your books they will instruct you." He directed them to spend their time studying, not in hunting husbands. Proud of their academic accomplishments, Lane felt they have enough time for marriage when they returned to St. Louis.

Both father and daughters knew full well that few employment opportunities for educated women of their class existed in St. Louis. Marriage offered the most security and status. Spinsterhood

Anne Ewing Lane. Ambrotype by Enoch Long, ca. 1858. MHS–PP usually left women dependent on relatives, never sure of their welcome or their future. Lane made every effort to insure that his daughters would never need to support themselves. Before Anne and Sarah returned from Philadelphia, he had promised to give each of them at least five thousand dollars to secure their economic independence.

When Anne and Sarah completed their formal educations in 1837, Anne was just eighteen, Sarah sixteen. They left Philadelphia with a reading list of historical classics, including Plutarch and Gibbon. Back in St. Louis, they joined the social round of local polite society–a whirl of formal calls, parties, and theatricals designed to encourage marriage proposals.

Sarah married at nineteen. Her husband, William Glasgow, Jr., had prominent Missouri family ties and had recently moved to St. Louis to join his uncle in real estate. William Carr Lane prepared a marriage contract for Sarah that gave her complete control over all the assets brought to the marriage and any she might acquire from her parents later on. Her mother did not return from Indiana for the wedding.

Anne turned twenty-two in 1840. She considered herself a failure, a spinster with no prospects. She wrote bitterly to her married sister, who had urged her to return to St. Louis from a long visit in Indiana, "You know you all came to the conclusion that I was neither useful or ornamental and only in your way."

Anne Ewing Lane never married, and her parents never quite let her forget their disappointment. She hoped she might fall in love but waited in vain for the right man. "Well Mama if I ever get a chance I intend to make you all happy. . . . They say no woman ever lived who had not one chance of getting married and if that is true I will not die an old maid for mine is to come yet and I am resolved to avail myself of it. Are you satisfied!"

She remained her father's devoted confidante and companion and, ironically, surrogate mother to several of her eventually invalid sister's ten children. She traveled extensively in later life, including trips to Europe. Although she always expressed strong private opinions on a wide range of social and political issues, she never gave them public voice. Anne Ewing Lane remained a person awkwardly out of place, unable to reconcile her independent spirit and intellectual abilities with the qualities of personality and female ambition both she and her culture valued.

Sources: This essay is based on the large and unusually rich collection of William Carr Lane Family Papers at MHS. Because the Lanes had close personal ties but often lived apart for long periods, their letters preserved interchanges between family members that would never have been recorded had they happened face-to-face. Nonetheless, the Lane papers require close reading and interpretation. Historians can never take personal correspondence at face value, because people write what they want others to read, not necessarily what they believe. Family letters also reflect internal family dynamics and broader contexts known best—or known only—to the correspondents themselves.

Although most accounts of St. Louis in the nineteenth century include information about William Carr Lane, the most comprehensive is an introduction to a selection of his letters: Stella Drumm and Isaac L. Lionberger, "Introduction to the Letters of William Carr Lane," *Glimpses of the Past* 7, no. 1 (January 1940). An article about Anne Ewing Lane published by a descendant makes no attempt to interpret the primary materials in the context of women's history: William Glasgow Bruce Carson, "Anne Ewing Lane," *BMHS* 21, no. 2 (January 1965).

Mary Easton Sibley

Spiritually awakened by a religious conversion in 1832, Mary Easton Sibley embraced her new calling. She believed it her duty to impart knowledge, morality, and Protestant Christianity to young people on the Missouri frontier. She pursued this mission ambitiously in three separate ways. She sought to Americanize European immigrants, especially Germans, by teaching them English through the Presbyterian Sabbath School. She established a separate African school to educate blacks, both slave and free, preparing them for colonization in Africa. Finally, she founded a boarding school in St. Charles, Missouri, for young, white women, which grew into Lindenwood College.

The eldest daughter of Rufus and Abby Easton, Mary grew up in the Missouri Territory. Her father, a prominent lawyer, became Missouri State Attorney General by 1821. Additionally, Rufus Easton left a permanent mark by founding Alton, Illinois, which he named after Mary's brother, Alton.

The man Mary chose as her husband had similarly serious ambitions. George Sibley, a thirty-three-year-old government Indian agent and friend of William Clark, surveyed the entire Santa Fe Trail and invested in large tracts of land in St. Charles. A new bride of fifteen, Mary accompanied George to

Fort Osage in western Missouri, where he served as a mediator between the United States government and the Osage Indians. Watching Christian missionaries promote Anglo civilization at the fort, Mary became convinced that the "country will never prosper unless the people get knowledge."

By 1828, the Sibleys moved back to St. Charles, and Mary's education project began to take shape. Through the Presbyterian Church, she offered to help teach English to German immigrants, whom she feared would otherwise become "the dupes of Political demagogues." The offer of free sectarian schooling attracted immigrants and also provided an opportunity to proselytize new members of the church.

Mary also sought to spread the gospel and teach free blacks and slaves how to read through her African school, founded in 1834. By educating blacks, she sought to mold them into future citizens and leaders of West Africa. Like many antislavery advocates, Mary was a member of the American Colonization Society, which favored the relocation of blacks to Africa. With gradual immigration, she believed that slavery would slowly end and racial strife diminish, thus creating a white American republic. The African School was well attended, and Mary recorded that she never felt happier or more confident that she was "doing some good." However, a critic leveled "misrepresentations" about the school, most likely accusations that she promoted ideas of freedom and encouraged slaves to revolt. Mary regretted that one by one, students "returned their books and said they were forbid [sic] to attend by their masters."

George did not share Mary's views about abolition. He owned at least five slaves and found slaveholding compatible with his religious beliefs. Infuriated with the antislavery rhetoric of Elijah Lovejoy, the well-known local abolitionist and publisher of the *Alton Observer*, George sparred regularly with him. Accusing Lovejoy of "insulting vituperation" of Christians, as well as printing articles "seriously injurious to the cause of truth, religion and sound philosophy," he ended his subscription and association with Lovejoy.

George's proslavery opinions seem to have had no effect on Mary's behavior. She continued to view slavery as a mortal sin and a national crime. Indeed, her views on slavery and women's education were linked. She believed that young southern women needed proper education in matters of domestic efficiency and Protestant values, thereby eroding both the practical need and moral excuse for human bondage.

Sibley accomplished this in 1832 when she launched her St. Charles school for white girls with six pupils. Her mission to rescue white southern girls through education was based on the notion that slavery rendered them dependent, useless, and weak, thereby unable to meet the challenges of the western frontier. She cringed at "the delicate girl who could scarcely bear the idea of helping herself to a drink of water," requiring a house servant to carry out that ridiculously simple task. These girls, she feared, were turned into objects of charity, dependent upon others for their own care. Thus, her school helped diminish the "enervating effects of slavery," as she saw them, by teaching domestic self-sufficiency, which in turn promoted strong republican virtue. If southern white women took responsibility for their own household chores, they would free themselves from their dependency on slave house servants and make slavery obsolete.

The second prong of attack included converting Catholic school girls to Protestant beliefs. The presence of Mother Philippine Duchesne and her order's Academy of the Sacred

Mary Easton Sibley. Painting photographed by Robert Goebel, 1910. MHS–PP

Heart in St. Charles no doubt troubled Mary. She frowned upon Catholic education, which she argued "turns upon the world thousands of my sex helpless dependent creatures, mere Doll babies dressed up for exhibition decorated with external accomplishment." Sibley felt that these girls were "very pretty to hold in the Drawing room or Ball room but of no manner of use either to ourselves or their fellow creatures, when called upon to take their station in society as wives, mothers, and heads of families."

Sibley's criticism of Mother Duchesne as well as her mission to instill Protestant faith and domestic skills in young women stemmed in part from her disdain of Roman Catholicism, a common Protestant American sentiment in her day. Perhaps the alleged "secret baptism" of her sister by a Catholic priest confirmed her worst fears of a sinister papist plot to subvert the American republic. She wrote newspaper articles condemning Catholic worship, hoping to "open the eyes of some of these poor deluded people who are led a stray [sic] to designing priests."

Mary also taught academic courses, and students filled their days learning French and German, music and art, and the Protestant virtues of piety and personal responsibility. By 1839 Sibley advertised that her school at Lindenwood offered tuition, board, and school supplies for three dollars a week. Enrollments increased in the 1840s requiring additional instructors and her full devotion to duties as "directress" of the school. In 1853, after George and Mary Sibley donated 120 acres of land to the college, Lindenwood Female College incorporated with a fifteen-man board of directors. The board had the power to appoint professors, teachers, and develop the school's curriculum.

Fervent Protestantism and fervent Catholicism, along with antislavery notions, spurred Mary Sibley to put her faith into action on the Missouri frontier. By the time she turned responsibility for her school over to men, she had created an enduring local educational institution for young women.

–*Sharra Vostral*

Sources: This essay is largely based on the Mary Easton Sibley Diary, MHS; the George Sibley Papers, MHS; and the Lindenwood College Papers, MHS and Lindenwood College archives. Sharra Vostral teaches at Indiana University.

Sisters of St. Joseph of Carondelet

In 1834 the Countess de la Roche-Jacqueline of France offered to send a small group of Sisters of St. Joseph from their motherhouse in Lyon to America "to convert the savages, to teach their children and those of the Protestant families." Founded in 1693, the Sisters of Saint Joseph had operated charitable and educational institutions throughout France until the French Revolution. Mother St. John Fontbonne, one of many sisters imprisoned during the Reign of Terror, barely escaped the guillotine. In 1807, she gathered a few remaining members of the disbanded convents and revived the order. Under her leadership, the nuns reestablished more than two hundred schools, orphanages, and hospitals. They looked to America as their next mission field, particularly the huge diocese of St. Louis that stretched from the Mississippi to the Rocky Mountains. The sisters who volunteered to come to St. Louis established the motherhouse of the Sisters of St. Joseph in America.

Sisters Febronic and Delphine, nieces of Mother Fontbonne, were among the first six nuns to arrive in 1836. Bishop Joseph Rosati directed three nuns to Cahokia, Illinois, and three to Carondelet, both rural villages where many residents still spoke French. In Carondelet they were greeted by Sisters of Charity, then preparing to move their boys' orphanage to a new building in St. Louis. They offered the Sisters of St. Joseph their two-room sparsely furnished cabin and two small sheds for a schoolroom and a kitchen. The three nuns promptly enrolled twenty day students.

Bishop Rosati had invited the Sisters of St. Joseph to St. Louis with the provision that some of the nuns be trained in the French Abbe Secard technique for teaching the deaf. Sisters Celestine Pomerell and St. John Fournier, who had remained in France to study sign language, arrived the following year to teach four deaf girls waiting for them in Carondelet. After the sisters began taking in orphans brought to the convent, they added several more rooms, a porch, and a second story to the building. In 1841 they replaced the primitive structure with a brick building and opened a boarding school as well as a day school. It became the cornerstone structure of a massive quadrangle constructed over the next fifty years at 6400 Minnesota Avenue.

Although much of the nuns' early funding came from French benefactors, they soon needed to become self-supporting. Mother Superior

Delphine Fontbonne could not rely on financial help from the diocese, which had no responsibility for the material needs of religious orders within its jurisdiction. She entered into financial agreements with Carondelet to educate all the town's female students and with the state of Missouri to teach sign language to the deaf. In the evening, the sisters sewed to supplement their income.

In addition to these financial concerns, the Sisters of St. Joseph, like most female religious orders, managed a complex set of relationships with the Catholic clergy. They lived under the administrative jurisdiction of the bishop, who appointed a local parish priest as their spiritual director. Whether teaching the deaf, nurturing orphans, or managing practical affairs, Mother Fontbonne filled a difficult leadership role in an inherently awkward institutional setting. Internal rivalries between parish priests and members of religious orders had a long history in the Roman Catholic Church. The sisters' delicate task was to maintain their autonomy, manage their internal affairs, and do their work without challenging the male authority of the church.

At the same time, the nuns enjoyed some advantages not available to benevolent Protestant women. Sisterhood gave them some degree of independence within the larger institutional structure of the church, a mutually supportive community in which to live and work, and a socially legitimate and valued role on the urban frontier. In 1838 Mother Delphine Fontbonne resigned as superior at Carondelet in order to teach at Cahokia. The capable and forceful Celestine Pomerell succeeded her.

Sources: Information from Sister Dolorita Marie Dougherty, *Sisters of St. Joseph of Carondelet* (St. Louis: B. Herder Book Co., 1966); Scharf, *History of St. Louis City and County*, vol. 1, 883–84; Marcella M. Holloway, C.S.J., "The Sisters of St. Joseph of Carondelet: 150 Years of Good Works in America," *GH* 7, no. 2 (fall 1986); the Reverend John Rothensteiner, *History of the Archdiocese of St. Louis: In its Various Stages of Development, from A.D. 1673 to A.D. 1928*, vol. 2 (St. Louis: Blackwell Wielandy, 1928); *St. Louis Globe-Democrat*, 14 February 1960. See Ewens, *The Role of the Nun in Nineteenth Century America*, for an analysis of the relationship between religious orders and local clergy. The Sisters of St. Joseph maintain an archive in their motherhouse at 6400 Minnesota Avenue.

St. Louis Association of Ladies for the Relief of Orphans

In December 1834 sixteen women, representing the city's four large Protestant churches—one Methodist, one Episcopal, two Presbyterian—met to organize the St. Louis Association of Ladies for the Relief of Orphans. Encouraged by the clergy, the wives of the city's leading Protestant businessmen adopted a constitution and bylaws limiting membership to women and fixed dues at fifty cents a year. Within the year, 190 women joined the association. The Board of Managers agreed "to solicit the council of several gentlemen" to arrange acquiring a house and to help them draw up a list of "the liberal gentlemen of the city" who might contribute funds. As in similar associations elsewhere, women volunteers provided the organizational impetus, leadership, and administrative skills. The only role for men was to raise money.

St. Louis faced a mounting orphan problem in the 1830s. The cholera epidemic of 1832 had wiped out 5 percent of the local population, leaving hundreds of children orphaned or with only one parent barely able to carry on. Immigrants, transients, and overland travelers heading west also crowded the community, further adding to the already desperate need for social services. Some who died left behind homeless children.

The new association responded by hiring women to board orphans in their homes; governing board members took others into their own homes. In the summer of 1835, however, the association purchased a lot on Seventh Street, between Morgan and Franklin, and constructed an orphanage for three thousand dollars. Most of the money came from appeals to liberal gentlemen.

Until the association incorporated in 1841, a member's husband served as legal guardian of all the children. The articles of incorporation stipulated that subscribers and managers must be women, but because Missouri law gave husbands control of their wives' money, a married woman who held any of the corporation's assets had to have her husband's consent. To avoid interference by potentially meddlesome husbands, the charter stipulated that the association's treasurer "shall always be a single woman of the age of twenty-one, or upwards."

The association raised most of the operating money. In addition to paying dues, members sewed for the children. The board members' social prominence gave the orphanage and its needs wide visibility. "Young gentlemen" offered to make it the beneficiary of a winter lecture series. Board members solicited money door to door, particularly at Thanksgiving. Because the association relied on donations, income fluctuated with the state of the local economy. Between January 1837 and the end of 1838, wages in St. Louis dropped as much as 50 percent, affecting not only donations to the orphanage but undoubtedly increasing the numbers of destitute children.

Local government assumed no responsibility for providing or supporting orphanages and imposed no regulations for their operation. In 1841, the board asked the mayor "for an annuity to assist the society in the support of the orphans," but no allocation appeared in the municipal budget. Legal incorporation made the board fiscally responsible and empowered them to make all decisions affecting how orphans were accepted, cared for, and placed in adoptive homes. No civic agency or governmental office oversaw its work or evaluated the results. By formally creating a charitable institution, the St. Louis Association of Ladies for the Relief of Orphans assumed the power to control the future of untold numbers of St. Louis children. In 1853 the association changed its name to the St. Louis Protestant Orphan Asylum to make it easier to receive bequests.

The St. Louis Protestant Orphan Asylum was technically nondenominational. But the association accepted Catholics only when no Catholic institution was available, and they transferred Catholic children as soon as possible. They would not place Protestant children in homes with a "Catholic influence." Although not immune to nativist bigotry in an era of rising anti-Catholicism, the association upheld the foundation upon which all charitable assistance rested: Protestants care for Protestants and Catholics for Catholics.

St. Louis men, who controlled the public purse, did not consider housing and educating orphans to be a public responsibility. Sectarian women, both Protestant housewives and Catholic nuns, stepped in to fill a community need. In doing so, the Ladies for the Relief of Orphans self-consciously made a space for themselves in the public sphere, where they could make significant decisions and act on them.

Sources: This essay draws on Ann Morris, "The History of the St. Louis Protestant Orphan Home," *BMHS* 36, no. 2 (January 1980) which was based on records of the institution, some of which are located at MHS. Quotations are from the association's charter and bylaws; additional information comes from annual reports. See also Hannah I. Stagg, *History of the Founding and Progress of the St. Louis Protestant Orphan Asylum* (St. Louis, 1891). For the impact of the Depression of 1837, see Gary M. Fink, "The Depression of 1837," *BMHS* 26, no. 1 (October 1969): 55–7. The Protestant Orphan Asylum moved to Webster Groves in 1869. Men did not serve on the Board of Managers until 1943, when the orphanage became the Edgewood Children's Center.

Although Catholic women founded the Catholic Orphan Association of St. Louis in 1841, men soon assumed the leadership roles, incorporating it in 1848 as the Roman Catholic Male and Female Orphan Asylum of St. Louis, as noted in Rothensteiner, *History of the Archdiocese of St. Louis*, 453.

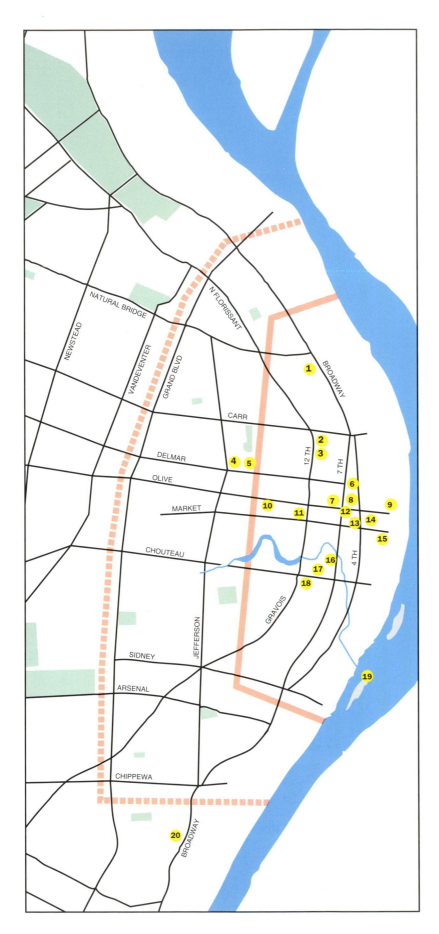

1840–1860

1. Episcopal Orphans' Home
2. St. Vincent's German Orphan Asylum
3. St. Ann's Widows and Orphans Home
4. Sisters of Mercy Convent
5. Girls' Industrial Home
6. City Jail, Lucy Delaney
7. Abigail Cranch Eliot Home
8. Elizabeth Sargent Home
9. Sarah Peale Studio
10. House of the Good Shepherd
11. St. Joseph's Half-Orphan Asylum
12. Old Courthouse, Harriet Scott
13. St. Philomena's Orphan Asylum
14. First St. Louis Public School
15. St. Joseph's School for African American Girls
16. St. Vincent's Institute for the Insane
17. Academy of the Visitation
18. Ursuline Convent
19. Quarantine Island
20. Home for the Friendless

▬▬ St. Louis City Limits 1841–1855
▪▪▪ St. Louis City Limits 1855–1876
▨ Parks

3

Women at the Gateway to the West

In October 1837, Abigail Cranch Eliot, a twenty-year-old bride, stepped off a steamboat onto the St. Louis wharf to begin a new life. She and her husband, William Greenleaf Eliot, a Unitarian minister recently graduated from Harvard University, were missionaries to the urban frontier, bent on promoting Protestant religious and civic culture in the gateway city to the West. "Although I had been told about the smoke and mud, I found it even worse than I imagined," Abby Eliot later recalled. Friends from Newport, Rhode Island, who had lived in St. Louis for several years, took the Eliots into their home on the western edge of town. "As a better class of

people were coming, each family who came with letters from friends was taken in as we were and kindly cared for."

In 1840, when Abby moved into her own home at Eighth and Olive Streets, sixteen thousand people lived in St. Louis. "We had no pavement, only cinder walks and the mud in the streets was fearful! I was fortunate enough in having a good colored cook, and we kept a cow. . . .

St. Louis, 26 August 1845, Fifth Street Toward Market. The artist made the street appear wider and cleaner than it actually was. Graphite on paper by Paulus Roetter. MHS Library

I could sit at my window and look at the courthouse with very little to obstruct the view." She wrote many years later, "Visiting among the sick and poor kept us very busy. Public schools just struggling with existence, one or two small dry goods stores, dark streets and muddy ways made life pretty hard for those of us charitably inclined."

The charitably inclined Eliots made a lasting mark on St. Louis. As minister of the Unitarian Church of the Messiah, the Reverend Eliot helped to shape the city's benevolent and educational institutions and became the spokesman for local civic Protestantism. Abby Eliot struggled with raising a family on the frontier—only five of her fourteen children survived to adulthood—and worked with other Protestant women to assist the casualties of the churning, rapidly growing community.

In 1837 the Eliots found themselves in an expanding, unstable city with no public social infrastructure in place or planned. Antebellum St. Louis was a raw boom town destined to grow in population from 16,000 to 160,000 in twenty years. Over time, St. Louisans came to rely on voluntary social services, organized along sectarian lines, supported and run for the most part by charitable women. Religious orders of nuns, summoned by the

city's Roman Catholic bishops, cared for and educated an expanding flock of Catholic immigrants. As St. Louisans became more divided over issues of religion, race, class, and sectional loyalties, women worked within those divisions to meet the human needs of a city growing too fast.

St. Louisans depended on charitable women because there was no organized citywide system of relief for the poor or permanently disabled, other than the county poorhouse. The county government allocated some public funds for this kind of institutional care. Certifiably disabled women with children could occasionally receive a few dollars of temporary aid if they petitioned the mayor directly. Most aid, however, was short-term and came directly from private individuals. In years with severe winters or disasters, such as the 1844 flood or the 1849 fire and cholera epidemic, the mayor organized businessmen to solicit private funds and distribute relief, but the committees disbanded when the crisis passed. In 1845 Catholic businessmen founded the St. Vincent de Paul Society to collect and distribute aid through the Catholic parishes. Jewish businessmen organized the Hebrew Relief Society.

There was no citywide organization with a nonsectarian mandate for charity until 1862, when Protestant businessmen under the leadership of William Greenleaf Eliot created the St. Louis Provident Association. Even then, the association did not assist people already receiving help from a church or other charitable organization. Poor St. Louisans could ask the privately supported association for food, clothing, or temporary shelter, but not money.

The Eliots came to St. Louis just as a wave of native-born and immigrant newcomers began to crowd the city. Although housing was scarce, Abby found food prices lower than she had expected, the effect of a depressed economy created by a nationwide panic in the late 1830s. But at the end of the 1840s the economy was growing again, drawing other more entrepreneurial New Englanders west. Thousands of immigrants from Ireland and the German states boarded steamboats in New Orleans for the trip upriver to St. Louis. In the 1830s, less that two thousand newcomers a year had settled in the city, but between 1848 and 1850 alone forty thousand people arrived. More than half the people in St. Louis at mid-century had lived there less than two years. The foreign-born outnumbered the native-born, and men outnumbered women 185 to 100.

Germans made up the largest group of foreign newcomers. In 1840, five thousand St. Louisans were

Abigail Adams Cranch Eliot. Photograph by J. C. Strauss of a painting by Charles Frederick von Salza, ca. 1894. MHS–PP

German-born; by 1860, fifty thousand immigrants from the German states lived in the city. Although political and religious freedom attracted both left-wing political radicals and Saxon Lutherans, a majority of Germans left home for economic reasons. Few, however, arrived destitute. Savings or cash proceeds from selling property in Germany allowed many newly arrived families to open small businesses. In the years between 1851 and 1856, Germans operated one-third of all new St. Louis businesses.

Most German immigrants had marketable skills. Single men settled into boardinghouses and looked for work as artisans and laborers. Those who needed help or encouragement could find it at the St. Louis German Emigration Society, founded in 1848 by German businessmen and cultural leaders. German wives organized within churches or male-led volunteer associations to aid the needy, seldom forming independent organizations.

By far the largest foreign-born group in the city, German immigrant women had less immediate contact with American culture. A housewife in 1850 could do all her shopping within a few blocks of her home and never need to speak English. She could read an excellent German-language newspaper, and she and her daughters might work in the family business or take in boarders. Unmarried immigrant women were also in demand as domestics, particularly as rising slave prices in the South reduced slaveholding in St. Louis. Whole families worked to make ends meet or to save for a home of their own.

In 1850 fewer than 7 percent of the city's immigrants owned land. But as house rents and the price of land rose in the booming economy, a significant number of German families found affordable building lots on the northern and southern edges of the city, and further afield in St. Louis County. They built brick homes in Bremen, a new town developed by German immigrants, and in the old French town of Carondelet. There, and in the city wards to the north and south, German homeowners typically lived in their own two- and four-family flats, collecting rent from their neighbor-tenants to pay the mortgage.

If most Germans moved out of hope, most Irish immigrants fled out of necessity. Famine and rapacious English landlords sent two million desperate people from Ireland to America between 1830 and 1860; more than thirty thousand ended up in St. Louis. Almost all Irish immigrants were Roman Catholic, unlike the German immigrants who were as diverse in their religion as in their skills. The Irish arrived with few urban skills and no money to buy farmland. Two-thirds of Irish men worked as manual

laborers in 1850. Their wives took in washing, sewing, and boarders. A few single women worked in the developing garment and shoe industries, but most looked for domestic work in private homes or boardinghouses, the latter, in lodging-short St. Louis, occupied by both the rich and the poor.

Although one St. Louisan in three lived in a boardinghouse in 1850, almost half the city's Irish rented rooms, mostly in densely crowded buildings on the near north side. A highly visible minority built "Kerry Patch," a colony of shacks on undeveloped land northwest of the city limits. The neighborhood name commemorated the devastated county in western Ireland from which so many refugees had fled. For the first generation of "famine" Irish, however, life in St. Louis was not much better. Being poor and unskilled in a strange and often hostile country frequently led to a downward spiral of hopelessness and contributed to the instability of domestic life. Irish immigrant women who found urban life a constant struggle often turned to the Roman Catholic Church for help.

Unlike Protestant eastern cities where native-born residents scorned the Irish for their ethnicity and their religion, St. Louis had a long tradition of Irish Catholicism. John Mullanphy, who had come from Ireland when St. Louis was still a Creole community, supported the city's first convent schools. He left his children wealthy. His son, Bryan, helped establish the St. Vincent de Paul Society and his daughter, Anne Mullanphy Biddle, gave much of her inherited wealth to Catholic institutions for women and children. Ann Lucas Hunt, whose parents acquired vast amounts of land in the territorial period, also gave generously to Catholic charities. These early philanthropists enabled religious orders to open orphanages, hospitals, and widows' homes, institutions already in place when the Catholic immigrant population exploded at mid-century.

Few Catholics lived in the United States in the early nineteenth century. The bishops of St. Louis looked to Europe and Catholic Maryland for women to teach and care for the poor, sick, and abandoned– the traditional responsibilities of the church. The European nuns who accepted the challenge of the St. Louis mission found that they had to adapt themselves and their organizations to the needs of the American environment.

European women who entered religious orders were usually middle and upper class. They chose to live in a community of women and dedicate their lives to God. When they left home, they brought a dowry to the order. This money, endowments, and the generosity of patrons enabled nuns to work among the poor without compensation. Contemplative orders and most teaching orders never went out into the world but lived cloistered in convents. They made solemn vows of poverty, chastity, and obedience to the rules of the order violable only with the pope's permission. The constitution of the religious community directed all areas of a woman's life: prayer, vows, works of charity, clothing, finances, and living arrangements. Class distinctions were acknowledged in the convent, just as they were in the culture. Some orders had two levels of membership: choir sisters who brought dowries and lay sisters from poor families who did housework and other chores.

With few exceptions, the nuns who came to St. Louis before the Civil War were foreign-born and arrived directly from European convents. The Religious of the Sacred Heart, a cloistered order of French upper-class women, were the first to adapt their rules to frontier life. Just finding someone to fetch water so they could stay in the convent presented a quandary, but the greater challenges entailed raising funds to continue their work and accommodating the rules of the order to the needs of the diocese.

In America the local bishop was responsible for charitable activity in his jurisdiction. His mission often conflicted, however, with the rules of a distant motherhouse that governed nuns living in his diocese. The fact that the constitutions of the Sisters of Charity and the Sisters of St. Joseph enabled them to go out into the community contributed to Bishop Joseph Rosati's decision to bring them to St. Louis. Concerned with the needs of the church and the shortage of religious workers, bishops encouraged sisters to adapt their rules to American culture. In 1843 Bishop Rosati argued that the "solemn" vows of the Religious of the Sacred Heart were unenforceable in America. Only "simple" vows, ones that could be modified by the local bishop, suited a country where the civil law did not respect vows of poverty and where no law could require women to stay in the convent.

These contentious issues proved difficult for nuns committed both to the rules of their religious orders and to the authority of the church. European sisters struggled as well to adapt to the contradictory culture in which they found themselves. Americans rejected traditional class distinctions but accorded status based solely on wealth. They professed equality but held slaves. American ideas of independence and individualism ran counter to the unquestioned obedience at the heart of convent life.

At the same time, the female heads of religious orders engaged in business affairs to a greater extent than most Americans were used to or approved of. Unlike most American female teachers, for whom the classroom was a stopover on the road to marriage and motherhood, nuns could anticipate practicing their profession for a lifetime. The orders that succeeded in America's cities either broke with European motherhouses or originated in the United States. As more American-born women joined religious communities, they made the communities into peculiarly American institutions.

"We are told . . . that the Catholics have evil designs," observed William Greenleaf Eliot when he first came to St. Louis in 1837. "Perhaps it is so; but until they exhibit such designs by other means than doing good, we do not feel authorized to join in preaching a crusade against them." Eliot did not join the anti-Catholic crusade that consumed many fervent Protestants, including publisher Elijah Lovejoy, in cities experiencing large influxes of Catholic immigrants. The nativism that fueled St. Louis election-day riots in the 1840s and 1850s targeted Irish voters. Anti-Catholic publications spun tales of international Catholic conspiracy and sexual improprieties within convents and Jesuit schools, including Saint Louis University. Although St. Louis did not experience the intensity of anti-Catholic rioting that swept some eastern cities, heightened emphasis on religious differences linked to ethnicity further separated the educational and charitable activities of Catholic and Protestant women.

Even though they worried about Papist proselytizing, Protestant parents in St. Louis often sent their daughters to schools run by Catholic sisters. After the city's first public schools opened in 1838, parents could chose between tuition-charging parochial schools and free public "common" schools. Most Catholic parents rejected secular schooling. Furthermore, most feared—not unreasonably—that the public schools were aggressively Protestant. The archbishops of St. Louis rapidly opened parish schools, staffed by nuns, that more than kept pace with the growth of public schools. Catholic schools educated more students than the public schools until 1850, when each instructed about twenty-five hundred pupils.

St. Louis public schools had never welcomed African Americans. After 1847, when Missouri law prohibited the teaching of black children, slave or free, none could attend. A few sectarian schools, both Catholic and Protestant, offered segregated classes for black students, but most St. Louis African Americans received no formal education.

St. Louis was a moderately antislavery city in an aggressively proslavery state. Many outstate Missourians, and a significant percentage of St. Louisans, would later sympathize with the Confederacy. Some white St. Louisans, particularly transplanted New Englanders and radical Germans, opposed slavery, but very few of them took action against it. The fate of Elijah Lovejoy, driven out of St. Louis and martyred in Alton, Illinois, for publishing an antislavery newspaper, served as instructive memory. Since slavery was both a system for exploiting labor and for regulating race relations, abolishing the former meant dealing with the latter. Like other white Americans, St. Louisans had no vision of an egalitarian interracial community.

For the most part white women did not extend their charity to black women or their children, nor did they join antislavery associations, as many similarly reform-minded women did in the Northeast. Abby Eliot was the white woman in St. Louis most likely to have actively campaigned against slavery. Unitarian women in New England were among the most fervent abolitionists. She and her husband abhorred slavery and extended personal benevolence to African Americans. But William Greenleaf Eliot publicly opposed direct political involvement. "I would hail with utmost joy the day which makes Missouri a free State," he declared. "But, there is no course which hampers the actions of those who would work for this ultimate end, so much as the unwise interference of societies and individuals." Whether intimidated by family objection and by the complexity of the slavery issue in Missouri, or simply unwilling to take a stand in opposition to the city's leading Protestant clergymen, white women with antislavery sentiments remained silent in the decade before the Civil War.

Some St. Louis slaves did not wait for reluctant liberators but simply freed themselves by running away. More did not, afraid of suffering the same fate as Elizabeth, the mother of William Wells Brown, who was sold downriver after a failed attempt to escape. Polly Wash, the mother of Lucy Delaney, and Harriet Scott, the wife of Dred Scott, fought slavery relentlessly in the courts. Powerless to challenge the legality of the system, they used the existing laws of Missouri and the United States to sue for their freedom.

By the eve of the Civil War, African American slavery was a dying institution in St. Louis, driven out less by moral revulsion than by a flood of cheap white immigrant labor. In 1860 fewer than 1,500 slaves lived in a city of more than 160,000. But slavery's broader context of ethnic, cultural, economic and social cleavages, ingrained habits, and haunting memories, remained to fracture St. Louis and the nation in Civil War. Whether she lived in a convent, a middle-class rowhouse, an immigrant boardinghouse, a four-family flat, an apartment above a small shop, or a slave cabin on a St. Louis County farm, no St. Louis woman could escape the conflicted legacies of the antebellum years or avoid the pain of the coming conflict.

Sources: Quotations from Abby Eliot's reminiscences are in the Henry Ware Papers, MHS. This essay draws on a number of published sources on antebellum St. Louis, including James Neal Primm, *Lion of the Valley: St. Louis, Missouri*, 3d ed. (St. Louis: MHS Press, 1998), and *SLAH*, Units 2, 3, and 4. For a rich, detailed, but biased analysis of social and economic turmoil in this period, see Jeffrey Adler, *Yankee Merchants and the Making of the Urban West: The Rise and Fall of Antebellum St. Louis* (Cambridge, Mass.: Cambridge University Press, 1991). Eliot quotation on Catholics is on page 54; on slavery, page 127 of this monograph. For information on nineteenth-century Catholic nuns and an analysis of their adjustment to America, see Barbara Misner, S.C.S.C., "*Highly Respectable and Accomplished Ladies*": *Catholic Women Religious in America, 1790–1850* (New York: Garland Press, 1988); Ursula Stepsis, C.S.A., and Dolores Liptak, R.S.M., eds., *Pioneer Healers: The History of Women Religious in American Health Care* (New York: Crossroad, 1989); and Mary Ewens, *The Role of the Nun in Nineteenth Century America* (Salem, N.H.: Ayer, 1984). Information on German immigration is from Audrey Louise Olson, C.S.J., "St. Louis Germans, 1850–1920: The Nature of an Immigrant Community and its Relation to the Assimilation Process" (Ph.D. dissertation, University of Kansas, 1970), and George H. Kellner, "The German Element on the Urban Frontier: St. Louis, 1830–1860" (Ph.D. dissertation, University of Missouri–Columbia, 1973). For public education, see Selwyn K. Troen, *The Public and the Schools: Shaping the St. Louis System, 1838–1920* (Columbia: University of Missouri Press, 1975). For Irish women, see Hasia R. Diner, *Erin's Daughters in America: Irish Immigrant Women in the Nineteenth Century* (Baltimore: Johns Hopkins University Press, 1983).

The history of German and Irish women's organizations, as well as the experiences of all immigrant women in the antebellum period, are important subjects for research. German churches and records of male-headed associations would yield valuable information to researchers with proficiency in German language, as would letters and journals in private collections in the United States and Europe. Irish women, most of whom were poor, left fewer traces, but a careful reading of St. Louis newspapers would produce clues to the female urban experience.

The Cholera Epidemic of 1849

"**W**hat a world of good these Sisters wrought, during the awful year of the Asiatic cholera," wrote Father John Kenny in the aftermath of the city's worst epidemic. For St. Louisans, 1849 was indeed an awful year, when more than 10 percent of the city's seventy thousand people died. During the height of the epidemic, thousands of residents fled the city while countless others lay dying. Local government was paralyzed; no one really knew what to do, and many municipal officials fled their posts. The Daughters of Charity and other religious women, however, never wavered in their mission to care for the sick and comfort the dying.

Although doctors suspected a relationship between fecal contamination, water, and cholera, no one knew for sure how the disease was transmitted until 1883, when the water-born bacterium that caused the disease was discovered. In 1849 most people believed the vapors, or miasma, rising from stagnant water caused cholera, especially in cities underlain with limestone. St. Louisans frantically removed liquid waste and decaying matter and lit bonfires of coal, tar, and sulfur to disinfect the air in a futile effort to halt the spread of cholera. Although the disease did not respect class, it seemed to fall heaviest on the poor, particularly recent immigrants who lived in low areas of the city where stagnant water collected.

Cholera had last visited St. Louis in the mid-1830s. Endemic in India, it followed trade and immigration routes through Europe to American ports. In 1849 it struck the nation's major eastern cities but was particularly severe in the Midwest. Since the cholera bacteria actually thrived in poor sanitary conditions and polluted water, it surprised no one that the disease arrived from New Orleans with immigrants who had crowded together for months on unsanitary steamboats.

Some frustrated and angry citizens held a public meeting to demand immediate action. Because the Board of Health had abdicated responsibility, they appointed a temporary Committee of Public Health, gave them extraordinary powers, and voted an appropriation of fifty thousand dollars to do the work.

Armed with administrative power, the committee immediately took action. They appointed a Quarantine Committee to stop and examine every northbound boat at Arsenal Island, renamed Quarantine Island, south of the city. Physicians consigned sick passengers to a hastily built hospital, where most died without ever reaching St. Louis. Quarantining newcomers, however, did not halt the spread of the disease.

Blue State of the Spasmodic Cholera, Sketch of a Girl Who Died of Cholera in Sunderland, November 1831. Lancet, vol. 1 (1831–1832). Bernard Becker Medical Library, Washington University School of Medicine, St. Louis. Death frequently came swiftly to victims of cholera. More than seven thousand St. Louisans perished of the disease in 1849.

The Daughters of Charity offered their services to the Quarantine Committee and requested an appropriation of three hundred dollars to cover expenses. Two nuns went to Quarantine Island to advise the committee on how to set up and run a hospital. They converted an existing building "and properly arranged for the sick, separating the males from the females," reported the committee. Supplies were arriving "and we have to state that the Sisters have secured their preparations by the volunteer labor of persons on the island."

While the committee organized additional temporary hospitals in public schools, appointed physicians, and assigned block inspectors, nuns did most of the practical work of caring for the sick. The Daughters of Charity were experienced health care providers willing to accept cholera patients, which made St. Louis one of the few cities in the nation prepared to hospitalize the indigent. As in earlier cholera epidemics, the sisters took patients into their hospital at Spruce and Fourth Streets. Their contract with the city specified the charges for accepting cholera patients: "42 67/100 cents a day for each patient. . . . No additional charge for the trouble of preparing the dead for interment. Payment to be made in cash at the end of each month." The nuns also provided nurses for temporary hospitals in the First, Fourth, and Sixth Wards. Their patients were mainly the poor, the old, and the alone. Most stricken St. Louisans stayed home to die quietly or recover slowly at their own expense. During the summer of 1849 two Daughters of Charity, two Sisters of St. Joseph, six Religious of the Sacred Heart, and one Visitation Sister died nursing victims of cholera.

Patient treatment consisted of a plethora of patent medicines and home remedies, most of which contained varying amounts of mercury, strong opiates, laxatives, and purgatives. The committee's inspector disparaged the poor for their distrust of hospitals and doctors, but in reality professional medical knowledge and practice was often no better, and sometimes worse, than home care and folk medicine.

While women at home cared for the sick, they also tried to keep cholera from entering the house. Physicians believed that cholera-tainted filth contaminated fresh fruits and vegetables, leading the Committee of Public Health to ban most produce from the public market. Elizabeth Wyman, a thirty-year-old housewife with young children, explained daily life during the summer of 1849 to her sister in Boston. "We live very plain, eat no vegetable, not even potatoes, no pies, no fruit, no rich cake. We do not go anywhere, for I am afraid to go from home, and we have no company, for visiting is out of the question." Middle-class families like the Wymans could escape cholera better than the poor. They lived in more salubrious conditions, had healthier diets, and could move away from infected areas. The members of the Committee of Public Health, who stayed to fulfill their civic responsibilities, however, suffered sickness and deaths in their own families.

By 1849, most Americans no longer believed that Asiatic cholera was a punishment sent by an angry God, but they did associate the disease with sloth, intemperance, and vice. Even though cholera struck both the rich and poor, they blamed the victims of poverty for harboring it. The Committee of Public Health requested the cooperation of the German Society of St. Louis to help with destitute immigrants living in "vast beds of putritidity," in shanties "half sunken in what was formerly the bed of Chouteau's Pond." Poor people whose streets and alleys stunk of uncollected garbage or whose dwellings had cellars and yards filled with standing water were somehow responsible for their appalling living conditions. The fact that more Irish and German immigrants fell victim to cholera than native-born Americans was perceived as further evidence of their ignorance, laziness, and moral laxity.

The measures enacted by the Committee of Public Health attest to the limited medical knowledge in the mid-nineteenth century. By the end of the summer, however, the committee realized that if traditional remedies could not cure the disease, cleanliness and improved public sanitation might prevent it. Although citizens had petitioned for storm sewers long before the epidemic, in 1850 the city appropriated funds for sewer construction, the first step in containing the water-born bacteria. Cholera returned briefly in 1866, but the city never again experienced as deadly an epidemic.

After the epidemic subsided in early August 1849, the Committee of Public Health acknowledged the work of Catholic nuns in its final report with "a debt of gratitude that can neither be measured nor canceled." In the fall a survivor wrote to his aunt in Illinois, "There are not many traces of the pestilence of last Summer that a stranger would notice. There are many people in mourning but all else looks as usual. In the graveyards however the sad story is told."

–Joan Cooper

Sources: The first and best social history of the nineteenth-century cholera epidemics is Charles E. Rosenberg, *The Cholera Years: The United States in*

1832, 1849, and 1866 (Chicago: University of Chicago Press, 1962). See also William M. McPheeters, "History of the Cholera Epidemic in St. Louis in 1849," *St. Louis Medical and Surgical Journal* 7 (1850). See also the Reverend John Rothensteiner, *History of the Archdiocese of St. Louis: In its Various Stages of Development, from A.D. 1673 to A.D. 1928,* vol. 2 (St. Louis: Blackwell Wielandy, 1928), 19; the Reverend John Rothensteiner, *Missouri Republican,* 3 August 1849; Committee of Public Health Records, MHS; Elizabeth Wyman Papers, MHS; and Paddock Papers, MHS.

Many family plots in local cemeteries hold cholera victims, but many more are interred in unmarked graves in Calvary Cemetery and in the Quarantine Island graveyard south of St. Louis.

Employed Women

"**A**unt" Mary Cleveland, a white St. Louis woman, earned her living as a seamstress. She did not work out of her own home or workshop but spent a few days a season with each of her clients. She cut and fitted new dresses for the women of the house, did alterations, and turned last year's gowns into the latest fashions by changing a sleeve here and a button there. She rarely stayed with a family long enough to finish anything before moving on to her next job.

Harriet Scott was a laundress, the job that white women most often left to black women. The most common occupation for free African American women in St. Louis was that of a washerwoman. Laundry workers worked for one family or washed for a number of clients, either in their homes or hers.

Sarah Miriam Peale was a portrait painter from a family of professional artists in Baltimore, where as a young woman she had maintained a studio. In 1847 she moved to St. Louis and continued to earn a living painting portraits.

Like these workers, women were employed nearly everywhere in antebellum St. Louis, but only a small percentage toiled in traditional male workplaces–stores, offices, factories, hotels, construction sites, or on riverboats. Most women worked as maids, cooks, and governesses in other people's homes or turned their own homes into schools, studios, laundries, brothels, or boardinghouses.

Although 1850s city directory listings for Sarah Peale, and later Harriet Scott, included their occupations, most St. Louis working women, like Mary Cleveland, left no record of their employment. The names of eighteen employed women appeared in the 1821 directory, all of whom used their domestic skills to earn a living. Three operated boardinghouses; one ran a tavern; one was a washerwoman; eight made clothing or hats; two were teachers; and three were midwives.

The 1840 directory listed 141 women with occupations, 54 of them African Americans. Most were single women living alone or female heads of households, since women in male-headed families seldom had their own directory listings. Only one listed black woman was not a washerwomen, and she was a chambermaid. Advertisements for 112 boardinghouses attested to the rapid growth of the city. Although only twenty-six boardinghouses appeared under women's names, undoubtedly women attended to the daily operation of most. Thirty-eight women were in the garment trades, six ran schools, and three were midwives.

Although most female employment remained unrecorded in official reports, in 1850 women appeared as 6 percent of the nine thousand workers reported by St. Louis manufacturers. Most female manufacturing jobs were in the shops clustered in the center of the city that produced men's clothing; only 68 of the 489 women listed worked south of Clark Avenue or north of Cass Avenue.

Unlike eastern cities that industrialized earlier, St. Louis did not have large water-powered textile mills in the 1840s employing thousands of young women. Local women sewed in the factory, just as they had in the home. A few worked for women who owned millinery shops. Nearly half held jobs in small tailoring shops where one or two women worked with four to eight men, at less than half their wages. Women typically did the finishing work: clipping threads, making buttonholes, sewing on buttons. They earned between eight and ten dollars a month, far less than public school teachers who made more than four hundred dollars a year. Women not employed in the garment trades toiled in candle factories, tanneries, drug manufacturing, and candy-making factories. Several set type for printers. Only twelve made shoes.

In 1860 St. Louis manufacturers reported 814 female employees. Manufacturers of men's clothing still hired the most women, 264. Steam-powered textile and cordage mills employed another 170; and 128 made bagging and awnings. Shoe manufacturing and tobacco processing, industries that would employ thousands of women at the turn of the century, had only begun to hire women in 1860.

With few exceptions, city directories only listed free women. The manufacturing census may have reported a few slave women, but their wages, like their persons, belonged to their masters. Skilled slave women, however, sometimes used the value of their labor to secure their own freedom. Elizabeth Keckley was a talented seamstress. She was owned by a Virginia family that moved to St. Louis around 1836 and immediately fell on hard times. When her master proposed to hire out Keckley's mother, Elizabeth suggested that her skill as a seamstress would bring a better return. For a time, Keckley supported her owner's household of seventeen persons, both black and white. In 1855 she bought her own freedom for twelve hundred dollars with money contributed by several wealthy St. Louis women she had sewn for. She remained in St. Louis until she repaid her benefactors and then moved to Washington, D.C., shortly before the Civil War. There she became a favorite seamstress in high society, counting among her clients Varina (Mrs. Jefferson) Davis and Mary Todd (Mrs. Abraham) Lincoln.

Most women workers in antebellum St. Louis earned their living with the skills they had learned from other women in the home. Like the work of men, who also practiced skilled crafts in the pre-industrial city, women's work would change dramatically by the end of the century. But some things would remain the same: their options would be fewer and their pay lower than those of male industrial workers.

Sources: For an overview of women's employment in this period, see Alice Kessler-Harris, *Out to Work: A History of Wage-Earning Women in the United States* (New York: Oxford University Press, 1982); Jacqueline Jones, *Labor of Love, Labor of Sorrow: Black Women, Work, and the Family from Slavery to the Present* (New York: Basic Books, 1985); and Barbara Wertheimer, *We Were There: The Story of Working Women in America* (New York: Pantheon Books, 1977). The scant information on "Aunt Mary" Cleveland is from "Abby Eliot Describes St. Louis," Henry Ware Papers, MHS. See this chapter's essay for more on Harriet Scott; See Karen McCoskey Goering, "St. Louis Women Artists 1818–1945: An Exhibition," *GH* 3, no. 1 (summer 1982) for more on Sarah Peale. Elizabeth Keckley wrote a memoir about her experiences in St. Louis and Washington, D.C., *Behind the Scenes; or, Thirty Years a Slave, and Four Years in the White House* (New York, 1868). For a contextual analysis of Keckley's life, see Benjamin Quarles, "Elizabeth Keckley," in *NAW* 2, 310–11. Other information is from John A. Paxton, *The St. Louis Directory and Register for 1821*; *St. Louis Directory for the Years 1840–1841*; and the 1850 Industrial Census for the City of St. Louis, all of which are available at MHS; and the Missouri Census of Manufacturers for 1860, 310–12.

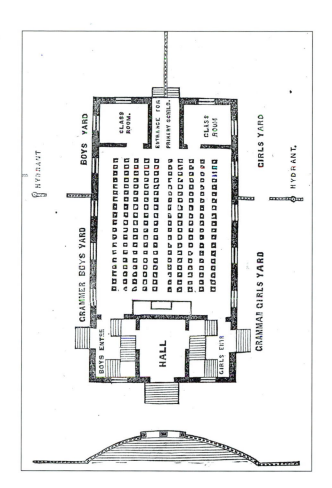

Arrangement of the Primary Department at Webster School. First Annual Report of the General Superintendent of the St. Louis Public Schools, 1854. The arrangement of the seats and platform for the teacher allowed for a very high student-teacher ratio, which kept costs down. MHS Library

Women and the Public Schools

On the first Monday in April 1838, Mary H. Salisbury started work as St. Louis's first female public school teacher. She was responsible for educating about one hundred girls in a new two-story brick building at the corner of Fourth and Spruce Streets. The school board designed the building around the Lancastrian system of education. Lancastrian schooling, a cost-cutting scheme, instructed large numbers of pupils with small numbers of teachers. A single teacher lectured classes of as many as two hundred students in a single room and trained older student monitors to lead follow-up small group drill sessions. Boys and girls attended class on separate floors. The system proved so cost effective that within the year the board opened another school for some 350 pupils on the north side at Fifth and Cherry. Twenty years later, when the city opened its first graded elementary school, ten thousand students attended day and night classes.

In 1850 St. Louisans voted to tax themselves for public schools. Until then all funding came not from taxes but from money collected on rental property owned by the school board. Mary Salisbury earned five hundred dollars in 1838; the male teacher in her school earned nine hundred dollars. Hard times immediately triggered lower salaries, and during the depression of the early 1840s salaries for female teachers fell to four hundred dollars. Even so, teaching was a high-paying job for an unmarried woman. In the 1850s, female teachers in the city's eleven public schools outnumbered male teachers two to one.

Before the first St. Louis public school opened in 1838, parents who wanted to educate their daughters had two choices, either private fee schools or free schools. Many working families considered free schools, usually run by religious groups, to be charity for the poor and opted to pay for their children's education. The proponents of public schooling, led by civic leaders and professional educators, envisioned a common education for all white children paid for by public funds. To attract the middle class to public education, the St. Louis school board opened an extravagant, well-equipped co-educational high school in 1855, near the city's wealthiest neighborhoods. Two years later the board added a teacher-training school in the same building. The decision to use scarce resources to educate a few secondary students meant that the school board turned away hundreds of elementary students for lack of space. However, middle-class participation, both as students and taxpayers, contributed to an annual increase of between one thousand and twenty-five hundred seats in the late 1850s. Public school enrollments passed those of Catholic schools, which until 1850 had educated more students. Because Missouri law prohibited African Americans in public schools, black parents had to find other ways to educate their children.

Sources: For a discussion of the history and philosophy of public schooling in the United States, see Lawrence A. Cremin, *Public Education* (New York: Basic Books, 1976). Some information for this essay comes from *Commemorative History of the St. Louis Public Schools, 1838–1988* (St. Louis: St. Louis Public Schools, 1988). The most comprehensive history of the St. Louis public schools is Troen, *The Public and the Schools*. Additional information is from William L. Montague, ed., *Saint Louis Business Directory, 1853* (St. Louis, 1854), and Raymond L. Breun, *Federal Land Laws and the Early Development of Education in St. Louis* (Ph.D. dissertation, University of Missouri–St. Louis, 1987). Annual Reports for the St. Louis public schools and some public school manuscript records, including payroll records, are located at MHS.

Polly Wash

On November 20, 1839, Polly Wash, an enslaved black woman, entered a plea in the St. Louis Circuit Court asking permission to sue slave trader Joseph Magehan for her freedom and five hundred dollars in damages. In the plea, Polly claimed she was legally free and that Magehan had unlawfully imprisoned and enslaved her. Four years later, a white jury awarded Polly her freedom and one dollar in damages.

Polly was born in Wayne County, Kentucky, in 1806 or 1807 and became the slave of Joseph Crockett at the age of seven. When she was fourteen, she moved with Crockett and his wife to Madison County, Illinois. Polly lived in the free state for several months that winter, which legally made her free. However, she continued to work as a domestic slave for the Crocketts, who also collected the two dollars a month Polly earned while hired out to neighbors.

Near the end of April 1821, Crockett sold Polly to Major Taylor Berry and his wife Fanny, residents of St. Louis. Polly worked as the Berrys' house servant, laundress, nursemaid, and seamstress. She married one of the Berrys' slaves, and they had two daughters, Nancy and Lucy. After Major Berry died, Polly and her daughters continued to live with and work for Fanny and her daughters. When Fanny married Judge Robert Wash a few years later, Polly, Lucy, and Nancy moved to the Wash Mansion. When not doing the Wash's housework, Polly worked as a chambermaid on a steamboat traveling on the Illinois River as far north as Peoria. Wash confiscated her wages of fifteen dollars per month. Following Fanny's death, Judge Wash sold Polly's husband to a slave trader, who took him to Mississippi.

Shortly afterwards, Fanny Wash's daughter married H. S. Cox of Philadelphia, and Polly's daughter Nancy accompanied them on their honeymoon to Niagara Falls, where she escaped to Canada. Lucy recalled her mother's reaction: "In her heart arose a prayer of thanksgiving, but outwardly she pretended to be vexed and angry. . . . I was a small girl at the time, but remember how wildly mother showed her joy at Nancy's escape when we were alone together. She would dance, clap her hands."

In 1839, Cox sold Polly to slave trader Joseph Magehan, who took her down the Mississippi River, but she escaped and walked to Chicago. When she arrived, she learned that slave catchers were searching for her. Fearing Cox would take his anger out on her daughter Lucy, Polly returned to St. Louis and sued Magehan for her freedom.

During Polly's trial, she lived in her own house and was probably hired out by the court. When Lucy washed her mistress's laundry in muddy water from the Mississippi and ruined it, Polly came over before dawn to help her rinse the laundry clean. In the fall of 1842, Lucy's owner decided to sell her downriver, but before he could, she escaped to her mother's house. The following morning, Polly had the sheriff accompany them to the city jail at Sixth and Olive Streets. Polly instigated a suit against Lucy's owner Robert Mitchell for possession of her daughter on the grounds that if she was free (which remained to be decided by the courts), her daughter was also free, as the child of a free woman could not legally be a slave.

Polly's trial showcased the contrasting and ambivalent views of slavery within a small white community in Illinois. At the trial, several of Polly's former neighbors spoke on her behalf, confirming that she had lived as a slave on free land for one winter twenty years earlier. A neighbor, Mary Moore, testified that Joseph Crockett knew upon his arrival that if Polly lived in Illinois for the entire winter, she would legally be free. Moore claimed to have heard Crockett say that "he would keep her there until spring [even] if she did get free. He said he wanted [Polly] with him for she was kinder to him than his own children and he intended when he and his wife were dead that she should be free." Another of her neighbors, Naomi Wood, testified that Crockett had arranged for his son and son-in-law to take Polly to St. Louis to ensure that she remained in slavery. Polly herself claimed she had been kidnapped and taken to Missouri.

Polly won her freedom in 1843 on the grounds that she had lived, traveled, and worked in Illinois while enslaved. By law, a slave's residence in a free state conveyed freedom, and that freedom was permanent, according to the doctrine "once free, always free" followed by the courts.

While engaged in the trial for her own freedom, Polly also cared for her imprisoned daughter, as the twelve-year-old Lucy spent seventeen months in jail before her case went to trial. After two months of imprisonment, Lucy's lawyer came to court to read a statement that she was "suffering from a severe cold occasioned as she believes from a deficiency of

clothing and the dampness of the room in which she is confined, and that had it not been for the careful attention of her mother, who visited her frequently, her sufferings would have been incalculable, and she believes that death would have been the consequence of such cruelty."

On February 7, 1844, Lucy entered the courthouse to begin the trial for her freedom. She later described her experience on that "bright, sunny day, a day which the happy and care-free would drink in with a keen sense of enjoyment. But my heart was full of bitterness; I could see only gloom which seemed to deepen and gather closer to me as I neared the courtroom. The jailer's sister-in-law, Mrs. Lacy, spoke to me of submission and patience; but I could not feel anything but rebellion against my lot." Polly won Lucy's freedom a few months later, and the court waived the seventy-eight dollars she owed as jailer's fees. Shortly afterwards, Lucy married, but her husband soon died in a steamboat explosion, and she moved back to her mother's home. Five years later, Lucy married Zachariah Delaney and remained in St. Louis, where she did charity work and had four children.

Despite their uncertain circumstances, Polly and Lucy maintained the strength of their family ties, even through the sale of Polly's husband, Nancy's escape to Canada, and the two separate trials. Polly persevered in her fight not just for her own freedom, but for that of the family members she unwaveringly supported. Her daughter Lucy

City Jail, Chestnut and Sixth Streets. Lucy Delaney, Polly Wash's daughter, was held here awaiting the decision of whether she was slave or free. Photograph by Emil Boehl, 1870. MHS–PP

displayed many of these values in her own life after she gained her freedom.

–*Katherine Douglass*

Sources: Most of the information in this essay is from the autobiography of Polly's daughter, Lucy A. Delaney, *From the Darkness Cometh the Light; or, Struggles for Freedom* (St. Louis, 1891). Although her memoir is a valuable source for Polly's life, outside verification shows that Lucy Delaney's memory of dates is faulty, understandable as she recalled the events more than fifty years after they occurred. However, these inaccuracies serve as a warning that the advantages of memoirs as sources are balanced by the pitfalls of poor memory and nostalgic sentimentality. Trial records from Polly's and Lucy's cases may be found at the St. Louis Circuit Courts Archives. Further information comes from Robert Moore, Jr., "A Ray of Hope, Extinguished: St. Louis Slave Suits for Freedom," *GH* 14, no. 3 (winter 1993–1994): 4–14, and a phone conversation with the author, November 1997.

Anne Lucas Hunt

Anne Lucas Hunt gave much of her inheritance from her father, John Baptiste Charles Lucas, to Roman Catholic institutions in St. Louis. Her money came primarily from the sale of land her father had purchased on the outskirts of town, long before

Anne Lucas Hunt. Photograph of drawing. MHS–PP

urban growth had increased its value. Anne Hunt attributed the decision to make these land investments to her mother, who died in 1811, but her father was one of the shrewdest land speculators in St. Louis. At one time, Anne and her brother James H. Lucas owned all the land between Market and Olive Streets from Twelfth Street west to Jefferson Avenue. Anne Lucas Hunt's generous gifts of money and building lots underwrote many of the charitable activities of religious orders in St. Louis.

Natives of France, Anne's parents settled first in Pennsylvania where J. B. C. Lucas practiced law and politics. In 1804 President Thomas Jefferson appointed him the commissioner of land claims and judge of the Louisiana Territorial Court. From the time they moved to St. Louis, the family enjoyed political and social prominence, despite Judge Lucas's notoriously unpleasant personality and violent passions. He made many enemies among the Creole elite for refusing to confirm their land titles granted by the Spanish colonial government. As a French-speaking, devout Catholic, Ann had more in common with her father's adversaries than with his brash American allies.

Educated at home by her mother, Anne married Captain Theodore Hunt, a former naval officer, at age eighteen. After Thomas Hart Benton killed her brother Charles in an 1817 duel, she and her husband avoided the politicized city and moved to the country south of town. Anne had eight children, but only three lived to maturity.

Four years after her husband's death in 1832, Anne married Wilson P. Hunt, a wealthy merchant not related to her first husband. Her father and her second husband both died in 1842, making her a rich woman.

Although she apparently had little interest in business before she was widowed, Anne managed her portion of the family inheritance. While she made shrewd commercial investments, she also gave away more than one million dollars in money and real estate, an amount well over sixteen million in current dollars. Her gifts included property at Tenth and St. Charles for St. Francis Xavier parish school for girls, at Third and Gratiot for Our Lady of Victories Church, at Seventeenth and Chestnut for the Convent of the Good Shepherd, and in the suburb of Normandy for St. Anne's Church.

Unlike the religious women who gave their time and talents to Catholic charity, Anne Lucas Hunt gave her money. As a rule, women had little access to large amounts of capital, but those who acquired it through inheritance and chose to give it away made a lasting and visible impact on the community.

Sources: Information on Anne Lucas Hunt's life is from Laura Jane Pace Crane, "Anne Lucas Hunt," in *Show Me Missouri Women: Selected Biographies*, vol. 2, eds., Mary K. Dains and Sue Sadler (Kirksville, Mo.: Thomas Jefferson University Press, 1989). See J. Thomas Scharf, *History of St. Louis City and County* (Philadelphia: L. H. Everts & Co., 1883), and Walter B. Stevens, *St. Louis, The Fourth City, 1764–1911* (St. Louis: S. J. Clark Publishing Co., 1911) for information on the Lucas and Hunt families, and William B. Faherty, S.J., *Dream by the River: Two Centuries of Saint Louis Catholicism, 1766–1967* (St. Louis: Piraeus, 1973), for Anne Lucas Hunt's Catholic charity. Although she wrote an account of her early years in St. Louis, Anne Lucas Hunt, "Early Recollections," *Glimpses of the Past* 1 (May 1934): 41–51, it reveals little of her personality except for her deep religious conviction, and even less about her daily life. Like many memoirs, it is descriptive rather than introspective and typically focuses on the hardships of the frontier.

Elizabeth Sargent

In the winter of 1846 a homesick twenty-four-year-old woman wrote from St. Louis to her family in Kennebunk, Maine. Elizabeth Sargent and her husband Haven had recently moved into a boardinghouse at 114 N. Fourth Street, one of eleven identical four-story brick buildings known as Glasgow's Row. They rented a twenty-by-twenty-six-foot room facing the river. From her third-floor windows, Elizabeth could see the sun rise over Illinois. "I am always looking to the east facing home, our dear New England home."

Haven came to St. Louis to open a business manufacturing and selling lard oil, then the major industrial lubricant, but Elizabeth, at least, was not committed to staying. "It is a good place to make money and I tell Haven he must make a fortune quick and go back east," she wrote. They were surprised to find hotels and boardinghouses scarce and expensive, but they could afford to pay Mrs. Braun thirty-five dollars a month to live in her "very respectable house." The Sargents' furniture arrived by steamboat from New Orleans a few weeks after they had moved in. "We have our portraits up, timepiece, piano forte so I feel quite at home," Elizabeth wrote to her family in February.

While Haven did business, his wife visited with the other boarders, including the families of three doctors and two lawyers. Mrs. Linn, the gregarious widow of a Missouri senator, occupied the room behind the Sargents, and Elizabeth "ran into her room often." In the evening Mrs. Linn entertained the guests gathered in the parlor with political gossip from the nation's capital. When Elizabeth was sick, the landlady and other women in the house brought broth and mustard plasters. Domestic chores were few at Mrs. Braun's. "I don't work hard," Elizabeth confessed to her mother. "I have not made my bed nor swept my room since I have been here but once or so, they keep a girl to do all the chamber work and wait on the ladies. I don't have to go down for drinking water unless I have a mind to. They dust and do all the work."

In April, Elizabeth assured her family that Haven's prospects were excellent. He was "making lard oil hand over fist" and had opened a bookkeeping office in a building at Pine and Levee. She, however, found St. Louis a lonely place. In June her room grew unbearably hot; in August the thermometer stood at 95 degrees every day, and one week twenty people died from the heat. "Bed bugs are plenty here, I find one or two every day. I strip my bed every morning and every other day take a sponge and cold water and wash it all over." The smoky, dusty streets were "as dull as the country compared to Boston . . . but I will be content awhile here if Haven can do well."

Although Elizabeth wrote that she intended to "live prudently and save all I can," the Sargents moved into a small house on the corner of Spruce and Main in the fall of 1846. She described it as a "French house built of stone with green shutters not blinds one story high–two large rooms and a kitchen and an attic, a piazza on the back part of the house which goes down 18 steps into a yard–a fine large yard shaded with trees, large old trees." The Sargents paid about $12.50 a month rent, and Elizabeth hired a German immigrant, a "great strong smart girl," for six dollars a month to live in and do housework.

Elizabeth was happy in her "snug, quiet little home," gaining fifteen pounds and spending most of her time sewing and doing housework, but by the following summer she and Haven had moved back to Mrs. Braun's. Although her landlady set a lavish table, "Day after day passes in the most monotonous manner." The Sargents' new room was on the fourth floor, above the one they had rented eighteen months earlier. She could still "see for 8 to 10 miles over in Illinois." Elizabeth had been sick and reported she was "extremely thin . . . and have a headache most of the time," but the summer was much cooler than the previous one. "Fourth of July passed very quietly. They don't understand getting up things as they do in New England."

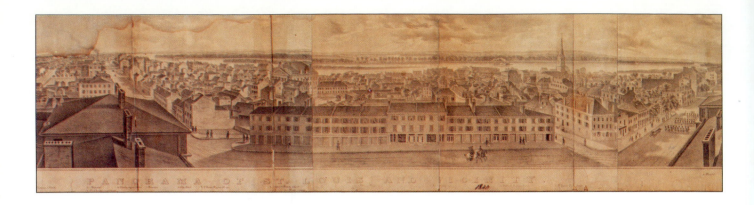

"I cannot tell whether we will stay here for a few years or not," Elizabeth wrote to her sister in August 1847. "It is just according to the opening of business. The place is getting overstocked.... But of St. Louis there is no stability. A man may be worth thousands today and tomorrow be worth nothing. Everything is fluctuating in trade so they say." Elizabeth and Haven Sargent did not stay in St. Louis; they left without a trace sometime after 1850.

Elizabeth Sargent typified many of the young wives who accompanied businessman husbands to antebellum St. Louis, staying only a few years. Isolated from family support and familiar surroundings, she tried to cope in a raw town of precarious fortunes. Because boardinghouses were safe social havens in a strange, unsettled world, they appealed to young, urban couples like the Sargents. In that respect, boardinghouse life resembled convent life for nuns on the urban frontier. While Haven strove to become a self-made man, Elizabeth stayed at home, cultivated domesticity, and seems never to have engaged in the life of the community, much less the social welfare charities that attracted some other eastern women.

Sources: The quotations and information about Elizabeth Sargent's years in St. Louis come from a small selection of letters she wrote to her family in New England: *The Letters of Elizabeth Sargent, 1846–47*, St. Louis History Papers, MHS.

While Elizabeth's correspondence with her mother reveals much about her daily life, she may have left out significant information and may have been discreet about other events and feelings. Her poor health, for example, may have been related to pregnancy and miscarriage. She and Haven might have disagreed bitterly over their St. Louis adventure. See Adler, *Yankee Merchants and the Making of the Urban West* for a good description of the letters' context. A lesson plan based on the letters appears in *SLAH*, Unit 3. The Sargents appear in the 1850 Federal Census for St. Louis but have not been found in other local records or city directories.

Harriet Robinson Scott

Harriet Robinson Scott is most commonly known as the wife of Dred Scott, the Missouri slave who sued for his freedom and lost in 1857. Less recognized is Harriet's impact on the famous case, one of the key events in the sectional conflict that led to the Civil War. Much of the legal process, which lasted eleven years, took place in the west wing of the courthouse on Market and Broadway. Although the suit became a test case for the expansion of slavery, Harriet and Dred Scott had motives of their own for suing to protect the freedom and integrity of their family.

When Dred Scott sued for his freedom as an individual man, Harriet also initiated her own case in 1846. The Scotts' lawyers and the Missouri courts consolidated the cases because they were thought to require similar legal reasoning. Harriet's motives for suing centered around her family.

Harriet was born a slave about 1820 in Virginia. In the early 1830s, her owner, an Indian agent named Major Lawrence Taliaferro, brought her with him to Fort Snelling, Minnesota, a military fort and fur-trading outpost on the upper Mississippi. Harriet worked as his house slave and lived among other slaves owned by members of the military, fur traders, and Indian agents, including a slave named Rachel who would later sue in the St. Louis courts for her freedom and win.

In 1836 Dred Scott arrived at Fort Snelling with his owner, Dr. John Emerson, an army

---

Glasgow's Row, Detail of Panorama of St. Louis and Vicinity. Elizabeth Sargent and her husband took rooms in the back of one of these rowhouses in the heart of St. Louis in 1846. Lithograph by J. C. Wild, 1840. MHS–PP

surgeon whom Dred worked for as a personal valet. Dred and Harriet were married in 1838 in a civil ceremony performed by Taliaferro, who was also the local Justice of the Peace. States customarily denied formal marriage ceremonies to slaves because a man could not be both head of his own household and subject to enslavement. Northern states tended to view marriage as emancipatory, while Southern states denied legal recognition of slave marriages.

Shortly after the wedding, the army transferred Emerson, and the Scotts moved to Jefferson Barracks, Missouri. En route to St. Louis by steamboat, Harriet gave birth to their daughter, Eliza. In St. Louis, Emerson hired out Harriet and Dred to Captain Henry Bainbridge, a relative of his wife, Irene. Harriet most likely worked as a laundress and domestic servant, while Dred probably served as Bainbridge's personal valet. Harriet bore another daughter, Lizzie, one or two years after they arrived; their two sons died as children. Harriet had friends in the St. Louis free black community and attended a black Baptist church. The pastor, Reverend John R. Anderson, was in a position to introduce the Scotts to their first lawyer, Francis Murdoch.

When Dr. Emerson died in 1843, he left his estate to his widow, Irene. Neither Harriet nor Dred appeared in his will. Shortly afterward, Irene left for an extended visit to Massachusetts. For three years, Harriet and Dred were hired out to Bainbridge and to Samuel and Adeline Russell, owners of the Russell and Bennett Grocery at 82 Water Street. Irene collected their wages.

In the spring of 1846, Harriet and Dred Scott filed two lawsuits in the St. Louis Circuit Court demanding their freedom. After an initial mistrial and subsequent retrial, the court decided in favor of the Scotts. The decision accorded with years of precedent in the Missouri courts, which repeatedly granted freedom to slaves who had established residency in free states with their owners' permission or knowledge.

Irene Emerson appealed the case to the Missouri Supreme Court in 1850. During the trial, she married Calvin Chaffee, a physician and antislavery congressman from New York, and transferred ownership of the Scotts to her brother, John F. A. Sanford. Harriet and Dred continued to live at 53 Third Street, between Pine and Olive.

When Sanford won his case, the Scotts appealed to the United States Supreme Court in the famous case *Dred Scott v. Sandford* [sic]. In 1857 the Supreme Court rejected Dred Scott's plea for

freedom. Just after the decision, John Sanford died and left the Scotts to Taylor Blow, who freed Harriet and Dred almost immediately. The next day, at the request of Irene Chaffee's lawyer, the court ruled that the Scotts' wages from the past seven years be paid to Irene.

The United States Supreme Court decision against Dred Scott nullified the Missouri Compromise of 1820, which set aside areas of "free soil" upon which slavery was illegal. The Court upheld owners' rights to take their slaves into free territory for travel or extended residence and thus dramatically increased tensions between slaveholders and Free Soilers.

The Court's decision came as a shock to many, for Harriet and Dred had reason to believe they would win their case. Legal precedent was on their side, as seventy-eight slaves had sued for wrongful enslavement and won their freedom from the St. Louis courts. In his dissent, United States Supreme Court Justice Benjamin Curtis argued that the marriage had freed both Harriet and Dred. No sale papers recorded the transfer of Harriet to Dred's owner, making the intentions of Harriet's owner unclear. He had hinted that he intended to free her with the marriage. If so, Harriet's two daughters were also free, as the children of a free woman could not be born slaves. Harriet had lived on free soil with her owner's permission for at least

Harriet Robinson Scott, Wife of Dred Scott. Wood engraving from *Frank Leslie's Illustrated Newspaper*, 1858. MHS–PP three years, and by Missouri law this made her a free woman. She also listed herself in the St. Louis City Directory for almost twenty years, which slaves generally did not do.

In 1858, Dred Scott died of tuberculosis. Harriet worked as a laundress and lived with her daughter Elizabeth and another middle-aged laundress named Ellen Knox at 811 North Eighth Street, between Franklin and Washington. Harriet listed herself in the city directory until 1870, when presumably she died. Elizabeth married Henry Madison, and their descendants still lived in St. Louis in the 1960s.

Harriet was twenty-eight years old in 1846 and faced the prospect of bearing more children into slavery. As a mother, she had a clear motive for suing for her freedom to keep her family together. Indeed, women initiated about 60 percent of slave suits for freedom in St. Louis, and Harriet's action for legal recognition of her family's right to freedom was not unusual. Had she not been caught up in the national crisis of sectionalism, she might well have succeeded.

–*Katherine Douglass*

Sources: Most of the information in this piece is from the extensively researched article by Lee VanderVelde and Sandhya Subramanian, "Mrs. Dred Scott," *Yale Law Journal* 106, no. 1 (October 1996–January 1997): 1033–122. Information on other lawsuits initiated by slaves is from Moore, "A Ray of Hope, Extinguished," and a phone conversation with the author, November 1997. For the Scotts' addresses and census data, see the St. Louis city directories from 1858 to 1873, and the U.S. Censuses of 1860 and 1870. Other information may be found in John A. Bryan, "The Blow Family and Their Slave Dred Scott," *BMHS* 4, no. 4 (July 1948): 223–31; Kenneth C. Kaufman, *Dred Scott's Advocate: A Biography of Roswell M. Field* (Columbia: University of Missouri Press, 1996); and Charles van Ravenswaay, *St. Louis: An Informal History of the City and Its People, 1764–1865* (St. Louis: MHS Press, 1991).

Harriet Hosmer

"**Y**ou know I was always obstinate," Harriet Hosmer wrote from Rome to St. Louis businessman Wayman Crow in 1858, declaring that "nothing will do but to let me have my own way." Hosmer's characteristically flippant tone does not reveal her serious approach to her art, or the effort it took her to be able to create at all. Although she spent little time in St. Louis, financial support and professional encouragement from Wayman Crow launched Hosmer's career as a sculptor and insured that two of her most important pieces would come to the city. An independent, unconventional woman, Harriet Hosmer became America's first professional female sculptor.

Born in Massachusetts in 1830, Harriet Goodhue Hosmer, the only surviving daughter of a widowed physician, grew up an athletic, energetic tomboy. She had decided at a young age to be a sculptor. Both she and her father realized that a knowledge of anatomy was a prerequisite for such a career. Although her male cousin could attend Harvard Medical School in 1850, Harriet could not. When her father asked the Boston Medical Society if she might attend their anatomy lectures, the impropriety of the request shocked the authorities. Typically, Harriet found a way to break through the gender barrier.

In the fall of 1850, she came to St. Louis, ostensibly to visit a former classmate, Cornelia Crow. She knew that Cornelia's father, Wayman Crow, was influential in St. Louis society. His influence gained Harriet admission to the Missouri Medical College in November 1850. Legend has it that Harriet packed a pistol to protect herself during her daily walk from the Crow home on Eighth and Olive to the medical school at Eighth and Gratiot. Whether or not this occurred, no one ever bothered her. Each morning, Dr. Joseph N. McDowell presented her with the abstract of his daily lecture and gave her an opportunity to study the day's specimens. Each day, wearing the brown bonnet which was her St. Louis trademark, she took her place on the hard bench in the amphitheater while Dr. McDowell presented his anatomical lecture to the entire class. In 1851, the college awarded her a diploma in anatomy.

Harriet Hosmer's next artistic stop was Italy, a common destination for aspiring American artists, especially sculptors. In Europe she could learn with the masters, study antique marbles, and observe live models—something still impossible in America. Also, the marble itself was there, and Hosmer felt a special affinity for that material. Both the setting and the substance reinforced her unwavering devotion to the neoclassical, which ennobles her two major St. Louis commissions, the statue of Thomas Hart Benton in Lafayette Park and Mercantile Library's *Beatrice Cenci*.

Harriet's eccentric nature contrasted sharply with the disciplined neoclassicism that characterized her work. Henry James, who appreciated her talent, wrote that "she was, above all, a character, strong, fresh and interesting, destined, whatever statues she made, to make friends that were better still." Nathaniel Hawthorne and his family visited Harriet's studio in Rome frequently. Although the sculptor's masculine working attire and forward manner initially put off the conservative Hawthorne, he respected her artistic talent. Perhaps Harriet's closest expatriate friendships were with the poets Robert and Elizabeth Barrett Browning. Reviewers praised her 1853 life-size cast of their entwined hands.

Harriet regularly reported the details of her life in Rome to the Crows, and she continued to flourish personally and artistically. In 1853 Wayman Crow became Harriet's patron, and Cornelia Crow announced her plan to marry. The divergence in the young women's lives prompted Harriet to write to her school friend that, even as a wife, she must retain her individuality: "It was never intended that a wife should *obey* a husband for that is the duty of a child toward a parent, but a husband is a friend, a companion and should be an equal." Harriet herself never intended to marry:

> I am the only faithful worshiper of celibacy and her service becomes more and more fascinating the longer I remain in it–even if so inclined an artist has no business to be married– for a man it is all well enough, but for a woman on whom matrimonial duties and cares weigh more heavily, it is a great moral wrong, I think, for she must either neglect her profession or her family, becoming neither a good wife and mother or a good artist. My ambition is to become the latter so I wage eternal feud with the consolidating knot. . . .

Harriet Hosmer's goal was individual freedom, not social reform. Not much of an outspoken women's rights advocate, she showed little interest in the women's suffrage movement.

Wayman Crow arranged for her to get the commission for the *Beatrice Cenci* statue, presented to the Mercantile Library Association of St. Louis in 1857. In a letter to her patron, Hosmer thanked the city, which had given her a chance to educate herself, that single woman's right she championed. She rejoiced that the statue was bound for St. Louis, "a city I love," not only because she began her studies there, but also because of her many friendships. Modestly bemoaning her lack of skill, she attributed to her patron any glory that her work might bestow. The statue, although classic in its graceful lines and symmetry, celebrated the story of the licentious Cenci family, which had caught the

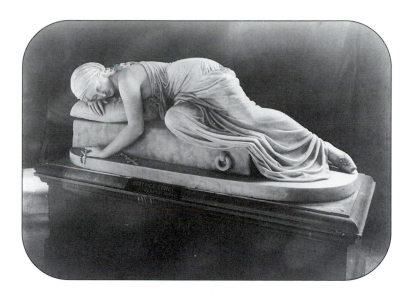

imagination of so many artists of the Victorian era and marked a departure from a classical subject for Harriet Hosmer. Her heroic statue of Thomas Hart Benton, commissioned by the state of Missouri, was erected in Lafayette Park in 1867.

Harriet Hosmer's last statue was a commission from a suffrage group, the Daughters of Isabella, for the 1893 World's Columbian Exposition in Chicago. In a controversy over the location for the statue of Queen Isabella, Harriet agreed with Susan B. Anthony that it should stand in a more prominent location than the Women Building. It was placed in the California Pavilion.

Harriet Hosmer was able to pursue a career in art because a St. Louis family helped her to circumvent the educational restrictions placed on female artists in antebellum America. She worked hard–and cheerfully–to establish her reputation as the "good artist" she had struggled to become. She died in Massachusetts in 1908. Her St. Louis work remains a testament to a woman who used her talent and advantages to secure a place in a profession which was at the time almost exclusively male.

–Kathleen Butterly Nigro

Sources: Biographical information on Harriet Hosmer comes from two works by Dolly Sherwood: *Harriet Hosmer: American Sculptor 1830–1908* (Columbia: University of Missouri Press, 1991), and "Harriet Hosmer's Sojourn in St. Louis," *GH* 5, no. 3 (winter 1984–1985): 42–8.

Additional sources include Cornelia Crow Carr, ed.,

Beatrice Cenci. Sculpture by Harriet Hosmer in the Mercantile Library, St. Louis. Photograph by Emil Boehl, ca. 1890. MHS–PP

Daughters of Charity of St. Vincent de Paul

The mission of the Sisters of Charity, who had first come to St. Louis from Emmitsburg, Maryland, in 1828 to found the Mullanphy Hospital, was to care for the sick and the destitute. In 1845 the order joined the French Daughters of Charity of St. Vincent de Paul. As immigrants crowded into the near north and south parishes, the Daughters of Charity, many of whom were immigrants themselves, established new institutions to care for women and children in need. Like most other religious and secular groups in antebellum St. Louis, the nuns dispensed aid only in institutional settings and only to people defined by the society as unable to care for themselves. However, despite the enormity of their efforts, the need always outran the available resources.

In 1842, Ann Mullanphy Biddle gave the Sisters of Charity property at Marion and Menard for an orphanage, three thousand dollars in start-up funds, and promised operating capital for three years. Within a year, the sisters had taken in forty-five orphan girls. Because the rules of the Daughters of Charity prohibited nuns from teaching boys over the age of five, after 1845 the sisters could no longer operate the boys' orphan asylum next to the St. Louis Cathedral on Walnut. They opened another school for girls at the southwest corner of Fifth and Walnut Streets. St. Philomena's Orphan Asylum and School was both a parish school and boarding school, but its most important function was the education of female orphans sent there from other institutions. The pupils learned to do fine needlework. The money earned from taking in sewing helped pay for the school.

In 1846 they also began caring for girls aged five to fourteen at St. Mary's Orphanage on the northeast corner of Biddle and Tenth, adjacent to the new St. Joseph's Church, built in 1844 for north-side German Catholics. This home was under the jurisdiction of the Catholic Orphans' Association, founded by six Catholic women in 1841 but administered by a board of prominent Catholic laymen.

In May 1853 four more nuns came from the motherhouse in Emmitsburg, Maryland, to start another asylum, this one for abandoned infants. They acquired a small house at Eleventh and Marion Streets, and on opening day they took in fourteen babies.

The sisters soon needed additional space as more foundlings, orphans, and dependent old people came under their care. Their benefactor,

Harriet Hosmer: Letters and Memories (New York: Moffat, Yard and Company, 1912), and Margaret Farrand Thorp, "Harriet Goodhue Hosmer," in *NAW* 2. Henry James quote from Henry James, *William Wetmore Story and His Friends: From Letters, Diaries, and Recollections,* vol. 1 (New York: Kennedy Galleries, 1969). The sculpture of the Browning hands is now in the Cloister of the Clasped Hands at Baylor University in Waco, Texas.

Quotations are from Hosmer's letters in the Hosmer and Lillie Devereux Collections, MHS, and Sherwood, *Harriet Hosmer,* 104, 124, and 163. Also of value is the collection of Robert J. Terry, "Recalling a Famous Pupil of McDowell's Medical College: Harriet Goodhue Hosmer, Sculptor," *Medical Alumni Quarterly of Washington University* 7, no. 1 (October 1943): 59–65.

Ann Mullanphy Biddle. Ann Biddle funded many charitable institutions in her lifetime, including the Visitation Convent, the Girls' Orphan Asylum, the Biddle Foundling Asylum, the Lying-In Hospital, and the Widows' Home. Watercolor on paper by J. H. B., 1847. Courtesy of Marion and Taylor Desloge.

Anne Mullanphy Biddle, willed land near St. Joseph's Church to build another Catholic charitable institution in the neighborhood. Earlier, her father, John Mullanphy, had left ten small houses and some money to the archdiocese for the care of ten aged widows. In 1857 Archbishop Peter Kenrick combined the two bequests to enable the Daughters of Charity to build a single institution. It served as a home for aged widows, a maternity hospital, and a foundling asylum.

In 1859 eleven members of the Daughters of Charity incorporated the new institution in a building at the southeast corner of Tenth and O'Fallon Streets. Officially the St. Ann's Infant Asylum, St. Louisans also called it St. Ann's Widows' Home, and St. Ann's Lying-In Hospital, and even the Biddle and Mullanphy Homes. Ann Biddle bequeathed an annuity of $3,600, but the five sisters designated as business directors also sought donations and other means of support.

In August 1858, the Daughters of Charity leased a former orphanage building from the archdiocese on the southeast corner of Marion and Ninth Streets. They opened St. Vincent's Institute for the Insane, where in 1860 twelve sisters cared for eighty-nine patients, with the help of seven servants and four male nurses. Like most of their patients who were German and Irish immigrants, none of the sisters were native St. Louisans. Mother Superior M. Veronica came from France, five sisters were Irish, three German, and the rest had come from the eastern United States.

Due to the generosity of Ann Mullanphy Biddle and their own ability as business women, the Daughters of Charity operated six essential social welfare institutions on the eve of the Civil War. The large number of foreign born under their care not only reflected St. Louis's burgeoning Catholic population, but also the fact that few recent immigrants had extended families in the city to care for them in times of need.

Sources: For additional information, see Scharf, *History of St. Louis City and County*, 858, 884, 1549; Faherty, *Dream by the River*, 66; Association of the Angels of the Crib, *Angels of the Crib* (St. Louis, 1897); and Rothensteiner, *History of the Archdiocese of St. Louis*.

For information on researching specific individuals who spent time in St. Louis orphanages, see Peggy T. Greenwood, "Beyond the Orphanage," *St. Louis Genealogical Society Quarterly* 24, no. 4; and 26, no. 1, available at MHS. Records of institutions operated by the Daughters of Charity are located at the archives, Marillac Provincial House, 7800 Natural Bridge Road, Normandy.

Sisters of St. Joseph of Carondelet

Soon after the Sisters of St. Joseph arrived in Carondelet in 1836, two motherless girls were left in their care, immediately expanding their teaching mission to include caring for orphans. After Celestine Pommerel assumed leadership of the religious order in 1839, waves of new immigrants entering the city escalated the need for trained personnel to organize and staff orphanages, hospitals, and schools. Under her direction, the order attracted young immigrant women to work locally and to go out from Carondelet to staff institutions in other dioceses.

In 1841, the sisters left the old log cabin that had been their first American home for a new brick convent, day school, and boarding academy at 6400 Minnesota Avenue. Three sisters opened a school for black Catholic girls at Third and Poplar Streets three years later. Although most were the children of free African Americans, a few were slaves whose masters permitted their enrollment. They received a basic education and lessons in French, sewing, and religion. Civil authorities closed the school in 1846, one year before the Missouri legislature made it illegal to educate African Americans, free or slave. The sisters quietly reopened it in the mid-1850s.

Mother Superior Celestine, still in her twenties, continued to train teachers of deaf children while administering a rapidly expanding commitment to staff parish schools for the St. Louis diocese. When

Convent of St. Joseph, Detail from Carondelet, Missouri. Lithograph by Th. Schrader, ca. 1859. MHS–PP

St. Vincent de Paul's Church opened in 1845 at Seventh Street, the Sisters of St. Joseph were asked to staff a parish school. The following year they took over a boys' orphanage at Third and Walnut, previously run by the Daughters of Charity. They later moved it to Thirteenth and Clark Streets. They ran a parish school for girls at St. Mary of Victories, a new church for German Catholics at Third and Gratiot Streets, and staffed the St. Patrick's parish girls' school at Sixth and Biddle Streets. Following the 1849 cholera epidemic, clergy and laity of the city's two German-speaking parishes opened the St. Vincent's German Orphans' Home at Twentieth Street and Cass Avenue, where Sisters of St. Joseph cared for the orphans.

In 1860 nearly all the sisters working in St. Joseph's Half-Orphan Asylum at Marion and Fulton Streets were immigrants from Germany or Ireland. The first eight Sisters of St. Joseph had been French, but in 1837, the daughter of a wealthy St. Louis Irish immigrant joined the order. Mother Celestine welcomed increasing numbers of young immigrant women as postulants and educated them to be teachers and administrators. From her experience in St. Louis, she knew that they needed not only professional training, but also confidence to work successfully with sometimes difficult and authoritarian local clergy. When American bishops requested sisters for their dioceses, she sent them only after she was convinced that the new location had the support of the clergy and Catholic community. Although the nuns came under the jurisdiction of the local bishop, Mother Celestine insisted they retain their identity as Sisters of St. Joseph. In 1857, at the age of forty-four, she died at the head a religious community that had grown from six pioneer nuns to more than 150 professional sisters. The Sisters of St. Joseph of Carondelet separated from the French motherhouse in 1877 to become an autonomous, self-sufficient Americanized order based in St. Louis.

Sources: For information on Celestine Pommerel, see Thomas Nickolai, "Celestine Pommerel," in *Show Me Missouri Women*. See also Sister Dolorita Marie Dougherty, et al., *Sisters of St. Joseph of Carondelet* (St. Louis: B. Herder Books, 1966); Rothensteiner, *History of the Archdiocese of St. Louis*; Marcella M. Halloway C.S.J., "The Sisters of St. Joseph of Carondelet: 150 Years of Good Works in America," *GH* 7, no. 2 (fall 1986); and the archives of the Sisters of St. Joseph–St. Louis Province, located at the motherhouse, 6400 Minnesota Avenue.

Episcopal Orphans' Home

In 1843 the bishop of the Episcopal Diocese of Missouri and the rector of St. John's Church met with a group of female parishioners to plan a home for orphans and destitute children. The women formed a voluntary association to fund and manage the Orphans' Home. In 1845 the Missouri General Assembly granted a charter giving "Emiline Hough and her associates" legal responsibility for the institution.

Emiline Hough, the driving force behind the Orphans' Home, had been a founding member of the Female Charitable Society in 1824. Unlike that organization, however, men had a role in the Orphans' Home. Changes in bylaws required the Episcopal bishop's approval. Only women could be members, but gentlemen could be honorary members by contributing five dollars annually. The Board of Managers, headed by First Directress Hough, had essentially the same responsibilities as the board of the Protestant Orphan Asylum, founded ten years earlier.

The Episcopal orphanage accepted "destitute persons" and children surrendered by their fathers in writing, or, in the absence of a father, by the mother. Most were not true orphans. The managers could "bind-out" children into "virtuous families until they came of age, or in the case of girls, until marriage under age." Most boys were apprenticed at age twelve. Girls, "being useful in the establishment," were frequently retained, although they might be sent out to be domestic servants. Parents had the right to reclaim children at any time, but they had to pay back the cost of the child's support. Managers arranged for adoptions only when parents had relinquished all claims. The Board of Managers made all decisions and rules affecting the children, who after 1848 were allowed visitors only on Tuesdays and Thursdays.

The first orphanage was a cramped alley house in the block bounded by Fifth, Sixth, Spruce, and Almond Streets, which they rented for ten dollars a month. During the first year, the board employed a matron and part-time servant and sometimes a teacher to care for twelve children. In 1848 the board rented a larger home on Franklin Avenue.

The matron and five of the children were the first St. Louisans to die in the 1849 cholera epidemic. The frantic managers took some of the remaining children into their own homes and sent the rest to City Hospital. For the next several years the organization struggled, moving its children from one rented house to another. In 1853, they opened a new building on donated land at Eleventh and Monroe in north St. Louis.

The membership was responsible for raising all the money for operating and building expenses. Female parishioners from each of the Episcopal churches paid annual dues of fifty cents. The dedicated, thrifty board members continually rounded up donations of goods—coffee, sugar, firewood, soap, ham—and held fairs and festivals to raise operating money. They solicited large donations and bequests from the city's businessmen, many of whom were their own husbands. Under the leadership of Mrs. Walker Carter, who succeeded Emiline Hough as first directress, the association succeeded in paying off the construction debt for the orphanage.

Sources: Information is from the Annual Report, *The Orphans' Home* (Episcopal Diocese of Missouri, 1855) and *The Church News*, July 1888, WHMC–UMSL. For the relationship of the Episcopal Diocese of Missouri to the home, see the archives at Christ Church Cathedral, 1210 Locust Street, St. Louis.

School Sisters of Notre Dame

In addition to vows of obedience, poverty, and chastity, women who joined the School Sisters of Notre Dame promised to educate youth. The founders, certified teachers trained in the progressive theories of Swiss educator Johann Pestalozzi, organized the Bavarian order in 1833. Six years later they opened one of the first kindergartens based on Frederick Froebel's philosophy of early childhood education in Germany. Encouraged by King Ludwig I of Bavaria, by 1847 there were 120 professed members educating girls and training teachers in the German states, Hungary, and England. That year Superior General Mother Theresa sent four nuns and a novice to the United States to teach the children of German immigrants. After first establishing a motherhouse in Baltimore, they moved in 1850 to Milwaukee, where Mother Caroline Freiss directed the expansion of the order into cities and small towns throughout the country. By 1860 the School Sisters of Notre Dame were educating two-thirds of all the St. Louis children enrolled in Catholic parochial schools.

From the beginning, the School Sisters of Notre Dame focused solely on religious life and teaching. They did not augment their income with sewing or other money-making projects; teaching

fees and donations covered their expenses. They were not permitted to sing in church choirs or give voice lessons. Like other European religious communities, however, the School Sisters of Notre Dame were a cloistered order when they arrived in Baltimore. Rules of enclosure permitted the sisters to communicate with the outside world only through grills. In Europe, convents, schools, and churches were all connected, enabling the nuns to fulfill their teaching mission without leaving the cloister. Immediately aware that these arrangements would be impossible for poor American churches, the nuns sent Mother Caroline back to Bavaria to negotiate modifications for their mission. Although Mother Theresa never agreed with the changes, she made Sister Caroline the head of the American branch. In her new position, Mother Caroline moved the motherhouse to Milwaukee, applied for American citizenship, and began sending sisters to teach in parish schools throughout the Midwest. Later modifications relieved the American nuns from waking at midnight to pray and permitted them to rise at 4:45 A.M. instead of the prescribed 4 A.M.

In May 1858, at the request of local Jesuits, Mother Caroline brought Mother Mary Seraphime and two teaching sisters from Milwaukee and arranged with Archbishop Peter Kenrick for them to teach girls in the parish school of St. Joseph's Church, the city's largest German Catholic church. At the end of the school year, clergymen and parents applauded the students' academic progress but were particularly pleased with exhibits of their sewing, darning, and crocheting skills. Pastors of Saints Peter and Paul, St. Liborius, and St. Lawrence O'Toole, all churches with large numbers of Irish and German parishioners, immediately requested the sisters. The next year more than one thousand children filled their classrooms. The churches provided living space in the school buildings or supplied a house nearby.

The School Sisters of Notre Dame did not limit their teaching to immigrants from Germany and Ireland. Although they spoke neither Bohemian nor Polish, they opened a parish school for ninety Bohemian children at St. John Nepomuk in St. Louis on the same day they established a school for Polish immigrants in Milwaukee.

Mother Caroline fought to keep control of the internal organization of the order as it expanded throughout America. She advocated for a strong central administration under a single female Superior General to protect the sisters and their schools from the whims of local clergy. Priests were

1928). See also Covelle Newcomb, *Running Waters* (New York: Dodd, Mead, and Co., 1947), and Mary Theola Zimmermann, S.S.N.D., *As a Magnet* (New York: Regina Press, 1967), both popular histories of the order. Like sources for the history of most religious orders, these are the works of members.

The motherhouse of the Southern Province is located at 320 East Ripa Avenue, where sisters also maintain an archive. In the twentieth century they enlarged the complex for Notre Dame College, now closed, and Notre Dame High School. In addition to the girls' high school, the sisters use the facility for a conference center, preschool, and other educational and social services for the surrounding community.

Ursuline Nuns

Answering a call from St. Louis Archbishop Peter Kenrick, three Ursuline nuns left their convent in Oedenburg, Austria, in the spring of 1848 on a mission to educate German-speaking children in Missouri. In order to serve the needs of the church in America, however, the Ursulines had to change the rules they had chosen to live under as religious women in Europe.

Since 1840 immigrants from the German states had flocked to Missouri, prompting Kenrick to recruit teachers abroad who could give proper educations to thousands of Roman Catholic children. After two months at sea, the three cloistered nuns and a postulant landed in Baltimore. Escorted by clergy to St. Louis, they went directly to the convent of the Visitation Sisters and the following month opened their own convent and school, housed in a damp, run-down building on Fifth Street purchased by Archbishop Kenrick.

The Bavarian convent sent more nuns the following year, and King Ludwig I of Bavaria, who funded many German Catholic activities in America, sent four thousand dollars to help build a new convent. The sisters also received regular donations from the Ludwig Mission-Verein, an association of Bavarian Catholics. With this money, the archbishop secured a lot on State Street, now Twelfth Street, between Russell and Ann Avenues, and in 1851 the Ursulines moved into a new convent. By 1855 Mother Aloysia Winkler was sending small groups of nuns out from St. Louis to open convent schools in other cities, including Alton, Illinois.

By 1860 the St. Louis community had twenty-five professed nuns and fifteen novices. There were 50 boarders and 120 day students. During the Civil War, the enrollment plummeted, as concerned parents refused to send their daughters into a war

responsible for religious services; bishops, parish priests, and school inspectors oversaw the running of schools. The common practice was to make local women's orders subject to the superior of the corresponding order of men or the diocesan bishop. The School Sisters of Notre Dame and the Religious of the Sacred Heart were the nineteenth-century orders most able to maintain their autonomy. During their first twenty years in America, the School Sisters of Notre Dame opened 126 parochial schools in 14 states and 17 dioceses. From the first four sisters who stepped off the boat in Baltimore, the American order grew to 669 professed nuns by 1870.

By the end of the nineteenth century, School Sisters of Notre Dame taught in more than one hundred parochial schools and a dozen high schools and academies in St. Louis and surrounding towns. In the 1880s, Mother Caroline chose St. Louis as the location of a motherhouse for the new Southern Province, although it was not established until after her death in 1892. The order purchased twenty-one acres on a bluff overlooking the Mississippi River adjoining Jefferson Barracks in 1894 and constructed Sancta Maria in Ripa, a large facility for training teachers, three years later.

Sources: Information is from Barbara Brymleve, S.S.N.D., "Ninteenth Century SSND Innovative Educators" (St. Louis: School Sisters of Notre Dame, 1983), and a two-volume history of the order written by an anonymous School Sister of Notre Dame, *Mother Caroline and the School Sisters of Notre Dame in North America* (St. Louis: Woodward & Tiernan Co.,

Former Ursuline Convent at Twelfth Street and Russell Avenue. Photograph by George Rothenbuescher, 1999.

zone. In 1862 wartime fears prompted the sisters to construct a wall in front of their building. Despite debts incurred during the war, in 1866 they enlarged the convent to accommodate both an academy and a day school.

Archbishop Kenrick, however, had requested the nuns because he needed teachers for the German parishes rapidly organizing throughout the archdiocese. The Ursulines, who were cloistered nuns, came to Missouri on a mission they could not possibly fulfill. Their rule prohibited them to leave the convent. Unless the order changed its rules, the sisters could not live in parish convents and teach in parish schools. Fortunately for the archbishop, the Ursuline constitution could be modified without papal permission to allow the sisters to appear in public for the purpose of attending school and church. At the end of the school term, however, the Ursulines all returned to the St. Louis convent.

Under this compromise, the Ursulines were able to open thirty-six schools in rural Missouri. By the end of the century, the St. Louis community included 155 nuns, many from the small towns where the sisters lived and taught nine months of the year.

Sources: For additional information, see Rothensteiner, *History of the Archdiocese of St. Louis,* 37; Faherty, *Dream by the River,* 77; Sister Ignatius Miller, O.S.U., *Ursulines of the Central Province* (Crystal City, Mo.: Ursuline Provincialate, 1983); and Mother Ambrose Duffy, *The Ursulines in St. Louis, 1848–1928* (St. Louis: A. B. Dewes Printing Co., 1928).
In 1912 the Ursulines opened St. Angela's Academy on Sappington Road in Kirkwood, and in 1925 they left the city for a new school constructed on the Oakland Avenue property. They sold the complex at Twelfth Street and Ann Avenue to St. Joseph's Croatian Church.

Sisters of the Good Shepherd

Most of the unmarried Irish women who immigrated to St. Louis in the 1840s found jobs as servants, but some of those unable or unwilling to do domestic work drifted into prostitution. Their redemption was the special mission of the Sisters of Our Lady of Charity of the Good Shepherd, who in 1849 opened an institution for "the reformation of fallen women and the preservation of young girls in danger." In addition to their vows of chastity, poverty, and obedience, the Sisters of the Good Shepherd committed themselves to the welfare of scorned and rejected women. Founded in France in the seventeenth century, they had convents in

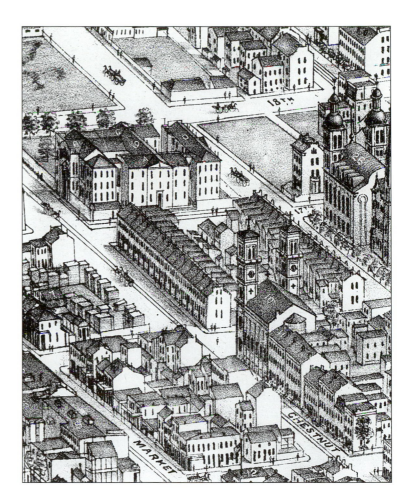

Ireland, Britain, and the United States. By the mid-nineteenth century, urbanizing America presented many opportunities for the sisters to do their rescue work. While most of the sisters were Irish, an Italian and German were among the five who came to St. Louis from Kentucky.

The sisters arrived penniless. Archbishop Kenrick met the nuns at the wharf and took them to a vacant house at Marion and Decatur, recently bequeathed to the archdiocese. He also provided another house nearby, since the sisters' constitution required that they live apart from the penitents they served. Within a year Anne Lucas Hunt, who supported many local Catholic institutions, donated land on the outskirts of town for a new building. Kenrick raised the funds to build a convent in 1852 on the block bounded by Sixteenth, Seventeenth, Chestnut, and Pine Streets. The cloistered sisters welcomed local "fallen women"

House of the Good Shepherd. Detail from Richard Compton and Camille N. Dry, *Pictorial St. Louis,* 1875, plate 42. Originally built in 1852, the complex saw the city grow around it. Lithograph by Camille N. Dry. MHS Library

Convent of the Visitation, Cass Avenue and Twenty-third Street. Wood engraving by F. Lamp from *St. Louis Illustrated*, published by Will Conklin, 1876. MHS Library

into a safe, structured environment that not only stressed their status as sinners, but also promised forgiveness and rehabilitation.

Some women came on their own to the convent; priests and parents brought others. Non-Catholics were admitted, but few came. Girls committed for prostitution to the House of Refuge, a public juvenile reformatory, sometimes came to the House of the Good Shepherd instead. The white-robed sisters separated their residents into distinct categories. Orphans left in their care lived apart from the "Class of Preservation," young women judged to be in danger of becoming prostitutes. Reformed prostitutes, called penitents, stayed as long as they wanted and could always return. Some chose never to leave and became nuns themselves, entering a separate contemplative order for reformed prostitutes called the Magdalens. Dressed in brown, Magdalens lived on the convent grounds but always separate from their protectors. Some residents, especially the Magdalens, earned money for the convent by doing much-prized sewing for layettes and trousseaus.

Women the sisters had cared for could never join the order, because virginity was a requirement for admission. Other young predominantly Irish women did join, however, and in 1859 the St. Louis convent became a Provincial House, a training center for sisters who in turn established convents first in Chicago and later in cities throughout the West.

Sources: For a study that could inform local researchers, see Suellen Hoy, "Caring for Chicago's Women and Girls: The Sisters of the Good Shepherd, 1859–1911," *Journal of Urban History* 23, no. 3 (March 1997). For additional information, see Scharf, *History of St. Louis City and County,* 1759; Rothensteiner, *History of the Archdiocese of St. Louis*; and the 1922 History of Sisters of the Good Shepherd, MHS. The archives of the Sisters of the Good Shepherd are located at the Provincialate, 7654 Natural Bridge Road, Normandy.

Academy of the Visitation

Agnes Brent was the daughter of a Maryland planter and niece of the archbishop of Baltimore. In 1815 she joined a new religious community modeled on the European Visitation Order, becoming directress five years later when she was only twenty-five. In 1832 she wanted to go west and open an academy for girls in St. Louis, but since the Sisters of the Sacred Heart had just moved their school to the city, Bishop Rosati suggested the Visitation Sisters settle instead across the Mississippi River in Kaskaskia, Illinois. Most of the nuns who moved to Kaskaskia were the daughters of Maryland planters and ill prepared for frontier village life. The region's wealthiest families, however, welcomed these new upper-class teachers and eagerly enrolled their children in Menard Academy. When the Visitation Sisters moved to St. Louis ten years later, they continued to educate the daughters of the Catholic elite.

In 1843, with the permission of Archbishop Peter Kenrick, Mother Brent brought six sisters from Illinois to St. Louis to open a school on Sixth Street near Pine. The following June, flood waters inundated the Kaskaskia school and convent. Sixteen sisters and twenty students fled to St. Louis where Anne Mullanphy Biddle welcomed them into her home on fashionable Fifth Street. In 1846 the two communities reunited in a spacious residence at Ninth and Menard Streets, a gift from the bishop.

The daughters of prominent Catholic, and some Protestant, families enrolled in the Academy of the Visitation. Mother Brent, after several years away from St. Louis, returned in 1850 eager to build on land given to the school by Ann Biddle. The location at the western limits of the city, away from smoke and congestion and near new subdivisions of substantial homes, put the academy close to the students it hoped to attract. Mother Brent borrowed $113,862 from the archdiocese to construct a three-story Federal-style building on Cass Avenue and Twenty-third Streets. The new school opened in 1858 and Agnes Brent, who lived to be eighty-one, retired from her administrative position shortly afterward.

Sources: For more on Mother Brent, see William B. Faherty, S.J., "Agnes Brent," in *Show Me Missouri Women*. Additional information is from the Centennial Souvenir, "The Academy of the Visitation," 1933. Archives of the Visitation Nuns are at Visitation Academy, 3020 North Ballas Road.

Home for the Friendless

In 1852 Charlotte Charless discovered that her former seamstress, an Irish immigrant, had died friendless and destitute in the St. Louis County poorhouse. Rachel Adams had been a proper, self-supporting maiden lady, and yet she suffered the same fate as the most irresponsible reprobate. Shocked by this seeming injustice, Charless went to her husband, the editor of St. Louis's leading newspaper, the *Missouri Republican*. She asked him and ten other businessmen for donations to open a home "to relieve the distress among that class for whom the ills of poverty add to the feebleness of age and sex." She collected nearly twenty thousand dollars. She and her socially prominent allies also convinced St. Louis County government to let her organization float public bonds with low rates of interest. From the beginning, the economic and social position of its founders insured the financial health of the Home for the Friendless. The

organizers had resources unavailable to Roman Catholic religious orders or most Protestant women's organizations who served the poorest St. Louisans.

Charlotte Charless and the wives of prominent St. Louis businessmen obtained a Missouri state charter, which made any woman who contributed to the institution a member of the corporation. The elected board of female trustees turned over responsibility for the group's financial affairs to a board of male advisors. They located a two-story stone building, which had previously been a boys' school, situated on eight acres of land four miles south of the city on Carondelet Road overlooking the Mississippi River.

At first the home accepted respectable Protestant and Catholic women over the age of fifty who had no other means of support. A thirty-dollar admission fee was the only charge. Residents worked in the garden, canned food, made clothing, and helped with the housework. While clearly not of the same social class as Charlotte Charless and her friends, women accepted into the home shared their benefactors' social universe–if only as seamstresses, teacher, companions, housekeepers, or as wives and sisters of tradesmen and small businessmen. The home also took in transient women in need of temporary assistance and helped them find jobs and lodgings. Until the 1860s, residents who were temporarily financially embarrassed outnumbered the permanent guests.

Antebellum local government gave no funds or other assistance to able-bodied men or women without family or resources. For elderly dependent women, the Home for the Friendless was one of the few alternatives to the county poorhouse, a dumping ground for the old and destitute.

Sources: Information is from Scharf, *History of St. Louis City and County*, 1760–61, and "The Home for the Friendless: A Century of Service," *BMHS* 10, no. 2 (January 1954): 186–91. The records of the Home for the Friendless, now called the Charless Home, are at WHMC–UMSL.

Girls' Industrial Home

In 1855 Mary B. Homes, the wife of the minister of Union Presbyterian Church, and Mary Ann Ranlett, whose husband was an insurance company executive and trustee of the Unitarian Church, joined with other Protestant women to incorporate the "Industrial School and Temporary Home for

Destitute Children." Their goal was "reclaiming and teaching habits of industry and educating orphan children, and children of depraved and destitute parents." Women who contributed at least three dollars annually became voting members of the corporation. In 1857 they renamed the institution the Girls' Industrial Home. The home and school were located in an old brewery building and ten-room house on a large lot at the southeast corner of Morgan and Nineteenth Streets. It offered poor girls and orphans a structured home life and a useful education. The managers also acted as an adoption agency for girls relinquished by their parents to the institution.

Like other middle-class Protestant women who directed similar orphanages in antebellum St. Louis, the Board of Managers set policy and raised money. They hired a matron and a teacher to run the institution with economy and discipline. Board members on the home's Visiting Committee sought out girls from nearby immigrant neighborhoods who were not attending public or parochial schools and offered them classes, shelter, meals, and clothing. When the members discovered children abandoned or battered by alcoholic parents, they tried to get them into the home. By 1858 they had rescued nearly five hundred girls. In that year, twenty girls lived in the home; on most days eighty girls ate their noon meal there.

While sympathetic to parents plagued by illness, the managers maintained that the majority of girls under their supervision were abused victims of "depraved" homes and tried to give the girls a clean break with their former surroundings. Unlike many orphanages, the home did not discipline with corporal punishment. They permitted the girls to have visitors one Friday a month but only with the matron or a board member present. Parents or guardians who could not retrieve a girl within six months had to relinquish custody to the institution. The board could then offer the girl for adoption or place her in a private home until she married or turned eighteen. Applicants wishing to adopt a girl submitted references and a statement defining her role in the family, the work she would be required to do, her opportunities for education, and the religious training she would receive. By 1858, fifty girls had been adopted or placed in homes, where most of them worked as domestic servants while attending school.

Motivated by concern for girls at risk, the managers of the Industrial Home nevertheless showed little concern for the parents or their wishes. Whether or not the managers believed only poor parents were depraved or abused their children, they certainly did not consider removing a middle-class child from her home. The poor in nineteenth-century St. Louis had few, if any, parental rights, just as abused children had few places to turn for help. In 1851 the State of Missouri opened the House of Refuge for indigent, orphaned, and delinquent girls and boys. Located south of the city at Gasconade and Osage Streets, it was a raw, underfunded, unpleasant place that, unlike the Girls' Industrial Home, belied its name.

Sources: Information is from the Fourth Annual Report, *The Girls' Industrial Home*, 1858, including charter and bylaws; and Scharf, *History of St. Louis City and County*, 1761–62. The Girls' Industrial Home moved to 5501 Von Versen Avenue, now Enright, and later merged with the St. Louis Protestant Orphan Asylum to become the Edgewood Children's Center at 330 North Gore Avenue. Microfilmed records and reports are available at WHMC–UMSL. Some records for the House of Refuge are at MHS.

Sisters of Mercy

By late 1856, the sight of two nuns walking briskly down the muddy streets of Kerry Patch no longer drew astonished looks. The sisters had come from New York several months before at the request of Jesuit Father Arnold Damen, pastor of St. Francis Xavier Church, at the corner of Ninth and Green Streets. Beginning in the 1840s poor Irish immigrants had moved into shanties in the largely undeveloped north side west of St. Xavier's, the college church for nearby Saint Louis University. Alarmed by the mounting poverty, sickness, and a "dangerous relaxation of moral principals" among his new parishioners, Father Damen asked Archbishop Peter Kenrick to send for some Sisters of Mercy to help him.

The Sisters of Mercy was an Irish order dedicated to serving the practical needs of the poor in their own homes. By leaving the cloister of their convent and working with the parish priest in the community, the Sisters of Mercy were the first organization in St. Louis, Catholic or Protestant, with a mission to care for the poor outside an institutional setting. During their early years in the city, their own lack of resources nearly defeated their efforts.

Led by Sister M. de Pazzi Bently, six sisters got off the steamboat in June 1856 and were delivered to a shabby makeshift convent at Tenth

Street and Morgan Avenue. They immediately began seeking out the sick and poor in the surrounding neighborhood. In July they made their first visits to the city jail and City Hospital. In August they opened a free parish school for girls at St. Xavier's Church and a Sunday school for black women and girls.

The nuns quickly realized that young, unemployed, and unskilled women faced domestic and sexual exploitation in the crowded chaotic tenements of the immigrant neighborhood. By year's end their convent housed the St. Catherine's Orphanage and Industrial School for Girls, and the House of Mercy, a free shelter for unemployed girls. The girls, many of whom were half-orphans and not eligible at that time for other Catholic orphanages, received a basic education as well as training in domestic skills and plain sewing.

Not even the energetic sisters could keep up with the runaway social needs of antebellum St. Louis. They quickly outran their resources and were themselves rarely much better off than the poor they served. Father Damen paid their transportation to St. Louis, found the old house for their convent, and gave them two other houses to rent for income. In the four years between 1856 and 1860, they lived on rents, donations (including nine hundred dollars from Archbishop Kenrick), and the proceeds from a bazaar and raffle. But their $5,670 income fell far short of their needs. By taking in laundry and sewing in the evening they made an additional $1,239, which enabled them to stay in St. Louis.

Despite the congregation's poverty, their numbers increased. By 1860 the nuns, the unemployed girls, and the orphans overwhelmed the old convent building. The archbishop gave the women a building lot at Morgan and Twenty-second, in the heart of Kerry Patch, and bought some of their old buildings to help fund a new one. Once St. Joseph's Convent of Mercy opened in 1860, wealthy Catholics began contributing to the sisters and their work. At the insistence of the archbishop, however, the sisters reluctantly opened a "select," or pay, school in the basement of the new convent. It was not a moneymaker since few Irish parents in the neighborhood could afford tuition. Although attending to the spiritual health of Catholics under their care was integral to their vocation, the Sisters of Mercy expended most of their energy and limited resources on the physical health and well-being of their poor neighbors.

APPENDIX 33

AGREEMENT BETWEEN ARCHBISHOP KENRICK AND THE SISTERS OF MERCY

1. When an application has been made for Sisters to found a convent on our order and it has been deemed advisable to accede to it, a copy of the following agreement is presented to the Bishop of the diocese requiring the foundation, for his approval and signature.

2. That the Right Reverend Prelate, as soon as the Sisters shall have placed themselves under his jurisdiction, become the guardian of their Rule, Constitutions' and Customs as at present existing in the Parent House, St. Louis, Mo., and by his canonical authority give force and vigor to their observances.

3. That the Right Reverend Prelate shall not introduce new practices of devotion or charity, however excellent in themselves, or abolish any of those already established as experience has amply demonstrated how admirably they are adapted to the attainment of the sublime end of this holy Institute, the sanctification of the members and the spiritual and temporal advantage of their fellow creatures.

4. That the Right Reverend Prelate shall by the appointment of a chaplain, secure to the Sisters, daily Mass in the convent.

5. That besides the ordinary confessor the Right Revereld Prelate appoint an extra-ordinary director to whom the guidance of the Sisters in the spiritual life shall be confided, but that neither of them shall be authorized to interfere with external obser-vances, customs or duties of the community.

(Signed) Sister Agnes O'Connor

Mother Superior

Agreement Between Archbishop Kenrick and the Sisters of Mercy. Typescript from *The Impact of Catholic Hospitals in St. Louis,* Appendix 33, ca. 1856. MHS Library

Sources: Information for this essay comes from Scharf, *History of St. Louis City and County*, 1555; Mary Constance Smith, *A Sheaf of Golden Years, 1856–1906* (New York: Benzinger Brothers, 1906); Mary Isidore Lennon, R.S.M., *Milestones of Mercy: Story of the Sisters of Mercy in St. Louis, 1856–1956* (Milwaukee: Bruce Press, 1957); and Rothensteiner, *History of the Archdiocese of St. Louis*. Archival records of the Sisters of Mercy are located at the motherhouse at 2039 North Geyer Road, St. Louis, Missouri 63130.

White Haven

In 1844 Ulysses S. Grant, a young army officer, gave his West Point class ring to Julia Dent on the front porch of White Haven, her family home. Her father, Colonel Frederick Dent, had bought the eight hundred-acre estate, located about twelve miles south of St. Louis, in 1820. Julia grew up on the farm with her parents, three sisters, four brothers, and about thirty slaves, many of whom were women. Like other substantial St. Louis County farms, White Haven was a place where black women and white women lived together, but for the female slaves it differed greatly from the place Julia Dent Grant called home.

Julia was born in St. Louis in 1826, the fifth of Ellen Wrenshall Dent's seven children. The family first used White Haven as a summer retreat to escape the heat and dirt of the city, but later made it their year-round residence. In her memoirs Julia described her home as the scene of a happy childhood. She recalled social gatherings in the family sitting room and formal parlor, but she remembered the front porch, or piazza, as the most pleasant place in the house. Her earliest recollection was her father lifting her from the piazza to see the locust trees blowing in the wind. She remembered the family listening to her sister play the guitar "as we sat on the piazza in the summer moonlight." She sat there with her mother and watched her four older brothers play games on the lawn in front of the house.

A year after Grant gave Julia his ring, he stood with her on the porch to see her father off on a business trip to the East. Grant rode with Colonel Dent to St. Louis and on the way asked for his daughter's hand in marriage. When Julia and Ulysses Grant married in 1848, Colonel Dent gave her eighty acres of the farm as a wedding present. Julia traveled with her husband while he was in the army, visiting only briefly at White Haven, but after Grant resigned in 1854 he built a log house on the property for his growing family. After her mother died three years later, Julia became the mistress of White Haven. The Grants were financially strapped until Ulysses reentered the army. Beginning in 1863, however, Grant began purchasing land from the Dent family; by 1865 he owned most of the farm. During the Civil War, when her husband served as a U.S. Army general, Julia acted as the farm's manager.

Although Julia, like her mother before her, was responsible for the domestic life of White Haven, she relied on slaves to do the housekeeping, prepare the meals, and provide daily child care. Kitty, Anne, and Suzanna, Julia's childhood playmates, took care of the four Grant children. Julia took her slave, Jule, with her during the Civil War to help with the children when she visited General Grant's various encampments. Jule reportedly slipped away to freedom on one of these trips. Years later, Julia Grant expressed regret over the loss of her emancipated slaves, believing they had been well cared for at White Haven.

The contrast between White Haven's open sunlit piazza and the dark enclosed basement kitchen illustrates the vast differences in the daily lives of the Dent women and their female slaves. Slave women worked in the winter kitchen, located under the west wing of the main house, and in the stone summer kitchen nearby. In the winter, they prepared food in the hot, dark basement and carried it out the back door into the cold yard. They took it up the steps onto the back porch and into the dining room three times a day. Mary Robertson, the slave woman Julia called "black Mary" in her memoir, was the head cook. She produced "loaves of beautiful snowy cake, such plates full of delicious Maryland biscuit, such exquisite custards and puddings, such omelettes, gumbo soups, and fritters." Mary probably spent her entire day in the basement preparing such delicacies to be served to the Dent family. "Old Aunt Eadie" made cornbread cakes for the slaves, and prepared their meals from the parts of butchered animals not considered suitable for the owner's family. Young slave girls assisted the women and did the serving. One slave woman probably slept in the basement to be ready to start cooking at daybreak.

The winter kitchen was rarely used after emancipation. During his presidency, Grant hired tenants to work the farm. With his permission, they enclosed a portion of the back porch to make a first-floor kitchen. The new caretakers, William and Sarah Elrod, moved into the house with their three daughters, who, unlike the Dent girls, were expected to do housework and to earn extra income by keeping chickens.

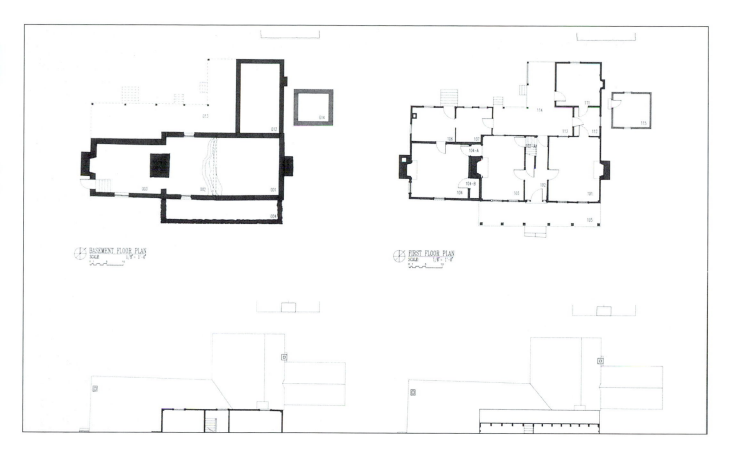

BASEMENT FLOOR PLAN
SCALE 1/8" = 1'-0"

FIRST FLOOR PLAN
SCALE 1/8" = 1'-0"

After Grant's presidency, the family lived in New York City and seldom returned to White Haven. In 1884 Grant had to sell the property to repay a loan. Profits from the former president's memoirs written just before his death in 1885 made Julia a wealthy woman. She lived in New York until her death in 1902.

–Pamela K. Sanfilippo

Sources: August A. Busch purchased White Haven and about 280 surrounding acres from private owners in 1903. The National Park Service (NPS) now owns the ten-acre core, including the house and four other historic structures. The NPS interprets the Ulysses S. Grant National Historic Site primarily as the home of the eighteenth president, but White Haven is also one of the few NPS properties with an explicit mandate to interpret women associated with the site. New programs for visitors are based on research developed in connection with the renovation of the house, now painted Paris Green as it was in 1870. Historians use archaeological artifacts, particularly those found in the kitchen, as evidence for interpreting the experiences of slave women. Other historic houses in the St. Louis area which are open to the public include the Campbell House Museum at 1508 Locust Street, the Eugene Field House at 634 S. Broadway, the Tower Grove House at the Missouri Botanical Garden, the Scott Joplin House at 2658 Delmar Boulevard, and the Bates House in Faust Park. Some provide programs that focus on the experiences of women and all are opportunities for research in the use of domestic space.

In addition to information from the National Park Service, sources for this essay include Julia Grant's memoirs, not published until 1975. John Y. Simon, ed., *The Personal Memoirs of Julia Dent Grant* (Carbondale: Southern Illinois University Press, 1975). See also Ishbel Ross, *The General's Wife: The Life of Mrs. Ulysses S. Grant* (New York: Dodd, Mead & Co., 1959); John Y. Simon, ed., *The Papers of Ulysses S. Grant*, vol. 1–20 (Carbondale: Southern Illinois University Press, 1967); and Emma Dent Casey, "When Grant Went A Courtin'," Grant Collection, MHS.

Pamela K. Sanfilippo is the NPS historian at White Haven. Sharra Vostral also provided information for this essay.

Historic Building Chronology, Phase IV: 1840–68 (detail showing first floor plan and basement) of White Haven. Drawn August 30, 1993 by L. M. Johnson. Courtesy of National Park Service Ulysses S. Grant National Historic Site.

Women at the Gateway to the West

75

1860–1865

1. Benton Barracks
2. Freedmen's Orphan Home
3. Ladies' Contraband Relief Society Refugee Home
4. St. Charles Street Prison
5. Mississippi Valley Sanitary Fair Building
6. Eighth Street Baptist Church
7. Margaret McClure House
8. Ladies' Union Aid Society Refugee Home
9. Ladies' Union Aid Society General Hospital and Western Sanitary Commission Office
10. Myrtle Street Prison
11. Gratiot Street Prison
12. Walnut Street Refugee Home
13. Fremont Headquarters
14. Floating Hospitals

━━ St. Louis City Limits 1855–1876

▢ Parks

4

St. Louis Women and the Civil War

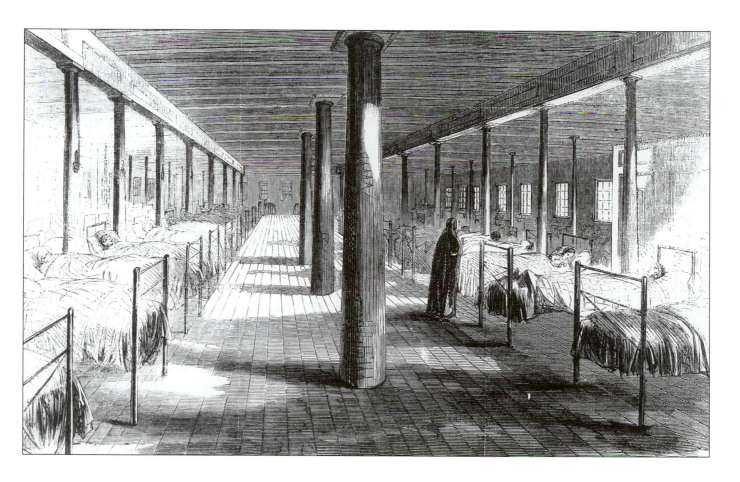

In December 1860, Sallie Case wrote from St. Louis to her cousin Sue King in Chicago. Amidst reports of family illnesses, Christmas preparations, and other domestic concerns, Sallie reflected on the political whirlwinds swirling outside her home: "There is a dreadful state of things now–times are so very hard, and the political trouble seems to be getting worse. Certainly we will have to render an account for our sins, if slavery is a sin we will have to bear the

punishment, and why should any one interfere if they would get up some good laws to protect the negroes, and limit the power of owners." She hoped for compromise to avert the impending crisis, for some way to preserve peace *and* the Union by containing slavery without freeing the slaves.

The Ward. Floating Hospital on the Mississippi. Wood engraving after Theodore R. Davis from *Harper's Weekly*, 9 May 1863. MHS Library

"We, the border states, will have all the trouble. Way down South and in the North it is easy enough to go either way, but what can we do but be pulled about by fanatics & fire eaters. . . . Well I wish it had happened after my time."

Sallie Case's position might seem morally untenable, but in 1860 it was commonly held by such politically diverse leaders as Democrat Senator Thomas Hart Benton and Republican presidential hopeful Abraham Lincoln. Sallie's anxiety and frustration also reflected her position as a woman caught up in political debates in which women had no formal voice. Like other St. Louisans, however, her race and class gave her a vested interest in their outcome.

As a slave owner, Sallie Case's domestic arrangements depended on preserving the slave system in Missouri. When six months later war came to St. Louis she sympathized with the Southern cause but did not take an active role. Other local women did, either in support of the Union or the Confederacy, and the conflict became the occasion for their stepping even further into public life. Partisanship spurred Unionists to use their organizational and fund-raising skills to care for needy St. Louisans, wounded soldiers, and refugees. Some Confederate women actively aided the Southern forces, while others watched their possessions sold for refugee relief. The war brought freedom to black women

but often put even greater burdens on poor women, particularly homeless ex-slaves and soldiers' wives.

In 1860, therefore, Sally Case had good reason to worry about the future. The sectional crisis over the extension of slavery was rapidly pushing St. Louis and the nation to war. For a few white and all black St. Louisans, the irreconcilable issue was the very existence of slavery, which denied African Americans their freedom. Some women and men, whose roots often lay in eastern Protestantism, believed slavery was a sin that corrupted whites as much as it oppressed blacks. However, they tended to favor moral persuasion over direct abolitionist action. Some would gladly have freed the slaves if they could have devised a way to remove freed African Americans from the country, either by sending them to Africa or to the Caribbean. Most local politicians, like most national leaders, cast the question in terms of the impact the slave system had on property rights, national unity, and territorial expansion.

Southerners argued that Congress did not have the power to deny slave owners the right to own property–slaves–no matter where they lived. Northerners argued that Congress could regulate slavery in the territories and require or prohibit slavery as a condition of statehood under the provisions of the Missouri Compromise. Popular Sovereignty, which would allow the white male residents of a territory to choose or reject slavery, seemed to many people a reasonable compromise in the early 1850s. Southern politicians could envision a time, however, when immigration and population growth in the North would eventually destroy the balance of free and slave states. The more populous North would win the battle for the West and control of Congress.

Slavery was legal in Missouri because slave owners held the state's political power in 1821. Since then, Northern businessmen, German and Irish immigrants, and settlers from all states east of the Mississippi had muddied the political waters. Politically radical Germans, who had fled repressive governments abroad to live in a democratic country, were strong Union supporters vigorously opposed to slavery.

By the 1850s some Missouri politicians had joined the new Free Soil Party. Free Soilers rested their main objections to slavery on economic rather than moral or religious grounds; they evidenced more concern about the harm slavery did to whites than it did to blacks. Under the banner of "Free Soil, Free Speech, Free Labor, and

---

Issuing Passes at St. Louis. Under martial law, women needed passes to visit and nurse prisoners. At least one who refused the oath of loyalty to the Union was able to get past the guards by flashing an old St. Louis high school tuition receipt. Wood engraving, 1862, from *Harper's Pictorial History of the Civil War.* MHS–PP

Free Men," they argued that entrenched slave power hindered economic growth by opposing tariffs, internal improvements, and the development of the West by white entrepreneurs and small farmers. The local Free Soil Party eventually adopted the slogan, "White Men for Missouri and Missouri for White Men."

The Dred Scott decision rendered the Missouri Compromise, which joined the state to the Union in 1821, unconstitutional. In effect, the U.S. Supreme Court supported the Southern position by ruling that Congress could not prohibit slavery in the territories.

By 1860, St. Louis Free Soilers, led by Congressman Frank Blair, had joined with antislavery Germans in supporting the developing national Republican Party. In the presidential election, Abraham Lincoln carried the heavily German wards in north and south St. Louis but lost in the middle wards comprising more Irish immigrants and wealthier Anglo-Americans. Statewide, Lincoln finished last. Missouri men also elected a proslavery Democrat governor, Claiborne Jackson.

Divisions within the city ran deeper than politics. Rapid native-born and immigrant population growth in the 1850s had reinforced long-standing ethnic and religious tensions. By the eve of the Civil War, St. Louis was already a divided community and increasingly alienated from Missouri as a whole. It was a predominantly pro-Northern city in a predominantly pro-Southern state. Sectional loyalties also strained business ties. Capital pulled St. Louisans north and east, while markets drew them south and west.

Although fewer than fifteen hundred slaves lived in the city by 1860, St. Louisans still actively engaged in the slave trade. Wealthy families with colonial or southern origins, especially in rural St. Louis County, depended on slave labor for domestic help and farm labor. Slaves, however, persistently ran away and resisted their bondage in more subtle ways. When immigrants began underbidding slave labor, it became more profitable to sell slaves than to hire them out.

A surface appearance of local elite solidarity masked deep social cleavages rooted in religion, ethnic identity, and family history. These factors contributed to the animosities that erupted in 1861, shortly after the Southern states seceded, formed the Confederate States of America, and fired on Fort Sumter. In May public response to the St. Louis "Battle of Camp Jackson"—where pro-Union forces, made up largely of German

immigrants, thwarted the pro-South Missouri militia's dream of delivering the state to the Confederacy—revealed how deep the divisions were. Not only families, but churches, clubs, and other civic institutions began splitting along partisan lines.

Although St. Louis became the Union stronghold in Missouri, both politically and militarily, women remained no less divided in their allegiances than men. In August 1861, General John C. Fremont, then the Union military commander in St. Louis, declared martial law in Missouri in an attempt to squash Confederate influence. Military rule remained in effect until March 1865. St. Louisans lived four years in a war zone, although no military action occurred in the city after the street violence following the surrender of Camp Jackson.

No St. Louis woman could escape the upheaval of war, even if she or her family members took no public political stance. Martial law protected citizens from violence but suppressed newspapers and required residents to sign loyalty oaths and carry passes. Husbands and sons enlisted in opposing armies. Authorities moved thousands of prisoners, wounded soldiers, and refugees into converted private residences and public buildings. War mobilization created more jobs for women, but the cost of living escalated. After Lincoln rescinded Fremont's 1861 Missouri emancipation decree, hundreds of black women were caught between slavery and freedom, until January 11, 1865, when the state legislature finally abolished slavery.

Sallie Case and her husband stayed in their Chambers Road home in rural north St. Louis County. George Case, a doctor who avoided service in the Union Army with a physician's deferment, was part-owner of an omnibus company. Throughout the war, Sallie struggled with ordinary domestic concerns: her own health and that of her large family; several new babies; and making clothes for herself, her children, and slaves.

The Civil War touched the domestic life of other women more directly. Most Union officers received regular pay, but enlisted men often went without paychecks for months, leaving their wives to support themselves and their children. Black men who joined the army often left enslaved families behind at the mercy of their owners. Missouri did not free the families of slaves who enlisted in the Union Army until 1865.

Because St. Louis attracted settlers from Northern and Southern states, local women often found themselves and their in-laws on opposite sides. William Carr Lane and his daughter Anne, both Confederate sympathizers, argued bitterly

Office of the Provost Marshal General,

OF THE DEPARTMENT OF THE MISSOURI,

ST. LOUIS, MO., *Jan 8th* 186*2*

Sir

You are hereby notified that, pursuant to General Orders No. 24 of 1861, and Special Order No. 18 of 1862, from the Head Quarters of the Department of Missouri, directing a levy upon the friends of the enemy for charitable purposes, you have been assessed the sum of *three hundred* Dollars, as your contribution in aid of the suffering families driven by the rebels from South-Western Missouri.

You will, therefore, pay the amount so assessed, or its equivalent in Clothing, Provisions or quarters to me within seven days after the service of this notice upon you; or, in default thereof, execution will be issued against your property for sufficient to satisfy the assessments, costs, and twenty-five per cent. penalty in addition. Should you elect to pay your assessment in Clothing, Provisions or quarters, you will give notice of such intention to this Office, accompanying the same with an inventory and description of the articles, or of the situation and value of the quarters tendered, which will be accepted, subject to an appraisement of the same by me.

Bernard G. Farrar

PROVOST MARSHAL GENERAL.

To *Dr. Wm. McPheeters*

Notice Sent by Provost Marshal to Dr. Wm. McPheeters, January 8, 1862. Sallie McPheeters's rosewood chest was seized to satisfy this levy while her husband served as a surgeon with the Confederate Army. In 1865 McPheeters and her children were banished to the South after a Union official took offense at a phrase in a letter she had written to her husband. McPheeters Papers, MHS Archives

with his daughter Sarah's husband, William Glasgow, who staunchly supported the Union. In the end, the Lanes' mutual affection proved stronger than their sectional loyalties, and the family remained united. It might have been different, however, had Sarah not been an invalid who spent most of the war in Europe while her sister cared for her older children in St. Louis.

Confederate supporters who did not leave the city after Fremont declared martial law found their personal possessions subject to seizure and sale to pay for refugee relief. Sallie McPheeters, the wife of a general in the Confederate Army, lost her rosewood parlor set and mahogany bedroom furniture. Federal authorities banished her and her two children from St. Louis for corresponding with General McPheeters in the field, in defiance of martial law.

As in all wars, the combat experience profoundly changed men. Casualties on both sides were appallingly high and many of those who did not die on battlefields, in hospitals, or in prisons returned home physically or mentally unable to resume their domestic lives. War also changed women who ran farms, earned wages, or kept families together for the first time on their own.

Middle-class women actually had expanded their domestic role years before the war to include philanthropic work by founding and operating orphanages and other charitable institutions. But with the exception of Catholic nuns like the Daughters of Charity, who established hospitals, women's organized charity had been largely directed to the needs of women and children. Moreover, women and men had done little of their charitable work together. During the Civil War, women's charity became more public, more political, and more intertwined with that of men.

In wartime the federal government neither funded nor assumed responsibility for securing most of the goods and services required for the care of wounded soldiers, refugees, or other civilian casualties. Following the August 1861 Battle of Wilson's Creek, General Fremont's wife, Jessie, and Dorothea Dix, superintendent of women nurses for the U.S. Army, persuaded the general to authorize a civilian organization to establish, outfit, and regulate military hospitals. The Western Sanitary Commission (WSC), although similar in organization and mission to the United States Sanitary Commission (USSC) already functioning in the East, was an independent agency. To lead the commission, Fremont appointed James Yeatman, a local banker, and a board of four other prominent men, including the Reverend William Greenleaf Eliot. Yeatman and Eliot, unlike the salaried USSC leadership, volunteered their time.

Concurrently, a group of prominent St. Louis women formed the St. Louis Ladies' Union Aid Society (LUAS), dedicated to aiding the Union by comforting and caring for wounded soldiers, traditionally women's responsibility. While technically independent, these two groups worked together to accomplish more than either ever anticipated. They eventually supplied fifteen hospitals in the St. Louis area; nearly fifty hospitals in Missouri and neighboring states; seventeen divisional hospitals; fifteen floating hospitals attached to the Mississippi fleet; and a number of hospital railroad cars for transporting the wounded. During the war, the WSC and the LUAS expanded services to freedmen, orphans, and Union war refugees and provided nearly $4 million in money and donated supplies.

Although the LUAS did much of the day-to-day work of raising money, distributing goods, and providing services, the WSC, as the official relief organization, controlled most of the funds and set policy. Eliot's Boston connections enabled him to work closely with the larger USSC and to solicit donations from as far as New England. Contemporary critics leveled charges of graft and poor management against the eastern organization but acknowledged that the WSC was honestly run and efficient.

If President Anna Clapp and the other leaders of the LUAS resented Yeatman and Eliot's paternalistic control over their work, they did not say so in public. James Yeatman held to the common assumption that women "volunteered to emerge from the seclusion of domestic life" to give both patriotic and philanthropic service to their country, not because they were personally ambitious or desirous of making independent decisions. Certainly, many women who volunteered for the LUAS agreed that "the noblest impulses of women's nature" drew them to comfort the wounded "by the tender ministrations of female hands." The practical experience of effectively administering much of the actual relief work and the public acknowledgment of their critical role in the success of the Mississippi Valley Sanitary Fair, however, pulled Anna Clapp and other leaders of the LUAS ever more decisively into the public life of the city. Shortly after disbanding the LUAS in 1866, they formed a new organization, the Women's Suffrage Association of Missouri, dedicated to winning the vote for women.

In a bitterly divided city, patriotic women's organizations such as the St. Louis Ladies' Union Aid Society, the Fremont Ladies' Aid Society, and the Ladies' National League publicly identified women with the Union cause, as they enabled them to support the war effort through fund raising, sewing, and other acts of benevolence. Women in established ethnic and religious organizations also visibly demonstrated their patriotism. Josephine Weigel took on the role of spokeswoman for German women in May 1861. "In keeping with our German custom, we women do not want to remain onlookers when our men have devoted themselves with joyful courage to the service of the Fatherland," she said as she presented a flag to Union forces. Local women sympathetic to the Confederate cause, on the other hand, had to remain quiet onlookers or face the consequences of martial law. Imposed silence gave the city the appearance of more Union loyalty than probably actually existed.

Most of the St. Louis women who volunteered for the war effort were middle-class women with domestic help. Women who had no one to look after the children or do the housework had little

Anna Clapp, President of the Ladies' Union Aid Society. Cabinet card photograph, ca. 1870. MHS–PP time to spend rolling bandages or visiting hospitalized strangers. Unmarried middle-class women discovered new opportunities for employment as nurses and teachers of refugee children. Women whose husbands served in the army had no choice but to seek paid employment. Because St. Louis was a military center filled with soldiers, women also supported themselves by working as prostitutes.

Women took low-paying jobs in St. Louis factories with contracts to supply food, clothing, and other supplies for the military. They packed hardtack crackers for field rations. They sewed hospital garments and washed them at John Brettell's steam laundry on Clark Street. Brettell contracted with the Western Sanitary Commission to wash all the clothes and linens used in the city's military hospitals. Wartime laundry needs undoubtedly expanded employment opportunities for African American women, who traditionally had done much of the city's wash.

Because few African American slaves lived in the city by the outbreak of the war, the Missouri emancipation ordinance of January 1865 actually freed only a small number of women. But the war nevertheless brought them liberation and the promise of legal marriage, education for their children, and personal freedom.

Women's most obvious wartime hardships in 1865 were dead and maimed husbands, sons, and fathers; other long-term consequences of the Civil War revealed themselves over time. The war was a profoundly disruptive event, a breaking point in the lives of men and women. For some, it brought unbelievable tragedy, for others new opportunities; for all it was a wrenching personal episode and the nation's central, collective emotional experience.

Partisan differences that seemed at the time beyond reconciliation proved easier to placate than deeper divisions of race, gender, or class. If white Americans fought the war in part to end slavery, they did not fight each other to end racism. Freedom would not bring equality for African Americans. Women's willingness to join in the war effort would not earn them entry into the voting booth. The ethos of individualism and materialism that underlay the Civil War politics of Free Soil would flourish in the Gilded Age; many families would prosper, but more would not.

After the war Sallie Case and her family continued to live in Ferguson. In 1871 her husband, George, became an owner of the Baden and St. Louis Railroad. He prospered as the city's streetcar system expanded to serve a growing population that began to leave the grimy industrial city for new homes beyond Grand Avenue. Postwar industrialization would provide more opportunities for women to be consumers, workers, and social reformers. It also brought into sharper focus the issues that divided them.

Sources: This essay draws on analysis by Jeanie Attie, "Warwork and the Crisis of Domesticity on the North," in *Divided Houses: Gender and the Civil War*, eds., Catherine Clinton and Nina Silber (New York: Oxford University Press, 1992). Additional information is from Steven Rowan, *Germans for a Free Missouri: Translations from the German Radical Press, 1857–1862* (Columbia: University of Missouri Press, 1983), 196; William G. B. Carson, "Secesh," *BMHS* 23, no. 2 (January 1967); Peter Bardagio, "The Children of Jubilee: African American Children in Wartime," in *Divided Houses*, 213–14, 226; Jacob Forman, *The Western Sanitary Commission* (St. Louis, 1864); and Hannah I. Stagg, "Local Incidents in the Civil War," *MHS Collections* 4 (1912–1923): 63–81.

Quotations are from James Yeatman, *Final Report of the Western Sanitary Commission*, 60. Information on the Case family is from "Builder of First Car Line in St. Louis Wed 59 Years," *St. Louis Globe-Democrat*, 28 October 1915; Sallie Case quotations from Sallie Case to Sue King, 23 December 1860, Case Family Papers, MHS; William McPheeters, "Private Banishment of My Wife," also included information on Missouri Southern Relief Association organized by Rebecca Sire, Sallie McPheeters, and other women sympathetic to the South for postwar Southern relief. The Mississippi Valley Sanitation Fair netted approximately $140,000, WSC Annual Reports, MHS; L. P. Brockett and Mary Vaughan, *Woman's Work in the Civil War: A Record of Heroism, Patriotism, and Patience* (Philadelphia: Zeigler, McCurdy & Co., 1867); Kris Runberg Smith, ed., "A House Divided: St. Louis and the Civil War," *SLAH*. An article on "Anna Carroll," in *NAW*, touches on her claim that she was an unacknowledged Union strategist operating for a time out of St. Louis but offers little evidence to support it.

For economic, social, and political history of the Civil War and events leading to it, see Eric Foner, *Free Soil, Free Labor, Free Men: The Ideology of the Republican Party before the Civil War* (New York: Oxford University Press, 1970); James McPherson, *Battle Cry of Freedom: The Civil War Era* (New York: Oxford University Press, 1988); and Page Smith, *Trial by Fire: A People's History of Civil War and Reconstruction* (New York: McGraw-Hill, 1982). See James Neal Primm, *Lion of the Valley: St. Louis, Missouri*, 3d ed. (St. Louis: MHS Press, 1998) for local context. For military history of conflict in St. Louis, see William C. Winter, *The Civil War in St. Louis: A Guided Tour* (St. Louis: MHS Press, 1994), and J. Thomas Scharf, *History of St. Louis City and County*, vol. 1 (Philadelphia: L. H. Everts & Co., 1883).

Jessie Benton Fremont

In July 1861 Jessie Benton Fremont and her husband, John, moved into the Brant mansion on the south side of Chouteau Avenue, between Eighth and St. Paul Streets. On taking military command of the Department of the West, Major General Fremont arranged to pay Jessie's aunt, Sarah Benton Brant, six thousand dollars annually to rent the palatial three-story villa for his Union headquarters. Local controversy over this expenditure was just the first of many that would surround the Fremonts in St. Louis. After only four months, President Lincoln ousted Fremont for overspending government funds, military incompetence, and attempting to free Missouri's slaves long before Lincoln's administration thought emancipation politically expedient.

Fremont was a man of many contradictions. Jessie, his intelligent, headstrong wife actively supported the antislavery cause and many of his decisions, only to undermine her credibility by publicly defending his poor judgment and erratic behavior. For a woman of Jessie Benton's talent and background, any marriage would have been a gamble. A loving husband might give her domestic happiness, but her public ambition could be realized only through playing a significant role in his successful career. By choosing the dashing John C. Fremont over her father's objections when she was only seventeen, Jessie Benton may have gambled and lost.

Jessie was the daughter of Missouri's first United States senator, Thomas Hart Benton. Though born in St. Louis, she grew up in Washington, D.C., surrounded by the men who would lead the nation to civil war. She was her flamboyant, overbearing father's favorite child, his secretary, confidant, and protégé. He gave her the kind of political education most national politicians reserve for their sons.

Jessie met John Fremont in 1840 when the young lieutenant in the Corps of Topographical Engineers had just returned from a western expedition. Awaiting reassignment in Washington, he courted the senator's rebellious daughter. Distressed, Senator Benton quickly had Fremont sent off to survey the Des Moines River. When Fremont returned in 1841 he secretly married Jessie. Benton quickly accommodated to the union, insisting that it was Jessie who married John, and threw his enormous political weight behind his new son-in-law's career.

Benton's influence and Jessie's driving intelligence

propelled Fremont onto the national scene. When Benton arranged for him to lead a western surveying expedition the following year, Jessie wrote his overdue report on the river survey and helped arrange the trip to the Rocky Mountains. She gave birth to the first of her five children in John's absence, and on his return they collaborated on the expedition's report. Jessie turned Fremont's field notes into a wildly popular descriptive narrative, for which she took no public credit. Considered the more capable of the pair by all who knew them, Jessie continued to promote and defend her husband's career through two more western expeditions and a messy court martial over Fremont's controversial conduct in California during the Mexican War.

Jessie Benton Fremont. Carte de visite photograph by E. Anthony, N.Y., 1862. MHS–PP

Despite Jessie's personal appeal to President Polk, John was forced to resign from the army. In 1849 the Fremonts followed the gold rush to California, and Jessie actually experienced frontier life for the first time. In California, John plunged into local politics, winning a seat as the state's first United States senator. In 1856 the new Republican Party chose him as their first presidential candidate. The popular campaign slogan, "Fremont and Jessie," reflected her public visibility in the losing campaign.

After their defeat, the Fremonts returned to California, discovered more gold on their land, and settled into San Francisco society. Jessie surrounded herself with bright, attentive young men but stayed devoted to John as he struggled to manage their finances.

When rumors of civil war began to escalate, John rushed east to secure a new army commission. Thrilled that they would be involved again in a great cause, Jessie joined him for the trip to St. Louis, but when they arrived in the summer of 1861, "it was a hostile city and showed itself as such" to her.

From the start, Jessie played an active role in her husband's efforts to hold St. Louis for the Union. She helped St. Louis women organize a soldiers' relief society and promoted William Greenleaf Eliot's plan to organize the Western Sanitary Commission (WSC). She was instrumental in bringing Dorothea Dix, a dedicated reformer with a temperament similar to her own, to St. Louis. Dix worked with the WSC to recruit women as paid nurses for the city's military hospitals.

Both Fremonts pressured Washington for supplies and troops and prepared for the coming military campaign. Because they lived on the second floor of the headquarters building, little if any space separated their public and private lives. Jessie attended to her husband's secret correspondence, participated in staff discussions, and intercepted his visitors. Critics began calling her "General Jessie."

John had little talent for administration, preferring to surround himself with cronies. He relied on his wife's organizational skills as much as he depended on her shrewd grasp of public issues. In spite of her best efforts, however, Fremont was in perpetual trouble. His apparent incompetence and autocratic temperament alienated Frank Blair, an equally ambitious and flamboyant Republican, but one with more local support and even stronger family ties to Washington. Fremont's military blunders did not inspire confidence, but his decision to emancipate Missouri's slaves on August 31, 1861, without consulting Lincoln verged on insubordination.

Lincoln quickly rescinded Fremont's Missouri proclamation; freeing slaves in a border state did not fit the president's political or military agenda. For all his personal failings, Fremont was an ardent foe of slavery. Respect for her husband's ideals and anger over this blow to his pride drove Jessie to action. She promptly left St. Louis for Washington, demanding a meeting with Lincoln to defend John's proclamation. Lincoln agreed to meet her the night she arrived. "I walked over immediately, just as I had been for two days and nights, in my dusty mourning dress." All her life she had been at home in the president's house; she went forward with all the confidence of the past. After she presented her husband's case, Lincoln gave her a long look: "You are quite the female politician," he said in what seemed to her to be a sneering tone. He seemed beyond all persuasion, but she pressed on, much to Lincoln's irritation. "Strange, isn't it," she wrote later, "that when a man expresses a conviction fearlessly, he is reported as having made a trenchant and forceful statement, but when a woman speaks thus earnestly, she is reported as a lady who has lost her temper." Jessie always blamed Frank Blair for turning Lincoln against her husband, but John's own blundering was reason enough for Lincoln to fire him on November 8, 1861.

After another unsuccessful tour of duty in West Virginia, the Fremonts settled in New York City, where Jessie volunteered for the U.S. Sanitary Commission and worked enthusiastically for the 1864 New York Sanitary Fair. She also began writing for publication under her own name.

In 1873 John declared bankruptcy. Romantic far-western trailblazer, military conqueror of California, one-time presidential hopeful, and perpetual abolitionist hero, Fremont never fulfilled his military, political, or financial dreams. Jessie supported the family by writing articles and books. The Fremonts returned to California in 1888. After John died two years later, Jessie moved to Los Angeles where she lived until her death in 1902, in a house presented to her by the women of the city.

Sources: See Winter, *The Civil War in St. Louis,* for information on the Fremonts' activities in St. Louis. For a full biography of Jessie Benton Fremont, see Pamela Herr, *Jessie Benton Fremont* (New York: Franklin Watts, 1987). Quotations are from Jessie Benton Fremont, *Souvenirs of My Time* (Boston: D. Lothrop, 1887), 166, and Herr, *Jessie Benton Fremont,* 337, 339. See also Allan Nevins, "Jessie Benton Fremont," in *NAW,* vol. 1, 668–71.

Ladies' Union Aid Society

When the first trains bearing the wounded from the Battle of Wilson's Creek began arriving in St. Louis on August 11, 1861, Adaline Couzins met them at the train station with a carriage-load of bandages and clean underclothing. She was a member of the St. Louis Ladies' Union Aid Society (LUAS), organized less than three weeks earlier by twenty-five women eager to demonstrate their national loyalty in a deeply divided border city. The carnage at Wilson's Creek in southwestern Missouri provided their first opportunities to serve the Union. Over the next four years, more than two hundred St. Louis LUAS volunteers, in cooperation with the male-run Western Sanitary Commission (WSC), provided supplies and care for wounded soldiers, prisoners, and refugees under St. Louis military jurisdiction.

The leadership of the LUAS was predominantly Protestant and middle class, and many had strong ties to the East. The organizational secretary was a teacher from New Hampshire. Vice President Frances H. Post had moved from Vermont to the Midwest after her marriage in 1834. Her husband, a Congregational minister, was one of the city's most vocal Unionists. Anna Clapp, the organization's president throughout the war, had been treasurer of the

Industrial School Association in New York City before moving to St. Louis with her merchant husband in 1860.

LUAS members were devoted Unionists, motivated as much by partisan patriotism as by concern for the sick and wounded. They emblazoned the slogan, "Union Forever," on their red, white, and blue stationery. In August 1861, when a Southern supporter threatened to tear down the Union flag that Alfred Clapp had raised over their house. Anna Clapp challenged, "You can only reach the flag over my dead body," as she barred the way.

Both the LUAS and the WSC occupied offices in the General Hospital, a military facility opened in September 1861 in a five-story building at the corner of Fifth and Chestnut Streets. Remaining independent organizations, the two relief agencies worked closely together. The women provided much of the volunteer labor from the outset, working twenty-four hours a day rolling bandages and helping to process tons of bedding, clothing, and other medical and sanitary supplies that poured into the WSC from all over the Union. They kept

---

Memorial [of the] St. Louis, Missouri, Ladies' Union Aid Society. This commemorative engraving shows the range of activities the Ladies' Union Aid Society engaged in during the Civil War. Steel engraving by Majors and Knapp, 1870. MHS-PP

detailed records of the funds and goods that they were responsible for. Although the value of much of their work was mingled with that of the Western Sanitary Commission, LUAS efforts generated about one-third of the more than $4 million in money and supplies received by the WSC during the war.

The first responsibility of the Ladies' Union Aid Society was to care for the wounded. Initially, volunteers assisted doctors directly, but after trained nurses took over, they focused on the patients' other physical and emotional needs. Because the government provided only basic food, shelter, and medical care, any amenities came from the women volunteers. They dressed wounds, bathed patients, read to them, and wrote their letters. They carried baskets on their daily visits to the fourteen area military hospitals to distribute "a bottle of cream, a home-made loaf, fresh eggs, fruit, and oysters . . . a flannel shirt, a sling, a pair of spectacles . . . a lively book." Many of the lively books were Protestant religious tracts provided by the U.S. Christian Commission.

Bettie Broadhead, a LUAS volunteer, organized a special diet kitchen in 1862 at Benton Barracks, a huge hospital complex located at the fairgrounds west of Grand Avenue. Volunteers prepared special meals of fresh food donated by sympathetic St. Louisans, offering patients selections from a new menu circulated every morning. Between May and October, the LUAS served 19,382 meals at Benton Barracks. The following fall, two volunteers took five hundred dollars and seventy-two boxes of supplies to Nashville, Tennessee, hoping to start a LUAS branch there. Although not successful, they enlisted volunteers from other aid societies to help organize a diet kitchen at a large military hospital.

In 1862 the LUAS contracted with the army to make hospital garments and bedding, which would provide work for needy soldiers' wives who applied at their office for aid. The women workers produced three to four thousand garments a week, and Anna Clapp herself traveled to Washington for assurance that the contracts would continue until the end of the war. Refugees and prisoners also requested aid from the volunteers. The society amended its mission in 1863 to include all "who suffer at the cause of Union, including sick and wounded prisoners of war." They added the Walnut Street Refugee Home and the Gratiot Street Prison to their rounds of daily visits, distributing clothing, food, and personal items to desperate people with no resources of their own.

To support their work and that of the WSC, the women organized concerts, bazaars, lectures, and elaborate social events. Their participation in the month-long Mississippi Valley Sanitary Fair helped raise more than a half million dollars, which paid for relief work for the final eighteen months of the war.

The Civil War disrupted the ongoing domestic and charitable activities of St. Louis middle-class women. Although they created the Ladies' Union Aid Society to meet a civic emergency and take a visible patriotic stand, the organization also gave them an opportunity to work closely with other like-minded women and men, to gain managerial experience in a large-scale public enterprise, and to envision a new place for themselves in the community. Anna Clapp, Rebecca Hazard, Lucretia Hall, and Virginia Minor all had positions of responsibility within the LUAS. Two years after the war, they were among the founders of the Women's Suffrage Association of Missouri.

Sources: Information on the St. Louis Ladies' Union Aid Society includes contemporary accounts: Brockett and Vaughan, *Woman's Work in the Civil War,* is the source of the quoted description of the items delivered to soldiers; a history of the Western Sanitary Commission written during the war is Forman, *The Western Sanitary Commission*; the quoted amended mission is found in the *Second Annual Report of the Ladies' Union Aid Society of St. Louis* (St. Louis, 1863); *Third Annual Report of the Ladies' Union Aid Society of St. Louis* (St. Louis, 1864). See also Paula Coalier, "Beyond Sympathy: The St. Louis Ladies' Union Aid Society and the Civil War," *GH* 11, no. 1 (summer 1990). See the MHS necrology files for information on specific members and the meager, fragmentary LUAS records in the MHS archives. Michael and Neatherly Fuller maintain a LUAS website at http://stlcc.cc.mo.us/mfuller/luas/.

Refugees of War

As the war in the West intensified in late 1861, civilian refugees began pouring into St. Louis from southwest Missouri. "Barefoot, half-clad, and in a destitute and starving condition," they were overwhelmingly white women and children displaced by guerrilla warfare or abandoned by men who had gone off to fight on both sides of the conflict. Although all St. Louisans considered refugees unwelcome temporary residents, local women rallied to their aid.

No one in St. Louis was prepared to help them. Private charities, municipal government, and the Union military command quickly decided that St. Louisans hostile to the Union should bear the

in her place

costs of refugee relief. In December, General Henry W. Halleck assessed sixty-four Southern sympathizers a total of ten thousand dollars in money and goods. Juliette Garesche, a descendant of a Creole founding family, saw her household furnishings sold at public auction. The Western Sanitary Commission (WSC) administered relief funds; the Ladies' Union Aid Relief Society (LUARS) organized to deliver food and donated clothing and made plans to shelter refugees.

An offshoot of the Ladies' Union Aid Society, the LUARS immediately acquired an old mansion on Elm Street, between Fourth and Fifth Streets, and furnished it with enough beds and bedding for sixty persons. They outfitted similar quarters in the rear of the house for black refugees. Within the first few weeks, nearly six hundred people passed through the facility. Most were fed, clothed, and sent on to Illinois or states further west. The women operated this facility for about eighteen months.

In 1863 President Lincoln suspended assessment levies, and the federal government assumed more of the cost of refugee relief. The Ladies' National League, a group of twelve hundred patriotic women loosely organized to raise money for Union causes, also allocated some money to refugee aid. When another surge of displaced people arrived in St. Louis that August, the WSC rented a house at 39 Walnut Street where volunteers cared for more than two thousand white refugees over the next year. The military paid for rent, food, and fuel for the Walnut Street Refugee House, but the voluntary relief organizations covered all other expenses. The WSC and the LUARS distributed thousands of coats, pantaloons, underclothing, women's dresses, shawls, shoes, and comforters.

In 1864 Confederate soldiers overran Union forces in southern Missouri. Displaced women and children streamed into Pilot Knob, Rolla, and Springfield. St. Louis businessmen organized to collect money for their relief. The WSC sent supplies and helped local women distribute clothing and open schools for refugee children. In St. Louis, hundreds of destitute soldiers' wives and widows moved into refurbished stables at Benton Barracks, where enclosed stalls were equipped with stoves for refugee families. At least forty more refugee children received care at the Mission Free School, an orphanage run by the Reverend William Greenleaf Eliot's Unitarian Church. Many children were later placed as indentured servants with St. Louis families.

The military command insisted that food and shelter be given only to people unable to work and who would starve without aid. This mandate motivated the WSC to relocate refugees away from the city as soon as possible. Between October 1863 and October 1864, the WSC sent more than fourteen hundred persons by rail or steamboat to free states further west. Only 202 of those dispatched were men.

However sympathetic middle-class, urban volunteers felt to the rural white refugees' plight, they regarded them as ignorant and barely civilized. WSC field reports from southern Missouri and Arkansas often mixed tales of brave

Union Refugees from Western Missouri Coming into St. Louis. Wood engraving from *Harper's Weekly*, 28 December 1861. MHS–PP

women struggling to find help for their children before dying themselves of starvation and exposure, with equally vivid accounts of peasant depravity.

Much of the rhetoric echoed the racist arguments of Free Soilers that the slave system hurt more whites than blacks. Reporters compared arrogant, lazy white women to hardworking black women who kept cabins swept and children neatly dressed. To Frances D. Gage, an eastern activist volunteer, white refugees were "victims of the institution of slavery, and degraded by its influence." The freedman, Gage wrote to the WSC, will sustain himself if protected "from the white man's injustice and cupidity." Poor white Southerners, however, would be productive citizens only when slavery no longer made honest labor a disgrace. Then "labor, the handmaid of virtue and prosperity, will take her place of honor, even among these."

In February 1865, the WSC, the LUARS, and the Ladies' Freedmen's Relief Association (LFRA) opened a home for white and black refugees in the Lawson Hospital building at the corner of Broadway and Carr. The former hotel and military hospital accommodated six hundred refugees in racially segregated quarters. Over the next six months, Anna Clapp, president of the LUARS, and Mrs. Lucien Eaton, president of the LFRA, saw to it that more than three thousand people received food, shelter, education, and medical care. Volunteers held separate classes for white and black children.

The WSC sent most refugees out of state, some back to the South once the war ended. The several hundred remaining when the home closed in July 1865 became wards of local government and charitable organizations. Sick and destitute adults went to City Hospital and the poorhouse. African American children went to the newly opened Freedman's Orphan Home on Twelfth Street. Other children moved to local white orphanages, including the Soldier's Orphan Home, which opened in 1865 in Webster Groves. Few refugees stayed in the area as permanent residents.

Sources: For a fuller description of refugee relief, see *Report of the Western Sanitary Commission of the White Union Refugees of the South* (St. Louis: Western Sanitary Commission, 1864). Frances Gage is quoted on pages 42–3. Additional information is in William Hyde and Howard Conard, *Encyclopedia of the History of St. Louis* (New York: The Southern History Company, 1899), 1210–11, and Scharf, *History of St. Louis City and County,* vol. 1, 414–17, 546–49.

Freedwomen in St. Louis During the Civil War

On the first day of January 1861, two thousand young men disrupted a slave auction on the steps of the Old Courthouse on Market and Broadway. Offering bids so unreasonably low that the auctioneer gave up, they ended what proved to be the last slave auction in St. Louis.

Exactly two years later, enslaved St. Louisans, free blacks, and sympathetic whites celebrated Lincoln's Emancipation Proclamation with a procession from the Eighth Street Baptist Church on Eighth and Lucas to Turner's Hall on Tenth Street between Market and Walnut. There, they "had a great thanksgiving and speaking service. . . . A wild blizzard howled outside and the snow lay deep on the ground, but that did not dampen the ardor of the happy people." The celebration was no less significant for being largely symbolic. Because the 1863 Emancipation Proclamation applied only to rebellious Confederate states, slaves in Unionist Missouri technically remained in bondage until the state legislature freed them in 1865.

As slavery began to disintegrate, slaves bore the brunt of harsh conditions caused by limited resources. Enslaved women strove to escape while keeping their families together and caring for them. Confederate owners treated their slaves worse than ever, forcing them to work for the secessionist war machine. Many slaves saw opportunity in the wartime upheaval and simply freed themselves. Freedwomen walked hundreds of miles with their children and all their possessions to reach Union ground or to reunite with relatives who had been sold. Border state cities like St. Louis became magnets for runaways. While some found friends and slipped unnoticed into the bustling urban scene, the cost of living exceeded what most former slaves could afford. Thousands sought refuge with Union troops, who called the former slaves "contraband" of war, considering them the property of rebellious Confederates and thus subject to confiscation by the Union.

After mid-1863 former slaves who joined the Union Army gained certificates of emancipation and wages, but when they went off to war, their relatives were often punished by angry slaveholders. Wives of black soldiers had to fend for themselves at home or follow their husbands to the dubious protections of contraband camps, where unwelcoming Union men called them prostitutes and idle vagrants. Slave owners intercepted mail from black soldiers to their families, took their

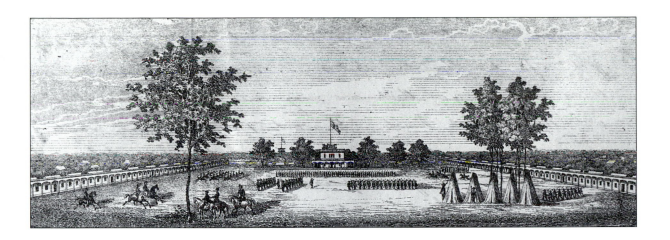

clothing at night to prevent escape, and compelled women to take over heavy manual labor previously performed by men. An enslaved woman named Martha wrote to her soldier husband at Benton Barracks from Mexico, Missouri: "You recollect what I told you they would do after you was gone. they abuse me because you went & say they will not take care of our children & do nothing but quarrel with me all the time and beat me scandalously the day before yesterday."

Before Union forces drove the Confederates from Missouri into Arkansas in February 1862, and after the Confederate Army invaded southern Missouri in the fall of 1863, thousands of slaves fled to St. Louis. So many left rural Missouri that in parts of the state crops rotted in the fields for want of harvest hands, and owners actually paid slaves to work.

Once slaves reached St. Louis, their status was unclear. Technically enslaved in the border states as a concession to proslavery Unionists, in reality slaves were subject to the whims of individuals. A ring of slave traders kidnapped freedmen and women from St. Louis, shipped them to Kentucky, and sold them back into slavery. The official federal policy was military noninterference in master-slave relationships, which local authorities oversaw, but in the absence of strong enforcement, officers and soldiers took matters into their own hands.

Despite the uncertainty of federal military protection, the brutal conditions of wartime slavery and the desire to keep families together led many former slaves to seek refuge in Union centers such as Benton Barracks, a military camp and training post in northwest St. Louis. There, former slaves lived in hastily constructed villages, often severely overcrowded and disease-ridden. An appalling 10 percent of the 947 slaves who appeared at Benton Barracks between January and March 1864 died.

Contraband camps were controversial for white Union troops and officers. Some welcomed the African American refugees in their midst, caring for them and protecting them from angry slaveholders. Others returned them and collected rewards. Many soldiers objected to "wasting" military resources on contrabands. One general admonished superintendents of refugees to "scrutinize and examine all applicants for aid . . . to see that the Government is not imposed upon by imposters, vagrants, idle loungers, and loafers."

Former slaves overwhelmed military resources at first, as one chaplain at an army base in Cairo, Illinois, noted: "The arrival among us of these hordes was like the oncoming of cities," he wrote. "There was no plan in this exodus, no Moses to lead it." Thus, the Union Army often cooperated with national charity and missionary groups (many of them actively abolitionist, such as the American Missionary Association and the National Contraband Relief Society) to transport former slaves to Northern states. There, freed families worked for wages as field hands or settled on homesteads that were privately sponsored or leased from owners, charities, or the federal government. Many became permanent residents.

When twenty-five hundred former slaves arrived in St. Louis from Arkansas in the spring of 1863, a Union general quartered them in the abandoned Missouri Hotel on Main and Morgan Streets and gave them military rations. Since more

Camp Benton, St. Louis. Benton Barracks served not only as a training and assembly camp for Union troops, but also as a facility for the displaced people of the Civil War. Freed African Americans and refugees turned out by the military actions in southern and western Missouri lived in converted stables. Letterhead engraving by Alex. McLean, 1862. MHS–PP.

than two thousand applications for field hands had arrived from Northern states by March, the Ladies' Contraband Relief Society helped escort the former slaves to those free states. By December, one thousand more had arrived.

Jobs for freedwomen were scarce and low in quality. Freedwomen received inadequate compensation for hard manual labor or lived as domestic servants in white homes, leaving them no private space, no room for children, and forced to face white prejudice every day. Mothers had a particularly hard time finding jobs, as employers of domestic servants did not want to care for their children as well. Former slaves of both sexes competed with free black St. Louisans for jobs. Many African Americans greased the wheels of the Union war machine, sustaining the city daily by preparing food and clothing for soldiers, caring for the families of Union citizens, moving cargo, tending horses, and driving as teamsters. Others worked as seamstresses, barbers, carpenters, shoemakers, blacksmiths, and tailors.

Most single freedwomen got jobs as domestic servants through the military, as Benton Barracks received more requests for servants than it could fill. They could expect to make five dollars a month. Former slaves hired by the Union Army worked as laundresses, commissary and quartermasters' employees, hospital attendants, officers' servants, and laborers.

Freedwomen contributed to the war effort by doing laundry aboard military hospital ships on the Mississippi. Some may have worked at J. K. Brettell's Steam Laundry on Clark between Sixteenth and Seventeenth Streets, which contracted to do all the military's laundry. Black artisans made crafts that were sold at the Mississippi Valley Sanitary Fair, freedwomen helped prepare the hall, and black soldiers stood guard throughout the event.

Federal authorities in Missouri generally refused to feed or care for "fugitive" slaves not employed by the army, many of whom were women. State and local governments had more pressing concerns, so the job of providing for former slaves fell to private groups. Racism often compromised the charitable efforts of whites who saw former slaves as lazy and ignorant, childish and in need of *white* help. In addition, white groups brought their own concerns to charitable projects: missionaries sought converts and expanded political influence, while abolitionists wanted to validate their own prewar efforts. While these groups performed valuable services, they generally did not understand or respect black St. Louisans' desires for autonomy.

Black-led charitable efforts suffered from white groups' refusal to let black groups run their own aid societies. On the other hand, the five thousand former slaves seeking refuge in St. Louis overwhelmed the free black community of fifteen hundred. There was simply not enough money to go around, which precipitated a tense atmosphere as black groups sought funding from white groups who had more money but expected to control the efforts they subsidized. White men administered and funded most efforts, white women organized and managed them, and black women's contributions, while unspecified in many accounts, entailed actual care.

Wounded black soldiers recuperating in segregated buildings at Benton Barracks enjoyed visits by members of the Colored Ladies' Contraband Relief Society, who "do all they can for their brethren. They visit them, teach them to read, read to them, and comfort them in many ways," wrote one white missionary. Providing such services was not easy; the black women rode the outer platforms of streetcars to Benton Barracks before March 1863, when they were allowed to sit inside–but only on Saturdays.

Most groups aiding former slaves assumed they would not become permanent residents of St. Louis but rather would move to the countryside and take up farming, as in fact most did. Several groups dealt exclusively with former slaves. The Ladies' Contraband Relief Society, organized in St. Louis in 1863 as an offshoot of the Ladies' Union Aid Society, cared for freedwomen and white refugees in two facilities: a hospital and small school in the Missouri Hotel, and also the Refugee and Freedmen's Home in the former Lawson Hotel on Carr and Broadway. There, between February and July 1865, more than three thousand freedwomen and white women refugees received lodging, food, medical care, clothing, and some school instruction. Both black and white residents of the racially integrated home cooked, laundered, and did housework. They earned moderate wages and according to the Western Sanitary Commission, which funded and administered the program, were "taught some of the first lessons of a better civilization" in classes presumably led by white teachers.

On July 10, 1865, the Refugee and Freedmen's Home closed, and some three hundred of its adult residents entered the city hospital or the poorhouse. Their children were transferred to the newly created Freedmen's Orphan Home on Twelfth Street between Cass and O'Fallon. The home opened with twenty-four African American "orphans," shortly joined by eighty others from Arkansas. The home was managed by the Freedmen's Orphan Home Association. Headed by white women, the association had some "intelligent and worthy colored women" as members whose names were not recorded.

As with children of white refugees of war, African American children at the home were sent to live with St. Louis families as indentured servants, provided the families agreed to send them to school or educate them at home for three months a year. If they attended school, they were not paid for their duties. Adolescents between the ages of fourteen and eighteen were not required to go to school, but their foster parents had to compensate them for their work. Those who adopted children had to return with them to the Freedmen's Orphan Home after three months to assure the directress that the arrangements were acceptable. The Western Sanitary Commission intended to reunite these orphans with their mothers when both mother and child could support themselves. The home operated until Congress created the Refugee and Freedmen's National Bureau in the winter of 1865.

While the majority of black families returned to rural areas in the years following the war, single women and single mothers remained in urban areas where they could get wage-work, since farm work was nearly impossible for an adult with several children. While urban life was difficult to negotiate, freedwomen ultimately contributed much to the cities they lived in, providing an economic and social base that nourished many black communities, bolstering them at a crucial time in their development after the abolition of slavery.

Emancipation wrenched African Americans out of slavery, casting them loose to seek greater economic and educational opportunities in a hostile white society. In the short term, charity could ease individual transitions from bondage to freedom, but long-term reconciliation would have to wait for changes of heart to prompt changes in public policy. In the meantime, former slaves followed their own initiatives, gathered up their scattered families, and got on with their lives.

–Katherine Douglass

Sources: For information on black-run aid groups, see George E. Stevens, *History of Central Baptist Church* (St. Louis: King Publishing Co., 1927). The Ladies' Contraband Relief Society was also sometimes called the Ladies' Freedmen's Relief Association. A good background article is Judy Day and M. James Kedro, "Free Blacks in St. Louis: Antebellum Conditions, Emancipation, and the Postwar Era," *BMHS* 30, no. 2 (January 1974): 117–35. For information on employment of former slaves in St. Louis, see Galusha Anderson, *The Story of a Border City During the Civil War* (Boston, 1908). For the quote from the chaplain in Cairo, see John Eaton and Ethel Osgood Mason, *Grant, Lincoln, and the Freedmen: Reminiscences of the Civil War with Special Reference to the Work for the Contrabands and Freedmen in the Mississippi Valley* (New York, 1907). Martha's description of her dire situation to her soldier husband is from Ira Berlin, et al., eds., *Freedom: A Documentary History of Emancipation, 1861–1867*, vol. 1 (Cambridge, Mass: Cambridge University Press, 1982), 244, 688; see volume 2 of this series for information on relocation and charitable projects involving former Arkansas slaves and on employment in St. Louis. The recounting of Union soldiers calling freedwomen idle vagrants and prostitutes and the analysis of former slave women building "enduring communities" come from Jacqueline Jones, *Labor of Love, Labor of Sorrow: Black Women, Work, and the Family from Slavery to the Present* (New York: Basic Books, 1985), 50, 76. For more on the Colored Ladies' Contraband Relief Society, see Theophilus Parsons, *Memoir of Emily Elizabeth Parsons* (Boston: Little, Brown & Co., 1880), 140. For more on the Freedmen's Orphan Home and indenturing of residents, see *Western Sanitary Commission Final Report*, no. 5 (St. Louis: R. P. Studley & Co., 1866), and Scharf, *History of St. Louis City and County*, vol. 1.

See also Donald G. Nieman, ed., *The Day of the Jubilee: The Civil War Experience of Black Southerners* (New York: Garland Press, 1994); Levi Coffin, *Reminiscences of Levi Coffin, The Reputed President of the Underground Railroad*, 3d ed. (Cincinnati: The Robert Clarke Co., 1898); Michael Fellman, "Emancipation in Missouri," *MHR* 83, no. 1 (October 1988): 36–56; Lawrence O. Christensen, *Black St. Louis: A Study in Race Relations, 1865–1916* (Ph.D. dissertation, University of Missouri–Columbia, 1972); Lorenzo J. Greene, Gary R. Kremer, and Anthony F. Holland, *Missouri's Black Heritage* (St. Louis: Forum Press, 1980); Joe M. Richardson, *Christian Reconstruction: The American Missionary Association and Southern Blacks, 1861–1890* (Athens: University of Georgia Press, 1986); and V. Jacque Voegeli, *Free But Not Equal: The Midwest and the Negro During the Civil War* (Chicago: University of Chicago Press, 1967).

Women Nurses in the Civil War

The Western Sanitary Commission's 1865 final report declared that "the army of faithful nurses" were the "true heroines of the war." This mostly female nursing corps served on the battlefield, on the hospital boats, and in the wards. Some received pay and others volunteered. They worked for various reasons: political commitment, patriotic fervor, humanitarian zeal, and the need for paid work. The female nurses, encumbered by prevailing attitudes about women's abilities and proper place, managed to work with and for men in the public, masculine arena of war. In serving their country, they also advanced women's entry into the traditionally male-dominated field of organized medicine.

Apart from midwifery, nursing before the war had been either a domestic duty performed by a woman or a servant, or a public social service performed as part of a religious calling. St. Louis medical facilities were ill-prepared to receive the influx of wounded soldiers when the first Missouri battles occurred in 1861. The United States Sanitary Commission, created in June, had been working with Dorothea L. Dix, the general superintendent of women nurses. With assistance from Dix, St. Louisans acted quickly to acquire nursing care. The job of selecting and placing female nurses in the city's hospitals was among the first duties of the Western Sanitary Commission (WSC).

Hiring paid nurses to staff military hospitals was a novel idea. But the work of Florence Nightingale in the Crimean War encouraged the United States government to place women in Civil War hospitals as an alternative to the usual practice of using convalescing soldiers to care for one another. Dr. Simon Pollak, a St. Louis surgeon working for the army, was not alone in suggesting, "Would it not be better economy to hire *well trained* male and female nurses. . . . Those who, by study and natural inclination have adapted themselves to this pursuit?" From the physician's perspective, the obvious disadvantages of the existing system and the need for trained personnel was more important than women's perceived natural sympathy and caring nature in the decision to bring paid nurses into military hospitals.

Initially, most of the women who cared for the sick and wounded in St. Louis were volunteers, but by the middle of 1862 there were enough paid nurses to replace all but the most experienced volunteers. Good physical and moral health were essential qualifications for the job. Applicants had to be between twenty-five and fifty years old, of good education, earnest but cheerful, and recommended by at least two responsible persons, preferably their clergyman and physician. Once accepted, nurses received assignments in military hospitals. They earned twelve dollars a month, plus room and board. Regulations required one nurse for every ten beds and no more than one female nurse for every thirty beds. However, many hospitals, like the Good Samaritan Military Hospital in St. Louis, did not hire any female nurses because the doctors would not employ them. This policy was not unique to St. Louis.

Whether the nurses were paid or voluntary, nothing could have prepared them for the job they had undertaken. Emily Parsons, a nurse whose talent and years of service earned her the position of supervisor of nurses at Benton Barracks Hospital, wrote home to Boston in 1863, "I am getting sadly familiar with death."

Parsons was a remarkable woman. Despite requirements that nurses be in good physical condition, she was blind in one eye, slightly deaf, and so lame in one foot that she could not walk or stand for long periods. She began her career as a volunteer nurse in Boston. By 1863 Parsons worked as a paid certified surgical nurse at the Lawton Hospital in St. Louis. When the WSC hospital boat left St. Louis to take supplies south and bring back wounded soldiers from Vicksburg and Memphis, physicians put her in charge of all nurses on board. She contracted malaria on the trip, but after her recovery, Dr. Ira Russell, the head surgeon at the enlarged Benton Barracks Hospital, requested her services. "He wishes me to be the lady supervisor of all the nurses male and female. . . . I never expected such a position as this—of so much responsibility," she wrote her mother in Boston. Parsons's responsibilities included organizing and running all the hospital wards, which after Vicksburg held more than one thousand patients. She supervised the male ward masters and the male and female nurses, reporting directly to Russell. Parsons hired nurses and supervised their training. Her work in St. Louis helped lay the foundation for nurses' training schools established later in Missouri and throughout the nation.

Professional female nurses such as Emily Parsons proved to male physicians that women could assist them with complex procedures and that they held up as well as men under the strain of wartime medical practice. As long as women did not challenge male control of the medical profession, they were welcome additions to the team. Civil War nurses created opportunities for the women who followed them into medical professions. Within a generation, nursing became a respected women's profession with prescribed training standards, certification, and relatively high pay compared to other female jobs.

–Joan Cooper

Sources: Information comes from Anderson, *A Border City During the Civil War*; Brockett and Vaughan, *Woman's Work in the Civil War*; Coalier, "Beyond Sympathy; J. E. D. Couzins Papers, MHS; Frank J. Lutz, ed., "The Autobiography and Reminiscences of S. Pollak, M.D., St. Louis, Mo.," *St. Louis Medical Review*, 1904; Parsons, *Memoir of Emily Elizabeth Parsons*; Kristie Ross, "Arranging a Doll's House: Refined Women as Union Nurses," in *Divided Houses*; Scharf, *History of St. Louis City and County*; Louise I. Trenholme, *History of Nursing in Missouri* (Missouri, 1926); Western Sanitary Commission Papers, MHS; and Mary Holland, *Our Army Nurses: Stories from Women in the Civil War* (Boston, 1897). For information on nursing by nuns, see Mary Denis Maher, *To Bind Up the Wounds: Catholic Sister Nurses in the U.S. Civil War* (Westport, Conn.: Greenwood Press, 1989).

Adaline Couzins

"**I**f there is anyone deserving of recognition for services rendered, it is Mrs. Couzins, and I hope that Congress will recognize these services, by granting her a pension," declared Michigan Senator Thomas W. Paler in his pension petition on behalf of Adaline Couzins, a middle-aged St. Louis volunteer who braved Civil War battlefields to gather up wounded soldiers and care for them on ships en route to St. Louis hospitals. She received her government pension, one of the few volunteer Civil War nurses officially recognized and rewarded.

Adaline Weston was born in England about 1815 and came to America at the age of eight. In 1834 she married John E. D. Couzins, a carpenter who later became St. Louis's chief of police and acting provost marshal during the war. Already active in charitable work before the war, Adaline volunteered her services as a nurse to Dr. Simon Pollak, a civilian St. Louis surgeon working for the army. In mid-August 1861, after the Battle of Wilson's Creek, she helped collect supplies and dress the wounds of casualties brought to St. Louis. Adaline became an active member of the newly formed Ladies' Union Aid Society (LUAS).

In the winter of 1862 the army asked the LUAS for volunteers to go to southwest Missouri battlefields in search of missing wounded. Adaline and a companion, Arethusa Forbes, braved sub-zero weather to locate hundreds of soldiers and bring them to St. Louis hospitals. Both women suffered frostbite; Forbes never fully recovered.

Shortly thereafter, Adaline Couzins volunteered to accompany Dr. Pollak to Fort Henry in Tennessee to bring back still more wounded. They were the first in the Civil War to use river steamers as floating hospitals. One volunteer on a boat at the Battle of Shiloh recoiled at the sight of wounded being carried on board and described the room where doctors amputated limbs as "a butcher's shamble."

Before the war, the only experienced hospital nurses in St. Louis were Catholic nuns. There was no formally organized medical training for either physicians or nurses. Few women considered paid nursing a respectable job. Dr. Pollak thought most amateur female nurses were an encumbrance rather than a service, citing "only two–Mrs. Couzins and

Adaline Couzins. Carte de visite photograph by Robert Goebel, MHS–PP

Mrs. Kershaw—who were worth anything." Subsequently, only nurses employed by the government were permitted on the boats. The physicians made exceptions for the experienced Sisters of Mercy from Chicago and a few highly regarded volunteers like Adaline Couzins. She was put in charge of nurses and medical stores on a hospital boat at the Battle of Shiloh, after which Dr. Pollak recognized Couzins's skill, reporting, "There were no amateur lady nurses present."

Despite the grueling work, emotional strain, and physical danger, Adaline Couzins continued to work, unpaid, on the hospital boats until the siege of Vicksburg in the summer of 1863. Her experiences there illustrated the perils of wartime nursing. Forbes later wrote to Adaline's daughter, Phoebe: "Did your mother keep that petticoat in which the rebels made a bullet hole firing at her from their fort?" Adaline had been struck in the knee, and while not serious enough to stop her work, the wound gave her problems in later years. She continued volunteer nursing until the end of the war.

After the war, Adaline Couzins returned to her peacetime charitable work and helped initiate the movement for woman suffrage in St. Louis. Like other female activists, she inspired her daughter to challenge traditional expectations for middle-class women. Phoebe Couzins became the first woman to enter Washington University Law School.

–Joan Cooper

Sources: Information about Adaline Couzins is from J. E. D. Couzins Papers, MHS. The Couzins collection includes a copy of the memorial submitted to the United States Senate in March 1888 by Thomas W. Paler, Senator from Michigan, on behalf of Mrs. Adaline Couzins, widow of the late J. E. D. Couzins, United States Marshal for the Eastern Division of Missouri, March 27, 1888, Washington, D.C. Also included in the collection is an excerpt from *Women Reformers*; Lutz, ed., *The Autobiography and Reminiscences of S. Pollak, M.D.*; *St. Louis Medical Review*, 1904; and Mark M. Krug, ed., *Mrs. Hill's Journal—Civil War Reminiscences* (Chicago, 1980).

"Battles of a Soldier's Wife"

In 1861 Mathilde Decker's husband, Robert, enlisted in the Union Army, leaving her alone and pregnant in St. Louis with a young son and only ten dollars in cash. Mathilde, a recent German immigrant and only twenty-one, had to rely on her own ingenuity to support herself and her children.

Although her husband served in the army until 1864, she could never count on any income from either the federal or local government. Like thousands of young mothers left behind to shift for themselves in wartime, Mathilde learned to be independent and self-sufficient.

A skilled seamstress, Mathilde's first plan was to decorate the best linens she had brought from Germany with fine embroidery and sell them. After a neighbor told her there were women living in certain areas of St. Louis who bought fancy linens, she began showing her work door-to-door in their neighborhood. One afternoon a woman welcomed her into a large two-story brothel, and within a few minutes the residents, all women wearing white negligees, bought everything in Mathilde's basket.

Unwilling to continue supplying houses of prostitution, Mathilde turned next to packing hardtack biscuits for soldiers' rations at night so she could care for her child during the day. From eight in the evening until two in the morning she left Frank asleep, watched over by a neighbor in the adjoining room. The hot hardtack burned her hands so bad, though, that she gave up the job shortly before the birth of her daughter. Because street fighting had delayed the midwife when she was in labor, Mathilde decided after Millie was born that the city was an unsafe place for a soldier's wife alone with two children.

Mathilde moved to a large farm in St. Louis County where she helped the farmer's near-blind wife do her chores. Although pleased that her children had plenty of fresh air and wholesome food, she often fell in bed at night too tired to get undressed. Robert filled his infrequent letters with war news, but sent no money, and neither did the army paymaster. Mathilde struggled with farm work until after the fall harvest but decided that she could safely return to St. Louis, now under martial law. She also wanted to be near her brother, who lived in the city.

Mathilde rented a room near the levee. Together with another soldier's wife, who had three children, she sewed during the day at home and packed hardtack at night. Little Frank watched over the baby, who slept in a dry goods box. In February all five children came down with small pox and Mathilde gave up her job to care for Frank and Millie. When health officials told her the children would have to go to the quarantine hospital, known to Mathilde as the "pest house," she brandished Robert's old pistol and ran the inspectors off. She nursed her children by giving them a strong laxative. To prevent scarring from the pox, she made masks of sweet oil medicine on their faces. Both her children recovered, but two of her neighbor's three children died in the quarantine hospital and the other was badly scarred.

Eventually Mathilde ran out of money for rent. After the landlord put her possessions on the street, Mathilde went to the army headquarters for help. She brought back two soldiers who forced the landlord to let her remain in her room. Then she went back to work packing hardtack and sewing by candlelight. That summer she moved again. Robert returned to St. Louis on a three-day pass, meeting his daughter for the first time. Mathilde's brother also enlisted in the Union Army, but before he left St. Louis, he brought his sister a lamp and some money to buy a sewing machine.

It took some time to master the sewing machine, but Mathilde kept at it. Soldiers' wives with sewing skills could go to the Ladies' Union Aid Society (LUAS) offices on Chestnut Street to pick up and return bundles of sewing. The LUAS distributed pre-cut materials to the wives who made hospital garments at home. Before women could sew for the LUAS, however, volunteers visited their homes to see if they truly needed and deserved help.

For exercise and a break from sewing, Mathilde often walked to the French market, leaving her children to play in the landlady's garden. A young man who lived in the neighborhood began to watch her on the street and, knowing she was a soldier's wife and alone, one night tried unsuccessfully to enter her room. The next time he came, Mathilde was waiting. She hit him over the head with a club as he climbed in the window. She also fought off the advances of a traveling daguerreotypist, who tried to convince her that Robert would never return from the war.

In 1864 Robert received a discharge for a medical disability. He returned home a sick man, hovering between life and death for six months. Finally, against his doctor's orders, Mathilde gave him a bowl of her landlady's sauerkraut. From that day Robert began his eventual recovery, which his wife attributed not to physicians, but to the natural healing powers of pickled cabbage.

The war had changed the Deckers and their relationship. After he recovered, Robert had difficulty finding work in St. Louis. Mathilde used two hundred dollars she had saved from her wartime sewing to support the family. They moved to Indiana where Robert returned to his trade as a painter and Mathilde opened a successful dressmaking business. After Robert's death in 1899,

she received a Civil War veteran widow's pension of eight dollars a month.

Sources: Louise Meyer wrote about the homefront struggles of Mathilde Decker, her great-grandmother, in a story titled "Battles of a Soldier's Wife," now in the MHS archives. Although she changed Mathilde's name to Helwig, Meyer described the young woman's experiences as told to her by family members. Whether or not the specifics are entirely accurate, Mathilde's story is similar to that of other women left alone to fend for themselves in wartime. Family stories placed in historical context are one way to learn about working-class immigrant women who left few written records. Information about the LUAS sewing project for soldier's wives is from Brockett and Vaughn, *Woman's Work in the Civil War*, 641, and Forman, *Western Sanitary Commission*, 133.

Gratiot Street Prison

During the Civil War, the McDowell Medical College building, located on the northeast corner of Eighth and Gratiot Streets, became the Gratiot Street Military Prison. The forbidding gray stone building, with its cupola, octagonal center section and two large wings, looked like a fortress. Dr. Joseph N. McDowell, who erected the building in 1847, was known as an intemperate man. He hated Catholics, abolitionists, and all black people. After he left St. Louis in 1861 to join the Confederate Army, the federal government confiscated his property to hold Confederate prisoners of war and civilians suspected of treason against the Union. St. Louis women sympathetic to the Southern cause spent time at Gratiot Street, some as volunteers bringing aid and comfort to prisoners, others as prisoners themselves. Although other local military prisons held women, they were not of the same class and did not engender the public sympathy accorded those at Gratiot Street.

Political prisoners usually spent only a few weeks at Gratiot Street. They were either released on bond, exiled to the Confederate states, or sent to a federal prison in Alton, Illinois. Living conditions at the Gratiot Street Prison were unpleasant enough for men accustomed to barracks life and battlefield misery; middle-class women found them appalling.

Women prisoners occupied space in the octagonal building reputedly once used for dissecting cadavers. Water drenched them every time the floors were washed in the hospital facilities in the rooms above. They slept on straw

Gratiot Street Prison. Photograph of a pencil sketch by M. M. Patterson, 1864. MHS–PP

pallets on the floor. Only daily food baskets from the Daughters of Charity saved them from disgusting prison rations. The taunts of surly guards made the experience even more humiliating for women accustomed to servants and deference.

Women were also imprisoned in the Myrtle Street Prison, formerly the city's largest slave pen, Mrs. McClure's Chestnut Street home, and the St. Charles Street Prison for Women. Conditions proved to be so bad in the St. Charles Street Prison that charges against Mrs. Dixon, the keeper's wife, prompted an official inquiry late in the war. Mrs. Dixon demanded bribes for favors, stole from prisoners, forced them to live in filthy conditions, and made inmates sew for her own family. Primarily poor women from rural Missouri imprisoned for guerrilla warfare, captives had little influence or power to improve their conditions.

However miserable, most rebel women prisoners were not innocent victims of war. They were partisans, most of them imprisoned for spying, transporting mail across enemy lines, and smuggling contraband goods in and out of the city. In 1863 Ada B. Haines was convicted of being a Confederate courier and banished to the South, but she returned to St. Louis when she learned one of her children was sick. After spending another five months in Gratiot Street Prison, she was released on bond and sent to New York State for the duration.

Imprisoned women remained active Confederates. According to Absalom Grimes, a convicted mail runner, four women held in the

room next to his in the Gratiot Street Prison helped him escape in 1862. The women were separated from Grimes by folding doors that had been nailed shut. They gave him some chloroform to use on his guards, but that plan did not work. Then one of the women passed him a dirk knife through a crack in the doors. He used it to make a hidden escape hatch in the floorboards of his cell. At night he crawled under the floor of the women's room and dug a hole in an outside wall bordering an alley. The women danced and moved the chairs above him to muffle the noise he made prying apart the bricks. To assure the guards that Grimes was still in his cell, they jerked a string through the folding door that was attached to a rocking chair. Grimes escaped with the women's help but was later recaptured and returned to prison.

Once martial law put an end to flagrant displays of allegiance to the Confederacy, the Gratiot Street Prison became a symbol of Southern sympathy for St. Louisans. Many more women entered the prison to bring food, clothing, and comfort to the prisoners than were themselves incarcerated. Young women promenaded on Eighth Street in view of prisoners to show their support. Military officials required women who wanted to help nurse the wounded in the prison hospital to sign an oath of loyalty to the Union. Many took the oath rather than be excluded from the hospital.

The imprisonment and exile of middle- and upper-class St. Louis women for their political activity during the Civil War evoked sympathy and outrage not only from Southern supporters, but also from women of their same class who supported the Union. This was true, in part, because they had known each other in social, volunteer, and religious groups before the war. Divisions of class, more ingrained than political or gender loyalties, prevented them from identifying with poor women who suffered far greater deprivations from the military prison system.

Sources: Information is from United Daughters of the Confederacy, *Reminiscences of the Women of Missouri During the Sixties* (Jefferson City, Mo.: The Hugh Stephens Printing Co., 1920s); Scharf, *History of St. Louis City and County*, vol. 1, 419–420, 448; Winter, *The Civil War in St. Louis*, 79–80; Michael Fellman, "Women and Guerrilla Warfare," in *Divided Houses*; Abbie Kennerly to John, 26 October 1862, Kennerly Papers, MHS; and Stagg, "Local Incidents of the Civil War."

Margaret Parkinson McClure

In the spring of 1863, Aline Taylor went with her mother to see a prisoner being held in a house on Chestnut Street just east of Seventh Street. Mrs. Taylor carried a special permit for the visit. Aline remembered that "there were guards at the door, also at the head and foot of the stairs. She was in the second-floor front room. I asked my mother why she went? She said the lady had been her friend and was in trouble."

The woman was Margaret Parkinson McClure, accused of using her home for dispatching Confederate mail, harboring escaped prisoners, and distributing contraband goods. Union officials placed her under house arrest on March 20, 1863, and turned her home into a prison. After selling her furniture and household goods, they set up cots for other women also arrested for aiding the Confederate cause.

On May 13, guards brought the prisoners from the McClure home, including Margaret's fourteen-year-old son, to the wharf at the foot of Pine Street. There, they joined thirteen secessionist men, also sentenced to deportation, to begin the long journey to Confederate territory in Mississippi.

The harsh treatment of women like Margaret McClure, who before the war had been a prominent, respected member of St. Louis society, separated old friends and contributed to the city's divisive environment. St. Louis was under martial law, however, and in a war zone the enemy was usually banished or imprisoned. The Confederate cause engendered as much patriotic fervor in some women as the Union cause did in others, and those who took political action understood the consequences.

Though born in Pennsylvania, Margaret McClure remained true to her family's Virginia lineage. A wealthy widow when the war began, she had moved to Missouri following her marriage in 1834 and had lived in St. Louis for twenty years. In addition to her townhouse, she had a large country home, Pine Lawn, northwest of the city. After her son Parkinson joined the Confederate Army, Margaret spent her days visiting captured soldiers in St. Louis prisons and hospitals.

Margaret's home became the dispatching center for Confederate mail and goods coming in and out of St. Louis. When her son Lewis was arrested as a Southern sympathizer, his poor treatment in prison only increased his mother's resolve.

Once banished, Margaret McClure spent the rest of the war as the guest of Confederate General Nathaniel Whitfield in Columbus, Alabama. She continued to visit wounded soldiers in Southern hospitals. At war's end she returned to her home in St. Louis, still an unreconstructed rebel. She became the first president of the St. Louis Daughters of the Confederacy in 1891 and a founder of the Confederate Home for Veterans in Higginsville, Missouri. In one of the ironic twists that so often marked the family histories of the Civil War generation, her son Charles eventually married the daughter of Mary Ann Boyce Edgar, an Alabama native and an ardent St. Louis Unionist during the war.

Although Margaret McClure was in fact an active Confederate sympathizer and probably a spy, other St. Louis women may have suffered arrest and exile on far less provocation. Military officials arrested women for aiding the South "by word or deed," whether their actions were active or passive. Women who displayed Confederate flags or pictures of Southern heroes, insulted Union troops, or communicated too freely with Confederate prisoners invited imprisonment or exile. The military often forcibly removed the families of Confederate officers from the city. When government officials assessed St. Louisans with secessionist leanings to fund refugee relief and the Missouri militia, some women who had taken no public political position at all saw their furniture carried out of their homes and sold.

As in all wars, men and women experienced the Civil War differently. Only a handful of women saw combat. On questions of political loyalty and subversive action, federally imposed martial law may actually have treated women better than men. Men, however, made political decisions for their families and, in most instances, they owned the family home and its furnishings. Whether or not a woman agreed with her husband, his politics affected her options in more ways than hers did his.

Sources: For additional information, see Mary K. Dains and Sue Sadler, eds., *Show Me Missouri Women: Selected Biographies* (Kirksville, Mo.: Thomas Jefferson University Press, 1989), 21; Mrs. P. G. Roberts, "History of Events Preceding and Following the Banishment of Mrs. Margaret A. E. McClure, as Given to the Author by Herself," in *Reminiscences of the Civil War*, ed., John B. Gordon (New York: Scribner's, 1903). Opening quotation is from Aline Sheafe Taylor Hicks, "Reminiscences During Civil War, St. Louis" (St. Louis History Papers, MHS Archives). See also Scharf, *History of St. Louis City and County*, and Winter, *The Civil War in St. Louis*.

Mississippi Valley Sanitary Fair Volunteers Preparing to Auction General Nathaniel Lyon's Last Letter. Stereograph photograph by Robert Benecke, 1864. MHS–PP

Mississippi Valley Sanitary Fair

During the spring of 1864, St. Louis women prepared for a huge public fair to benefit the Western Sanitary Commission (WSC). Some had organized hospital kitchens or coordinated relief activities at the office of the Ladies' Union Aid Society (LUAS) since the first year of the war. Others had visited wards or sewed in their homes for the wounded and refugees. Now they were doing fancy needlework and knitting mittens, soliciting donations of china, art, and flowers, and planning a children's fish pond. In May the city's most prominent citizens mingled with ordinary St. Louisans, black and white, in a huge temporary building on Twelfth Street between Olive and Washington Avenues. During the three-week fair, they bought and sold enough donated goods to each other to finance the work of the WSC through the end of the war.

Volunteer groups in many Northern cities mounted extravagant fairs to raise money for war relief. They were called "sanitary fairs" for the hospital supplies, or sanitary goods, purchased with the profits. Sanitary fairs gave everyone an opportunity to do good by having fun. Typically, everything but publicity and building construction was donated; profits were nearly 90 percent. St. Louis Unionists decided early in 1864 to hold a fair to replenish their rapidly diminishing funds.

Although the Mississippi Valley Sanitary Fair was a cooperative project of the WSC and the LUAS, its organizational structure and operation gave men all the top leadership positions. Men's political and business connections proved invaluable in negotiating shipping and construction contracts, but much of the daily effort required to pull off the huge event fell to women. The hours of work and organizational expertise they brought to the project, however, did not gain LUAS members seats on the policy-making executive committees.

Women made up more than half of the six hundred people who did committee work for the fair. Committee membership followed traditional gender lines, although both men and women served on the Fine Arts, Floral, and Public Amusements Committees. Men volunteered for Shoes, Arms and Trophies, Iron and Steel, Stoves and Tinware, Swords, Tobacco and Cigars, and Finance. Women handled Jewelry, Ladies Furnishings, Millinery, Shirts, Children's Activities, and most refreshment concessions—except for wine and beer.

The Executive Committee of Ladies made few formal requests of fair officials, but they did protest plans for liquor sales in or near the building. Supported by James Yeatman and William Eliot of the WSC, they voiced all the traditional female arguments for temperance: possible disagreeable scenes of intoxication, temptation for morally weak men, and opposition to the will of God. The men conceded the liquor sales but not beer and wine, in part because they wanted the participation of St. Louis Germans, many of whom were ardent Unionists. In the end, the WSC reported that German organizations "patriotically sold lager beer and a host of people patriotically drank it."

Women also encouraged African American participation in the fair. Eliot, Galusha Anderson, and other Protestant ministers gave their support for integrating the building. Fair officials paid black soldiers stationed at Benton Barracks to guard the entrances. One sales booth raised money for the Committee for Freedmen and Refugee Relief. No black women, however, appear to have held leadership positions.

The Executive Committee of Ladies was charged with coordinating the work of women volunteers. Many had experience planning church bazaars, but this may have been their first major public endeavor. In addition to months of preparation, women produced and sold a newspaper during the run of the fair. *The Daily Countersign* directed visitors to the various booths and amusements and printed feature articles, poems, and patriotic literature. Women provided the creative spark and sales force for dozens of attractions designed to make parting with a few dollars an enjoyable experience as well as a patriotic duty. Volunteers charged visitors a dollar to vote for their favorite general. They raffled off three bars of silver and sold lottery tickets on a donated St. Louis County farm. Dressed up as "Aunt Mahitable" and "Dr. Emerson," they sold Boston baked beans in the New England Kitchen. Volunteers sorted, priced, and sold clothing and other merchandise donated from as far away as New York and Philadelphia.

When the fair ended on June 12, the fair had grossed $618,782.28 and made a net profit of $554,591. Of that, the Ladies' Union Aid Society received $50,000 for its work in hospitals and with soldiers' families, as well as $1,000 monthly to the Ladies' Freedmen's Relief Association for activities in aid of black soldiers and freedmen, women, and children.

St. Louisans had a good time at the Mississippi Valley Sanitary Fair. It was a unifying experience for Unionists after three years of debilitating wartime sacrifice and confusion. Although the fair's paternalistic male leadership attempted to keep them in their place, women gained from the successful community event a renewed confidence in their ability to work together for a common goal.

Sources: See Jasper W. Cross, "The Mississippi Valley Sanitary Fair, St. Louis, 1864," *MHR* 46, no. 3 (April 1952) for a description of the fair's organization and activities. *The Daily Countersign* (17 May–12 June 1864) is available at the MHS library. Scharf describes the fair in *History of St. Louis City and County,* vol. 1, as does Anderson, *A Border City in the Civil War.* For insight into women's position in the fair's organizational structure, see "Minutes of the Executive Committee of the Mississippi Valley Sanitary Fair," MHS Archives, and Yeatman, *Final Report of the Western Sanitary Commission.*

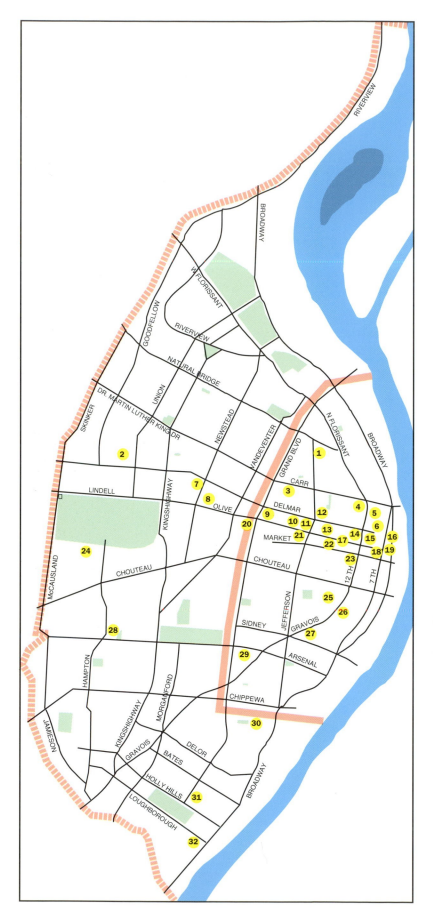

1865–1900

1. Little Sisters of the Poor
2. Academy of the Visitation
3. WCA White Cross Home
4. Colored Orphans' Home
5. Carrie Smith's Boardinghouse
6. Mission Free School
7. Religious of the Sacred Heart City House
8. Kate Chopin Home
9. Virginia Minor Home
10. Mary Institute
11. Liggett & Myers Tobacco Factory
12. St. John's Hospital
13. WCA Women's Christian Home
14. Lucy E. Tilly Working Girls Club
15. Prostitution District
16. WCA Training School
17. Bell Telephone Office
18. St. Louis Normal School
19. Famous Department Store
20. Women's Exchange
21. Loretto Academy
22. WCA Traveler's Aid at Union Station
23. St. Mary's Infirmary
24. Forest Park College
25. City Hospital Nursing School
26. South Side Day Nursery
27. Fruth House
28. Social Evil Hospital
29. St. Elizabeth's Academy
30. Maryville College
31. Des Peres School
32. Women's Christian Temperance Union Hall

— St. Louis City Limits 1855–1876
--- St. Louis City Limits 1876–Present
■ Parks

5

Women in the Industrializing City

In the decades after the Civil War, signs of vigorous economic growth appeared everywhere in St. Louis—in new factories and railroad terminals, warehouses, public buildings, streetcar tracks, telegraph and telephone lines, and homes. In 1875, flush with booster enthusiasm and eager to draw boundaries between urban and rural space, St. Louis voters moved the city limits west of Forest Park and withdrew from St. Louis County. In 1880 nearly 350,000 people lived within the expanded city. Building on their prewar commercial success, entrepreneurs courted new customers in the southwestern states to replace the midwestern and southern markets lost to the war or to upstart Chicago. No longer

content to merely wholesale eastern goods, local industrialists began manufacturing clothing, shoes, and other consumer products. In 1880 the city ranked sixth in the value of its manufactured goods, claiming the world's two largest tobacco factories as well as the largest brewery. Civic leaders, still hopeful of surpassing Chicago as the Future Great City of the Midwest, envisioned a million prospering St. Louisans by the early twentieth century.

St. Louis, Missouri. Hand-colored wood engraving by Schell and Hogan after C. A. Vanderhoof, 1876, from *Harper's Weekly*, 8 July 1876. MHS–PP

Industrial capitalism created immense wealth for a few St. Louis families. Their mansions rose on private streets west of Grand Avenue, guarded by pretentious gates and restrictive deeds. North and south of the central corridor, new subdivisions of brick townhouses lined the western extensions of older downtown thoroughfares. The families who lived here were members of a small but steadily expanding urban middle class. Further east and nearer the river stood a jumble of large factories, small manufacturing shops, warehouses, churches, schools, saloons, and working-class flats on muddy macadam streets. The poor crowded together at the edge of the central business district or near the river.

These visible patterns of Gilded Age expansion held clues to less obvious social and economic changes. Population pressures, unregulated industrial growth, and the reluctance of property owners to tax themselves for municipal services overwhelmed serious efforts to provide an adequate urban infrastructure. Decisions made by a few affected not only land use and air quality, but also the quality of life for both longtime residents and newcomers.

Many of the newest St. Louisans were African Americans escaping rural poverty. Between 1860 and 1900 the city's black population increased tenfold, from three thousand to more than thirty-five thousand. They lived in every city ward. Along with recent Eastern European immigrants, poor

black families crowded into dense east-central neighborhoods, segregated as much by class as by race. Other African Americans, however, both newcomers and descendants of old families, were as middle class in their values and ambitions as their white counterparts. Except for schooling and marriage, racial discrimination functioned by custom and contract, not by law, but increasingly the racist policies of white St. Louisans restricted African Americans' access to jobs, education, and better housing.

In St. Louis, as in other American cities, white women from all social classes found they had more options. A significant number of families moved into the middle class. By the 1880s many of the children of earlier German and Irish immigrants could rent or purchase postwar homes with indoor plumbing and central heat. Until then, most women, even those with servants, had spent their days sewing, cooking, and caring for children and the sick. Now, commercially produced food and ready-made clothing reduced time spent in the kitchen and at the sewing machine. More healthy mothers with fewer children reflected a declining birth rate and improved medical care. Abby Cranch Eliot, married in 1837, devoted most of her life to caring for her family, but only five of her fourteen children survived to adulthood, while her daughter-in-law, Charlotte Stearns Eliot, married in 1869, became an active club woman and writer. Six of her seven children lived to old age. Young women in particular took advantage of their new options to work in an office, factory, or department store, rather than in their homes. Paradoxically, as the distinction between a male public world and a female private world began to erode, the rhetoric of gender difference and separate spheres grew more insistent.

The division of labor in marriage, always structured by gender, became rigidly defined in moral terms by the prospering urban middle class. The concept of "separate spheres" linked differences in individual personality and abilities to innate gender traits and harshly judged deviant behavior. Middle-class St. Louisans came to view their homes as private havens that separated their families from the complex, confusing public world outside their doors. Home was the focus of family life and the setting where women preserved and nurtured the virtues necessary for survival in the morally dangerous industrial city.

Nationally published social reformers such as Catherine Beecher urged women to make homemaking a career and their homes classrooms

Parlor at the Women's Christian Home. Halftone from the Thirtieth Annual Report of the St. Louis Women's Christian Association, 1899. MHS–PP

for training children, especially their daughters, in proper behavior. One of the effects of this proscriptive literature was that it raised a higher standard for cleanliness, taste, etiquette, and child rearing. Playing on genuine fear of family disintegration and social chaos, manufacturers of household furnishings encouraged visions of domesticity that made home embellishment a moral imperative. Retailers advertised mass-marketed consumer goods in newspapers and catalogs and showcased them in downtown department stores. Men usually left home management to women; they expressed manly virtue by competing successfully in the ruthless marketplace.

Postwar prosperity brought fewer changes to poorer women, who were never far from the perils of urban life that most middle-class families tried to ignore or escape. Working-class women also aspired to attractive, well-furnished homes but worried more about having enough money from their own labor and that of other family members for basic food, clothing, and shelter. Graniteware cookware, bakery bread, store-bought clothing, and indoor plumbing were luxuries beyond the reach of most St. Louis women in the Gilded Age. Heavy housework still consumed their domestic time and energy. In all nineteenth-century American cities, at any given time between one quarter and one half of all working-class housewives took in boarders.

Women had the greatest opportunities and faced the greatest risks during the years between schooling and marriage. Between 1860 and 1900, the number of American women in the labor force grew from 10 percent to 21 percent. Forty percent of all single women, but fewer than 5 percent of married women, worked outside their homes. While these figures did not give an accurate accounting of women's paid work–they did not include part-time workers or married women who did laundry or piecework for clothing manufacturers in their homes–they did show that the majority of working women were between the ages of sixteen and twenty-four, primarily either domestic workers or factory workers.

By the end of the century, 37 percent of all St. Louis women workers were either domestic servants or laundresses; another 34 percent worked in factories. But both locally and nationally, the ratio between domestic workers and factory workers declined as more women took manufacturing jobs. All other occupations–teaching, office, and retail–accounted for only 29 percent of female workers.

By 1900, 16 percent of St. Louis women workers held sales or clerical jobs, about twice the national average.

Industrial cities offered women real alternatives to domestic service. The independence that wage work made possible, however, directly challenged the ideology of domesticity and women's dependent position in the family. In 1893 a local tobacco factory worker told an interviewer why she preferred factory work to domestic work: "I commence work at a certain hour and at a certain hour I quit. All work is by the piece, and there is no fault-finding and scolding. My Sundays and evenings are my own. My services are appreciated, and my pay is according to the work done." Given the opportunity, this factory worker had chosen a job that gave her some control over her time, was impersonal, and put money in her pocketbook. But it enabled a precarious independence that gave little protection from unhealthy working conditions, seasonal layoffs, and the gulf between earnings and living costs.

Unlike domestic workers who earned less money but received room and board from their employers, most factory workers lived at home and contributed to the family income. All but 58 of 851 St. Louis female factory workers surveyed in 1890 lived at home. One-third of these families lived in two-room flats. Even if their parents did not need their help, few women could afford to live independently. The average wage of a tobacco worker was slightly less than the basic weekly expenses of a self-supporting single person. Women employed in tobacco and shoe factories

Platt and Thornburgh Paint Factory, Interior of Vat Room. Industrial jobs were segregated by gender; women seldom did the same work as men, and female jobs paid less. Photograph by Otto Laroge, 1898. MHS–PP

made the highest wages. Those who made clothing and bags earned much less. With the exception of professional occupations like teaching, most jobs for women in late-nineteenth-century St. Louis paid too little to live on.

Prostitution, a growth industry in cities like St. Louis, was a constant threat to young single women without adequate income or family support. Commonly labeled the "fallen woman problem," prostitution and unwed motherhood were serious issues for desperate poor women, for working-class women at risk, and for concerned middle-class women. Beginning in the 1830s, St. Louis women of means had aided destitute women and children by establishing orphanages, homes for the aged, maternity hospitals, and vocational training schools. As more females entered the job market, middle-class women interpreted the problems of working women, and their growing independence, in the context of their highly sexualized Victorian society.

Women, considered natural guardians of virtue, protected other women from men, regarded as natural sexual predators. Men might exploit a fallen woman but never willingly wed her. The presumption of virginity was essential for proposals of marriage, and marriage was the one option women did not want to lose. For most, it provided the only real possibility for financial security.

Benevolent women established institutions to help untarnished working-class women retain their virtue and learn domestic and marketable skills. Strategies included affordable, chaperoned boardinghouses, retail outlets for handiwork, industrial schools, inexpensive day care, and girls' clubs. Episcopalian women established two branches of the Girls' Friendly Society, one for whites and one for blacks, to help virtuous young women striving for a "pure and modest life . . . stand firm against the frequent opportunities and strong temptations to an opposite course." A girl who lost her virtue forfeited her membership card. Other institutions offered shelter and training to sexually active single women, including unwed mothers. Middle-class women organized clubs and libraries for working women to encourage self-improvement, rather than self-indulgent leisure activities. Working-class women were ambivalent about these new facilities. Not only did most prefer to manage their own social lives, but they also resented the moral judgments that accompanied offers of assistance.

Distinguishing between the worthy and the unworthy poor was important to middle- and upper-class St. Louisans. They believed that giving aid to the unworthy only encouraged their natural sloth and intemperance; worthy, able-bodied individuals did not need, and in fact would resist, offers of assistance. The tendency to blame the poor for their poverty was doubly ingrained in Protestantism and in the capitalist ideals of individualism, hard work, and personal responsibility. The model of nineteenth-century benevolence, Protestant or Catholic, was an institution that sheltered dependent, unemployable poor people.

May Harrington, Prostitute. Photograph by St. Louis Police Department, 1897. MHS–PP

Bertillon Identification and Arrest Record for May Harrington. St. Louis Police Department, 1897. MHS–PP

In 1870 St. Louis had more than sixteen hundred institutionalized children. Before 1900 nearly eleven thousand would pass through the city's privately supported orphanages and public reformatory. Only about one in twenty was a true orphan. More than one-fourth were either mentally or physically disabled or judged incorrigible by municipal authorities. Half-orphans accounted for one-fourth; another fourth were boarded by parents unable to care for them. The rest had been abandoned, abused, or neglected. Nuns and middle-class Protestant women sheltered and cared for most of these children, and for the destitute, ill, and aged. The city's small Jewish population aided dependent Jews.

Although they left most institutional care to women's organizations or to underfunded public facilities, whenever natural disasters struck, St. Louis businessmen acted quickly to help innocent victims. After the 1849 cholera epidemic and great fire, they organized to solicit and distribute emergency aid. German and Irish groups sometimes gave temporary help to countrymen new to the city. Individuals aided relatives down on their luck and passed out food or clothing to occasional beggars who came to the door.

As long as St. Louis had a small population and enough jobs for most able-bodied workers, this unorganized, private charity worked effectively. But when St. Louis's population neared 160,000 in the late 1850s, a severe economic slump prompted William Greenleaf Eliot and banker James E. Yeatman to consider establishing a citywide relief organization. These civic leaders, who also organized the Western Sanitary Commission for Civil War relief, incorporated the Provident Association in 1863 to solicit private donations directly from businessmen. Though legally nonsectarian, the agency was staffed largely by ministers and mainly aided Protestants. In cooperation with its co-religious counterparts, the Catholic St. Vincent de Paul Society, organized along parish lines, and the Hebrew Relief Organization, the Provident Association collected and distributed all citywide relief until the 1930s.

In 1871 the Provident Association warned of "certain dark portents on the horizon; certain terrible questions in the relation of capital and labor that should add a motive to all holders of prosperity to do all they can to help the sons of toil, especially when want of work drives men to ruin or starvation or crime." Prospering St. Louisans who benefitted from the expanding economy could not ignore the paradox of poverty in the midst of progress or the

desperate victims of postwar industrial capitalism. The threat of social disorder, always just below the surface, made helping the poor of vital importance to civic leaders and businessmen for the first time. Charity, properly administered, now became good social policy.

Always wary of being hoodwinked by the undeserving poor, the staff of the Provident Association carefully investigated all requests for aid. James Yeatman created the agency after a beggar woman who was receiving charity from a church had asked him for aid as well. The Provident Association only rewarded work and opposed the concept of "outdoor relief"–giving money directly to needy people. Men chopped wood for a day in the agency's wood yard before receiving any food, clothing, or shelter. In 1892 the association established the Women's Division, a separate branch that offered job training and similar assistance to women and girls. Although female volunteers served on the board of the Provident Association, it was from the start a bureaucratic relief organization administered largely by men. They rationalized citywide benevolence and shifted the locus of giving from women's groups to male business and professional organizations with greater access to resources. Men became more involved in supporting charity, but women still provided most direct assistance through their female-run organizations.

Women's organizations reflected the postwar growth in female education. After the Civil War,

Yes, On Condition That You Buy Me a "Domestic," with New Wood Work and Attachments. Manufacturers and retailers promoted products for the home by suggesting that they were the key to a woman's heart and a guarantee of domestic bliss. Chromolithograph advertising card, ca. 1880. MHS–PP

middle- and upper-class girls attended secondary schools, and even colleges, in greater numbers but still small by modern standards. Only 3 percent of St. Louisans of high school age enrolled in public high school before 1900. The daughters of prospering businessmen more often attended private schools. To meet the rising demand, religious orders opened new academies or enlarged and modernized old ones. Hosmer Hall and Mary Institute, both located on fashionable Locust Street, prepared young Protestant women for college and the professions. Phoebe Couzins graduated from Washington University Law School in 1871. A few graduates like Mary Hancock McLean even pursued degrees in medicine at out-of-state schools.

Most educated St. Louis women and others who moved to the city after graduating from eastern schools did not pursue careers. Married women, along with some single professional women, organized clubs where they met in the afternoon to read original papers on topics in literature and art history. The Shelley Club, founded in 1888 to study England's Lake Poets, evolved by 1890 into The Wednesday Club, which soon broadened its agenda to include social and political issues.

By the turn of the century, dozens of active women's clubs operated in St. Louis, although they were not the most prevalent type of women's organization. More women, particularly working-class wives, joined groups affiliated directly with churches or fraternal organizations. The members of secular women's clubs were overwhelmingly middle class, and like nearly all social organizations in urban America, women's clubs were racially segregated.

A few St. Louis club women took political action beyond meeting-room or parlor discussion. After studying the effects of air pollution, Wednesday Club members collaborated with men from the Engineers' Club to lobby for local smoke abatement regulations. Other women joined Frances Willard's Chicago-based Women's Christian Temperance Union (WCTU), founded in 1874, in a crusade against alcoholism and the liquor industry. The WCTU became the largest women's organization in the nation. Despite the fact that the organization held its 1882 national convention in St. Louis, the local branches were probably less active than other female reform groups. Most Missouri WCTU members lived in small outstate towns.

The most politically active women in Gilded Age St. Louis gathered at the Mercantile Library in May 1867 to organize the Woman Suffrage Association of Missouri, the first organization in America dedicated solely to gaining the vote for women. Virginia Minor, elected the first president, had been active in the Ladies' Union Aid Society during the Civil War, as had founding members Anna Clapp and Rebecca Hazard. Their ardent support for the Union cause and their successful, if limited, partnership with the male leadership of the Western Sanitary Commission drew these elite women into public life and allied them with Radical Republicans. Reform-minded men, like William Greenleaf Eliot and Virginia's attorney husband, Francis Minor, joined them in support of suffrage for women. The Minors argued that the Fourteenth Amendment that granted citizenship to African Americans gave all United States citizens, both women and men, the right to vote. They pursued their ultimately losing case all the way to the U.S. Supreme Court.

The Minors' views were similar to those of Susan B. Anthony and Elizabeth Cady Stanton, founders of the National Woman Suffrage Association (NWSA). The NWSA refused to support the Fifteenth Amendment, which gave the vote to black men, unless the amendment enfranchised all women as well. In 1869 the national suffrage movement split over this issue. Virginia Minor served as vice president of the NWSA in the 1870s and 1880s, having resigned from the St. Louis organization when a majority of its members joined with the new American Woman Suffrage Association (AWSA), founded by Lucy Stone and other former abolitionists. The AWSA members feared that linking female voting rights to the Fifteenth Amendment would jeopardize suffrage for African American men. They supported Republicans in promoting the federal amendment to enfranchise black males, while still working on the state level for legislation to give women the vote. When the two organizations reunited in 1890, Virginia Minor became president of the state affiliate.

The range of arguments women put forth in support of suffrage illustrated the complexity of their changing place in industrial America at the end of the nineteenth century. When elite women sometimes implied that educated, white, taxpaying women deserved the vote more than naturalized immigrants and poor black men, they reaffirmed the racial and ethnic prejudices that had long set urban populations against each other.

Women who demanded suffrage as a right of citizenship expressed a developing understanding of themselves as individuals, not simply as female dependents of a patriarchal household. Encouraged by both Protestantism and democratic capitalism, individualism was an American virtue men could no longer keep exclusively for themselves. The old idea that a man voted for his household conflicted with a growing belief in every individual's right to think and act independently.

Women had already made valuable, acknowledged contributions to the public life of their communities. Their record in social service and skill in managing charitable institutions was proof to some women and men that they not only had earned the vote but that they would use it to further the general welfare.

Largely ignored by suffrage organizations, few working-class women lobbied for the vote. Many other women opposed suffrage because they feared it would upset the supposedly natural complementary relationship between men and women. However, industrialism had already upset not only gender relationships, but also much of what Americans believed was true about their cities. St. Louisans lived surrounded by evidence that rapid urban growth created as much poverty as progress, as much ugliness as civic beauty, more chaos than order.

With a population approaching six hundred thousand at the turn of the century, St. Louis was no different from other American cities whose citizens sought ways to contain the excesses of industrial capitalism. In the post–Civil War years women expanded their place in the city as workers and activists. Now, even more middle-class women were eager to be "municipal housekeepers," a popular expression that reflected confidence in their ability to help set things right. Working-class women, too, organized on their own behalf, demanding higher wages, better jobs, and safer workplaces. Women would be as active as men in the reform movements of the twentieth century.

Sources: For information on Gilded Age St. Louis, including reasons behind the city/county separation, see James Neal Primm, *Lion of the Valley: St. Louis, Missouri*, 3d. ed. (St. Louis: MHS Press, 1998); Katharine T. Corbett and Howard S. Miller, *St. Louis in the Gilded Age* (St. Louis: MHS Press, 1993); and William Hyde and Howard Conard, *Encyclopedia of the History of St. Louis* (New York: The Southern History Company, 1899). Rich J. Compton and Camille N. Dry, *Pictorial St. Louis* (St. Louis: Compton, 1876) not only shows nearly every building in 1875 St. Louis, but also provides contemporary descriptions of women's institutions and work places. Other sources include

Sara M. Evans, *Born for Liberty: A History of Women in America* (New York: The Free Press, 1989), 119–43; Lawrence O. Christensen, "Black St. Louis: A Study in Race Relations, 1865–1916" (Ph.D. dissertation, University of Missouri–Columbia, 1972), 89; Bureau of the Census, Special Reports, Occupations at the Twelfth Census, Table 43; and Missouri Bureau of Labor Statistics, 1891 report.

Millinery and dressmaking afforded opportunities for female self-employment. Millinery shops were the most common female-headed small businesses. See Wendy Gamber, "The Female Economy: The Millinery and Dressmaking Trades, 1860–1930" (Ph.D. dissertation, Brandeis University, 1990), and Doris Weatherford, *Foreign and Female: Immigrant Women in America, 1840–1930* (New York: Schocken Books, 1986). The tobacco worker surveyed about her work is quoted in Lawrence O. Christensen and Gary R. Kremer, *A History of Missouri, 1875 to 1919*, vol. 4, ed., William E. Parrish (Columbia: University of Missouri Press, 1997), 50.

For information and analysis of the Women's Christian Temperance Union, see Anne Firor Scott, *Natural Allies: Women's Associations in American History* (Chicago: University of Illinois Press, 1992), and Ruth Bordin, *Woman and Temperance: The Quest for Power and Liberty, 1873–1900* (Philadelphia: Temple University Press, 1980). For a national perspective, as Scott notes that although Catholic and Jewish women were active organizers, most research and analysis has focused on Protestant women. See Elizabeth Cady Stanton, Susan B. Anthony, and Matilda Joslyn Gage, eds., *History of Woman Suffrage* (New York: Fowler and Wells, 1922) for more on the national movement and internal conflicts.

Information on institutionalized children is from Edward Olds, *Trends in Child Dependency in St. Louis, 1860–1944* (St. Louis: Social Planning Council of St. Louis and St. Louis County, 1946). For attitudes about the poor in America, see Michael B. Katz, *In the Shadow of the Poorhouse: A Social History of Welfare in America* (New York: Basic Books, 1986). See Carroll Smith-Rosenberg, ed., *Disorderly Conduct: Visions of Gender in Victorian America* (New York: Knopf, 1985) for more attitudes about sexuality and gender. See Stuart Blumin, *The Emergence of the Middle Class: Social Experience in the American City, 1760–1900* (Cambridge: Cambridge University Press, 1989) for development of the urban middle class.

See also Peggy Pascoe, *Relations of Rescue: The Search for Female Moral Authority in the American West, 1874–1939* (New York: Oxford University Press, 1990), and Estelle Freedman, "Separatism as Strategy: Female Institution Building and American Feminism, 1870–1930," *Feminist Studies* (fall 1979). For analysis of the interaction between working women and middle-class reformers, see Joanne Meyerowitz, *Women Adrift: Independent Wage Earners in Chicago, 1880–1930* (Chicago: University of Chicago Press, 1988). A similar study of St. Louis women awaits a historian.

Susan Blow

On a September morning in 1873, Susan Blow welcomed sixty-eight boys and girls to her cheerful kindergarten room in the new Des Peres School on 6303 Michigan Avenue in Carondelet. Recently annexed to the city, the old French village was now an industrial town of foundries and factories and home to large working-class families. Carondelet was an ideal location for testing new ideas in urban socialization and public schooling.

Blow convinced William Torrey Harris, superintendent of the St. Louis public schools, to let her expose the neighborhood's unruly, poor preschool children to creative play and great literature. She was sure that if they learned to restrain their "basal instincts" and develop "higher natures" the children would grow into productive workers and good citizens. A member of Harris's circle of intellectuals, Blow volunteered to train teachers in the Froebel method of German education if the school district would support the kindergarten. While not the first kindergarten in the United States, Blow's was the first successfully and permanently integrated into a public school system. Susan Blow's work became a pedagogical model, earning her a national reputation among educators.

Susan Blow. Photograph by Emil Boehl of crayon drawing by C. F. Maury, ca. 1870. MHS–PP

Born June 7, 1843, in St. Louis, Susan Blow was the oldest daughter of Minerva Grimsley and Henry T. Blow, a wealthy industrialist and civic leader. Both parents were staunch Presbyterians. In 1850 the Blows built an impressive home in Carondelet where they gave Susan the appropriate education for an intelligent girl of her social status: instruction by tutors, attendance at a private female seminary, and access to her father's extensive library. At age twenty-five, Susan served as her father's secretary and as his Portuguese translator during his brief tenure as United States Minister to Brazil. Following his diplomatic tour, the family visited Europe, where Susan observed the German kindergartens developed by Friedrich Froebel.

Blow family values, class interest, and faith in industrial capitalism underlay Susan Blow's confidence in her educational goals. As a young women, she had studied the philosophy of Frederick Hegel with William Torrey Harris. Both she and Harris subscribed to a Hegelian vision of an ideal society in which citizens voluntarily tempered their individual will for the good of the state. Since children were born uncivilized and amoral, public education must be the foundation of a good society. Harris believed that children had to learn how to distinguish the good from the bad and to willingly make the choices that would guide them toward perfection. Kindergarten, Blow argued, was essential to this developmental process. It caught children early, before they acquired too many bad habits. "The formation of character is the chief end of education," she wrote, "and recognizing this truth we are logically forced to admit the necessity of utilizing the period of early childhood for the purpose of stirring healthy affections and shaping the will into forms of healthy activity." Trained teachers using proper instructional methods could help children learn how to make themselves moral, productive citizens.

The importance of education for an industrial economy and the recognition that most children left school after a few years led Superintendent Harris to support Susan Blow's proposal to open a public kindergarten. In 1870 only half of St. Louis's school-age population regularly attended any classes at all. The majority completed just a few early grades and left the system by age fourteen. Educators had to work fast and efficiently. Harris only agreed to implement Blow's plan, however, after she offered to work without salary. Although her father was willing to fund the whole project, Susan insisted that the school district make some financial commitment. After a year of training in

New York, she returned to educate one primary teacher, Mary Timberlake, and two unpaid apprentices in the Froebel method before opening the Des Peres kindergarten.

Blow agreed with Harris in the importance of teaching "regularity, punctuality, and attention"–all attributes of good workers and good citizens–but she also envisioned the kindergarten as a place where children would be happy, active learners. The pedagogical goal was development rather than instruction. The Froebel method of education was predicated on Friedrich Froebel's belief that play improved children's intelligence and personalities. Although Blow offered the children pleasurable activities appropriate to their physical and cognitive abilities, it was structured fun with a purpose. Students sat at tables, not desks, in a cheerful classroom and learned by singing and working with "the gifts"–teaching aids developed by Froebel. Using colored blocks, balls covered with colored yarn, and cardboard perforated to be sewn with yarn, the children learned colors, shapes, and fractions. They folded and wove paper strips into intricate designs to develop motor skills, equally useful for creative writing and factory work. Blow also introduced preschoolers to great literature– Greek and Roman myths as well as traditional folk tales and Bible stories. While the heart of her program was self-expression, she purposefully encouraged only those forms of expression she believed helped children learn to make the right moral decisions. The most important aspect of the kindergarten method was the guiding role of selected teachers trained in the activities.

Susan Blow insisted that the first-grade students who had attended her kindergarten were more intelligent than those who had not. Whether or not they were brighter, they behaved better. Teachers and parents enthusiastically supported the program. Over the next two years Blow trained twelve teachers and thirty unpaid assistants, and by 1878 the district implemented kindergarten classes throughout the system. She worked for eleven years with the school district as a volunteer teacher and instructor in the Froebel method. Under her direction the kindergarten program reached an enrollment of nearly nine thousand students.

The St. Louis kindergarten became a national model, creating a demand for Susan Blow as a lecturer and educational theorist. Her national success, however, brought her less satisfaction at home. She lost her strongest advocate and intellectual mentor when Harris left the superintendent job in 1880 for a better position in Massachusetts. A volunteer, Blow lost control of the kindergarten program once it was integrated into the regular school system. Although she had trained Mary McColloch to take over as paid director, Blow frequently disagreed with her successor's policies, fearing that the St. Louis kindergartens would become pre-primary classes rather than developmental laboratories.

Frustrated and suffering from a thyroid condition later diagnosed as Graves' Disease, Blow moved to Cleveland in the mid-1880s to be with family members. After her health improved, she published five books on educational theory and taught briefly at Columbia University's Teachers' College in New York. In 1895 she became a member of the Advisory Board of the International Kindergarten Union, remaining active in the organization until her death in 1916.

Susan Blow was a pioneer in urban education whose work contributed significantly to St. Louis's nineteenth-century national reputation for excellent public schools. Because her educational theories were based on Hegelian moral philosophy, however, she failed to integrate them with the instructional methods favored by later progressive educators with different theories of childhood development. Regardless of the philosophy that inspired it, the St. Louis kindergarten movement fulfilled its social mission. The evidence existed in the careful, disciplined work of the city's future industrial workers.

Sources: Quotation is from Susan Blow to Mrs. Edwin De Wolf, 15 November 1909, The Wednesday Club Archives. For additional information, see Susan Blow, "Commentaries on Froebel's Kindergarten Theories," unpublished manuscript, St. Louis Public Library; Louise Boyle Swiniarski, "A Comparative Study of Elizabeth Palmer Peabody and Susan Elizabeth Blow by Examination of Their Writings" (Ann Arbor: Xerox University Microfilms, 1976); Dorothy Ross, "Susan Blow," in *NAW*, vol. 1; NiNi Harris, "Susan Blow," in *Show Me Missouri Women: Selected Biographies*, eds., Mary K. Dains and Sue Sadler (Kirksville, Mo.: Thomas Jefferson University Press, 1989). See also Susan E. Blow Papers, Blow Family Papers, and William Torrey Harris Papers, MHS. For a listing of all Susan Blow sources at MHS, see Beverly Bishop and Deborah Bolas, eds., *In Her Own Write: Women's History Resources in the Library and Archives of the Missouri Historical Society* (St. Louis: MHS, 1983). The former Des Peres School, now the home of the Carondelet Historical Society, has a large collection of archival and artifactual materials related to Susan Blow and the St. Louis public schools.

Private Schools for Young Women

Passengers traveling north by steamboat in 1872 knew they were approaching St. Louis when they spotted the domed cupola of a five-story building overlooking the Mississippi River. Maryville Academy, a Catholic boarding and day school for girls run by the Religious of the Sacred Heart, sat on a bluff four miles south of the courthouse. It was only one of many new private schools for women constructed in the last quarter of the nineteenth century, when growing numbers of young women extended their school years.

Parents were eager to send their daughters to schools that reinforced their family's values. In the late nineteenth century, nearly one-third of all St. Louis students attended private schools, primarily Catholic or Lutheran parish elementary schools. Fewer than 10 percent of all St. Louis children enrolled in high school, but the majority of those attended private schools.

Private schools were safe zones that brought together young people of the same social class, religion, and ethnic group. Secondary education for girls, available only to the privileged few before the Civil War, mushroomed afterward, as more families were willing and able to pay private school tuition.

Mary Institute. Stereograph photograph by Boehl and Koenig, 1890. MHS–PP

Improved public transportation in postwar St. Louis not only made it easier to get around the increasingly diverse and sprawling city, but it also threatened parental control over children's social lives. Private schools ensured that young women would be courted by acceptable young men. Only a few schools were co-educational; most girls' schools joined with similar boys' schools for social activities.

Maryville was an outgrowth of the Young Ladies' Academy of the Convent of the Sacred Heart, founded by Philippine Duchesne and the French order of the Religious of the Sacred Heart in 1818. Relocated from Florissant to St. Louis in 1827, the convent school remained at the order's "City House" at Broadway and Convent Street until after the Civil War. By then the neighborhood had become less desirable for the daughters of St. Louis Catholic businessmen fleeing south and west to escape the grit of the city. In 1874 the sisters opened a new boarding and day school on twenty-one acres of land at Meramec and Pennsylvania Avenues in south St. Louis. Eighty tuition-paying boarding students and seventy poor children enrolled in the free school moved to the new building. The sisters added another wing and a handsome Gothic chapel in the 1880s.

The Religious of the Sacred Heart exposed their American students to French culture, including domestic arts and traditional European social customs. The students wore long, black wool uniforms with white collars. The Maryville curriculum retained its original French emphasis on manners, history, and literature but added algebra, science, and philosophy.

Protestants also established private schools for girls of the same social class. Business and civic leaders created the Mary Institute, a nonsectarian private school on Lucas Street, for the daughters of men like themselves. William Greenleaf Eliot, along with other founders of Washington University, opened Mary Institute in 1859 and named it for his and Abby Cranch Eliot's oldest daughter, Mary Rhodes, who had died at age sixteen four years earlier. Like the older Smith Academy for boys, Mary Institute was a branch of the university, but unlike the male secondary school, it initially did not prepare girls for college.

In 1878 the successful school moved west to a new building on the corner of Beaumont and Locust Streets with space for four hundred day pupils. Staffed by eastern educators, Mary Institute developed a college preparatory program in the 1890s, enabling graduates to attend prestigious women's colleges as well as Washington University.

At the turn of the century, the school followed its clientele and students to the West End, relocating in 1902 at the corner of Lake and Waterman Avenues.

By the 1890s many of the families of day pupils who attended the elite Catholic female academies had also moved to the West End, and the schools followed them. In 1893 the Religious of the Sacred Heart closed City House and relocated the convent and the Academy of the Sacred Heart to a new building at Taylor and Maryland Avenues. The Visitation nuns purchased eleven acres in Cabanne Place in 1891. Their new building, completed in 1894, accommodated 115 pupils. Over time, the arrival of private schools helped define the central corridor of the city as the domain of upper-class St. Louisans.

All of the city's private schools for girls, however, did not gravitate to the West End. The Sisters of Loretto opened Loretto Academy in 1874 at Pine and Jefferson. The Loretto sisters had come from their Kentucky motherhouse to Florissant in 1847. Six nuns established a convent and school there in buildings previously occupied by the Religious of the Sacred Heart. During the twenty years before they opened Loretto Academy, the order ran a girls' school in Florissant and staffed parish schools throughout the city. In 1882 they enlarged the Florissant buildings, but by the mid-1890s, Mother Praxedes Carty wanted a suburban location further south. In 1897 she purchased, in the name of the Sisters of Loretto, seven acres of land and a large home from Ben V. Webster in Webster Groves. Loretto Seminary opened the following year and remained in the old Webster home until it burned down in 1905. The order constructed a new school on the site.

Some schools in south St. Louis continued to draw students from neighborhoods of prospering middle-class Germans. Ursuline Academy, operated by German nuns, remained on Twelfth Street, between Russell Boulevard and Ann Avenue. The Sisters of St. Joseph enlarged their academy at Minnesota and Kansas Avenues. The Sisters of the Most Precious Blood opened St. Elizabeth's Academy in a convent on Arsenal Street formerly owned by the Sisters of St. Mary. St. Elizabeth's emphasized the housekeeping skills prized by German housewives.

Most private schools owed their existence to the passions of their founders. Anna Sneed opened a school for girls in Kirkwood in 1861 because the St. Louis Public Schools would not let her use the Bible as a textbook. The daughter of a New England abolitionist minister, she modeled her curriculum after eastern preparatory schools, which combined liberal arts, Bible study, and strict Protestant morality.

In 1891 Sneed married John C. Cairns, a St. Louis architect who designed a new campus for the school, renamed Forest Park University, on six acres of land south of the park. The school offered both college preparatory and college courses, enrolling an average of 150 pupils a year, many from other states. Pursuing the lifelong passion for women's rights and Christian morality that underlay her educational goals, Anna Cairns became an active member of the Missouri Equal Suffrage Association and the Women's Christian Temperance Union. Cairns never relinquished control of the institution or its curriculum, and enrollments declined after the state refused to accredit Forest Park University as a junior college in 1915.

Anna Sneed Cairns vowed that her students would learn to be "cultured, useful, honorable women . . . rather than butterflies of fashion." All St. Louis private girls' schools aspired to similar goals, even as they envisioned marriage, motherhood, or sometimes religious life as their students' future vocations. Committed to preserving class, religious, and ethnic values, private female schools also raised the aspirations of their students. By spending the interlude between childhood and marriage in a challenging female environment, women developed the skills and confidence that they would later bring to public, as well as private, endeavors.

Sources: For additional information, see Dorothy Garesche Holland, "Maryville: The First Hundred Years," *BMHS* 29, no. 3 (April 1973); The Reverend Earl K. Holt III, "Lengthening Shadows: Mary Institute's 125 Years," *GH* 5, no. 2 (fall 1984); J. Thomas Scharf, *History of St. Louis City and County*, vol. 1 (Philadelphia: L. H. Everts & Co., 1883), 882–84; vol. 2, 1890; the Reverend John Rothensteiner, *History of the Archdiocese of St. Louis: In Its Various Stages of Development, From A.D. 1673 to A.D. 1828* (St. Louis: Blackwell Wielandy, 1928). For information on Anna Sneed Cairns, see Anne Johnson, *Notable Women of St. Louis* (St. Louis: Woodward, 1914), 43–50.

Women and the Public Schools

Between 1870 and 1895 St. Louis built more than seventy new public elementary schools, most of them identical twelve-room buildings. Since the majority of St. Louis students in the postwar years were female, these schools educated thousands of girls.

Central High School Graduating Class, 1905. The predominance of female graduates noted by William Torrey Harris persisted after the turn of the century. Photograph by the Gerhard Sisters, 1905. MHS–PP

They also provided employment for hundreds of women, most of whom graduated from the St. Louis Normal School, located within Central High School.

The daughters of skilled immigrant workers were just as likely to attend normal school as girls from middle-class families. All students received free tuition if they promised to work two years for the St. Louis public schools. Teaching was a high-paying, respectable occupation for a woman and a way to escape either the factory floor or the servants' quarters. In 1875 elementary school teachers earned between $2.50 and $3.75 a day; more than twice the pay of salesclerks or female factory workers.

Due to a national economic depression, more women were graduating from normal school in the early 1870s than there were teaching jobs available in St. Louis. In 1877 Irish-American members of the Board of Education introduced a resolution that would have replaced married teachers with young single graduates of the normal school, many of whom were the daughters of Irish immigrants. Although reluctant in hard times to employ married teachers with husbands to support them, board members overwhelmingly defeated the resolution to dismiss them. By appearing to deliberately reject teachers from the Irish Catholic working class, board members reinforced the traditional Protestant biases of the public schools. This attitude was consistent with the policies of

St. Louis Superintendent William Torrey Harris, whose ideas of public education had been influenced by Protestant New England schools. Harris thought middle-class women made the best teachers, even if they were married.

Harris, who headed the St. Louis public schools from 1868 until 1880, believed that public education should provide "careful training in habits of regularity, punctuality, industry, cleanliness, self-control and politeness," values clearly identified with the feminine middle class. Harris's support for female education in general led him to include women at every level of his administration. Although most female employees taught in the district's elementary schools, women also held positions as high school teachers, principals, and administrators. Anna Brackett, who earned an annual salary of twenty-eight hundred dollars in the 1870s as the principal of the normal school, was one of the highest paid female educators in the country. In 1878 Harris and the school board raised the salaries of all women teachers to the same level as those of men.

However, the salaries of female educators were generally lower than those of their male colleagues. Although school board policy stipulated equal pay for equal work, the average salary for male teachers in 1891–1892 was $1443.77, while female teachers received $554.27 on average. The wage difference reflected the fact that many women were assistants, and relatively few worked as principals or in administrative positions with higher pay.

In addition to offering women social status and more employment options, the coeducational high school symbolized the changing relationship between women's domestic role and their expanding public place. The city's pioneering high school, first opened in 1853, moved in 1856 to an imposing new building at Fifteenth and Olive Streets. The curriculum was not vocational; students chose either a classical or general course of study. Although admission was by formidable examination until 1884, nearly three-fourths of all admitted students dropped out before graduation. Boys, particularly, left to go to work. In that year, 425 of the school's 638 students were girls.

Harris had argued earlier that women need a high school education "if they are to earn a living in the work-a-day world . . . and in their roles as guardians of education, the family, charity, morality, purity, and all interests not directly connected with money-getting." Businessman Almon Thompson justified the public expense of secondary education for women in 1884: "If men are to be saved from the wild dissipations of outside life it must be done by making homes . . . and if we are going to have men grow up around us who are to be a pride to this community, we must have homes where there will be mothers trained to these higher thoughts."

High school students represented only 2 percent of all students in public schools, and the majority were girls. Despite the success of the overcrowded secondary school, taxpayers were reluctant to increase public funding. In the 1890s, the Board of Education revised the curriculum to attract more boys by adding business courses and other vocational subjects. The first printing class attracted six girls and only four boys.

In 1893 the board moved the school, later called Central High School, to a new sixty-room building at Grand and Finney. Branches operated in some of the city's elementary school buildings. By the turn of the century, about 30 percent of pupils entering public high school graduated, and 20 percent went on to college. However, only 3 percent of all high school–age St. Louisans enrolled in the public high school. Although most boys and girls finished their education at eighth grade or sooner, a significant number attended the city's many private and parochial secondary schools.

Some working women, particularly immigrants, enrolled in elementary school evening classes. Beginning in 1875, young working people under the age of twenty could attend classes four times a week for sixteen-week terms. By 1878, the district's 4,539 night students far outnumbered those enrolled in the high school. Beginning in 1889, adult workers under the age of twenty-six could also attend night school for a $6.50 tuition fee. Until then, charitable organizations provided the only educational opportunities for young working women over the age of twenty.

From the earliest days of public schools until the U.S. Supreme Court struck down school segregation laws with *Brown v. Board of Education of Topeka* in 1954, St. Louis's African American students attended racially segregated schools. Though educating African Americans had been outlawed in Missouri in 1847 and remained illegal until the Missouri state legislature repealed the ban in February 1865, determined slaves circumvented the ban, and by the war's end there were at least four "colored" schools in St. Louis.

In the aftermath of the Civil War, African Americans viewed education as the key to their successful advancement in American society. In late 1863, St. Louis African Americans held a mass meeting and organized the Board of Education for Colored Schools to raise funds and run free schools in the city. The black-controlled board, comprising ten black men and three white men, received funding and administrative assistance from the American Missionary Association (AMA) and the Western Sanitary Commission (WSC). This led to tension between the AMA, WSC, and black community groups, which needed financial help from these organizations but resented their assumptions that African Americans could not effectively run their own schools.

In 1866 members of the St. Louis Board of Education began converting and creating black schools, which they numbered rather than named. The High School for Colored Children opened in 1875, and the Board of Education later named it Charles Sumner High School, in honor of the Massachussetts senator who was the first prominent politician to advocate full emancipation of slaves.

White teachers staffed local African American schools until 1877, when a group of black parents organized the Colored Education Council to get African American teachers for their children. The council petitioned the Board of Education to certify black teachers as well as white ones. The board agreed. Black teachers, many of them women, began working at Sumner and other local schools the following term.

In addition to being a respectable and relatively lucrative occupation, teaching required talent and education but no capital investment, making it an attractive career choice for African Americans of limited means. Teaching held high status for black women because they had such limited job opportunities. However, black women faced tougher competition for teaching jobs in black

Missouri Remarkable Exodus of Negroes from Louisiana and Mississippi Incidents of the Arrival. Support and Departure of the Refugees from St. Louis. Detail, "Feeding the Refugees at one of the colored churches." Wood engraving from *Frank Leslie's Illustrated Newspaper*, 19 April 1879. MHS Library

After the Compromise of 1877, Southern Democrats regained a powerful majority in many state governments. They began to dismantle civil rights that black Southerners had gained under Radical Republican rule, solidify the sharecropping system, and violently impede African Americans from voting. In March 1879, about four thousand blacks left the South in several waves bound for Kansas. Often by the hundreds, the migrants lined up on the banks of the Mississippi to board steamboats bound for St. Louis, but from there many could not afford transportation to Kansas. The city of St. Louis provided medical care only for the migrants, and under pressure the Mullanphy Emigration Board contributed one hundred dollars. However, the black community provided the vast majority of aid. Migrants stayed in Union Hall, Second (formerly Eighth) Street Baptist Church, Lower Baptist Church, St. Paul's A.M.E. Church, Happy Hollow, and the homes of black parishioners. When a reporter for the *Missouri Republican* visited the Second Street Baptist Church, he found that "there were nearly two hundred [migrants] inside the church. . . . A portion of the floor near the front door and in the aisles was covered with the mattresses, upon which whole families slept, while the young ladies and gentlemen stretched themselves upon the pews. . . . During the evening the immigrants were visited by a large number of the churchgoing colored people, who brought large baskets of provisions and came with encouraging speeches to cheer their new acquaintances."

–Katherine Douglass

schools than white women did for jobs in white schools, because more black men sought teaching positions as a result of their own limited job opportunities. In contrast to their white counterparts, and possibly as a result of black men's limited job options, students at black public schools were roughly half male and half female during this period. Of the seventy-two women who graduated from Sumner between 1885 and 1892, all but one went on to teach in St. Louis city schools, evidence that a high school education gave black women a chance to enter or stay in the middle class.

While 95 percent of the teachers in white schools were female, women filled roughly half of the teaching positions in black schools before the turn of the century. In 1891 women headed half of the white schools, while at the African American schools the majority of assistants were women and all of the principals were men. The excellent educations of the black men on the faculty reinforced the higher status of teaching jobs in the black community but also made teaching jobs open to women rarer than in white schools. Sumner recruited many educators, both men and women, from prestigious colleges such as Harvard, Mount Holyoke, Oberlin, Howard, and Vassar.

In 1889 the Board of Education established a normal department at Sumner to train teachers for black elementary schools. At first the program operated out of the old buildings at Fifteenth and Walnut Streets, then it followed Sumner to the Ville, where it remained in operation until 1929, when the department became Harriet Beecher Stowe Teachers College, an independent institution. The teachers college moved into rooms in the Simmons Elementary School at 4306 St. Louis Avenue, between Lambden and Newstead. With national school desegregation in 1954, Stowe merged with the all-white Harris Teachers College to become Harris–Stowe State College.

–Katherine Douglass and Katharine Corbett

Sources: For additional information, see Selwyn K. Troen, *The Public and the Schools: Shaping the St. Louis System, 1838–1920* (Columbia: University of Missouri Press, 1975); Stephen L. McIntyre, "'Our Schools Are Not Charitable Institutions': Class, Gender, Ethnicity, and the Teaching Profession in Nineteenth-Century St. Louis," *MHR* 92, no. 1 (October 1997); *A Century of Achievement in the St. Louis Public High Schools* (St. Louis, 1885); Payroll book for teachers in the St. Louis public schools, 1875, St. Louis Board of Education Collection; and Report of the High School, 1883–1884, MHS.

Women Physicians and Nurses

After the Civil War and into the early years of the twentieth century, the domestic nature of medical care gradually gave way to treatment by specialized professionals. Until then doctors, midwives, nurses, and other healing professionals learned through apprenticeship and had little scientific basis for their work. Midwives and practitioners of folk medicine, usually women, probably had better records of success than most male physicians. As medicine became more scientific, however, it became more male dominated. Men denied women entry into medical schools and withheld professional recognition from healers without proper certification. Nursing, which also developed new standards, became a middle-class, female profession, subservient to the male medical establishment. St. Louis women who became physicians and nurses in the nineteenth century had to be strong-minded to overcome discrimination and physically strong to overcome the working conditions and grueling labor.

Women physicians faced decades of educational discrimination and professional exclusion, as men made internships, residencies, and medical society memberships increasingly hard to acquire. By the end of the century, women constituted only about 5 percent of all certified physicians. As increasing numbers of women applied for medical training, however, some medical schools began to accept them. A supportive network of female connections aided women new to the profession.

The first woman doctor with a professional degree in medicine arrived in St. Louis in 1866. Dr. Nancy Leavell had trained at the Women's Medical College of Pennsylvania. She was fortunate in having a St. Louis physician, Dr. Simon Pollack, for a patron. He not only gave her an internship in his clinic at the Mullanphy Hospital, but also helped her get started in private practice. Although the St. Louis Medical Society denied her membership, she became physician-in-charge at the St. Louis Female Infirmary in 1880. She also joined the St. Louis Woman Suffrage Association.

By the mid-1880s, a number of female physicians practiced in the city. The most effective route to acceptance for a woman doctor was to treat other women. Dr. Mary McLean, born in Washington, Missouri, and a graduate of the University of Michigan Medical School, returned to St. Louis in 1884. She became the first female intern (and the last until about 1940) at the city's

Female Hospital. In 1885 she was the first (and last until 1903) woman elected to the St. Louis Medical Society. The 1890s saw more women practicing in St. Louis. Their influence spread as they encouraged and helped other women entering the profession.

Women received training in St. Louis in the 1870s from colleges that taught homeopathic medicine, but local professional medical schools did not admit women until the 1890s. Washington University Medical School, however, did not admit its first two female students until 1918. Saint Louis University was even later, denying women admission until 1948.

While always one of women's domestic duties, nursing generally had not been considered suitable employment for middle-class women. The example of Florence Nightingale in the Crimean War and the experiences of some American women in the Civil War launched a movement to turn nursing into a skilled profession. One way to make the job more respectable was to replace the untrained but experienced domestic worker. "The trained nurse can not be made in the private house," a contemporary source noted. "Hospital training does not make nurses callous or unsympathetic. . . . Her

St. Louis Training School for Nursing, First Graduating Class, 1886.
St. Louis City Hospital #1 School of Nursing Collection, MHS–PP

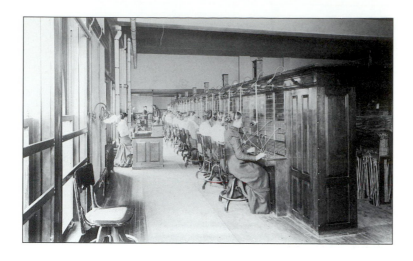

Nursing proved to be a popular career for women. Nurses' training was more accessible and cheaper than medical school. Aspiring nurses needed only a good secondary school education, sound health, and good character. A graduate of the St. Louis Training School for Nurses could expect to earn as much as three dollars a day year round. The gradual shift from home care to hospital care created a growing demand for trained nurses.

Nurses made greater progress than female doctors, because nursing fit pre-existing ideas about women's work. They received less training, less respect, and lower pay than physicians. Nurses, as helpers of men, were in no position to challenge male control of the medical profession.

–Joan Cooper

Sources: See Ruth J. Abram, ed., *"Send Us a Lady Physician": Women Doctors in America, 1835–1920* (New York: Norton, 1985) for context. For the impact of professionalization of the medical profession in St. Louis, see Kenneth Ludmerer, *Learning to Heal: The Development of American Medical Education* (New York: Basic Books, 1985). For more information on local female practitioners, see Martha R. Clevenger, "From Lay Practitioner to Doctor of Medicine: Woman Physicians in St. Louis, 1860–1920," *GH* 8, no. 3 (winter 1987–1988): 12–21. Although the St. Louis City Directory lists the names of midwives, there is no study of midwifery in the city. See also Dains and Sadler, eds., *Show Me Missouri Women*; Louise Marion Hunt, "Woman's Place in Medicine: The Career of Dr. Mary McLean," *BMHS* 74, no. 4 (July 1980): 255–63; Frank J. Lutz, ed., "The Autobiography and Reminiscences of S. Pollak, M.D., St. Louis, Mo.," *St. Louis Medical Review* (1904); Louise I. Trenholme, *History of Nursing in Missouri* (Columbia: Missouri State Nurses Association, 1926); YWCA Archives; and St. Louis City Hospitals Schools of Nursing Collection, MHS.

calling is a noble one and worthy of the best efforts of refined and cultivated women." Appeals that characterized nurses' training and work as appropriate for middle-class women helped to make nursing a female profession.

The first training schools for nurses opened in the East in 1873. The first in St. Louis opened in 1884, when Mrs. William H. Pulsifer, a non-practicing physician, started the St. Louis Training School for Nurses at the City Hospital. William Greenleaf Eliot and James Yeatman, organizers of the Western Sanitary Commission during the Civil War, backed the project.

Filth, bad food, run-down accommodations, and insufficient help characterized City Hospital when the nursing school opened. The students received a small monthly allowance from the city in return for working on the wards and attending lectures. They worked from 7 A.M. to 7 P.M. under appalling conditions. In addition, the first students also had to contend with male doctors and interns who resented their presence. The first class graduated in 1886. By 1891, nurses from the training school staffed all but two wards of the hospital.

As many as nine more training schools opened before the end of the century. Many were sectarian, including the Catholic Daughters of Charity School at Mullanphy Hospital that trained both nuns and lay women. In 1898 the Provident Hospital, a small facility run by black physicians for their patients, opened a training program for African American nurses.

Female Operators Seated at Kinloch Telephone Company Switchboard Number One. Until 1924, both the Kinloch and Bell Telephone Companies served the St. Louis area. Photograph by Otto E. Laroge, 1899. MHS–PP

Telephone Workers

New technologies brought men and women together in late-nineteenth-century offices. Women as well as men operated telegraph equipment, typewriters, stenographic machines, and telephone switchboards. In 1884, both women and men worked at the St. Louis Bell Telephone central telephone office at 1417 Olive Street. All calls came through a single switchboard where Rose Farrell and Frances Overbeck, the company's first female operators, connected customers to each other.

Telephone companies first employed office boys to work the switchboards, but once they reorganized the job for efficiency, managers determined that men were not suited for the work because "they were in the habit of following their own operating practice and assuming their own responsibilities." Managers reported that women made better operators because they took orders and adapted well to the systematized, sedentary, and repetitive work. Women soothed irritated customers and in stressful situations held their tempers in check better than men. By offering women an opportunity to work with other women in a clean, safe environment away from the public, telephone companies competed successfully with factories and retail stores for female workers.

Men aspired to better, more challenging positions in the telephone industry and could reasonably expect to move beyond the switchboard. Because they had fewer options, women adapted to the requirements of the operator's job. One young St. Louis woman who went to work as an operator in 1883 remembered that she came to the job by accident. "The only positions open to women on the outside were as salesladies or school teachers, and I did not want to be either," she said. "I had a friend who walked past my home on her way to work every morning, and I wanted to be like her. . . . Until the day I went to work for the telephone company, I had never seen or used a telephone."

The switchboard became a woman's place with women's wages. In 1907 telephone operators made seven dollars a week, not enough to live independently. However, women could move into better positions supervising other women. Neither Frances Overbeck nor Rose Farrell married, but they made successful careers with the telephone company. Overbeck became chief operator at the main office after it moved to Tenth and Pine Streets in 1898. For many years, she was the principal of the operator's school, located at the Lindell office from 1902 to 1925. Farrell became a supervisor and was chief operator until the manual office closed in 1927.

Source: For additional information, see Jordan C. Singleton, "Telephone Comes to St. Louis," *BMHS* 10, no. 1 (October 1953); "The History of the Southwestern Bell Telephone Company from 1878 to 1940," unpublished manuscript, MHS library; R. T. Barrett, "A Sound Mind and a Sound Body," *Southwestern Bell News* (autumn 1935); and Bureau of Labor Statistics of the State of Missouri, 1907. Quotes are from R. T. Barrett, "Watching the Years from a Switchboard," *Southwestern Bell News* (spring 1935): 10–11.

Women Tobacco Workers

In 1892 Carrie Smith left her boardinghouse at 1303 Biddle Street six days a week to work ten hours a day in a nearby tobacco factory. Tobacco processing, a major local industry, had made Missouri the nation's leading manufacturer of tobacco products. Thanks to the labor of St. Louis women like Carrie Smith, the value of tobacco products produced in the state increased from just over $2 million in 1872 to $23 million in 1892.

Nearly twenty-five hundred women and girls worked in the city's chewing tobacco factories, turning out twice the annual production of any other American city. Liggett & Myers, the nation's largest manufacturer of plug tobacco, was located at St. Charles and Thirteenth Streets until 1896. Six large tobacco factories and several smaller ones operated in the city at the turn of the century.

Using some Missouri-grown leaves, but importing more from the other tobacco-producing states, St. Louis manufacturers processed tobacco into increasingly popular plugs for chewing. The manufacturing process required workers to strip out the leaf's center stem, sweeten, flavor, and roll the tobacco, and then wrap the lumps of rolled tobacco in colored paper. Hydraulic presses forced the rolls into flat blocks called plugs, which the workers then packed into boxes for shipment.

Although men operated the presses, girls and women did most of the other work. In 1890 most St. Louis tobacco workers were immigrants, primarily from Germany, Bohemia, or Eastern Europe. Many of the native-born 10 percent were African Americans. In 1890 the average female worker earned just over five dollars a week, but wages ranged from two to eighteen dollars for the various jobs. Stemmers and strippers, whose average age was fifteen, earned about eighty-five cents a day; more skilled lump wrappers made $1.65. Female tobacco workers earned more than most women in the garment trades, in part because the work was not seasonal.

Women entered the tobacco factories as young girls and stayed until they married. In 1890 the Bureau of Labor Statistics of the State of Missouri surveyed working women as part of its annual inspection of factory conditions. Of 201 female tobacco workers interviewed, only eight were married. The average informant was 21, earned $271 a year, and had been working for five years. Half had started before the age of fifteen; only ten were over forty. Older women only chose to strip tobacco leaves when they were no longer physically able to work at washing, scrubbing, or ironing. Only 26 of the 195 workers who lived at home did not help support their families. The few, like Carrie Smith, who lived independently spent about 60 percent of their income on room and board.

Tobacco workers worked hard, made decent wages by contemporary standards, and spent much of their disposable income on entertainment. Whether or not they lived at home, tobacco workers went on excursions and attended the theater more frequently than other surveyed workers. In 1888 federal labor surveyors characterized St. Louis tobacco workers as "foreigners, whose habits of life are often riotous."

The independence that young, single tobacco workers exhibited alarmed middle-class women. Concerned that factory workers with frivolous interests and little formal education might stray from respectability, they organized working women's clubs to encourage constructive use of leisure time. The Lucy E. Tilly Working Girls Club, located in three rooms at 1322 Washington Avenue, specifically recruited employees of the nearby Liggett & Myers tobacco factory. Designed to be self-supporting and self-governing, the club had about forty-five members in 1890, each paying twenty-five cents a month in dues. A double parlor contained space for classes in dressmaking and physical culture, as well as a piano and small library, where the women held weekly "book talks." Only a small number of tobacco workers, who worked forty-four hours a week in a factory, chose to spend their leisure time participating in club activities.

Although the work paid well enough to give some tobacco workers disposable income, working conditions were deplorable. The Missouri Bureau of Labor Statistics reported in 1990 finding children between the ages of nine and fifteen "closeted in rooms stemming tobacco in a temperature of 80 to 83 degrees and every window closed." Ten years later the bureau attributed low absenteeism by female workers to the factory owners' diligence in sweeping the factory floor several times a day and installing exhaust fans to remove the tobacco fumes and particles from the air. Other observers, however, considered tobacco factories to be filthy and unhealthy workplaces.

Inspectors in 1900 considered jobs in tobacco factories to be some of the more desirable female factory jobs in the city, either because working conditions were no worse than in other industries or because they believed the benefits outweighed the costs to employees. Noting that the largest firm gave its workers an annual steamboat excursion on company time, inspectors detected "an air of contentment among the employees" in the tobacco factories.

Sources: Carrie Smith is listed in the St. Louis City Directory, 1892. Because city directories list only heads of households and people living independently, the names of most female factory workers, including tobacco workers—young women living at home— seldom appear. Assessment of factory conditions from the father of tobacco worker arrested for participating in 1900 transit strike is from *Scientific American* (January 11, 1970). For additional information, see Hyde and Conard, *Encyclopedia of the History of St. Louis*, vol. 4, 2278–80; Second Annual Report, Bureau of Labor Statistics of the State of Missouri, 1880; Thirteenth Annual Report, Bureau of Labor Statistics of the State of Missouri, 1891; Sixteenth Annual Report, Bureau of Labor Statistics of the State of Missouri, 1894; 1900 Annual Report, Bureau of Labor Statistics of the State of Missouri; Fourth Annual Report of the Commissioner of Labor, 1888, U.S. Government Printing Office, 1889. Statistics and analysis found in reports from the Bureau of Labor Statistics are frequently biased. Some bureau heads were more sympathetic to labor than others. In general, Missouri reports from the turn of the twentieth century are more biased toward the owner than those from the late nineteenth century.

Domestic Workers

As in other American cities, young women who needed jobs in St. Louis could usually find work as domestic servants. Even though Irish and German immigration swelled the number of unmarried women seeking employment, there were never enough domestic workers to fill the demand. Women of means had always relied on domestic help, either slave or free. In the post–Civil War years, when more urban families entered the middle class, a married woman who might have been a domestic in her own youth could afford a live-in servant to help with the housework, sewing, and child care. In 1880, 58 percent of all St. Louis women wage earners were in domestic service. Employers usually hired German girls over Irish or African American applicants. By the 1890s, however, St. Louis employment agencies received as many as three times the number of requests for domestics as they had women to fill them. Employers referred to the persistent shortage of acceptable, reliable household workers as "the servant problem."

Working women characterized "the servant problem" differently: the problem was in being a servant. Throughout the nation, women considered domestic service a dead-end, low-status job when compared to sales or office work, or even to factory labor. They resented the long hours, lack of privacy, and constant surveillance. Although they lived with families, they felt like outsiders banished to lonely, sparsely furnished sleeping rooms when their work was done. Many complained that they had no place to entertain friends and little time off. It was customary for domestics to be on duty all week except for one half-day and one other evening. Frequently, a servant's evening off was on Sunday, after she had prepared and cleaned up a big noon meal. In 1885 a St. Louis domestic worker wrote to a friend, "I will try to come out and see you. Would ask you to come in but have no time for company and then this is not my house and I don't exactly feel at liberty to ask people here. It is hard to be poor and to have to earn your living in other people's houses." With more new factory jobs available for women, many domestic workers began to consider other options.

Women who preferred domestic work over other jobs often chose it because the tasks were familiar and required no special training. They liked living away from their parents' homes, but in a family setting. Because they received room and board, domestics could often save more money than factory or clerical workers. Young unmarried women from rural areas in Missouri and Illinois answered newspaper ads placed by employment agencies or responded to recruitment notices posted in small-town stores and post offices. Domestic service offered a respectable way to leave the farm for St. Louis.

The financial records of a St. Louis German middle-class family that employed a succession of ten live-in servants over ten years reveal some of the patterns of these young women's lives. Whether or not Caroline and Andrew Fruth or their employees believed they had a "servant problem" can only be inferred from the existing records.

In 1880 Louisa Hofmeister, then sixteen, worked for the Fruths at their home at 2032 Sidney Street, in a developing middle-class neighborhood in south St. Louis. Louisa helped Caroline do the housework and care for the Fruths' two boys, aged four and five. Louisa's parents were Bavarian immigrants, but she had been born in Illinois. She may have taken the job with the Fruths as a way to get to St. Louis. She also may have developed a friendship with fourteen-year-old Amelyn Bergmann, who lived next door and worked for the Buchroeder family of three adults and two young children.

Louisa and the domestic servants who came after her lived in the attic room of the Fruths' two-story rowhouse. In 1880 she earned eight dollars a month, which included room and board. Although Andrew Fruth raised her pay to ten dollars the next year, Louisa left in October 1881.

Iris Spiesback replaced Louisa at the same wage, but Andrew Fruth held her wages without interest. He gave her cash when needed, and by the time she left in August 1884, she had saved fifty-five dollars. Josephine Isselhardt, who replaced Iris, also made ten dollars, but she left within two months, perhaps because of illness. (Andrew Fruth paid a doctor $3.50 from her wages.) The Fruths' next servant, Mary Sattler, earned eight dollars for less than a month's work. In November 1884 Victoria Reinovsky worked at 2032 Sidney. She collected her ten dollars wages monthly until July 1885, but over the next six months she withdrew only ten dollars. When Victoria left in March 1886, she took eighty-four dollars in savings with her.

Josephine Herbstreit began working for the Fruths in April 1886 and received an increase to twelve dollars in November. Josephine typically took half of each month's wages, but in August 1887 she withdrew $107.80 in back pay. Josephine probably left the Fruths' employ, since they immediately hired Mary Ferkel, who worked for only one month.

In 1888 Josephine again worked for the Fruths, but her employment may have been erratic. Andrew Fruth began paying Anna Brockschmitt in August, and the following May employed Tillie Orth. In June 1889 Josephine Herbstreit received fifty dollars in back wages and left an additional two hundred dollars with Andrew Fruth at 4 percent interest, payable in one year. Since Andrew Fruth, a successful businessman, had sufficient funds, Josephine probably decided to invest her money with him rather than with a bank. Fruth never paid his servants interest on their wages, but he paid interest to Josephine rather than give her the due amount in full. The following August, Fruth had paid Josephine $204 and settled the account. At the end of 1890, Lotte Ague, who had replaced Josephine in 1889, worked for the Fruths at twelve dollars a month.

In a period of ten years, Caroline and Andrew Fruth had employed ten different domestic servants. They paid wages consistent with the average for white domestics in midwestern cities. The women who stayed more than a year accumulated savings.

Servants' Wages from Fruth Family Account Book. Fruth Family Papers, MHS Archives

Although the number of servants employed in America continued to rise until 1910, the percentage of women wage earners in domestic service dropped to 26 percent by 1900. Commercial laundries replaced the laundress who came to the house or the woman who took laundry into her home. Servants no longer baked bread; grocers delivered commercially baked goods to the back door. New household appliances may not have reduced the amount of housework, but they did make cleaning and washing easier and more efficient, and more pleasant for middle-class women.

Sources: For domestics' opinions about their work as well as comparative information on wages and working conditions, see David M. Katzman, *Seven Days a Week: Women in Domestic Service in America* (New York: Oxford University Press, 1978), still the standard study of domestic labor. Andrew Fruth's detailed record of all his household expenses between 1878 and 1890 has been preserved in the Fruth Collection, MHS. See also Annual Report of the Bureau of Labor Statistics of the State of Missouri, 1891, 1894; 1880 Manuscript Census for St. Louis; Eleventh Census, Population, Part II, 724–25; Twelfth Census, Occupation, 706–8; St. Louis domestic worker's letter from Magill Papers, MHS. See also Faye Dudden, *Serving Women: Household Service in Nineteenth-Century America* (Middletown, Conn.: Wesleyan University Press, 1983).

Ella Barstow's Journal

On August 13, 1878, Ella Gale Barstow wrote the first entry in a journal she kept about her domestic life at 3643 Lindell Boulevard. A thirty-year-old housewife and mother of five children, Ella had been married for nine years to Charles Barstow, a partner in the successful firm of Barstow & Whitelaw Paint and Oil Company. Her father, Daniel Gale, had moved to St. Louis from New Hampshire in 1838 and had become one of the city's first wholesale grocers. Her mother, Caroline Gale, was active in church and charity work. Ella grew up in exclusive Lucas Place and attended Mary Institute. She and Charles lived with her parents until after the birth of their fourth child. In 1877 they moved to a new neighborhood of substantial homes just west of Grand Avenue, about one mile from her widowed mother's house.

Ella kept her journal for less than two months. It reveals not only the pleasure she took in her home and family, but also the frustrations of daily domestic life. Despite her privileged position, she

The Fruths' servants were probably all white women. Many more white than black women sought work in late-nineteenth-century St. Louis, even though the work force comprised a greater percentage of black women. Ninety-two percent of African American women working in St. Louis in 1890, however, held domestic service jobs. Most did not live in but earned $1 to $1.50 doing day work. Although national figures showed that less than 7 percent of all servants were married, nearly one-fourth of black domestics had husbands and families to care for at home. They earned more doing housework three or four days a week than they could earn working six days in a factory.

By 1900 many of the domestics' tasks had transferred to the commercial or industrial sectors.

struggled with child care, sewing, and housekeeping. Ella Barstow was typical of affluent young women who made homemaking a career and tried to live up to cultural norms for wives and mothers of her class.

August 13, 1878: Just one year tonight since we took our first meal in our new home. But I must first say who we are. First there is Charles P. Barstow whom we call Papa. Ella Gale Barstow who is called Mama. Then there are two little boys, Theodore Gale Barstow who is called Teddie, aged 8 years, Charles Warren Barstow Jr. who is called Warnie aged 7 years, Daniel B. Gale Barstow who is called Dannie aged 3 years 10 months, and two little girls. Caroline Barstow who is called Calla, Sister, Bridgie, etc. aged 2 years and Ella Barstow who is called Jessamine–aged 6 mos.

I, Mama, fully intended writing or commencing to write a year ago a brief sketch of our from day to day life, but getting settled in our new home took some time, then Teddie had scarlet fever, then little Jessie made her appearance, which caused the cook to leave and it was not until the fifth cook came that anything was brought on to the table decent; and by that time I was so worn out and nervous that Papa had to take me away to see Gramma Barstow. We took our two little girls and our faithful nurse Lena. It is not long that I have been feeling well but long enough to appreciate good health. . . . Grandma Gale is spending the night with us and it is ten o'clock. . . .

August 16: Early this morning I gathered flowers for library, parlor, and my room. It was nearly twelve o'clock before I finished my housework and just then the lunch bell rang. After lunch I went to work on some new shirtwaists for Teddie and Warnie. I had the boys with me most all the afternoon. They came to me soon after breakfast and asked permission to go up to Carpenters as all the boys were making a wagon. I said yes, but be home by ten thirty.

I saw no more of the scamps until I sent for them to come home to lunch. Their excuses were numerous, but I told them they could not go outside of the front gate this afternoon or evening. They did not take their punishment very hard. They blew soap bubbles, played marbles. . . . Tonight Charlie has gone to the "Merchants Meeting." [Merchants' Exchange]

August 19: I had to sing "Oh do not be discouraged" all day today. Dannie not very well, baby with such a bad cold, which made her fuss so much. Things to get ready for the wash, and in the midst of all mother came for me to go downtown with her. So I was obliged to shove babies and all off my mind, dress myself and go. Was gone till nearly twelve.

The afternoon I spent with the little folks. This evening I am pretty tired, but I still continue to sing, "Oh do not be discouraged."

August 20: Have been down to mother's spending the day and as usual have had a very nice time. Eat just lots of dinner, everything tastes so good at mother's.

It is very pleasant for me to go down and spend one day of every week with my mother, but now the Lena [the nursemaid] is away, to get my house in order, all the children, to get the basket ready, to order supper–my head's nearly crazed. I lay it back in a chair and don't speak, and in a few minutes I am all right again.

August 21: As I am to have a dressmaker tomorrow and know that I would not have another free moment in which to sweep or dust for the remainder of the week, I determined to do as much as possible today. I swept until my hands were blistered, then mother came about twelve o'clock, so I stopped, and after sponged an old black silk dress. I wish I never had to have a dress made over, maybe someday I won't.

Teddie got up feeling better, but looking pale. When Papa went out this morning, he said, I wouldn't let the boys run so much today Mama, but I would just like to see him prevent it, unless he tied them somewhere. They are like flies, you just think you have got them, when they are gone. They had a grand time getting dressed this afternoon, I told them I guessed I should have to get a stick tomorrow and see if that would help them any. They played football with the sponge, made faces at each other. . . . But they are such precious boys and I love them dearly.

August 23: My dressmaker came this morning, and she went to work with such good will that it brightened me wonderfully. I helped her all morning and then divided the time between Jessie who has a bad cold and making bows of cardinal and pale pink ribbon for my dress that I wore to Mary's tonight. Everything at Mary's table went off very nice. We first had fried chicken and fried Irish potatoes with hot rolls and coffee. Then the plates were removed, coconut cake with lemon ice, vanilla and chocolate cream, then the plates removed and fruit brought in.

August 25: My Sabbaths are not what the ought to be, I fairly realize it. They are not like the Sabbath days I passed when a child, or a young girl, or a young lady.

Now it is hurry to get the boys off to Sunday School, then hurry to get the housework done, and I know more than getting myself dressed before they come in from church, or if Lena is home I am obliged to hurry to get ready for church. After dinner we sit around and tell stories to the children, read to them, etc., etc., and that is about all. But I wish it was different.

I wish there could be a prayer, a reading of the Scripture, and quiet talk with each other. Maybe it will be so when the children get a little older. . . .

August 27: A horrid, horrid day! I was obliged to punish my boys, and it nearly kills me, but the trouble was all talked over with Papa this evening and made right, and altho I did the punishing, no one but mama would do to put them to bed, they said they must have mama. Darling boys how I love them but they must mind.

August 31: Oh what a busy day this has been. The corn-beef didn't come, neither had the butcher attended to it. Consequently I had to put on my things and go way down to market [in her own carriage], and as I am obliged to pass mother's, I can't resist going in, so of course it is late when I get home, and that was the way it was this morning. I had my work to do when I got home.

September 10: Charlie went to drill [Ransom Post, G.A.R.] last night and Mrs. Perkins and I sewed in the sewing room until half-past ten, or until we heard Charlie coming, and then . . . we put up our work and turned off the gas and act as if we had been doing nothing but engaging in pleasant conversation all the evening. Charlie hates the sight of a needle and dislikes dreadfully to have me sew, but I can't hire everything, and the children must not go in rags.

September 24: Have been spending the day with mother, and it has been the pleasantest day that I have spent there since we came out here to live. The boys were at school, Dannie and Bridgie played so well together, and Emma [mother's maid] had the baby so that mother and I talked and sewed in peace in the morning and went downtown this afternoon. Papa came for us at half-past five and after we had the children safely housed, we went to the park [probably Forest Park] alone.

Lena had a nice supper ready for us and tonight the boys are having a grand time playing Parcheesi. Dannie is playing with the wheelbarrow Grandma brought him and Bridgie with the dolls I got for her. Little Ella sits on the floor playing with her shoes and attempting to escape, Precious little Jewels.

Ella Barstow had another son, Edward, after she stopped writing this journal. Her daughter, Caroline, died before 1900. In 1890 Ella Barstow had become one of the founders of The Wednesday Club, an organization of upper middle-class women seeking cultural enrichment and self-improvement. The family later moved to Glendale, in St. Louis County. Charles Barstow, who served as a director of the Mercantile Library and the St. Louis Provident Association and as

vice president of the St. Louis public schools, died in 1914. Ella lived until 1931 and died at the home of her daughter Ella Simmons, at 46 Westmoreland Place, a private street in the Central West End.

Sources: Excerpts from Ella Gale Composition Book, Daniel B. Gale Papers, MHS archives. Additional information from Compton and Dry, *Pictorial History of St. Louis*; Hyde and Conard, *Encyclopedia of the History of St. Louis*, vol. 1, 112–13, and vol. 2, 859–60. See also necrology scrapbook, vol. 11, 223, and vol. 11C, 55, for obituary notices for Charles and Ella Barstow. The necrology scrapbooks at MHS library are a particularly valuable resource for information about women married to prominent businessmen. For more on Gilded Age domesticity, see Susan Strasser, *Never Done: A History of American Housework* (New York: Pantheon Books, 1982).

Women Go Downtown

In 1879 St. Louis women flocked to the opening of Barr's, a new department store at the corner of Sixth and Locust Streets. "Sales ladies," hired to sell the products of Gilded Age industrialism, greeted middle-class women who had the means to buy the latest home furnishings and fashions in ready-to-wear clothing. The department store brought together in one building merchandise previously available only in separate specialty stores. When old established dry goods companies like the William Barr Company opened department stores, they created female space in the heart of central business districts. These new marketing organizations underscored the growing importance of women in the consumer economy.

Like department store owners in other cities, Barr designed the store specifically for female shoppers. The customers received personal attention from trained saleswomen in separate merchandising departments. The store's seamstresses custom altered a woman's ready-to-wear clothing purchases, which were delivered later to her home. She met her friends for lunch in the store's well-appointed tearoom, attended special promotional events, and enjoyed amenities like elevators and attractive fashion displays that made shopping easier and more pleasurable.

Department stores not only encouraged women to be more active consumers, they also created new female workplaces. Although some women worked behind the counters of neighborhood stores or sold millinery in their own shops, selling had been primarily a male occupation until department stores revolutionized urban retailing. By the 1890s large downtown St. Louis stores had created hundreds of jobs for female sales clerks, waitresses, elevator operators, clerical workers, bundle-wrappers, and seamstresses.

Male managers hired women to persuade other women to buy consumer products. Skilled in social interaction, women quickly became effective sales clerks. Domestic life had prepared them to function effectively in a complex social hierarchy where they exercised little visible authority or direct economic power. The organization of a department store required daily interaction between managers, saleswomen, and customers, each dependent in some way on the other for success. Women used their experience from private situations to fashion a workplace culture that could maximize their autonomy and control over their daily lives.

Because authority in department stores was fragmented, women did gain some leverage over their working conditions. The department store, unlike the factory, was an ambiguous, flexible workplace where constant direct supervision was neither practical nor desirable. Managers relied on saleswomen to assist each other. Saleswomen knew that managers depended on their initiative and social skills to move the merchandise. Buyers needed the cooperation of the sales force to keep them informed of customer needs and preferences. Managers, who encouraged saleswomen to be manipulative on the salesfloor, also wanted them to identify with middle-class customers. While customers did not let saleswomen forget their class difference, female bonds between clerk and customer had the potential to subvert store policy. When a saleswoman, for example, steered her customers away from shoddy goods, she fostered personal loyalty over loyalty to the store and its management.

Saleswomen also resisted male authority over what they saw as female ways of doing things. When the selling floor became female space, women treated men as interlopers, much as they did in the kitchen. Salewomen frequently ignored or subverted petty bureaucratic rules, regulations about dress, and required ways of displaying or storing merchandise. Saleswomen banded together to control their space and working conditions in many of the ways women did in their domestic lives.

Store managers responded to worker solidarity by initiating policies designed to make women more competitive with each other. While this did increase competition, it also encouraged saleswomen to make collective decisions affecting tasks that would keep them off the selling floor.

Although managers recognized and exploited saleswomen's interpersonal skills, they valued them less than the skills men brought to the workplace. Managers paid low wages and were quick to fire women, in part because they believed these skills were natural to all women and could easily be replaced. Union organizers, who also treated women as temporary unskilled workers, believed department store saleswomen's identification with middle-class customers and nonconfrontational approach with managers would make them poor union members.

Department store managers, like employers in other industries with growing numbers of female workers, adopted paternalistic employment policies but seldom paid women enough to live independently. In 1915 a female buyer made $10 a week, and a bundle-wrapper made $3.50. A saleswoman employed at Nugent's Department Store at 500 N. Broadway earned six dollars a week for selling goods valued at $140. The company withheld twenty cents a week for health benefits and paid her ten dollars for the three weeks she missed work due to illness. She estimated that she would need at least eight dollars a week to live independently. Like most department store workers, she lived at home with her parents.

Scruggs, Vandervoort and Barney . . . The Leading Dry Goods House of St. Louis. Wood engraving by Compton Litho Company from the Official Program, Veiled Prophet's Sixth Annual Autumnal Festival, 1883. MHS Library

The culture of the department store combined elements of the male world of business and the female world of the home. Owners designed the stores to appeal to the domestic values and concerns of their female customers. Managers recognized and exploited the interpersonal skills saleswomen brought to the workplace. As workers, women sometimes used their domestic social skills to improved their working conditions. As customers, they used their buying power to help change the way Americans shopped.

Sources: Analysis of department store female work culture is from Susan Porter Benson, *Counter Cultures: Saleswomen, Managers, and Customers in American Department Stores, 1890–1940* (Urbana: University of Illinois Press, 1986). Information on wages and benefits in St. Louis department stores is from *Report of the Senate Wage Commission for Women and Children in the State of Missouri to the Senate of the 48th General Assembly* (Jefferson City, 1915). See Hyde and Conard, *Encyclopedia of the History of St. Louis*, for more information on nineteenth-century St. Louis department stores.

Red Light Districts in St. Louis

In florid Victorian rhetoric, reporters J. A. Dacus and James Buel summed up the moral degradation of their hometown in 1878: "St. Louis is truly a great, seething, sinful city, where shameless bawds are to be enumerated by the thousands." Prostitution "is found in the gentleman's kitchen" and, they admitted, "not unfrequently in the gentleman's parlor," concluding, "in all circles of society the poisonous infection has found a lodgement." While acknowledging that prostitution took place in the presence of "gentlemen," Dacus and Buel held "shameless bawds" responsible. Middle-class St. Louisans viewed prostitution as a necessary evil that provided men an outlet for their sexuality, and the city used the red light districts in order to contain illegal sexual activity. The effects of these districts, however, placed a strain on the reputations of women in these areas, prostitute or not.

Before 1870, St. Louis police allowed illegal prostitution to flourish in red light districts through selective enforcement of the law. Near the wharf along Almond Street, prostitutes, their customers, police, and reformers often crossed paths. The other concentration of commercial sex was in the tenement district north of the central corridor, between Washington and Wash, and Sixth and Eighth Streets. Here, many laborers, single working women, and immigrant families crowded together in flats and alley houses. Dacus and Buel called these districts "the plague spots of the proud metropolis" and claimed that "those who dwell in them are moral lepers, who would contaminate the vilest wanderer over the footstool of God."

Most prostitution occurred in these red light districts. While the general public hardly approved of them, the designated areas kept prostitution away from middle-class neighborhoods. Brothels fell into a descending hierarchy, from the well-appointed homes of kept women and houses of assignation, where illicit lovers trysted and women engaged in casual prostitution, to bordellos, brothels, and rooms above saloons. Elite houses stood along Green and South Sixth Streets, while bawdy houses lined Almond Street. Prostitutes who could not afford houses or rooms worked in back streets like Wild Cat Chute, reputedly the center of local black prostitution.

Prostitution extended beyond recognized districts, usually into places where transient men congregated, such as the wharf or military camps. At Benton Barracks commanding officers in the Union Army tried to limit soldiers' access to prostitutes by banning all civilians from coming within a mile of the barracks, but with little effect. In 1866 Missouri infantryman Thomas Bevel wrote to an old friend that the camp was "always filled with the fair ones of the Earth, both decent and indecent," and reported that "venimous old hoars [sic] of the city comes out to see us but not often." The military also tried but failed to extend its influence onto civilian ground, as the reverse side of one soldier's leave pass shows. While the pass permitted F. M. Johnson to go into the city to play music, it also warned, "If found on Almond Street under any circumstances, in any low saloon where 'beer jerkers' are kept, dance house, or house of ill fame," military officials would revoke the pass, imprison its holder, and report him to his commanding officer. Every pass was printed with this warning, suggesting that the offense was a common violation of military code.

The experiences of prostitutes themselves depended on a host of circumstantial factors. In St. Louis, between the Civil War and the turn of the century, nearly all prostitutes were subject to sporadic and arbitrary control by police, condemnation by reformers, and the vagaries of their pimps and customers. Most were career prostitutes, but some women entered and left the trade during periods of poverty or unemployment. In a time when the weekly wage of a seamstress was $1.50

and the monthly rent on a room in a respectable boardinghouse was $3.50, casual prostitution was one of few economic options for working women who needed to supplement their incomes or women in seasonal employment who scraped to get by in the off-season. Though figures for prostitutes' fees are unavailable, the practice could be quite lucrative; in the 1870s, madam Kate Clark and her three roommates paid twenty-five hundred dollars in rent for their house.

The middle class tacitly allowed red light districts to exist in St. Louis for at least half a century. In a period when American society was increasingly and rigidly divided along class lines, red light districts helped establish middle-class standards of respectability, which by definition did not include visitors or residents of such districts. Their existence also gave the police and middle-class citizens a measure of control over the working-class women and immigrants living in the tenements just north of downtown.

The official policy toward prostitution was total suppression, but corruption, uneven enforcement, and arrests of prostitutes for catchall offenses like vagrancy compromised the policy. Police interference in the trade varied from year to year, sometimes in response to public outcries that prompted periodic crackdowns.

While prostitution commonly referred to the exchange of sexual favors for money, it was difficult to define in legal terms and still more difficult to prosecute. As early as 1835 St. Louis city ordinances made it illegal to own or operate brothels and prohibited taverns from employing "lewd" women as entertainers. Under city statutes, prostitutes themselves, or women suspected of being prostitutes, were prosecuted as vagrants, identified as "any prostitute, courtesan, bawd, or lewd woman, or any female inmate of any bawdy-house . . . who shall be found wandering about the streets in the night-time, or frequenting dram-shops or beer taverns . . . or any such lewd woman, having the reputation of a prostitute, who shall be found employed as a beer-carrier." "Lewdness" was as hard to define legally as it is now, and it often fell to the courts to determine the crime. Most likely, judges knew it when they saw it. Easiest to prosecute was the crime of keeping a bawdy house, which constituted physical evidence and could be said to disturb the neighborhood.

Lawyers for Anna Clementine, prosecuted for keeping a bawdy house, argued in 1851 that her character or reputation should not be used against her, because "character is what the public think and express . . . concerning others, and is full of perils if it is to be received of crime." Clementine's lawyers claimed public opinion "would convict an asylum of Magdalens [reformed prostitutes]. It is unknown to the law." However, the judge in Clementine's case agreed to hear testimony about her character. The fact that reputation was admissible as evidence in a lawsuit for prostitution gave all women reason to worry about their neighbors' perceptions of them. Single working women who lived alone or in boardinghouses were particularly suspect, especially in red light districts.

The districts supposedly protected the virtue of middle-class women outside them by containing the influence of vice. St. Louis's red light districts limited contact between white middle-class women and immigrant and working-class men, whose sexuality the native middle class saw as a threat to respectable women. The fact that many were young and unmarried was especially threatening.

In theory, the districts also protected middle-class domestic life by providing an outlet for male sexuality, an overabundance of which would corrupt the home, the bastion of middle-class life, and threaten the sanctity of marriage. Prostitution normally was not discussed; like other taboo subjects, it was thought too indelicate for public conversation. However, denying it did not erase its existence, which persisted as long as men were willing to pay for sex. Many middle-class men could afford to and did, justifying the practice as an outlet that diverted the corrupting influence of male sexuality from virtuous women.

Middle-class norms harshly condemned prostitutes themselves. In part, this judgement was an outgrowth of the sexual double standard, which held women to a high standard of virtue while withholding censure of men's extramarital sexual behavior. Therefore, while many considered visiting a prostitute natural and morally acceptable, prostitutes were seen to have "fallen" from their natural state of female purity, if they had ever been pure.

Dacus and Buel argued that some prostitutes came from "the lowest ranks of sinful humanity; they are illiterate, vulgar, rude, and wanting in all the graces usually attributed to the sex." They had been "bred in hot-beds of sin from earliest infancy, and never learned the significance of the word purity." Lost in sin from the beginning, these women "perhaps are not amenable to censure for remaining sinful. How could they be otherwise?" Dacus and Buel absolved working-class women for

their immorality, whether they chose a life of sin or were born into it.

In Victorian American society, what was variously called female virtue, chastity, or purity carried a heavy weight in determining a woman's status, which had a variety of implications for women living in St. Louis's red light districts. Women who were not prostitutes were suspected of immorality because they lived in the area or walked its streets at night. Such subjective perceptions and moral judgments, in turn, limited their ability to leave the districts. In addition to legal ramifications, women with reputations as prostitutes found it hard to get a respectable job. Proper and private employers often required moral certification in letters of reference, particularly for potential domestic servants. Because they were considered the unworthy poor, women suspected of immorality could not expect to receive private charity in times of need.

By 1870 the red light district had become so widely accepted that the city council legalized prostitution, which they regarded as a necessary evil, to regulate and contain it. Codifying in law what was commonplace in fact, the passage of the Social Evil Ordinance began an experiment that had dramatic implications for all St. Louis women.

–Katherine Douglass

being born sinners but shared the prevailing sentiment that fallen women were forever lost to decent society. Repentance and improved moral behavior could not cleanse a stained reputation, no idle matter when a woman's reputation could be used as legal evidence against her.

Dacus and Buel believed that many prostitutes were country girls who arrived in the city only to be seduced by wealthy and urbane suitors who then abandoned them. Already compromised, the women fell "victim to their own folly." These "high-toned prostitutes," though really no better than "their rude and barbarous sisters," came from a different social class and had "more art, if less scruple in their career of sin and crime." While conceding that irresponsible or corrupt men played some part in women being seduced and abandoned, the real problems were the greed and folly that had led women to the city. In each case, Dacus and Buel castigated prostitutes and held them responsible for

Sources: Historians of prostitution have the most access to the perspectives of reformers whose beliefs were codified in law. The experiences of prostitutes themselves are the most inaccessible; we do not know how prostitutes felt about their work or how they saw themselves. It is also difficult to gauge working-class perspectives on middle-class reformers, and to what extent members of the working class strove to meet or reject middle-class norms. Nearly all sources on prostitution are thirdhand; women in the trade and their customers did not frequently publicize their activity or record it because of the social stigma attached to it.

Much of the information comes from Duane Sneddeker, "Regulating Vice: Prostitution and the St. Louis Social Evil Ordinance, 1870–1874," *GH* 11, no. 2 (fall 1990): 20–47, and Jeffrey Adler, "Streetwalkers, Degraded Outcasts, and Good-For-Nothing Huzzies: Women and the Dangerous Class in Antebellum St. Louis," *Journal of Social History* 25, no. 4 (1992): 737–55. Other sources include Mayor's Annual Message; Hyde and Conard, *Encyclopedia of the History of St. Louis*; and Kathy Peiss, "'Charity Girls' and City Pleasures: Historical Notes on Working-Class Sexuality, 1880–1920," in *Powers of Desire: The Politics of Sexuality*, eds., Ann Snitow, et al. (New York: Monthly Review Press, 1983), 74–87; Christine

Scene on Almond Street. This image conveys Dacus and Buel's belief that prostitutes, not their customers, were responsible for the trade and its negative social consequences. Wood engraving from J. A. Dacus and James W. Buel, *A Tour of St. Louis*, 1878. MHS Library

Stansell, *City of Women: Sex and Class in New York, 1789–1860* (New York: Knopf, 1986). This study has set the standard for much of the scholarship on female sexuality and prostitution in the nineteenth century. J. A. Dacus and James W. Buel, *A Tour of St. Louis; or, the Inside Life of a Great City* (St. Louis: Western Publishing Co., Jones and Griffin, 1878).

Arguments on middle-class tacit acceptance of vice districts, perceptions of immigrant male sexuality, and the double standard are from Neil L. Shumsky, "Tacit Acceptance: Respectable Americans and Segregated Prostitution, 1870–1910," in *The Other Americans: Sexual Variance in the American Past*, ed., Charles O. Jackson (Westport, Conn.: Praeger Publishers, 1996).

St. Louis Social Evil Hospital and House of Industry

In March 1870, the city of St. Louis legalized prostitution in order to regulate it. Hoping to reduce the spread of venereal disease, the city built the Social Evil Hospital to provide medical treatment for infected prostitutes. The hospital sat on eleven acres of land at Arsenal and Sublette in the complex containing the insane asylum and the new poorhouse. Just inside the complex's gate stood a two-story frame building reserved for African American patients. Two plainclothes policemen stood watch at all times, and visitors could enter only with a permit. Dr. E. M. Powers, the resident physician, Mr. and Mrs. J. R. Bollinger, the steward and matron of the hospital, and their young daughter lived in the brick hospital building. Patients slept in wards with eight beds per room, despite original plans to build individual cells for them.

The Social Evil Hospital opened in 1873 after delayed construction. Meanwhile, infected prostitutes endured the crowded conditions at City Hospital, where they slept three to a bed for some time; in 1871 and 1872, they lived at the Women's Guardian Home. Proceeds collected from prostitutes and madams financed doctors' salaries and the construction and maintenance of the facility.

Doctors had some success treating venereal disease, but since their patients represented a fraction of sexually active St. Louisans, the overall effect was limited. Some treatments may have caused more harm than good. Doctors treated venereal diseases with mercury compounds which caused excessive salivation, loose teeth, and rotting of the soft parts of the mouth and cheeks.

In addition to medical treatment, reformers attempted to "save" prostitutes in the House of Industry, a companion building where they hoped "the benign influence of christian charity may throw its protecting mantle around those erring and wayward daughters of Eve." However, prostitutes did not want to adjust their lives to middle-class norms and resented reformers' attempts to impose their beliefs on them. Reporters from the *Missouri Republican* who visited the House of Industry found that its inmates did not work, and several expressed frustration with their enforced idleness. Most of them were not debilitated by disease, and they spent time reading newspapers, knitting, sewing, playing cards, chatting, and playing croquet on the hospital grounds. Reform efforts stopped short of religious instruction because reformers feared kindling resistance from prostitutes. The *Republican* and the head doctor agreed that while religion might do them good, the inmates were of different faiths and had "some funny notions of their own about these things, and a religious enthusiast among them might create serious trouble."

Prostitutes resented being patronized and penalized by reformers. The *Republican* reported that patients at the Social Evil Hospital "are all grown and responsible. They understand perfectly that their money supports the institution and feel that they should be treated as ladies, so long as their pockets pay for it."

The hospital was part of a larger program modeled on European trials of similar programs designed to reduce venereal disease among soldiers. St. Louis was the first American city to undertake the experimental project. The Union Army briefly legalized prostitution in Nashville during the Civil War, but Congress quickly stepped in and prohibited soldiers from visiting brothels.

The Boards of Police Commissioners and Health initiated the Social Evil Ordinance to reduce the spread of venereal disease, to give prostitutes an opportunity to reform, and to control their residences and public behavior.

However, few prostitutes wanted to reform, and they actively resisted police. In fact, the ordinance gave police a great deal of control over the trade and over women suspected of being prostitutes, while removing legal consequences for male customers. Repealed amid great controversy four years later, the ordinance exposed radically different perspectives on women and morality in Victorian St. Louis.

The ordinance required police to register all prostitutes and brothels with the Board of Health. Once a week, doctors appointed by the Board of Health examined all registered prostitutes and, upon payment of their monthly hospital dues of six dollars, issued them certificates of inspection. Infected women had to report to the Social Evil Hospital for treatment within twenty-four hours. Madams also paid a monthly fee of ten to fourteen dollars on their brothels. Police could close any house of prostitution at any time, and their permission was required to open new ones. The police also gained legal control over prostitutes in public areas. For instance, "Registered women were forbidden to solicit on the street by 'word, sign, or action,' or in public places (such as saloons), or at the doors or windows of their rooms or houses." Police charged women who solicited customers with a misdemeanor.

During the three-odd years of the Social Evil Ordinance, the police department registered a total of 2,052 prostitutes. These women did not represent all the prostitutes in St. Louis, which the police chief estimated at five thousand–though a generous count was in his interest as a backer of the ordinance. Within two months of the ordinance's passage, however, several prostitutes refused to pay medical fees and seven escaped from City Hospital–doctors later took away patients' shoes upon admission. After one year, the number of registered women had fallen by nearly half. Though police claimed that the decline represented women leaving the profession, more likely many had decided that registering was unnecessary, as enforcement was irregular and fees were high. Police may have accepted bribes for leaving women off the rolls.

Prostitutes themselves were a varied group, as police statistics show. In 1873 the police found that of the 766 prostitutes registered that year, two thirds reported having entered prostitution by choice, while 18 percent claimed poverty motivated them. The remaining 17 percent put themselves in the categories of 'seduced,' 'family trouble,' 'abandoned by husband,' or 'bad company.' While the survey depended on subjective responses, it revealed some of the ways prostitutes viewed themselves. Far from striving to meet the standards middle-class reformers set for them, prostitutes viewed themselves as independent women and clearly felt their choices should be respected. Before entering the trade, one third of respondents were unemployed, another third were servants, 14 percent were married, and

the rest worked as teachers, clerks, saleswomen, milliners, dressmakers, and actresses. For many of these women, prostitution was an antidote to poverty, not a willful descent into immorality.

The Social Evil Ordinance created controversy from the moment it was signed. Prostitutes vigorously objected to the high fees and forced medical inspections. The *Republican* found while talking with "several intelligent courtesans" that they saw the Social Evil program as "an outrage upon their liberties" and a violation of their rights, but they admitted that the system had some medical benefits. However, the *Republican* concluded, "They are not paupers, and they are not criminals, and they fully understand it, and feel that they have no right to be used in any other way than such as they may desire, so long as it is compatible with sanitary principles."

As supporters of the ordinance, police and public health officials viewed the total suppression of prostitution as an unrealistic goal, arguing instead that its ill effects must be mitigated and the vice strictly controlled. By 1872 police reported that they had successfully contained the trade. Prostitutes were behaving in ways acceptable to middle-class reformers, as police commissioners claimed, "Public women . . . are more decorus in their manner in public [and] the plying of their wicked trade upon the public streets has been almost entirely discontinued." The commissioners cited successful efforts to reform some prostitutes, who had been "restored to respectable life." Claiming to have reduced casual prostitution, commissioners proudly noted that "clandestine, or private prostitution, which often develops into open vice, has been materially checked."

The ordinance's effects were paradoxical. While it gave police more power over individual women on the street, the ordinance also provided legal protection and a stable business climate for prostitutes and madams who registered, which in turn increased the visibility of prostitutes. This was evident on Mardi Gras in 1874, when leading prostitutes and madams accompanied prominent St. Louis men to a masked ball. The chief of police even skipped the annual meeting of the Police Board of Commissioners to attend. Men who hired prostitutes did not face consequent arrest or publicity if caught in a brothel.

Critics of the ordinance objected that legalizing prostitution failed to counter its spread and public acceptance. They believed that the best way to solve problems with the trade was to outlaw it and prosecute offenders. Others argued that since so many crimes unrelated to prostitution took place in bordellos, legalizing them would raise the crime rate. Unitarian minister and civic leader William Greenleaf Eliot indignantly complained that the ordinance failed to decrease the number of prostitutes and the incidence of venereal disease, threatened the institution of the family by condoning married men's visits to prostitutes, and "created a class of women who are to be permanently held as the instruments of the legalized lust of habitually profligate men." He further argued that it was unjust for men, "equally culpable and often times more diseased" to be able to "quietly assert the freedom as an American citizen and go on in their unimpeded course" while the registered women were permanently branded by society.

Prostitutes probably agreed with Eliot's view of reformers as hypocrites who penalized women for being prostitutes but did not punish their male customers. The *Republican* reported that patients at the Social Evil Hospital "have a feeling, which is easily discerned though they seldom can frame it in words, that society has marked out their path for them; the world keeps them in it; and the rebuffs, unkindness and insults met with in trying to get out of it would be about as bad as the woes of the present, without any of the present's enjoyments."

Pressure for a repeal mounted in January 1873, led by Mayor Joseph Brown, William G. Eliot, and Rebecca Hazard, who had helped found the Women's Guardian Home and the Woman Suffrage Association of Missouri. Several unsuccessful attempts at overturning the ordinance were made in the St. Louis Circuit Court on the grounds that it was inconsistent with state law, unconstitutional, and unjust because it did not apply to both sexes. After receiving a massive wave of petitions opposing it, the city council finally nullified the ordinance in April 1874.

The Social Evil Hospital continued to operate for several years after the repeal, though the House of Industry emptied almost immediately and voluntary admissions to the hospital dwindled considerably without compulsory inspection. The Social Evil Hospital, later renamed the Female Hospital, continued to treat unwed mothers and patients with venereal diseases. The head doctor reported that patients were treated "with medicine and not dosed with lectures on female virtue and goodness by overzealous laymen."

The Social Evil Ordinance failed to alter existing attitudes toward "fallen women." Rather, it

briefly institutionalized social and legal control over the public behavior, finances, and bodies of prostitutes and of women suspected of prostitution. Simultaneously, the Social Evil experiment removed the legal consequences for men who hired prostitutes, codifying in law what many tacitly approved of in fact. While men gained increased freedom from prosecution, prostitutes simply exchanged periodic police crackdowns and jail time for costly fees, compulsory gynecological examinations, and internment in a police-guarded hospital and reformatory.

–*Katherine Douglass*

Sources: For additional information, see "Social Evil Hospital. Its Inmates and Management, How It Works . . . Compliments, Complaints, and Comparisons. What the Inmates Think of It," *Missouri Republican*, 29 December 1872; Dacus and Buel, *Tour of St. Louis*; Mayor's Message: Report of the Board of Police Commissioners, 1872. Sneddeker, "Regulating Vice"; John C. Crighton, *The History of Health Services in Missouri* (Omaha, Neb.: Barnhart Press, 1993).

St. Louis Female Hospital (originally the Social Evil Hospital). Stereograph photograph by Boehl and Koenig, 1880. MHS–PP

The Suffrage Movement

The first recorded appearance of the suffrage movement in St. Louis occurred in December 1854. Clarinda Nichols of Vermont gave two lectures on women's rights, one in a hall rented at her own expense and another at a Universalist church. She later reported that the audiences were "intelligent and respectful," but there is no evidence that her efforts spurred them to action. St. Louis women did not begin to organize a movement for full rights of citizenship until after the Civil War.

In the years immediately following the war, passage of the Fourteenth and Fifteenth Amendments affirming the citizenship and voting rights of former slaves energized the national women's movement. St. Louis had many connections to the East, where the movement was strongest, and the city was a natural stopping place for suffrage leaders on their way to Kansas, which in 1867 considered the inclusion of a suffrage amendment into its state constitution. In March of that year, St. Louis women presented a petition with 355 signatures to the Missouri State Legislature, suggesting that the elimination of the word "white" from the voting qualifications in the state constitution did not go far enough. "We believe that all persons who are subject to the law, and taxed to support the government have a voice in the selection of those who are to govern and legislate for them. . . . We therefore pray that an amendment may be proposed striking out the word 'male' and extending to women the right of suffrage." The all-male legislature, unmoved by their rhetoric, rejected the plea by a vote of eighty-nine to five.

In May 1867, Rebecca Hazard, Lucretia Hall, Penelope Allen, and Anna Clapp held a meeting at the Mercantile Library and organized the Woman Suffrage Association of Missouri (WSA), electing Virginia Minor as their first president. They chose Allen as vice president and Hazard and Hall as secretaries. At the second meeting, they adopted a constitution affirming their mission: "The sole object of this association shall be to secure the ballot for women upon terms of equality of men." Later that year, Susan B. Anthony, in one of several visits she made to the city during the Kansas campaign, addressed a large audience at the Mercantile Library.

The association's work in 1868 as reported to the *Revolution*, the national suffrage publication, included the preparation of a second petition for suffrage, which members presented to the state legislature; it died in the Committee on Constitutional Amendments. By 1869 the organization had attracted the support of a few liberal clergymen and businessmen as well as a core of dedicated female members, and it held regular meetings twice a month.

Newspaper reporters did not take the women seriously: "A debate arose as to whether a good talkist or a good-looking delegate would be most influential with the tyrants in Washington and Jefferson City who make laws to trample down women." At a January 1869 meeting, members described by the press as "daintily habited in black" or "arrayed in purple" earnestly discussed plans to involve working women in the movement and to advocate equal wages for men and women. One speaker argued that women's inclusion in the political process would "bring a higher intellectual and moral element upon the legislation." This theme, drawing on a cultural belief that women were by nature more moral and nurturing than men, would dominate as the movement expanded.

The concern of these women, members of St. Louis's upper middle class, for the "moral improvement" of the city led them to hold evening meetings for working women. The women linked suffrage to the issue of equal wages and also to their fear of "the fallen woman." Arathusia Forbes, chair of the WSA's committee on working women, addressed one of the meetings: "Underneath unjust class law and this narrowed down, poor paid sphere of woman, lies the root from whence spring the greatest degradations and crimes and agonies the world ever knew, of both sexes; for now, as in the beginning, if woman fall, man must." The WSA continued to sponsors meetings for the workers until the formation of the Working Women's Protective Union.

When Anna Clapp addressed the regular membership in February 1869, she heightened the moral tone of the crusade. Employing biblical quotations, she asserted that the masses of women seeking the vote found nothing in the Bible denying their equality. Two male ministers in attendance affirmed her remarks. That same assembly tabled a resolution that described a man who enjoyed any right denied a women as "contemptible," calling its wording "too injudicious" for the sensibilities of the members.

Their sensibilities appeared unaffected by the undercurrent of racism and classist sentiment that marked the arguments of many suffragists. Such individuals were indignant that the Constitution now permitted former slaves to vote but not women. The National Woman Suffrage Association

(NWSA), which refused to support the Fifteenth Amendment because it did not include women, held its annual convention in St. Louis in October 1869. Julia Ward Howe and Susan B. Anthony were among the national leaders who addressed the convention. Virginia Minor, president of the local suffrage organization, anticipated the constitutional argument that later became the basis of her suit against the election board of the city: "I ask you, can a woman or negro vote in Missouri? You have placed us on the same level. . . . Women of the State, let us no longer submit to occupy so degraded a position! Disguise it as you may, the disenfranchised class is ever a degraded class. Let us lend all our energies to have the stigma removed from us. Failing before the Legislatures, we must then turn to the Supreme Court of our land and ask it to decide what are our rights as citizens, or, at least . . . give us the privilege of the Indian, and exempt us from the burden of taxation to support so unjust a Government."

The high-profile event attracted attention and generated enthusiasm among the faithful, but the number of suffrage supporters remained small and largely ineffectual. The record of the next twenty years showed consistent action but little progress. St. Louis County women established a suffrage association in 1870, but the original Woman Suffrage Association of Missouri split in 1871 when officers voted to affiliate with the American Woman Suffrage Association (AWSA). Virginia Minor, a member of the competing National Woman Suffrage Association, resigned in protest, and a number of others followed. Rebecca Hazard of Kirkwood remained with the state organization, was active in the national AWSA, and became its president in 1878. The Missouri association continued to focus on action in Jefferson City, petitioning and lobbying legislators. It held regular meetings until 1886.

In May 1879, the NWSA held its national convention in St. Louis, with Susan B. Anthony presiding. Fifty St. Louis women promptly organized a local branch of the group. They elected Virginia Minor as president and Eliza Patrick, Caroline Todd, and Phoebe Couzins as vice presidents. Minor's reports to the national conventions indicate that the group seldom met but felt they had "planted a seed" and attracted publicity for the cause. By 1890, the St. Louis group and the WSA of Missouri, following the lead of the two national organizations, merged into one, the Missouri State Equal Suffrage Association. This new association lobbied successfully for women's right to vote in school

elections and to run for school boards. It also won the mandatory appointment of women physicians to public institutions incarcerating women, and it continued to press for total suffrage.

Under the able leadership of Frances Willard, who argued that women's votes were critical to the passage of a prohibition measure, the national temperance movement gained considerable political influence in the 1880s. The Women's Christian Temperance Union (WCTU) submitted petitions for a Missouri suffrage amendment in 1885 and for municipal suffrage in 1889. While membership between temperance and suffrage organizations overlapped, their basic philosophies led to differences in strategies and goals. The Equal Suffrage Association (ESA) focused only on suffrage because "justice demanded equal rights," while the WCTU saw the vote as a means to achieve their goal of prohibition. Because the powerful brewing interests and heavily German population of St. Louis solidly opposed prohibition, the suffragists understandably wanted to keep the issues distinct.

Tensions between the WCTU and the St. Louis branch of the state ESA (which by the mid-1890s also had chapters in Kansas City and smaller cities throughout Missouri) culminated at the state convention in St. Louis in 1896. Victoria Conkling Whitney, the first woman attorney to practice before the St. Louis Court of Appeals, believed that the convention had been stacked with delegates from rural areas where the temperance group was strongest. She claimed that many of these delegates were not members of legitimate suffrage organizations and that the incumbent state president was simply a pawn of the WCTU. The St. Louis organization, denied proportional representation, declared itself the true Equal Suffrage Association, whereupon the state officers and other backers of the WCTU left and called for a separate convention to be held later that year. National suffrage leaders Susan B. Anthony and Carrie Chapman Catt endorsed the temperance faction and attended the second meeting. Stung by this rebuff, the embittered Whitney called for the formation of a new national organization that would focus, as did the St. Louis group, solely on the issue of suffrage. She failed in this effort, and the splintered Missouri movement never recovered from the rift.

The national movement also floundered in the period from 1896 to 1910. The first generation of suffragists was dying and new leaders had not yet taken command. Despite the unification of the two national groups in 1890, members were divided on strategies and lacked organization at both the national and local levels. Conservative businessmen and politicians concerned about women's impact on their domains joined the liquor interests in opposing suffrage. In the years after male voters in Colorado (1893) and Idaho (1896) approved suffrage for women, only four states held referenda on the issue; it failed in all four. An amendment to the federal constitution also appeared to be a dead issue.

In 1899, Anna Sneed Cairns, one of Whitney's backers, reported that "the logic of events is moving forward in Missouri, and we can see great progress. . . . It helped Missouri women to see how superior their Colorado sisters were . . . that wielding the power for the ballot had only made women larger in capacity, more efficient in executive detail, without in any way taking from their nobility, their loveliness of character, or their exquisite grace as hostesses, as dispensers of hospitality in their own homes, as mothers of bright happy children, or as wives of the most proud and devoted husbands."

Cairns may have been justified in her pride in the "true womanhood" of her voting sisters in Colorado, but no evidence appeared of "great progress" in Missouri at the turn of the century. While suffrage organizations existed in name and in memory after 1900, they held no conventions after 1901 and presented no petitions to the state legislature. A decade passed before a new generation of women picked up the banner, organized themselves anew, and carried the fight for the vote to its successful conclusion.

–Susan Beattie

Sources: The best chronology of the early period of the suffrage movement is detailed in Monia Cook Morris, "The History of Woman Suffrage in Missouri, 1867–1901" (master's thesis, University of Missouri–Columbia, 1928). An abbreviated version of this thesis appeared in the *MHR* 25, no. 1 (October 1930). Additional information from third-generation suffragist Christine Orrick Fordyce, "Early Beginnings," *MHR* 14, nos. 3–4 (April–July 1920). See also the letters of Victoria Whitney and Anna Sneed Cairns, in the Blake Collection, MHS.

Available histories of the national suffrage movement include Stanton, Anthony, and Gage, eds., *History of Woman Suffrage*; Eleanor Flexner, *Century of Struggle: The Woman's Rights Movement in the United States* (Cambridge, Mass.: Harvard University Press, 1975); and Anne Firor Scott, *One Half the People: The Fight for Woman Suffrage* (Philadelphia: Lippincott, 1975). This essay draws on them for discussion of the Women's Christian Temperance Union and in explaining the "doldrums" of the late nineteenth century. Ellen Carol DuBois, *Woman Suffrage and Women's Rights* (New York: New York University Press, 1998), offers a multifaceted analysis of suffrage and the ways in which its history has been written.

The persistence of this small group of women in petitioning the legislature is intriguing and deserves further research, particularly in developing biographies of key figures and their connections to one another and other organizations. While St. Louis did not have an active abolitionist movement prior to the Civil War, many of these women participated in relief efforts during the war, and others were also WCTU members. Another area of interest is the involvement of the liberal church groups, which lent their buildings for suffrage meetings. See also Ann Braude, *Radical Spirits: Spiritualism and Women's Rights in Nineteenth-Century America* (Boston: Beacon Press, 1989) for the influence of spiritualism had on the national women's movement.

Virginia Minor

"**I** believe that the Constitution of the United States gives me every right and privilege to which every other citizen is entitled; for while the Constitution gives the States the right to regulate suffrage, it nowhere gives them power to prevent it." With these opening words, Virginia Louisa Minor, a soft-spoken southern gentlewoman, electrified an audience that had gathered in St. Louis in October 1869 for a convention on woman suffrage. She continued with an impassioned argument that the Fourteenth Amendment, ratified the previous year to confirm the citizenship of former slaves, had in fact also enfranchised women.

Her husband, attorney Francis Minor, had drafted three resolutions detailing the legal foundations of the argument. Virginia's speech and the convention's adoption of these resolutions received national attention. Elizabeth Cady Stanton published the resolutions in the *Revolution* and used the argument in testimony before a Senate committee in 1870. Victoria Woodhull, a journalist and financier, lobbied Congress on the point in 1871 and urged women to elect her president in 1872, although she remains better remembered for her scandalous advocacy of free love. More than one hundred women had cast ballots that year. One of them, Susan B. Anthony, used the Fourteenth Amendment case in her unsuccessful attempt to force prosecution for unlawful voting in New York.

On October 15, 1872, Virginia Minor put her legal claim to the test at the county courthouse at

Fourth and Market Streets. She tried to register to vote as a citizen of the city of St. Louis in the upcoming congressional and presidential election. The registrar, Reese Happersett, turned her away, citing the Missouri Constitution's inclusion of the term "male citizen" in its qualifications for voting. Since a married woman was not allowed to sue on her own behalf in Missouri, Virginia and Francis Minor filed suit against Happersett on November 8, asking damages of ten thousand dollars. Their brief followed the lines of the resolutions put forth three years earlier, adding that Missouri had violated the Thirteenth and Fourteenth Amendments by placing women "in a position of involuntary servitude." Happersett countered that no cause for action existed, since he simply followed the laws of the state. The circuit court dismissed the Minors' suit.

The Minors then submitted the same plea to the Missouri Supreme Court, which held that the Fourteenth Amendment had been passed particularly for the protection of slaves; since Minor had not been a slave, it did not apply to her case. The Minors likely anticipated and hoped for this negative ruling, which allowed them to move their case to the national arena by appealing to the United States Supreme Court. On March 29, 1875, the Supreme Court unanimously rejected the Minors' definition of the constitutional privileges of citizenship. It acknowledged the citizenship of women under the Constitution but concluded that voting was not necessarily a right of citizenship. Individual states could deny women the vote as they did children or criminals. If women were to gain the franchise, it would have to come through legislative action.

From her background Virginia Minor seemed an unlikely person to take such a public stand. She was born in 1824 into a well-connected Virginia family of plantation owners and lawyers. Except for a brief period at a "ladies academy" in Charlottesville, Virginia, she was educated at home. She married Francis Minor, a distant cousin, at age nineteen and lived with him in Mississippi for a year before moving to St. Louis in 1845. They had only one child, a son born in 1852, who died in a shooting accident at age fourteen.

Despite their Southern origins, the couple supported the Union during the Civil War, and Virginia became an active member of the St. Louis Ladies' Union Aid Society. James Yeatman of the Western Sanitary Commission wrote to Francis Minor in 1863 thanking the couple for supplying fresh fruits, vegetables, canned goods, and milk to hospitals and to soldiers in the field.

Rebecca Hazard, another early St. Louis suffragist, recalled a chance meeting with Minor in 1866 in which they confided to one another their opinions in favor of Negro suffrage: "I expressed myself . . . 'And go farther—I think women also should vote.' She grasped my hand cordially, saying, 'And so do I!' We had each cherished this opinion, supposing that no other woman in the community held it." Other women did share their opinion and signed a note Minor wrote thanking Senator B. Gratz Brown for his support of suffrage. Perhaps energized by that experience, she drafted a formal petition, gathered more than 350 signatures, and presented it to the state's general assembly in March 1867. In it she argued that all persons subject to the law and taxed to support the government should have a voice in the selection of public officials as a simple act of justice. The document was the first of its kind in Missouri; it met with no more success in the legislature than the many others submitted over the next thirty years.

In May 1867, Minor joined a group of women who met at the Mercantile Library and resolved that "we will make all suitable exertions to obtain

Virginia Minor. From E. C. Stanton, S. B. Anthony, and M. J. Gage, eds., History of Woman Suffrage, *vol. 2. Saint Louis University Library*

such an amendment to our state constitution as shall confer rights of suffrage on women . . . we will organize ourselves in an association to be called the Woman Suffrage Association of Missouri." The membership elected Virginia Minor the first president of the organization. Although the court case bearing her name became without question her most lasting legacy, Minor remained in the vanguard of the suffrage movement in Missouri as one of its most tireless workers.

Minor made repeated trips to Jefferson City, bearing new petitions and seeking audiences with legislators and governors. She served as a delegate to conventions of the National Woman Suffrage Association (NWSA), founded by Susan B. Anthony in 1869, and as a national vice president in the 1870s and 1880s. In July 1876, on the 100th anniversary of the Declaration of Independence, she was one of twenty-eight women who joined Susan B. Anthony, Lucretia Mott, and Elizabeth Cady Stanton as signatories to the "Declaration of Rights for Women." In an obvious reference to her recently lost court case, this document underscored its significance: "When the constitution was so amended as to make all persons citizens, the same high tribunal decided that a woman, though a citizen, had not the right to vote. Such vacillating interpretations of constitutional law unsettle our faith in judicial authority, and undermine the liberties of the whole people."

Standing on her own interpretation of constitutional law, Minor refused to pay property taxes, addressing the St. Louis Board of Assessors in a letter dated August 26, 1879: "The principle upon which this government rests is representation before taxation. My property is denied representation and therefore can not be taxable. . . . I refuse to become a party to this injustice . . . as clearly the duties of a citizen can only be exacted where rights and privileges are equally accorded."

When her St. Louis organization affiliated with the rival American Woman Suffrage Association in 1871, she resigned both her presidency and her membership but continued to speak and lobby for the cause. In 1879, after a convention of the National Woman Suffrage Association in St. Louis, a second local group organized as the St. Louis Branch of the NWSA, and Minor immediately became its president. When the two competing national organizations consolidated in 1890, she was elected to head its state affiliate, a post she held until 1892 when she resigned for "reasons of health." The health in question may not have been her own; her husband Francis died within a week of that resignation.

Virginia Minor died in 1894. The executor of her will was Minor Meriwether, a cousin of indeterminable degree, whose wife, Elizabeth Avery Meriwether, had argued for suffrage on national speaking tours with Susan B. Anthony. Elizabeth Meriwether, her daughter, and granddaughter were beneficiaries of Minor's estate. A committed suffragist apparently even beyond the grave, Minor bequeathed one thousand dollars to Susan B. Anthony and five hundred dollars each to two nieces—but only if they remained unmarried. Her obituaries in local newspapers noted that while several hymns were sung as her body was removed from her home, she did not attend church regularly nor did a minister conduct a religious funeral service, "because she felt they were opposed to her cause."

–Susan Beattie

Sources: Virginia Minor left no journals or personal writings that hinted at the influences that shaped her dedication to the cause of women's rights. Little is known of her early life. Biographical material is from Dains and Sadler, eds., *Show Me Missouri Women*; "Suffragist Heroine," *Post-Dispatch*, 7 February 1975; and obituaries in the *Post-Dispatch* and *St. Louis Star*, 15 August 1894. Virginia Louisa Minor is buried with her husband and son in Bellefontaine Cemetery.

Details of *Minor v. Happersett* appear in Laura Staley, "Suffrage Movement in St. Louis During the 1870s," *GH* 3, no. 4 (spring 1983), and Stanton, Anthony, and Gage, eds., *History of Woman Suffrage*. See also Kathleen Peterson, "The Dawn of Her Deliverance," unpublished paper, WHMC–UMSL. Information on Minor's suffrage activities is in Morris, "The History of Woman Suffrage in Missouri." Helen R. Pinkney, "Virginia Minor," in *NAW*, vol. 2, 550–51. Stanton, Woodhull, and Anthony's use of the Fourteenth Amendment argument is discussed in Elisabeth Griffith, *In Her Own Right: The Life of Elizabeth Cady Stanton* (New York: Oxford University Press, 1984) and Ellen Carol DuBois, ed., *Elizabeth Cady Stanton, Susan B. Anthony: Correspondence, Writings, Speeches* (New York: Schocken Books, 1981). In retrospect, the Minors' argument seems unsound, but there is no evidence to suggest that they were not themselves convinced of its logic. DuBois's essay "Outgrowing the Compact of the Fathers," in *Woman Suffrage & Women's Rights*, argues that their approach, although new, was well founded in legal precedent and consistent with the Reconstruction Era approach to women's rights.

St. Louis Women's Christian Association

In May 1876, a group of Protestant church women announced they would build a new Women's Christian Home at 1814 Washington Avenue for unprotected employed women whose pay was "too scant to afford them a decent living." One of the most active women's organizations in postwar St. Louis, the Women's Christian Association (WCA) opened its first residence home in a rented building at Fifth and Poplar Streets in 1868. At various times over the next fifty years, the women operated four homes for working women, a girls training school, a home for the aged, a maternity home for unwed mothers, a home for blind girls, a retail outlet for women's handicrafts, and an aid station for female travelers in Union Station.

According to Catherine Springer, a volunteer for the Ladies' Union Aid Society during the Civil War, the inspiration for subsidized boardinghouses in St. Louis came from her work with two young refugees. Springer easily found jobs for the girls but could not find them clean, decent housing. "I saw my life work ahead of me," she recalled later.

After the war, other Protestant church women became alarmed over the "working girl problem." As increasing numbers of daughters of war widows and hard-pressed farmers left rural Missouri and Illinois for jobs in the city, upper middle-class women organized to help them avoid the perils of urban life. Like similar women in other cities, they founded a local branch of the Women's Christian Association, with the encouragement of the national Young Men's Christian Association. Their goal was to aid young, white female newcomers by looking after their moral, spiritual, and physical safety. By creating specialized residential institutions, the WCA addressed the real needs of young working women, while still reinforcing existing divisions of class, race, and culture.

The officers of the WCA were the wives and daughters of civic and business leaders. They opened the first home with donations from members of twelve local churches. The rented building had thirty rooms, including a sewing room where temporarily unemployed residents could work for their keep. In 1875 Catherine Springer became president and immediately initiated a drive for a new larger building. Springer, whose personal motto was "Up and Doing," quickly solicited seventeen thousand dollars in contributions, including a ten thousand-dollar donation of leftover Civil War relief funds from the Western Sanitary Commission.

Opened in 1880, the new brick residence on Washington Avenue accommodated more than one hundred boarders in fifty bedrooms. There were bathrooms with hot water on each of the three floors, a library, and a large attractive dining room. The association set strict rules for admission, which they hoped would separate the "wheat" from the "tares." An employed woman or student presented a Certificate of Morality attesting to her virtue and good character. Once admitted, she paid between $3.50 and $5 a week, depending on her accommodations. Since few urban working women made more than five dollars a week, most would have found living at the Women's Christian Home beyond their means. The majority of residents were newcomers to the city with jobs as nurses, teachers, office workers, and saleswomen.

In 1882 the Women's Christian Association opened another residence specifically for working-class women. Initially located at 1801 Olive Street, the Women's Christian Home and Training School soon moved to 807 North Fourth Street, nearer to the factories and shops bordering the north business district. Like boarders at the Women's Christian Home, training school residents were young women of certified virtue. Under the direction of a board of managers headed by Mrs. C. C. Rainwater, the combined school and home offered "industrial girls" instruction in marketable skills and a safe place to live.

Cooking Department, Women's Training School. Halftone from the Thirtieth Annual Report of the St. Louis Women's Christian Association, 1899. MHS–PP

The training school's small bedrooms were plain but comfortable. The matron expected residents to speak softly and not loiter in the vestibules and halls. Although not as well appointed as the other WCA residence, the building had a library to encourage self-improvement.

Employed women paid between $3 and $4.50 a week to live at the home, but domestic day workers paid only $2.10. Unemployed servants could live in the home for thirty cents a day until they found work. Young working women paid tuition for night courses in dressmaking, shorthand, typewriting, bookkeeping, and domestic skills. A series of dressmaking lessons cost as much as thirteen dollars and cooking lessons ranged from eight to fifteen dollars. With the exception of business courses, tuition included room and board.

The training school used the 150-seat dining room to operate a lunchroom for young women employed in the neighborhood. Business students waited on tables to earn their tuition. A hot, healthy lunch cost from five to fifteen cents. The working girls who ate in the lunchroom were also encouraged to use the school's library. In 1892 the training school served 80,836 lunches, an average of more than 250 each working day.

Like the affluent women who organized domestic training programs in orphanages or ran informal employment services for mothers of children in day nurseries, WCA members combined charity with self-interest to solve their own servant problem. Training school residents learned to be laundry workers and housemaids. Several times a week they received instruction in cooking and dressmaking. When they successfully completed the course, students received certificates and help in finding work. The association's large middle-class membership appreciated the well-trained workers.

The training school later moved to 3434 Morgan Street. Rainwater, a leader in the local volunteer social service movement, headed the board of the training school until it merged with a new organization, the Young Women's Christian Association, in 1905. The WCA continued to use the building for a working girls' clubhouse.

In addition to the Women's Christian Home and the Women's Training School, the WCA supported at least six other facilities. Each had a separate all-female board of directors devoted to the association's mission to protect the virtue of white urban women while helping them to become self-sufficient.

For several years the WCA also assisted some women who had lost their virtue but needed help and a place to live. The White Cross Home, at 1335 North Garrison Avenue, was a home for deserted pregnant women, characterized in WCA reports as a "reformatory home to aid tempted and betrayed women, and redeem the fallen." Opened in 1888, the staff cared for deserted wives, unwed mothers, and their infants. Many of the residents were new to the city, afraid or unable to return home. According to the WCA, two-thirds of the women admitted to the White Cross Home were domestic servants, and the remainder "never worked at anything." A matron managed the home, assisted by residents able to work. During their "time of trial" residents received donated medical care and support but were required to attend daily religious devotionals. Women physicians delivered babies and treated mothers. Of the 156 babies born at the White Cross Home in its first four years, 50 were adopted, 26 placed in orphanages, and 19 died. Presumably, the other 61 left with their mothers.

The Blind Girls Home, another WCA project, operated at 1731 North Twelfth Street in the 1880s and later at 1828 Wash and 1335 North Garrison. Young female graduates of the Missouri State School for the Blind organized the home in 1877 to live cooperatively in a safe setting. They helped support themselves by knitting and performing for the public as the Blind Girls Industrial Band. Philanthropist James Yeatman assisted them through several changes in location until the WCA assumed responsibility for the home in 1884. At the turn of the century, the WCA purchased a lot at 5235 Page Avenue and an association member donated the money to build a residence "suitable to the needs and life of the blind." The WCA used the building on North Garrison for a new women's residence, the Russell Home for "middle-aged ladies, alone and yet engaged in some industrial work." This home later moved to 3217 Washington Avenue and became a home for the aged.

In 1882 the WCA opened the Women's Exchange in the training school building with support from St. Louis merchants. The exchange helped poor women earn money by providing a retail outlet for their needlework. Immigrant women were particularly skilled in producing embroidered linens, layettes, and trousseau lingerie. WCA members staffed the exchange and sold the handiwork to women like themselves. They also ran a lunchroom to attract women shoppers. In 1884 the exchange moved to the heart of the retail district at 617 Locust Street and opened separate lunchrooms on the second floor for female shoppers and male businessmen. After moving again to 510 North Grand, in 1917 the exchange followed its customers to the Central West End first with a store and later a tearoom at 390 North Euclid Avenue. The Women's Exchange became an independent organization affiliated with twenty-eight similar enterprises in the National Federation of Women's Exchanges.

In the fall of 1890 the WCA embarked on yet another project to protect poor young women who came to the city alone "to seek their fortunes." Convinced that people waited at "the station, in the street, even on the train . . . to lure them from virtuous lives," the WCA sought the cooperation of the Terminal Railroad Association (TRRA), which operated the old Union Station at Twelfth Street. They received permission to place a matron in the Women's Waiting Room. She offered to assist children traveling alone and inexperienced young women "perfectly ignorant of the temptations of a large city." In 1894 the TRRA constructed a separate room for the Traveler's Aid in the new Union Station at Eighteenth and Market Streets. For twenty-five years the ladies' guilds of local churches contributed ten dollars a month to pay the matron's salary and to send stranded women and children back to their homes. The TRRA later took over the service with financing from the Mullanphy Fund, a local charitable trust.

At the turn of the century, many young single women new to St. Louis benefitted from the Traveler's Aid helping hand, but few sought the class-bound, maternal protection of the WCA residences. Their earnest benefactors never quite understood that the appeal of the big city went beyond employment. Women not only came looking for work, but also for independence, excitement, and to escape the restrictions of home, church, and propriety. Those who did want a structured Christian environment, however, found it with the Women's Christian Association.

Although the mission of the WCA was to help young female newcomers to St. Louis, one of its first, and ultimately most successful, projects benefitted older couples. One of few homes for the aged founded specifically for married couples, the Memorial Home opened in 1882 in the Rene Beauvais Mansion at the northwest corner of Grand and Magnolia Avenues. George Partridge, an organizer of the Western Sanitary Commission and trustee of the Soldier's Orphan Home, arranged for the orphan home to buy the property for the WCA with money left over from the Civil War relief organization. The women raised an additional twenty thousand dollars and put much of their own labor into making the private home suitable for aged residents. Handsomely furnished with donated furniture, the Memorial Home offered gracious living to couples who turned over their assets for guaranteed life care. The WCA added four wings to the building between 1885 and 1916. Although in the mid-twentieth century the home broke from the Women's Christian Association, the all-female board continued to offer high-quality care for the aged.

In 1919 the WCA considered opening residence homes for working women in the northern and southern parts of the city but concluded that female workers in those neighborhoods were primarily St. Louis residents who lived with their parents. Instead, they opened the Catherine Springer Home in a three-story hotel building at the corner of Spring and West Pine and named it in honor of the woman who had guided the organization for forty years. Catherine Springer died in the Memorial Home in 1920. Reminiscing about her life's work four years before her death, she refused to associate her efforts for women with the suffrage movement, asserting that "woman exerts her greatest influence in the home." Catherine Springer, proud that she was "not much of a radical," exemplified the energetic and committed women who tried to mitigate, if not challenge, those aspects of urban industrialism most threatening to young women.

Sources: Quoted material is from the First Annual Report of the St. Louis Women's Christian Association, December 1868; Thirty-fourth Annual Report of the WCA, 21 January 1903; Mrs. John N. Booth, "Short History of the St. Louis Women's Christian Association," December 1935; and an interview with Catherine Springer, *St. Louis Republican*, 31 January 1916, MHS vertical file. Additional information is from Annual Report of the Women's Training School, 25 January 1893; Helen Vollmer, "The History of Beauvais Mansion and the Memorial Home," from the papers of the Memorial Home, now known as Beauvais Manor on the Park; the Thirteenth Annual Report of Labor Statistics of the State of Missouri, 1893; and St. Louis city directories. For the Women's Exchange, see *BMHS* 8, no. 2 (January 1952): 204, and the *St. Louis Post-Dispatch Magazine*, 12 June 1988. For a national perspective on Protestant women's organizations, see Scott, *Natural Allies*. Mary Toothill contributed research for this essay.

In 1927 the Women's Christian Home moved from 1814 Washington Avenue to a new building at 2709 Locust Street, which became the home of the Phyllis Wheatley YWCA in 1941. The relationship between the WCA and the YWCA is complex, but the two organizations retained separate identities. Some records of the Women's Christian Association are at the Memorial Home complex at Grand and Magnolia Avenues.

Charitable homes for women operated by women of all faiths proliferated in turn-of-the-century St. Louis. In addition to the WCA and YWCA homes and the Girls' Industrial Home and School at 5501 Von Versen Avenue (later Enright) founded in 1854, at various times there existed the Women's Home of the Female Guardian Society at 1731 North Twelfth Street, Young Women's Christian Home at 603 South Sixth Street, Women's Training School at 703 North Garrison Avenue, Hephzibh Rescue Home at 3014 Morgan Street, Queen's Daughters at 111 North Sixteenth Street, Working Women's Home at 2654 Locust Street, Young Girls' Industrial Home at Twenty-first and Morgan Streets, House of Protection for Servant Girls Out of Situation at Morgan and Twenty-third Streets, Worthy Women's Aid at 1005 Howard Street, and Working Women's Home and St. Louis Female Infirmary at 1407 North Twelfth Street.

Mary Ellen Tucker and the Mission Free School

On the evening of October 28, 1880, after all the children were in bed, Mary Ellen Tucker sat down to record the day's events in the matron's diary of the Mission Free School. It had been a quiet day. The only visitor had been a women seeking to have two children boarded for the winter. Mary had sent her to the St. Louis Protestant Orphan Asylum in present-day Webster Groves. Only poor, abused, or homeless children were eligible to live at the Mission Free School. Some eligible children were turned away for lack of space. Several of the little children had the mumps but fortunately didn't seem too ill. She had given a pair of old shoes to a woman who appeared at the door.

For Mary Tucker this was a typical day at the children's home and school at the southwest corner of Ninth and Wash Streets. Organized by members of William Greenleaf Eliot's Unitarian church, the school functioned like other St. Louis orphanages with a female board of managers. The Mission Free School, however, also operated as a neighborhood settlement house and informal referral center for St. Louisans with no other place to turn for help. In addition to running the orphanage, nearly every day Mary Tucker gave food, clothing, or assistance to poor neighbors or others who came to the door. With the backing of her volunteer board, she used every available resource to help those she believed worthy of aid.

The Mission Free School started in 1852 when the Charitable Society of the Unitarian Church of the Messiah began teaching poor children practical skills in the basement of the church. By 1860 the school had outgrown the church basement and had moved to a house on Eighth Street. Under Eliot's guidance it evolved into a more comprehensive facility—an orphanage, day nursery, employment agency, and temporary homeless shelter. Incorporated as an orphanage by male church members in 1863, operation of the home and school devolved to a female board of managers in 1879. In 1881 the institution moved to a five-story building on Ninth Street, with school rooms in the basement, dormitories on the first three floors, and a chapel seating five hundred on the top floor. The home remained there until after the turn of the century.

Children were usually brought to the home by a relative, frequently the mother, who could no longer care for them. Authorities had removed others from abusive home situations. Mothers sometimes left their children temporarily so they could take jobs as live-in domestic workers. The children stayed at the school until their relatives returned for them. Mary Tucker arranged for children without guardians to be adopted or bonded out to work. If a child was deemed incorrigible, she petitioned the mayor to incarcerate him in the city reformatory. The school released all children by the age of fourteen.

Mary Ellen Tucker persevered as matron of the Mission Free School from 1875 to 1888, when she resigned, exhausted. In 1891 the school added a day nursery, which probably enabled some working mothers to keep their children at home.

The following selection of entries from Mary Ellen Tucker's diary illustrates the kinds of problems she faced daily, the roll of association members in the affairs of the school, and the network of private and public agencies she solicited for help. Her entries also reveal the ethnic stereotyping and moral judgments that underlay Gilded Age benevolence, along with Mary's obvious frustration with the community's inadequate charitable resources. Despite her many connections, she could find no place other than the poorhouse for the epileptic Mrs. Duignan. Although organizations like the Provident Association tried to rationalize and coordinate citywide public assistance, most direct help still came from overworked women like Mary Ellen Tucker and the volunteer boards of charitable institutions like the Mission Free School.

Thurs., Oct 14, [1880]. Mrs. McKittrick [Board Member] *called & sent up material for the Sewing S[chool]. 2 women came wanting children & a German man wanting to get 4 children boarded. Sent him to the German Home* [The German Protestant Orphans' Home on Natural Bridge Road] *or to Webster* [St. Louis Protestant Orphans' Home in Webster Groves].

Sat., Oct. 16. Grew cold. Went out in morning. Little Willie Davis went away. 2 people came for girls. 2 women came for help were drunk so sent them away. A woman & little baby came for shelter, kept them all night. A bundle of clothing sent in.

Mon., Oct. 18. Busy in house all morning. Made two calls in afternoon. 2 women came for girls. The Father of the Johnson boys turned up. Says he will take them to Chicago. The Unity Church people sent a lot of vegetables & apples here, their Harvest Sunday.

Thurs., Oct. 28. The ladies met to sew upstairs. Several came to see the house. A woman with 4 children came & wanted to be taken in. Could not take her, have 25 already.

Fri., March 3, [1882]. . . . A woman here with two little children mere babies. She seemed in such trouble I told her I would keep them until Monday. They cried so she did not want to leave them. So I sent her to Mrs. Evans [Mary A. Evans, matron of the Working Women's Home on North Twelfth Street], *who was full & sent her back. I told her she might stay all night with the babies, & I would write to the Mayor to give her a pass* [paid transportation to leave the city] *to Cairo where her Mother is, but while I went down to the childrens supper she went off with the children.*

Thurs., March 16. Went to see Mrs. Eliot [Abby C. Eliot] *about Lilly & woman brought a little boy, the same woman who went off so strangely on the 3rd. Says she has earned enough to take her to her friends and only wants him to stay to night. He has cried himself almost sick. Gave away a pair of old shoes to a poor woman who came to the door.*

Tues., June 13. A Mr. & Mrs. B. F. Smith from Terra Haute Indianna. Came to get a little child to adopt. Gave references & were so anxious to take Louis & I was so well satisfied with their appearance & so I let him go, hope & think it is best. We hate to loose him. Took Mary Anne to the Dr. Gave Mrs. Moran a pair of shoes.

Sat., June 17. A warm fine day. A lady here who wants a little girl for a friend in the country. Thought she would like to take Sara. We all miss Louis so much we wish he was back. . . . Ben Duignan got a place with a dairy man.

Sun., June 18. Took the children to the [Eads] bridge in the evening. Mary Anne feels very weak & miserable. Mr. Snyder called to say the school was invited to a Matinee at the Pickwick [Theater] on Wednesday.

Sat., June 24. A very hot day. A woman wanted to put in three small children–refused to take them. She was a big impudent Irishwoman. Gave a coat & pair of shoes to a sick man & shoes to his old mother. Rosina Robbinson went away with her Mother. Mary Anne seems much better. Lessie the cook is sick again.

Tues., June 27. Lessie is in the kitchen again & the children are better. Gave clothing for herself and sick baby to a nice looking Englishwoman.

Fri., Jan 7, [1887]. Very cold, went with Mrs. Duignan to Sisters Hospital, but they will not take her in there. I have tried nearly all the Catholic homes & Hospitals & no one will have her on account of the Epilepsy poor woman. Had to have a plumber to open the drain from the bathroom sink. A Mrs Car came to ask me to take a little boy. She will bring him Sunday. Alfred Chapman cannot read.

Sat., Jan 8. Went to the Protestant Hospital to see if I could get Mrs. Duignan in there, met with more encouragement than anywhere else I have been, will have to see Mrs Arnold. . . .

Wed., Jan 12. Gave some clothes to a poor woman who was sent here & a large bundle to Mrs Caldrone the Mexican woman whose children were here last summer. They have all been sick. Went to see Mrs Arnold about Mrs Duignan. She could do nothing for me but sent me to Mrs. Patterson a rich & charitable Catholic lady but she refused. What shall I do? . . .

Thurs., Jan 13. Mrs. Patterson sent her companion "Miss Jones" here to ask me about Mrs Duignan. She thinks they can find some place for her. . . .

Fri., Jan 14. Went to see a poor family advertised in paper 815 Franklin Av. They ought all to be taken away from the vile neighborhood they are in but I could not persuade the older girl to let me take the little ones. . . . Miss Jones was not successful in finding a place for Mrs. Duignan, the poor woman is quite discouraged. I shall have to keep on taking care of her.

Sat., Feb. 12. A large Sewing School. Sent Reena Schulze to the Hospital. Mrs Duignan here all bruised up from falling in a fit. Mrs Shay took her children home to spend Sunday. Gave breakfast to an old man. A woman here about finding a home for a boy of 13. Will speak to Mrs Tilden about him. She also wants a place for a deaf & dumb girl of 6 yrs.

Mon., Feb. 28. Bought a lot of children's shoes at the Mound City Shoe Store sale. A lady & Gentleman here to get a girl of 12, had none. Went with Mrs Tom Lynch to St. Vincents Assylum to see if they would take Mrs Duignan–got a promise from the Mother of a place soon to be vacant. Mrs. Malloys sister came here with a story, it is the same woman & I will not help her. She deceived us & many who helped her in a very barefaced way. Her children ought to be taken from her for she is making beggars of them.

Tues., March 22. Mrs Brown came to see Barney, brought him some clothes & left $2.00. I went to St Lukes Hospital as a last resort for Mrs Duignan but no use; the moment I say Epilepsy every door is closed against her & she can be so useful. . . .

Wed., March 23. Gave a few clothes to Mrs Hill for her sick grandchild. Went to the Health Office about Mrs Duignan & to see Mrs McKittrick. Got a postal from Mrs Howell who says she will call for Richard on Friday morning.

Thurs., March 24. Sallie McGary, or Alice Carey as she is now called arrived early this morning much to my surprise & sorrow. Mrs Insiepen sent such an ambiguous letter I cant tell by it why she sent her back & alone too. I don't like it at all. I wrote to her. Went to the Health Office again & all they will do for Mrs D is to send her to the Poor House–went to see Mrs Moran & Mrs Quin.

July 4. A quiet day in the house but the noise in the street dreadful. Several of the children went out for the day. I bought fire crackers & torpedoes for those who were here. Ida went to a Picnic. So did William. Let the children stay up until nearly ten to see the sky rockets & baloons.

Mon., Jan 30, [1888]. A Mrs Hoffman [an applicant for Tucker's job] *whom Mrs McKittrick had spoken to came to see me about the place; said she would think about it. I am very tired & wish someone would come soon. I sleep from 8 to 9 until midnight while the others are some of them up; then I partly dress & watch the rest of the night. Sleeping some again towards 5 A.M. getting up at 8:15 to be ready to see that all are right before breakfast.*

Mary Ellen Tucker left the Mission Free School soon after making the last entry.

Sources: The diary excepts are from Elizabeth Chapin Carson, "The Mission Free School," *BMHS* 9, no. 4 (July 1953): 351–71. The archives of the First Unitarian Church of St. Louis preserves the school's surviving records. Additional information is from Hyde and Conard, *Encyclopedia of the History of St. Louis*, vol. 3, 1544–45 (erroneously identified as Missouri Free School), and Bureau of Labor Statistics of the State of Missouri, 1891.

South Side Day Nursery

On March 17, 1886, fifteen Unitarian women gathered at the home of Mrs. George Durant, whose husband was the manager of the St. Louis Bell Telephone Company. Residents of the city's south side, her guests lived on the new middle-class blocks that stretched west of Twelfth Street toward Grand Avenue. That day, however, they were concerned with the plight of women and children in the working-class neighborhoods of the industrial area to the east. They met to organize the South Side Day Nursery for "infants belonging to poor women whose daily labor compels them to leave their children in incompetent hands and in unwholesome surroundings." The nonsectarian privately funded nursery opened two months later at the corner of Tenth and Julia Streets. The city's pioneer day-care facility gave working mothers a safe place to leave their preschool children for only five cents a day.

The all-female board of the association rented an old school building and hired a matron, who for twenty dollars a month came with her own furniture to operate the nursery six days a week. The board circulated notices printed in English, German, and Bohemian throughout the neighborhood.

Before accepting a child, the Visiting Committee interviewed the mother in her home and questioned her employer about her "worthiness." It was just as important to the association that the mothers work and be worthy as it was that their children be cared for. If a worthy mother had no money, one of the association members paid the initial fee. At the first meeting the board voted to admit African Americans. They were more reluctant to accept the children of unwed mothers but finally agreed to treat each case individually.

The nursery accepted babies as young as six weeks and children as old as eight. The director and her assistants received preschool children at 6:30 A.M. and promptly washed and dressed them in clothing owned by the institution; their own clothes were "put to air." The children ate bread and milk in the morning and had dinner at noon. In the late afternoon they had more bread and milk just before the assistants re-dressed them in their own clothes. Older children came for after-school care. Alert to the danger of infectious diseases, the staff insisted on strict rules of hygiene, which they emphasized with the mothers as well. Association members financed the nursery by assessing themselves twenty-five cents a month, holding fund-raising events, and sewing much of the clothing and linens.

The nursery quickly became more than a day-care facility. Once board members and their friends began hiring mothers as domestic day workers, it functioned as an employment agency. With the nursery "in the hands of ladies who believe that the most effective way of aiding the poor is to help them help themselves," employers could do good while solving their servant problem. Daily attendance ranged from twelve to forty, but more children came on Mondays and Tuesdays, the traditional washing and ironing days.

Because the nursery was within an easy walk of thousands of working people, in 1889 the board decided to buy the rented building and make a long-term commitment to the neighborhood. The board believed that "families in which the working factor is a mother, sometimes a widow, sometimes the wretched partner of a sick or lazy husband," would live there for years to come. In 1891 the nursery had four employees and room to care for sixty children. Because the association no longer paid rent, the nursery reduced the cost of keeping a child to seventeen cents a day. A mother who earned one dollar a day could leave two children at the nursery for ten cents, because the association members contributed the other twenty-four cents.

Fanny Woodward, whose husband Calvin founded the Washington University Manual Training School, headed the board for twenty years. She reported in 1892 that the reputation of the nursery was "spreading over this part of the city. . . . The moral influence of our institution must be considerable. It sanctions neither idleness or vice." She wished, however, that the nursery could make the mothers more employable, "for many of them lack training even in laundry work." If somehow they could be organized into classes in washing and ironing, she said, they would benefit from "the spirit and methods of the new idea in education, which is to put scientific thought into the everyday work of life." Although the South Side Day Nursery continued primarily as a child-care facility, its mission reflected the philosophy of the emerging settlement house movement, which addressed the interconnected social problems of the poor in America's cities.

Sources: For additional information, see *South Side Day Nursery History, 1886–1986*, published by the association and compiled largely from annual reports; *Thirteenth Annual Report of the Bureau of Labor Statistics of the State of Missouri, 1891*; Hyde and Conard, *Encyclopedia of the History of St. Louis*, vol. 4, 2105–6; and *Register of Charities, 1892*. See Allen Davis, *Spearheads for Reform: The Social Settlements*

Little Sisters of the Poor. Halftone from *The Notable Catholic Institutions of St. Louis and Vicinity*, 1911. MHS Library

The Little Sisters of the Poor operated a home for the aged in north St. Louis. Founded in 1839 in Brittany, France, the order came to the city at the request of Archbishop Peter Kenrick in 1869. The following year, charitably inclined St. Louisans gave them a house at Twenty-third and Herbert Streets. Distinguished by their white bonnets, the seven French-speaking women begged door to door for food and money to support themselves and the home's aged residents. They took in only the destitute, tracking down homeless old people in the immigrant neighborhood surrounding their convent. Unlike many of the city's nineteenth-century religious orders with broad urban agendas, the Little Sisters of the Poor had only this one mission. They were unusual also in that they depended entirely on charity; the order had no endowments or income-producing activities. By 1890 the nuns were caring for 268 elderly people in their expanded facility. They are still serving the poor at the same location.

and the Progressive Movement, 1890–1914 (New York: Oxford University Press, 1967), for the reform philosophy of Chicagoan Jane Addams and the rise of the neighborhood settlement house movement at the turn of the century.

St. Louis Colored Orphans' Home

In 1896 Mary Ford Pitts, president of the St. Louis Colored Orphans' Home, lauded the women whose work made the organization function. "Too much cannot be said in praise of these few consecrated women who are sacrificing their home, their pleasures, their all, for the sake of poor motherless children. Surely many will rise up and call them blessed." Since its founding eight years earlier, a small cadre of African American women who belonged to the city's Harper Women's Christian Temperance Union (Harper WCTU) worked tirelessly to secure the safety and build the moral character of homeless black children. The fifteen women who composed the board of directors, including teachers and ministers' wives, raised all the funds needed to operate the house at 1427 North Twelfth Street, where as many as forty children resided at one time.

Like similar facilities started by African American women elsewhere, the Colored Orphans' Home began as the charitable act of an individual, grew to encompass a small group, and finally became a community project with a permanent building and expanded services. Sarah Newton founded the organization in 1888. A graduate of Oberlin College, a former teacher in the St. Louis public schools, and later the wife of the Reverend J. S. Cohron of the Central Baptist Church, Newton allegedly took a young orphan girl from the streets of St. Louis, placed her in a private home, and paid for her care. But Newton understood that her act constituted only a short-term measure. She induced the temperance union to establish a permanent home that could compensate for the lack of provision made by the city for African American orphans or children whose impoverished families could not provide for their needs. They sought to protect such children from "demoralizing influences" and humiliation if left to the streets or the poor house. As temperance activists, the women operated in a female reform culture that emphasized Christian duty and invoked an expanded notion of women's role in bettering society. The Orphans' Home provided members of the Harper WCTU with a specific project designed to impress the local community with their competence, inspire other women to take up reform causes, and act on their concern for children and racial uplift.

That nearly half the original board members continued to work with the organization in 1894 attested to their devotion and drive. Fannie M. Oliver, a graduate of Lincoln Institute and one of the first black women teachers employed in the St. Louis public schools, was one such member. Because the center was not endowed, Oliver, Newton, and the other board women shouldered the responsibility for raising money to meet annual operating costs. The home required a monthly income of at least one hundred dollars to cover the expenses of housing thirty to fifty children, along with the salary of a live-in matron, a nurse, and a cook. Although the managers believed the home was better for young children than the poorhouse, they preferred to move children into adoptive families, "as we know the individuality of each child can better be preserved, its character studied and molded and more freedom granted in a private home than in an institution." The home, as well as the Harper WCTU were nonsectarian, although decidedly religious. "While we try to meet the physical and mental wants of our children, we also give them religious instructions and a reverence and love for God's word." In keeping with this philosophy, the home sent children to school during the week, conducted a weekly Sabbath school, and brought them to church on Sundays.

Despite the best efforts by its devoted board, by 1919 the Colored Orphans' Home faced a multitude of problems from its continued precarious financial state. That year, the facility at 4316 Natural Bridge Road, where the home moved in 1905, housed thirty children. The building was "quite free from debt" but was "old, out of repair, lacking in proper heating facilities and adequate plumbing. There is little furniture, and the children are often without food." When the president resigned, entrepreneur Annie Malone took the helm of the organization. Between 1919 and 1943, Malone devoted her considerable management skills and resources to the home. Her ten thousand-dollar donation allowed the home to relocate in 1923 to 2612 Goode Street (now Annie Malone Drive), adjacent to Homer G. Phillips Hospital in the Ville. In 1946, in recognition of her contributions, the board renamed the facility the Annie Malone Children's Home.

—Anne Valk

Sources: For additional information, see George B. Mangold, "Children's Institutions in St. Louis," *Bulletin of the Central Council of Social Agencies* 1 (March 1919);

Annual Statement of the Colored Orphans' Home, 1894, in Nina P. Lewis Collection, WHMC–UMSL; Seventy-fifth Diamond Jubilee Annual Report of Annie Malone Children's Home, Panorama of Growth, 1888–1963, in Afro-Americans in St. Louis Collection, WHMC–UMSL; and "A History of the Club Movement Among the Colored Women of the U.S.A.," in *Minutes of the National Association of Colored Women*, 1895, 1896.

See also Dorothy Salem, *To Better Our World: Black Women in Organized Reform, 1890–1920* (New York: Carlson Publishing, 1990); Anne Firor Scott, "Most Invisible of All: Black Women's Voluntary Associations," *Journal of Southern History* 56 (February 1990): 3–22; and Patricia A. Schechter, "Temperance Work in the Nineteenth Century," in *Black Women in America: An Historical Encyclopedia*, eds., Darlene Clark Hine, et al., (Bloomington: Indiana University Press, 1993).

Convent of the Good Shepherd

In 1895 the Sisters of the Good Shepherd moved into a new building still under construction on an eleven-acre site at 3801 Gravois. Since the sisters opened their first local convent and women's reformatory in 1849, St. Louisans had delivered more than three thousand women and girls into their care for rehabilitation and training. Primarily incarcerated for their sexual activity, including but not limited to prostitution, their numbers increased with the mounting poverty and social dislocation that characterized the post–Civil War industrial city. Like the Social Evil Hospital constructed earlier, the imposing new Good Shepherd reformatory was material evidence of St. Louisans' attempts to control sexual activity by institutionalizing "fallen women."

The huge new complex cost four hundred thousand dollars to construct. The Sisters of the Good Shepherd had always relied exclusively on income from sporadic donations, work performed in the convent, and contributions from inmates' parents. In 1880 they sought support from the public, which by then considered the institution a community resource. An anonymous woman's seventy-five thousand-dollar bequest provided initial funding for the new building; beer baron Adolphus Busch gave the land. By the time of its completion, more than three hundred St. Louisans were making annual donations to the reformatory.

According to the sisters' fund-raising literature, women strayed from virtue because of "defective moral training, instability of character, innate laziness, a love of idling about from place to place, and cowardly shirking of honest toil in any form."

The institution's task was to reform their "whole moral nature." The majority of the women in the reformatory were sixteen and seventeen years of age. The sisters reported that 75 percent of the inmates had reformed before they left, and that fewer than 10 percent had escaped or been dismissed as incorrigible. To prevent irresponsible parents and relatives from removing wayward girls before they were reformed and trained in employable skills, the sisters encouraged courts to commit and pay for their incarceration.

Inmates learned skills that would give them viable alternatives to prostitution. Training included chair-caning, sewing for "some of the largest shirt manufacturing houses in the city," and doing private laundry. Income from the inmates' labor paid for all the institution's food and clothing.

By 1898, 285 women were living under the supervision of 85 nuns in the new building on Gravois. The nuns kept 42 orphans in their care separate from the reformatory's 185 "fallen women." Fifty-eight Magdalens, reformed prostitutes, chose to remain cloistered on the grounds as well.

Sources: For additional information, see chapter 3; Hyde and Conard, *Encyclopedia of the History of St. Louis*; *Convent of the Good Shepherd, An Appeal* (St. Louis, 1880); and Bureau of Labor Statistics of Missouri, 1891. The reformatory and convent were demolished for a commercial building. The records of the Sisters of the Good Shepherd are preserved at their motherhouse, 7654 Natural Bridge Road.

St. John's Hospital

Founded in 1871 by the Sisters of Mercy, St. John's Hospital was the first hospital in St. Louis to provide medical treatment and nursing care to both private and charity patients. Patients boarded at the hospital while being treated by physicians and students of the Missouri Medical College. By assuming responsibility for hospital administration and nursing services, the Sisters of Mercy created an institution that would make them partners with male physicians in providing health care to St. Louisans for generations.

Planned originally as a female infirmary, the hospital began with twenty-five beds in a wing of the sisters' Industrial School and Home for Girls at Twenty-second and Morgan (now Delmar) Streets. In 1873 the faculty of the Missouri Medical College constructed a large, well-equipped building at Twenty-second and Lucas Streets, directly behind the hospital. A passageway connected patient

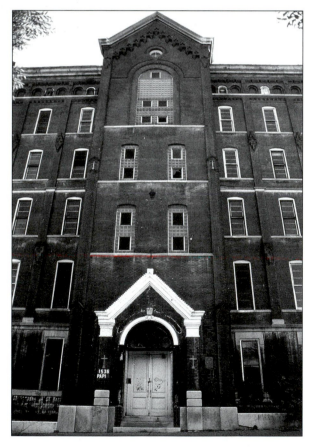

The Missouri Medical College and Adjoining St. John's Hospital.
St. John's, seen here behind the medical school, served as a teaching hospital from 1873 to 1893. This complex was in use from 1873 to 1890. Stereograph photograph by Emil Boehl, ca. 1880. MHS–PP

St. Mary's Infirmary. Photograph by George Rothenbuescher, 1999.

rooms with the school's clinical amphitheater. Fees paid by the physicians' private patients subsidized both the nuns' charity patients and the free dispensary, an outpatient clinic for the neighborhood poor. By 1874 St. John's was a fifty-bed general hospital, incorporated by the Sisters of Mercy as a separate institution.

In 1890 the nuns' crowded complex included a convent, orphanage, industrial school, and night refuge for poor women, as well as the hospital which by then had outgrown the building it shared with the girls' home. The sisters sold forty acres of Clayton farmland, a dowry from a nun who had entered the religious order many years earlier, to purchase a building lot at Twenty-third and Locust Streets. The new hospital was in a more prosperous neighborhood a few blocks south of the old building. The Sisters of Mercy bore all construction costs with the exception of some rooms furnished by staff doctors and friends.

Most patients paid hospital fees that ranged from seven to fourteen dollars a week depending on their accommodations. Outpatients received free care at the dispensary, which in 1895 moved from Morgan Street to a new wing of the hospital. A separate, adjacent infirmary cared for African American women and girls.

St. John's Hospital ended its affiliation with the Missouri Medical College when the faculty sold its school building in 1893 and moved next to the St. Louis Polyclinic on Jefferson Avenue. However, in 1903 the Sisters of Mercy formed a partnership with the medical school of Saint Louis University. The hospital remained on Locust Street until 1912, when the sisters replaced it with a new facility at 307 North Euclid. By the twentieth century, the Sisters of Mercy not only owned a modern facility, but also had become professional hospital administrators as essential to the city's medical resources as its male physicians.

Sources: Information is from Sister Mary Isidore Lennon, *Milestones of Mercy: Story of the Sisters of Mercy in St. Louis, 1856–1956* (Milwaukee: Catholic Life Pubs., 1856). See also the St. *Louis Star, One Hundred Years of Medicine and Surgery in Missouri* (St. Louis, 1900); Dacus and Buel, *A Tour of St. Louis*; Rothensteiner, *History of the Archdiocese of St. Louis*; and Conference on Catholic Charities (St. Louis, 1912). Archives are located at St. Joseph's Convent of Mercy, 611 S. New Ballas Road, 63141. See also Ursula Stepsis and Delores Liptak, ed., *Pioneer Healers: The History of Women Religious in American Health Care* (New York: Crossroads Publishing Co., 1989).

St. Mary's Infirmary

In 1872 Mother Mary Odilia Berger, a forty-nine-year-old Bavarian nun, immigrated to America with five other religious sisters, all refugees from the Franco-Prussian War. Members of a Franciscan order that nursed the sick in their homes, they arrived in St. Louis just as smallpox was overtaking the city. They immediately began visiting the afflicted in the immigrant neighborhoods near the river, south of Mill Creek. Because the rules of their order prohibited the nuns from charging for their services, they solicited donations for all their needs. By 1873 they had enough money and supplies to build a convent adjoining St. Mary's Church on Third and Gratiot Streets.

Although the nuns formed a new order and took the name Sisters of St. Mary, they continued to be called "the smallpox sisters." Their poor neighbors welcomed the nursing sisters into their homes during annual outbreaks of smallpox, diphtheria, and cholera. By 1875 the community had grown to twenty-three nuns and had expanded its mission. They opened the St. Joseph's Home for orphans in a donated building at Arsenal and Arkansas Avenues. They also started "La Creche," a home for unmarried mothers in north St. Louis financed by wealthy Catholic matrons. In 1878 five sisters died in Memphis nursing victims of yellow fever.

In 1877 Mother Odilia concluded that the sisters could serve poor St. Louisans better if they opened a hospital. In the late nineteenth century, hospitals were still largely institutions for the destitute. Most Americans only went when they were too sick to nurse themselves and had no one else to take care of them. They established St. Mary's Infirmary in the former home of Missouri senator Carl Schurz, located on a large lot at Fifteenth and Papin Streets. In 1884 it became the order's motherhouse as well.

By the 1880s, physicians had some understanding of germ theory and of the ways infectious diseases spread. When contagious diseases swept through dense city neighborhoods, public health officials tried to prevent citywide epidemics by institutionalizing indigent victims. Physicians could give little medical treatment to patients, even those with private care. Hospital nursing largely involved feeding, bathing, comforting, and cleaning up after suffering and dying poor people.

The Sisters of St. Mary became the city's primary providers of public health care. In 1883 the St. Louis health commissioner asked them to nurse smallpox patients at the city Quarantine Hospital. Over the next two years they cared for nearly fifteen hundred hospitalized charity patients. Diphtheria patients filled their hospital wards in 1886 when the Board of Health asked the sisters to take in poor victims, mostly children.

The hospital soon outgrew its converted residence. In 1889 the Sisters of St. Mary completed a new five-story building in front of the old house at 1536 Papin Street. By 1898, sixty-five members of the religious community nursed the poor and solicited donations for the hospital. They added an addition to the west side of the hospital in 1896 and one to the east side in 1906.

Sources: For additional information, see Sisters of St. Mary's motherhouse, *Seventy-Five Years of Service* (St. Louis, 1947); Conference of Catholic Charities, 101–3; Rothensteiner, *History of the Archdiocese of St. Louis*, 334–39; *West End–Clayton Word*, 5 June 1997; and Hyde and Conard, *Encyclopedia of the History of St. Louis*, vol. 2, 1055. The archives of St. Mary's Infirmary are located at Our Lady of the Angels, motherhouse of the Sisters of St. Mary.

The 1896 Tornado

On May 28, 1896, a shocked Bertha Scott noted in her diary: "What masses of ruin! We pass poles blown down, wires hanging in masses, then roofs of houses, finally we come to where block after block of houses have been blown down, churches, schools, powerhouses, warehouse are masses of ruin, the streets in many places impassable. . . . I hope and pray I may never see such a sight again."

The previous day a devastating tornado struck St. Louis at 5:15 P.M. near Hampton Avenue, moved along Arsenal Street, swung eastward through Tower Grove Park and on towards Compton Hill. Then it swept through Jefferson and Grand Avenues, causing damage to Lafayette Park and City Hospital, and reached the river about 5:35 P.M. It blasted across the Mississippi River, damaging Eads Bridge as it passed, and littering the riverbanks with twisted wreckage from trains, tenements, hotels, and businesses on its way to East St. Louis. Torrential rain followed the tornado. After dark, fires spread through the collapsing buildings and around downed power lines.

In 1896 no municipal, state, or national emergency relief organizations existed to aid disaster victims. But even so, St. Louisans were better prepared than they had been for the cholera epidemic nearly fifty years earlier. In the interim they had mobilized for war and established citywide private, sectarian relief organizations. This time municipal officials and civic leaders organized to provide immediate temporary assistance. The response to this community crisis, however, revealed the assumptions and biases that underlay social welfare in St. Louis. It also illustrated women's changing role in charity at the end of the nineteenth century. The scale and complexity of effective relief efforts in the industrial city required resources more readily available to men than women.

According to the official report, 138 St. Louisans died and the health department treated 92 injured people. Undoubtedly, many more received treatment at home or from private physicians. The tornado damaged nearly eight thousand homes and four thousand buildings.

Far more people suffered losses than the official forty to fifty thousand initially assisted by the Merchants' Exchange Relief Committee. Victims came from all social classes, the affluent and the poor, from fashionable residences and tenement buildings. Bertha Scott, who lived well out of harm's way on Washington Avenue, observed that the worst areas hit were "the blocks of little homes, in the German quarter, with the broken-hearted women and men." Lafayette Park itself was absolutely "laid waste."

Particularly hard hit were people, mainly widows and the elderly, whose assets were tied up in damaged property. Most of the large businesses were insured, but smaller businesses and home owners lost everything. Temporary closure of stores, offices, and factories put people out of work. The storm damage created temporary day labor, but it did not help most displaced workers. Some families recovered quickly; others, coping with death, injury, and property damage, suffered long-term heartbreak and financial distress.

In the absence of an official federal disaster relief agency, Congress passed a bill on May 28, authorizing the mayors of St. Louis and East St. Louis to borrow enough tents to shelter the homeless temporarily. Municipal aid was more complicated because it involved assessing responsibility. The city council was accountable to its taxpayers for upkeep of roads, sewers, parks, and public health. The city was also responsible for citizens incapable of self-support, but not for those suffering "temporary distress and misfortune, from whatever cause arising." That was left to private benevolence.

City workers started clearing the debris fairly quickly. Although residents castigated Mayor Cyrus Walbridge for incompetence and tardiness, the city accomplished much under extraordinarily difficult conditions. An initial lack of departmental coordination and labor slowed efforts to retrieve the dead, clear roads, and repair power lines. Bad weather and the overwhelming number of sightseers added to the confusion. South siders, who already believed city hall slighted their immigrant neighborhoods, called the Municipal Assembly callous and incompetent for passing a relief bill that benefitted city institutions over needy victims.

Because city authorities disclaimed responsibility for relieving the temporary distress of its citizens, they left the task to others. The morning after the tornado, the Merchants' Exchange began soliciting funds and distributing relief to victims. In cooperation with the three main St. Louis charities–the St. Vincent de Paul Society, the Provident Association, and the Hebrew Relief Society–the Merchants' Exchange Relief Committee divided the stricken area into three districts. Under normal times these organizations served mainly their own constituents. Because it had its infrastructure in place, the Merchants' Exchange worked through them to distribute clothing, food, bedding, and rent money to worthy applicants.

Two weeks after the tornado, the committee concluded that "every known sufferer of the storm had been fed, clothed, and housed." The hundreds of people who did not apply, however, received no direct benefit from the $267,000 disbursed. Additional help came from collections at public schools and people outside St. Louis. Families, friends, and neighbors contributed an estimated one hundred thousand dollars. Counting large quantities of donated clothing, bedding, food, and services, an estimated four hundred thousand dollars in aid reached victims.

The Merchants' Exchange decided to mount a large-scale relief effort in part because they had rejected offers of organized aid from communities outside St. Louis. Businessmen feared that accepting assistance would reflect badly on the local business community and imply that the city was shut down. The Merchants' Exchange collected money and delegated most of the work to established charities. The organizations, however, resented the control the businessmen exercised over their work. They criticized the Merchants' Exchange for believing only temporary relief necessary or desirable, and for making no financial provision for situations that required long-term funding.

Women played a less visible but crucial role in relief operations. Newspapers reported hundreds involved in relief work. Informally, they aided family, friends, and neighbors by supplying bed and board, caring for the sick, and helping with clearing up. Women's groups, especially those connected with churches, organized help, raised money, and collected and distributed food and supplies. A public school relief committee made each school in the stricken area a distribution center for clothing and shoes. Teachers visited the homes of all their pupils to see what was needed. Nurses in the ruined City Hospital helped move patients to the old reformatory owned by the Sisters of the Good Shepherd. The Sisters of Mercy at St. John's Hospital took in many seriously injured victims. The Provident Association's new visiting nurses department employed three nurses to visit tornado victims. Two of St. Louis's women physicians, Dr. Ella Marx and Dr. Adelheid Bedal, offered their services to the Provident Association relief operations.

Many other women helped with official relief operations organized by the citywide charities. They collected and distributed goods, sewed and repaired clothing, cooked meals for victims, worked on application forms and then went to check out the details. They canvassed neighborhoods for reluctant charitable recipients. Bertha Scott recorded in her diary: "Mrs. Tuttle comes to ask me to collect clothing and bedding for the tornado sufferers. Collect quantities. People give very liberally." She took what she had collected to St. Stephen's Mission and the Soulard Police Headquarters. On June 4, she stayed all day at one of the distribution stations on Lafayette Avenue. "I find my German most useful–many can speak no English at all–many are Bohemian and speak through German interpreters." Whether affluent housewives like Bertha Scott, or nurses, or the neighbor next door, women were indispensable to tornado relief.

Tornado relief did not escape the class tensions inherent in all Gilded Age charitable work. Volunteers complained that affluent donors gave working-class tornado victims evening wear and dirty bedding. "The garments which the applicants are offered are sometimes worse than the ones they have on," observed a *Post-Dispatch* reporter, "I know of friends who live near me in the West End who made separate bundles of their old clothes. The inferior articles were sent to the depots east of Ninth Street because it was said the naturally poor were not accustomed to anything better, while the

bundle of fairly good clothes was sent to the Union Club depot for sufferers of a higher social order." The crusading newspaper accused organizers of being stingy in their distribution of money and goods because they were businessmen "set in their ways, and accustomed to doling out aid among people who are poor and needy every winter."

Critics assailed the St. Vincent de Paul Society, the Catholic relief organization, for using the same criteria for tornado victims as it did when dealing with chronic indigents. They considered the standard procedures too humiliating for respectable people suffering hardship through no fault of their own. All agencies used investigative reports, application forms, and home visits to ensure that only the worthy received aid. All relief groups made moral distinctions between those deserving help and those who did not. Victims themselves sometimes refused help because they believed that acceptance might indicate a lack of individual responsibility and moral fiber.

The tornado of May 27, 1896, was a major catastrophe for the city and its inhabitants. While most help came quickly, the process of returning to normal took a long time. Businessmen were pleased with relief operations, which showed St. Louisans to be responsible and self-sufficient. Many of the victims repaired their homes and lives within a few months. Some experienced long-term consequences: death of children or parents, disabling injuries, loss of home or business, and

Wreckage on Lafayette Avenue after the 1896 Tornado. Photograph by J. C. Strauss, 1896. MHS–PP

unemployment. Some upper middle-class women who assisted with tornado relief returned to their West End social lives, but others became even more involved in the larger concerns of their city and its people.

–Joan Cooper

Sources: Information on legal responsibility of government and estimates of damages and dollar amount of relief are from Hyde and Conard, *Encyclopedia of the History of St. Louis*. The *Post-Dispatch*, the *Globe-Democrat*, and the *Republic*, May and June 1896. Criticism of relief work is from the *Post-Dispatch*, 5 June 1896. The *Post-Dispatch* was a crusading newspaper often critical of the business elite. See also Julian Curzon, *The Great Cyclone* (St. Louis, 1896); *The Great Tornado at St. Louis on the Evening of May 27, 1896* (St. Louis, 1896); Mary K. Dains, "The St. Louis Tornado of 1896," *MHR* 66, no. 3(April 1972); and the *St. Louis Post-Dispatch Magazine*, 26 May 1996.

Kate Chopin

In 1899 Katherine O'Flaherty Chopin published *The Awakening*, a short novel that critiqued the strict gender roles of Victorian society. Although the story took place in Louisiana, Kate Chopin wrote this and most of her other fiction in St. Louis. Born in 1850 to Thomas O'Flaherty, an Irish immigrant, and Eliza Faris, a Creole aristocrat, Kate left the city in 1870 after marrying Oscar Chopin, a Louisiana businessman. She returned to St. Louis after her husband's death in 1882, living first at 3317 Morgan Street and finally at 4232 McPherson Avenue in the West End. As independent as the characters she created, Kate Chopin refused to bend her will and vision of truth to convention. Her most powerful stories addressed female independence, women's sexuality, and the tensions just below the surface of middle-class domestic life in the Gilded Age.

Eighteen-year-old Katherine O'Flaherty wrote confidently in 1869 about freedom in the allegorical tale, "Emancipation. A Life Fable." In the story, a strong and beautiful caged animal is nurtured by "an invisible protecting hand," and all his needs are met. Although nourished physically, his life is empty. One day, the cage stands open, and after much hesitation he escapes. The animal's life will never again be as easy, but he does not return: "So does he live, seeking, finding, joying and suffering."

Although her early tale does not reveal the skill and finesse of the later writer, it does reveal a theme that recurs throughout Chopin's works: abhorrence of restraint and confinement and devotion to freedom, regardless of cost. In fact, Chopin would reconfigure the hero of "Emancipation" thirty years later in her masterpiece, *The Awakening*, in Edna Pontellier, a woman with the same characteristics and behaviors.

Chopin spent her childhood in a large Southern-style home on Eighth Street between Gratiot and Chouteau, then a fashionable address. Her father became a wealthy merchant and a stockholder in the Pacific Railroad. The young Katherine O'Flaherty's rides with him along the St. Louis waterfront strengthened their relationship and stimulated "a lasting love of place." In 1855, her father died in the train wreck following the collapse of the Gasconade River Bridge.

The St. Louis of Chopin's fiction is often a reflection of the writer's resentment of its social conventions and class divisions. Her mother belonged to the old French Creole aristocracy and her ancestors were among the founders of St. Louis and Kaskaskia. Kate attended the prestigious St. Louis Academy of the Sacred Heart on Fifth Street. Later in her fiction, she questioned and criticized the values and conventions she had observed in her youth.

Kate Chopin's upbringing taught her to admire great writers and to be a keen observer. Her maternal great-grandmother, Madame Victoria Verdon Charleville, told her stories from the founding days of Creole St. Louis. From those colorful tales, Kate gained insight into human character and motivation, and she learned tolerance for conduct, which deviated from the narrow norms of the Gilded Age. She learn to face life without hesitation or embarrassment, trusting that only God could judge other people's behavior.

"The Maid of Saint Phillippe," a story set in a small village across the river from St. Louis, reflected the impact of these early Creole tales. Chopin portrayed her heroine, Marianne, as a tall, strong French girl, more like a handsome boy in her buckskin clothes. She rebels against the female stereotype when she refuses the dashing French Captain Vaudry's proposal to marry and return with him to France. What could possibly be left for her, he wonders, after denying allegiance to England, Spain, and France? "Freedom is left for me!" she cries, shouldering her gun.

Kate's writing gained its color and sensuality while she lived in Louisiana with her Creole husband Oscar Chopin. Although she lived there for the duration of her marriage, from 1870 until Oscar's sudden death in 1882, Kate retained close ties with her family in St. Louis, and three of her five sons were born there. Shortly after Oscar's death, Chopin returned to the city to live with her mother.

Chopin became a serious writer after she returned to St. Louis. During the ten years between 1889 and 1899, she became a popular local author, hosting a literary salon which proved both entertaining and thought-provoking. She also felt free there to be unfeminine, smoking cigarettes and crossing her legs.

Fewer than a dozen of Kate Chopin's stories appeared originally in the periodicals of her native city. In October 1889, the *St. Louis Post-Dispatch* printed her first local publication, "A Point at Issue." National periodicals such as *Vogue* or magazines published in New Orleans were bolder than St. Louis periodicals, printing her more daring works. One of these stories was "The Story of an Hour," which *Vogue* published in December 1894. *St. Louis Life* reprinted it a month later.

In the story, Louise Mallard, whose face "bespoke repression and even a certain strength," learns of her husband's untimely death. Yet rather than becoming distraught, she welcomes her second chance at freedom: "Free! Body and soul free!" is the refrain she whispers to herself. When her husband returns, not really dead at all, Louise Mallard dies from shock, which the doctors ironically attribute to "the joy that kills."

Although Chopin's own marriage was apparently happy, "this possession of self-assertion," which Louise Mallard recognizes as "the strongest impulse of her being," stronger even than love, recurs consistently in the author's work, figuring most prominently in *The Awakening*. Chopin considered the novel to be a true representation of a young woman's growing awareness of her sexual nature. Edna Pontellier's personal quest leads her to rebel against traditional roles of wife and mother.

The Awakening shocked the reviewers and the public, although many recognized the quality of the work. They disparaged the subject of a woman's newfound sexual awareness. The *St. Louis Globe-Democrat* observed that the "poison of passion seems to have entered her system with her mother's milk." That Edna Pontellier no longer loved her husband Léonce was bad enough, but that she loved another man—and submitted to the sexual advances of yet another—was scandalous. The *Post-Dispatch* reviewer admired the style of

Kate Chopin. Photograph, 1899. MHS–PP

Chopin's Home at 4232 McPherson Avenue. Photograph by George Rothenbuescher, 1999.

The Awakening but felt that it contained observations too "disturbing–even indelicate" to discuss when "we have all agreed [they] shall not be acknowledged." Kate Chopin's exploration of the female consciousness which had begun thirty years before in her fable of the sleek animal resurfaced in the "graceful severity of poise and movement, that made Edna Pontellier different from the crowd."

Kate Chopin was distressed by the critical reception of the novel with which she identified so profoundly. Literary legend has it that *The Awakening* wrecked her career. Magazines which had once praised her work now refused to review it; local libraries, including the St. Louis Mercantile Library, banned her book; the St. Louis Fine Arts Club refused her membership. However, most of these stories were apocryphal. In fact, the prestigious Wednesday Club invited her to speak in 1899.

Like Edna Pontellier, Kate Chopin was "different from the crowd." She told her critics that if she had known what Mrs. Pontellier was going to do when she began writing, "I would have excluded her from the company. But when I found out what she was up to, the play was half over and it was then too late." Edna says in the novel that she would give up the "unessential"–her life or her money–for her children, but she would never give her self. Kate Chopin stubbornly maintained that same integrity.

On August 20, 1904, Kate Chopin attended the St. Louis World's Fair. She suffered a cerebral hemorrhage that night and died two days later at the age of fifty-three. The *St. Louis Hesperian* reported that St. Louis had lost its foremost author. The *Post-Dispatch* was not so generous, noting that since *The Awakening*, the author had published nothing of importance.

–Kathleen Butterly Nigro

Sources: Quote from Chopin on "love of place" is from Daniel S. Rankin, *Kate Chopin and her Creole Stories* (Philadelphia: University of Pennsylvania Press, 1932), 31; "A Point of Issue," published in the *Post-Dispatch*, 27 October 1889; "Story of an Hour" in *St. Louis Life*, 5 January 1895; the *Post-Dispatch* review of *The Awakening*, 20 May 1899; and the *Globe-Democrat* review, 13 May 1899. Most of the biographical information is taken from Emily Toth, "St. Louis and the Fiction of Kate Chopin," *BMHS* 32, no. 1 (October 1975); Emily Toth, *Kate Chopin* (New York: William Morrow, 1990); or Per Seyerstad's introductions to *The Storm and Other Stories with the Awakening* (New York: The Feminist Press, 1974) and *The Complete Works of Kate Chopin* (Baton Rouge: Louisiana State University Press, 1969). Also helpful for background and criticism is the Norton Critical Edition of Margaret Culley, ed., *The Awakening/Kate Chopin* (New York: Norton, 1976). Early background can be found in Rankin, *Kate Chopin and her Creole Stories*. See also Steve Nissenbaum, "Kate Chopin," in *NAW* vol. 1, 334–35, and Emily Toth, *Unveiling Kate Chopin* (Jackson: University of Mississippi Press, 1999).

If this is Womanly—

Why not this?

These two lantern slides, drawn by Mary Ellen Sigsbee, were produced by Smith Slide Manufacturing Company, St. Louis, Missouri, in 1914. They are from a set of slides used to illustrate a lecture promoting suffrage and equal opportunities for women. MHS–PP

By the end of the nineteenth century, women's place extended beyond the home, but their underpaid work was still largely domestic. In the twentieth century, some St. Louis women would become "municipal housekeepers," determined to tackle the social problems of the expanding city with skills acquired managing homes and charitable organizations.

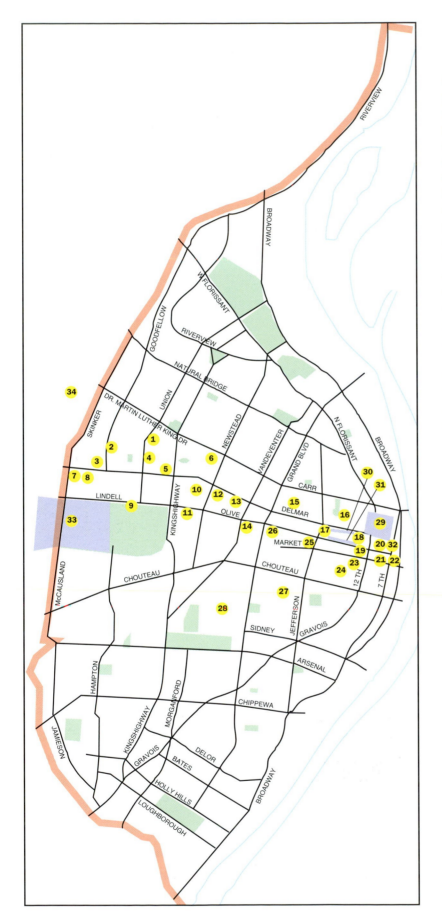

1900–1920

1. Cabanne Branch, St. Louis Public Library, ESL
2. Fannie Hurst Home
3. Mary Bulkley Home
4. St. Philomena's Technical School
5. Charlotte Rumbold Home
6. St. Francis's Colored Orphan Home
7. Lillie Rose Ernst Home
8. Pearl Curran Home
9. Confederate Memorial
10. The Wednesday Club
11. St. Louis Women's Club
12. Dr. Mary Hancock McLean's Home and Office
13. Helpers of the Holy Souls Mission
14. Queen's Daughters Residence Home
15. Phyllis Wheatley Branch YWCA
16. Dr. McLean's Evening Dispensery
17. Suffrage Convention, Coliseum
18. Marx and Haas Clothing Factory
19. YWCA Building
20. Bell Telephone Building
21. Missouri Equal Suffrage Association
22. *Rip-Saw* Office
23. Josephine Baker Home
24. Queen's Daughters Home for Self-supporting Women
25. St. Louis Children's Hospital
26. St. Rita's Boarding School
27. Barr Branch, St. Louis Public Library
28. Kate Richards O'Hare Home
29. Area of 1907 Housing Report
30. Washington Avenue Garment District
31. Golden Lane Route
32. Suffrage Convention, Statler Hotel
33. 1904 World's Fair Site
34. Wagner Electric Company

- St. Louis City Limits 1876–Present
- Parks
- Sites

6

Progressive Era Women

Arsania Williams attended the Louisiana Purchase Exposition in Forest Park shortly after it opened in the spring of 1904. The eager young St. Louis public school teacher studied the educational exhibits, listened to John Philip Sousa's band, and marveled at the piles of consumer products displayed in the huge exhibit palaces. She and her friends watched cascades of sparkling water rise from the Grand Basin and glisten in the light from thousands of electric bulbs outlining Festival Hall. But Williams was more than a casual visitor to the 1904 World's Fair. An active club woman, she was a local delegate to the National Association of Colored Women (NACW), which was preparing to hold its annual convention on the fairgrounds. She was also the only woman on a

committee of black St. Louisans that had invited Booker T. Washington to speak to thousands of African Americans coming to the fair August 1 for Negro Day.

Neither the NACW convention nor Negro Day actually took place at the World's Fair. Driven by a desire to increase attendance, exposition officials adopted an official nondiscrimination policy and invited black St. Louisans to sponsor events that would bring African Americans to the fairgrounds.

View of Downtown St. Louis with Smoke. St. Louis hoped World's Fair visitors would judge the city by its sparkling Forest Park fairgrounds, not by its grimy, smokey downtown. Detail of panoramic photograph, ca. 1910. MHS–PP

They did not, however, require all concessionaires to serve black fairgoers. Persistent evidence of racial discrimination at the fair convinced leaders of both African American groups to cancel their events at the last minute. In boycotting the fair they not only protested racial discrimination, but also protected their guests from possible humiliating incidents on the fairgrounds.

The mixed message that white St. Louisans sent to Williams and her African American colleagues was only one example of the deep divisions that characterized St. Louis at the turn of the century. Black St. Louisans negotiated a complex racial terrain everyday in a city segregated more by custom than by law. Racism fostered distrust and resentment, but tensions also grew between ordinary working-class people and the wealthy residents of the West End. More and more St. Louisans came to believe that their civic leaders not only flaunted but also misused tightly held political and economic power. Industrialization had created an urban landscape fractured by race and class.

By the turn of the century, people in American cities no longer could deny that social problems caused by industrial capitalism drove residents apart as they overwhelmed social services and public resources. Affluent white men and women, usually with ties to the community's business leadership, formed a movement known as progressivism to address what most perceived as an urban crisis.

Progressivism, usually identified with a short-lived political party, was a broad but rarely coordinated national social movement. Various groups, with sometimes conflicting priorities, sought to contain the energy of industrialism without sacrificing material progress. They focused on cities, because there the dynamics of industrialism were most obvious and its tensions most visible. The progressives' goal was "reform," and they pursued it with religious zeal. They envisioned a twentieth-century urban America that was democratic, expansive, prosperous, and just, but also disciplined, efficient, and loyal to the traditional pyramid of social status and political power. Progressive containment welcomed change, but not too much or too fast; democracy within the bounds of deference; and social justice within the existing social order. Progressive idealism was a genuine heartfelt urge to do the right thing tinged with hypocrisy, nativism, racial bigotry, and class interest. Like other American middle- and upper-class women at the turn of the century, St. Louis women threw themselves into a wide range of progressive activities, motivated by compassion and

a familiarity with urban problems acquired through years of organizational experience.

In 1892, women representing fifty-eight charitable institutions met to discuss what they were doing for "women and humanity at large." In welcoming the delegates, the host minister declared that "one of the loveliest moral spectacles" of the age is the "gradual enlargement of woman's sphere" to include community betterment. Volunteers from Protestant, Catholic, and Jewish charities spent three days reporting on their work. They tried to identify the city's most pressing social problems and their plans for the future. At the final session, they formed a committee to investigate rising homelessness and unemployment among boys and recommended legislation to raise the female age of consent from fifteen to eighteen. They also endorsed women's suffrage.

The resolutions passed at the 1892 conference showed that at least some women were ready to use overt political tactics to advance their moral mission. In the first two decades of the twentieth century, the separate spheres of women's benevolence and men's political action began to converge. Always more ideological than behavioral, this gender separation nevertheless described a nineteenth-century reality where women created and administered their own social service institutions and men organized and ran government.

Women social reformers in St. Louis had always had the support of some influential men. William Greenleaf Eliot and Albert Todd, a prominent local lawyer, even allied themselves with nineteenth-century suffragists. Protestant ministers preached a "social gospel" that propelled religion into social action. Rabbis of reformed Jewish congregations pressed their female members to apply their ethical standards to community service. For the most part, however, male St. Louis progressive reformers were business and professional men distressed by graft and ineptitude in local government and appalled by the ugly, dirty city they had helped build. At the turn of the century the interests of these men and their reform-minded wives and daughters came together in a common strategy to use the power of government to effect change.

Throughout the nineteenth century, America's economic system relied on positive government action, which operated under the philosophy that it must help but never hinder private enterprise. Government had been particularly active in cities, building infrastructure like wharves, roads, and sewers to facilitate commerce. Business leaders fulfilled their civic responsibilities through public office: William Carr Lane, physician and real estate speculator, was mayor of St. Louis for five terms before 1850. However, as immigrants swelled the size of industrial cities and new technologies drove up infrastructure costs and profits, the opportunities for graft escalated as well. Although corrupt politicians and their political machines received the most publicity, they were not always the greatest abusers of the public trust. Elected officials in St. Louis, and other cities, made sweetheart deals with leading businessmen over utility contracts and transit franchises that reached into the most exclusive neighborhoods. By the turn of the century, St. Louisans were frustrated by a city that did not work and embarrassed by "muckraking" journalists who told its sordid stories in the national press.

Paradoxically, in St. Louis the biggest "boodlers" and the most ardent reformers were neighbors in the exclusive West End. Unlike coalitions in other cities that included grass-roots leadership, St. Louis's reform movement was generated by the local elite. Determined to usher in a "New St. Louis" with the new century, they called for the election of "good men" to municipal office, democratic revisions in the city charter, the creation of a rational city plan, and an international World's Fair. David R. Francis, the driving force behind the fair, was a former Missouri governor and mayor of St. Louis, wealthy grain broker, and West End resident. He and reform Mayor Rolla Wells used fair planning as a strategy for revitalizing the city's economy, appearance, and tarnished national reputation. Civic boosters hoped that visitors to the Louisiana Purchase Exposition in 1904 would be dazzled by an attractive, well-functioning city on their way to see exotic wonders in Forest Park.

St. Louis was a smoky, dirty city. With a population of nearly six hundred thousand living largely east of Grand Avenue, it was no uglier than other industrial cities fueled by coal at the turn of the century. Rising concern over urban aesthetics had created the nationwide City Beautiful movement, a progressive effort to improve cities by making them more attractive. Faith in the morally and socially uplifting power of beautiful surroundings led to campaigns for impressive public art and architecture, and for modern parks and boulevards. The City Beautiful impulse also encouraged more mundane projects like planting trees, picking up trash, and removing unsightly billboards. Municipal well-being required not only cleaner government and surroundings, but also healthier people. The new germ theory offered an explanation of how disease actually spread, and although St. Louis could claim the lowest death rate of America's five largest cities, improving public health became a reform priority. Concerned citizens called for better sanitation, better air, public baths, and rigorous inspection of foodstuffs like milk and meat.

In St. Louis, as in other cities, prosperous club women were among the earliest and most effective champions of the City Beautiful. Many were the daughters and nieces of women who had been active in religious charity work and Civil War relief. Although some were unmarried teachers, most were native-born high school or college graduates with growing families who had the time, and servants, to pursue their own interests in the afternoon. They formed social clubs for self-improvement. In the 1890s women began to ally their local organizations with similar groups in other cities. The National Federation of Women's Clubs rationalized the club movement and set an agenda that broadened the topics for study from art, literature, and music to civic improvement and social economy. Members of The Wednesday Club of St. Louis, the most prestigious of the local groups, were instrumental in setting this national agenda.

Club women did not usually identify themselves as feminists, a term popularized early in the century by radical young women demanding full equality with men. Many did not even support suffrage until the 1910s. Their activism grew out of the goals of progressivism that they shared with their businessmen husbands and from their own experience in urban benevolence. In 1893 Wednesday Club members joined with the St. Louis Engineers' Club to push through the city's first clean air ordinance, although lax enforcement in city hall rendered it ineffectual. Over the years The Wednesday Club study topics and weekly meetings with guest speakers became increasingly focused on civic problems, while still giving attention to literature, art, and music. Members studied and discussed at the club house; they acted in other organizations. Mary McCall was a founding vice president of the national City Beautiful organization, the American League for Civic Improvement. Charlotte Rumbold became a leader in the national parks and recreation movement through her work with the St. Louis Civic League and her position in the city's Parks Department. Some club women, such as Mary Bulkley who worked for a time at Chicago's Hull House, were ambivalent about the movement and criticized its elite conservatism.

Still others retained a primary involvement with religious organizations. Whatever their means, the impact of club women on progressive reform in St. Louis was enormous.

Elite white women were not the only women to form enrichment clubs before 1900. African American teachers like Arsania Williams led the movement for black women's clubs in St. Louis and elsewhere. Stung by white stereotyping of black women as inherently immoral and determined to provide benevolent institutions for African Americans equal to those whites created for themselves, black women's clubs addressed both literary and social concerns from the start. The National Association of Colored Women, founded in 1896, brought local clubs together in one national organization. Social services and institutions created by African American women developed an infrastructure to sustain their community through

Statler Hotel, 822 Washington Avenue. In March 1919, the National American Woman Suffrage Association held its Golden Jubilee convention at the Statler. Missouri women gained the right to vote in presidential elections on the convention's last day. Photograph by George Rothenbuescher, 1999.

segregation and later provided a base to challenge racial discrimination. Like white women reformers, however, elite black women imposed their values and activities on those they sought to help.

At the turn of the century, suffrage took a back seat to this more broad-based reform agenda. Since progressives believed the salvation of cities lay in substituting business and professional expertise for politics as usual, elite women could take part in civic life without the vote. Instead of insisting that women deserved the franchise as equal citizens, they stressed the natural and proper extension of women's influence from the home into the community. "Municipal housekeeping" did not threaten established relationships between men and women or suggest the radical potential of the ballot for women. Although a new generation of St. Louis suffragists mounted a vigorous campaign for the franchise after 1910 and sought to widen their appeal to working-class women, they did not challenge hierarchies of race, class, or ethnicity. They offered the educated white woman voter as a political counter to the African Americans or Southern European immigrants then streaming into cities like St. Louis. By convincing men, and other women, that patriotic female voters would help insure a more stable, traditional America in the post–World War I years, they finally won the ballot in 1919.

By 1900 upper- and middle-class women were not only integrating their traditional women's activities with active public roles, but they were also becoming better educated and more professional in their occupations. Well-trained, unmarried teachers in private girls' high schools and women's colleges, while not necessarily advocating alternatives to marriage, served as powerful role models for their students. Teachers in Catholic religious orders offered alternatives to marriage—a life of service to God and to their communities. Between 1890 and 1920 the number of female college graduates increased 225 percent. Progressive Era women were journalists, secretaries, domestic scientists, and child psychologists. They were better trained teachers, doctors, nurses, and artists than they had been a generation earlier.

In 1903 the St. Louis Provident Association began its own "School of Philanthropy" to train volunteer workers. Six years later it became the School of Social Economy, affiliated with Washington University, after Roger Baldwin, Washington University's first teacher of sociology and leading figure in the city's progressive movement, took control. The new name reflected the school's professional approach to social work, which, according to Baldwin, "was preventative rather than remedial, social rather than individual, civic rather than sympathetic, and scientific rather than sentimental."

The trained social worker, a professionalized version of the nineteenth-century charity worker, was more likely to be a woman than a man. New professions like social work that recruited a large number of women, tended to be in the nonprofit or social service areas, a distinction used to justify their lower pay scales. Between 1909 and 1915, more than half the masters degrees awarded by Washington University were in social work.

The "New Woman" who came of age after the turn of the century was more self-confident in the company of men because there were more opportunities for men and women to do things together on an equal basis. They shared leisure activities like tennis, bicycling, and photography. In these situations women felt comfortable being assertive, active, and collegial. Young single women, particularly, began thinking of themselves as individuals with their own career aspirations and personal goals, in much the same way young American men had always viewed themselves. Too often, however, the New Woman ran up against the old man if she attempted to take a leadership role in newly integrated businesses, civic organizations, or political associations.

Working-class women also made more urban spaces female places. They filled new jobs in offices and factories that previously had been male preserves. In 1890, 19 percent of American women were in the paid work force; by 1920 the number had risen to 23 percent. St. Louis percentages were higher: 22 percent of females over the age of ten held jobs in 1890, 30 percent in 1920. For all but African American women, the shift from domestic labor to office and factory work that started in the late nineteenth century accelerated in the twentieth. Only 10 percent of the one hundred thousand women employed in St. Louis in 1920 held professional jobs. The rest were nearly evenly divided between domestic and personal service (which included such nondomestic jobs as waitressing and hairdressing), factory work, and jobs in stores or offices.

As in the case of professional women's occupations, working-class women's jobs paid less than men's. By 1900 unions were giving men leverage in the workplace, but the American Federation of Labor excluded women from most trades and showed no interest in organizing female

workers. Women traditionally supported striking male workers in their roles as wives and daughters–some of the most disruptive activity in the 1900 St. Louis transit workers strike was the work of women–but less than 2 percent of St. Louis's female workers were themselves members of any union.

In 1902 young female garment workers formed their own United Garment Workers Association local. In 1907 Hannah Hennessey, president of Local 67, sought support from the Women's Trade Union League (WTUL), a national organization of working women and progressive upper- and middle-class reformers. One of the few women's organizations that crossed class lines, the WTUL brought local working women together with St. Louis progressives like Mary Bulkley. The WTUL supported telephone operators on strike in 1913 and helped other female workers organize and fight for better wages and working conditions. Unlike maternalistic groups such as the Young Women's Christian Association that merely instructed or protected working-class women, the WTUL tried to bring women together as equals.

Many working women were immigrants or, more often, the daughters of immigrants. Among large American cities, only Baltimore had fewer foreign-born residents than St. Louis in 1910. The city failed to attract large numbers of Italian, Slavic, Greek, or Russian immigrants at the turn of the century. But many of the women in the local labor movement were politically radical immigrants from eastern and Southern Europe, particularly young

First African American Social Workers in St. Louis. The workers were trained at the St. Louis School of Social Economy by arrangement with the Provident Association, 1917. Halftone from *Your St. Louis and Mine* by Nathan B. Young, ca. 1937. MHS Library

Jewish women employed in the garment industry. The most influential socialist in St. Louis, however, was the daughter of Kansas farmers. The devastating impact of industrial capitalism on traditional agriculture politicized Kate Richards O'Hare's family in the 1880s; her contact with labor organizer Mary Harris (Mother) Jones made her a socialist as an adult. In St. Louis, O'Hare and her husband edited a socialist newspaper, the *National Rip-Saw*, in the years before the First World War. An ardent pacifist, O'Hare spoke out against America's entry into the conflict in 1917 and served fourteen months in the Missouri State Penitentiary for publicly opposing the draft.

The Great War affected St. Louis women in many different ways. Sons and husbands left for France with the 35th Army Division. Nearly twelve hundred residents of St. Louis City and County did not come back, dying of wounds or disease before Armistice Day. Sixty-five St. Louis nurses served at a base hospital in France with the American Red Cross. Back home an intensive government propaganda campaign against all things German forced thousands of St. Louis women to suppress their Germanic cultural heritage in the name of American patriotism. Hundreds of women went to work making cartridges at Wagner Electric Company. Twenty-eight thousand others registered with the Red Cross to knit for soldiers and refugees.

Look At These Homes Now! Save Your Home! Vote For Segregation! Flier distributed during the campaign on the segregation ordinance of 1916 featured homes in the 4300 block of West Belle Place, many of which had recently been purchased by African Americans. Race Relations Collection, MHS Archives

America was probably more overtly racist in the early twentieth century than at any time since slavery. African Americans confronted organized white resistance as they moved out of the rural South and into northern cities looking for work. In St. Louis, white racism steadily intensified as African Americans arrived in greater numbers after the turn of the century. The percentage increase was small, from 6.2 percent in 1900 to 9 percent in 1920, but between 1910 and 1920 the black population grew more than four times faster than the white population. Neighborhood associations, real estate agents, and bigoted individuals managed to keep most African Americans in designated residential Negro Districts, mainly on the east end of the central corridor. St. Louisans living nearby feared that black population pressure would push the Negro District into their all-white neighborhoods. They responded by passing the most restrictive residential segregation ordinance in the nation, one that was *not* enforced only because it was declared unconstitutional.

The Segregation Ordinance of 1916 was a blow to St. Louis's progressive leadership, who had campaigned vigorously against it. Although they blasted the law as un-American and detrimental to civic progress, they failed to convince voters, who endorsed the proposal in all but four of the city's twenty-eight wards. Voters perceived West End reformers as hypocrites removed from the problems of ordinary St. Louisans. The ordinance was only on the ballot because voters had insisted that the new city charter include a provision for grass-roots referendums.

Despite appeals to civic cooperation, most progressive reformers, protected by their wealth from black incursions into their own neighborhoods, had no better record of race relations than other white St. Louisans. Two years earlier, reformers mounted the Pageant and Masque, a huge civic festival in Forest Park. The theme of the Pageant and Masque was good government, citizenship, and cooperation. Charlotte Rumbold proclaimed its goal: "If we play together, we will work together." Seven thousand St. Louisans participated in the extravaganza and four hundred thousand more sat on the grassy slope of Art Hill to watch its five-day run. The organizers made no effort to recruit black organizations or to provide roles in the production for African Americans.

The faith in expertise and rational organization that characterized progressive values benefitted women because these were skills one could gain through education and experience. Women's successes undercut theories of innate gender differences and helped to break down barriers between men and women. Modern life in all its political, social, and psychological dimensions, however, encouraged individualism at the expense of communal bonds. It eroded the culture of women expressed in voluntary, private female efforts. This happened less with religious women who continued to develop their own women's culture within the patriarchal framework of the church. Moreover, Progressive Era men were generally more willing to acknowledge women's right to a larger place in public life and to accept the evidence of their intellectual abilities when doing so did not entail relinquishing economic or political power.

With few exceptions, neither progressive men nor women challenged traditional domestic roles. Most Americans believed that domesticity was women's first responsibility, breadwinning men's. Entrenched gender expectations did not change. Perennial complaints about low pay and status for feminized professions and the absence of women in high-salaried, decision-making jobs fell largely on deaf ears, male and female. "Domestic science" rationalized and systematized domestic work, but despite an explosion of prepackaged foodstuffs prepared with new gas and electric appliances, the family kitchen remained exclusively woman's space.

The St. Louis progressive reform movement was in many ways a triumph for white women. Their collective power, building since the middle of the nineteenth century, reached its climax in a massive push for civic reform and woman suffrage. The white middle-class character of the movement, however, meant that for the most part women allied themselves with white middle-class men rather than with working-class or African American women. Sincere, committed reformers like Charlotte Rumbold, who lived in the exclusive West End, were no more able than less enlightened St. Louisans to transcend the biases of race or class.

Sources: The best analysis of progressivism in St. Louis is in Howard S. Miller, "The Politics of Public Bathing in Progessive St. Louis," *GH* 10, no. 2 (fall 1989): 2–21; Scott McConachie, "The 'Big Cinch': A Business Elite in the Life of a City, Saint Louis, 1895–1915" (Ph.D. dissertation, Washington University, 1976); Edward C. Rafferty, "Orderly City, Orderly Lives: The City Beautiful Movement in St. Louis," *GH* 11, no. 4 (spring 1991): 40–62; Elizabeth Noel Schmidt, *Civic Pride and Prejudice: St. Louis Progressive Reform, 1900–1916* (master's thesis, University of Missouri–St. Louis, 1986); and David Glassberg, *Historical Pageantry: The Uses of*

Tradition in the Early Twentieth Century (Chapel Hill: University of North Carolina Press, 1990). See James Neal Primm, *Lion of the Valley: St. Louis, Missouri* (St. Louis: MHS Press, 1998), 327–95, for both a description of the 1904 World's Fair and a clear account of the politics of local corruption, as well as Lincoln Steffens, *The Shame of the Cities* (New York: McClure, Phillips and Co., 1904). No one yet has done in-depth research into the public and personal relationships between St. Louis's leading progressive reformers or assessed the impact of women on the local movement. See also Charlotte Rumbold, *Housing Conditions in St. Louis: Report of the Housing Committee of the Civic League of St. Louis* (St. Louis: St. Louis Civic League, 1908) for living conditions on the near north side, probably the worst in St. Louis at the time but similar to areas of dilapidated housing on the south side.

Information on the 1892 conference is from the *Journal of Proceedings of the Conference of Charitable and Philanthropic Institutions of St. Louis, 1892.* Included with a record of the proceedings are descriptions of the fifty-eight participating charitable institutions. A comparison with the *Social Service Conference Yearbook, 1911–1912,* shows the impact of professionalism and greater male involvement on local benevolence administration. For professionalization of social work, see Robyn Muncy, *Creating a Female Dominion in American Reform, 1890–1935* (New York: Oxford University Press, 1991). See Ann Douglas, *The Feminization of American Culture* (New York: Noonday Press, 1998) for Protestant women's influence on social gospel ministers and vice versa. See Walter Ehrlich, *Zion in the Valley: The Jewish*

New Women. The turn-of-the-century New Woman was more confident and assertive than her Gilded Age mother. Photograph, ca. 1900. MHS–PP

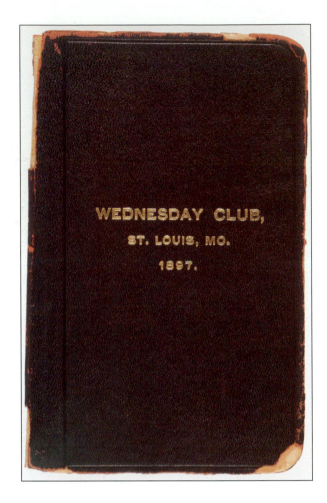

Community in St. Louis, 1807–1907, vol. 1 (Columbia: University of Missouri Press, 1997) for the role of Jewish leadership in benevolence.

Scholarship on the women's club movement includes Karen Blair, *The Clubwoman as Feminist: True Womanhood Redefined* (New York: Holmes & Meier Publishers, 1980). See also Noralee Frankel and Nancy S. Dye, eds., *Gender, Class, Race and Reform in the Progressive Era* (Lexington: University Press of Kentucky, 1992). The archives of St. Louis women's clubs are rich with sources for studying their internal history as well as the impact of clubs and club women on civic life. The WHMC–UMSL holds the papers of many twentieth-century women's organizations. See specific essays in this chapter for sources for Charlotte Rumbold, Mary Bulkley, Kate Richards O'Hare, Arsania Williams, NACW, and the St. Louis suffrage movement. *The Missouri Woman*, published from March 1915 to August/September 1919 by the Missouri Equal Suffrage League, and available at MHS, is a rich resource for the activities of suffragists and other progressive reformers. "Missouri Women and Womanhood," six scrapbooks compiled by MHS

Cover of The Wednesday Club Bylaws and Membership List, 1897. Printed by R. P. Studley & Co., 1897. MHS Library

from newspaper articles about women provide glimpses of hundreds of St. Louis women and women's organizations that were the subjects of feature stories and occasional news reports in local newspapers beginning at the turn of the century.

National statistical information on female education and employment is drawn mainly from Sara M. Evans, *Born for Liberty: A History of Women in America* (New York: Free Press, 1989). See also Clara Menger, "An Analysis of Women Workers of St. Louis, Mo, Census of 1930," an unpublished report that includes information on working women in 1920, WHMC–UMSL, and the 1900 and 1910 federal census reports.

Provident Association information is from the archives at MHS. Their reports are a window on the evolution of social service in St. Louis and would be a good source for research on women both as deliverers and recipients of social services. Roger Baldwin, like William Greenleaf Eliot earlier, played a central role in St. Louis reform movements in the early twentieth century. Research to assess his influence on local women reformers, and theirs on him, would make a valuable contribution to scholarship of this period. The Baldwin quote is from Ralph E. Morrow, *Washington University in St. Louis: A History* (St. Louis, MHS Press, 1996), 192.

The mass marketing of consumer goods and the creation of national brands changed how women cooked and cleaned in the twentieth century. See Susan Strasser, *Satisfaction Guaranteed: The Making of the American Mass Market* (New York: Pantheon Books, 1989); Susan Strasser, *Never Done: A History of American Housework* (New York: Pantheon Books, 1982); and Ruth Cowan, *More Work for Mother: The Ironies of Household Technology from the Open Hearth to the Microwave* (New York: Basic Books, 1993).

The Wednesday Club

On April 4, 1908, the members of The Wednesday Club of St. Louis laid the cornerstone for a new clubhouse at the corner of Taylor Avenue and Westminster Place in the Central West End. Designed by Theodore C. Link, architect of Union Station, and financed by the membership and their husbands, it was the club's first permanent home. The items members placed in the cornerstone that day documented the evolution of The Wednesday Club since its founding in 1890. A literary essay on Dante by Mrs. L. W. Learned lay next to a Playground Report prepared by Charlotte Rumbold for the Practical Work Committee in 1906. During the first two decades of the twentieth century, St. Louis women set much of the city's reform agenda in this building.

The Wednesday Club became a stimulus for reform because many of its members were talented, energetic women with social standing and social consciousness. Founded as a literary club where upper middle-class white women could engage in self-improvement with their peers, The Wednesday Club created an organizational structure in its first decade that encouraged members to take an activist role in civic reform. At the same time the club was able to retain its more conservative members. What appeared on the surface to be organizational rigidity was, in fact, a carefully devised strategy for maintaining the club's professed political neutrality and educational agenda. Unlike most Progressive Era reform groups, The Wednesday Club survived into its one hundredth year by becoming a forum for many ideas, but a proponent only of those that did not attract controversy.

Fifty women responded in the fall of 1889 to Cordelia Sterling's invitation to meet in her home to study the poetry of Percy Shelley. Since the Civil War many of these same women had been meeting in each other's homes for mutual cultural enrichment and creative learning. Only a few were college graduates like Amelia Fruchte, a Central High School literature teacher, but they enthusiastically joined in a self-prescribed course of study. The Shelley Club met fortnightly into the winter of 1890, discussing ideas and reading their own "stimulating papers."

The following April, half of the seventy members of the Shelley Club voted to reorganize into a women's club. The Wednesday Club, with a constitution, bylaws, and membership fee, was "to be an organized center of thought and action . . . to promote the usefulness of its members." An elected board would arrange "the program of work," and each member pledged to do her assigned share. The constitution explicitly prohibited bandage rolling or service projects that might take time and energy from serious study.

The rapid transformation of the informal Shelley Club into the highly structured Wednesday Club reflected the impact of the emerging women's club movement on upper middle-class American women. Eva Perry Moore, an 1873 graduate of Vassar College and founding member, moved to St. Louis in 1890 and brought with her an enthusiasm for club work. The same month that The Wednesday Club organized, representatives from ninety-six other clubs met in New York to form a federation of women's clubs. The Wednesday Club of St. Louis joined the General Federation of Women's Clubs in 1891 and incorporated in 1892.

Founder and First President, Cordelia S. Sterling. From Dorothea A. Maxwell, *The Wednesday Club of Saint Louis: The First Hundred Years 1890–1990.* Courtesy Landmarks Association of St. Louis.

The St. Louis Women's Club, 7600 Lindell Boulevard. Founded by affluent white women at the time of the World's Fair, the St. Louis Women's Club offered its members space for socializing and did not adopt the same educational agenda as The Wednesday Club. The membership still uses this Central West End clubhouse. Photograph by George Rothenbuescher, 1999.

The Wednesday Club met from 3 to 5 P.M. on alternate weeks. The unusual late-afternoon meeting time accommodated members who taught school; eleven of the twenty-seven women identified as charter members were unmarried and most of these were teachers. The rest had servants at home to prepare dinner. Most lived clustered between the 2500 and 4000 blocks of the West End, as befitted the wives and daughters of the city's business elite. The club limited membership for the first year to one hundred; the board accepted an average of ten women each month. Bylaws instructed the board to allocate all money collected for club purposes only. Until 1893, the club met in members' homes. Unlike some women's clubs, The Wednesday Club served only simple refreshments and held few social events. From 1896 to 1908, when the new building opened, the club rented meeting rooms at the YMCA building at Grand and Franklin Avenues.

During the first year under the new Wednesday Club structure, former Shelley Club members prepared essays on the Lake Poets, but the board also chose Christian Socialism, child labor, compulsory education, and "The Fellowship of Women" as program topics. Martha Fischel, the wife of a prominent physician and a founder of the Ethical Society, was influential in broadening the "scope of work" beyond English poets.

Discussion topics documented members' broad range of interests and rising social consciousness. They debated the wisdom of compulsory education in 1891 (the Missouri Legislature did not pass a compulsory education law until 1905). The author of one paper extolled the German compulsory system; another opposed both education and child labor laws on the grounds that the child belonged to the parent, not the state. Another argued that Germany's repressive government was cause enough to oppose its education policies. Charlotte Ware Eliot, the daughter-in-law of William Greenleaf and Abby Cranch Eliot, favored compulsory education because a democracy required informed, educated voters. No one raised economic arguments on either side of the issue.

Over the next several years the club attempted to forge a balance between literary topics and contemporary issues suggested by the membership. As the club grew larger, its membership diversified within its acknowledged homogeneity of class and race. Women who had been active in charitable organizations were usually more interested in discussing social issues than in preparing literary papers. Following the example of larger eastern clubs,

The Wednesday Club adopted standing committees, or sections, that met independently to study and prepare papers. Each section became responsible for a stated number of programs on topics chosen by the members and approved by the board. The club required every member to join a section.

Sections formed to study literature and history, science, art, current topics, education, and social economics. Social economics was originally proposed as domestic science, but after Martha Fischel assured members that social economics still applied to domestic subjects, they approved the change. The move from a literary to a departmental club gave The Wednesday Club the necessary structure for its members to develop specialized skills and knowledge for social activism—often conceptualized as "municipal housekeeping."

The Wednesday Club quickly established a structure for dealing with social action projects that enabled members to take an active role in public affairs without embroiling the club in controversy. The Practical Work Committee, composed of one representative from each section, built consensus for new projects or implemented projects on which there already was consensus—typically noncontroversial social service. In 1900 the Practical Work Committee ran a variety of small clubs and classes at 1223–1225 North Broadway, in the heart of the city's worst slums. Under the supervision of Della La Beaume, volunteers taught sewing, dancing, and deportment and ran weekly clubs for boys, working girls, and mothers. The modest budget came from club funds and donations.

In 1904 the Practical Work Committee, now under the chairmanship of Charlotte Rumbold, worked with a consortium of organizations to publicize a list of respectable boardinghouses for single women visiting or working at the World's Fair. Among its many projects, the Practical Work Committee and its successor, the Civics Section, lobbied against child labor and for juvenile protection laws, initiated an underage kindergarten, and provided penny lunches at the Lincoln School. During four months in 1915, two to four volunteers, aided by a paid cook, served lunch to nearly one hundred children a day. Children paid a penny, the Board of Education provided space and equipment, and The Wednesday Club spent $123 from its treasury.

Early on, The Wednesday Club recognized the need to separate projects they sponsored, projects they endorsed but did not sponsor, and projects undertaken by individual club members. The 1892 project with the St. Louis Engineers' Club to clean up the city's smoke-choked air forced them to confront the possibility of fatal internal conflict. Wednesday Club members averted dissension developing strategies that enabled women of the same social class but with very different interests to work within one organization.

In the 1890s St. Louis was acrid and heavy with soft coal ash that choked the lungs, blackened wash on the line, and often nearly obscured the sun. Belching domestic chimneys and factory stacks, signs of material progress in the Gilded Age, were now becoming signs of social irresponsibility. The brick company of which Cordelia Sterling's husband was president undoubtedly contributed to the pall of smoke enveloping the city. Nevertheless, in the winter of 1892 when the St. Louis Engineers' Club spearheaded a campaign for smoke abatement, The Wednesday Club sent three representatives to the organizational meetings. The Wednesday Club Smoke Abatement Committee recommended the club spend five dollars to join the Smoke Abatement Association and suggested that interested members make voluntary contributions to the cause. The board later agreed to pledge $175–one dollar for each member–and authorized the committee to invite an expert from the Engineers' Club to speak to the membership. The club made up the difference between the members' donations and the amount pledged.

The following week the members met to approve a resolution prepared by the club's Smoke Abatement Committee. Since smoke endangered health, particularly of infants and school children, and added "to the labor and expense of housekeepers," the resolution declared it had become "a nuisance no longer to be borne with submission." Club members pledged to study the issue and "by our own personal influence to urge passage of the smoke ordinances and their enforcement." The membership voted to send the resolution to the local newspapers and to dissolve The Wednesday Club Smoke Abatement Committee. The club received thirty-six votes in the Smoke Abatement Association by virtue of the $175 donation. These were distributed by lot to those members who had made individual contributions.

In 1893 the Smoke Abatement Association's efforts resulted in the first city smoke abatement ordinances, which were later declared unconstitutional. Smoke still bellowed from city chimneys, and Wednesday Club members continued to be interested in smoke abatement. In 1910 the now five hundred-member club called a mass meeting of "the women of St. Louis" at the clubhouse. At the meeting, 250 women paid to join the Women's Organization for Smoke Abatement. By 1912 that group had thirteen hundred members. Members of The Wednesday Club took leadership roles in the Women's Organization for Smoke Abatement, which continued to meet at The Wednesday Club building. But the club was a facilitator, not an active participant.

In handling the smoke abatement issue, The Wednesday Club created a policy for the club's involvement in public issues and with other organizations. At the same time they were considering smoke abatement in 1892, the board gave the Education Committee permission to open a free kindergarten at the Bethel Mission under the auspices of the club, an action, however, which assumed "no financial or other responsibilities." During the 1893 depression, the Women's Emergency Guild, made up of club members and "others invited to join with them," provided sewing work at the clubhouse for unemployed women. During World War I members met at the clubhouse to do "war work" six days a week and permitted the Red Cross to use the building as a temporary headquarters.

In the Progressive Era and beyond, members of The Wednesday Club were active in civic life in far greater numbers than could be attributed simply to their wealth, education, and social position. They continued to emphasize culture as well as civics, adding a poetics section in 1907 and a dramatic study group in 1921, to insure that the club serve the interests of all the membership and not lose sight of its original purpose. Although the literary club made the departmental club possible, ultimately the subject of study was less important than the act of study–the opportunity to exchange ideas on serious subjects with one's peers; to develop plans of action to meet specific goals; to have rooms of one's own.

Sources: The primary sources for this essay are the records of The Wednesday Club, located at the clubhouse at 12589 Ladue Road and available to scholars by written request. Specific materials consulted were board minutes; Report of the Practical Work Committee, 1904; Report of Clubs and Classes, 1900–1901; Report of the Penny Lunch Room, 1915; Dorothea Andrews Maxwell, *The Wednesday Club of St. Louis: The First Hundred Years, 1890–1990* (St. Louis: The Wednesday Club, 1990); Katharine T. Corbett, "Thought and Action: The Early Years of The Wednesday Club," unpublished paper; club yearbooks; and biographical material on members at MHS. The Wednesday Club deserves a comprehensive historical study that would explore further the two themes suggested in this essay on the early years of the club: the impact of the club and its members on St. Louis and ways in which the club adapted, or did not adapt, to social change in the twentieth century.

In addition to The Wednesday Club board minutes, information on the smoke abatement campaign is from Richard E. Oglesby, "Smoke Gets in Your Eyes," *BMHS* 26, no. 3 (April 1970); Robert Dale Grinder, "The War Against St. Louis's Smoke, 1891–1924," *MHR* 69, no. 2 (January 1975); Ernest R. Kroeger, "Smoke Abatement in St. Louis," *American City*, no. 6 (June 1912); and Joel Tarr and Carl Zimring, "The Struggle for Smoke Control in St. Louis," in *Common Fields: An Environmental History of St. Louis*, ed., Andrew Hurley (St. Louis: MHS Press, 1996).

For more on the women's club movement, see Blair, *The Clubwoman as Feminist*; Theodora Penny Martin, *The Sound of Our Own Voices* (Boston: Beacon Press, 1987); and Anne Firor Scott, *Natural Allies: Women's Associations in American History* (Urbana: University of Illinois Press, 1991). For a personal and revealing insight into the dynamics of a small-town Wednesday Club in Cape Gerardeau, Missouri, see Elizabeth Dierssen, "The Wednesday Club in Person—A Diary," at the WHMC–Columbia, and the annotated excerpt in Carla Wall and Barbara Korner, eds., *Hardship and Hope: Missouri Women Writing About Their Lives, 1820–1920* (Columbia: University of Missouri Press, 1997).

National Association of Colored Women

In 1895, a statement by a Missouri journalist prompted the formation of one of the longest-lasting and largest of all African American organizations. In a letter to the secretary of a London anti-slavery society, James Jacks, the white male president of the Missouri Press Association, charged that "the Negroes of this country are wholly devoid of morality, the women are prostitutes and are natural thieves and liars." African American women leaders throughout the United States gathered in Boston to coordinate a response. As one outcome of this meeting, they the formed the National Association of Colored Women (NACW), whose motto "Lifting as We Climb" recognzied the task these women believed lay before them.

The NACW brought together individuals and local organizations who, by setting examples of respectability and taking on matters of moral and social reform, attempted to transform the public image of black womanhood. Approximately one hundred women, representing twenty clubs and ten states, had gathered in Boston, including Mary Ford Pitts from St. Louis. She attended the conference as a delegate of the Women's Club, the Harper Women's Christian Temperance Union (WCTU),

and the Citizens of St. Louis. Bringing greetings from other St. Louis women, and provoked by Missourian Jack's disparaging words, Pitts contended that the time had come to "vindicate the womanhood of our race through the example of women's work: To ourselves, and ourselves alone we must look for progress in the future, and that progress must come through the cultivation and exercise and virtues proper to a Christian civilization."

Jack's comments were not atypical. It was common for whites to commit such indignities. Locally, for example, the Banner Buggy Company insulted African Americans with advertising campaigns that used images of "little pickaninnies" to sell carriages to white businessmen. Outraged by such affronts to their race, middle class African Americans sought to challenge prevailing white opinions about blacks by presenting themselves publicly as individual representatives of the race and as persons above reproach. Focusing on personal appearance, character, and public actions, E. M. Woods handbook, *The Negro in Etiquette* (published in St. Louis in 1899) not only provided instruction in manner and morals, but also offered an African American male's perspective on the proper deportment in relationships, for example, between women and men and between domestics and their employers. But many African American men and women viewed the activities and character of women as central to changing white attitudes and to improving the condition of the race. In St. Louis and nationally, women in particular mobilized into organizations to encourage self-development and to bring increased visibility to their reform work.

St. Louis women responded to the initial call from the NACW with moral and financial support. They also assumed leadership roles from the beginning. Pitts served on the nominating committee, but turned down a nomination to serve as a secretary for the convention. The following year, she attended the 1896 convention in Washington, D.C., along with Libbie C. Anthony, a member of the Wheatley Club and the Woman Suffrage Association, and Haydee Campbell, a public school teacher. Pitts served as second recording secretary from 1910-1912, Campbell chaired the Kindergarten Department, and Anthony held the post of NACW treasurer from 1901-1906. Proceedings from the first two meetings recorded the following St. Louis organizations as members of the national association: the Phyllis Wheatley Club; the Woman Suffrage Association; the Harper WCTU; and the Young Married Women's Thimble Club.

At the 1896 meeting Pitts shared her view of the verity of women's contribution toward racial advancement, "Never before in the history of the world has the capacity of woman been more recognized than now. It is her era of promise, a vivid reflection of exultation." And anticipating a criticism that would plague the NACW, she warned, "Women must become more considerate of their sisters, as never before." NACW women advocated a sisterhood among black women that prevailed despite their differences, but at times class divided them. NACW members believed that, as women, they shouldered the responsibility for homes and families and that they must strive for purity, wisdom, patience, and perseverance. Self-appointed representatives of black womanhood who too often emphasizing lifestyle, these privileged women frequently were accused of failing to recognize the complex issues that shaped other women's choices. Pitts took a slightly different tact. "The home must be made simpler and less an object of care and anxiety. Our dress must be determined by taste, health and utility rather than fashion and caprice. We must try to bring about freedom for the women because it will elevate them politically, socially, financially, and morally." To that end, Pitts encouraged women to start reading clubs or debating societies that would provide mental stimulation "to every careworn, tired housewife . . . so you get the women to express themselves and take her outside of herself and of the care with which her life is filled." Thus, according to Pitts, the way to relieve the burdens of life that some women struggled against was through self-improvement and institution building with the insight and means to "lift as we climb."

Building on the coordinating efforts of women's benevolent, church, and self-improvement groups, Missouri women formed the Missouri Association of Colored Women's Clubs. On July 21, 1900, Maria L. Harrison, Mary Ford Pitts, and Susan Paul Vashon organized the association in Harrison's home at 2107 Walnut Street. Seven clubs enrolled in the statewide organization, including the Harper WCTU, the Wednesday Afternoon Sewing Club, and the Orphans' Home Association, all from St. Louis. St. Louis frequently hosted the state conventions and Vashon, a former school teacher and school principal, served as president of the state association from 1901 to 1903.

Locally the members undertook an array of activities. The Harper WCTU and the Wednesday Afternoon Sewing Club established and maintained institutions, the St. Louis Colored

Orphans' Home and the Colored Old Folks' Home, respectively. The St. Louis Women's Club, over which Vashon presided, coordinated a range of activities, including raising funds to support a charity where women presented papers and attended poetry readings. For yours after the state group formed, St. Louis women coordinated a city group, the St. Louis Association of Colored Women's Clubs (SLACW). The city association, headed by Harrison, comprised some twenty-four separate clubs. In a major undertaking for a fledgling organization, the SLACW hosted the convention of the national body, which brought more than two hundred delegates and visitors to St. Louis in July 1904.

Originally, the NACW had scheduled their second day's meeting at the World's Fair, but when they heard reports of discrimination against African American women who applied for jobs at the exposition, as well as the failure to serve African Americans who sought to buy refreshments, they reconsidered their plan. One convention delegate, Hallie Q. Brown of Ohio, tested the rumors and applied for employment on the Pike but was refused a job. Margaret Murray Washington, the

"Pickaninnies" 3 for $100. Racist images such as this spurred African American club women to publicize their ongoing efforts for reform. Broadside advertisement ca. 1900. MHS Archives

wife of Tuskegee Institute president Booker T. Washington, introduced a resolution to boycott the fair. Ironically, only two weeks earlier, Washington's husband had spoken at the fair to several thousand members of the National Education Association. When a large majority of the delegates to the NACW convention supported Washington's resolution, the meeting moved to St. Paul's A.M.E. Church. During the following days, delegates heard papers on the state of African American women and reform activities of various clubs. Reaffirming their commitment to the eradication of discriminatory and humiliating behavior towards African American women, NACW speakers maintained their stance. In order to change white attitudes, they contended, black women must stress their respectability. Some of the speakers criticized trends among African Americans that the club women believed demeaned the race and violated their notions of propriety. NACW members condemned women's practice of wrapping their hair with thread to straighten it, and suggested that they realize, "God had seen fit to make [their hair] kinky." In addition, several women attacked "rag time, coon songs, and cake walks as disgraceful, vulgar, and destructive of good taste and self respect in all Colored people who indulged or tolerated them."

The affirmation of women's work in racial advancement and admonitions to women to act with respectable manners and morals characterized the dual emphasis of the NACW and its local affiliates. NACW members recognized that as women, mothers, and educators, they possessed an important capacity to influence racial advancement. On a national, state, and local level, NACW clubs and members played a significant role in challenging white prejudices, creating opportunities for African Americans, preparing black women to undertake leadership roles in their communities, and establishing networks of organizations that supported black communities. In St. Louis, these groups and the institutions they built provided a foundation for social life, political activism, and economic endeavors within African American communities even beyond World War II.

—Anne Valk

Sources: For additional information, see "A History of the Club Movement Among the Colored Women of the United States of America," Minutes of the 1895 and 1896 Convention (NACW, 1902); Elizabeth Lindsay Davis, *Lifting as They Climb* (Washington, D.C.: NACW, 1931), 42–46, 345–51; and E. M. Woods, *The Negro in Etiquette: A Novelty* (St. Louis: Buxton and Skinner, 1899). Autobiographical information on Vashon from Hallie Q. Brown, *Homespun Heroines and Other Women of Distinction* (Xenia, Ohio: The Aldine Publishing Company, 1926). See also Dorothy Salem, "National Association of Colored Women," in *Black Women in America: An Historical Encyclopedia*, eds., Darlene Clark Hine, et al. (Bloomington: Indiana University Press, 1996), 842–51; Deborah Gray White, *Too Heavy a Load: Black Women in Defense of Themselves, 1894–1994* (New York: W.W. Norton & Co., 1999); *St. Louis Republic*, 13 July 1904; and *St. Louis Palladium*, 16 July 1904, 9 May 1903, 6 June 1903, and 11 July 1903 (reports of St. Louis clubs and 1904 convention).

Arsania M. Williams

In April 1940, the Missouri State Association of Negro Teachers honored Arsania Williams with a distinguished service medal. A Testimonial Banquet, held at the Pine Street YMCA, appropriately focused on the theme "Service Along the Way." Friends, colleagues, and coworkers from professional, women's, African American, and church-related organizations presented Williams, "The Human Dynamo," with bouquets, leather traveling cases, and a book of poetry. Williams accepted the accolades and gifts with grace and expressed her view that her service offered its own rewards. She stated that she enjoyed doing some "little things because I have got the joy of giving service for fellowmen for the common good."

Williams was born in Baton Rouge, Louisiana, the third of five children of George and Julia Williams. As an infant, she moved with her parents to St. Louis. In 1895 she graduated from Sumner High School's Normal Department and began a teaching career that lasted approximately fifty years. Segregation in St. Louis necessitated the employment of African American teachers to work in schools for black children. Williams taught at L'Ouverture, Simmons, and Marshall Elementary Schools.

Teaching provided one of the few opportunities for African American women to work in a professional position under the immediate supervision of black principals and away from white men. As a result of their position of privilege relative to the majority of black men and women, many teachers, including Williams, felt called to extend their job beyond the classroom. Williams answered this call through a life of service in women's clubs, church groups, professional associations, and participation in organizations focused on the creation of opportunities for African Americans. Starting at an early age, she directed her organizational and teaching skills and seemingly boundless energy to a variety of causes.

In 1904 Williams served as the only woman on the committee charged with arranging Negro Day at the Louisiana Purchase Exposition. Ironically, Williams was also an active member of the National Association of Colored Women (NACW), an organization that decided to boycott the exposition. Williams attended and spoke at the NACW meetings in St. Louis during the World's Fair. In 1911 she participated in the establishment of and became the first chair of the Board of Directors of the Phyllis Wheatley Branch of the YWCA. She worked with women's groups at the local, state, and national levels. She served as president of the St. Louis Association of Colored Women and president of the Missouri Association of Colored Women. In the 1930s Williams took her experience and prominence in these groups to the national level, where she was elected the recording secretary and the vice-president-at-large of the NACW.

Many of the causes and issues with which Williams became involved focused on the teaching profession and, in particular, the creation of groups that would address the problems that black educators faced and assist in bettering their work. On a statewide basis, Williams became an active member of the Missouri State Association of Negro Teachers (MSANT); she served twice as president of that organization, in 1909 and 1931, in addition to holding numerous other offices. During her 1931 term as president, Williams reformed election procedures and created new offices and committees, including the post of MSANT historian. Locally, she organized the St. Louis Grade School Teachers' Association in 1917 and helped reorganize it in 1938.

As a long-time member of the Union Memorial Methodist Church, Williams tied her religious faith to her dedication to education. In 1922 she organized the St. Louis Standard Leadership Training School for church school teachers and other religious leaders and worked as the accredited dean for two decades. She also served as dean of the Women's Home Missionary Society of Missions and chair of the Interdenominational Committee of the Central West Conference of the Methodist Episcopal Church. For more than twenty-five years, she sat

on the Board of Directors of the St. Louis Christmas Carols Association.

Although service brought its own rewards, Williams received recognition for her efforts throughout her lifetime. In 1937, the Central West Lay Conference of the A.M.E. Church honored her with a Sun-Gold Plaque Achievement Award for meritorious service. The following year, Douglass University awarded her an honorary Masters of Arts degree. On March 24, 1954, Williams died at Homer G. Phillips Hospital. A woman of monumental achievement, Williams's contributions are perhaps best recalled in the 1943 *Metropolitan St. Louis Negro Directory*, which glowingly stated: "MISS WILLIAMS IS WORTHY OF THE HALL OF FAME. She is an IMMORTAL."

–Anne Valk

Sources: For information on Arsania Williams, see the *Metropolitan St. Louis Negro Directory*, 1943; the *St. Louis Argus*, 26 April 1940, and 25 March 1954; the *St. Louis Palladium*, 16 July 1904; and Arsania M.

Arsania Williams. This photograph shows Arsania as a young teacher. Halftone from *Your St. Louis and Mine*, by Nathan B. Young, ca. 1937. MHS Library

Williams's obituary in the verticle files, UMSL. See also Stephanie J. Shaw, *What a Woman Ought to Be and Do: Black Professional Women Workers During the Jim Crow Era* (Chicago: University of Chicago Press, 1996).

Working-Class Women and the WTUL

At age thirteen, Hannah Hennessey left school to work in a St. Louis garment factory. In 1902 she sewed at one of the two Marx & Haas clothing factories located at Fifteenth and Washington and at Sixteenth and Market, in what was fast becoming the city's garment district. Hennessey recruited coworkers for Local 67, a new all-female local of the United Garment Workers of America (UGWA). In 1907 she founded the St. Louis Women's Trade Union League (WTUL). Although most local WTUL chapters attracted more progressive reformers than working-class women, the St. Louis chapter was the exception. Hannah Hennessey, in cooperation with her middle-class "allies," spearheaded efforts to organize St. Louis wage-earning women in the early twentieth century.

More than six thousand women made clothing in St. Louis factories in 1907, the year Hannah Hennessey attended her first national conference of the WTUL in Richmond, Virginia. Founded in 1903 by a small group of trade unionists, social workers, and club women meeting in Chicago, the WTUL strove to bring women into the union

Women Textile Workers at the Ely-Walker Plant at Cherokee and Texas Streets. Photograph, 1918. MHS–PP

movement. The American Federation of Labor (AFL) viewed women workers as temporary and unskilled and took little interest in organizing them, even though they made up one-fifth of the nation's work force.

Progressive reformers wanted to help female workers gain entrance into AFL unions, particularly in the garment industry. They sought a cooperative relationship with working-class women, one that supported their right to fight for workplace rights and even to strike. One of the few organizations that brought women of different classes together as equals, the WTUL envisioned a membership equally divided between working-class women and their middle-class allies, who provided assistance, expertise, and support.

Hennessey returned from the Women's Trade Union League conference in Richmond determined to organize a chapter in St. Louis that would serve as a focal point for organizing efforts. Only 1,199 women belonged to the city's 204 unions, although nearly forty thousand St. Louis men were union members. The Washington Avenue garment industry, where Hennessey sewed for Marx & Haas, employed the greatest number of local female factory workers, and Local 67 became the organizational base for the WTUL in St. Louis. Hennessey and her coworkers recruited recently arrived Italian and Russian Jewish immigrants in surrounding factories to the cause.

In 1910 male and female union members struck Marx & Haas after the company locked them out for walking off the job in support of an aggrieved worker. The company brought in strikebreakers and obtained an injunction against picketing strikers, but the union fought back. Anna Sandweiss, a twelve-year-old Russian Jewish garment worker, took the platform at fund-raising meetings to tell about deplorable working conditions in the Marx & Haas factories. The local WTUL chapter supported the strikers by finding jobs for some of the women in other factories.

One month into the strike, Hannah Hennessey died of tuberculosis. Fannie Sellins, from an Irish immigrant family, became president of Local 67. She campaigned nationally for a boycott of Marx & Haas products that forced the company to close one factory and finally settle the strike. After the 1911 settlement, Sellins encouraged garment workers at Schwab Clothing at 2649 Locust Street to join the UGWA and promoted boycotts against companies that resisted worker attempts to unionize. Sellins left the UGWA when the union refused to support illegal boycotts. She was murdered in 1919 while working for the United Mine Workers of America.

In addition to organizing St. Louis garment workers, the WTUL initiated union campaigns among women in the brewing and shoe industries. There were more than four thousand female shoe workers in the city; the printing, chemical, and tobacco industries also employed large numbers of women. By 1912, 200 packers and labelers in brewery bottling departments, 400 shoe workers, and 540 garment workers were among women enrolled in fifteen St. Louis locals.

In 1913 the WTUL mounted a national campaign to organize telephone operators. St. Louis telephone operators, who belonged to a sub-local of the International Brotherhood of Electrical Workers (IBEW) Local 1, discussed strategies with other union women when the national WTUL held a convention in the city. St. Louis operators later participated in an IBEW strike against Southwestern Bell, but when Local 1 leadership settled the strike without consulting the striking telephone operators, the women moved to separate. With the support of the WTUL, they organized the Telephone Operators' Department as an independent organization within the IBEW.

Working-class women may have been drawn to the local Women's Trade Union League chapter because their middle-class allies were themselves serious activists. Two women heavily involved in league activities were Mary Bulkley and Kate Richards O'Hare, political women who scorned elite society reformers. O'Hare was an ardent socialist who had worked in a machine shop. Bulkley, a suffragist and social activist friend of Jane Addams, was also a skilled bookbinder. More of an artist than a craftsman, Bulkley never joined a union, but she understood the work of women employed in St. Louis's large bookbinding and printing industry, 489 of whom were union members by 1912.

St. Louis middle-class WTUL members contributed their time and money to initiate investigations into working conditions. They lobbied successfully for protective labor legislation that prohibited Missouri women from working more than nine hours a day and more than fifty-four hours a week. New laws also required employers to provide seats for women when they were not busy, a particular concern of department store workers. In 1915 the St. Louis WTUL chapter pressured the employers to reduce fire hazards in factories.

Both Bulkley and O'Hare advocated minimum wage legislation at hearings held in 1915 at the Planter's Hotel by the Missouri Senate Wage Commission for Women and Children. Bulkley, chairperson of the Industrial Relations Committee of the Central Council of Social Agencies in St. Louis, spoke for the nut pickers, women who removed the nut kernels from shells and were among the lowest paid female factory workers in the city. O'Hare presented the findings of her wage survey of waitresses, workers in department stores and telephone companies, and meatpackers. She determined that a working girl required at least eighty dollars a year for clothing, and that room and board in "comfortable places" cost at least five dollars a week. Nearly half the women surveyed took home less than six dollars a week. After hearing from dozens of working women, employers, and social workers, the commission determined that the minimum weekly cost of living for women in St. Louis was $8.53. Since nearly 60 percent of the workers surveyed made less than eight dollars a week, commissioners recommended minimum wage laws for women by industry.

Missouri lawmakers did not pass legislation guaranteeing women a living wage. Political lobbying and union organizing by working women and middle-class reformers of the WTUL did not dramatically improve conditions and pay for factory workers. In 1915 women were still less than 5 percent of all union workers, and those at Marx & Haas were little better off than the majority of non-union garment workers. But in 1918, when orders for war-related merchandise created a demand for labor, nearly twenty thousand St. Louis workers struck for union recognition, higher wages, and shorter hours. More than ten years of effort by the WTUL helped to insure that working women were on the picket lines with men.

Sources: Rose Feurer has done the most research on the St. Louis labor movement. See particularly her essays, "Washington Avenue Garment District," *The St. Louis Labor History Tour* (St. Louis: Bread and Roses, Inc., 1994), and "Shoe City, Factor Towns: St. Louis Shoe Companies and the Turbulent Drive for Cheap Rural Labor, 1900–1940," *GH* 9, no. 2 (fall 1988). There are few records of local branches of the Women's Trade Union League. Information consists almost entirely of WTUL convention reports that contain brief accounts of the activities of local leagues. Information about Hannah Hennessey is from Feurer, "Washington Avenue Garment District," and Nancy Schrom Dye, *As Equals and As Sisters: Feminism, the Labor Movement, and the Women's Trade Union League of New York* (Columbia: University of Missouri Press, 1980). Dye concluded that the St. Louis branch was unusual in its percentage of working women members, but more research is needed on the relationship between working- and middle-class women as well as the division of labor and responsibility in the organization. Statistics on local union membership are from the Missouri Bureau of Labor Statistics, 1901, 1908, 1916–17; Katherine L. Sandweiss, "'Among My Own People,' An Oral History of Anna Lincors's Involvement in the Men's Clothing Unions" (bachelor's thesis, Yale University, 1980) is the source for Anna Sandweiss's strike activities. Excerpts are from the Report of the Senate Wage Commission for Women and Children in the State of Missouri to the Senate of the 48th General Assembly (Jefferson City, 1915). See also Carolyn Daniel McCreesh, *Women in the Campaign to Organize Garment Workers, 1880–1917* (New York: Garland Publishing, Inc., 1985), and Margaret Ann Spratt, "Women Adrift and Urban Pioneers: Self-Supporting Working Women in America, 1880–1930" (Ph.D. dissertation, University of Kentucky, 1988).

Charlotte Rumbold

"It would be a serious mistake to minimize the personal responsibility of each man for his own conduct and environment," observed Charlotte Rumbold in 1906. "But it seems unlikely that from the ends of the earth, thirteen thousand people of all sorts of heredity and racial and national tradition should gather together in one little section of this city and deliberately choose to be dirty and diseased and lazy and criminal and poor." As a progressive reformer, Rumbold held all St. Louisans responsible for deplorable living conditions and social problems, not just the poor people who lived in the decaying tenements of the city's slums. Upper middle class, well educated, and unmarried, Charlotte Rumbold was an extraordinary example of the New Woman of the early twentieth century, who by creating new agendas for themselves helped to reshape their communities. And like other New Women, Rumbold discovered that when she challenged men's political and business interests they did not hesitate to use her gender against her.

Charlotte Rumbold was born in 1869, the daughter of a prosperous St. Louis physician, Thomas Frazier Rumbold, and Charlotte, his second wife. Two of their four daughters chose professional careers over marriage. Caroline, eight years younger than Charlotte, earned a Ph.D. in plant pathology from Washington University in 1911 and had a distinguished research career with the U.S. Department of Agriculture. Charlotte studied in Europe and New York, probably at the social work school later affiliated with Columbia University, before returning to the family home at 3862 Washington Avenue. She worked as a professional social worker and manager of the St. Louis School of Housekeeping at 1023 North Grand Avenue. Bearing all the proper West End credentials, Charlotte joined The Wednesday Club. In 1900 she helped organize a summer playground in a slum neighborhood as a project of the club's Practical Work Committee.

Convinced of the moral and social value of recreation, Charlotte joined the League for Civic Improvement's playground committee in 1902. That summer thirty-five thousand children participated in recreation programs at three Civic League playgrounds, where they also enjoyed free showers in temporary bathhouses donated by St. Louis businessmen. Along with a genuine sympathy for the poor, Charlotte shared the bourgeois conviction that cleanliness was next to Godliness. Eager to make bathing readily available to children year-round, Charlotte collaborated with Dwight Davis, another recreation enthusiast from a prominent family, to rally support for municipally financed public bathhouses. Rumbold delivered talks, illustrated with lantern slides, to civic groups in her "plain, straightforward style . . . unrelieved by quip or jest." Public health and recreation were becoming her lifework.

Charlotte Rumbold and a small group of zealous women and men succeeded in their strategy to turn a private pilot project into publicly financed urban infrastructure. Over a period of five years, St. Louis created a progressive system of free neighborhood playgrounds. Spurred by the urgent need to present a clean, healthy city to World's Fair visitors, city government authorized construction of several public baths in 1902. The city also took over the expenses for one Civic League playground in 1904 and later assumed responsibility from the Civic League for the World's Fair model playground. The following year, the city's Parks Department equipped and maintained four new playgrounds. The St. Louis Playground Association, a merger of the various voluntary playground committees, established nine more playgrounds on schoolyards and vacant lots in poor neighborhoods.

While working with the Civic League and the St. Louis Playground Association, Charlotte Rumbold was also chairing The Wednesday Club section on social economy. The 1905 topic for study and discussion was "Applied Sociology–with reference to St. Louis Activities." In November the group covered public sanitation and civic centers; in

December they took up bathhouses and housing conditions. They read the published work of Jane Addams, Charlotte's professional colleague and founder of Chicago's Hull House. Addams extolled the benefits of free playground programs that taught children democratic values through supervised group play.

In 1907 Rumbold became the first secretary of the new Public Recreation Commission, a division of the Parks Department. After the city took over the work of the St. Louis Playground Association, Rumbold became an active member of the Playground Association of America, a new national organization founded by Jane Addams and other social progressives. After 1911 Rumbold worked directly under her old public bathhouse ally, Dwight Davis, a former director of the Civic League and now St. Louis park commissioner.

Charlotte also took the study of St. Louis housing conditions out of The Wednesday Club clubhouse and onto the streets. In 1907 the Civic League Housing Committee surveyed forty-eight blocks of the worst slums in the city, a near north side area bounded by Seventh and Fourteenth Streets, Lucas Avenue and O'Fallon Street. Charlotte Rumbold wrote the committee's report based on field work conducted by graduate students from the Missouri School of Social Economy.

Filled with appalling statistics, Rumbold's report was the St. Louis echo of Jacob Riis's more famous New York exposé, *How the Other Half Lives*. Thousands of people had no bathing facilities; 134 people used four privies in one filthy tenement yard. Poignant photographs of hollow-eyed children playing in rubbish supported reformers' conclusions that community irresponsibility was as much to blame for social ills as personal deficiencies. Rumbold's text was both descriptive and interpretive; it reflected her ability to see both the benefits and perils of urban life for the city's immigrant poor. She concluded with detailed recommendations for new municipal ordinances to regulate builders and landlords.

Shortly after publication of the league's report, Charlotte drafted successful legislation requiring higher standards of tenement house construction. The greatest impact of her work, however, was to focus attention on deplorable living conditions in St. Louis and to bolster Civic League efforts toward city planning, particularly for neighborhood health and recreation services.

Because Charlotte had her own West End apartment, she understood the need for privacy denied to unmarried working women living with

their large families in cramped quarters. She argued that overcrowded apartments drove young women to seek entertainment away from home. "If the daughter of the house wants to see one of her men friends . . . she must go to a dance hall or a theater," or, what is very popular, make a trip "down the pike, Franklin Avenue from Twenty-second Street east"—a reference to the similarity between the busy north side artery and the amusement strip at the World's Fair as places where young women gathered to meet men. The choice of dance hall, Rumbold observed, determined the character of a girl's acquaintances and, quite probably, the man she would marry. She understood that everyone needed recreation and hoped to improve commercial entertainment through regulation.

Franklin Avenue was a notorious vice district, where saloon owners, ward politicians, and police collectively organized and profited from prostitution. Like nineteenth-century reformers, Rumbold feared that poor women would be lured into brothels, but rather than blaming the victims, she put the blame squarely on men engaged in "white slave traffic" and on the community that

Charlotte Rumbold. Halftone from the *Missouri Woman*, February 1916, MHS Library

Crowd on Art Hill for the Pageant and Masque of St. Louis.
Photograph, 1914. MHS–PP

allowed it to exist. In 1912 she sought to extend the jurisdiction of the Public Recreation Commission to dance halls, moving picture shows, and other places of public recreation by proposing the Rumbold Recreation Bill. The bill gained broad support from a coalition of suffragists, civic reformers, and temperance advocates but failed to pass. Her campaign, however, alienated powerful brewery, vice, and political interests who would not forget.

Under the leadership of Charlotte Rumbold, now city recreation supervisor, and Roger Baldwin, the city parks had become thriving centers of public activity by 1912. She drew inspiration for innovative programs like children's theatricals from the Playground Association of America, embracing the association's philosophy of social and moral reform through public recreation.

Many Progressive Era cities produced civic pageants in an effort to encourage community cohesion. Reformers believed that citizens who cooperated in celebrating their city's heritage would then work together to solve urban problems like vice and slum housing. Grass-roots opposition to a number of Civic League initiatives, including a bond issue for parks and a much needed new city charter, combined with increasing labor strife and racial discord to convince Charlotte Rumbold that 1914 was the right time to stage a massive public pageant on the lagoon at the foot of Art Hill in Forest Park.

Under the supervision of the Parks Department, the volunteer Pageant Drama Association hired Percy MacKaye, a professional civic theater writer, to prepare a script. MacKaye, who subscribed to Rumbold's belief in the educational value of constructive leisure, specialized in allegorical drama. The association asked him to produce a symbolic masque to follow a more traditional historical pageant by Thomas Wood Stevens. Unlike the directors of the 1904 World's Fair who involved only a narrow strata of businessmen and social leaders in meaningful roles, the Pageant and Masque organizers mounted an intense publicity campaign to draw in white ethnic groups from every part of the city. Stevens's historical pageant depicted a sanitized version of local history; MacKaye's masque was a heavy-handed morality play that showed good government vanquishing greed and corruption.

The Pageant and Masque was a stunning success. When voters passed a new city charter soon afterward, reformers believed they had finally generated grass-roots support for their reform agenda. But more likely it was the provision that permitted citizens to initiate referendums that voters endorsed, not civic cooperation or West End leadership. Segregationists immediately proposed an ordinance that would effectively make it illegal for white and black St. Louisans to live on the same blocks.

In 1915, as part of their campaign of fear, supporters of the Segregation Ordinance booked D. W. Griffith's inflammatory film, *Birth of a Nation*, at a St. Louis theater. When African American community leaders protested to the St. Louis police commissioner, he turned the problem over to Charlotte Rumbold, who as city recreation supervisor was also the city movie censor. Concluding that the timing "might be planned with diabolical ingenuity," she condemned the film's content and managed to secure a temporary injunction banning the film from opening. Once the court lifted the injunction, however, *Birth of a Nation* played to packed houses. St. Louis's black newspaper, the *Argus,* praised Rumbold's spirited, if unsuccessful, assault on segregationists. She became publicly identified with opposition to racial discrimination.

In the midst of rising public uproar, Rumbold asked the Board of Aldermen to increase recreation department salaries, including raising her own from $1,800 to $2,400. The Ways and Means Committee, composed mostly of aldermen from brewery wards, denied her increase. A public outcry forced the Board of Aldermen to hold a public hearing, which drew five hundred people. Representatives of St. Louis women's clubs and civic interest groups spoke on her behalf. Rumbold had opened public baths, a municipal dance hall, park comfort stations, and nineteen new city playgrounds in her eight years as city recreation supervisor, as well as spearheading a host of other civic improvement projects and perhaps preventing a local race riot. None of these accomplishments, however, were enough to overcome male resentment against this New Woman. A representative of the Tenth Ward Improvement Association opposed the increase for "woman material" because he knew many men who would work for seventy-five dollars a month and "could support Miss Rumbold on the salary" as well. By a vote of twenty to six the board sustained the committee's decision. One justification for the decision–that "Miss Rumbold is no voter and when she has jobs to give she never favors Republicans"–revealed the power of a gender-based political system to dismiss women's public aspirations in spite of their public accomplishments. Without the vote, women like Rumbold had no recourse against the likes of Alderman Adam Wackerman, who stormed out of Rumbold's hearing, shouting, "Woman's place is in the kitchen."

Publicly humiliated, Charlotte Rumbold resigned her position with the Parks Department in 1916 and left St. Louis for a second social service career in Cleveland, Ohio. St. Louisans passed the Segregation Ordinance by an overwhelming majority. Had the court not issued a permanent restraining order against the ordinance, progressive St. Louis would have been the largest officially segregated city in the nation.

During a national conference on civic reform held in connection with the Pageant and Masque, Charlotte Rumbold had declared that "there is nothing wrong with the citizenry of the cities; that is to say, we have good material. We only have to organize the machinery." Her belief in the essential goodness of ordinary people and in the responsibility of upper middle-class progressives like herself to set the civic agenda exemplified the best and worst of progressivism. Rumbold tried to use the power and resources of government to make daily life better for the masses of urban dwellers, but her progressive idealism also led her to underestimate the power of deeply felt class, race, and gender biases to thwart her personal and professional goals.

Sources: Charlotte Rumbold left no personal papers related to her work in St. Louis. Sources for this essay include Miller, "The Politics of Public Bathing in Progressive St. Louis"; Schmidt, *Civic Pride and Prejudice*; Glassberg, *Historical Pageantry*; Oglesby, "Smoke Gets in Your Eyes"; Donald Bright Oster, "Nights of Fantasy: The St. Louis Pageant and Masque of 1914," *BMHS* 31, no. 4 (July 1975); Daniel T. Kellener, "St. Louis' 1916 Residential Segregation Ordinance," *BMHS* 26, no. 4 (July 1970); Rumbold, *Housing Conditions in St. Louis*; Mayo Fesler, "The Municipal Outlook in St. Louis," *The American City* 2, no. 3; Report of the Housing Committee of the Civic League of St. Louis, 1908; and Report of the Public Recreation Commission, 1911–1912. Further information is available in the vertical files at MHS.

Kate Richards O'Hare

Kate Richards O'Hare was one of the most visible–some would say notorious–women in St. Louis in the years between 1911 and 1919. "In a loud, clear, carrying tone, sometimes ironical, often sneering, and generally sarcastic," she confronted St. Louisans on the steps of city hall, on the platform at political rallies, and in the witness box at public hearings. O'Hare spoke for victims of oppression, especially poor working women, and against entrenched economic and political interests. She worked tirelessly with local progressives for social change, but unlike most middle-class women she did not cast her reform agenda in nonpartisan terms. O'Hare was a socialist and editor of the *National Rip-Saw*, a socialist monthly published in St. Louis. Imprisoned in the Missouri State Penitentiary for protesting America's entry into the First World War, O'Hare's distress over conditions for female prisoners sparked a life-long crusade for penal reform. Her radical critique of America's political and economic institutions, however, did not extend to traditional domesticity. She tried, not always successfully, to integrate her career as a public activist with her responsibilities as a wife and mother.

Born the daughter of liberal Kansas farmers in 1876, Kate Richards moved to the slums of Kansas City, Missouri, when drought forced the family off the land in 1887. Her father found work as a machinist and became an ardent unionist. Although Kate earned a teaching certificate from Pawnee City Academy in Nebraska, she chose to work in the machine shop with her father rather than in the classroom. Already politicized by her childhood experiences and her family's commitment to democratic activism, nineteen-year-old Kate

embraced socialism after hearing Mary Harris (Mother) Jones, a radical labor organizer, speak in 1895. She joined the Socialist Party of America in 1901.

The following year, Kate Richards married Frank P. O'Hare, a party activist, and began her long career as a political writer and speaker. Socialism, a serious political force in the first decades of the twentieth century, attracted primarily disenchanted workers and intellectuals. Although most Americans were reluctant to support open attacks on capitalism, Socialist Party candidate Eugene Debs drew four hundred thousand votes for president in 1904 and received nine hundred thousand, about 10 percent of the vote, in 1912.

Kate O'Hare was an immediate success as a speaker on the Socialist Party circuit, traveling the

Kate Richards O'Hare with Thomas Mott Osborne in the Office of the National Rip-Saw. *Photograph, 1922. Frank P. O'Hare Collection, MHS Archives*

country with Frank to address coal miners, factory workers, and crowds of western farmers at camp meetings. During those nomadic years she had four children. In 1909 the family settled down in Kansas City where Frank found steady employment and the children attended city schools. Unlike other couples active in the Socialist Party, it was Kate, not Frank, who kept up the pace of political activity. A particularly popular speaker in Kansas, where women had long been active in left-wing causes, she soon overshadowed her husband as a party leader. In 1910 Kate ran for the United States Congress and made a creditable showing.

"Red Kate" was a fiery feminist who denounced women's economic and sexual exploitation, but she did not reject traditional marriage and the primacy of woman's domestic role. Neither did she consider abandoning, nor even limiting, her commitment to her political career. With the help of an assortment of live-in relatives, Frank took on most of the daily child-rearing chores. Whenever possible, the O'Hares integrated family life with the socialist community, whose political rallies, picnics, and educational activities made it function as an extended family. The O'Hares deliberately exposed the children to a variety of people and ideas, sending them to both public and private schools, including a Catholic boarding school.

The O'Hare family moved to St. Louis in 1911 when Kate accepted the associate editorship of the *National Rip-Saw*. Frank became the magazine's business manager. Published at 403 Olive Street, the *Rip-Saw* attracted primarily rural subscribers. Kate not only wrote for the magazine, but also sold subscriptions on her annual speaking tours. The O'Hares lived briefly at 4202 Cook and later at 3955 Castleman, both addresses in then solid middle-class neighborhoods west of Grand Avenue. They were active in the heavily German local branch of the Socialist Party; the whole family participated in its social and cultural activities. The leadership, however, considered Kate an outsider. While in demand as a featured speaker at rallies and as a spokesperson at citywide meetings, she never had great power within the St. Louis branch.

Kate's radical political views and the reformist agenda of St. Louis progressives were inherently contradictory. Reformists pushed for a new city charter that would limit the political power of the inner-city wards and the very people who were O'Hare's socialist constituents. These differences, however, did not prevent her from working with mainstream reformers on issues of common concern or from tailoring her message to their interests and sensibilities. In 1912 she assured a meeting of the Equal Suffrage League that she was "sickened by politics, but it is the only way for women to protect the home." She told West End women their own health was in danger because "a sick child in a dirty tenement" had shelled the nuts in the candy they bought for one dollar a box. By telling women their children's clothes were "stitched by a girl with a fatal disease," she appealed both to middle-class benevolence and fear of poor people.

Other St. Louisans may have disagreed with the goals of the Socialist Party, but party members were neither political nor social outcasts; by 1915 Kate O'Hare was a respected, articulate, public figure in St. Louis, as well as a nationally known political radical. She joined with members of the Women's Trade Union League, the Civic League, the Equal Suffrage League, and even The Wednesday Club to lobby against prostitution and for better working conditions, improved housing, and women's suffrage. She ran unsuccessfully for the St. Louis Board of Education. Shortly afterward in 1914, Republican Mayor Henry Kiel appointed her to a municipal committee to make recommendations for reducing local unemployment.

Everything changed when the United States entered the World War in 1917. Kate's *Rip-Saw* had been opposing possible American involvement for several years. Her anti-war protests, like those of other American socialists, escalated as the nation moved closer to combat. In April 1917, she took a leading role at a Socialist Party meeting in St. Louis that denounced President Woodrow Wilson's decision to enter the war. The government limited dissension and free speech as a means to build support for the war. Arrested in North Dakota on July 17 for giving an anti-war speech in violation of the newly passed federal espionage act, she was tried and sentenced to five years in prison.

Because there were no federal prisons for women, Kate O'Hare served fourteen months in the Missouri State Penitentiary in Jefferson City before President Wilson commuted her sentence in 1920. Appalled by the state's treatment of female prisoners, she mounted a reform campaign to improve their food, working conditions, and health care. She kept up a steady attack on the prison system while, like other female prisoners, she sewed in the prison workshop nine hours a day. Emma Goldman, the Russian-born anarchist also incarcerated in the Missouri prison for protesting the war and the draft, initially criticized Kate for her middle-class reserve and reformist politics but soon came to admire her.

Although heavily censored, her carefully crafted letters to the family became powerful testimonials and effective propaganda after Frank sent them to the *St. Louis Post-Dispatch* for publication. Her letters also revealed the complexity of her commitment to traditional family relationships, her intellectual critique of American capitalism, and her passion for institutional reform:

I hope none of you are worried about me, for I am really having a most interesting time. In Emma Goldman, and the dear little Italian girl, I have intellectual comradeship, and in my little 'dope' [drug addicted prisoner] some one to mother; in the management of the institution very interesting study, and in the inmates a wonderful array of interesting fellow-beings.

If it were not for being deprived of my loved ones, I could fully enjoy the new and unusual experience. If I could have my typewriter, and write more often to my darlings, I would be quite content to do my work here for a time. It seems so needlessly stupid that I should be deprived of the opportunity to write, when I have paid my last ounce of flesh demanded by the state at the sewing machine. There is so much I want to write while the impressions are vivid.

If I were outside today I might be speaking to a great crowd. Perhaps my empty place and silent voice will serve my comrades and my cause better than my presence.

So do not worry about me and do not be sad. I am all right and will come back to you a better wife, a more tender mother, and a wiser and more efficient comrade.

After her release from prison, Kate O'Hare found it difficult to be either a better wife or a more efficient political comrade. Although two thousand St. Louisans crowded into the Odeon Theater to welcome her home, within two weeks she was off again on a speaking tour. But the Socialist Party, decimated by the war and government persecution, was in disarray. Kate, who had never allied herself with the party's radical wing, rejected the communist alternative. She never lost her faith in socialism, however, or her disdain for capitalism, which she held responsible for the nation's inequalities and the human suffering she battled all her life.

Kate O'Hare threw her energy into humanitarian causes. In 1922 she led a trainload of wives and children of imprisoned war protesters to Washington, D.C., in the Children's Crusade for amnesty. In 1923 she published *In Prison*, the story of her incarceration, which exposed conditions in the Missouri Penitentiary and furthered her campaign against the state's policy of exploiting prison labor to underbid private firms.

The O'Hares lost their jobs with the *Rip-Saw* and left St. Louis together, living for a while in a socialist educational commune in Louisiana. In 1928 Kate divorced Frank and married a successful engineer, moving with him to California. There, as assistant state director of penology, she implemented prison reform at San Quentin. In the 1930s, she joined Upton Sinclair's End Poverty in California movement. Frank lived in St. Louis until his death; none of their children entered politics.

The most radical public figure in pre–World War I St. Louis, Kate O'Hare was never really "Red Kate," even though the contemporary press linked her views to those of anarchist "Red Emma" Goldman. Kate O'Hare was a middle-class socialist who believed Americans could build a just and more humane society by reforming their political, economic, and social institutions.

Sources: The information for this essay comes mainly from Sally Miller, *From Prairie to Prison: The Life of Social Activist Kate Richards O'Hare* (Columbia: University of Missouri Press, 1993). Since Frank O'Hare destroyed most of his ex-wife's papers, this comprehensive biography, which includes an excellent bibliography, is based largely on secondary sources and Kate's extensive body of published work. See also Bonnie Stepenoff, "Mother and Teacher as Missouri State Penitentiary Inmates: Goldman and O'Hare, 1917–1920," *MHR* 85, no. 4 (July 1991). The quote describing O'Hare's speaking style is from the *Missouri Republican*, 27 June 1915. Letter excerpted from Kate Richards O'Hare, *Selected Writings and Speeches*, eds., Phillip Foner and Sally M. Miller (Baton Rouge: Louisiana State University Press, 1982), 208–9. See also Report of the Equal Suffrage League meeting, 29 May 1912, Barbara Blackman Scrapbook, MHS, and Marla Martin Hanley, "The Children's Crusade of 1922," *GH* 10, no. 1 (summer 1989). For information on socialism in St. Louis, see Socialist Party Papers, WHMC–UMSL.

Board of Lady Managers at the 1904 World's Fair

When the Louisiana Purchase Exposition opened in 1904, women were everywhere on the Forest Park fairgrounds. They waited on tables and performed in theatrical attractions on the Pike; at least a dozen held the contracts for concessions and managed their operations. Women worked as clerks and secretaries for the Louisiana Purchase Exposition Company (LPEC). They created sculpture and designed landscapes for the fairgrounds. Nearly half the press corps was female; photographer Jessie Tarbox Beals captured the most sought-after images of the fair. They served as hostesses for the state buildings and on the commissions that built them. Women exhibited their work next to that of men and were judged by the same standards. Men and women together planned and ran the Model City exhibit, where they promoted progressive theories of city planning, social welfare, and early childhood education. Ironically, in spite of such extensive female participation at the fair, the record of the official Board of Lady Managers (BLM) was probably the least noteworthy.

In tune with women's growing participation in public life, fair organizers planned to exhibit women's work along side that of men and judge it by the same standards, but when the national commission for the 1904 World's Fair appointed twenty-four women to a Board of Lady Managers in 1901, they gave the group responsibility for "all the work pertaining to women." Board members struggled among themselves, with fair administrators, and with the press over what that work should be. Their failure to fashion a meaningful role for the board at the World's Fair reflected, in part, their own ambivalence about the place of women in turn-of-the-century America.

The powerful precedent for women's work at world's fairs was set by the Board of Lady Managers for the 1893 Chicago fair. There, the 117-woman board constructed a building where women exhibited their work and met to discuss women's issues. Led by the dynamic and very rich Bertha Potter Palmer, the Chicago BLM used the fair to celebrate women's culture as defined by the wealthy volunteer board members. Palmer's financial resources and contributions from women's organizations made the Women's Building possible. While the press patronized the BLM and gleefully reported any sign of internal dissension, they respected the millionaire Palmers. Most people, particularly women, considered the Chicago Women's Building a success.

The St. Louis Board of Lady Managers met for the first time in New York in 1902. They elected Appoline Blair, the only St. Louisan, as president. Appoline's husband James was the grandson of Frank Blair, a local Civil War hero whose wife had been a founder of the St. Louis Children's Hospital. James was chief legal counsel for the LPEC. Not prominent in civic betterment or club work, thirty-five-year-old Appoline owed her appointment to her own social status and her husband's position. The Wednesday Club proposed for membership Eva Perry Moore, former club president, president of the Missouri Federation of Women's Clubs (MFWC), and a leader in the national federation, but David R. Francis, president of the LPEC, refused to appoint her. Many of the other board members, however, were accomplished women with years of women's club or business experience. Their first act as a board was to take a public stand against the "debauched" entertainment that had drawn millions to the Chicago Midway in 1893. The national press relentlessly ridiculed the board's opposition to "Hoochee Coochee" dancers, setting a dismissive tone that persisted in subsequent coverage of their activities.

The most important question the board debated at their first meeting was whether or not to have a Women's Building. None of the board members supported a separate building for women's exhibits, believing firmly that men's and women's work should stand together in the exhibit halls. They voted to construct a Hall of Philanthropy, however, as a meeting place and showcase for women's social services activities. The Wednesday Club spearheaded a drive by the MFWC to cooperate with the Board of Lady Managers in creating the Hall of Philanthropy. The idea for the building originated in a 1901 committee, headed by St. Louisan Charlotte Stearns Eliot, to develop ideas for MFWC participation at the fair. After considering "southern scenes of plantation life" and a model tenement, they rejected both ideas in favor of a building to showcase exemplary projects in "practical sociology" and to provide a forum for discussing new theories of institutional care. Although The Wednesday Club preferred to sponsor a historical pageant, they supported the Hall of Philanthropy because it could also serve as a women's building and be a lasting memorial to the fair. In 1902, when the BLM and a committee from the MFWC met to endorse the Hall of Philanthropy, The Wednesday Club assumed responsibility for soliciting funds from members of the national General Federation of Women's Clubs. They raised only four thousand dollars, far short of their goal. The MFWC abandoned the project and used the money to entertain visiting club women and other dignitaries on the fairgrounds.

Without the Missouri Federation of Women's Clubs' support the BLM had no money to build

anything. The Louisiana Purchase Exposition directors gave them a small entertainment budget but made no provision for building funds. Moreover, unlike the Chicago BLM, the St. Louis BLM did not have a wealthy benefactor, and Francis's refusal to appoint Eva Moore probably discouraged wealthy local women from becoming more involved. Unwilling to raise its own funds, the Board of Lady Managers accepted the offer of rooms in the Eads Physics Building on the new Washington University campus, leased to the LPEC for the fair. The little classrooms, suitable only for offices and small gatherings, were inappropriate for the meetings and displays planned for the unrealized Hall of Philanthropy. Recognizing that by limiting their space the LPEC had effectively limited their activities, BLM president Appoline Blair complained: "It has taken 50 years of hard work to put women on an equality with men . . . yet we will have no building." Despite the BLM's clear statements to the contrary, the press failed to understand that the women did not want a separate exhibit building, but as men's equals, they expected to have some of the LPEC resources to spend as they saw fit. Men controlled more than $15 million appropriated or raised for the fair. The BLM controlled only the three thousand dollars that men had granted them.

The BLM did have two uncontested responsibilities: selecting female judges for

Board of Lady Managers, Louisiana Purchase Exposition. Photograph, 1904. MHS–PP

integrated exhibits and serving as official hostesses for the fair administration. With their small classroom building and smaller budget, they turned their attention to planning social functions—and too often turned on each other. Bickering among the board members delighted the press. Despite her administrative inexperience, However, Appoline Blair was a dedicated promoter of the fair, speaking to civic groups while she searched for a meaningful role for the BLM. And while she publicly criticized the fair's directors, she never defied them.

Appoline Blair's term as BLM president ended abruptly when her husband, a vocal proponent of good government and business integrity, was forced off the exposition's Board of Directors for robbing a client's trust fund for personal gain. The Blairs left St. Louis in disgrace before the fair opened. Margaretta Manning from Albany, New York, replaced Appoline as board president.

An experienced club woman with political connections in Washington, Manning successfully lobbied key congressmen to withhold a loan to the LPEC unless it included one hundred thousand dollars earmarked for the Board of Lady Managers. With sufficient money in hand, the BLM decorated their meeting rooms, entertained hordes of dignitaries, and discussed sponsoring a drop-in nursery on the fairgrounds. Instead of taking on child care, however, they helped fund the Model City nursery facility.

The BLM's only other official duty was to select female judges for gender-integrated exhibits. Manning recruited an impressive list of distinguished women. Jane Addams of Hull House evaluated exhibits in social economy. Respected women scientists judged electricity and horticulture exhibits. She appointed four members of The Wednesday Club to judging committees, but because the Louisiana Purchase Exposition Company exacted no penalty from exhibit organizers for failure to identify female entries, all-male juries evaluated much of the work of women. Only thirty-two of two hundred juror positions actually went to women.

The Lady Managers of the 1904 World's Fair were not the foolish, squabbling women ridiculed in the press for having no greater purpose than to entertain and be entertained. Neither were they as effective as the energetic, committed women whose Chicago Women's Building celebrated women's culture in 1893. There were not enough of them; they had few local connections; they were unwilling to raise money. They even returned some of their federally mandated appropriation.

As twentieth-century New Women, the St. Louis Board of Lady Managers found themselves in two predicaments that the nineteenth-century woman had not faced. First, they believed in greater equality. If they were to be judged equally with men in integrated exhibits, they felt entitled to a more equitable share of the fiscal and political power. The St. Louis BLM conceived of integration as a means to equality, while Chicago BLM stressed women's and men's differences. They had no expectations of equality and drew naturally on their own resources and female connections for support.

Secondly, if the women were clear about what they gained by integration, they were less clear about what they gave up. They recognized the need to promote some kind of women's culture, even if it was just a place where women could come together. Without a special place for women, there was no way to call attention to their achievements, no opportunities for informal discussion, no role models—no celebration of women's culture. This was particularly important in the face of the scorn, ridicule, and misrepresentation that the BLM and their efforts received in the press. The Board of Lady Managers did not understand or articulate their needs as well as they might have, but they struggled to balance the benefits and drawbacks of the first gender-integrated world's fair.

Sources: Information is from Louisiana Purchase Exposition Company Papers, MHS, and the published report of the Board of Lady Managers, as well as the *Post-Dispatch* and *Globe-Democrat* in years leading up to the exposition. See Jeanne Madeline Weimann, *The Fair Women* (Chicago: Academy Chicago, 1981) about the Chicago Board of Lady Managers; Mary F. Cordato, "Representing the Expansion of Women's Sphere: Women's Work and Culture at the World's Fairs of 1876, 1893 and 1904" (Ph.D. dissertation, New York University, 1989); and Virginia Grant Darney, "Women and World's Fairs: American International Expositions, 1876–1904" (Ph.D. dissertation, Emory University, 1985). Information about the Missouri Federation of Women's Clubs' and The Wednesday Club's participation at the fair is from The Wednesday Club Archives at the clubhouse. Little or no published research exists about female concessioners or other women who worked on the fairgrounds, with the exception of Jesse Tarbox Beals.

See also Robert Rydell, *All the World's a Fair: Visions of Empire at American International Expositions, 1876–1916* (Chicago: University of Chicago Press, 1984); Kathleen Moenster, "Jessie Beals: Official Photographer of the 1904 World's Fair," *GH* 3, no. 2 (fall 1982); and Alexander Alland, *Jessie Tarbox Beals: First Woman News Photographer* (New York: Camera/Graphic Press, 1978).

Florence Hayward

Assertive and ambitious, Florence Hayward was a successful freelance writer in 1901 when St. Louisans began planning a world's fair. She considered herself a New Woman, equal in ability to men of her race, education, and experience. Determined to play a role in the Louisiana Purchase Exposition, Hayward negotiated a position on the all-male Board of Commissioners. A self-styled, self-made woman, Hayward rejected women's collective efforts for equality, arguing instead that individuals receive equal treatment based on merit and self-promotion. Although she made valuable contributions to the success of the fair, in the end the male leadership did not reward her with the power and recognition she felt she had earned.

In 1901 Florence Hayward, a graduate of Mary Institute and Washington University, lived with her parents at 348 North Spring Avenue in the West End. A freelance journalist specializing in magazine travel articles, she was seldom home. Hayward prided herself on her ability to write on everything from "pig iron to grand opera" and to sell her stories. She used her own success as evidence that women could achieve equal pay and status with men through their own talent and hard work. A founding member of the gender-integrated St. Louis Artists League, Hayward was not a club woman, did not identify herself with women's issues, and professed no interest in woman suffrage.

Through her business connections Hayward was able to warn the Louisiana Purchase Exposition Company (LPEC) directors that a potential contractor had an unsavory reputation. As a reward for this information, she requested an appointment as a roving commissioner to European countries. David R. Francis, the president of the LPEC, agreed, asking her to use her personal and professional connections to promote the fair overseas, particularly with women.

Neither Francis nor Hayward consulted the fair's Board of Lady Managers (BLM) before making the appointment. The BLM, who believed they had jurisdiction over all women's activities at the fair, protested. Hayward had already alienated them by insisting on full credit for the decision to integrate the exhibits of men and women. Dismissing the BLM's objections, Hayward left for England in 1902.

Although Hayward traveled throughout Europe promoting the fair, her major accomplishment was acquiring for exhibit gifts Queen Victoria had received for her Golden Jubilee

in 1887 and historical items, mostly manuscripts, from the Vatican. She sent businesslike, but deferential, reports to Francis. When she returned to St. Louis, Francis put her in charge of the historical exhibits in the fair's anthropology division, a responsibility originally assigned to Pierre Chouteau III. Apparently, Chouteau had made little progress. Hayward took over with characteristic drive and self-assurance. She delivered exhibits celebrating the progress of man in the Mississippi valley from prehistory to 1904 that not only emphasized the positive impact of European culture, but also supported evolutionary theories of social progress promoted in exhibits throughout the fairgrounds.

The only woman on the fair's governing board, and often documented in photographs of LPEC officials, Hayward appeared to be a major figure in the administration. Her influence, however, was far less than the historical record seemed to show. She had no administrative or managerial role other than publicizing the fair, acquiring exhibit items, and organizing several successful exhibits. She did not achieve any more equality with male administrators than the women who served on the ineffectual Board of Lady Managers.

Rolla Wells, Frank D. Hershberg, Florence Hayward, David R. Francis, Archbishop John Glennon, and Vatican Commissioner Signor Coquitti at the Opening of the Vatican Exhibit at the Louisiana Purchase Exposition. Photograph by Frances Benjamin Johnston, 1904. MHS–PP

Hayward took away bittersweet memories of her fair experience. She thought her work the high point of her career but resented the fact that she had little to show for it. She became obsessed with her belief that David R. Francis had not publicly credited her with acquiring the Queen's gifts. The local press had indeed acknowledged her efforts at the time, praising her pluck and negotiating skills, but the credit that counted, credit from the men who ran the fair, never came. When Francis published his history of the fair in 1913, he did not mention Hayward's role in acquiring the Queen's gifts. She never forgave the slight.

In 1904, twenty million people came to the World's Fair to get a glimpse of the future, to see what changes the twentieth century might bring. They were more open to technological change than to social change and its consequences. For all its progressive promises, on balance the fair did as much to justify the status quo as it did to energize reform. The New Women at the fair knew they were the equals of men, and by 1904 many of the men agreed. The problem was not in the proposition but in its interpretation and implementation.

Sources: For additional information, see Johnson, *Notable Women of St. Louis*; David R. Francis, *History of the Louisiana Purchase Exposition*; and the LPEC Collection, MHS. See also *Post-Dispatch*, 14 February 1904, and *World's Fair Bulletin* (December 1902), 22.

Lillie Rose Ernst

When she elected to not marry, Lillie R. Ernst threatened a social order based around patriarchal families and an economic order based on the primacy of men's work. Ernst, an accomplished educator and administrator whose work for the St. Louis public schools spanned more than forty years, succeeded through ambition, talent, and with the support of women allies. Her life illuminates aspects of the New Women of the early twentieth century. That cohort of middle- and upper middle-class women born in the late nineteenth century were among the first generations to benefit from expanded access to higher education. Ernst and her colleagues were ambitious professionals who chose to place work, social reform, and relationships with women at the center of their lives. Many lived in "Boston Marriages" with other professional women who shared their households and built intimate partnerships that were widely accepted yet seldom discussed. As they moved into professional careers,

such women challenge existing gender relations through their growing public presence as teachers, reformers, and government workers. Ernst and her colleagues also challenge historians who sought to understand the relationships that such women shared with each other.

Born in St. Louis on September 14, 1870, Ernst attended St. Louis public schools and Washington University. Beginning as a botany teacher at Central High School, Ernst slowly rose through the ranks to hold the position of principal at Cote Brilliante School from 1907 to 1920. As an educator, Ernst encouraged students to find moral and spiritual fulfillment through their appreciation of nature and art. She told students in an 1920 address, "It is our playtime that should net us re-creation, enthusiasm for work, joy for living, ever-widening fields for thought, deeper thrillings of the soul, reverence, and an ever growing consciousness and comprehension of truth and beauty and law." With such an appreciation for the importance of artistic self-expression, Ernst became a mentor for the Potters, the small group of young women who produced the monthly literary and artistic magazine, *The Potter's Wheel*.

In 1920 Ernst overcame opposition to become the first woman appointed as Assistant Superintendent of Instruction for the St. Louis public school system. Some St. Louis educators considered Ernst's views, her outspokenness, and her very presence as a woman threatening. As the male principals who organized to oppose Ernst's nomination as assistant superintendent noted, the promotion of a woman principal was objectionable because "such a promotion would tend to disrupt the school system." Yet with the support of the League of Women Voters and members of the school board, her nomination held. After six years of service Ernst was demoted to the principalship of Mark Twain School. She served as assistant superintendent again from 1929 to 1934, and again was demoted to principal of Blewett High School, a position she held until her retirement in 1941. Although the reasons for her movement in and out of the job of assistant superintendent are not known, it was perhaps due to the controversy she caused as an unmarried professional woman. Despite the occasional setbacks, throughout her career, she worked to improve the city's schools, advocating reforms of the Board of Education, instituting procedures to improve the retention of high school students, and pushing for the creation of a pension plan for retired teachers.

For New Women like Ernst, a successful career provided excuses not to marry and brought financial independence that freed them from marrying as a matter of economic necessity. For many years she lived with her two unmarried sisters at 6058 Kingsbury Avenue. Released from the responsibilities of marriage and motherhood, Ernst made a life-long commitment to social reform and civic activism. Her numerous activities included involvement as a founding member and one-time vice president and president of the Washington University Alumnae Association; a board member of the St. Louis Children's Hospital and the St. Louis Urban League; and a member of the Humanity Club, Wednesday Club, and the League of Women Voters. An avid naturalist, Ernst helped lead the St. Louis Bird Club and climbed mountains even in the last years of her life. Throughout her career, Ernst received recognition for her efforts in the field of education. Washington University granted her an honorary degree in 1907 and in 1931 the Women's Advertising Club honored Ernst as one of the ten most achieving women in St. Louis.

Part of Ernst's notoriety in her hometown derived from her appearance. At the same time that St. Louisans looked to Ernst as a leader in education, newspaper articles that covered her career seldom failed to mention her "mannish dress." Photographs that accompanied such articles depict Ernst in spectacles, ties and suit coats, and with hair pulled closely to her head. But while the newspaper writers perceived Ernst's appearance as masculine, it is impossible to know what impression Ernst intended to convey through her dress. By her unconventional demeanor Ernst proclaimed her difference from other women of the time. While contemporary readers might interpret Ernst's behavior as sexually transgressive, little evidence directly addresses Ernst's sexuality.

Ernst's private life is shrouded in secrecy, but provocative snippets reveal the intimate relationships Ernst shared with other women. The Potters, some of whom knew Ernst from their days as Central High School students, adoringly described their mentor as a "Blond Brute and Star-of-our-Existence," and themselves as "idolatrous females worshiping a yellow-haired Amazon." While the Potters' statements indicate that Ernst served as a figure of intrigue and adoration, other historical records hint at the possibility of lesbian love. Leonora B. Halsted, a St. Louis author and fellow member of the Humanity Club, willed her estate to Ernst upon her death in 1929, in "appreciation of her devoted care for many years,

and of my abiding love." In turn, when Ernst died fourteen years later, she willed part of her estate to another woman friend (an unmarried school teacher), with a provision that when her beneficiaries died, the remainder of the estate would go to Washington University to establish the Leonora B. Halsted Fund to aid needy students. In an era before the gay liberation movement, prejudice and women's own lack of self-definition as lesbians conspired to keep Ernst and her contemporaries silent about their personal lives. Thus we can only extrapolate as to how Ernst understood her own sexuality and characterized the passionate relationships she enjoyed with other women.

–Anne Valk

Sources: Quotation of the Potters' description is from Carolyn Risque, "The Pursuit of the Ideal"; other quotations from Leonora B. Halsted's will, #70230, Probate Court, St. Louis Civil Courts Building; Lillie Ernst's 1920 speech is reprinted in *The Potter's Wheel* 3, no. 9; and male teachers' opposition to Ernst's appointment is from the *Post-Dispatch*, 14 April 1920.

Lillie Rose Ernst. Photograph by the Parrish sisters, ca. 1910. MHS–PP

For additional information, see Official Proceedings of the St. Louis Board of Education 36, 186–87; 50, 839–40; Beverly D. Bishop, "The Potter's Wheel: An Early Twentieth Century Support Network of Women Artists and Writers" (master's thesis, University of Missouri–St. Louis, 1984); Margaret Haley Carpenter, *Sara Teasdale: A Biography* (New York: Schulte Publishing Company, 1960); Leonora B. Halsted and Lillie R. Ernst wills; *Lillie R. Ernst Memorial Tribute*, St. Louis Bird Club, 1944. See also the *Post-Dispatch*, 13–14 April 1920; 7 September 1926; and the *Globe-Democrat*, 4 May 1931; 1 September 1934; 7 December 1943; and 11 December 1943.

Despite the paucity of information about lesbian lives in St. Louis before World War II, a growing body of historical literature now illuminates broader aspects of lesbianism during this period. General sources regarding women's romantic friendships and lesbian life in the early twentieth century include Lillian Faderman, *Odd Girls and Twilight Lovers: A History of Lesbian Life in Twentieth-Century America* (New York: Columbia University Press, 1991); John D'Emilio and Estelle B. Freedman, *Intimate Matters: A History of Sexuality in America* (Chicago: University of Chicago Press, 1998); Elizabeth Lapovsky Kennedy, "'But We Would Never Talk About It': The Structures of Lesbian Discretion in South Dakota, 1928–1933," in Ellen Lewin, ed., *Inventing Lesbian Cultures in America* (Boston: Beacon Press, 1996).

Lucille Lowenstein and the Missouri Children's Code

The daughter of a prosperous Jewish businessman and civic leader, Lucille Bernheimer began life in a luxurious home at 3421 Washington Avenue. Before she was ten her mother died and her father lost his business. Lucille contracted tuberculosis and never finished high school. Her father died suddenly in 1912 when Lucille was twenty-four. She married Maurice Lowenstein the same year, only to see him die two months after the wedding. At age twenty-six Lucille became a wealthy widow with no children or parents to care for, no education or career aspirations, and no financial need for a job. She retreated to her sister's St. Louis home convinced her life was over, but only five years later, Missouri reformers thanked Lucille Lowenstein for coordinating a successful campaign for child welfare legislation.

Years later, after a distinguished career in social service, Lucille Lowenstein Milner attributed the redirection of her life to advice she received from Rachel Stix Michael, a family friend and older woman who had turned to volunteer work after the death of her only child in 1894. "I have never forgotten that first talk with Mrs. Michael," Lucille recalled. "She told me of a world which to that moment never existed for me—the world of the poor, the hungry, the out of work." Rachel Michael encouraged Lucille to leave St. Louis and study social work at the New York School of Philanthropy. Although Lucille returned to St. Louis after graduation in 1916, she moved permanently to New York in 1919, where she helped found the American Civil Liberties Union (ACLU). She was the executive secretary of the ACLU for twenty-five years.

During the three years Lucille Lowenstein spent in St. Louis before joining the ACLU, she became an effective lobbyist who could unite women's organizations with other progressive groups in a common cause. As executive secretary of the Children's Code Commission, she lobbied the Missouri Legislature to adopt a comprehensive program of child welfare laws and coordinated the grass-roots effort that resulted in some of the most advanced child welfare legislation in the nation.

In 1915, responding to pressure from welfare, civic, and labor leaders, Governor Elliot W. Major appointed the first Missouri Children's Code Commission. Six women were among the twenty-four volunteer members, a who's who of Missouri social progressives headed by Roger Baldwin, St. Louis juvenile court officer and former faculty member of the Washington University School of Social Work. Other St. Louisans included Eva Perry Moore, prominent both locally and nationally for her work with the Federation of Women's Clubs, and Josephine Poe January, secretary of the Missouri Consumer's League. As volunteer executive director, Lucille Lowenstein coordinated the work of the commission's subcommittees charged with collecting data on conditions affecting children throughout the state. The commission drafted fifty-two bills to bring before the legislature in 1917.

The Children's Code included a bill to give every county a juvenile court. Others authorized special care for retarded and disabled children, free use of public schools as community centers, and free medical examinations for all school children. The code affirmed the right of unmarried women to raise their own children under the mother's pension program first enacted in 1911. Missouri had enacted child labor and compulsory school attendance laws in 1905, and the commission proposed strengthening both. Members recommended compulsory full-time school attendance to age sixteen for all children. They advocated raising the age of consent for girls from twelve to fifteen. The code covered all areas of child welfare and if adopted would have made Missouri a leader in protective legislation for children.

As chief lobbyist for the Children's Code Commission, Lucille Lowenstein moved to Jefferson City for the 1917 legislative session. An active suffragist, she shared a hotel room with Edna Gellhorn, who was lobbying the legislature for the vote. She quickly learned the intricacies of state government and the methods politicians used to subvert unpopular bills. Although the Missouri State Teachers' Association and the Missouri Federation of Women's Clubs endorsed the nonpartisan child welfare bills, the General Assembly rejected most of the significant proposals. Proponents realized they had not generated broad enough statewide support and made plans to arouse the public before the next legislature assembled in 1919.

Lucille Lowenstein and the Code Commission sought the help of influential women's organizations. By fall 1918 the Women's Christian Temperance Union, with chapters in small towns all over Missouri, had endorsed the code. Representatives of the Women's Trade Union League spoke to unions statewide and initiated a letter-writing campaign. The Missouri Federation of Women's Clubs, the Missouri Women's Committee on National Defense, and the Equal Suffrage League all publicized the code. In the six months before the General Assembly convened in January 1919, the Missouri Children's Code Commission and its allies–churches, civic groups, and women's organizations–blanketed the state with publicity.

This time the legislature passed twenty-five of the most important recommendations, including establishment of a state Division of Child Hygiene. Missouri became one of only three states with compulsory education for mentally retarded children. The new code was a model of legislation emulated nationally by child welfare experts.

While Lucille Lowenstein lobbied for child welfare, she also protested United States' involvement in the First World War. She gave encouragement to her friend Roger Baldwin, imprisoned in New Jersey for his anti-war stand. In 1919 she decided to leave St. Louis and study the labor movement firsthand by making artificial flowers in a New York sweatshop. Her venture into working-class life ended with her marriage in 1920 to Joseph Milner, a university professor.

Although she was the mother of newborn twins, in 1920 Lucille accepted the position of executive secretary to the newly founded American Civil Liberties Union from its director, Roger Baldwin. Her wealth enabled her to pay for child care, live in the suburbs, and commute to New York City. She remained with the ACLU for twenty-five years. In 1954, when McCarthyism had made civil liberties a national issue, she published her memoirs, *Education of an American Liberal*, in which she chronicled many of the ACLU's court battles from an insider's perspective.

Lucille Lowenstein Milner began her national civil rights career as a St. Louis progressive reformer. Her work on the statewide campaign for the Children's Code taught her the political power of coalition. The fight for the Missouri Children's Code also demonstrated the ability of organized women to effect change when they agreed on an issue like child welfare that crossed boundaries of class, religion, and ethnicity.

Sources: Information on the battle for code is taken from Peter Romanofsky, "'The Public is Aroused': The Missouri Children's Code Commission, 1915–1919," and the quotation is from Lucille Milner, *Education of An American Liberal* (New York: Horizon Press, 1954), 28. See also "25 Years of 'Adventure for Freedom,'" *Globe-Democrat*, 6 June 1954; Lucille Lowenstein Milner obituary, *Post-Dispatch*, 18 August 1975; and John W. Leonard, ed., *The Book of St. Louisans* (St. Louis: The St. Louis Republic, 1906). Any extant Lucille Lowenstein Milner Papers were in the possession of Peter Romanofsky in 1974. For further information on the Missouri Children's Code legislation passed in 1917 and 1919, see Missouri Statutes, available locally at the Saint Louis University and Washington University Law Libraries.

Missouri was the first state to adopt a mother's pension law, but benefits were initially limited to widows in St. Louis and Kansas City. The legislation also created the St. Louis Board of Children's Guardians to administer the program and to regulate child placements in foster homes and orphanages. See *Proceedings of the National Conference of Charities and Corrections* (National Council of Social Work Practice, 1914).

Young Women's Christian Association

Shortly before the Louisiana Purchase Exposition opened in the spring of 1904, young women began arriving in St. Louis from rural Missouri and Illinois looking for work and an opportunity to participate in the excitement of urban life. Dr. Mary McLean

YWCA Building. Halftone of a photograph by Ashen-Brenner, ca. 1928. From *Missouri's Contribution to American Architecture* by John Albury Bryan. MHS–PP

convinced a group of women from local Protestant churches to open a temporary home to shelter female transients "from temptation in all its forms." After the fair closed, several of the founders decided to keep the home open and broaden its mission by affiliating with the Young Women's Christian Association (YWCA), an eastern-based organization dedicated to Christian social action. Motivated by the same religious zeal that had led similar women to open homes for working women in the nineteenth century, the founders of the St. Louis YWCA joined a highly structured national organization dedicated to serving the educational, physical, social, and spiritual needs of "industrial girls." In 1912, after several years in a renovated house at 709 Garrison Avenue, they opened a modern facility at 1411 Locust Street designed to implement their fourfold mission. As the needs of girls and women changed in the twentieth century, so did the programs of St. Louis YWCA.

The YWCA movement began in the United States in 1858, when a Prayer Circle and Ladies Christian Association in New York established a boardinghouse for the "temporal, moral and religious welfare" of working women. In other cities, middle-class churchwomen founded organizations with the same goals, including in 1868 the St. Louis Women's Christian Association (WCA). When a national YWCA governing body formed in 1871, the

local WCA did not affiliate with it. The organization inspired by Mary McLean in 1904, joined the national movement in 1907, but its activities and administrative structure followed the YWCA program from the beginning. By the turn of the century the national YWCA was training organizers and administrators, called secretaries, to staff local branches. This meant that a professional staff, working with volunteers, implemented the comprehensive range of services dictated by the mission. Also, by affiliating with the national association, YWCAs in segregated cities like St. Louis found themselves in an organization that had African American branches in northern cities and espoused interracial cooperation.

The St. Louis YWCA opened its first facility in 1905 in a house donated by Samuel M. Dodd at the corner of Garrison and Lucas Avenues. Lillian Trusdell, the first resident secretary, was joined by General Secretary Hester McGaughey, who was charged with running the four specialized departments—educational, physical, social, and spiritual—under the direction of a volunteer board. The following year they opened a cafeteria and restrooms in the Holland Building for women working in the business district and an Extension Department to work directly with female factory workers. Although YWCA personnel sought to be a moral influence on the workers, they also pledged to study wages and working conditions to "procure needed improvements." Within several years, the Extension Division was doing service work in the Bemis Bag Factory and the Home Cotton Mills.

In 1907 the WCA released its training school, which united with the YWCA's Education Department. Mrs. C. C. Rainwater, who headed the school since its inception, joined the YWCA board and helped to expand its class offerings. To fulfill its commitment to physical education and health, a special concern of Mary McLean, the YWCA built a gymnasium in the Dodd building. McLean also sponsored instruction in posture, health, and sex-hygiene. In 1910 the YWCA added an Employment Department and a Clerical Division, both geared toward raising the skills of job applicants and helping them find employment in healthful workplaces with living wages.

By 1910 it was obvious that the YWCA needed a new building. Board members solicited an initial gift of fifty thousand dollars from prominent industrialist James Gay Butler and a free lot from the St. Louis Union Trust Company. Within twelve days they raised five hundred thousand dollars, primarily from businessmen but with broader public support as well. In May 1912, when they moved into the new building at 1411 Locust Street, the 8,159 members made the St. Louis YWCA the largest in the nation. That same year the board sponsored the Phyllis Wheatley Branch for African American women, which opened in a donated house but moved in 1915 to the old Dodd house vacated by the white YWCA.

The new ash-brick Italianate five-story building was designed to facilitate the organization's fourfold plan of health, education, religion, and sociability. It had a two-story wing with a swimming pool in the basement. The main building had two gymnasiums on the first floor, with offices, a boardroom, and a prayer room on the mezzanine overlooking a spacious foyer. The third floor held classrooms, an auditorium for religious gatherings and lectures, and a memorial chapel to Rebecca Sire, active in Civil War relief and the early St. Louis suffrage movement. Twenty-one rooms for transient women were on the fourth floor. The cafeteria and roof garden for socializing and girls' club meetings were located on the top floor. The following year the board opened an annex to provide more rooms for boarders and young women in need of temporary, safe housing, a service YWCAs began to offer nationally and internationally. The association's Friendly Visitor, a trained social worker, supervised this residence and a later expansion at the old St. Charles Hotel at Fourteenth and St. Charles Streets.

Club work for younger girls focused on religion, practical instruction, and physical education. The emphasis on physical fitness set the YWCA apart from other religious groups that offered leisure activities with training in marketable skills. In addition to a gym and pool, the new facility had tennis courts and playground equipment. Beginning in 1913, they sponsored summer camps for students and "industrial girls." McLean received board permission for girls to wear bloomers at camp "on the condition that if any outsider appeared on camp grounds the girls should have their skirts in readiness to don immediately over their bloomers."

During the First World War the national YWCA board established an Industrial Service Center at Eighteenth and Washington to assist women war workers and encouraged the local association to offer recreational programs, known as hostess houses, for soldiers at Jefferson Barracks. Although these projects were successful, tensions between the local and national agendas would surface in the future as the YWCA adapted to meet new needs and coexist with other service and social organizations. The product of social gospel religious zeal and Progressive Era efficiency, the YWCA became an important and ever-changing resource for St. Louis women.

Sources: Historical information comes primarily from two booklets printed by the St. Louis YWCA, "History of the Young Women's Christian Association of Saint Louis, 1905–1916," the source of the quotation on the founders original mission, and "Y.W.C.A. Silver Jubilee, Central Building, 1937," both in the extensive, well-organized local YWCA Papers at WHMC–UMSL. Quotation regarding bloomers is from Elva Norman, notes of conversation with Gertrude Prack, 1951, YWCA Papers, WHMC–UMSL. Mary Toothill provided research assistance.

See Scott, *Natural Allies*, for more information on the national YWCA movement and its relationship to similar nineteenth-century and Progressive Era women's organizations. The standard history of the YWCA is Mary S. Sims, *The Natural History of a Social Institution: The Young Women's Christian Association* (New York: The Woman's Press, 1936). See also Nina Majagkij and Margaret Spratt, *Men and Women Adrift: The YMCA and the YWCA in the City* (New York: New York University Press, 1997). The organization deserves a modern interpretive study, one that places the YWCA in the context of the co-educational program developed by the YMCA after World War II. See also Joanne Meyerowitz, *Women Adrift: Independent Wage Earners in Chicago, 1880–1930* (Chicago: University of Chicago Press, 1988) for analysis of the interaction between middle-class women and young working women in organizations such as the YWCA. The national magazine of the YWCA, sequentially titled the *Association Monthly* (1907–1922), the *Women's Press* (1922–1950), and *YWCA Magazine* (1951–1973), provides insight into the changing role of the organization.

Mary Hancock McLean, M.D.

Although few female physicians practiced medicine in St. Louis at the turn of the century, poor women living in the immigrant neighborhoods on the city's north side knew how to find a highly trained, sympathetic woman doctor. Between 1893 and 1912 Dr. Mary McLean ran an evening clinic, first at 1607 Wash Avenue and later a few blocks west at 1900, assisted by young female physicians she mentored. Although her family's wealth and influence enabled her to receive the education she needed to become one of St. Louis's first woman physicians, McLean used her advantages to promote health services for poor women and Protestant social welfare programs.

Mary McLean was born in 1869 in Washington, Missouri, the daughter of Elijah McLean, a

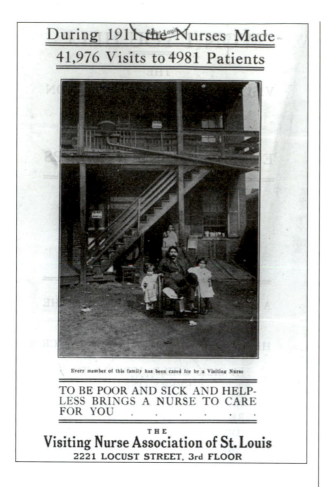

During 1911 the Nurses Made
41,976 Visits to 4981 Patients

Every member of this family has been cared for by a Visiting Nurse

TO BE POOR AND SICK AND HELP-
LESS BRINGS A NURSE TO CARE
FOR YOU . . . . .

THE
Visiting Nurse Association of St. Louis
2221 LOCUST STREET, 3rd FLOOR

Visiting Nurse Association of St. Louis. Pamphlet, 1911. MHS Library

Spurred by the discovery in the 1880s of the role of germs in disease, sanitation and preventative medicine became important public health issues by the turn of the century. Reformers went into the St. Louis slums not only to help the poor, but also to protect all city residents from diseases lurking in filthy alleys and contaminated wells. Under the auspices of the Provident Association, Eva Perry Moore, a local reformer and national leader of the Women's Club movement, organized a committee in 1895 to send trained nurses into the homes of the poor. A national movement, Visiting Nurse Associations were operating in more than 120 cities by 1905.

The Provident Association employed three visiting nurses in 1905. They quickly expanded their efforts beyond the health needs of individuals to community public health issues. They worked with the Pure Milk Commission, circulated a petition for the closure of polluted wells and cisterns, and organized diet kitchens and infant welfare classes. In 1905, the Provident Association employed three visiting nurses. The visiting nurses initially funded their charitable work solely from donations and fees charged patients who could afford to pay, but in 1909 they strengthened their financial base by contracting with Metropolitan Life Insurance Company to provide care for policy holders. The Visiting Nurse Association became a separate agency in 1911 with offices at 2221 Locust Street.

—Joan Cooper

prosperous local physician. Tutored at home until she was thirteen, she went to St. Charles for three years of secondary education at Lindenwood College. She studied two years at Vassar College in New York before enrolling in the University of Michigan medical school. Not yet twenty-five, Mary McLean, M.D., came back to Missouri in 1883 and to a city that offered few opportunities for women with her training and ambition to practice medicine.

McLean used her family connections to get a foot in the door of St. Louis's male medical establishment. In 1884 a friend managed to get her a one-year internship at City Hospital, a position no other woman would hold until 1940. In 1885 Simon Pollak, the city's most prominent physician, sponsored her for membership in the St. Louis Medical Society. Surprisingly, she was accepted, probably because Pollak listed her as M. H. McLean on the application. The society did not admit another woman until 1903.

After completing her internship, McLean opened a private practice in obstetrics and gynecology. She joined the staff of the new Bethesda Hospital and used inherited money to help support it. In 1893 she and another woman physician, Ella Marx, opened the Evening Dispensary for Women, a female clinic at 1607 Wash Avenue offering medical advice and treatment to working women. They charged a small fee to women who could afford to pay, but most services were free.

McLean's concern for female health extended beyond medical care. As a devout Protestant, she joined other church women in their efforts to provide a safe, healthy environment for working women, particularly young, rural migrants to the city. She initiated plans for the Emmanus Home for Girls, a residence for women employed at the 1904 World's Fair. Her religious convictions spurred her to go to China in 1905 as a medical missionary, but poor health forced her return within a year. In St. Louis, McLean opened her home to Chinese students, particularly those studying health care.

After returning from China, McLean took an active role in making the Young Women's Christian Association (YWCA) responsive to the needs of working women. Under her leadership, the YWCA took its programs into factories and department stores. She offered female employees physician examinations, exercise classes, and health education. McLean introduced sex education into the YWCA program of preventative health.

Mary McLean never married and lived with her sister at 4339 Delmar Boulevard, where she maintained a medical office from 1914 until shortly before her death in 1930. She was an energetic, dedicated advocate of social change, motivated by strong religious conviction. A highly trained and skillful surgeon who commanded respect from her male peers, she used her influence to assist other women entering the medical profession. Her concern for the physical and moral health of young working women made her a pioneer in St. Louis public health.

–*Joan Cooper*

Sources: A good brief biography of Mary McLean is Marion Hunt, "Woman's Place in Medicine: The Career of Dr. Mary Hancock McLean," *BMHS* 36, no. 4 (July 1980). The YWCA Papers, WHMC–UMSL, include a portrait from Anne Johnson, *Notable Women of St. Louis* (St. Louis: Woodward, 1914). The papers also contain Dr. Ellen Loeffel's account, *History of Women Doctors in St. Louis*, and the reminiscences of Miss Gertrude Prack, who worked with Dr. McLean at the YWCA. The obituary in the *Globe-Democrat*, 18 May 1930, and Dr. Frances Bishop's obituary in the *Weekly Bulletin of the St. Louis Medical Society* 24, no. 2 (June 27, 1930), are also useful guides to her life and career. For background reading on the medical profession in St. Louis, see Frank J. Lutz, ed., "The Autobiography of S. Pollack, M.D., St. Louis, Mo.," *St. Louis Medical Review*, 1904. See also Martha R. Clevenger, "From Lay Practitioner to Doctor of Medicine: Woman Physicians in St. Louis, 1860–1920," *GH* 8, no. 3 (winter 1987–88).

Phyllis Wheatley Branch YWCA

Early in 1911 nearly 150 St. Louis black women gathered at Berea Presbyterian Church to discuss opening a residence home for single young African American women. Imbued with the same religious conviction that had spurred local white churchwomen to affiliate their facility for white working girls with the national Young Women's Christian Association (YWCA) movement four years earlier, they too hoped to offer newcomers to St. Louis a safe place to live, help in finding employment, and a morally uplifting, Christian-focused social life. The need for decent housing, however, was particularly critical for black women who were part of the Great Migration of African Americans leaving the rural south in the early decades of the century. The church women were also concerned about young black women and girls already living in segregated St. Louis who had few opportunities for organized after-school activities or recreation.

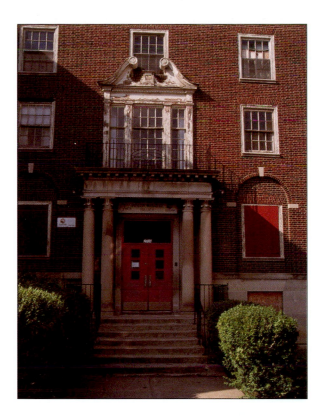

Middle-class black women founded homes for working women in many cities, frequently naming them in honor of the colonial slave poet, Phyllis Wheatley. Some affiliated with the National Association of Colored Women (NACW), others with the YWCA. The national board of the YWCA encouraged black branches of local white associations but did not have a clear policy for implementing interracial cooperation. The Phyllis Wheatley Branch of the St. Louis YWCA, like the city's African American public schools and hospitals, succeeded because its leaders worked to build their own institution within a segregated organizational structure controlled by white St. Louisans with far greater resources.

Most of the women who founded Phyllis Wheatley were public school teachers or the wives of ministers, educators, and doctors. Led by Arsania Williams, a teacher in her early thirties active in club and church work, they began by soliciting support from local African Americans, the national YWCA board, and the local white YWCA, which agreed to help only in an advisory capacity. The national board's representative for "Colored Work," however, intervened and asked the St. Louis YWCA to make

Former Phyllis Wheatley YWCA, 2709 Locust Street. Photograph by George Rothenbuescher, 1999.

the black women's home a branch of their own organization. They reluctantly agreed on the condition that they have legal control over the branch's finances and general management, an arrangement adopted by YWCA associations in other cities as well. Ruth Coleman, a white YWCA member, served on the new branch's Committee of Management and represented the branch as an *ex officio* voting member of the Board of Directors.

Without sufficient funds to secure and equip an adequate building, the black women were in no position to reject the terms of affiliation with the white facility. Louise Chapman, a former member of the YWCA board, offered to lend the branch organizers an old house if they would pay taxes and insurance; other women helped with furnishings. The board, unwilling to spend any of its own money on the branch, gave the black women permission to solicit gifts of furniture from selected dealers. Busy preparing to move into their own new five-story building, the Central YWCA agreed to give the "Colored Branch" any furnishings that remained after retaining "all that would be useful to us."

Located west of Jefferson Avenue, the Chapman house stood in a neighborhood of middle-class African Americans near the center of the city's "Negro District," which extended west to Grand and east to the area around Union Station now rapidly filling with rural newcomers. In 1912 the facility took the name, Phyllis Wheatley Branch, but the YWCA insisted that a sign also identify the building as a colored branch.

In 1912 May Belcher, a trained black YWCA worker, arrived from New York to help organize the branch. Belcher was appalled at the poor condition of the borrowed building, and after calling the lack of affordable rooms for young black women "a mountain of insufficiency" she set out to make Phyllis Wheatley a welcoming, supportive haven for young women. The new residents plastered and papered the bedrooms; volunteers supervised activities and helped plant a garden on an adjacent vacant lot. The growing membership, however, included more young mothers and girls from the neighborhood than newcomers. Unlike the Central YWCA, which had the resources to offer secretarial courses and teach other marketable skills, Phyllis Wheatley concentrated on affordable housing and wholesome recreation. Later that year Belcher and the volunteers, aided by a Special Worker for Colored Work sent by the national board, organized a fund-raising campaign that attracted even more members but few donations

from black St. Louis business and professional men, many of whom were staunch supporters of the Pine Street YMCA for African American boys.

The Phyllis Wheatley Committee of Management had to negotiate continuously for funds from the Central YWCA, which had fiscal responsibility for the branch but no mandate to provide financial assistance. In 1913 the Central YWCA began paying May Belcher's salary. Although this enabled the committee to spend more of its limited money on programming, it reinforced the branch's subordinate status, since there were no black women on the YWCA governing board. After the Chapmans sold the Phyllis Wheatley building, the Central YWCA appointed a committee of white women to locate a new home for the branch. After they discovered the original home of the white YWCA at 709 Garrison Avenue was again for sale, several white women made personal donations toward its purchase. The most generous donor, Mary Ranken Jordan, was an active churchwoman and a leader in the Women's Christian Association and The Wednesday Club.

The Phyllis Wheatley Committee of Management formed a building committee to oversee renovation of the old building, its gymnasium, and swimming pool. The Central YWCA insisted on adding five white members to this committee. As committee members participated in the daily activities of the branch, however, they managed to convince the board to be more generous in its financial support.

The Phyllis Wheatley volunteers continued to solicit money in the community as they filled the new facility with young black women. Resident girls slept in dorms and, in the summer, on sleeping porches. They played tennis on the old tennis court and learned to swim in the pool. Everyone used the gymnasium for athletics, plays, concerts, and social events. May Belcher and Elizabeth Moore, her newly hired assistant, began outreach work with women employed at two local bag factories and the Funsten Nut Company. They served hot lunches to students at the nearby Banneker School. Not only did the Mullanphy Traveler's Aid and the St. Louis Provident Association regularly send stranded or destitute girls to the branch, but refugees from the 1917 East St. Louis race riot also found a temporary home in the gymnasium. During the First World War, black women who wanted to volunteer for the Red Cross came to the branch. The Employment Department, which placed women in domestic work, found them better positions once white women moved into defense work.

May Belcher left the branch in 1917 for a job with the YWCA's War Work Council, never having been invited to a professional meeting at the Central YWCA. Always short of money for repairs and programs, the Committee of Management ran the branch for more than twenty years under the leadership of Arsania Williams, overseen by the board's representative. By the 1930s, however, the national board was making interracial cooperation a greater priority. St. Louis African American women pressed for more voice in decision-making both at the branch and in the association. By 1939 the three branches of the YWCA–Central, Phyllis Wheatley, and Carondelet–each had representatives on the board. Still committed to segregation, the white-run St. Louis YWCA, nevertheless, gave its black branch more autonomy and initiated more interracial contact in line with national board guidelines. The city condemned the Garrison Avenue building in 1937, but an interracial committee made the decision to move the Phyllis Wheatley Branch in 1941 to the former Women's Christian Association residence at 2709 Locust Street, a modern building only fourteen years old.

Sources: This essay draws heavily on Jean Mongold, "Vespers and Vacant Lots: The Early Years of the Phyllis Wheatley YWCA," unpublished manuscript, WHMC–UMSL. Quotations from the YWCA board minutes are cited there. The fragmentary records of the Phyllis Wheatley Branch are in the YWCA Papers, WHMC–UMSL. Because most information about the early years of the branch comes from the YWCA board minutes, the perspective is usually that of the white board members. Many activities of the Phyllis Wheatley Branch, however, were reported in the *St. Louis Argus*, the city's middle-class black weekly, making the newspaper microfilm a good source for the role of the branch in the black community. Secretaries of black branches filed regular reports with the National YWCA, which also are available on microfilm. These records contain information about the St. Louis Phyllis Wheatley Branch and would also provide a context for them. See also Adrienne Lash Jones, "Phyllis Wheatley Clubs and Homes," in *Black Women in America*, eds., Hines, et al., and Majagkij and Spratt, *Men and Women Adrift*.

St. Philomena's Technical School

By 1900, technical, or manual training, schools taught marketable skills to increasing numbers of urban children. In 1910 the Daughters of Charity, who began teaching orphans to sew before the Civil War, moved their training school from Clark and Ewing Avenues to an imposing red brick building at Union and Cabanne Avenues. With the move to the city's West End, the nuns took on a one hundred thousand-dollar mortgage, changed the name of the institution to St. Philomena's Technical School, and no longer restricted enrollment to orphans.

Originally founded as an orphanage, St. Philomena's Industrial School for Girls became a separate facility for teaching white girls needlework and dressmaking in 1864. When girls in the city's Catholic orphanages reached the age of twelve, they were eligible to live at St. Philomena's. The school placed graduates in private homes as seamstresses. In 1891 the sisters were boarding sixty-five girls in the building at Clark and Ewing Avenues, while also staffing a parish school for St. Malachy's Church across the street. Since there was a growing demand for both elementary education and vocational training, the sisters moved the training school to a new larger building.

The new St. Philomena's Technical School took in properly recommended poor girls and made them "self-reliant, good members of society." They learned to be skilled domestic workers. Along with a basic education and instruction in Catholicism, students learned general housework, plain cooking, laundry work, and especially hand and machine sewing. The school's reputation for fine handiwork produced by the nuns and their pupils created a demand in the Catholic community for their work. In 1912, about one hundred girls supported themselves at the institution by making fancy garments for women and children, but their mundane training in the practical arts proved to be more valuable after graduation when they became garment workers, domestic workers, and housewives.

Sources: J. Thomas Scharf, *History of St. Louis City and County* (Philadelphia: L. H. Everts & Co., 1883); Bureau of Labor Statistics, 1891, Reports of Catholic Charities of the City of St. Louis, 1912, 1914, 1921. See also the Daughters of Charity for records of ethnicity, age, associations, etc., of girls who attended the school. This would be a good opportunity for oral history research, as many former students and their families still live in the St. Louis region.

Queen's Daughters

In 1913 the Society of the Daughters of the Queen of Heaven, an organization of Catholic lay women, opened a boardinghouse for self-supporting women at 3730 Lindell Boulevard. Concerned that some Catholic working women were "boarding

turn of the century they also operated a Home for Self-Supporting Women and Young Girls at 111 North Sixteenth Street, in a neighborhood of second-generation Irish and German factory girls and domestic workers. Boarders paid $3.50 a week; young women temporarily unemployed could live for free in a protected Catholic environment. Between 1897 and 1912, 736 boarders lived in the home. Their rent paid most of the home's expenses, enabling the Queen's Daughters to save five thousand dollars from membership dues and fund raisers to use for a separate residence for middle-class working women in the city's central corridor.

The Lindell Avenue home accommodated twenty-four women who paid between $3.50 and $5 a week. In 1914, seventy women stayed there, including eight who were temporarily unemployed and did not pay. By 1920 the addition of an annex enabled eighty-two women to live in the home and participate in social activities of a "strictly Catholic nature."

Although it operated within the St. Louis archdiocesan structure, the Queen's Daughters was an independent organization of lay women organized by Catholic parishes. Representatives of each affiliated group served on the organization's Diocesan Council. For the first twenty years, their most extensive work was the Saturday Sewing School, sessions held in parish halls, where members taught girls to sew and helped them make clothing for themselves and their families. By 1912 more than twelve thousand girls had made twenty-one thousand garments. The membership, however, was growing reluctant to commit their Saturday mornings. The Queen's Daughters closed all the schools except those at St. Patrick's and Guardian Angel Settlements, both in poor immigrant neighborhoods.

The Queen's Daughters also cooperated with other public agencies. In 1906, at the request of Roger Baldwin, probation officer of the juvenile court, they began looking after the welfare of Catholic girls who came before the court. They supplied them with clothing, found them homes and jobs, and visited them in institutions. At the request of Tuberculosis Society visiting nurses and the chaplain of the State Penitentiary, the Queen's Daughters also assisted the families of hospitalized patients and prisoners.

In his introduction to the 1914 Report of the Catholic Charities, Archbishop John Glennon lamented a situation where the courts committed children to institutions but did not pay for their

among strangers" at the new Protestant YWCA, the Queen's Daughters acquired a spacious private residence near Saint Louis University in the West End. They hoped to attract Catholic office workers and young professionals to a residence that, like the YWCA, offered "every convenience for relaxation, sociability, and instruction."

Since the mid-nineteenth century, Catholic women had responded to the changing needs of working women by establishing the same kinds of institutions founded by Protestant women. Although St. Louis was more than one-third Roman Catholic, there were fewer institutions run by middle-class Catholic women. Religious orders operated most of the city's Catholic orphanages, industrial schools, and homes for women at risk.

The Queen's Daughters organized in 1889 to run sewing schools for girls in poor parishes. They took on a variety of charity projects in cooperation with parish women's guilds, including collecting and distributing mountains of shoes, clothing, and bedding to the poor. By the

Queen's Daughters Residence, 3730 Lindell Boulevard. Recently restored, the building is now part of the Saint Louis University campus. Photograph by George Rothenbuescher, 1999.

upkeep. As with the city's similar Protestant and Jewish institutions, Catholic institutions received no regular city, county, or state money. At the turn of the century, charitable Catholic women, organized either by parish or religious order, worked to meet very different and rapidly changing needs of hundreds of young Catholic women living on their own in St. Louis.

Sources: For additional information, see the Report of Catholic Charities of the City of St. Louis, 1912, quotation from page 77; 1914, 1921. The first conference report gives a brief history of each organization. It lists all Catholic organizations that women either ran independently or operated for the archdiocese.

These reports are a good source for descriptions and statistical information on Catholic orphanages, settlement houses, and day nurseries operated by women's groups, Catholic layman's groups, the archdiocese, and religious orders. Jewish women also organized for benevolence. Historical records of the local chapter of the National Council of Jewish Women are located at the WHMC–UMSL.

St. Francis's Colored Orphan Asylum

In 1912 sixty-one African American orphans lived in St. Francis's Colored Orphan Asylum in the northwestern suburb of Normandy. Nine nuns of the Oblate Sisters of Providence cared for them. Also living in the orphanage were twenty-five young African American women, primarily domestic day workers whose board helped defray some of the institution's operating costs.

The Oblate Sisters of Providence came to St. Louis in 1880 at the invitation of Jesuits who seven years earlier had established St. Elizabeth's Church, the citywide parish for African American Catholics. Four sisters taught parish children in the church basement and later in a converted social hall at Fourteenth and Morgan Streets. Because the only orphanage in the city for black children was the Protestant Colored Orphan Home, operated by members of St. Paul's A.M.E. Church, Catholic African Americans began bringing destitute children to the Oblate Sisters' convent. With the help of Mary E. Boyce and other women from prominent white Catholic families, the sisters expanded their convent and schools on Morgan Street.

In 1887 a donation from the local clergy and the promise of one thousand dollars from the annual archdiocesan collection for Negro and

St. Vincent's Hospital. Postcard by St. Louis News Company, ca. 1908. MHS–PP

In 1896 the Daughters of Charity moved their hospital for the insane from the city's south side to this impressive building constructed on a ninety-three-acre site near the Wabash Railroad tracks in suburban Normandy. Unlike most mental hospitals, St. Vincent's was more like an institutional home than a prison. The four-story brick building, surrounded by gardens and attractive natural grounds, had two wings of private rooms and wards for five hundred patients. There, the nuns gave mental patients the same humane care they had been giving them for more than twenty-five years. In the twentieth century, St. Vincent's retained its reputation as a leader in treating the mentally ill.

Although the Daughters of Charity took in some charity cases, most inmates were paying patients from the middle class. Families throughout Missouri brought mentally ill relatives to the nuns and left them for long-term custodial care. In 1896, when the Daughters of Charity moved their inmates, many of whom had been incarcerated for years, they took them to Normandy in a long line of carriages under cover of night. At the new building, patients were guaranteed space and privacy. They kept violent patients segregated from the rest, reducing the use of locks and bars. The nuns provided a library and recreational facilities for patients who were permitted access to the landscaped grounds. They introduced a program of occupational therapy in 1922, but the institution was, like most mental hospitals at that time, dedicated to giving life-long custodial care to incurables. Being a patient at St. Vincent's, however, was far preferable to the hard life most poor mentally ill St. Louisans experienced in the public Insane Asylum and Poor House on Arsenal Street.

children. Because they worked in white homes, the orphans were not treated as family members, as white orphans sometimes were. They continued to think of St. Francis as their home. Girls could return to the home if their live-in work situations were unsatisfactory, or they could board there when they became young adult day workers.

As the only African American religious order in St. Louis, the sisters tried to provide the same kinds of services to black girls that white Catholic and Protestant women were offering white girls. Some members of the order continued their classes for St. Elizabeth's parishioners. When the church moved to an old mansion at 2731 Pine Street, they stayed behind to teach domestic skills to African American girls in the Morgan Street neighborhood.

In 1912 the Oblate Sisters opened St. Rita's Boarding School for girls at 3000 Pine Street, moving in 1914 to 3128 Laclede Avenue and later to 4650 South Broadway. A large house with a barn and outbuilding stood on the South Broadway site on the bluffs overlooking the Mississippi River. African American girls came from many states for an education with a curriculum similar to Catholic high schools for white girls.

Indian missions enabled the sisters to purchase the Taylor Mansion at 4538 Page Avenue, on the outskirts of town. They named the new orphanage in honor of St. Francis of Rome, the patron saint of the Oblate order.

The oldest and one of only a few religious orders for African American women, the Oblate Sisters were a teaching order founded in 1828 by French-speaking refugees from Santo Domingo. The sisters established schools in Baltimore, which, like St. Louis, had a significant number of black Catholic residents, and later in Philadelphia and New Orleans before coming to St. Louis.

Under the leadership of Superior Mary Dominsia, the orphanage had outgrown the building on Page Avenue by the time white residential development reached the area. In 1897 the sisters made enough profit on the sale of the valuable property to buy several brick buildings on eight acres in rural Normandy. In 1905 the Oblate Sisters constructed a large new building there.

The nuns accepted orphans and half-orphans aged between two and twelve. The children received the education and training typically offered to African American children at the turn of the century. Although they provided a basic elementary school education, the nuns were most anxious to cultivate habits of economy, thrift, and industry. As soon as the children were old enough, fifteen or sixteen years of age, the sisters placed them in domestic service or housekeeping jobs. Few orphans were adopted. It was a rare black family that could afford to adopt unrelated

Sources: Statistics are from the Conference of Catholic Charities, 1912, 1914. See also Grace Sherwood, *The Oblates: One Hundred and One Years* (New York: Macmillan, 1931); William Barnaby Faherty, S.J., and Madeline Oliver, *Religious Roots of Black Catholics of St. Louis* (privately printed, copy at MHS); William B. Faherty, S.J., *Dream by the River: Two Centuries of Saint Louis Catholicism, 1766–1967 (St. Louis: Piraeus, 1973),* and the Reverend John Rothensteiner, *History of the Archdiocese of St. Louis: In Its Various Stages of Development, From A.D. 1673 to A.D. 1828* (St. Louis: Blackwell Wielandy, 1928).

Mary Seematter, who contributed research for this essay, has interviewed former residents of the St. Francis's orphanage and St. Rita's School for a study of local African American religious orders. The Oblate Sisters, who also staffed other black parish schools in the city and in Kinloch, closed St. Rita's in 1958 and sold the property to the La Salette Fathers. The school building burned down in 1969. The sisters closed the Normandy orphanage in 1965 and left St. Louis in 1992. Their records are located at the Oblates's Motherhouse Archives, Our Lady of Mt. Providence Motherhouse, 701 Gun Road, Baltimore, Maryland 21227.

Other local religious orders who served black St. Louisans were the Helpers of the Holy Souls, a French order who arrived in 1903 to provide direct aid to the poor and in later years connected people in need with available social services. Located for many years at 4012 Washington Avenue, they also opened a

St. Francis's Colored Orphan Asylum. The Oblate Sisters sold this building in 1897 and moved the orphanage to Normandy. Photograph by Emil Boehl, ca. 1890. MHS–PP

facility at 3950 West Bell Avenue, known as St. Benedict's Center, because their Washington Avenue neighbors complained about African Americans visiting the convent. The Helpers of the Holy Souls sold the Washington Avenue property in 1965 and lived at 4485 Westminster Place for twenty years. They left St. Louis in 1988, leaving some records at the Archdiocesan Archives. The biracial Sisters of the Blessed Sacrament opened a mission on Pine Street near St. Elizabeth's in 1914 and continued to teach at the black parish until it closed in 1949.

St. Louis Children's Hospital

At the opening of the new St. Louis Children's Hospital building on Kingshighway in April 1915, Dr. Borden Veeder commended its affiliation with Washington University. "The day has passed," he said, "in which a hospital restricted to the care of the sick alone justifies its cost and existence, . . . the university connection implies the development of the scientific and research side of the hospital's work." Veeder's remarks reflected the enormous changes in medical care that had taken place since a small groups of committed women founded the hospital in 1879.

By the end of the nineteenth century, advances in knowledge, technology, education, and technique necessitated widespread changes in medical practice. The need for better-trained staff reformed medical training and led to the establishment of nursing schools. As public respect for science increased, so did the demand for more specialized treatment. Hospitals grew in acceptance and numbers, forcing them to operate more like businesses than as traditional charitable institutions.

Powerful philanthropic foundations began to take an interest in health care expansion and reform. The Carnegie Foundation funded an investigation into the medical education system and in 1910 published the *Flexner Report*. The report established educational guidelines that if met by medical schools would lead to large foundation grants. The schools that met the conditions became prestigious and profitable institutions. Reflecting these changes, the 1915 annual report of the St. Louis Children's Hospital stated that "it seems as if ages of time and a continent of effort must separate the splendid new Children's Hospital, so immaculate and efficient, from the old house . . . where the work began."

In late 1879, St. Louis Children's Hospital admitted its first two patients to a small rented house at 2834 Franklin Avenue. The previous winter, Appoline Blair, the widow of Civil War

general and U.S. Senator Frank Blair, had discussed with friends the need for a hospital dedicated solely to the care of poor children. The women may have been inspired by the well-publicized concerns of homeopathic physicians about the health of children made sick by "reason of the poverty, ignorance or neglect of their parents." Certainly, the same concerns motivated the establishment of the hospital.

For women like Appoline Blair, helping poor, sick children was an ideal cause. Whether or not they had children of their own, they empathized with the problems illness created since they knew that women assumed most of the responsibility for the physical and moral health of children. They also emotively portrayed poor children as innocent, helpless victims of negligent parents. Shocked by the lack of order and morality they perceived in poor families, middle-class women feared that this influence would infect vulnerable children and create a generation of delinquents and scroungers. They presumed that many physical ailments stemmed from a lack of domestic order. Therefore, to help the sick, poor child was for many middle- and upper-class women a practical method of improving the poor and ensuring civic health.

Social and demographic trends also contributed to a growing concern for the welfare of children. The falling birth rate placed new emphasis on ensuring the survival of smaller numbers. Pediatrics, specific medical care for children, became a recognized professional specialty.

Appoline Blair and others encouraged their friends to support the hospital financially and maternally. A female Board of Managers undertook the daily administration of the hospital, and a "gentleman's advisory board" took care of the financial and legal side. After renting for a year, they bought a building on Franklin Avenue with solicited funds. The first hospital had fifteen beds. A medical staff from the homeopathic medical college treated the children with small doses of drugs. The hospital cared for children between two and fourteen years old. Patients with chronic, incurable, or infectious diseases were not admitted. However, since it proved difficult to keep out children with infectious diseases, the women soon added an isolation ward.

Within a few years it was apparent that the building was too small. The managers raised money to build a new hospital, which opened in 1884 on the corner of Jefferson Avenue and Adams Street with accommodations for sixty patients and a ward for infectious cases. In 1894 the Board of Managers established a kindergarten in the hospital.

Although the managers recognized the need to keep children constructively occupied from the start by visiting the wards to teach simple songs and prayers, the opening of the school formalized the hospital's commitment to the whole child.

A dispensary treated outpatients and served as a way to determine whether or not to admit a child. Mothers who worked nearby as washerwomen, domestics, or in factories used the dispensary. The hospital reported that "half of the mothers are separated from their husbands, others have unfortunate or worthless husbands, and some are widows." The dispensary, but probably not the hospital, treated African American children.

Partly due to national social, economic, and political trends, the turn of the century saw an accelerated change in health care. Some changes were in response to scientific knowledge about germ and disease relationships that resulted in more professional and public attention to preventative medicine and public health issues. Indicative of this was the opening of a Pure Milk Station in the hospital in 1904. Proof of the connection between contaminated milk and high infant mortality from intestinal infections resulted in a national campaign for the distribution of safe milk in large cities. The dispensary station distributed milk to patients and neighborhood children. By 1910, the Pure Milk Station was part of a citywide service that gave out twenty-five thousand bottles annually and helped to save many infants before pasteurization and refrigeration made safe milk readily available.

The hospital also responded to other scientific advances. Application of new antiseptic and isolation procedures made operations safer. A department of pathology opened and produced its first report on disease-causing organisms in 1905. The hospital acquired incubators, an x-ray apparatus, a new sterilizer, and hot and cold distillers. With the introduction of more scientific methods and technologically sophisticated equipment, the hospital felt compelled in 1907 to establish a training school for nurses. Until then, the hospital had not employed properly trained nurses. Three years later, it closed the nursing school and moved it to Washington University.

Washington University played a vital role in the future of Children's Hospital, one that by 1915 had transformed the charity hospital run by women into a large, modern teaching hospital run by professional male administrators. In 1909 Abraham Flexner visited St. Louis and gave Washington University Medical School a poor rating. Invited back by Robert Brookings, the university president,

Flexner laid down the conditions that would make the medical school eligible for a foundation grant—a full-time faculty and affiliated teaching hospitals.

As Mrs. Robert Jones, the president of the Board of Managers of Children's Hospital, later remarked, "It was the most opportune time for the Children's Hospital to affiliate." The Homeopathic Medical School that had staffed the hospital since the beginning had closed. The Martha Parsons Free Hospital, a children's hospital specializing in orthopedic care, wanted to associate with Children's. As the dispensary attendance increased, they had added a feeding clinic. The facilities on Jefferson were stretched beyond their limits. For this problem, however, there was a solution. Mrs. John Fowler donated $125,000 to build a new hospital. Affiliation with Washington University Medical School helped solve the problem of medical staff for Children's Hospital, and the combination of orthopedic and pediatric hospitals in a new facility helped meet Washington University's need for an affiliated teaching hospital.

Affiliation proceeded quickly. A chairman of the new department of pediatrics was appointed in 1910, and the medical school took over the clinical care of patients. By 1911 the board had purchased a lot on Kingshighway, which put the new hospital close to both the medical school and the new Barnes Hospital. Plans included private rooms for paying patients, a new direction for the hospital. The 1911 report justified this change: "The prosperous need [hospital care] for the sake of their own carefully guarded children, as much as those handicapped by poverty and ignorance. . . . Disease in the slums spreads into the best and cleanest homes." Reflecting the increased interest in public and preventative health, the hospital established a social service department.

Although the Board of Managers remained female until 1950, it is clear that from the time of the affiliation with Washington University the power of the women managers steadily diminished, as professionals, the majority of whom were men, took over most of their duties. Trained social workers dealt with the welfare aspects, the medical school faculty appointed staff and ran the medical side of the hospital, and a professional administrator supervised the rest. By the time the new hospital building opened, the female Board of Managers no longer had the responsibility of administration. The thirty-six years that separated the "old house" on Franklin Avenue from the "splendid new hospital" on Kingshighway were about more than physical change. They reflected changes in the economics and politics of health care that had reduced the influence of the female volunteers who had first recognized the need for a children's hospital in St. Louis.

–Joan Cooper

Sources: For a history of the hospital, see Marion Hunt, *"A Goodly Heritage": St. Louis Children's Hospital Centennial History, 1879–1979* (St. Louis: St. Louis Children's Hospital, 1980), and Marion Hunt, "Women and Childsaving: St. Louis Children's Hospital 1879–1979," *BMHS* 36, no. 2 (January 1980). Addition information on the early days is in the Missouri Bureau of Labor Statistics, 1891; William Hyde and Howard Conard, *Encyclopedia of the History of St. Louis* (New York: The Southern History Company, 1899); and *St. Louis Globe-Democrat*, 30 October 1936, 22 November 1959. For the history of medical education and care reform, see Morrow, *Washington University in St. Louis*. For a good general background on women and the medical profession, see Barbara Ehrenreich and Deirdre English, *For Her Own Good: 150 Years of the Experts' Advice to Women* (New York: Anchor Press, 1978).

The Suffrage Movement

In March 1910, Florence Richardson and her mother, Florence Wyman Richardson, invited eight friends to meet at their home at 5737 Cates Avenue to talk about woman suffrage. The St. Louis suffrage movement, weakened by internal dissension and the aging of first- and second-generation activists, had been largely dormant in the early years of the Progressive Era. Activist women had turned their energies instead to the "municipal housekeeping" of civic improvement and to literary and social welfare organizations. The national suffrage movement floundered in similar disarray and provided little leadership. By 1910, however, spurred by the success of their English compatriots and empowered by their civic experience, a second wave of suffragists began to form. In St. Louis, nineteen-year-old Florence Richardson received the suffrage banner from her mother and the few diehard women who had kept it afloat.

Richardson later recalled a 1909 meeting with Victoria Conkling Whitney and Elizabeth Meriwether, "two untiring and dauntless women who kept the cause alive, single handed and alone, when it lay forgotten and neglected." Prompted by a newspaper report stating that Whitney planned to present a suffrage petition to the state legislature in the week following, Richardson met with the two in Meriwether's sickroom. She never forgot the words they spoke to her: "We two have met from time to time to keep this from actually dying out, but perhaps it may fall to you to help build another organization with new blood and vitality, which will see the things about which we have dreamed and for which we have worked and sacrificed. If so, we have not met together all these years in vain."

The ten women meeting at the Richardson home in 1910 agreed to ask English suffragist Emmeline Pankhurst to speak in St. Louis. Pankhurst accepted but was called back to England before she could fulfill the engagement. The organizers, however, discovered while publicizing the event that St. Louis women were far more interested in suffrage than they had suspected. A follow-up meeting on April 10 attracted fifty women, who formed the St. Louis Equal Suffrage League (ESL) and elected the elder Florence Richardson as president. To forestall any misconceptions that the "suffragettes" would engage in the outrageous antics of their English sisters, the league positioned itself as a purely educational club. Its object was "to bring together men and women who are willing to consider the question of Equal Suffrage and by earnest co-operation to secure its establishment." The ESL met regularly at the Cabanne Branch Library at Kingshighway in the West End. The sub-group met at Barr Branch Library on the south side and at the Crunden Branch at 500 N. Fourteenth Street.

The ESL affiliated with the National American Woman Suffrage Association (NAWSA). The national organization had changed its earlier tactics of lobbying state legislators for the vote to pressing for a federal amendment to the Constitution. The ESL mounted an educational campaign through lectures, newspaper publicity, and citywide demonstrations. Although Sylvia and Emmeline Pankhurst, Ethel Arnold, and other English and American suffrage speakers came to St. Louis, they avoided any hint of militancy. In 1911 Sylvia Pankhurst engaged prominent St. Louisan Isaac Lionberger in a lively debate at Mary Institute. Suffrage advocates stressed, however, the refinement women would bring to the political process.

Barbara Blackman O'Neil, who succeeded Florence Richardson as ESL president, connected "woman's sphere" to the public arena. "No one believes with greater sincerity than the suffragist that woman's place is in the house," Blackman insisted. Not only did eight million working women need the protection of the vote, she argued, but homemakers must follow the duties they once performed in the home out into the public arena. "Questions of water supply, the milk

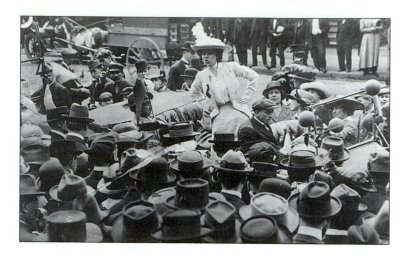

the General Assembly to submit the suffrage issue to Missouri voters in 1914, but the senate tabled the discussion. Undaunted, the women, led by Barbara O'Neil and state ESL president Mrs. Walter McNab Miller, immediately began planning for a second petition campaign. By February 1914, they had ten thousand signatures from St. Louis alone. After receiving the petition signed by thirty-four thousand women across the state, the legislature agreed to put the matter on the ballot that November.

On National Suffrage Day in April 1914, a parade of suffragists in yellow-bannered automobiles traveled downtown from Edna Gellhorn's West End home, circled the courthouse and then headed west to a meeting in front of the Jefferson Memorial in Forest Park. Thereafter, the campaign intensified; national leaders Anna Howard Shaw and Jane Addams joined local speakers in arguing the benefits of suffrage.

In November, the statewide measure failed, with only 182,000 "yes" votes to 322,000 in opposition. Only thirteen Missouri counties voted in favor of suffrage. The male voters of St. Louis overwhelmingly rejected the amendment by a margin of nearly three to one.

In 1916 the National Democratic Convention met at the St. Louis Coliseum. Emily Newell Blair of Carthage suggested a dramatic demonstration to publicize the cause. More than two thousand women, carrying yellow parasols and wearing white dresses draped with yellow sashes emblazoned with suffrage slogans, formed a "Golden Lane" along Locust Street between the Coliseum at Twenty-third Street and the Jefferson Hotel at Twelfth Street, the hotel for the majority of convention delegates. The "walkless, talkless parade" forced delegates to walk a symbolic gauntlet and sought to shame them into giving women a political voice. The official participants took turns standing and sitting in camp chairs; reportedly five times as many paraded the adjoining streets and sidewalks. The event was sponsored by the NAWSA and national officers Anna Shaw and Carrie Chapman Catt reviewed the throng by car.

Midway along the Golden Lane route, suffragists performed a tableau titled "Up to Liberty" on the steps of the old Art Museum building between Eighteenth and Nineteenth Streets. Women clad in black mourning garb with shackled wrists, representing those states where women had no vote, stood to the right. On the left, in gowns of lavender for "second mourning," stood figures representing the states with partial suffrage. Thirteen women clad

and foods generally, the problem of the clean street and clean alley, garbage and ashes collections and a hundred . . . other things—she can no longer control without a voice in the making of laws affecting such matters."

Suffrage ignited women across Missouri. Suffragists created a new state organization in 1911; its headquarters and much of its backing was in St. Louis. Affiliated groups formed in Kansas City, Warrensburg, Sedalia, and other towns. On the political front, the Farmers' Alliance, State Teachers' Association, and the Prohibition and Single Tax parties all supported the vote for women. Encouraged by this support and that of local newspapers, the ESL petitioned

A Woman Addresses the Crowd on National Suffrage Day, May 2, 1916, in Downtown St. Louis. MHS–PP

The Golden Lane at the Walkless-Talkless Parade, June 1916. Courtesy WHMC–UMSL

in white and crowned in gold symbolized the twelve states and one territory that gave women full voting rights. At their head under a gold canopy on the top step, Barbara Blackman O'Neil stood costumed as a triumphant Spirit of Liberty.

The demonstration was impressive political theater and attracted enthusiastic press coverage, just as a similar march had the previous week in Chicago. There, five thousand suffragists marched in the rain to convince delegates to the Republican convention to support the vote for women. Both parties added vague, noncommittal suffrage planks to their party platforms and received major party endorsement for the first time.

The following year, suffragists supported a successful bill for presidential suffrage in the Missouri legislature. St. Louis League President Christine Fordyce reminded the gentlemen that "fifty years ago my grandmother came before the Missouri legislature and asked for the enfranchisement of women; twenty-five years ago, my mother came to make the same request; tonight I am asking for the ballot for women. Are you going to make it necessary for my daughter to appear in her turn?"

Fordyce's daughter did not have to make a similar trip to Jefferson City. When the United States entered World War I, most of the suffragists supported the war effort through sales of war bonds, participation in Red Cross and knitting clubs, fund raising for overseas hospitals, directing food conservation plans, and other patriotic activities. The state suffrage magazine, *Missouri Woman*, devoted a great deal of its editorial space to the effort. President Woodrow Wilson and the major political parties supported suffrage more because of women's demonstrated patriotism than from either a sense of justice or a fear of black and immigrant male voting power, although these were factors.

The National American Woman Suffrage Association held its Golden Jubilee Convention at the Statler Hotel in St. Louis in March 1919. In her opening address, President Carrie Chapman Catt urged the delegates to "raise up a league of women voters" as a memorial to the hard work and sacrifices of the pioneers of the suffrage movement. The convention passed a resolution to establish such a league as a separate unit within the NAWSA, with membership drawn only from those states where women were allowed to vote. They defined the league's duties as the completion of the campaign for full suffrage and consideration of legislation affecting women in those states where they did have the vote.

On the convention's final day, word came from Jefferson City that the Missouri senate passed a measure allowing women to vote in presidential elections, as well as a resolution to submit a constitutional amendment for full suffrage to the electorate. Edna Gellhorn, speaking for the St. Louis ESL, pointed out that a state amendment was unnecessary, since it appeared certain that their aims would soon be achieved at the federal level. In June, at the urging of President Woodrow Wilson, Congress passed the Nineteenth Amendment: "The right of citizens of the United States to vote shall not be denied or abridged by the United States or by any State on account of sex." Missouri was one of eleven states to ratify the amendment in the first month; another year passed before approval by the thirty-sixth state made it a binding part of the federal constitution.

The St. Louis Equal Suffrage League continued to operate under that name until it adopted a new constitution in November 1919, following the lead of the state organization at its convention in October. Both groups had worked in the months since Carrie Chapman Catt's challenge at the Jubilee Convention to fulfill her goals for education through the establishment of Citizenship Schools for Missouri Voters, particularly the foreign-born, women as well as men. Each would now be known as an affiliate of the League of Women Voters.

Board Meeting of St. Louis Equal Suffrage League in Their First Headquarters. Photograph, 1912. MHS–PP

The public-spirited New Woman launched the twentieth-century suffrage movement. The leadership came from the local, well-educated women's elite. A majority of the founders were members of The Wednesday Club; at least half were residents of the affluent West End. A number were graduates of the prestigious Mary Institute. Nevertheless, significant representation came from groups that would have been considered radical by standards of the times. Mary Bulkley, Cynthella Knefler, Althea Somerville, Anna Sheldon, and the mother-daughter team of Edna Fischel and Edna Gellhorn were connected to the Ethical Culture Society, its Self-Culture Halls, and the Women's Trade Union League, all of which espoused varying degrees of socialist political thought. Many belonged to the liberal Unitarian church, which had supported the original suffrage organizations of the mid-nineteenth century. There was also overlapping membership with the St. Louis Business Women's Suffrage League, founded in April 1912, which included attorneys, doctors, and other professional women. The league also sponsored a junior ESL for college students.

Despite the range of their political affiliations, the St. Louis suffragists were overwhelmingly middle class. Their record on issues of class and race is mixed. Responding to a poll conducted by the *Post-Dispatch* in 1908, several suffragists made it clear that they were appalled and indignant that men of lesser status and education than they, implying recent European immigrants and African Americans, had the vote while they did not. Alice Paul's Congressional Union, a national suffrage organization, argued that woman suffrage would negate the rising black vote in southern states.

It was apparent, however, that from the beginning the Equal Suffrage League made some attempts to cross lines of color and class. Florence Richardson Usher spoke to women at the Negro Self-Culture Hall, another Ethical Society spin-off, encouraging them to organize under their own leadership. Cynthella Knefler addressed both managers and workers at six local breweries, where German traditions and anti-temperance feeling had produced a strong anti-suffrage backlash. Knefler assured the brewery workers that suffrage was not a partisan party issue. By the end of the league's first year, members were holding regular meetings at the Crunden and Barr Libraries to serve the northern and southern parts of the city. The ESL sponsored two more separate groups: the Jewish Alliance League and the Wage-Earners' Suffrage League, with membership drawn primarily from the WTUL.

Another indication of outreach was a Rally Day held in November 1912 to support the vote in 1914 that included activities in every ward of the city. The ESL tailored events to a wide variety of interests. There was not only a citywide baby contest, a rally at Forest Park University, speeches at the Ethical Society's Sheldon Memorial and the exclusive City Club, but also addresses in Yiddish as well as English at settlement houses in immigrant neighborhoods and an evening meeting for working women sponsored by the WTUL. There were afternoon teas in the West End's luxurious homes, as well as in German homes on the south side. The St. Louis Artists' Guild featured a concert and poster contest; a musicale at 3502 North Grand attracted a primarily German-American audience.

Progressive Era idealism was framed by a social Darwinian notion of racial progress that moved from primitive to advanced civilizations. St. Louisans got a heavy dose of this world view at the 1904 World's Fair, which was explicitly organized to demonstrate the superiority of white Euro-American cultures. It is, therefore, not surprising that suffrage had serious overtones of racism and class bias. What is surprising is how often St. Louis suffragists cut through the pervasive bigotries of their time and place in pursuit of common polity and humanity.

–Susan Beattie

Sources: Dina M. Young, "The Silent Search for a Voice," *GH* 8, no. 4 (spring 1988) is a good summary of the formation and activities of the Equal Suffrage League. First-person accounts (including the story of Christine Fordyce's address to the legislature and the founding of *Missouri Woman*) by Florence Atkinson, Althea Somerville Grossman, and Florence Weigle were published in a collection edited by Mary Semple Scott in *MHR* 14, no. 3 (April 1920).

The League of Women Voters Papers, which include early ESL records, WHMC–UMSL; scrapbook compiled by Florence Richardson Usher, WHMC–UMSL; and scrapbooks of Barbara Blackman O'Neil and Mrs. John Green, MHS, are invaluable sources of contemporary newspaper accounts of the movement. MHS also has a full set of the *Missouri Woman* from 1915 to 1919. Archives of the Ethical Society of St. Louis (sponsor of the Self-Culture Halls) are at WHMC–UMSL.

Phoebe Couzins

On December 6, 1913, Phoebe Couzins died destitute in a sparsely furnished room of an unoccupied house at 2722 Pine Street. She was mourned only by her brother and a few friends who had come to her aid at the end of her life. Couzins, however, had been a well-known St. Louis woman—the first female graduate of Washington University, one of the first female American lawyers, and the first woman appointed a United States marshal. She was a nationally known writer and lecturer for woman suffrage and later a well-paid lobbyist for the United Brewers Association. In her early seventies and in poor health for many years, her death was not unexpected. The circumstances in which she died underscored the perils of old age for single women without money or family before the advent of the welfare state. Phoebe Couzins, however, was not a typical sick old woman without resources. A complex and contradictory New Woman, she was unable to use her many advantages to create a lasting place for herself.

Phoebe Couzins's life began very differently from the way it ended. She was born in 1839, the daughter of prominent St. Louisans, Adaline and John E. D. Couzins. Her father was the city's chief of police during the Civil War. Her mother was active in local charity work and a respected volunteer wartime nurse. Adaline and Phoebe belonged to the Ladies' Union Aid Society, and after the war both women joined the St. Louis Woman Suffrage Association, where Phoebe first drew attention as a public speaker. Encouraged to apply for admission to the law school at Washington University in 1869, she was the university's first female graduate, earning her LL.B. degree in 1871. Although licensed to practice law in the federal courts and in Missouri, Arkansas, Utah, and Kansas in the 1870s, she chose the lecture circuit over a legal career. She vigorously campaigned for woman suffrage and temperance all over the northern United States. She was an attractive, vibrant, and outspoken advocate for women's rights who drew large crowds to her lectures.

Phoebe Couzins was in her early forties when, in 1884, her father became U.S. marshal for the Eastern District of Missouri. He made her one of his deputies. After the death of Phoebe's father in 1887, President U.S. Grant appointed her interim U.S. marshal, the first woman to hold that position, but two months later she was replaced by a man. Her father's death gave Phoebe an opportunity for public recognition, but it also left the family in financial straits. John Couzins left no pension or savings for his wife and daughter. Phoebe successfully helped her mother petition the federal government for a war service pension and probably lived in the family home for most of the 1880s. By

1889, however, she was living in Washington, D.C., supporting herself by writing articles for newspapers and periodicals.

Personality traits that made her later life difficult surfaced after she moved to Washington, D.C. The very attributes that brought her success—ambition, determination, and self-confidence—offended people who could have helped her. When the National Woman Suffrage Association (NWSA) and the American Woman Suffrage Association (AWSA) merged in 1890, Phoebe's outspoken support of the NWSA leadership antagonized women in the reorganized movement both locally and nationally. The St. Louis suffrage group had been affiliated with the AWSA. Couzins also offended colleagues while serving as a Missouri representative on the Board of Lady Managers for the 1893 World's Columbian Exposition in Chicago. She held a salaried position as secretary of the board but lost her job when her efforts to dominate the meetings alienated the board and its powerful chair, Bertha Potter Palmer. She sued for reinstatement but lost.

Phoebe Couzins. Photograph, ca. 1904. MHS–PP

Failing health contributed as much to her misfortunes as her personal shortcomings. Severe attacks of rheumatism (or arthritis) often required her to use crutches or a wheelchair. The painful, debilitating attacks curtailed her mobility and made it hard for her to work. She spent a lot of money searching for a cure, which compounded her mounting financial problems. After her mother's death in 1892, Phoebe, now in her fifties, had only her ailing younger brother to help her.

In the midst of her health problems, Phoebe abruptly changed direction and renounced woman suffrage and the temperance movement—actions that were widely publicized in 1897. The reasons for her reversals were never adequately explained, but financial concerns must have been a factor. She became a national lecturer and lobbyist for the United Brewers Association, actively protesting prohibition.

She also turned for help to the network of women who had helped her further her career, writing to at least one old acquaintance for aid. While she had alienated many, she still had some friends in the suffrage movement. "We are very busy getting up a benefit for Miss Cousins (sic)," a local suffragist reported in 1898. "All her old friends are rallying to her support. . . . She has many friends in the city of St. Louis of the highest position."

Although she continued to speak out against anti-liquor legislation, in 1908 Couzins lost her job with the United Brewers Association, which proved to be a personal disaster. Phoebe was about sixty-eight years old, unemployable, and disabled when she returned to St. Louis from Washington, D.C. She needed sheltered care but refused to go to a home for the aged or to City Hospital. With the specter of the poorhouse before her, she applied in desperation to the federal government for a job and to the Brewers Association for aid. When the few friends she still had in 1913 rallied to her support, it was too late. Only six people attended her funeral.

The obituaries that recounted Phoebe Couzins's achievements attributed her poverty to spending money "unwisely." Even so, there were places in St. Louis for destitute women like Phoebe. The Charless Home for the Friendless, founded as a private refuge for elderly middle-class women without family or funds, might have accepted her despite her difficult personality and physical disabilities. The specter of institutional living may have been such an anathema to Couzins that she chose independence at any price. Her brother reported that her last words were, "If I can get back to Washington, John, and get to work again, things will be all right."

—Joan Cooper

Sources: Phoebe Couzins left very few personal writings, but some can be found in the J. E. D. Couzins Papers at MHS, which also includes the Lillie Devereux Papers that contain references to Phoebe's suffrage lecture tours in the 1870s. Obituaries are in the *Globe-Democrat, Post-Dispatch,* and *New York Times.* For articles about Phoebe, see St. Louis and Missouri Womanhood Scrapbook, vol. 2: 38, 103–4; vol. 3a: 24; vol. 7: 124; vol. 8: 183. See also Phoebe Couzins Newspaper Clippings, MHS vertical file; and *The Spectator,* 8 April 1982; 3 March 1983. Short biographies are in Mary K. Dains and Sue Sadler, eds., *Show Me Missouri Women: Selected Biographies* (Kirksville, Mo.: Thomas Jefferson University Press, 1989), and Carla Waal and Barbara Oliver Korner, eds., *Hardship and Hope: Missouri Women Writing About Their Lives, 1820–1920* (Columbia: University of Missouri Press, 1997), which also contains a reprint of the gracious speech Phoebe Couzins gave in 1871 thanking Washington University for admitting her and the law faculty for their encouragement and courtesies during the two years she spent getting her Bachelor of Law degree.

For information on her complex relations with the Board of Lady Managers at the 1893 Fair, see Weimann, *The Fair Women.* For her suffrage activities, see Elizabeth Cady Stanton, Susan B. Anthony, and Matilda Joslyn Gage, eds., *History of Woman Suffrage* (New York: Fowler and Wells, 1922). See also Dorothy Thomas, "Phoebe Wilson Couzins," in *NAW,* vol 1.

Mary Ezit Bulkley

In the first decades of the twentieth century, Mary Ezit Bulkley made a place for herself in nearly every reform activity in St. Louis. When she was ninety years old, she looked back on her remarkable career of social activism. "During all [the] years when I was coquetting with benevolence and general 'uplift,' with settlements and trade union auxiliaries, with pacifism and charity hospitals," she wrote in a memoir, *Grandmother, Mother and Me,* "I did not see that what I really wanted was to help to bring about some measure of social justice, in which everyone might have a fighting chance to develop himself." Bulkley may have characterized herself as a Progressive Era dilettante, but the record of her activities and opinions suggest otherwise. A West End resident from an upper middle-class family, Bulkley was a typical club woman involved in the arts, civic reform, and woman suffrage. But she always cast a critical eye at "do-gooders" and was by the end of her life considerably to the political left of most of her reformist compatriots.

Mary Bulkley was born in New York City in 1856 to Peter and Mary Moody Bulkley. Her father's real estate business afforded the family a comfortable life, which continued after the family moved to St. Louis when Mary was ten. Her father lost heavily in the Panic of 1873. However, Bulkley had expected to attend Vassar College after her high school graduation, but lean years and family obligations required her to manage the house and nurse her invalid mother. The Bulkleys were clearly not destitute. Their reduced circumstances did permit the family to hire one maid, because Mary's "young shoulders were really too slight to keep house and nurse unassisted." There was money enough to send her younger brother to college.

The source and size of Bulkley's income for much of her life is unclear. Like many middle-class families forced by financial reversals to accept a reduced, but adequate, standard of living, Bulkley had to help support herself. As a young woman she tutored younger students. She studied design briefly at tuition-free Cooper Union in New York but left the school to care for her brother, who was in Asheville, North Carolina, recuperating from an illness. She was engaged to a young lawyer for a period of two years, but the relationship waned and she never married. Although she was not consistently employed, she maintained an independent middle-class lifestyle, which suggests she must have had at least a modest regular income from family resources. She worked as a secretary to the Board of St. Louis Children's Hospital shortly after its founding in 1879 but moved back to New York at one point to serve as governess to the children of a cousin. She first observed the art of hand bookbinding on a European trip with this family and decided that it would be a perfect occupation for a young woman in her circumstances. After studying the craft with several teachers, she moved to Chicago to study under Ellen Gates Starr, a master bookbinder and cofounder with Jane Addams of Hull House. She paid for her lessons with Starr by teaching English classes in the settlement house. When she returned to St. Louis, Bulkley opened a studio and practiced bookbinding for more than fifteen years.

Working at Children's Hospital and at Hull House, she saw poor people up-close for the first time. "Up to that time I had always thought that 'shiftlessness' and drunkenness were the causes of poverty. This was a kindergarten course for me, giving me some sense of community responsibility," she recalled. She completed her education in St. Louis when she became involved in political and social reform. However, from the start she saw that "the selfish manipulations of industry made a spectator who was an 'Uplifter' more than a little romantic about an abstraction called 'Labor.'" By her own admission, she slowly moved beyond easy answers to hard problems, taking "step after step into a very disagreeable terrain. I went through all the states: There ought to be a law: . . . Put the good men in office' et cetera. 'Uplifting' is a very contagious disease."

Despite her proclaimed aversion to uplifters, she was involved in middle-class reform for the rest of her life. She was a founding member of The Wednesday Club, recalling it as "a University for Gray-Haired Women." She became active in the Ethical Culture movement (today known as the Ethical Society) and was a board member and teacher at their Self-Culture Hall, which sponsored musical events, lectures, and classes for the working poor and served as a meeting place for a variety of grass-roots organizations. Bulkley later dismissed this neighborhood association because, she said, it was instituted in the organizers' misguided belief that by sharing their joy in Shakespeare and musical classes with the less privileged they could really help the poor. She ultimately rejected the philosophy of the society as too cold and "scientific."

It was, however, at the Self-Culture Hall that she hired as director young Roger Baldwin, who later became a Washington University professor and founder of the American Civil Liberties Union. Despite a twenty-year age difference, they became lifelong friends and greatly influenced one another. She recalled later that when the Civic Improvement League hired Baldwin, she "tagged along and got myself elected to the Governing Board." While she was involved in the Ethical Culture movement, she was also active in the Women's Trade Union League of St. Louis, which used the hall as its meeting place.

As might have been expected, Bulkley was one of ten women who met in the spring of 1910 to organize the St. Louis Equal Suffrage League, (ESL). For the next decade, she was one of the foremost workers for the franchise. While she disclaimed any talent as a speaker, a local writer described her as a "forceful talker . . . illuminating and skillful in her comparisons and figures of speech." She illustrated her arguments with stories and experiences from real life. Bulkley served as treasurer of the state suffrage organization for most of its existence and was key in founding its monthly publication, *Missouri Woman*. She regularly contributed articles, often sparked with her wry humor and always provocative in content and tone.

Bulkley's writing talents were not limited to journal articles. In 1919 she wrote a play for the Equal Suffrage League. Titled "The Trial: What's the Constitution Among Friend?" it described Susan B. Anthony's legal battle following her attempt to vote in 1872.

She wrote a booklet "Aid to the Woman Voter in Missouri" in anticipation of the passage of the suffrage amendment, which the ESL sold as a fund raiser and used in voter education classes. A revised version, issued by the League of Woman Voters in 1920, dropped the word "woman" from the title. It had become the authoritative guide and educational text for all Missouri voters.

Bulkley was an artist as well as a civic reformer. Her bookbinding may or may not have been profitable, but it was definitely a form of artistic expression. She displayed her work in the Artists' Guild exhibit at the World's Fair. A founder and first president of the Municipal Art League, she worked to supply artworks to the public schools. She taught art classes at the Self-Culture Hall.

In 1920 a serious heart condition forced Bulkley to retire from public life. She left her West End home at 5906 Clemmens Avenue and moved to California. She bought and renovated an old house in Carmel-by-the-Sea, where she took up weaving and metalwork. She continued to write, publishing a book of poetry *Speaking at 70* (she was actually seventy-five) in 1931. That same year, she put forth her ideas for getting America out of the Great Depression in a pamphlet titled "A Primer of Social Credit." While specifically rejecting communism, she called for a guaranteed monthly income for all Americans and for manufactures to sell goods below cost.

Mary Ezit Bulkley had many faces: artist, activist, club woman, and feminist. Her final work was an autobiography, written the year before her death in 1946 at age ninety-one. While it is sometimes the vague, disorganized self-conscious musings of an "elder," the biting wit and turn of phrase are those of an ironic, perceptive woman who played an active role in St. Louis progressive reform.

–*Susan Beattie*

Sources: Much of the biographical material for this essay is found in Bulkley's unpublished autobiography, *Grandmother, Mother and Me*. A typescript of this work, along with copies of Bulkley's published books are at MHS. Bulkley's involvement in the Self-Culture Halls, Equal Suffrage League, and Wednesday Club is included in records of those organizations, MHS and elsewhere.

Mary Bulkley was a fascinating individual whose life spanned nearly a century. She was connected to virtually every reformer and reform organization in the city before her retirement in 1920, as well as many in the arts. While her autobiography gives a good picture of many of her activities, it is not organized chronologically, seldom gives dates, and often omits names of organizations and people. In many ways a representative of the single woman activist of the Progressive Era, she was certainly more radical than most of her compatriots and seemed to become more so as she aged. Researching her associations with Roger Baldwin and Kate Richards O'Hare and her work at Hull House and St. Louis's Self-Culture Hall and an in-depth study of her writings might shed light on her political thought and its origins.

Josephine Baker

Born to a laundress on June 3, 1906, Josephine Baker–nicknamed "Tumpy" as a child–spent her early years at 212 Johnson Street (formerly Targee Street), in the Mill Creek Valley neighborhood near Union Station. Poverty-stricken as a child, she stole food from garbage cans at Soulard Farmer's Market and fallen coal from the Union Station rail yards. Josephine attended Lincoln Elementary School through the fifth grade and worked as a live-in maid and as a waitress at the Old Chauffer's Club at 3133 Pine Street.

Mill Creek Valley was a mixed white and black neighborhood, the latter scattered in segregated pockets. Many of its buildings dated from the Civil War. While their condition depended on the efforts of individual owners, many were dilapidated. Poor African Americans moved into some of the area's most decayed and overcrowded structures as white residents moved west.

Mill Creek Valley was home to several vaudeville venues that often doubled as movie houses, including the Jazzland, Booker T. Washington, and Comet Theaters. Visiting any of these or the valley's many juke joints would have exposed Josephine to show business at an early age.

As she wrote in her autobiography, "I spent most of my time wandering around the colored quarter. . . . Everyone seemed to own an accordion, a banjo or harmonica. Those without enough money for real instruments made banjos from cheese boxes. . . . As soon as the music began, I would move my arms and legs in all directions in time to the rhythm or make the beat with my friends on the treasure we pulled from the trash: tin cans, battered saucepans, abandoned wooden and metal containers."

At age thirteen, Josephine married Willie Wells, a black foundry worker in his late twenties. After less than a year, she left the failing marriage and joined the Dixie Steppers, a vaudeville group traveling across the South and East, performing minstrel shows in threadbare plaid dresses. She moved to New York in 1921 and joined the traveling musical *La Revue Négre*, where her signature was the "*Danse Sauvage.*" When the show closed in Paris the *Folies Bergere* hired her, and she became an instant sensation in France.

Josephine soon had an international audience that flocked to hear her melodious voice and watch her fluid, athletic, and sensuous dancing. Josephine was famed for her daring presentations; in one number, she arrived on stage atop a man's shoulders, doing the splits and wearing nothing but an artfully placed flamingo feather. In another famous piece, she danced the Charleston clad only in a skirt made of bananas.

Josephine was an integral part of the expatriate American community in Paris between the world wars, often performing to music by black American groups and contributing to the popularity of jazz in France. There, Josephine was able to live lavishly, and her popularity lessened the impact of racial discrimination on her daily life. She had access to a wider variety of performance roles as well, though French audiences interpreted her exoticism in the light of African and Cubist art and their own stereotyping of "primitive" beauty and sexuality.

Josephine eventually transcended racial stereotyping and transformed her image from an exotic vaudeville dancer to a continental lady, frequently performing in lavish designer ball gowns. She never, however, abandoned the eroticism that her audiences found so alluring. In the 1930s she appeared in several films, including *Zouzou* and *Princess Tam-Tam.* As flamboyant in real life as she was on stage, Josephine often walked the Champs-Elysées with her pet leopards. She routinely received marriage proposals from smitten fans. While she married five times, Josephine had no children of her own. Between World War II and the 1960s, she adopted twelve children of different races whom she called her "Rainbow Tribe."

After becoming a French citizen in 1937, Josephine spied on Italian fascists, eavesdropping on diplomats at cocktail parties who thought they were merely talking with an exotic dancer. During World War II, she relayed information on Axis forces to the Allies by writing in invisible ink on her musical scores. Later in the war, she worked for the Resistance in North Africa, where she entertained

JOSÉPHINE BAKER
dans

troops and drove an ambulance, earning her the Croix de Guerre and the Legion of Honor.

After the war, Josephine used her fame to support the American civil rights movement. During her American tour in 1951, Josephine would perform only for integrated audiences; she turned down a twelve thousand dollar-a-week run at the Chase Hotel in St. Louis when the management refused to admit African Americans to the audience. She participated in the March on Washington and made speeches on school integration for the NAACP. She also paid for the funeral of a black man executed (unjustly, Josephine felt) for raping a white woman, and she made speeches on American race relations all over the world. The FBI and the State Department branded Josephine a communist and investigated her.

Just after opening her comeback tour to standing ovations, Josephine died in Paris in 1975. Thousands of Parisians thronged her funeral, which featured a twenty-one-gun salute. At her death, she

Josephine Baker. Halftone from Your St. Louis and Mine, by Nathan B. Young, ca. 1937. MHS Library

was bankrupt; poor financial management, providing for a family of twelve, and a dwindling income after she was informally blackballed in America had eaten up her fortune. Josephine was an astounding performer of international repute who found fame abroad more easily than at home; a social justice reformer and anti-fascist activist branded a subversive by her home country; and an adored star who died broke.

–Katherine Douglass

Sources: In France, Baker invented herself from the ground up, circulating fabulous and conflicting stories about her past. For this reason, many of her memories should be taken with a grain of salt—as is often the case with memoirs and autobiographies. Cited below are sources which historians generally regard as trustworthy. Josephine's childhood recollections are taken from Josephine Baker and Jo Bouillon, *Josephine*, trans., Mariana Fitzpatrick (New York: Harper & Row, 1977).

General sources include Jean-Claude Baker and Chris Chase, *Josephine: The Hungry Heart* (New York: Random House, 1993); Lynn Haney, *Naked at the Feast: A Biography of Josephine Baker* (New York: Dodd, Mead & Co., 1981); and George Lipsitz, *The Sidewalks of St. Louis: Places, People, and Politics in an American City* (Columbia: University of Missouri Press, 1991).

The quote about French audiences in confusion comes from Anna Kisselgoff, "Josephine Baker's Unfulfilled Dance Career," *St. Louis Post-Dispatch,* 29 March 1987. Information on Josephine's civil rights activity comes from George Lipsitz, "Le Jazz Hot," *St. Louis Magazine* (September 1984), and Michael Bronski, "Harlem on her Mind," *Gay Community News* (St. Louis) 15, no. 32 (Feburary 28–March 5, 1988). Many of these articles are included in the vertical file on Josephine Baker at MHS.

Pearl Curran, Spiritualist Medium

On the evening of July 8, 1913, Pearl Curran sat down to a table with three other women in her West End apartment at 6031 Kingsbury Avenue to ask questions of a Ouija board while her husband played pinochle with his friends in the next room. The Currans were a sociable, childless, middle-class couple from southwestern Missouri. Pearl's father had been a bookkeeper for railroads and mining companies. Pearl gave piano and voice lessons before marrying John Curran in 1907. They moved to St. Louis after John resigned a state government position. Supported by John's land development projects and investments, both Currans enjoyed writing but more as a hobby than a vocation.

Pearl and her friends frequently spent an evening at the Ouija board. The ancient device used by spiritualists to communicate with the dead had become a popular parlor game by the early twentieth century. The women rested their fingers lightly on the supposedly spirit-directed, heart-shaped pointer while it slowly spelled out answers to the questions they posed. Like the majority of Progressive Era Americans, thirty-year-old Pearl Curran did not believe supernatural forces spoke through Ouija boards, but when the pointer quickly moved to spell, "Many moons ago I lived. Again I come Patience Worth my name," she unexpectedly found herself at the center of a sensational local mystery story. Over the next twenty-four years Pearl Curran insisted that Patience Worth, the spirit of a seventeenth-century Puritan woman, dictated the books, plays, and poems she produced in rapid succession. For nearly two decades Patience Worth was St. Louis's best-known local author.

Although the creative method and the literary context of the work defied rational explanation, the experience itself had historical precedent in nineteenth-century spiritualism, which had given otherwise reticent middle-class women articulate and often radical public voices. By the turn of the century, however, spiritualism had lost its reformist zeal. For Pearl Curran and the other St. Louisans caught up in her story, Patience Worth was a baffling literary phenomenon, not the champion of social or political change she might have been had she spoken fifty years earlier.

Spiritualism resonated with nineteenth-century Americans' changing attitudes about death and their growing individualism. By then, most Protestant Americans felt more comfortable with doctrines of universal salvation than with older Calvinist predestination that consigned most souls to hell. If all who accepted Christ would be saved, then believers could imagine family reunions in heaven. Spiritualist mediums offered evidence of the soul's immortality by contacting dead loved ones in the spirit world. In 1853 St. Louisan Flora Byrne consulted a local medium who relayed a message from her dead son that he was living in heaven and waiting to "meet her again where there is no sorrow." Her long lost brother reported that he had been "knocked off a boat in the New York harbor" and was now living where there was no fear of death. Flora wrote her skeptical mother in Baltimore that "a great many more believe every day and to me it is an unspeakable joy."

Spiritualists also rejected traditional lines of religious authority. The independent medium sought truth directly from spirits without human intermediaries or interpreters. Although many believers integrated conventional religious doctrine with spirit summoning, committed spiritualists did not regard themselves as Christians. They espoused no theology, rejected formal organization, and established no hierarchical governing bodies. This stance was a religious heresy with a history in America going back to Anne Hutchinson and Roger Williams, who defied the religious authority of colonial New England clergy. Spiritualism gave believers a religious rationale for questioning all authority and led some to advocate women's rights and other radical political and social reforms.

Spiritualism was a growing movement that terrified traditional churchmen. The St. Louis clergy mounted vigorous opposition. In 1853, the Second Baptist Church of St. Louis tried a parishioner for heresy. The same year a committee of seventeen male St. Louis spiritualists challenged the Reverend Dr. N. L. Rice, a Presbyterian minister, to a public debate pitting spiritualist beliefs against Christian theology. He declined.

Spiritualism attracted many St. Louisans, but their fervent individualism made them difficult to count or locate. Traveling spiritualist lecturers, however, drew large crowds. When the Fox sisters, mediums from Buffalo, New York, who allegedly had communicated with the spirit world since 1848 by interpreting mysterious rapping noises, visited the city in 1859, Dr. John McDowell, the eccentric head of the McDowell Medical College, conducted "scientific experiments" that proved to him they were not charlatans. Years later they admitted that they were.

Several St. Louisans regularly contributed to the *Banner of Light*, a national radical newspaper that printed letters from spiritualists and reports from the field. In 1868 the *Banner of Light* reported that Mathalda A. M'Cord opened a room at 513 Chestnut Street, where "spiritual and liberal" books, pamphlets, and periodicals could be procured. In 1870 Warren Chase, a well-known spiritualist lecturer and advocate of women's rights, reported opening a liberal bookstore at Fifth and Washington, financed in part by two unnamed "middle-aged females, with a small capital left them by a deceased father." Mrs. P. E. Bland, whose lawyer husband had headed the 1853 spiritualist committee, was a practicing medium. The Spiritualist Association of St. Louis was founded in 1882 and held meetings at the Mercantile Library. Although the movement had peaked earlier, in 1890 there were still an estimated forty-five thousand spiritualists in thirty-nine states.

Women were particularly drawn to spiritualism, only in part because it promised domestic life beyond the grave. The emphasis on reunion without judgment encouraged belief in a deity who was gentler and more feminine than the traditional vengeful masculine God. The role of a spirit medium was consistent with qualities associated with women: passive, nurturing, and ethereal. But the most appealing aspect of spiritualism for women was its insistence on absolute self-determinism regardless of gender. The concept of self-ownership which underlay the movement's individualistic philosophy made spiritualists among the earliest and most outspoken advocates for women's rights. Suffrage leader Elizabeth Cady Stanton considered spiritualists the only religious sect in the world on the right side of the woman question.

Trance spiritualists who performed in lecture halls before large crowds were some of the first American women to lecture in public. They sidestepped entrenched opposition to women as public speakers because the words they spoke were really not theirs; the speaker appeared to be in a trance, unconsciously delivering a message from the spirit world. A number of nineteenth-century female reformers began as pre–Civil War spiritualist lecturers.

Pearl Curran. Photograph. MHS–PP

Spiritualists supported women's rights as part of a larger reform agenda that put them at the center of nineteenth-century American radicalism. They vigorously opposed slavery and crusaded for marriage reform, children's rights, vegetarianism, dress reform, socialism, and other causes that advanced social justice and individual freedom.

In 1867 Emma Hardinge, a popular spiritualist lecturer, spoke in St. Louis to help the Western Female Guardian Society raise funds for a home for outcast women. She chastised business leaders and denounced William Greenleaf Eliot, the city's most prominent liberal minister and a supporter of the project, for giving less to finance the home than to renovate the burned-out Lindell Hotel.

Severely criticized for their anti-institutional stance, spiritualists took the most heat for espousing "free love," which their detractors interpreted to mean advocating promiscuity over marriage. In fact, most spiritualists supported monogamous relationships but denounced the widely held and legally sanctioned belief that husbands had a right to demand sex from their wives. Spiritualists held that a woman's body was her own to be freely given or withheld. Spiritualist Stella Campbell, who lived at 1108 Olive Street in St. Louis, was a frequent contributor to *Lucifer*, a leading national anarchist periodical. In 1889 she argued that men make their wives prostitutes when they "pay the church or state for the privilege of living with women in the sex relation."

Like nineteenth-century spiritualists, Patience Worth, who in 1913 began speaking through the voice of Pearl Curran, professed immortality and human goodness. She also showed their same fierce independence and opposition to women's oppression. Most of the literary output attributed to Patience, however, consisted of detailed historical epics, many with Biblical settings, and poetry written in antique or pseudo-English dialect but structured like contemporary twentieth-century fiction.

Respectable middle-class St. Louisans were intrigued by the mysterious presence that emitted from Pearl Curran, first through the Ouija board and later directly through the medium's own voice. The Currans held regular seances in their home and invited ever-more prominent visitors. They posed questions to Patience who answered sometimes sharply, sometimes teasingly, but always with authority. Between 1916 and 1930 Pearl, a high school dropout from a small Missouri town, produced a large body of literature in these living-room sessions. Admirers published at least three novels and several volumes of poetry.

Like nineteenth-century female trance mediums who performed in public, Pearl received the spirit communication but let others handle the logistics of recording, publishing, and promotion. John Curran transcribed most of the medium's words in notebooks as she spoke. Major local journalists, including William Marion Reedy, publisher of *Reedy's Mirror*, and Casper S. Yost, editor of the *St. Louis Globe-Democrat*, promoted Patience Worth and published her work.

In 1918 Casper Yost invited Lucille Lowenstein to join a "sitting" with Pearl Curran. Seven other people attended, including "a Washington University professor, a social welfare leader, two women active in the woman's suffrage movement, a society woman, and two businessmen of note." Lowenstein reported that Patience dictated poetry through Pearl with "never a second's hesitation over choice of word or phrase and with never an alteration." Patience offered to compose a poem for each guest. As Lowenstein rested her hands on the pointer with Pearl Curran, the Ouija board spelled out:

> I am a harbor, a home,
> A porting place upon the shore
> Of eternity, and the waves
> Of all wisdom press upon me.
> Little crafts come idly in
> And I toy with them,
> watching them disport themselves
> Upon the little lapping wave-tongues.
> When they depart and I wait,
> Wait, wait, until a greater hulk
> Comes, heavy laden through
> Troublous waters. And I eagerly
> Unhold her of her store,
> Greedily eating my fill of her riches.
>
> Then as I become
> Stronger and my voice assume
> Assuredness and I make certainties
> Which I have created.
> And I doubt, yet they are mine
> And I send them forth as mine.
> Oh, I am a port, a home
> upon the shore of eternity.

Lucille Lowenstein, who had not met Pearl Curran before that night, was amazed that the poem captured the significant events of her life: a sheltered childhood, the death of her husband as a young bride, the decision to study social work, and the self-confidence and satisfaction she found in her work. In the tradition of earlier spiritualists, Pearl Curran delivered a message that celebrated women's autonomy and self-determination.

Pearl Curran communicated with Patience Worth until her own death in 1937, although she dictated less each year. The Currans spent the income they received from Patience's writings transcribing and publishing works most people found too arcane to read. After John Curran died, Pearl remarried and moved to California. She wrote some magazine short stories under her own name, but none displayed the broad knowledge of history and literature that underlay Patience's writing.

Patience Worth remains a mystery. Contemporaries were convinced that Pearl Curran was not a fraud. Unless she did communicate with the spirit world, Pearl's writings were somehow her own. More recent critics have been less impressed by the quality of the writing than were Reedy and Yost, but they still could not reconcile the work with the woman. Like the female spiritualists who preceded her, Pearl Curran found her voice and made her public place as a persona separate from the one she presented to the world as her own.

Sources: The most detailed account of Pearl Curran's life and experiences as a spirit medium is Irving Litvac, *Singer in the Shadows: The Strange Story of Patience Worth* (New York: Macmillan, 1972). See also Laurel E. Boeckman, "Pearl Lenore Curran (Patience Worth)," in Dains and Sadler, eds., *Show Me Missouri Women*. The Patience Worth Collection at MHS contains twenty-nine volumes of writings recorded by John Curran and attributed to Patience Worth. For reactions of Marion Reedy and Casper Yost to the phenomenon, see *Reedy's Mirror* (October 20, 1910) and Casper Yost, *Patience Worth: A Psychic Mystery* (New York: Patience Worth Publication Company, 1925). Daniel Shea, professor of English at Washington University, has researched the case in the context of nineteenth-century spiritualism, literary analysis, and recent psychological theory. His unpublished essay, "A Psychic St. Louis Woman," is the most comprehensive analysis to date.

This essay draws on Ann Braude, *Radical Spirits: Spiritualism and Women's Rights in Nineteenth-Century America* (Boston: Beacon Press, 1989) for information about the spiritualist movement and analysis of the relationship between spiritualism and the nineteenth-century women's rights movement. For more on the connections between spiritualism, anarchism, and women's rights, see John C. Spurlock, *Free Love, Marriage, and Middle-class Radicalism in America, 1825–1860* (New York: New York University Press, 1988), and Ann Russo and Cheris Kramarae, eds., *The Radical Women's Press of the 1850s* (New York: New York University Press, 1991).

Quotations from Flora Byrne's 1853 letters are in the Meyer Collection, MHS. See "Correspondence of the St. Louis Spiritualists and the Rev. Dr. Rice" for their local dispute, MHS. Information on Dr. McDowell and the Fox sisters as well as names of local spiritualists and accounts of her own activities in St. Louis as a traveling lecturer are found in Emma Hardinge, *Modern American Spiritualism*, 4th ed. (New York: New York Printing Co., 1870), 353–80. See *Banner of Light*, 13, 20, and 27 April 1867, for Hardinge's St. Louis visit and her efforts to raise funds for fallen women. Stella Campbell's correspondence is in *Lucifer*, 9 June 1893, and 31 December 1898. See both *Banner of Light* and *Lucifer* for notices of meetings of St. Louis spiritualists and reports on the local scene by traveling spiritualists and anarchists. Warren Chase's announcement of his bookstore in the *Banner of Light*, 10 September 1870, and his *Forty Years on the Spiritual Rostrum* (Boston: Colby and Rich, 1888). See also Scharf, *History of St. Louis City and County*, vol. 2, for announcement of the Spiritual Association. Lucille Lowenstein Milner's account of the seance with Pearl Curran and Patience Worth's poem is from "An Evening with Patience Worth," in the Milner Papers, MHS.

The Potter's Wheel

In 1904 five St. Louis women, all recent high school graduates with an interest in art and literature, declared themselves members of the Self and Mutual Admiration Society. Their announced objective was the advancement of their individual and collective talents. In the introduction to the first issue of *The Potter's Wheel*, a hand-made magazine produced by the group, Williamina Parrish wrote:

> By "admiration" we do not mean vanity and egotism; it stands for self-respect, self-appreciation, for that element which makes us recognize that we can and must do and think our very best at all times, and "admiring" ourselves thus . . . it becomes possible for our confreres to admire us also.

The women of the Self and Mutual Admiration Society soon called themselves the Potters, but the original tongue-in-cheek name of the group revealed the essential emotional link between the members: a positive image of the woman as artist and a commitment to the highest critical standard for themselves.

White upper middle-class young women, they did not see themselves dabbling in watercolors or making seed paintings to fill the time before they committed themselves to the serious business of marriage and family. Art was a vocation, not a hobby. Between 1904 and 1907 they nurtured their talents and their friendships by creating *The Potter's Wheel*. *The Potter's Wheel* was a magazine made entirely by hand, with blank pages at the end for critical comments by the members.

The Potters met at a member's home every other Friday afternoon. Each one took home several sheets on which to make her contributions and brought the completed work back to the group. Initially published on the first Friday of each month, contributions were due on the final Friday of the preceding month. The original magazine was 8" x 10," produced in brown, tans, and grays. Later, they expanded the size of the magazine to 10" x 12" and produced a volume every other month until 1907.

They circulated the completed magazine for the members to record their critiques. As serious artists they did not hesitate to criticize each other's work. They did not feel compelled to be polite or diplomatic; such traditionally "lady-like" behavior would not improve their skill as artists or enhance the quality of their production.

Williamina "Will" Parrish, considered a "born tyrant," made her fellow contributors' lives "miserable," observed Frances Porcher, "but the 'Wheel' always comes out." Williamina made the sequencing decisions, pegged the pages together, and did most of the binding.

Without the help of her talented friends, however, Parrish would not have had anything to produce. Each founding member of the group had her special gifts: Williamina's sister Grace was a talented photographer like Williamina herself. Vine Colby and Celia Harris were writers; Caroline Risque was an accomplished sculptor. Later, members of group included Guida Richey, Inez Dutro, Edna Wahlert, Petronelle Sombart, and Sara Teasdale. Each member made a contribution for each issue, and each issue circulated around the group.

The aesthetic sensibilities and the serious commitment of the members were evident in their production; myths and legends appealed to them, as well as Lewis Carroll's *Alice in Wonderland* and the work of the Pre-Raphaelites, mid-nineteenth-century British artists who were committed to a new vitality and individualism in art. This was the driving philosophy behind the Potters as well. Years later, Edna Wahlert remembered that the Potters "simply came together as a matter of temperament–the elusive type of mind which holds only the inner spirit of importance."

In addition to the shared artistic philosophy, however, was a commitment to friendship: the women depended upon each other for emotional and critical support. In *The Potter's Wheel* 1, no. 4, dated February 1905, Williamina Parrish composed "The Rubaiyat of Friendship," celebrating the relationship of the group's members. "Our group was a spontaneous agglomeration," Edna Wahlert recalled, "which respected individuality when self-disciplined and in the process of emerging into awareness of the creative potential." The intensity of their friendships and passionate attachments sometimes caused conflicts within the group, but they remained devoted to each other personally and professionally. Lillie Rose Ernst, a teacher some of the young Potters became acquainted with at Central High, was an important influence and unifying force. An assertive, independent woman who later served as the first female assistant superintendent of the St. Louis Public Schools, Ernst was a natural mentor for the group.

The Potters emerged at the end of the nineteenth century when a gender-segregated culture encouraged close female relationships and fostered female solidarity. In their commitment to personal goals, however, they were representative of the New Woman of turn of the century urban America.

In the twentieth century, white middle-class women like the Potters could reasonably aspire to both a career as an artist and a conventional marriage. Only a few decades earlier, the sculptor Harriet Hosmer had felt she needed to chose between her art and her personal life. Nevertheless, it was not always easy to resolve conflicts between domestic roles and individual interests outside the home.

Some of the Potters found this combination of responsibilities difficult to manage. Edna Wahlert's husband was "turned out of his own house by a mob of Potters" for their 1910 reunion, but he took it in good humor; all of the married Potters enjoyed an unusual degree of personal freedom. Still, the constraints of trying to live both lives well took its toll. Caroline Risque, although married to an artist, felt that her marriage interfered with her work.

Ultimately, most of the members of the group found success with their art. Caroline Risque's talent as a sculptor was finally recognized in 1954 when the *St. Louis Post-Dispatch* described her busy studio on Henderson Avenue in Clayton and reported that a statue to be placed in Forest Park was "distinguished for its movement and spiritual qualities and the excellent drawing for which this sculptor's work always is notable." Risque also established and ran the art department at the John Burroughs School until her death in 1952. In 1901 a reporter for the *Post-Dispatch* hailed the Parrish sisters of 5607 Cabanne Place as "two of the cleverest young amateurs" whose work "Equals Work Done by Professional Photographers of Many Years' Experience." He was particularly impressed with the "stained window-glass effect," a technique Williamina also used in the magazine illustrations. "We have a wild desire to try everything we can think of," Williamina told the reporter, who declared that their attempt "vies with the results obtained only in the best galleries in the city." The sisters frequently exhibited their work and were published in leading photographic magazines.

In 1923 the *Post-Dispatch* recognized the Parrish sisters for their ability to produce photographs which "consistently [are] exhibited in collections restricted to the fine arts." Vine Colby McCausland praised the Parrish sisters and Caroline Risque in a review for *Reedy's Mirror*. "It is the work of artists who have something to say, and who have said it." Celia Harris, Edna Wahlert, Petronelle Sombart, Vine Colby, and Sara Teasdale all published their writings after the Potters disbanded, but only Teasdale gained national recognition for her work.

When the members decided to end publication of *The Potter's Wheel* in 1907, they gathered together all the issues and drew lots to determine who would receive each volume. The Missouri Historical Society eventually obtained sixteen issues and ten critical notebooks.

–Kathleen Butterly Nigro

Sources: The majority of the biographical information for this entry is taken from Bishop, "The Potter's Wheel: An Early Twentieth Century Support Network of Women Artists and Writers." See also "The Potter's Wheel," an article which Mamie Teasdale Wheless, Sara's sister, prepared for the Yale University Library, MHS. Kathleen Butterly Nigro is working on a larger study of the Potters.

Fannie Hurst

Fannie Hurst grew up at 5641 Cates Avenue, a quiet St. Louis house "of evenly drawn shades, impeccable cleanliness, geometrically placed conventional furniture, middle-class respectability." She became America's highest paid author, however, because her magazine stories and novels resonated with the lives of millions of ordinary women. Her best-remembered novels, *Imitation of Life* and *Back Street*, were the stories of working-class women who, despite wrenching rejection and

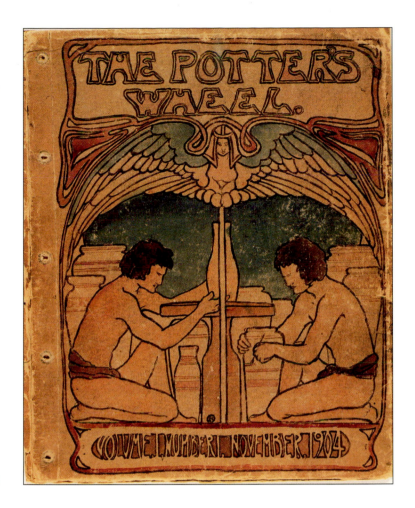

hardship, got what they wanted through sheer determination and savvy decision-making. Although Rose Hurst insisted that her daughter only associated with "the best" people at the family's West End home, and the author herself denied being influenced by her "Missouri environment," Fannie Hurst's empathy for women painfully out of place in their surroundings originated in her turn-of-the-century St. Louis childhood.

Fannie Hurst lived in the Cates Avenue house until she left for New York in 1910, a twenty-one-year-old graduate of Washington University determined to be a writer. Although Samuel Hurst was a successful shoe manufacturer, he and his wife did not participate in the city's Jewish social and religious culture. Rose felt too insecure and envious to socialize with her wealthier local relations. Fannie, who adored her emotional, indulgent mother, was a lonely child, confused by her parents'

The Potter's Wheel *I, no. I (November 1904)* [front cover]. Watercolor on paper by Caroline Risque, 1904. *Potter's Wheel* Collection. MHS Archives

University. They too took themselves seriously as women and as artists, but they rejected Fannie as a colleague. With the exception of Sara Teasdale, the Potters stayed in St. Louis to pursue local careers or to raise families. After college, Hurst left for New York over the objections of her parents to write and "study people" and to eventually become a commercial success as a writer of women's fiction.

As an adult, Fannie Hurst seldom wrote sympathetically about women of wealth and status. If she drew on her St. Louis experiences, it was to champion struggling working women victimized by traditional expectations. In New York she quickly immersed herself in working-class culture, briefly taking waitress and retail sales jobs. Her fiction not only reflected the needs of ordinary women for romance and happiness, but also for justice and fair treatment. Throughout a fifty-year career she published seventeen novels, nine books of short stories, three plays, and innumerable magazine stories. Women wept through twenty-nine screen adaptations of her published work.

The critics were less approving of her efforts than were her many readers; scathing reviews accompanied each new publication. In her autobiography, she acknowledged her limitations as a writer. The judgment of a St. Louis Potter who said, "I would rather be a classic failure than a popular success like Fannie Hurst," still stung.

Fannie Hurst also demonstrated an early concern for social causes, particularly those related to Jewish interests and the welfare of working women. After *Lummox*, the story of a domestic worker exploited by her employer, caught the attention of Eleanor Roosevelt, the two women became friends. Hurst actively supported New Deal policies and chaired committees on housing and workman's compensation. She served on a national committee of the Works Progress Administration and on the board of the National Urban League.

While her assimilated parents had avoided identification with Jewish causes, Fannie sought them out. During World War II, she raised funds for victims of Nazi Germany and afterwards was an active promoter for the state of Israel. She left money in her will to Washington University and to Brandeis University in Massachusetts, established by Jews in response to anti-Semitism in eastern universities.

As a child Fannie had felt smothered by conventional family life; as an adult she advocated restructuring marriage to give women more freedom within it. She and her husband often maintained separate residences; she kept her own name; they had separate social lives. But she wrote

tensions over their Jewish heritage. "We were Jews. Almost everybody else was not," she wrote later. "I was fat and all the other girls in the world were thin . . . everybody else had sisters or brothers." Fannie's teenage response to being different at St. Louis's Central High School was to draw attention to herself with unconventional clothing and theatrical mannerisms and to write stories.

After high school graduation Fannie resisted her mother's efforts to find her a husband, enrolled in Washington University, and continued to write. She sought out William Marion Reedy, publisher of *Reedy's Mirror* and a mentor to many aspiring young writers. He accepted the ambitious college junior's story, "The Joy of Living," for his literary magazine. While still a student, Fannie unsuccessfully submitted dozens of manuscripts to magazines, receiving thirty-five rejections from the *Saturday Evening Post* alone.

Fannie Hurst was a contemporary of a group of affluent young St. Louis women who called themselves the Potters, some of whom also attended Central High School and Washington

Fannie Hurst. Halftone of a photograph by Kajiwara, 1914. From *Notable Women of St. Louis*, 1914. MHS Library

to him weekly and always wore a calla lily, the first flower he had given her. Unlike the Potters who either rejected marriage or struggled to combine it with careers, Hurst boldly advocated a new style of marriage. She and Jacques Danielson remained married until his death in 1952. She died in 1968 and was buried in the family plot in New Mount Sinai Cemetery in St. Louis.

Dismissed as a sentimental writer of women's fiction, Fannie Hurst reached her female audiences because her stories spoke to their basic concerns for love, family, security, and fairness. Like many other creative people who left St. Louis, Fannie believed her childhood had given her an outsider's perspective. A former Potter, Edna Wahlert acknowledged that Hurst might have been "chased out" by the shallowness of St. Louis society but believed that "Miss Hurst should not feel hurt. . . . She is a link and a bridge, and we all loved her and were proud of her."

–*Kathleen Butterly Nigro and Katharine Corbett*

Sources: This essay is based on information from Fannie Hurst, *Anatomy of Me: A Wonderer in Search of Herself* (Garden City, N.Y.: Double Day, 1958), which includes quotations on her early family life; and Antoinette Frederick, "Fannie Hurst," in *NAW*, vol. 2, 359–61. Waal and Korner, *Hardship and Hope*, contains an except from *Anatomy of Me* about Hurst's childhood in St. Louis. The Edna Wahlert quote is from the *Post-Dispatch*, 12 November 1958. Quotes are from Cynthia Ann Brandimarte, "Fannie Hurst: A Missouri Girl Makes Good," *MHR* 81, no. 3 (April 1987), and Catherine Crammer, "Little Visits with Literary Missourians—Fannie Hurst," *MHR* 19, no. 3 (April 1925). See also Brooke Kroeger, *Fannie: The Talent for Success of Writer Fannie Cook* (New York: Random House, 1999).

In addition to Fannie Hurst, William Marion Reedy published poet Sara Teasdale and playwrite Zoe Akins. See chapter 7 for Sara Teasdale. Akins, a St. Louis writer who garnered more critial acclaim but far less remuneration than Hurst, corresponded with Edna Wahlert and Thekla Bernays, another Hurst contemporary. Their letters, in the Thekla Bernays Collection, MHS, along with information about Akins in *Notable Women of St. Louis* reveal undercurrents of both support and competition between St. Louis women struggling to establish careers in the arts.

Confederate Memorial

On December 5, 1914, three hundred St. Louis members and friends of the United Daughters of the Confederacy (UDC) dedicated a monument just south of Lindell Boulevard in Forest Park, culminating years of effort by a determined group of women to commemorate the Southern cause defeated nearly fifty years earlier. St. Louis had been a Union stronghold in a slave state and a bitterly divided wartime city governed by martial law. The impressive monument was material evidence that St. Louisans with personal and ideological ties to the Confederate South had strong sentiments and long memories.

Women had been particularly ardent in their support for the Confederacy and particularly resentful of their treatment by St. Louis Unionists. Margaret McClure, a Southern sympathizer imprisoned in her own home and later banished from the city, founded the UDC in St. Louis, and the national organization was still located there in 1914.

Officials in St. Louis objected to any public memorial commemorating rebel forces. To placate public opinion and induce the city to place their monument in Forest Park, the Ladies Confederate Monument Association of the UDC held a competition for a design that would depict neither a Confederate soldier nor an object of modern warfare.

Three sculptors accepted the challenge to represent the spirit of the militant Confederacy without any military motifs. Models of their submissions displayed in the St. Louis Public Library during the contest set off spirited public debate. One entrant surrounded a shaft with allegorical figures of Glory, History, Poetry, and Sorrow. Another presented an allegorical figure of patriotism bestowing the palm of heroism on the heroes of the South. The winning design, submitted by George Julian Zolnay, featured a bronze relief of a Southern man dressed in civilian clothes setting forth to fight for the cause, encouraged by three figures who appeared to be his wife, mother, and child. An allegorical figure of the *Angel Spirit of the Confederacy*, sculpted in stone, hovered above the group. Dedicated to the memory of the soldiers and sailors of the Southern Confederacy, a quotation from Robert E. Lee was etched on the back of the thirty-two-foot shaft designed by Wilbur Trueblood.

The UDC raised the twenty-three thousand-dollar cost of the monument. Responding to a national movement of conciliation and wanting not to offend southern businessmen, the city accepted the women's gift. But nervous councilmen, reluctant to spend any public money on a monument to disloyal Americans, passed a special ordinance requiring the UDC to pay for maintaining it.

At the dedication ceremony, Mrs. H. D. Spencer, president of the monument association, spoke passionately of the members' "love and loyalty to the traditions of the South." Although the rededication ceremony in 1965 emphasized the "many charitable works of the Sons and Daughters of the Confederacy," the monument continued to acknowledge the deep divisions that still existed between St. Louisans. The sentimental family tableau, conceived to make the statue less controversial, was in itself a dramatic reminder that both men and women wage war.

Sources: For exact location of the Confederate Memorial in Forest Park, see Caroline Laughlin and Catherine Anderson, *Forest Park* (Columbia: University of Missouri Press, 1986), 134–35. See also Confederate Memorial Dedication, *BMHS* 21, no. 2 (January 1965): 136; John F. Veirling Scrapbook, MHS; St. Louis Beautification Commission, *Public Art in St. Louis* (St. Louis: St. Louis Beautification Commission, 1969), 125–38; and the *Post-Dispatch*, 14 November 1912, and 4 December 1914. Lee Ann Whites, *The Civil War as a Crisis in Gender* (Athens: University of Georgia Press, 1995), and Kirk Savage, *Standing Soldiers, Kneeling Slaves: Slaves, Race, War and Monument in 19th-Century America* (New Jersey: Princeton University Press, 1997) discuss turn-of-the-century Civil War memorials and the way they reconstructed the war to deny the centrality of slavery and instead focused on white male honor and defense of family.

Women, Work, and World War I

The Wagner Electric Company, at 6400 Plymouth Avenue in Wellston, contracted to make detonators and firing pins for World War I munitions. Many women seized the opportunity of the labor shortage to participate in the wartime economy by working at defense plants like Wagner. These women were among the seventeen thousand St. Louisans who initiated a wave of strikes early in 1918. Like other workers determined to use their bargaining power in a tight labor market, Wagner employees demanded union recognition, higher wages, and shorter hours. The presence of women in union meetings and on pickets lines testified to their active participation in the local wartime economy and to their highly visible, if limited, union membership.

Women had worked in St. Louis factories since the Civil War, although they seldom did the same jobs as men. The gender division of labor persisted even as the number of female factory workers grew

in the first two decades of the twentieth century. By 1915 the war in Europe had created a market for military hardware that accelerated after the United States entered the conflict in 1917. St. Louis industries benefitted not only from defense contracts, but also from demand for consumer products, particularly chemicals previously imported from Germany. Just when orders for war-related material burgeoned, the armed services began to draw men out of the work force. Wagner Electric and Mallinckrodt Chemical Company were among local employers who solved their labor problems by hiring more female workers.

In 1918 nearly one quarter of St. Louis's 155,000 factory workers were female. Fewer than forty-three hundred women belonged to a union, however, even though the city's manufacturing work force was more than half unionized. Male union leaders showed little interest in organizing women and most manufacturers treated women as cheap, easily replaceable workers. Women earned between seven and fifteen dollars a week for working six nine-hour days; male workers averaged between twelve and twenty-four dollars for the same hours.

On March 6, 1918, an estimated one thousand men and women walked off the job at Wagner Electric's plant to protest the dismissal of men who had attended a Machinist Union organizing meeting. Within a week nearly twenty-one hundred men and seven hundred women were on strike. In addition to union recognition, Wagner workers demanded higher wages and shorter hours. Male workers at Wagner made less than half the union rate for similar work; women's earnings were half those of their male coworkers. The strikers charged Wagner with violating defense contracts that stipulated eight-hour days and equal pay for equal work.

Because Wagner made vital munitions for the U.S. and British governments, the War Department brokered a settlement. Most workers returned to work on March 18, assured that Wagner would not penalize union members and would negotiate wages and hours. The agreement fell apart, however, when Wagner failed to address grievances and required workers to sign loyalty pledges to the company. In April more than twelve hundred workers, supported by veteran labor organizer Mary Harris (Mother) Jones, walked out again. The War Labor Board took over negotiations in July but could not effect a settlement between the company and the union. Labor unrest continued at Wagner into the postwar years.

Workers at Wagner Electric were not the only women who tried to use the wartime economy to better their own working conditions. The International Tobacco Workers Union sought to unite the city's four thousand tobacco workers, about half of whom were women. By March 1918, organizers had enrolled more than four hundred women. When the union struck the Liggett & Myers factory on Fulsom Avenue, organizers told them to stay at home. Instead, they joined men on the picket lines outside the company's three St. Louis factories. Some Italian and Polish women continued on the job until interpreters explained the strike and worker demands. The tobacco workers won a 10 percent wage hike, a reduction in the work day from ten to nine hours, and a promise that Liggett & Myers would not discriminate against union members. In the same month, garment workers, the majority of whom were women, struck five local factories. The strike ended when the employers agreed to submit employee grievances to the War Labor Board and to reinstate strikers without recrimination, but only one of the companies recognized the union. Women were also heavily represented in strikes against biscuit companies and bag manufacturers.

One of the year's most visible strikes was the month-long walkout by department store workers in July. Although low-paid female salesclerks made up more than half of department store workers, less than one-third of the strikers were women. The Women's Trade Union League (WTUL) and other concerned women's organizations, however, organized an open meeting of strikers and owners at the St. Louis Public Library. When the department store owners refused to attend, Edna Gellhorn, social activist and suffrage leader, blamed the WTUL's public endorsement of the strike. Gellhorn later became a founding member of the League of Women Voters, a civic organization that took a nonpartisan position on most controversial issues. Department store workers, who did not have the same leverage with employers as defense workers, failed to gain either shorter hours or higher wages, but they did get union recognition and reinstatement without penalty.

Girl's Hand Screw Machine Department, Work on Mark 3 Detonators. Photograph by Oscar C. Kuehn, 1918. Wagner Electric Company Collection. MHS–PP

Pontiac playground in Soulard. Photograph, ca. 1916. MHS–PP

Mary Margaret Ellis was born in 1911 and grew up in the Soulard neighborhood of St. Louis. Her mother's parents were Irish immigrants. This excerpt is from her unpublished memoir, "That's the Way It Was," which is preserved in the WHMC–UMSL. A longer excerpt and biographical information about Mary Margaret Ellis appears in Waal and Korner, *Hardship and Hope.* Mary's family lived in a four-family flat at 2111 South Fourth Street from the mid-1910s until the 1920s.

"Our flat had three rooms. . . . Three other families lived in the building; we were on the first floor. Along with offering some room for playing, the back yard had four wood sheds, one for each family, an ash pit and two toilets. There was no inside plumbing in that neighborhood, and of course no house had hot water. Everybody used coal for heating, so everybody had ash pits in their yards. Coal lamps supplied light. People either used coal or wood for cooking.

"I got a good slap from Mom one day and I don't think I deserved it. It was wash day and we had two tubs sitting on the wringer bench on the back porch. The night before we had filled the wash boiler with water and put it on top of the cook stove. While Mom was cooking our breakfast, the water would get boiling hot and we would transfer it to the tub, add some cold water, put in the washboard and start scrubbing the dirty clothes. . . .

"Lisa, the girl from upstairs, came down one wash morning to watch us. She said to me, 'You didn't turn the socks inside out when you washed them.' Without thinking, I said, 'Oh, my Mom never turns the socks. We only wash them on one side.' When I went in the kitchen to get more soap, Mom grabbed me, and slapped me hard, saying, 'Don't you ever tell the neighbors we don't turn our socks when we wash them.' I said, 'But Mom we don't.' She said, 'Even if we don't, you don't have to tell the neighbors about it.'"

When the war ended in November 1918, women lost the skilled factory jobs that had been exclusively male before the war. Companies like Wagner had no more military contracts, and there were plenty of men, including former servicemen, to meet postwar needs. Although they returned to gender-segregated jobs, women did not rush to leave the manufacturing work force. Despite employers and unions who still characterized them as marginal and temporary, St. Louis women took themselves seriously as workers and continued their steady advance onto the factory floor.

–Joan Cooper

Sources: For a detailed analysis of industrial production, union activity, and labor unrest in the war years, see the Missouri Bureau of Labor Statistics, 1916–1919. See also Gary M. Fink, *Labor's Search for Political Order: The Political Behavior of the Missouri Labor Movement, 1890–1940* (Columbia: University of Missouri Press, 1973). For local media coverage of the individual strikes, see the February to July editions of the *Post-Dispatch, Globe-Democrat,* and *St. Louis Republic.* Useful background information about the wartime period is from Floyd C. Shoemaker, "Missouri and the War," MHR 12, no. 3 (April 1918); 13, no. 1 (October 1918), and Lawrence O. Christensen, "World War I in Missouri," *MHR* 90, no. 3 (April 1996); 90, no. 4 (July 1996)

For information on women and work, see the Report of the Women's Committee, Council of National Defense, Missouri Division, 1 June 1918 to 27 February 1919, MHS, and *The Missouri Woman,* 1918. Photographs from Wagner Electric Company are in MHS collections, and photographs of women working during the war can be seen in Rockwell Gray, *A Century of Enterprise: St. Louis 1894–1994* (St. Louis: MHS Press, 1994).

St. Louis's World War I Nurses

On October 9, 1917, Julia C. Stimson described the daily routine of nurses at St. Louis Base Hospital Unit 21 in Rouen, France, in a letter to her family in New York. The nurses slept with "helmets over their faces and enamel basins over their stomachs," she wrote. "Wearing men's ordinance socks under their stockings," they stood in frosty operating rooms "doing such surgical work as they never in their wildest days dreamed of." Stimson, chief nurse at the unit, had headed the Department of Nursing and Social Service at Barnes Hospital before leaving for war-torn Europe. After the armistice, Julia Stimson became superintendent of the Army Nurse Corps and dean of the Army School of Nursing. Most of the women under her charge, however, went back home to their jobs in St. Louis hospitals, changed forever by the sights, sounds, and smells of trench warfare.

The local chapter of the American Red Cross had recruited most of the unit's 28 doctors, 65 nurses, and 141 enlisted men from St. Louis hospitals in 1916. One of six mobile hospitals organized and equipped by the Red Cross, the St. Louis unit was the second to go overseas under the command of the War Department. Base Hospital Unit 21 arrived in France in June 1917 to relieve exhausted British medical personnel.

The base hospital was no modern facility on Kingshighway. The nurses worked in a vast sea of fifteen hundred tents, each holding fourteen beds. Their patients were not like those they had cared for at Barnes, St. Luke's, or City Hospitals. Most were British soldiers suffering from massive combat wounds and the choking effects of poison gas. Nurses changed dressings on skin burnt by gas and on the stumps of amputated limbs. They drained the festering wounds of men in agonizing pain. "Two of our men have died and we were so glad to have them die," Stimson wrote home in March. The task of writing the families of dying patients fell to her assistant, Mance Taylor, who became head nurse at the unit when Stimson was promoted to chief nurse of the American Red Cross in April 1918. Taylor had been superintendent of St. Luke's Hospital's nursing school before the war.

The most harrowing experience for the nurses was to be a member of the small surgical teams sent to the casualty clearing stations on the front line. "What with the steam, the ether, and the filthy clothes of the men, which they had to cut off before they could start," Stimson reported, "the odor of the operating room was so terrible that it was all any of them could do to keep from being sick." Constance Cuppaidge, supervisor of operating rooms at St. Luke's Hospital, was cited by the British for her work on the front lines.

Stimson worried constantly about the mental, emotional, and physical stress of combat nursing on the women under her command. "I have about a dozen of them weeping," Stimson reported in August, "and I am hunting about for more forms of diversion." She organized entertainment and games, played her violin, and had sheet music sent from home to encourage group singing. Although the nurses were entitled to leave after six months, most stayed on duty until the war ended.

Several months after the armistice, some St. Louis nurses went to Germany with the Army of Occupation but most came back to their peacetime jobs. Although they were in France for less than a year, during that time the women at the St. Louis Base Hospital Unit 21 had treated 62,400 casualties of war. Nothing in the nurses' medical experience had prepared them for the horrors they faced during their wartime service. The harsh reality made a mockery of the "ministering angel" image depicted in recruiting posters. They had to be physically strong to deal with exhausting hours on duty under appalling conditions and mentally strong to cope with the suffering and pain they witnessed. They nursed amid threats of air attack and sounds of battle. "These weary, dirty, splendid women of mine," Stimson wrote in praise of the St. Louis nurses, "one need never tell me that women can't do as much, stand as much, and be as brave as men."

–Joan Cooper

Sources: Julia Stimson's letters about her experiences as chief nurse of Base Hospital Unit 21 between June 1917 and April 1918 were published by her family in 1918 in *Finding Themselves: The Letters of an American Army Chief Nurse in a British Hospital in France*. More information about her background and her time at Washington University can be found in Morrow, *Washington University in St. Louis*.

For background on the war period, see Shoemaker, "Missouri and the War"; Christensen, "World War I in Missouri"; and David March, *History of Missouri* (Missouri, 1967). The *Globe-Democrat* and the *Post-Dispatch* covered the departure of the base hospital in May 1917. For general information on nurses in World War I, see Philip A. Kalisch and Margaret Scobey, "Female Nurses in American Wars," *Armed Forces and Society* (winter 1983), and Lyn MacDonald, *The Roses of No Man's Land* (New York: Atheneum, 1980). See also Louise I. Treholme, *History of Nursing in Missouri* (Missouri, 1926).

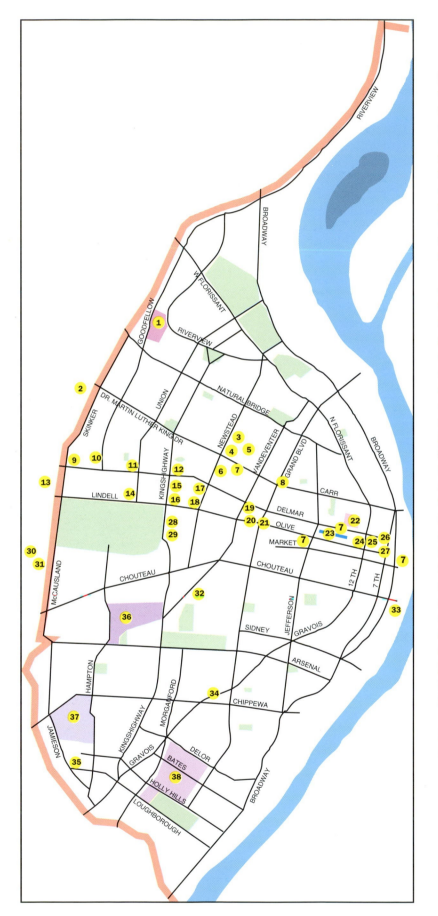

1920–1945

1. U.S. Cartridge Small Arms Plant
2. Wagner Electric Company
3. Turner Open-Air School for Crippled Children
4. Poro College
5. Homer G. Phillips Hospital
6. Booklovers Club
7. Funsten Nut Company (4 locations)
8. Mullanphy Hospital
9. Miss Hickey's Training School for Secretaries
10. Irma Rombauer Home
11. St. Louis College Club
12. Chase Hotel—Five State Regional Conference on Birth Control
13. Fannie Cook Home
14. Clara Pendleton Home
15. Maternal Health Association of Missouri
16. Junior League
17. Rachel Stix Michael Home
18. Edna Gellhorn Home
19. People's Art Center
20. Jessie Housley Holliman Mural
21. Sara Teasdale Home
22. Carr Square Village
23. Washington Avenue Garment District
24. Hahn Fountain in Lucas Park
25. The Town Club
26. Stix, Baer & Fuller Sit-in
27. Famous-Barr Sit-in
28. Elias Michael School
29. St. John's Hospital
30. Jewish Orphans Home
31. St. Mary's Hospital
32. Liggett & Myers Tobacco Company
33. Hooverville
34. House of the Good Shepherd
35. Louise Venverloh Home
36. The Hill Neighborhood
37. St. Louis Hills Neighborhood
38. Holly Hills Neighborhood

St. Louis City Limits 1876–Present

Parks

7

Changing Places

Pregnant with her sixth child in 1926, Louise Schmidt Venverloh was preparing to move into her own home at 5426 Lisette Avenue in southwest St. Louis. The daughter of a German immigrant, she had left school at age thirteen to care for her motherless siblings. She married her stepbrother in 1914. Louise's world centered on her family, church, and south side neighborhood.

Only a few years younger than Louise, Clara Pendleton replaced a drafted draughtsman at the Wagner Electric Company after graduating from Soldan High School in 1917. She did not marry but took advantage of every opportunity to learn new skills. By the late 1930s, she was the Assistant St. Louis City Engineer, supervising fifty people on a New Deal–funded study of local land use.

Washington Avenue, Southwest Corner of Seventh Street. Swekowsky Collection. MHS–PP

The different experiences of Clara Pendleton and Louise Venverloh caution against easy generalizations about flappers in the roaring twenties or unemployed girls a decade later. Few St. Louis women drank bathtub gin in the 1920s, but many experienced greater independence in an expanding consumer economy, even if Louise did not. Single women were often more employable than men or married women during the depression years, although Clara was particularly fortunate to have a job funded with federal money. In a time of falling national birthrates, Louise Venverloh's large family was consistent with the Roman Catholic faith she shared with many St. Louis women. Pendleton's success in a traditionally male job went against a national trend of gender-segregated jobs, but she was one of an increasing number of individual St. Louis women who achieved success in business and the professions in the interwar years.

Between 1920 and 1945, Louise Venverloh and Clara Pendleton made different places for themselves in St. Louis. Their individual stories, like those of thousands of other women, illustrate the complex interplay between race, religion, class, and ethnicity operating within the broader contexts of profound changes in the economy, governmental policy, and national culture after 1920. By 1945 there were far fewer places completely closed to women than there had been twenty-five years earlier. But there were also fewer exclusively female spaces than there had been at the turn of the century. Ironically, new tensions accompanied the benefits of the narrowing gender gap. In a society of separate spheres, women's individual aspirations often overlapped with women's collective goals. In a more open society, individual and collective agendas more easily diverged.

For many St. Louisans the defining image of the 1920s was Charles Lindbergh, the Lone Eagle, soaring over Art Hill in Forest Park after completing his transatlantic flight in the *Spirit of St. Louis*. Lindbergh symbolized the individualism and independence later generations would associate with the decade. But self-reliance had been an American male virtue even before the mid-nineteenth century, when Horace Greeley urged young men to go west and grow up with the country.

A virtuous American woman did not seek to be an independent individual. She acted in the world as a wife, mother, or daughter. The post–Civil War women's rights movement and the successful suffrage movement of the early twentieth century, however, had made women political individuals. The growth of industrial capitalism also eroded

traditional assumptions about female dependence; women increasingly bought, sold, and produced goods as individuals in the market economy. By the 1920s many women thought of themselves both as self-reliant individuals and emotional centers of nuclear families, a potentially conflicting self-image.

Other powerful forces of change were evident by the 1920s. The automobile, the new symbol of independence, gave Americans more choices of where they lived and worked and how they spent their leisure time. Cars also gave them opportunities for personal mobility and privacy at a time when Freudian theories of human psychology made sexuality a major source of personal identity—for women as well as men. While these innovations had a liberating effect on women, they also changed the ways men and women interacted socially and challenged deeply felt religious and ethnic values. Advertisers exploited the growing emphasis on romantic love and personal attraction in their appeals to female shoppers, whom they now estimated purchased 75 percent of personal consumables.

Mass marketing, a factor in American life since the late nineteenth century, helped create an image—part reality, part fiction, and part aspiration—of a sexy, youthful urban culture in the 1920s. New communication technologies launched the city's first sound movies and commercial radio station. Women encountered images of femininity at the Fox or American movie theaters that were different from their mothers' generation; those images were reinforced in slick women's magazines and romantic radio dramas on KSD Radio. The fashions of the 1920s stripped away yards of bulky fabric and made women appear younger. The new ideal woman had short hair and a slim boyish figure, in a short, straight dress. Ten years earlier, her mother had pinned up her long hair and worn a corset under ankle-length skirts.

Fashion changed more radically, and more quickly, than social, economic, and emotional realities. St. Louis industries had employed women in gender-segregated jobs since the late nineteenth century. There were always more local women in the work force than the national average, only in part because traditionally more women held paying jobs in urban areas. In the 1920s, after a short post–World War I recession, the national economy began to grow again, making St. Louis the nation's seventh largest manufacturing center by 1930. Other economies had grown faster—St. Louis's had been fourth in 1890—but much of the expansion was in light industries employing women. By the end of the decade, 28 percent of all St. Louis workers were women over the age of ten; the national average was 22 percent. Women still worked primarily in racially and gender-segregated jobs.

The chemical and electrical equipment industries expanded significantly and both had sizable female work forces. Some old industries, like meatpacking and metal fabricating, moved their traditionally male jobs across the river into Illinois, but clothing and shoe companies held their own as the area's largest industrial employers. In 1922 the majority of women in manufacturing made clothing and shoes. Female jobs in tobacco processing declined as companies moved to eastern cities and began making cigarettes rather than plug tobacco. But new St. Louis factories for shelling nuts created similar jobs. Over 50 percent of local black women in manufacturing worked in low-wage food processing, the majority in nut picking.

The highest paid women in St. Louis industries were the 149 pieceworkers in the manufacture of electrical products; their median weekly wages exceeded sixteen dollars, which compared favorably to the average manufacturing wage for men. By 1925 only the shoe, clothing, and bag-making manufacturers employed more St. Louis women than the electrical and drug industries. These rankings remained constant throughout the decade.

Fewer than one-third of St. Louis's 106,583 women workers, however, were employed in manufacturing in 1930. White collar jobs accounted for much of the 20 percent statewide increase in working women over the decade. Between 1920 and 1930 the number of Missouri women in clerical positions more than doubled, and professional positions, a much smaller number, increased nearly 100 percent. Clara Pendleton's office job, if not her engineering career, was in line with national and local trends.

In St. Louis, as well as nationally, three of four employed black women were domestic workers. Eleven percent of the city's work force, African Americans were denied most sales, clerical, and manufacturing jobs. They were only 117 of the more than 10,000 women employed in the clothing and shoe industries. The tobacco and food processing industries and commercial laundries were the largest employers of black women in the city. African American women held more than 80 percent of the private laundry jobs in the city.

A larger percentage of African American women worked outside their homes than white women. Nationally, less than 12 percent of all married women were in the labor force in 1930, up only a few percentage points from 1920.

While Louise Schmidt might have been expected to work before her marriage to Bernie Venverloh, it would have been very unusual for her to have been an employed housewife, even if she had not had nine children to care for.

Louise Venverloh's only job was caring for her home and family, which was true for nearly 90 percent of St. Louis married women. When Louise married Bernie Venverloh he had a good job as a stenographer in a car factory. The south St. Louis flat she moved into as a bride in 1914 had indoor plumbing, a coal stove in each room, an ice box, and a blue enamel gas stove in the kitchen. The consumer economy that was responsible for much of the post–world war economic growth depended on the purchasing power of housewives like Louise. Electric washing machines and refrigerators were readily available to St. Louis families in the 1920s if they had the money or the credit to buy them, but most did not. Relatives helped the Venverlohs buy their first home in 1926. Although Bernie had a good-paying job, supporting such a large family used up most of the cash. Louise did the laundry the old-fashioned way, with a scrub board, wash tubs, a wash boiler, and a hand-powered wringer.

St. Louisans had been able to buy on credit since the Singer Sewing Machine Company introduced installment buying in 1856, but in the 1920s retailers made buying-on-time an acceptable and easy way to acquire home furnishings. Radio

Women Workers with Mica Gauging Segment for Electrical Motor Commutators. Wagner Electric Company. Wagner Electric Collection, MHS–PP

"Star Brand Shoes Are Better"

class families. In 1912 only 7,752 motor vehicles were registered in the city; in 1920 about 50,000, a decade later more than 179,000. Although the population of St. Louis City increased until mid-century, St. Louis County grew at a much faster rate once automobiles opened land to residential development. In 1920, 772,897 people lived in the city and just over 100,000 in the county. The population of the county doubled in the next decade and nearly doubled again in the depression decade of the 1930s. Although more than twice as many people lived in the city in 1940 as in the county, the suburbanization of St. Louis County was well underway before World War II.

St. Louis County suburbs did not draw people equally from all parts of the city or from all groups within the urban population. New suburban houses were expensive. In spite of wage increases in the 1920s, most St. Louisans could not afford down payments, car payments, or even the newly popular self-actualizing home mortgages. A number of St. Louisans who could most afford to move in the 1920s, wealthy Central West End families for example, chose not to leave. The new booming suburbs, like University City, attracted the families of independent professionals, office workers, or business owners. In 1930, when 60 percent of University City families owned or were buying their own home, only 30 percent of city dwellers were homeowners.

Not all St. Louisans, however, aspired to home ownership. The apartment buildings constructed in the Central West End and University City in the 1920s appealed not only to young married couples saving for their first homes, but also to unmarried professional women like Clara Pendleton, women who were no longer as willing to live with their parents or in supervised boardinghouses and were now financially able to live independently. Clara lived in the Branscome apartment hotel at 5370 Pershing Avenue, where she admitted to cooking only "spasmodically," and not very well.

Discrimination denied black St. Louisans who aspired to home ownership access to most of the city's residential neighborhoods. By the 1920s some middle-class black families had left the central wards to live near Sumner High School in the north side Ville neighborhood west of Grand Avenue. They had no choice but to remain east of Kingshighway because restrictive deed covenants in the new western subdivisions prohibited sale or rental to nonwhites. In cooperation with homeowners' associations, the St. Louis Real Estate Exchange kept black neighborhoods like the Ville hedged in by the color line. Although the residential segregation

and newspaper advertising of national brands encouraged buyers to buy now and pay later.

Consumer credit was even more essential to automobile sales than to home appliances. Few people could afford to pay cash for a luxury costing half the yearly wage of the typical working man, who made less than one thousand dollars a year. The cost of private transportation restricted the housing choices of white families who wanted to leave crowded city neighborhoods. The earliest suburbs had, for good reasons, grown up along railroad and streetcar lines. Southwest St. Louis and much of St. Louis County remained undeveloped until buses and private cars became commonplace. In the late 1920s, developers of Holly Hills and St. Louis Hills subsidized private buses that linked their southwest St. Louis subdivisions to existing city streetcar lines.

During the 1920s St. Louisans, already major car producers, became car consumers as well. Suburban living became a practical ideal for middle-

"Star Brand Shoes are Better," Roberts, Johnson & Rand Shoe Company Catalog, Fall-Winter 1925–1926. Halftone, (colored). MHS Library. The difference between women's clothing in the 1920s and the dress this stylish model's mother would have worn before the First World War was one indicator of rapid social change.

ordinance approved by voters in 1916 was never enforced and proved to be unconstitutional, the courts would uphold restrictive deed covenants until the 1947 *Shelley v. Kraemer* U.S. Supreme Court declared them unenforceable.

Meanwhile, the greater Ville area, where the earlier rural population had been racially mixed, became the institutional center of African American St. Louis, home to Homer G. Phillips Hospital, Stowe Teachers College, Poro College, Annie Malone's Children's Home, and the Turner public school for black children with disabilities.

When second- and third-generation white immigrant families like the Venverlohs became homeowners in the 1920s, poorer St. Louisans moved into rental property in the neighborhoods they left behind. Black southern rural migrants poured into a narrow band of central wards bordering the Mill Creek Valley, the area designated as the Negro District, even faster than the old residents moved out. The Great Migration of African Americans who came north after World War I to escape sharecropping, violence, and racial oppression avoided neither segregation nor discrimination in St. Louis.

Before federal legislation virtually ended immigration in 1924, Czech-speaking Bohemians and other Eastern Europeans moved into other declining inner-city neighborhoods. An area of the near south side between Cherokee and Park, Broadway and Eighteenth became known as Bohemian Hill, with St. John Nepomuk Catholic Church as its community center. The city's small Jewish population grew from ten thousand to over fifty thousand in the first decades of the century, when many immigrants from Eastern Europe settled on the near north side. They were the city's largest new immigrant group. Tensions arose between the poor, primarily Orthodox newcomers and the largely assimilated and better off German Jews who had come to the city earlier. As in the nineteenth century, immigrant women juggled domestic responsibilities with caring for boarders or piecework sewing to supplement the family income. Before marriage, young Jewish and Polish women frequently worked in the garment industry.

In the late nineteenth century, Italian immigrants had clustered with other newcomers on the near north side. In the 1920s a new isolated Italian community developed south of Forest Park and north of Arsenal Street. Men from Cuggiono in the Lombardy province of northern Italy settled on the Hill, which overlooked the clay pits and brick kilns that had drawn them to St. Louis early in the twentieth century. The settlement's male to female ratio was six to one, until the men began arranging marriages with "picture brides" from Cuggiono. Women brought with them Catholic piety, village traditions, and family bonds, which helped keep Hill residents separate from the surrounding American culture. Like immigrant women in mid-nineteenth-century ethnic neighborhoods, the Italian women on the Hill did not need to learn English to care for families and boarders in the self-contained community.

Discrimination, physical isolation, and poverty also made Hill residents look inward. Parents, intent on home ownership, took both boys and girls out of school at age fourteen to work. In 1930 most of the girls processed tobacco at the Liggett & Myers plug tobacco factory on Tower Grove Avenue until they married. An old resident remembered that "they came home dirty, smelling of tobacco and then they had to cook meals and do their housework. All economics. To buy their home." Lacking the opportunity for education and expected to marry within the community, the daughters of immigrants stayed in their place.

The Hill, arguably St. Louis's only surviving European ethnic neighborhood, was not typical of the city's immigrant enclaves. Most were mixed in ethnicity and experienced high turnover when residents or their children were able to move up. In the 1920s and 1930s, few immigrant communities rejected American values of individualism, education, and mobility in order to maintain the stability of their traditional cultures.

While the average Hill resident had barely a fifth-grade education in 1940, the average St. Louisan graduated from eighth grade. In 1920 only 28 percent of all sixteen- and seventeen-year-old children in St. Louis attended school. Louise Schmidt Venverloh had dropped out of school in 1906 at age thirteen to care for her motherless siblings—a common practice at the time. An achieving, upwardly mobile German immigrant, Ludwig Schmidt probably would have wanted his daughter to complete eighth grade but not to enter high school.

By 1920 men and women graduated from high school and entered college in nearly equal numbers. Nationally, fewer than 17 percent of seventeen-year-olds graduated from high school, but 60 percent of them were women. Like Clara Pendleton, most went to work not to college, but nearly half of those who did enroll were women.

Most women who attended college, like less well-educated women, entered female-dominated

professions after graduation. Nearly a third of all college professors in the 1920s were women, but their numbers declined in the depression decade that followed. Those who did not become teachers more likely became social workers and librarians than doctors or lawyers. A significant number of St. Louis women with post-secondary educations were Catholic nuns who trained other nuns and lay women to be teachers.

Earlier, female college graduates often chose employment over marriage. But as their numbers grew, fewer educated women made that decision. Many did not enter the work force at all before marriage, which began to take on status as an occupation in itself. Freudian theories placed family relationships at the center of human psychological and sexual development. Experts emphasized the importance of informed child rearing, admonishing middle-class mothers not to let servants rear their children. Bombarded with advertising directed to the consuming nuclear family, growing numbers of middle-class women became convinced that their college educations prepared them first and foremost for domestic careers. Rather than preparing a young woman for a profession, a college education made her a better wife and mother and provided personal enrichment and "something to fall back on" in the event of divorce or a husband's death.

The daughters of upper middle-class women who had founded women's charitable organizations in the 1890s now had college degrees, but the nature of benevolence work had changed since women began doing "municipal housekeeping."

St. Louis NAACP Officers and Board, 1957. Both men and women served on the governing boards of nonprofit civic organizations, but corporate boards were still predominantly male. Courtesy WHMC–UMSL

Some of the leaders of nineteenth-century charitable organizations and women's clubs had been college graduates, but most had not. They had educated themselves through their club work and in many cases applied what they learned to solving social problems in the community.

In the twentieth century, some women-run institutions lost favor; experts now considered even a bad home environment preferable to an orphanage. The professionalization of social work and institutional administration squeezed out skilled volunteers or reduced their responsibilities. Large bureaucracies, staffed by women but usually headed by men, assumed much of the benevolence work that women had done on their own or in cooperation with other Progressive Era reformers.

College-educated women joined new volunteer organizations such as the League of Women Voters (LWV), where they studied issues to make themselves informed citizens. The prestigious Wednesday Club focused more on personal enrichment than on the civic issues that had made it so influential in the Progressive Era. St. Louisans also founded social organizations specifically for college-educated women, such as the College Club, the local chapter of the American Association of University Women, the African American St. Louis College Club, and sorority alumnae groups. The Jewish Scholarship Foundation raised money to send other young women to college. The Junior League, a new organization of young, well-educated, upper middle-class women, attempted to give volunteerism professional status.

The pattern of men and women doing community service together that began with the progressives now reached into more areas. Women ran for public office and served on school boards with men; they sought volunteer leadership roles in gender-integrated social service and civic organizations.

Accomplished women such as Edna Gellhorn, a founding member of the LWV, Emily Proetz and Margaret Hickey, both successful businesswomen, and novelist and social activist Fannie Cook, served on commissions and civic committees. But unless they came from very wealthy families or controlled other resources, women frequently faced rejection from male-dominated organizations where a place at the table depended on one's personal influence in business and political circles or on the ability to raise large amounts of money.

Social organizations were less likely to be gender-integrated than professional and civic groups. Businessmen's social clubs did not admit women, just as women's clubs stayed exclusively female. Business and professional women organized their own service clubs for collegiality and contacts. The Town Club, located in a twelve-story building at 1120 Locust Street, had three thousand members in 1925. Called "The House That Jill Built," it served businesswomen as an athletic and social club in much the same way the City Club and the Missouri Athletic Club served businessmen. Beginning in 1931, the Women's Advertising Club gave annual public recognition to St. Louis "Women of Achievement." Chosen originally by a committee of prominent men and later by men and women, individual women were honored for their success in a variety of areas—business, education, social service, the arts and homemaking. Although weighted heavily to traditional women's paid and volunteer jobs, the awards acknowledged individual female achievement that otherwise would have gone unrecognized.

Women had won their place in the voting booth in 1919, but in St. Louis, as elsewhere, they did not have a clear vision of how to exploit this victory. By the time women could vote, the nineteenth-century political and legal reform agenda, central to the movement for women's rights, no longer had the same relevance. The battles to eliminate the most egregious legal inequities between men and women had been won. Women now had the right to their own wages, to an education, and, if they were willing to take less pay, to practice most professions. The newly enfranchised women whom some had believed would form a gender-based voting bloc either explicitly abandoned women's for citizen's issues or interpreted political issues from class or racial biases rather than from a female perspective. The barriers of race and class that had always separated women took on new significance when African Americans and working-class women demanded to be treated as enfranchised equals rather than as beneficiaries of middle-class charity.

The debate over the proposed Equal Right Amendment (ERA) revealed tensions that had been just beneath the surface of feminist social action for decades. Introduced into the U.S. Congress in 1923 by the National Women's Party, the ERA tried to focus women's political agenda solely on ending legalized discrimination. Women reformers and workers had lobbied state legislatures relentlessly for laws that regulated working conditions for women in offices, stores, and factories. They refused to renounce collective protective legislation in the name of equality for individuals. One problem was that the demand for equality with men in all areas ignored real, physical differences between men and women, and between women themselves. The debate revealed the potential conflict between securing the rights of individual women and meeting collective needs of all women.

The debate over the ERA took place in the context of an increasingly gender-integrated urban culture. In education, politics, employment, and social activities men's and women's places were converging, reducing the opportunities and sometimes the need for women to work together for their own interests. Women had not achieved equality in any of these areas, however, and they still needed to think of themselves as a group separate from men if they were to transcend barriers of class and race. At the same time, women celebrated their individualism and aggressively sought personal choice and freedom of expression. The factor that most undermined women's collective strength in the 1920s may have been women's integration into the individualistic ethos of a consumer economy.

By the close of the decade, the consumer economy was in serious trouble and the country was headed for economic depression. Although the causes of the Great Depression were complex and global, 1920s prosperity both in the United States and in Europe ultimately depended on ordinary people having enough income to purchase the country's mounting output of goods and services. When the ability of producers to produce outran the ability of consumers to consume, the economy eventually choked on its own success. Chronic under-consumption caused by maldistribution of wealth was a major factor in the country's plunge into economic depression at the end of the decade.

The income of St. Louis workers had increased in the early 1920s, but as the dollar value of local manufacturing output rose later in the decade both employment and wages drifted downward.

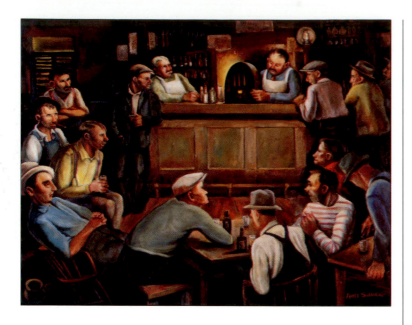

President's Fire Side Chat, by Aimee Schweig. Oil on board, ca. 1938.
MHS Art Collection

An art teacher at Mary Institute for twenty-five years, Schweig was an advocate for avant-garde and experimental artists. She helped found the St. Louis chapter of the National Society of Arts and Letters, People's Art Center, and an art colony and school in Ste. Genevieve, Missouri. This depression-era painting reflects her lifelong interest in social problems and regional subjects.

This was particularly true in the competitive garment industry that employed the most local women, but even male blue-collar workers in St. Louis who earned close to the national average male manufacturing wage could not adequately support a family of five. Often, their wives' paid work or thrifty home management made the difference between subsistence and security.

Between 1929 and 1933 the value both of St. Louis manufactures and wages fell by half. At the end of 1931 one quarter of the local labor force was unemployed and four out of ten black workers had no jobs. There were no federal or local funds earmarked for unemployment relief. Mayor Victor Miller appointed a committee of businessmen to raise money for the privately funded Provident Association, now swamped with applicants seeking aid. Despite additional infusions of city funds, in June 1932 the association stopped accepting new relief applications and reluctantly dropped ten thousand families from its rolls.

The St. Louis Communist and Socialist Parties organized out-of-work men and women into the Unemployed Council, a grass-roots protest group. In July they rallied at City Hall to protest relief cuts and demand public money to re-employ the jobless. Faced with an empty city treasury and mounting unemployment, voters approved a $4.6 million relief bond issue in November 1932, and they swept Democrats into local, state, and national office. Mayor-elect Bernard Dickman promised to use some of the money to begin construction of the long-overdue hospital for African Americans, which voters had approved in 1923.

Shortly after President Franklin Roosevelt took office, Congress passed the first legislation authorizing outright federal funds to poor people. Unemployment relief was the most impressive and best-remembered accomplishment of the administration's New Deal programs of economic aid. The St. Louis Provident Association, which had long been opposed to the dole, reluctantly became a public agency in order to distribute direct federal aid. Inabel Burns Lindsey, an African American social worker employed by the Provident Association in the early 1930s, recalled the difficulty the association had integrating the paternalistic yet flexible practices of the private agency with the more liberal but rigid government guidelines. What remained constant was the agency's inability to meet the overwhelming needs of poor people, despite its greater resources.

In October 1933 nearly one hundred thousand St. Louisans—one in eight—were on the relief rolls.

By then Bernie Venverloh had been out of work for over a year, having lost his job when the National Freight Company folded. The family was receiving some government aid, and Louise used all her energy and ingenuity to keep the household functioning, but even without a large family to care for she would have been reluctant to look for work outside her home. Like many unemployed men, Bernie resented married women who took jobs when male breadwinners like himself had none.

Throughout the depression the unemployment rate for St. Louis women in the work force was somewhat lower than the rate for men, largely because the hardest-hit local industries had traditionally refused to hire women and those that did, such as the garment industry, fared better. Although clothing manufacturers payed low wages for irregular work, employers continued to hire women throughout the 1930s. In many instances whole families depended on a garment worker keeping her job.

In 1933, when the National Industrial Recovery Act (NIRA) guaranteed workers the right to unionize, the International Ladies Garment Workers Union (ILGWU) began organizing the St. Louis garment industry. Many women found themselves caught between their desire to take collective action on their own behalf as workers and the need to support their families. Like the black women who struck the Funsten Nut Factory earlier in the year, most chose to support the movement for union recognition.

New Deal programs like the NIRA ushered in the modern welfare state, with its greatly expanded role for the federal government in the lives of all Americans. The 1935 Social Security Act was a start at providing Americans with a social safety net.

Although the immediate grass-roots impact of New Deal legislation was dramatic, the results were mixed because programs were administered unevenly, often worked at cross-purposes, and operated in the context of local politics and custom, which in St. Louis included entrenched racism. The local chapter of the Urban League became a clearinghouse for black grievances against New Deal policies and practices.

New Deal employment programs directly aided many more St. Louis men than women. The two major New Deal relief programs, the Public Works Administration (PWA) and later Works Progress Administration (WPA), created traditionally male jobs. The PWA underwrote large-scale construction projects such as Homer G. Phillips Hospital, the Soldiers' Memorial, and the Kingshighway viaduct;

Unemployed March on Pine Street. Women were actively involved in protests for aid and jobs. MHS–PP

Women WPA Workers at the Courthouse in Clayton, Missouri. Photograph by W. C. Persons, ca. 1940. MHS–PP

Mary Ryder Home, 4361 Olive Boulevard. Founded by Mary Ryder in the 1930s to aid homeless women, this modern facility now provides nursing home care for poor elderly women, most of whom are African Americans. Photograph by George Rothenbuescher, 1999.

the more labor-intensive WPA projects employed hundreds of men paving streets, building Lambert Field runways, and digging sewers.

Women's WPA work also followed traditional patterns: clerical, research, recreational, and health-related services. More than half of all women employed with WPA money worked in sewing rooms. There, they repaired old garments and made new ones from donated fabric for distribution to families on relief. In St. Louis the WPA funded a large sewing room in the old Merchants' Exchange Building at Third and Chestnut Streets.

New Deal legislation that reinforced the sexual division of labor also supported traditional family norms. Women made up 13 to 19 percent of all WPA workers only in part because so few suitable jobs existed. Only one member of a household was eligible for a WPA job, and women who had able-bodied husbands did not qualify. The Social Security Act made access to aid contingent on family status, and women's benefits came primarily through their husbands. Married working women who paid social security tax on their income received the same amount as non-working wives. New Deal legislation made most entitlements wage-based, strengthening the role of man as breadwinner and woman as dependent homemaker.

The New Deal and the expansion of government in the 1930s created new opportunities for experienced businesswomen and also social workers, 67 percent of whom were women.

Under pressure from Eleanor Roosevelt, FDR appointed women to high-level positions in his administration and in New Deal agencies. Margaret Hickey, who ran a successful secretarial school in St. Louis, met Secretary of Labor Frances Perkins while serving on an advisory committee for the Office of Emergency Planning. Perkins later recommended her for the chairmanship of the Women's Advisory Committee of the War Manpower Commission. The increased participation of women in government declined with the end of New Deal programs, however, and did not carry over into electoral politics. Between 1918 and 1940 only twenty-eight women served in Congress; none were from Missouri. More women held local and state offices, however, largely due to the efforts of the League of Women Voters to involve women in political life. The first women elected to the Missouri House of Representatives was Mellcene Thurman Smith of University City, who served one term from 1922 to 1924. Elsie Langsdorff, the first St. Louis female state representative, was elected in 1943, but local women had served on school boards and in municipal government much earlier.

The depression may have disrupted women's lives less than men's, since a smaller percentage had been in the paid work force and many had worked sporadically at temporary low-paying jobs. But family life was tense when male breadwinners could not find work and women bore much of the responsibility for keeping families healthy, fed, and together. The two best-selling novels of the late 1930s, *The Grapes of Wrath* and *Gone With the Wind*, shared a similar theme: when hard times come men either run off or collapse into helplessness, leaving women to keep families together and carry on.

Although he wanted to support his family, Bernie Venverloh did not work regularly for three years. Louise canned homegrown vegetables to supplement food purchased with government coupons and made bread from government-issued wheat. She cooked meals for a neighbor and took in ironing to keep the family going. When she thought they would lose the house, she tearfully dug up her rose bushes and gave them to friends. Only the Home Owners Loan Corporation (HOLC), a federal program that helped homeowners with equity keep their homes, saved the Venverlohs from foreclosure.

Louise got emotional support at an afternoon ladies' group at her church, where over cards and coffee she shared her troubles with other depression-stressed housewives. She had three more children in the 1930s. By the time the Venverlohs celebrated their twenty-fifth wedding anniversary in 1939, they were recovering financially, and Louise was looking forward to her grandchildren.

Although the Venverlohs were already back on their feet before 1940, World War II pulled many other St. Louisans out of the depression. High unemployment, idle factories, and low consumer spending had crippled the city for a decade. In 1940 St. Louis had the highest percentage of substandard housing of any major city in the country. The city's first two federally subsidized low-income housing projects, Carr Square Village on the near north side for African Americans and Clinton-Peabody Terrace on the near south side for whites, enabled only a lucky few poor St. Louisans to have new homes with central heat and indoor plumbing.

However tragic in other respects, World War II spending revitalized the local economy, funded an expansion of the industrial base, and created new jobs, especially for women. Approximately 150,000 women held jobs in the St. Louis metropolitan area in 1940. However, 15 percent of the St. Louis work force of 622,000 still remained unemployed, including about 25,000 women. In November 1943, at the peak of wartime employment, 600,000 people had jobs in the St. Louis area, about 220,000 of them women. The number of women engaged in manufacturing more than doubled, from 40,000 to 100,000. Many of these new manufacturing jobs went to women in the normal St. Louis work force who moved into factories from unemployment or other types of work. Fully one-third of the new jobs for women were at the U.S. Cartridge Plant on Goodfellow Avenue in north St. Louis.

Dorothy Gronmeir's wartime experiences were similar to those of many St. Louis women. A married nineteen-year-old native of south St. Louis, in 1942 she worked as a salesclerk in a Cherokee Avenue dry goods store. That June she took a one-hour bus ride to the U.S. Cartridge Company's Small Arms Plant and applied for a new job. For more than a year she worked with a team of seven women inspecting .50-caliber machine gun bullets. In 1943, she had a baby and her husband entered the service. She left the Small Arms Plant and took a job making army tents in a factory closer to her home while her mother took care of the baby.

The majority of St. Louis women war workers were local, like Dorothy Gronmeir. Although the city received millions of dollars in defense contracts and produced 40 percent of all small arms used by U.S. forces in the war, it was never a boom town on the scale of Detroit or Seattle-Tacoma. The wartime civilian population grew only 4 percent in the metropolitan area, and plans to accommodate thousands of newcomers proved largely unnecessary.

Concerned that naive, outstate women with defense jobs in the northwest industrial area of St. Louis would frequent the region's mushrooming number of bars, bowling alleys, and dance halls, the YWCA opened a center for working women on Easton Avenue in Wellston. It attracted few women. St. Louis female war workers proved to be a more married, more resident, and more childrened group than had been anticipated. Young single women preferred to spend their leisure time in their own neighborhoods, at the servicemen's USO center at Lambert Airport, or downtown, where newspapers reported that war workers negotiated with bartenders "in a manner you would expect buying eggs instead of liquor." For the most part, the war did not change women's values and aspirations as much as it gave them opportunities for independence and good-paying jobs.

While female war workers, particularly white women, had generally positive work experiences, they did not receive unqualified community support. Bars and movie theaters stayed open late to attract servicemen and shift workers, but few grocery stores opened at night to accommodate women with homemaking responsibilities. But the most pressing unmet need for working women was for child care. In 1943 the federal Lanham Act supplied some money for day-care centers, but it provided space for fewer than two thousand children in public day-care facilities. In St. Louis, as in other defense areas, community resistance and lethargy combined with bureaucratic red-tape to deny mothers and children necessary services. Like Dorothy Gronmeir, working mothers generally left their children with relatives or neighbors.

Black women took advantage of the wartime labor shortages to move into better jobs through individual and collective effort. In her novel, *Mrs. Palmer's Honey*, Fannie Cook chronicled the experiences of African American women, encouraged by union organizers, who left domestic service for work in defense industries. Far more black women moved into better civilian jobs vacated by white women who had taken higher-paying positions. Supported by federal mandates, black women joined with black men and concerned whites in fighting discrimination in defense jobs and in public accommodations. Marion O'Fallon, a Sumner High School student, spent her Saturdays protesting the American Theater's racist admission policies.

While women did not breach the traditional barriers of race and class that historically divided them, some did work together for common goals. In 1944 Pearl Maddox, a black middle-class St. Louisan, led a sit-in at the Stix, Baer & Fuller department store lunch counter that refused African Americans service. Fannie Cook, a white member of the Mayor's Race Relations Commission, tried to convince the commission to put pressure on department stores to serve their black customers. Neither was successful, but they helped make African American civil rights a public issue.

Each woman who made a place for herself in St. Louis during the interwar years had a different experience. Their individual stories, however, illustrate some of the changes and continuities in women's lives since the city's founding nearly two hundred years earlier. Although a few women, like Clara Pendleton, literally worked their way into successful professional careers, more, like Dorothy Gronmeir, still balanced home responsibilities with sex-segregated low-paying work. After the war, Dorothy's husband came home, and she had another child. She stayed out of the work force for several years and then returned to retail sales, the same type of job she had left in 1942. At Famous-Barr on South Kingshighway, she worked for low pay and no benefits because the company's flexible hours made it possible for her to combine child care with employment.

Women still had primary responsibility for domestic life and family care. But while most married white women were homemakers, many, like Louise Venverloh, helped their daughters get better educations that would lead to more options in the future. Although Louise's religious faith had led her to reject birth control, by the postwar years even some Roman Catholic women were actively seeking family planning information.

Black women still faced daily social and economic discrimination in St. Louis. Inabel Lindsay left her job at the Provident Association and the city about 1937 for educational opportunities not available to African Americans in St. Louis. She later became dean of the School of Social Work at Howard University. But Marion O'Fallon Oldham stayed to become a St. Louis public school teacher and a local civil rights leader in a movement born of wartime protest.

For every woman who made her place in St. Louis, there were others, like Inabel Lindsey, who did not. They may have gone west with their husbands and fathers, returned to Germany, been transferred to a convent in another city, or struck out on their own. Some, like Clara Pendleton, who left the City Planning Department in 1944, simply slipped through the cracks in the historical record.

Sources: See James Neal Primm, *Lion of the Valley: St. Louis, Missouri*, 3d ed. (St. Louis: MHS Press, 1998), and Katharine Corbett, Alex Yard, Howard Miller, and Mary Seematter, "The New St. Louis in Boom and Bust," *SLAH,* for information on the St. Louis economy and local New Deal programs. For a national context and analysis of ERA debate, see Sara M. Evans, *Born for Liberty: A History of Women in America* (New York: The Free Press, 1989), 175–241. Information and analysis on family economics and the Social Security Act is from Stephanie Coontz, *The Way We Never Were: American Families and the Nostalgia Trap* (New York: Basic Books, 1992). For domestic consumerism, see Susan Strasser, *Never Done: A History of American Housework* (New York: Pantheon Books, 1992) and *Satisfaction Guaranteed: The Making of the American Mass Market* (New York: Pantheon Books, 1989). For a discussion on women's civic virtue, see Evans, *Born for Liberty,* and Linda Kerber, *No Constitutional Right To Be Ladies: Women and the Obligation of Citizenship* (New York: Hill and Wang, 1998). For Bohemian Hill, see Patricia L. Jones, "What Ever Happened to Bohemian Hill," *GH* 5, no. 3 (winter 1984–1985). For the Hill, see Gary Mormino, *Immigrants on the Hill: Italian-Americans in St. Louis, 1882–1982* (Urbana: University of Illinois Press, 1989). Information on declining birthrates, national education statistics, and labor statistics for 1920 is from Nancy Woloch, *Women and the American Experience*, 2d ed. (New York: Knopf, 1984).

Although some single women could afford to rent apartments, many others could not. Mary Ryder established several homes for homeless women in the 1930s; see Mary Ryder Papers, WHMC–UMSL. "Women and Womanhood" scrapbooks at MHS include newspaper clippings of feature stories on women and their activities, including information on every woman who had been selected a "St. Louis Woman of Achievement." Like other newspaper scrapbooks compiled by volunteers, these are invaluable because St. Louis newspapers were not indexed before 1975. These and other MHS scrapbooks are indexed in the library's information file.

Additional sources include *Black Women Oral History Project*, Interview with Inabel Burns Lindsay, May 20–June 7, 1977, 271–333; Katharine T. Corbett, "St. Louis Women's Employment in World War II," unpublished paper delivered at the St. Louis Women Historians Conference on St. Louis Women and World War II, 1984; and Susan Ware, *American Women in the 1930s: Holding Their Own* (Boston: Twayne Publishing, 1982). Information on Louise Venverloh is from Karen Venverloh Bewig, *Memories of a Century in St. Louis* (Manchester, Mo.: KAVV Publishing Co., 1993). See also the State of Missouri Annual Reports,

Bureau of Labor Statistics, 1920 through 1926; State of Missouri 58th Annual Report of the Labor and Industrial Inspection Department, also 51st and 52nd Reports, 1929 to 1931; Clara Pendleton feature story, *Post-Dispatch*, 27 July 1941; Katharine Darst, "The Girls Kept Their Shoes On," *BMHS* 14, no. 1 (October 1957); Susan Hartmann, *The Home Front and Beyond: American Women in the 1940s* (Boston: Twayne Publishing, 1982); "Interview with Dorothy Gronmeir," Women in World War II Oral History Project, WHMC–UMSL; Women's Advertising Club Papers, WHMC–UMSL; YWCA Papers, WHMC–UMSL; Margaret Hickey Papers, WHMC–UMSL; and Priscilla A. Dowden, "Over This We Are Determined to Fight: African American Public Education and Health Care in St. Louis, Missouri, 1910–1949" (Ph.D. dissertation, Indiana University, 1997).

The League of Women Voters

Carrie Chapman Catt's challenge to "raise up a league of woman voters" was fulfilled in February 1919 with the formation of the National League of Women Voters at a Chicago convention. St. Louis women, however, did not wait for national passage of the suffrage amendment. They spent the summer of 1919 rallying support for ratification in Missouri and then began a statewide program of citizenship schools, enrolling thirteen thousand prospective members. On November 13, 1920, the Equal Suffrage League formally disbanded and created the League of Women Voters of St. Louis (LWV). Once ratification of the Nineteenth Amendment secured women's place in the voting booth, suffrage leaders such as St. Louisan Edna Gellhorn asked, "How are we going to use it?"

A major disagreement arose at the national level on the implications of women's use of the vote. In 1916 a minority of suffragists, who advocated a separate political party to pursue a broader agenda of women's rights, organized the National Women's Party under the leadership of radical activist Alice Paul. Its more militant suffrage tactics and the National American Woman Suffrage Association (NAWSA) leadership's personal dislike of Paul helped motivate the moderate majority to redefine their goals. Not only concerned with women's issues, the group sought to make good citizens, an endeavor that placed them above the political fray. The NAWSA executive council made this clear in one of its policy recommendations at the 1919 Jubilee Convention in St. Louis: "Resolved, that the NAWSA shall not affiliate with any political party nor endorse the platform of any party, nor support or oppose any political candidates." The council insisted that nothing in the resolution limit the right of any member "to join or serve the party of her choice in any capacity whatsoever as an individual."

The St. Louis LWV, despite this policy, backed candidates in a local judicial election, considered a special case warranting the league's involvement. After the election, members found that the public perceived them as a Democratic organization, particularly since the local president's husband was a leader of that party. To regain its neutral standing, the St. Louis LWV for several years chose co-presidents representing Republican, Democratic, and Independent Parties, creating an unwieldy system that dissolved in 1926.

The St. Louis LWV also selected and endorsed candidates in several school board elections in the early 1920s. The national organization disapproved of this, noting that the divisiveness of political campaigns could impede the LWV's fundamental activities, which most members agreed lay in the realm of citizen education. Members found participation in the political process educational and invigorating, but by 1925 the group turned its efforts toward a systematic investigation of political issues and candidates and published the findings in the first of its many voters' guides. This painstaking selection and study of a LWV "program" through a system of committees became the hallmark of the national organization as well as its local chapter.

In the first decade after suffrage, the national and local LWV backed legislation that applied specifically to women, notably the federal Sheppard-Towner Act, which established clinics to reduce infant mortality; the Cable Act, which protected the citizenship of American women who married non-citizens; child labor legislation; and the Civil Service Reclassification Act, which included "the principle of equal compensation for equal work irrespective of sex." Local members lobbied the state legislature to eliminate the word "male" from the Missouri constitution, abolish common-law marriage, provide for women factory inspectors, and give equal representation to women on political committees. This feminist agenda lost strength during the 1920s. Differences with the National Women's Party intensified when Alice Paul introduced the Equal Rights Amendment in 1923. The moderates of the league could not bring themselves to support a constitutional provision that could erase the protective legislation they had struggled to win. By the end of the decade, a unilateral women's voting bloc, which some Americans had feared, clearly did not exist.

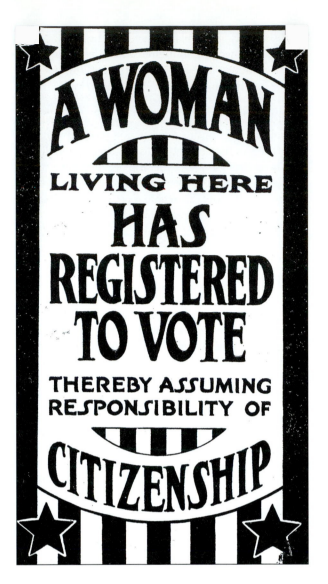

A WOMAN LIVING HERE HAS REGISTERED TO VOTE THEREBY ASSUMING RESPONSIBILITY OF CITIZENSHIP

The depression forced both national and local leagues to regroup and refocus their efforts. The membership of the St. Louis organization fell from 2,840 in 1927 to a low of 500 in 1934; several smaller leagues in St. Louis County dissolved completely. Delegates to the national convention of 1934 reorganized LWV programs under six major departments focusing on issues of government. Edna Gellhorn served as national chair of a major effort to end the political spoils system in federal employment. During the decade, St. Louis members tried unsuccessfully to push a merit charter amendment through the Board of Aldermen. They continued their lobbying until the board agreed in 1941 to submit the issue to a public vote.

Sign Distributed to Potential Voters by the League of Women Voters, ca. 1925. Courtesy WHMC–UMSL

The league played a critical part in the success of the subsequent campaign, organizing 500 women to make over 125,000 phone calls to voters across the city. Other 1930s programs focused on relief efforts, public housing, and the improvement of the St. Louis public schools.

Two major programs dominated the league's work in the World War II "War Service Units," which met regularly to distribute government information and discuss ways that residents could help the war effort. Members also organized a speakers bureau and produced a series of radio programs to increase the flow of information. Simultaneously, the league played a key role in the campaign to draw up a new Missouri constitution. In 1941 they began preparing and distributing study kits, organizing study sessions, and campaigning for a constitutional convention. When the convention met in 1944, the league monitored its work, headed a petition drive to add key provisions to the working draft, and spearheaded the final campaign for its acceptance in 1945.

The League of Women Voters of St. Louis differed from most affiliates of the national LWV in its inclusion of African American women. While most cities formed separate black and white affiliates, the local group from its beginning accepted black women as full members. The leadership established a "Colored Division," a standing committee with representation on the executive committee of the St. Louis LWV. Over the years, the league actively supported reforms affecting the black community that did not challenge the racial attitudes of its white members. For example, it endorsed health care and housing issues, the expansion of Lincoln University, and improvement of the city's public schools, but it did not oppose school segregation.

Within the organizational structure, the St. Louis league protected the rights of its African American members. Local delegates refused to be seated at the first national convention until it recognized the nonwhite delegates. The St. Louis LWV also resigned in 1921 from the Advisory Board, a local confederation of women's groups that insisted that the league change its membership policy. The league refused to hold meetings in hotels or other facilities with segregated dining or other services; the leadership moved its headquarters from the Kingsway Hotel in 1941 after incidents of discrimination against African American members.

Nevertheless, the league did not challenge St. Louis's racist social climate. Edna Gellhorn acknowledged to a league officer of another city in

1937 that "there are certain social meetings where the colored members are not included, not because the league wishes to have it so, but just because it is better that we should not offend too many of our prejudiced groups." She reported that African American members received invitations, but that they did not attend because "they never wish to intrude where they have any reason to believe their presence would embarrass anyone."

Although the St. Louis LWV had an integrated membership, African American women conducted their own study groups in housing, education, and other areas of interest until 1946, when the Interracial Committee disbanded in an effort to include black women in the larger committee system. In the postwar period, the league generally gave its support to the growing civil rights movement in St. Louis, but as one officer admitted in 1950, real integration of the organization had not yet occurred.

Both nationally and locally, the League of Women Voters was a reformist organization that, despite its direct link to the suffrage movement, was committed to the broader social welfare goals identified with progressivism. Progressive Era women did "municipal housekeeping" without the franchise and outside of the party system. They used self-education, organizational savvy, and nonpartisan persuasion to effect change, primarily governmental reform. For these women the vote was one more powerful tool to further that agenda. The white middle-class members often had the same patronizing attitudes about black and working-class women that had characterized Progressive Era reformers, but the league opened its membership to African American women when no similar organization would. League members were not feminist radicals, but they sought justice and opportunity for all women. While taking a leadership role in promoting hundreds of local reform efforts, the St. Louis League of Women Voters trained and encouraged women who would move into the partisan political arena in the post–World War II period.

–Susan Beattie

Sources: The resolution on nonpartisanship was reported in the *Globe-Democrat,* 26 March 1919. Edna Gellhorn's quote on racial attitudes in St. Louis is from a letter, 15 November 1937, to Mrs. Carter Harrison, contained in the League of Women Voters Archives. WHMC–UMSL holds an extensive and underutilized archive of records for the state and city leagues, and for the Kirkwood and North County chapters. These include correspondence, minutes, photographs, and scrapbooks of news clippings, as well as audiocassette interviews made with early members in the 1970s. For an understanding of the formation and development of the local organization, start with league member Avis Carlson, *The League of Women Voters in St. Louis: The First Forty Years, 1919–1959* (St. Louis: League of Women Voters of St. Louis, 1959); her article "The First Decade of the St. Louis League of Women Voters," *BMHS* 26, no. 1 (October 1969); and Ruth Pruett, *A History of the League of Women Voters of St. Louis, 1919–1936* (St. Louis: R. Pruett, 1937); Priscilla Dowden, "Over This Point We are Determined to Fight: African-American Education and Health Care in St. Louis, Missouri, 1910–1949" (Ph.D. dissertation, University of Missouri–St. Louis, 1990) provides an excellent analysis of the league's participation in African American social organization in St. Louis.

For background on the national League of Women Voters, see Louise M. Young, *In the Public Interest: The League of Women Voters, 1920–1970* (New York: Greenwood Press, 1989), and Robert B. Fowler, *Carrie Catt: Feminist Politician* (Boston: Northeastern University Press, 1986). Few recent examinations of twentieth-century women's history discuss the league in depth; Naomi Black, *Social Feminism* (Ithica, N.Y.: Cornell University Press, 1989) argues against most feminist scholarship that the league is a continuation of the historic women's movement and should be viewed as both a feminist and political organization.

Junior League

The Junior League of St. Louis has its roots in the Progressive Era suffrage movement. A subsidiary of the local suffrage organization, the Junior Equal Suffrage League was formed in 1912, with seventy-five members under the leadership of Margaret McKittrick and Ann Drew. They represented "The Junior League of St. Louis" at a state suffrage convention in April 1913. The chronology of the group's transition from suffrage to volunteer activities is sketchy, but the modern organization recognizes a meeting in November 1914 at McKittrick's home as its official beginning. McKittrick later said that many girls' families objected to their suffrage work and that some members had joined out of curiosity, without a commitment to the suffrage campaign. When members encountered the Junior League movement in other cities, they decided to continue their association but with an altered mission.

The first Junior League was founded in New York City in 1901 by Mary Harriman and Nathalie Henderson, both privileged members of the inner circles of high society. Harriman, whose parents were actively involved in a variety of philanthropies,

in-law of Edna Gellhorn and member of both the Equal Suffrage League and the Junior League. The group's sponsor, Josephine Poe January, was also a leader in the St. Louis League of Women Voters.

Like the New York Junior League, the St. Louis chapter's early projects included the distribution of flowers to hospitals and the staging of theatrical performances, rummage sales, and balls as fund raisers for charity. From the beginning, the group instructed members to work in other volunteer organizations. It also established its own endeavors, including the Occupational Therapy Workshop, founded in 1917 as a part of relief efforts in World War I, and a lunchroom at the Neighborhood Association that served free meals to poor children. Members worked with the Red Cross both at home and in Europe.

As membership grew in the 1920s, the league established its first official headquarters in the West End and opened a shop called "The Open Door" as a fund-raising project. A tearoom for members began in 1927; it later opened to the public as another way to fund the league's projects and to contribute to other agencies like Miss Gregg's Settlement House and the Grace Hill House Nursery School.

In the 1930s the league made great strides toward the professionalization of volunteerism with the establishment of a training program in social work for new members, called "provisionals." As the depression deepened, the group also created a Placement Committee to evaluate the city's increased welfare needs and to work with organizations like the Red Cross, Children's Aid Bureau, County Welfare Office, and the YMCA to identify the areas most in need of volunteer help.

During World War II members worked with the Red Cross, USO, Salvation Army, and other organizations in formal and informal support of soldiers and their families. Some even joined the movement of American women into paid employment. As the war ended, the Junior League turned its attention to children's issues, establishing the Forest Park Children's Center, a psychiatric study home. The league supported the home with volunteers and financial aid, which continued after its merger with the Edgewood Children's Center in 1955.

Until relatively recently, only elite socialites belonged to the Junior League of St. Louis. The first group of prospective members in 1915 came from that year's list of debutantes, and members had the right to blackball nominees who did not meet their standards. The key qualification for membership

Junior League Rummage Sale, 7 April 1949. Junior League members not only held traditional fund raisers, but also trained to be effective volunteers for social service agencies. Courtesy WHMC–UMSL

had heard a report on the work of the College Settlement House on New York's Lower East Side and decided that supporting it would give her contemporaries "a definite purpose" for their debut season. She and Henderson brought eighty debutantes together to form the Junior League for the Promotion of Settlement Houses. In that first year, they staged tableaus to raise funds and distributed masses of party flowers to area hospitals. Some members volunteered in the settlement house. Harriman continued to oversee the group as it added new members in following years, and the idea spread to other cities. The St. Louis chapter formed in 1915, becoming the eleventh member of the national organization.

Despite this redirection, the St. Louis group continued to reflect the suffrage influence in the early years. Junior League members acted as pages at the National American Woman Suffrage Association Jubilee in St. Louis, and several were convention delegates. The chapter was one of the first groups to sign up for an Equal Suffrage League "Citizenship School" in 1919, scheduling ten classes under the direction of Mrs. Walter Fischel, a sister-

was the willingness to give both time to the league and "congeniality to the other girls." The degree to which Junior League membership added to a young woman's social standing varied nationally; in large cities like New York, other women's clubs were more exclusive, more prestigious. In St. Louis, membership was simply a matter of course for women of the city's leading families; it solidified their social standing and marked a rite of passage into the adult responsibilities of their class. Although the Junior League in recent years has lifted its membership restrictions and broadened its base, it is still widely perceived more as an elite social club than a progressive volunteer organization. Its history shows it was both.

–Susan Beattie

Sources: The Junior League of St. Louis is in the process of transferring its archives, currently housed at its building on Clayton Road, to WHMC–UMSL. This extensive collection includes board minutes from the group's founding in 1914, yearbooks from 1918, and numerous scrapbooks and photos from the early period to the present.

Information on the Junior Equal Suffrage League of St. Louis is included in the League of Women Voters Archive at WHMC–UMSL (in files covering the Missouri and St. Louis Equal Suffrage League groups) and in the Suffrage Collection at MHS.

The Junior League is generally omitted from discussions of women's organizations founded in the Progressive Era, presumably because of the exclusionary membership policies that marked much of its history. Janet Gordon and Diana Reische, *The Volunteer Powerhouse* (New York: Rutledge Press, 1982) is a comprehensive history of the national Junior League organization, written by two of its members.

Edna Fischel Gellhorn

"**W**e just knew we wanted to get something done and we did our darndest to get it done." On her eighty-fifth birthday, Edna Gellhorn's typically offhanded explanation of the effort she and her friends expended to gain the vote for women understated the role she herself had played. Gellhorn is best remembered for her leadership in the suffrage movement and the League of Women Voters, but for more than sixty years she "belonged to every white-hat organization in town." She brought a combination of energy, charm, and good humor to each new campaign of civic reform; she also brought intelligence, compassion, a fine talent for organization, and a firm conviction in the rights and responsibilities of citizenship for all Americans.

Edna Gellhorn was born into a prominent and socially active St. Louis family in 1878. Her father, Dr. Washington Fischel, was a professor of clinical medicine at Washington University, and a founder and first president of Barnard Skin and Cancer Hospital. Her mother set a standard of social involvement for her four children. Martha Ellis Fischel was a pioneer of the women's club movement, a founding member of the Adelphi Club, The Wednesday Club, the Women's Club of St. Louis, and the Missouri Federation of Women's Clubs. She and Dr. Fischel were charter members of the Ethical Society of St. Louis; she later served as president of both the local society and its parent group, the American Ethical Union. She participated in the Humanity Club, the Provident Association, and the St. Louis Emergency Aid efforts following the tornado of 1896, and she chaired the Board of the Charity Commissioners of St. Louis. An exemplar of the "municipal housekeeping" ethic of her generation, Martha Fischel developed a system of training in homemaking skills, cajoling friends to join her in teaching at her School of Domestic Economy at the Self-Culture Hall settlement house she founded with Ethical Society leader Walter Sheldon in 1888. In 1900 the St. Louis Board of Education incorporated her program into its curriculum of

Edna Fischel Gellhorn. In her late eighties, Edna Gellhorn reflected on a lifetime of public service. Photograph by Thelma Blumberg, ca. 1965. Edna Fischel Gellhorn Papers, Washington University Archives.

manual training and hired two women trained by Fischel as its first teachers. She remained active in a number of organizations until her death in 1939. Edna grew up in a household that was intellectually stimulating and that regarded civic responsibility and "doing our darndest" as facts of life.

Edna Gellhorn demonstrated leadership qualities early in life. Her classmates elected her president at Mary Institute and life president of the Bryn Mawr College class of 1900. Returning to St. Louis after graduation, she met Dr. George Gellhorn, a recent immigrant from Germany and her father's medical protégé; they married in 1903. Together they raised a family of four—journalist and novelist Martha; law professor Walter; medical educator Alfred; and international businessman George Jr. Edna balanced the needs of her children and husband with her civic duties. She always credited good household help and the enthusiastic support of her husband as critical to the success of her own work. The family lived at 4366 McPherson Avenue in the Central West End from 1911 to 1948.

As a newlywed, Gellhorn had been involved in pre–World's Fair efforts to clean up St. Louis's water supply and worked alongside her mother in other civic campaigns, but she found a cause to make her own in the suffrage movement. From 1910 until the passage of the Nineteenth Amendment in 1919, she was an officer in both the St. Louis and Missouri State Equal Suffrage Leagues, leading demonstrations, lobbying officials, speaking to organizations all over the state, and rallying her colleagues in the face of repeated legislative defeats.

When full national suffrage was won in 1920 and the women's organization was reborn as the League of Women Voters, Carrie Chapman Catt asked Gellhorn to serve as its first national president, calling her "the best suited to the task of any woman I know in the country." She refused the position, citing family duties, but accepted the first vice-chairmanship of the national group, as well as the presidency of the state organization. In later years she served another term in that position, as well as three terms as president of the St. Louis branch. To her friends and to her community, Edna Gellhorn *was* the League of Women Voters, representing the organization in speeches before a myriad of other groups, chairing committees, volunteering for even mundane tasks like envelope addressing, and hosting countless strategy sessions. The league recognized her efforts by electing her to both their state and national Rolls of Honor.

The St. Louis League of Women Voters was atypical of the national movement in its inclusion of African American women as representatives to its board from the beginning, a fact that Beatrice Grady, the first black officer, attributed to a tie-breaking vote cast by Edna Gellhorn in 1919. Under her leadership, the league withdrew in 1921 from the Advisory Board, a confederation of St. Louis women's groups, rather than change its policy of admitting African Americans as members. Gellhorn was president of the St. Louis league when they moved from the Kingsway Hotel in 1941, after black members experienced discriminatory treatment by hotel employees.

In a city with engrained racial prejudice, Gellhorn's actions consistently demonstrated her commitment to equal treatment of African Americans. Her speaking calendars of the 1930s and 1940s included many engagements before black women's clubs, churches, and civil rights organizations; league members recalled organizational meetings of young black women held in Gellhorn's home in the 1920s, an occurrence unheard of for the time. When the College Club split in the 1940s over the issue of admitting blacks, she joined the group advocating open membership and lent her name as the club's founder to a lawsuit over the disposition of club property. She also served on the Mayor's Race Relations Commission, the Homer G. Phillips Advisory Committee, and the boards of the Urban League and the People's Art Center. Mayor Bernard Dickman appointed her to the committee to mediate the Funsten Nut Company strike.

A politically savvy and tireless reform campaigner, Edna Gellhorn chose not to run for public office herself. Adlai Stevenson, presidential hopeful in 1952, was the only candidate she ever openly supported. Instead of running for office, she used her administrative skills in numerous appointed positions, including regional director of Herbert Hoover's food program in World War I and food rationing during World War II. She also served on the Social Security Commission, Slum Clearance Commission, the mayor's committee to resolve the International Ladies Garment Workers Union organizing strike, the governor's Commission on the Status of Women, and the Commission to Revise the Missouri Constitution.

Gellhorn reduced her league activities in her later life, dividing time between her family and lobbying for world peace. She joined her friend Eleanor Roosevelt in support of the United Nations Association and helped found the local Citizens

Committee on Nuclear Information. Injuries from a fall left her a semi-invalid for the last two years of her life, but she continued to entertain and delight visitors at her home until her death in 1970 at age ninety-one. Her obituaries applauded her many public achievements; friends and family remembered her many small kindnesses, the dozens of brief notes she scrawled off each day, her abiding honesty, and her infectious laughter.

In her lifetime, Gellhorn repeatedly proved her ability to change. She became the epitome of the "Modern Woman" who led her colleagues to "use their rights once they had them," and she met new challenges with the same enthusiasm as those she had conquered. Speaking to a new generation of league members in 1957, she said, "The only value of the past is that it's the foundation . . . the jumping off place for the future."

Edna Gellhorn's activist roots lay in the Progressive Era of her birth and early womanhood. Her profound sense of social justice was rooted in a family tradition of public service and nurtured by their participation in the Ethical Culture movement, which held social activism as a creed. In an interview given shortly before her death, Gellhorn said, "I was inspired by the message that women had something to contribute." To her, it was that simple. Perhaps her greatest contribution was that through the strength of her own beliefs and the force of her personality, she brought out the very best in others.

–Susan Beattie

Sources: Edna Gellhorn's life and work deserve further research and a full biography. Ample material documents both her public and private lives. Her papers are in the Washington University Archives. Included is information on the dozens of organizations that she was involved in, letters and clippings on both Gellhorn and Fischel family members, and personal correspondence files, including copies of letters exchanged with Eleanor Roosevelt, the originals of which are at the Hyde Park Library.

The Fischel family's involvement in the Ethical Culture movement was a critical influence on Gellhorn. Details can be found in the Ethical Society of St. Louis Archives, WHMC–UMSL.

The Western Historical Manuscripts Collection also holds the archives of the League of Women Voters, which includes Gellhorn correspondence, biographical material, and scrapbooks devoted to her work in the league. Personal correspondence and an audio recording of her memories of the suffrage movement and the league are part of the Genevieve Nelson Collection, WHMC–UMSL.

Profiles of Gellhorn appear in *NAW,* and in Mary K. Dains and Sue Sadler, eds., *Show Me Missouri Women: Selected Biographies* (Kirksville, Mo.: Thomas Jefferson University Press, 1989). Other biographical articles from local newspapers and magazines are in the vertical files at MHS. Carl Rollyson, *Nothing Ever Happens to the Brave* (New York: St. Martin's Press, 1990) is a biography of Edna's daughter, the writer Martha Gellhorn, which includes several chapters that offer insight on the Gellhorn family.

College Alumnae Organizations

"**I**n those days if a girl ever expected to acquire a husband and a home of her own she had to be careful for the man must not know that she could even recite the alphabet." Despite her later evaluation of the perils of obtaining a college education, Bryn Mawr graduate Edna Gellhorn and one hundred other young women founded the College Club of St. Louis in 1901 as a way to maintain the sense of community, identity, and purpose they had acquired on university campuses. This was particularly important to the growing number of graduates who, unlike many alumnae of the preceding generation, intended to marry and feared losing themselves completely to the roles of wife and mother.

The college graduate of the turn of the century was a member of an elite group: only about 5 percent of all eighteen to twenty-one year olds in the country were full-time students. While more than a third of these were women, they received only one-fifth of the undergraduate degrees awarded. Women graduates had formed the Association of Collegiate Alumnae (ACA) twenty years earlier to continue their education and to encourage other young women to attend college. A St. Louis branch may have existed as early as 1893.

The focus of the St. Louis group was identical to that of the national alumnae; they met regularly in literary study groups, sponsored purely social teas and dances, and increasingly raised money to establish scholarships to help other young women earn a college diploma. By 1980, the St. Louis College Club had provided over $100,000 in scholarships and loans to 345 students.

In 1920 the College Club merged with the local chapter of the Association of Collegiate Alumnae, and, when the national organization changed its name to the American Association of University Women (AAUW) the following year, it followed suit by adding "St. Louis Branch of AAUW" to the original title. The merger, together with the increasing numbers of women enrolling in colleges, gave the group a membership of several hundred and the financial strength to consider buying a building to eliminate the frequent turnover in borrowed or rented meeting spaces.

In 1922 they purchased a residence at 5428 Delmar Boulevard, that provided not only comfortable meeting and dining rooms on its first floor, but also added a source of club income through use of the second and third floors as a boarding facility for members. This building housed the club through twenty-plus years of growth and expansion of its scholarship programs; it also became the focus of a dispute that later split the membership permanently.

While the AAUW was nominally nondiscriminatory from its inception, the reality of legalized segregation made it in fact a white organization. African American women, responding to the same needs as white college graduates, formed their own alumnae associations. St. Louisan Ethel Hedgeman Lyle founded Alpha Kappa Alpha as an undergraduate social sorority at Howard University in 1908. In 1920 Felicia Stevens Alexander founded a graduate chapter of the sorority Gamma Omega in St. Louis to promote cultural and educational uplift in the black community. Other St. Louis women were members of the National Association of University Women, organized by renowned clubwoman and educator Mary Church Terrell in 1910. Although they also provided financial aid and encouragement to students, these groups expanded their scope of activities beyond those of their white counterparts. They established community institutions to fill the gaps left by the white establishment and worked with other organizations like the Urban League, Housewives' League, and the National Association for the Advancement of Colored People (NAACP) to fight economic and political inequality, lead consumer boycotts, and take part in demonstrations against employment discrimination.

In highly segregated St. Louis, the parallel racial groups operated without question of integration or even cooperation until an event outside the city brought previously unarticulated racial policies to a test. In 1946 Mary Church Terrell applied for membership in the Washington, D.C., branch of the AAUW and was refused admission. In response, the national board adopted and published a resolution of nondiscrimination, and the Washington branch filed suit to establish its right to set membership qualifications locally. The court decided in favor of the local organization.

At the national convention in June 1949, delegates adopted a revision of the AAUW bylaws that limited restrictions to purely educational standards and effectively opened membership to all graduates of qualified institutions, regardless of race. St. Louis delegates had been instructed to vote against the revision and reported to the membership that they had done so. The official College Club position was that they simply wanted to protect the autonomy of the local clubs against imposition of national rules. The record makes it clear that race was in fact the primary issue. Correspondence leading up to and accompanying a ballot taken to determine if the College Club would withdraw from the national association accentuates that retention of the affiliation would mean adherence to the policy of "admitting qualified negro women." And in St. Louis, that would mean not only integrating the clubhouse meeting rooms, but also the possibility that an African American member might expect to live in the boarding area, something that was unthinkable to many white St. Louisans, even college-educated women.

When the ballots were counted, a narrow majority of voters (but not of the total membership) favored withdrawal from the AAUW. A sizable minority, including most of the elected officers, opposed that move. Two distinct groups, with separate slates of officers, claimed to be the legitimate College Club with rights to the name and ownership of assets including a ten thousand-dollar treasury and the clubhouse itself. Mary Ellen Conway Nardin, who had played an active role in the groups' merger and in the purchase of the clubhouse, organized and led the opposition to the disaffiliation and chaired the Legal Advisory Committee. When the backers of the national nondiscriminatory policy sued the opposing group, Edna Gellhorn, first president of the original College Club, lent her name to the lawsuit and also served on the Legal Advisory Committee until shortly before the conclusion of the case.

The legal battle lasted until March 1956, when an appeal of the original suit was also decided in favor of the faction that had disaffiliated and was in possession of the clubhouse. At that time, the losing group, which had continued to call itself "College Club St. Louis Branch of AAUW," was forced to drop "College Club" from its name.

The court's decision had almost nothing to do with issues of racial discrimination, nor did it address the separation of powers between the national organization and the local affiliate. It was decided instead on arguments regarding the sequence by which the ACA and College Club had merged, its chartering under Missouri corporate law, and subsequent affiliation with the national group. By the 1960s, the all-white College Club found itself the owner of a deteriorating property in a neighborhood rapidly changing in racial composition, and it began looking for a new home. The last meeting at the Delmar location was held on June 27, 1967; in the fall of that year, the club moved into rented quarters in the original University Club building at Grand and Washington Avenues. In 1975, the College Club joined the University Club in its move to a new building in St. Louis County.

–Susan Beattie

Sources: Archives of both the College Club and the St. Louis branch of the AAUW since the split in 1949 are housed at the WHMC–UMSL. The College Club Collection consists of microfilmed scrapbooks of newspaper clippings and programs for social and fund-raising activities as well as a copy of a brief history of the club, written in 1982 by member Henrietta Gummels. The AAUW collection contains records and correspondence from 1949 to 1973, including depositions and correspondence pertaining to the lawsuit, along with board minutes for the period. The Edna Gellhorn quote is from an article in the *Post-Dispatch*, 12 May 1933.

Archives and publications of the Alpha Kappa Alpha Sorority are also at WHMC–UMSL. For additional information on African American sororities in St. Louis, see Suzzana Maupin Long, "I Made It Mine Tho the Queen Waz Always Fair" (master's thesis, University of Missouri–St. Louis, 1988). For a history of African American Alumnae organizations, see Paula Giddings, *In Search of Sisterhood: Delta Sigma Theta and the Challenge of the Black Sorority Movement* (New York: Morrow, 1988).

For an overview of the political and economic issues of the period, see Woloch, *Women and the American Experience*, which includes a bibliography and an appendix with graphical representations of statistics on education, marriage, childbearing, and the labor force.

Booklovers Club

On a Saturday afternoon in April 1925, Josephine Stevens welcomed the Booklovers Club to her home at 4219 West Finney Avenue, on the southern edge of the city's black middle-class enclave known as the Ville. The wife of George Stevens, pastor of Central Baptist Church, she had founded the club in 1907 with Carrie Bowles, another young African American teacher. Since then, the Booklovers had gathered in each other's homes twice a month to discuss literature, the arts, social sciences, and current events.

On this day the topic was W. E. B. Du Bois's new book, *The Gift of the Black Folk*. Du Bois, a passionate advocate for African American intellectual leadership, was an appropriate choice for these educated women intent on personal growth. Over the next two decades, the Booklovers studied a wide variety of cultural topics but most often grappled with current African American social and intellectual issues. Their dual identity as women and African Americans led them to embrace the self-education typical of middle-class clubwomen, as it shaped their intellectual interests and drove their social activism.

The two founders modeled the Booklovers on a similar group in Kansas City. Carrie Bowles, born in Selma, Ohio, in 1873, graduated from a Chicago normal school and taught in southern cities before moving to East St. Louis in 1902 and later to St. Louis's Ville neighborhood. Bowles, who became one of the Provident Association's first professional case workers, joined the Colored Committee of the League of Women Voters (LWV) in 1919. Josephine Stevens was also active in the LWV, as well as the Phyllis Wheatley Branch of the Young Women's Christian Association (YWCA).

The Booklovers Club's original eight members had grown to twenty-five by 1912, and the group decided that admitting any more would crowd their living rooms. In 1925 at least sixteen Booklovers, or their husbands, were St. Louis public school teachers or principals, six at Sumner High School alone. The six unmarried women were all teachers.

Booklovers Club on Their 25th Anniversary. Booklovers Club Scrapbook, ca. 1933. MHS Library

The husbands of the others included a minister, realtor, physician, post-office clerk, and two porters who probably worked on Pullman sleeping cars. One woman, Clara Shaw, ran a hotel.

Like similar clubs organized by white women, the Booklovers' only stated goal was study. The members, actively engaged in religious, charitable, and social work elsewhere, endorsed "all movements for civic and social improvement and race betterment" but intended to meet only for intellectual stimulation. During the first five years they studied anthropology and sociology, particularly the relationship between race and culture. Members presented papers, reviewed new books, and discussed current events at each session. At the first meeting in September, they reported on summer vacation trips to places as distant from St. Louis as Latin America or Europe.

Until the 1920s, the Booklovers focused on topics in western civilization. In 1912 members surveyed art history, adding both an annual visit to the St. Louis Art Museum and an open lecture meeting for guests. Sculpture was the topic for 1915–1916, world literature in 1916–1917, and modern drama between 1917 and 1919. Although the membership was exclusively African American, the Booklovers occasionally invited white speakers, used study material developed by the General Federation of Women's Clubs, and called on the directors of the St. Louis Art Museum and the School of Fine Arts for assistance in planning programs.

Although opera was the topic of study in 1919, the Booklovers began to combine cultural enrichment with the study of civic issues. When the St. Louis LWV recruited Beatrice Grady to start a "colored division," the Booklovers allied themselves with the league and its educational programs. Like the League of Women Voters, they endorsed a new school tax in 1919. In 1922 the Booklovers program included LWV citizenship lessons and lectures on "How a Bill Becomes a Law," along with members' papers on "Egypt" and "The Phoenicians."

As educators and members of the local black elite, the Booklovers promoted education on all fronts. The subject for study in 1925–1926 was "The Negro Problem as Seen in Current Literature." While discussing poetry, social commentary, history, and drama by black authors, they actively lobbied for a second high school for African Americans. They urged the LWV to request that the new school for African Americans, under construction on Laclede Avenue, open as both a junior and senior high school. High school classes in the new building would relieve overcrowding at Sumner High School and maintain the middle-class character of the Ville institution. Vashon High School was planned primarily to serve the black district east of Grand Avenue, which was rapidly filling up with poor migrants from the rural south.

The Booklovers remembered 1925 as "a year of self-searching and research which left us strong in our own self-regard." The following year, they studied "The Psychology of the Color Line." They agreed with Du Bois that "in matters of Race the power of error masquerading as truth was greater than the power of truth itself." Convinced that there is "no characteristic typical of race," they began exploring the origins and possible solutions to America's social problems. In 1926–1927 they explored "social trends, labor problems, marriage laws and family problems."

In 1927 the club discussed these issues as expressed in "modern literature and the field of race relations." They read novels by Sinclair Lewis, Dorothy Canfield and Fannie Cook, a local social realist who spoke to the group in 1927. The annual report for 1927–1928 mentioned a 20th anniversary celebration at Poro College but not a tornado that tore through their streets in September, damaging homes, killing neighbors, and destroying the West Belle School where several Booklovers taught.

Maggie Cannon, one of the most active members of the Booklovers, became the Industrial Secretary of the segregated Phyllis Wheatley Branch of the YWCA. The Booklovers later met at the Wheatley Branch and organized a library there for black girls.

In 1932 the club program ignored the national depression and took an international turn in response to mounting world tensions. Russia, China, Japan, and India each received attention, followed by fascism, Marxism, and the position of Jews in Germany. Because the membership was increasingly active in social welfare work, during the depression years they began meeting only once a month. "Revolution and Revolt," the topic for 1937–1938, led to discussions of sharecroppers in southern Missouri and Mexican revolutionaries. The following year the club wrote to commend Eleanor Roosevelt for arranging Marion Anderson's performance at the Lincoln Memorial after the Daughters of the American Revolution refused to let her perform for them. The Booklovers ended the decade by discussing the historical experiences of ethnic minorities in America, the European dominance of African cultures, and the meaning of cultural pluralism.

During World War II, Booklovers became even more visible social activists. They protested defense contractors denying black women jobs on government contracts. They also supported the March on Washington Movement and appointed a committee to investigate inadequate recreational facilities for black soldiers stationed in St. Louis, all the while reading on subjects as varied as psychology and world peace. In 1944–1945, like thousands of other Americans, they read and debated Gunnar Myrdal's controversial bestseller, *The American Dilemma: The Negro Problem in American Democracy.*

For nearly forty years, twenty-five black women had met regularly to pursue a diverse program of self-education in world culture and politics, which included studying some of the most significant scholarship in African American culture. Not only did this extended conversation between peers benefit the women intellectually, but the lively discussions at Booklovers meetings gave them insights into their own place in St. Louis and the confidence to act publicly on that knowledge.

Sources: The history of the Booklovers Club is drawn from a scrapbook compiled by the club and donated to MHS. Other information comes from the 1925 St. Louis City Directory and Dowden, "Over This Point We Are Determined to Fight."

The historical role of book clubs, both highly organized groups like the Booklovers and more informal ones, in women's self-education and female consciousness is an important, underresearched topic for study.

Annie Turnbo-Malone and Poro College

Dressed in crisp white blouses and dark skirts, dozens of young African American women arrived each weekday morning in the 1920s at a three-story brick building on the southwest corner of Pendleton and St. Ferdinand Avenues in the Ville neighborhood. Some were learning to dress hair at the Poro Beauty College; others were packing cosmetic products for shipment to Poro saleswomen throughout the country; still others were training to be Poro distributors. They came to earn and learn from Annie Turnbo-Malone, the black entrepreneur who constructed the building in 1917 to house her successful cosmetics firm. Turnbo-Malone envisioned the Poro building as a place where ambitious women could acquire more than just the entrepreneurial skills that had made her the among the wealthiest businesswomen in Missouri.

"Dignity, grace, beauty, industry, thrift, efficiency, godliness–that these ideals be held aloft for the glorification of women and girls of my Race, Poro College is consecrated," she declared in 1925. Through her beauty culture business and private philanthropies, Annie Turnbo-Malone not only returned much of her wealth to the community, but she also helped to make her neighborhood the center of St. Louis middle-class African American culture.

The tenth of her mother's eleven children, Annie Turnbo was born in Metropolis, Illinois, in 1869. After her parents died, she lived with her older siblings and became interested in cosmetology as she helped her sisters dress their hair. Because African American women were always looking for better treatments to promote healthy, stylishly long hair, Turnbo knew that a ready market for effective products existed. After experimenting with various chemical formulas, she produced Wonderful Hair Grower, designed to strengthen hair and improve its sheen and texture. For two years she manufactured and sold an expanding line of hair products in Lovejoy, Illinois, but in 1902 she decided to seek new customers from the thirty-five thousand African Americans living in St. Louis and the thousands more who would be coming for the World's Fair.

From a four-room flat at 2223 Market Street, then in the heart of the black commercial and residential district, Annie Turnbo and three assistants canvassed the neighborhood, offering a free treatment to every woman who answered her doorbell.

Advertisement: Concert by Marian Anderson at Poro College. St. Louis Argus, *22 February 1923. MHS Library*

Turnbo increased door-to-door sales by advertising in the black press, but her real success came after she recruited women to be independent franchised agents. Sarah Breedlove McWilliams, a St. Louis laundry worker who would later market her own competing line of beauty products under the name of Madame C. J. Walker, was one of her first sales agents. By 1910, when Turnbo acquired a copyright for the trade name "Poro," agents were selling her products throughout the United States.

The Poro company offered a variety of new employment opportunities for African American women whose traditional job options had been limited to domestic service or a few professions, such as teaching, that required a least a high school diploma. At the company headquarters women found clerical and light factory work and a supportive environment, but jobs as sales agents had the greatest potential. An ambitious woman could with little capital investment make a good living selling Poro products through her own network of family and friends. She could combine selling with her other responsibilities or make her distributorship an independent business. Annie Turnbo trained her agents to become respected, successful entrepreneurs.

In 1910 she moved the headquarters of her expanding company to a large house at 3100 Pine Street. After her 1914 marriage to Aaron Eugene Malone, a former teacher and traveling salesman, she began planning for an even larger facility to accommodate her complex operation. She chose a residential area in western St. Louis across the street from the city's only high school for African Americans.

Annie Turnbo-Malone's choice of the Ville neighborhood as the site of her new distribution and training center reflected her middle-class concerns and her determination to make the institution "a constructive force in the development of the race." In 1917 upwardly mobile African Americans could buy homes in only one small area of the city's western suburbs. Originally called Elleardsville after a white horticulturist who lived in the area, the Ville had attracted black residents in the wake of Sumner High School's relocation in 1910. In 1920, however, blacks made up only 8 percent of the Ville's population; by 1930, 86 percent of the residents were African American. These newcomers were not descendants of the nineteenth-century black elite who still lived on the south side but were more typically members of an emerging black middle class eager to move west as poor migrants from the south crowded into older black neighborhoods east of Grand Avenue. Annie Turnbo-Malone's decision to call the new building Poro College and to promote it as a cultural community center contributed significantly to the Ville's emergence as a black middle-class community.

Completed in 1920, the new building and an annex covered an entire block. In addition to housing the company's force of clerical, manufacturing, and distribution workers, Poro College trained out-of-town beauticians to use Poro products and sales agents to market them. Turnbo-Malone made her refined, well-equipped, and tastefully decorated facility a community social center as well as a factory and training school. Agents, who might spend several weeks in St. Louis, stayed in hotel-style rooms, ate in the company's attractive dining room, and graduated in a fully equipped five hundred-seat auditorium. Students lived in two large dormitories and ate with employees in a cafeteria that also served the public. The facility had its own laundry, bakery, and tailor shop for making employee uniforms. African Americans in the city for business or pleasure, who would have been turned away from white-only hotels, booked rooms at Poro. Black artists who did not want to perform in saloons and vaudeville theaters gave concerts in the auditorium. Turnbo-Malone also used the room for daily employee devotionals and offered it as a meeting space for religious, fraternal, social, and civic groups.

Poro's nearly two hundred local employees worked under Turnbo-Malone's watchful eye. She stressed cleanliness, good grooming, thrift, and industry, rewarding workers who invested in real estate or helped their parents buy homes. She promoted race pride by featuring exotic African hairstyles in her advertisements and fostered personal growth by organizing a girls orchestra that played in the rooftop garden adjoining her own penthouse.

By 1924 Turnbo-Malone was one of the wealthiest self-made women in Missouri. She donated generously to black institutions: the St. James A.M.E. Church, the Pine Street YMCA, Howard University Medical School, and Wilberforce University in Ohio. In 1919 she donated land on Goode Avenue in the Ville for a new building for the St. Louis Colored Orphans' Home and raised much of the construction money. She served as the orphans' home board president from 1919 to 1943, returning annually for the May Day celebration after she moved to Chicago in 1930. In 1945 the institution was renamed the Annie Malone Children's Home in her honor.

In 1927 Aaron Malone sued Annie for divorce and demanded half of her business. Some prominent African Americans supported Malone, a well-known local black Republican politician, but the black press, clergy, and her own employees sided with Annie. In a costly out-of-court settlement, she retained sole ownership of the Poro company. In 1930, bitter over the divorce and looking for more business opportunities, Annie moved her company to Chicago but retained the St. Louis building, which served as a hotel and movie theater in the 1930s. In 1939 it became the site of the Lincoln University Law School, created in response to the *Gaines v. University of Missouri* Supreme Court ruling that required the state law school to either admit black students or open a separate, segregated facility. The St. James A.M.E. Church bought the Poro College building in 1965 and replaced it with a residence for the elderly.

By any standard, Annie Turnbo-Malone was a successful entrepreneur. At one time she provided work for more than seventy-five thousand women who sold her products in North and South America, Africa, and the Philippines. In 1957, at the time of her death in Chicago at age eighty-seven, there were Poro Colleges in thirty American cities. Although she and her company had been gone from St. Louis for many years, her accomplishments and example still shaped the culture of the Ville.

Sources: Information is from Jean Coney Mongold, "Annie Turnbo-Malone," in *NAW*, 700–2; Dowden, "Over this Point We Are Determined to Fight"; Mary Bartley, St. *Louis Lost* (St. Louis: Virginia Publishing, 1994), 104–6; and Mary A. Mosley, "Madam C. J. Walker," in *Show Me Missouri Women*, vol. 2. Quotations are taken from Annie Turnbo-Malone's promotional booklet, "Poro" in *Pictures with a Short History of Its Development* (St. Louis: Poro College, 1926). See Kathy Peiss, *Hope in a Jar* (New York: Henry Holt & Co., 1999) for a study that places Turnbo-Malone in the context of the 1920s beauty culture.

Marie Meyer's Flying Circus

Three years before Charles Lindbergh's solo flight across the Atlantic, another barnstorming pilot dazzled St. Louisans by riding the wing of her airplane above the streets of the city. Like Lindbergh, Marie Meyer was a pioneering aviator. Her love of flying led her to attempt daring feats that helped awaken Americans to the airplane's potential. Very few women learned to fly in the early days of aviation, and even fewer traveled the country

performing aerial stunts in their own planes. She was the same age as Charles Lindbergh and had strong ties to St. Louis and Lambert Field as well. Although she earned her flying license and owned her own plane before Lindbergh, they both barnstormed around Illinois and Missouri about the same time. For reasons of temperament, ambition, opportunity, or gender their careers took different turns.

Marie Meyer was born in 1902 or 1903 in St. Louis, near the site of the old airmail field in Forest Park. As a child she watched pilots take off and land and knew that she wanted to fly more than anything else. About age seventeen she began taking lessons. William Robertson of the Robertson Aircraft Company was one of her teachers. In August 1921 the *Globe-Democrat* reported that Miss Marie Meyer of 5021A Cates Avenue, St. Louis, was expected to complete her final hour of the flying requirement at the Missouri State Fair in Sedalia. She passed the Aero Club of America licensing test later that year.

When she was about twenty years old, Marie Meyer bought her own plane. Accompanied by two other flyers, she flew to small towns where she gave demonstrations and sight-seeing trips. "We went to many towns where the people had never even seen a flying machine," she later recalled. Realizing the additional commercial possibilities and attractions of stunt flying, she assembled a group of daring trick flyers, sometimes including Charles Lindbergh, and formed Marie Meyer's Flying Circus.

Marie Meyer and Her Husband, Charles Fower, Standing by Their Standard J-1 Plane. Hangge Collection photograph by Russell Froelich 1924. MHS–PP

In 1924, Marie Meyer and her new husband, Charles Fower, gave a spectacular performance in front of a hometown audience. "Lambert-St. Louis Field was in its infancy. The hangars hadn't even been built," she told a reporter. "We were invited by the St. Louis Flying Club to give a performance on July 4 to raise money for the upkeep of the field." But the promoters asked her to buzz downtown St. Louis before the event. On June 24, several thousand people lined the city streets, crowded at windows, and stood on rooftops to watch the advertised stunt. With smoke flares trailing, Marie Meyer climbed onto the top wing as the plane swooped down to pass between the Railway Exchange and the *Globe-Democrat* Building at just above the eighth-story level. She managed to wave briefly for the press photographers before turbulence disrupted her ride and nearly caused the plane to hit a smokestack. On July 4, she performed a different and more spectacular stunt at Lambert-St. Louis Field. This time she stood on the upper wing and held onto a rope while the plane looped-the-loop. She repeated the stunt with her feet in stirrups so she could wave to the crowd while looping. She finished with a parachute jump from the lower wing span.

For the next four years, Marie Meyer, her husband, and her circus traveled the country, ever expanding their range of stunts and publicity gimmicks. In planes with tails painted with slogans like, "She's a Jazz Baby!" and "I'll Say She Is!" they performed "Death Defying Stunts on an airplane traveling 100 miles per hour." They also took couples up to be married in an airplane. Not just a stunt pilot, Marie Meyer also competed in international air races in St. Louis and Dayton.

Meyer ended her hectic barnstorming career in 1928 at about age twenty-six. "We continued until shortly after Lindy made his famous Paris flight, and by that time airplanes were no longer oddities." She stopped stunt flying and settled down with her husband to run a chain of gas stations and later candy stores in and around Macon, Missouri. They continued to fly, owning a plane until 1938 and giving away free airplane trips as sales promotions. In 1956 Marie Meyer died in an automobile accident.

–*Joan Cooper*

Sources: For a brief biography, see Dains and Sadler, eds., *Show Me Missouri Women*, vol. 1. A scrapbook on Marie Meyer Fower is in the public library in Macon, Missouri. Also in Macon, see the *Macon Daily Chronicle Herald*, 12 June 1923, and 24 May 1956. Quotations from a *Globe-Democrat*, 26 November 1944 interview. For St. Louis media accounts and

articles, see the *Globe-Democrat*, 15 August 1921, 24 June 1924, 29 June 1924, and 26 November 1944; and the *Post-Dispatch*, 25 June 1956. For information on flying in St. Louis, see James J. Horgan, *City of Flight: The History of Aviation in St. Louis* (Gerald, Mo.: Patrice Press, 1984). See also biographies of Charles Lindbergh, including Reeve Lindbergh, *Under a Wing: A Memoir* (N.Y.: Simon & Schuster, 1998), and A. Scott Berg, *Lindbergh* (N.Y.: G. P. Putnam's Sons, 1998).

The 1927 Tornado

In the early afternoon of Thursday, September 29, 1927, a tornado tore through the city of St. Louis. Moving from west to east, the funnel took a northerly route, touching down to the southwest near Manchester and Taylor Avenues and moving northeast through Lindell and across Olive, Washington, and Delmar. It continued to Page and Sarah, along Grand, crossing the river east of Fairgrounds Park. Since the 1896 tornado hit the south side, great changes had occurred in the city, some of which were reflected in the ways St. Louisans responded to the 1927 tornado. In 1896 an ad-hoc group of businessmen, local relief agencies with religious affiliations, and scores of female volunteers assisted the damaged neighborhoods, primarily consisting of poor white immigrants. In 1927 a more efficient government, professional relief organizations and trained social workers, many of whom were women, aided the devastated areas–primarily middle-class black neighborhoods in the city's northwest.

The 1927 tornado caused a great deal of property damage, many injuries, and eighty-seven deaths, including six schoolgirls. The death rate was lower than the 138 reported in 1896, but the damage was greater due to increases in population and housing. The city's emergency disaster services, under the central control of the Red Cross, dealt efficiently with the physical damage and quickly issued an appeal for funds to help the victims. The appeal raised more than $1 million, contributed primarily by St. Louis residents, and provided immediate relief and rehabilitation for 5,534 families, more than 22,000 people.

The city's highly coordinated response to the disaster contrasted sharply to the "terrorized and unorganized St. Louis of 1896," which the *Post-Dispatch* reported "took days to put into the field those defenses which this time sprang into being over night." Using many of the technological advances made since the last tornado, the Red

Cross and the city departments summoned their workers and volunteers by telephone, the radio station KMOX, and messengers sent out in automobiles and motorcycles to notify off-duty personnel. Within hours, the roads were being cleared to facilitate the removal of the dead and injured. They established a multitude of relief stations and field kitchens. Police, the army, and the militia guarded and patrolled the stricken area. Advances in medicine and public health increased awareness of disease spread by the consequences of damaged infrastructure–broken sewers, ruptured water mains, damp damaged dwellings–and the injured received free anti-tetanus injections.

St. Louis had become far more racially segregated since 1896, and the tornado ripped through the heart of black St. Louis–a section bordered by Lindell and Page, and Newstead and Vandeventer. This area contained boardinghouses, tenements, and a number of large elegant residences, as well as businesses, churches, and schools, many of which suffered great damage. The district housed a cross-section of black St. Louisians, who resided within boundaries established by real estate covenants and practices.

The *Argus*, the city's African American newspaper, reported that the Red Cross headed the relief operations with considerable assistance from many local black groups like the American Legion and the Boy Scouts. Annie Malone threw open the facilities of Poro College at Pendleton and St. Ferdinand Avenues, which became the official Red Cross distribution and relief station for African Americans, feeding and caring for nearly five thousand victims. The paper issued an appeal for funds, and a black relief committee organized to distribute the money. Initially, black St. Louisans viewed the Red Cross with suspicion, based on its racial discrimination during Mississippi River flood relief operations earlier in the year. However, editorials in the *Argus* stated that the tornado temporarily made black and white sufferers equal. The Red Cross received high accolades from all, and two local exclusively white hospitals, Deaconess and the Baptist Sanitarium, were praised for their care of black victims. The Red Cross and the white press also acknowledged the well-organized black relief efforts, although it was tempered with stereotypical astonishment at their efficiency.

Besides giving an insight into St. Louis race relations, the accounts of the 1927 tornado illustrate dramatic changes in charity work since 1896. Female volunteers were no longer at the center of disaster

relief, but the Red Cross and other agencies employed both black and white female social workers in their relief programs. The role of the female volunteer had contracted during the intervening thirty years. After 1900, American corporations adopted impersonal business methods that emphasized efficiency and profit. This trend in corporate management accounted for many of the changes in charity work, particularly in the creation of the Community Fund, which St. Louis charities had established in 1922 to efficiently raise money for forty separate charitable organizations. The money funded private organizations, covering virtually the whole field of non-governmental social welfare services in St. Louis City and County. Because of this consolidation, charities could concentrate on improving and expanding their services. Even more importantly, the regular income permitted many agencies to employ professional staff rather than rely on untrained volunteers.

Black and white female social workers played an important role in tornado relief and rehabilitation programs and were indicative of the changes in the social service field. When the charitable agencies became professionalized, much of the policy-making and managerial work of the female volunteers was taken over by trained, paid staff. For the most part, men dominated the management

Apartment House, 4200 Maryland Avenue, Damaged by 1927 Tornado. Devastation was heavy in the Central West End and on streets with African American homes just to the north. Photograph, 1927. MHS–PP.

of these organizations, even though social work remained a largely female profession.

–Joan Cooper

Sources: The best sources for the 1927 tornado are the reports of the *Globe-Democrat,* the *Post-Dispatch,* and the *St. Louis Argus.* For the changes within the field of social work and other professions, see Woloch, *Women and the American Experience,* and Daniel J. Walkowitz, "The Making of a Feminine Professional Identity: Social Workers in the 1920s," *American Historical Review* 95, no. 4 (October 1990): 1051–75. For information on the Red Cross and disaster relief programs during this period, see John M. Barry, *Rising Tide: The Great Mississippi Flood of 1927 and How it Changed America* (New York: Simon & Schuster, 1997).

Roman Catholic Women Religious

There were twenty-seven congregations of religious women in St. Louis in 1927 nursing the sick, caring for the homeless, and educating elementary school children. Fifteen years earlier, Archbishop John Glennon had laid the cornerstone for the Sisters of Mercy's new hospital building at Parkview and Euclid Avenues with the observation that "in the fifty-six years the Sisters of Mercy have been engaged in the work of love in St. Louis, I don't believe there have been fifty-six words printed about their good deeds." Every day St. Louisans passed by huge brick institutional buildings where hundreds of anonymous figures in dark, flowing garments were busy at work. Religious sisters administered or staffed orphanages, homes for the aged, and three major hospitals. Without nuns in the classroom, the entire system of Catholic education would have collapsed, throwing thousands of students into already crowded public schools. No one seriously calculated the value of all this unpaid skilled labor. When after mid-century fewer women entered religious life, St. Louisans had to address the true cost of the educational and social services nuns had provided for more than one hundred years.

In 1911 Catholic Charities of St. Louis, which later became the coordinating body for all Catholic social service agencies, estimated the value of the work performed by the ninety-five nuns at the three major hospitals operated by Roman Catholic religious women in St. Louis at $60,000. Much of this unpaid work was in administration and skilled nursing. The three hospitals–St. John's, St. Mary's, and Mullanphy–also employed a total of sixty-one lay persons, but nuns at other Catholic institutions such as the Sisters of the Good Shepherd reformatory, St. Mary's orphanage, and the Little Sisters of the Poor's home for the aged often made do with only one or two handymen to assist them.

After the Sisters of St. Mary opened their nursing school in 1907, trained nuns did the skilled nursing and all the laboratory work for St. Mary's Infirmary. The sisters cared for eight hundred hospitalized charity patients at the infirmary at Fifteenth and Papin Streets in 1911. They estimated the total cost for a ward patient at eighty cents a day. Working with physicians who donated their services, the sisters also operated a free walk-in clinic where, during the first six months of 1911, nearly six thousand poor south side residents received treatment. The Sisters of St. Mary financed their expanding health care facilities with fees from the eighty hospital beds reserved for private patients and from donations.

In 1924 the Sisters of St. Mary opened a new one million-dollar convent, hospital, and nursing school on Clayton Road just west of the city limits. They continued to operate the old facility as a teaching hospital for Saint Louis University until 1930, when they entered into an agreement with the university to jointly own and operate the new Firmin Desloge Hospital at 1325 South Grand Avenue. In 1945, one hundred and sixty Sisters of St. Mary worked at the two hospitals.

In 1933 the sisters rededicated the Papin Street Infirmary as a hospital for African Americans. At the time no other Catholic hospital in the city accepted black patients. Three years later the order opened the St. Mary's Infirmary School of Nursing for Colored Nurses there. The old motherhouse later became a convent for young African American women preparing to join the order.

Known as the Smallpox Sisters in the nineteenth century for their work with victims of infectious diseases, the Sisters of St. Mary continued that tradition after the discovery of the tubercle bacillus confirmed that bacteria, not "weak lungs," caused tuberculosis. In 1900 they opened Mount St. Rose Sanitarium at 9101 South Broadway for the treatment, prevention, and study of tuberculosis. In the 1920s they also operated hospitals in St. Charles and Jefferson City, Missouri.

The Sisters of Mercy moved St. John's Hospital and Nursing School to the Central West End in 1912. The old hospital complex at Twenty-third and Locust Streets became the Mercy Home for Working Girls, and their buildings at Morgan and Twenty-second Streets remained a convent, orphanage, and industrial school. In 1918 the sisters built a new motherhouse and modern facility for St. Catherine's Home for Girls in Webster Groves. They continued to use the old hospital buildings as a working women's residence until 1936, when they converted David R. Francis's former home on Newstead Avenue, between Pershing and Maryland Avenues, into McAuley Hall, a place for Catholic working girls to live economically in a "refined and religious atmosphere."

The Daughters of Charity of St. Vincent de Paul, who had opened the first St. Louis hospital in 1832, operated Mullanphy Hospital at 3225 Montgomery Street from 1874 until the building was destroyed by the 1927 tornado. They replaced it in 1930 with a new 410-bed general hospital at 2415 North Kingshighway, later called DePaul Hospital.

The day before the 1896 tornado destroyed the St. Vincent's Asylum on the city's south side, the Daughters of Charity had removed mental patients under cover of night to their new home in suburban Normandy. Renowned for its beautiful landscaped grounds, attractive living accommodations, and supportive staff, St. Vincent's gave patients excellent custodial care but, like other insane asylums, offered little treatment. Although three out of four patients were classified as incurables, in 1925 the nuns renamed the facility St. Vincent's Sanitarium to reflect a new emphasis on treatment and cure.

In 1936 the Daughters of Charity hired a full-time psychiatrist as medical director. Within a few years the hospital had become a treatment center where most patients stayed less than three months. Those requiring long-term care were transferred out, usually to the State Hospital. St. Vincent's, one of the first institutions to use music therapy, stayed current with new methods of treating the mentally ill, adopting insulin shock therapy in 1937 and electroshock and lobotomy in the 1940s. In the early 1930s, the sanitarium established a four-month course in psychiatric nursing for area nursing students and in 1939 opened its own training school for psychiatric nurses. Like other hospitals administered by religious orders in St. Louis, St. Vincent's offered nurse training to nuns and lay women.

While most of the health care institutions Catholic religious women had founded in the nineteenth century grew and expanded in the twentieth century, the same was not true for orphanages. By the 1920s, social service professionals believed that dependent children should be placed in foster homes whenever possible. The number of children at St. Catherine's Orphanage peaked at 150 in 1923 and declined to 62 by 1945. Since coming to

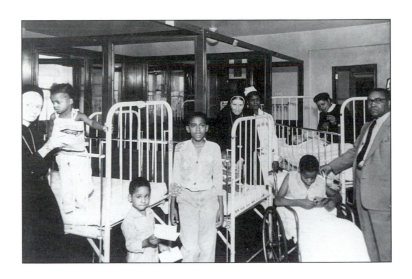

St. Louis in 1869, the Sisters of the Good Shepherd had opened fifty-two institutions for female orphans, delinquent girls, and reformed prostitutes throughout the United States. In the 1920s they supervised about four hundred girls and women in their convent reformatory at 3801 Gravois, but in 1934 social workers recommended that the orphans not be housed there too. The Convent of the Good Shepherd became a female reformatory exclusively for "maladjusted" teenage girls referred by the juvenile court or other agencies. Other Catholic and Protestant residential orphanages and industrial schools gradually changed their missions from caring for all dependent children to caring for children with emotional, physical, or social disabilities. At one time the Sisters of St. Joseph of Carondelet operated ten orphanages in the St. Louis Province of nine midwestern states and Hawaii; seven eventually closed and the remaining three became specialized institutions. The shift to foster care had many benefits but required new resources to replace the care provided by the nuns and their institutions.

In 1905 the Missouri legislature passed a compulsory education law requiring children to stay in school until age fourteen, which greatly increased the need for teachers in the city's parochial schools. In 1903, 24,430 students attended parish schools in the city, in 1927 there were 31,205, and by 1947 the archdiocese's 277 Catholic parishes in eastern Missouri were educating more than 50,000 elementary school children a year.

Sister Colette de Galzain and Mother Flora Sapart, Society of the Helpers of the Holy Souls (Now Called Society of Helpers) with Mr. Virgil McKnight at Homer G. Phillips Hospital, 1952. Courtesy WHMC–UMSL

Nuns taught in most of the parish classrooms. A Polish-speaking order of nuns, the Franciscan Sisters of Perpetual Help, came to teach in St. Stanislaus parish on the near north side in 1901 and five years later ran six parish schools. St. Louis was the headquarters for the Southern Province of the School Sisters of Notre Dame, a teaching order with a St. Louis motherhouse, Sancta Maria, at 320 East Ripa. In 1947 the school sisters staffed fifteen schools in the city of St. Louis alone and many more throughout eastern Missouri.

Both the Sisters of St. Joseph and the Sisters of Loretto answered the call to teach in parish schools. As late as 1960, the Sisters of St. Joseph staffed thirty-two elementary and four high schools for the archdiocese in the immediate St. Louis area, in addition to operating St. Joseph's Academy for Girls, St. Joseph's Hospital in Kirkwood, St. Joseph's Institute for the Deaf in University City, St. Joseph's Orphan Home, and Fontbonne College in Clayton. The Sisters of Loretto began teaching in parish schools in 1869 when St. Michael's opened at Eleventh and Clinton Streets. Over the next one hundred years the teaching sisters moved often, as old schools closed and new ones opened in response to the westward movement of the city's population. At the same time, the Sisters of Loretto taught private pupils at Loretto Academy, which moved to 3407 Lafayette Avenue, and at Webster Academy in a new building constructed in Webster Groves in 1915. In 1924 the academy's preparatory department moved to a nearby site and became Nerinx Hall High School; the collegiate department became Webster College. Not only did thousands of St. Louis girls benefit from the education provided by nuns, but as teaching standards rose, many of the nuns also benefited from college educations at Webster College, Fontbonne College, and at Maryville College, run by the Sisters of the Sacred Heart. Maryville became a four-year college in 1922; three of its first five graduates were nuns.

Many reasons accounted for a decline in the number of young women who chose to join Roman Catholic religious orders in the second half of the twentieth century. Greater opportunities in education and in the workplace gave women more options. The American culture of individualism also made religious life less appealing. Fewer young women were willing to remain celibate or to accept the unquestioned authority of their religious superiors and the strict rules of their religious communities. Most orders, particularly those engaged in health care, social service, and teaching, modified their codes of dress and living conditions as part of a larger reform movement within the Catholic Church in the 1960s. Nuns who still could not find a place for themselves within religious life left. They did not always break with their orders and frequently became social activists in secular or Catholic organizations. Hospitals and schools began hiring more lay people to do the work nuns left behind.

For those nuns who stayed and those who left, the spiritual component of religious life that drove their nineteenth-century forbearers to serve needy St. Louisans remained an enduring legacy. For most St. Louisans, however, the work of thousands of women religious remained an unknown aspect of the city's history.

Sources: See the *Conference on Catholic Charities, First Annual Report, 1912.* Delegates to the first conference of Catholic social service organizations compiled the statistics for the report. The conference led to the formation of Catholic Charities of St. Louis, a coordinating organization for Catholic social work and the office responsible for raising money in the community and allocating it to the member charities. Annual reports located at MHS are useful for tracking various agencies over time. For more information, see the Archives of Catholic Charities, St. Louis. For information on women-run Catholic hospitals, see Mother Anne Kathryn Webster, *The Impact of Catholic Hospitals in St. Louis* (Ph.D. dissertation, Saint Louis University, 1968), and the Archives of the Catholic Hospital Association. For more information on the Sisters of St. Mary (now called the Franciscan Sisters of Mary), see *Seventy-Five Years of Service* (Sisters of St. Mary, 1947). The archives of St. Mary's Infirmary, St. Mary's Hospital, and Mount St. Rose Hospital are located at the Archives of Our Lady of the Angels, motherhouse of the Sisters of St. Mary. For Sister of Mercy, St. John's Hospital, St. Catherine's Home for Girls, and McAuley Home, see Sister Mary Isidore Lennon, R.S.M., *Milestones of Mercy: Story of the Sisters of Mercy in St. Louis, 1856–1956* (Milwaukee: Bruce Press, 1957) and the archives of the motherhouse of the Sisters of Mercy, 2039 North Geyer Road, Kirkwood, Missouri. The Sisters of Mercy constructed a large modern hospital in St. Louis County in the 1960s, which they administered until 1999. See the Archives of the Marillac Provincial House, Daughters of Charity of St. Vincent de Paul for information on Mullanphy Hospital, DePaul Hospital, and St. Vincent's Hospital. See *Convent of the Good Shepherd,* pamphlet ca. 1925, at MHS, and Archives of the Sisters of the Good Shepherd Provincialate, 7654 Natural Bridge Road, Normandy.

Information on the archdiocesan parochial schools is available at the Archdiocesan Archives, Kenrick Center, Laclede Station Road. For an overview of nuns educational work in St. Louis, see the Reverend John

Rothensteiner, *History of the Archdiocese of St. Louis: In Its Various Stages of Development, From A.D. 1673 to A.D. 1828* (St. Louis: Blackwell Wieland, 1928), and William B. Faherty, S.J., *Dream by the River: Two Centuries of Saint Louis Catholicism, 1766–1967* (St. Louis: Piraeus, 1973). Unpublished information on Sisters of Loretto courtesy of Mary Seematter. See also Sister Mary Mangan, "The Sisters of Loretto, St. Louis 1847–1997," *GH* 18, no. 3 (winter 1997–1998), and the Sisters of Loretto Archives, 590 E. Lockwood, Webster Groves. For information on the Sisters of St. Joseph, see Marcella M. Holloway, "The Sisters of St. Joseph of Carondelet, 150 Years of Good Works in America," *GH* 7, no. 2 (fall 1987); Sister Dorita Marie Dougherty, et al., *Sisters of St. Joseph of Carondelet* (St. Louis: B. Herder Books, 1966); and the *Globe-Democrat,* 14 February 1960. The Sisters of St. Joseph of Carondelet founded many educational and health institutions outside the St. Louis region. For more information, see the Archives at the St. Joseph Provincial House, 6400 Minnesota Avenue, St. Louis. For a history of Maryville College, see Dorothy Garesche Holland, "Maryville—The First Hundred Years," *BMHS* 29, no. 3 (April 1973).

There is no body of secular literature on the female religious orders in St. Louis. The work of the nuns in the community and its relationship to the history of education and social service needs to be integrated into historical studies of the city. As more historical research focuses on the experiences of women religious, the extensive archives of St. Louis orders will prove to be valuable resources.

Rachel Stix Michael

In September 1925, the first students enrolled in the Elias Michael School for Crippled Children at the corner of Forest Park Boulevard and Euclid Avenue. Although named for the former president of the Rice-Stix Dry Goods Company, the pioneering school owed its existence to his widow, Rachel Stix Michael. Only the second woman elected to the St. Louis Board of Education, Rachel Michael promoted progressive education and worked to improve the St. Louis public schools for more than sixteen years. Her lasting legacies were the Michael School and the Charles Henry Turner Open-Air School for Crippled Children, a similar facility for African American children located at 4235 Kennerly Avenue in the Ville. Like other accomplished female volunteers who served on gender-integrated boards in the interwar years, Rachel Michael encountered strong opposition when she challenged the power structure and aspired to the board presidency in 1929.

Born in Cincinnati, Ohio, in 1866, Rachel Stix was twenty years old when she married Elias Michael, who had worked his way up in her father's dry goods company and was, at thirty-one, the head of the St. Louis branch. Their only child, born the next year, died in 1894. For the next fourteen years, Rachel managed their home at 4383 Westminster Place and threw herself into volunteer work at the Jewish Day Nursery. Her husband served on civic committees, charitable boards, and the St. Louis Board of Education until his death in 1913.

Elias Michael's death devastated Rachel, but it also presented the wealthy young widow with new social service opportunities. She studied for two summers in Boston, then enrolled in the School of Social Economy in St. Louis. Until 1922 she worked at the Washington University Dispensary and St. Louis Children's Hospital. As a member of the Missouri Women's Committee of National Defense during World War I, she chaired the committee that trained women to take jobs vacated by servicemen. She was a founder of the Missouri Association for Occupational Therapy. An educated, experienced volunteer, she became a national leader in the movement to teach occupational skills to people with disabilities.

Rachel Stix Michael Receiving an Award for Child Welfare Work from Governor Henry S. Caulfield, 1933. Photograph. MHS–PP

In 1921 Rachel Michael ran for the St. Louis Board of Education, hoping to become its first female member. She lost, but Mayor Henry Kiel promptly appointed her to the board of the St. Louis Public Library, and to an unexpired term on the Board of Education the following year. The League of Women Voters, the Republican Women's Club, and the Board of Religious Organizations endorsed her candidacy. Two years later she was elected to the board by a large majority, again with the support of civic organizations.

Rachel Michael brought professional expertise and knowledge of progressive education to her volunteer position on the school board. She observed classes, attended national professional meetings, and took education courses at Columbia University. She worked tirelessly to open the two public schools for children with disabilities.

When she ran for board president in 1929, she had the backing of civic organizations and the assurance of victory from fellow members. However, male members did not vote for her. They might have cited her liberal views as the reason for not supporting her but, instead, unhesitatingly attributed her loss to her gender. "Women should not expect such honors," said one. "The reason I did not vote for her is because she went after the job too hard," said another. The League of Women Voters angrily contrasted Michael's record of service to that of less distinguished male board members. It publicly denounced the cronism of a nonpartisan body for rejecting one of their most qualified colleagues simply because she was a woman.

Although Rachel Stix Michael was denied the board presidency, she was reelected in 1931, the same year the Women's Advertising Club named her one of the ten most achieving St. Louis women in the first of its annual recognition events. Governor Henry Crawfield presented her with the second Governor's Medallion for distinguished civic service. She served on the school board until her death in 1936 at the age of seventy and willed $150,000 to Washington University to establish a professorship in occupational therapy.

Sources: Information about Rachel Michael's career comes from the *St. Louis Post-Dispatch*, 7 September 1922, 9 April 1925, 30 October 1929, 14 April 1930, and 9 September 1936; the *Globe-Democrat*, 7 January 1933, and 9 September 1936; *The Book of St. Louisans* (St. Louis, 1906); and *Official Proceedings of the St. Louis Board of Education,* vols. 31, 231, 378; and Burton A. Boxerman, "St. Louis Jewish Leaders," *GH* 6 no. 4 (spring 1986). See St. Louis Jewish Federation Archives for information on the Jewish Day Nursery. MHS holds the records of the Missouri Women's Committee of National Defense.

The faculty of the Elias Michael School placed a plaque honoring Rachel Michael in the building in 1938. Both the school building and the practice of segregating students with disabilities were obsolete by 1997, when Washington University purchased the building and tore it down. Portraits of Rachel and Elias Michael are displayed at the new Michael School, now part of the Gateway Educational Complex on Jefferson Avenue.

St. Louis Jewish women, who had first organized to raise money for Jewish Hospital in 1895, re-established a local section of the National Council of Jewish Women in 1917. Committees on religion, philanthropy, education, and service created a program that focused both on the study of Judiasm and social action issues, including housing discrimination and suffrage. Between 1917 and 1920 they operated milk stations for poor children in city schools; in 1926 they inaugurated English and Americanization classes for immigrants. In 1934 they opened the Council House, a community center for children and adults that pioneered the area's first program for senior citizens. The council obtained federal funding to open Delcrest Apartments for the elderly in 1947. The records of the St. Louis Section of the National Council of Jewish Women are located at WHMC–UMSL.

Jewish Orphans Home

On February 3, 1929, the Jewish Orphans Home Society dedicated a complex of four new buildings at 6630 Oakland Avenue across from Forest Park. Under the leadership of Fannie Shank and with the assistance of a temporary men's auxiliary, the society's membership of twenty-five hundred St. Louis women had raised more than two hundred thousand dollars for a home "on the cottage plan, adequate to the needs of our community." The orphanage was the culmination of twenty years of effort by Jewish women, many of whom had been poor immigrants from Eastern Europe at the turn of the century, to rear Orthodox orphans in their own St. Louis religious community.

A small group of Orthodox Jewish women had organized the society in 1909 in protest over what they believed to be unfair treatment by the secular United Jewish Educational and Charitable Associations, under which St. Louis's privately organized relief system provided social services for the city's Jewish population. The charity's policy of sending poor school-age orphans to out-of-town asylums and boarding those under six in non-Orthodox homes denied the children religious training in their own Eastern European immigrant community. This disagreement over the care of orphans reflected a split between the established assimilating German Jews, who had immigrated before 1890 and had few destitute children, and the later, much poorer *shtetl* Jews from Eastern Europe, who by now comprised most of the city's Jewish population of forty thousand. Not a local phenomenon, this split reflected deep divisions between American Jews involving class and ethnicity as much as religion.

The Jewish Orphans Home Society hoped to open an Orthodox orphanage financed with weekly dues of five cents contributed by families in the immigrant neighborhoods. The society collected only eight thousand dollars in the first eight years. By 1917, however, some Eastern European Jews were prospering in St. Louis. That year Fannie Shank, the energetic wife of a successful tailor, became president of the society. The women raised enough money in two years to open a debt-free twenty-five thousand-dollar orphanage at 3117 Lafayette Avenue. Membership increased from five hundred to two thousand women, whose donations supported the work of the institution. A junior auxiliary of young volunteers also raised money for a laundry and playground equipment. In 1924, aided financially by the men's auxiliary, the society purchased a three-acre site between Oakland and Clayton Avenues near Forest Park. On this property they equipped a large playground and constructed a boy's cottage, a girls cottage, a small children's cottage, and an administration building. Fannie Shanks, now widowed but still the society's president, lived in a large new home only a few blocks away.

In building an institution for children without special physical or psychological needs, Fannie Shanks and the members of the board knew they were going against a national trend to reduce the number of institutionalized children. Social service experts now believed a child placed in a foster home was happier and better adjusted than one consigned to an orphanage. After much reflection, the board had decided against placing orphan children in private Orthodox Jewish homes, a growing practice in other cities. They noted that second-generation Orthodox families were succumbing to "the tendency in American life to simplify home life by occupying small apartments" with little room for extra children. But they also feared that even in a religious home a child might not receive a proper upbringing in keeping with strict Orthodox traditions. By rejecting home placement for orphans, the society sought to strengthen and preserve the Orthodox community. In planning the new facility, however, they rejected the nineteenth-century dormitory style of housing for more modern cottages, where older children could live in home-like surroundings and sleep only three to a room. The children attended public schools and received religious education at the home. They belonged to the YWHA and the YMHA, participated in cultural activities, and had their own scout troops. The board guaranteed each child two years of high school, permitting those with the aptitude to complete four years, a common practice of many working-class parents in the 1920s.

Later renamed the Jewish Children's Home, the institution merged with Jewish Family and Children's Service, which is now located at 9385 Olive Boulevard.

Sources: All quotations are from *The Jewish Orphans Home of Saint Louis* (St. Louis: Dedication Booklet, 1929). For information and archival records of the successors to the Jewish Orphans Home, see the St. Louis Jewish Community Archives located at the Jewish Community Center Association, 11001 Schuetz Road. See the *Globe-Democrat*, 10 July 1959, concerning the 50th anniversary of the Jewish Children's Home. For more on the tension between German and Eastern European Jews and a history of the Jewish Community of St. Louis to 1907, see Walter Ehrlich, *Zion in the Valley: The Jewish Community of St. Louis, 1807–1907*, vol. 1 (Columbia: University of Missouri Press, 1997). For a national study of Jewish orphanages, see Reena Sigman Friedman, *These Are Our Children: Jewish Orphanages in the United States, 1880–1925* (Hanover, N.H.: University Press of New England, 1994).

The Varieties of Domestic Life

In the twentieth century, many residents of St. Louis's nineteenth-century ethnic neighborhoods moved west. With the exception of an Italian enclave on the Hill south of Forest Park, neighborhoods more often reflected race and class than the ethnicity of the residents. Poor Southern European immigrants and southern American migrants, black and white, moved into the downtown flats that second- and third-generation Germans and Irish left behind. The relatively easy geographical mobility did not apply to African Americans, however. Restrictive covenants, realtor practices, and governmental policy limited their choices irrespective of income or desire. Attitudes about race and class clearly shaped the appearance

of four new St. Louis neighborhoods constructed after 1920. As domestic space, however, Holly Hills, St. Louis Hills, Hooverville, and Carr Square Village also reflected prevailing ideas about gender and women's place in the home.

In the 1920s, Hollywood signified dreams fulfilled. The Federer Realty Company, developers of Holly Hills, hoped this image would entice upwardly mobile south St. Louisans to move out of their identical brick flats on narrow city lots into their own suburban homes on the north side of Carondelet Park. Holly Hills' promotional material envisioned "The Cornfields of Yesterday as the Dream City of Today." The subdivision took its name from the California movie capital, and its architecture reflected scaled down versions of movie star's pseudo-English estates and German castles, as well as popular Arts and Crafts–style dwellings.

Holly Hills was located beyond the reach of the city's streetcar lines. Federer could not have transformed cornfields into homesites without bus service, a 1920s innovation. The company subsidized a bus extension to existing Grand Avenue streetcar lines. Holly Hills attracted south side Roman Catholics who in 1926 initiated construction of St. Stephen Protomartyr Church and School several years before a public school opened in the neighborhood.

In 1928, building on the success of Holly Hills, Cyrus Crane Willmore, a successful developer of affluent neighborhoods in suburbs on the western edge of St. Louis, opened a new subdivision on the largest tract of undeveloped land in southwest

St. Louis. He planted thousands of pin oaks and hundreds of roses on the flat, barren landscape and called it St. Louis Hills. Willmore targeted the same prospering south side families that Holly Hills courted for his single-family homes, each unique and laden with architectural details. By 1928, Willmore could assume that his buyers were or soon would be one-automobile suburban families, but he knew that urban Americans expected public transportation for work, shopping, children's activities, and transporting domestic servants. He, too, provided bus service from the subdivision to an existing streetcar line.

Like promoters of St. Louis subdivisions dating from the 1890s, Willmore extolled the virtues of suburban living for maintaining healthy, stable families. There were no "death dealing germs" in the St. Louis Hills' "clear crystal air." His advertising literature emphasized the home, and particularly the kitchen, as the center of family life. He filled the company magazine, *News of St. Louis Hills,* with pictures of idealized family life that showed women decorating their homes, cooking, and entertaining. Although the country plunged into depression soon after St. Louis Hills opened, Willmore continued to build and sell houses, assuring prospective buyers that the contentment and values St. Louis Hills homeowners shared would make the subdivision a sanctuary against an uncertain future. In February 1938, *News of St. Louis Hills* featured on its cover a happy young housewife taking heart-shaped cookies from the oven.

In contrast to the carefully contrived domestic environment created by suburban developers, an unplanned neighborhood of shanties sprang up along the riverfront in the early 1930s. Constructed of scrap lumber and old crates by out-of-work St. Louisans, Hooverville was named in scornful honor of the incumbent president, whom many blamed for the depression. Although "Hoovervilles" appeared throughout the United States in the 1930s, St. Louis had the largest; at its peak more than three thousand people lived there in about six hundred shacks. The haphazard arrangement of buildings on the riverbank expanded from an old houseboat settlement south of the Municipal (now McArthur) Bridge near the mouth of the Mill Creek sewer. Comprising four neighborhoods beginning with "Happyland" north of the bridge, Hooverville stretched south to "Merryland," "Hooverville," and "Hooverville Heights."

Unlike most St. Louis neighborhoods, Hooverville was a racially integrated community. Residents laid out regular streets, fenced in their

The Office for Cyrus Willmore's St. Louis Hills Development in 1928. Photograph by Sievers Photographers, 1928. MHS–PP yards, and planted gardens. They built four churches and the Welcome Inn, a combination community center, city hall, and post office. They established an ad hoc municipal government headed by "Mayor" Gus Smith. Ruth Homby, a sixteen-year-old student at Beaumont High School, almost single-handedly opened Ruth's Haven, a social service center that offered cooking classes, free entertainment, a kindergarten, and meals supported by donated funds.

Most Hooverville residents were people struggling to preserve family and community life in a time of economic collapse and social stress. Hard times, however, fostered both cooperation and conflict. When a local company donated boxes of macaroni to the Ark of Safety Church, some women fought with Mayor Smith to have them distributed to church members only. Hooverville residents worked odd jobs when they could find them, including selling popcorn to sightseers. During the day men took two-wheeled carts and "rustled" in nearby neighborhoods, searching for discarded items to trade for cash or household necessities. Most employed women left the community each day to work as domestics.

Hooverville had no city utilities. Housewives carried water from a street pump. They fed their families with produce donated by merchants at nearby Soulard Market. Despite the grim living conditions, curtains could be seen in windows of shanties that women had made into homes. By 1933, however, the community had begun to change. As some families found steady work and moved out, more transients moved in. In 1934 the Works Progress Administration used land clearance money for the Jefferson National Expansion Memorial to begin destruction of Hooverville. Most buildings came down immediately, but some remained and were occupied for years. When in 1959 the city of St. Louis agreed to buy out the forty-three families still living in Hooverville for $21,154 each, one elderly women who had lived there for twenty-one years expressed reluctance to leave her home and garden.

In 1939 St. Louisans broke ground for more permanent housing for the city's poor. Two federally subsidized low-income housing projects opened in 1942. Carr Square Village, on the near north side, was designated for African Americans, while Clinton-Peabody Terrace on the near south side was for white tenants. Both were a welcome change for their new residents, most of whom had never enjoyed central heat or indoor plumbing.

Bounded by Fourteenth, Eighteenth, O'Fallon, and Cole Streets, Carr Square Village was a complex

of 558 living units in identical low-rise buildings. Cookie Jones, who grew up in the complex, recalled her childhood in those "sterile as they come" buildings with nostalgic affection. She remembered walking to Kellerman's Drugstore to buy Evening in Paris cologne for her mother, crossing Fifteenth Street every Sunday to attend Greater Brown A.M.E. Zion Church, dancing at the Capri Center, and shopping with her mother at Biddle Market. Her memories were of a safe, secure childhood where teachers and parents knew each other and discipline was reinforced by community norms.

As a child, Cookie Jones could not have known the adult world her parents inhabited, the hard work her mother may have done, the sacrifices she may have made to assure her daughter a secure childhood, or the problems she may have kept to herself. The 1940s low-rise public housing complexes were much more livable than the postwar high rises, which had poor design, insufficient tenant screening, and inadequate maintenance. Even so, Cookie's mother's story would have differed from her daughter's.

Domestic life varied greatly in St. Louis as it did elsewhere, but whatever the setting, women were the primary care givers, just as they had been throughout the city's history. Whether a suburban housewife, working mother, or an unemployed worker, a woman was expected by her community and family to make a house a home.

–*Kathleen Butterly Nigro and Katharine Corbett*

Hooverville. Housewives hung decorative curtains at the windows of their Hooverville homes. Photograph by Isaac Sievers, 1934. MHS–PP

Sources: Information on Holly Hills is from NiNi Harris, A *History of Carondelet* (St. Louis: Patrice Press, 1991), and "Landmarks: St. Louis Neighborhoods," in *Landmarks 7*, eds., Rosemary Hyde Thomas and Martha Baker (Kirkwood: St. Louis Community College at Meramec, 1993). Much of the information on St. Louis Hills is from "News of St. Louis Hills," *St. Louis Magazine* (October 1965): 19, and various promotional pamphlets available at MHS. Hooverville information comes from Martin Towey, "Hooverville: St. Louis Had the Largest," *GH* 1, no. 2 (fall 1980). Some interviews with individuals directly concerned with Hooverville are located in the Archives and Oral History Center, Saint Louis University, and the *Post-Dispatch*, 22 January 1932, and 3 August 1959. Information on Carr Square Village, from Cookie Jones, "A Look at a Neighborhood: Carr Square Village," *Proud Magazine* 9, no. 1 (1978). A video produced by MHS, *Through the Eyes of a Child*, includes the reminiscences of African Americans who grew up in Carr Square Village.

The domestic lives of women are best explored through letters and oral interviews. In this instance, interviews with women who lived in Holly Hills or St. Louis Hills in the 1920s and 1930s would make an interesting contrast to the images of these neighborhoods promoted by their developers. Towey's article is a descriptive narrative history of Hooverville; women who lived there could give a richer picture of domestic life in the community and a different story than might be gleaned from newspaper articles. Interviews with women who moved with their families into public housing would give valuable context to the memories of their children. Most women who were housewives in the prewar years are over eighty years old. Their stories may be lost.

Maternal Health Association of Missouri

Early in December 1935, birth control advocates, physicians, and social welfare workers convened at the Chase Hotel in St. Louis for the Five State Regional Conference on Birth Control. For two days, national and regional speakers discussed the problems of organizing maternal health clinics and the coordination of clinics with other social service agencies. Sessions focused on the social and economic problems of family limitation, the relationship between the birth rate and unemployment in the United States, and religious and moral concerns associated with birth control. The conference was coordinated by the St. Louis–based Maternal Health Association of Missouri (MHA), an organization whose membership of more than eight hundred contributed to the support of maternal health clinics and public education efforts. As conference attendees swarmed the meeting place, they confronted religious activists who protested the gathering by speaking out on the radio and in lecture halls and distributing handbills in front of the hotel. Opponents argued that the birth control movement promoted "race suicide" and had caused the United States to suffer "a falling birth rate, the dying off of the best elements of our population, broken homes, more divorces than any other nation in history, gigantic selfishness."

The confrontations during the 1935 conference revealed the attitudes toward family planning and contraception prevalent in St. Louis throughout the mid-twentieth century. Protests by Catholic priests and other religious activists neither shut down the conference nor deterred women who sought assistance at MHA's four St. Louis clinics. Indeed, in the aftermath of the 1935 conference, the volume of patients increased, with doctors and resources stretched beyond their limits. The Wednesday night clinic, which served those women whose work or family responsibilities prevented them from attending during the days, was particularly stressed. In 1936, 4,220 patients visited MHA clinics, an increase over the previous year of more than 500 women. MHA records noted Protestant, Catholic, and Jewish women among their clients. An overwhelming majority reported that economic need compelled them to prevent the birth of additional children. Despite the objections of Catholic and some Protestant church leaders and the theological opposition to artificial family planning, for many women and their families, economic and practical factors strongly motivated women to use the services of the Maternal Health Association.

The birth control movement in St. Louis got off to a shaky start in May 1916 when protests by Catholic priests led to the cancellation of a lecture by birth control crusader Margaret Sanger. Sixteen years later, however, changes in St. Louis's social and economic landscape helped revive the movement. Advocates of birth control embraced the national concern for "race suicide," that is, the declining birth rate among native-born, middle-class Americans relative to the size of immigrant, poor, and African American families. After the country plunged into economic depression in 1929, growing numbers of political, religious, and medical leaders in St. Louis expressed the belief that birth control among poor families would gradually decrease dependence on the public dole. The MHA formed in April 1932, with inspiration from Margaret Sanger and under the local guidance of physicians and elite women. The organization concentrated primarily on issues of maternal health and educated the public on the medical, social, economic, and ethical importance of birth control to women and their families. With the encouragement of Sanger's American Birth Control League, Missouri's MHA established clinics in St. Louis to provide contraceptive prescriptions and medical services.

In their quest to give women the freedom to choose not to reproduce, the MHA initially aimed to reach a population of poor, married, white mothers; later, they extended their services beyond those women already with children. Although MHA staff and directors made occasional efforts to address the maternal health concerns of African American women in St. Louis, an overriding interest in strengthening the bonds and resources of white families determined the MHA's priorities. Women with monthly family incomes under two hundred dollars paid fifteen dollar fees for services that included consultation with a doctor and social worker, a prescription for contraception, and a follow-up home visit by a social worker. Until 1935, the organization located its office at 396A North Euclid Avenue, a three-room facility they rented monthly for thirty-five dollars and furnished with donated equipment. The small number of clients served within the first months convinced the center to open new locations, closer to women who needed their help. By 1935, the MHA operated clinics four times a week: two at the main facility at 4817A Delmar Boulevard, one at Kingdom House, a Methodist social center in the southern part of the city, and one at the Episcopal church's settlement house, Holy Cross Dispensary in north St. Louis. Volunteer doctors and paid social workers, primarily women, staffed each facility. In addition to the clinics, the MHA focused on educating the public regarding its work and family limitation approaches in general. MHA representatives spoke throughout the region. In 1935 speakers addressed "one religious, five colored, six social service, three educational and two factory groups, and nine public school mothers' meetings." Furthering its public education efforts, the MHA operated a library where clinic patients could borrow books. Women shared borrowed books with neighbors and friends, expanding the MHA's reach beyond those clients who visited its clinics.

A variety of motivations drove the founders and directors of the MHA, including deplorable maternal health conditions, the economic depression, the rising number of children on public welfare, and the nebulous concept of race suicide.

In a 1933 fund-raising letter, the MHA articulated its essentially conservative view of the need for birth control. "In times like these, when the very existence of our social structure is menaced by economic depression and social unrest, the health of the mother is all important. Necessary and proper contraceptive advice to her is help of the most fundamental sort, birth control is preventive and not palliative. This help is not only immediate but it is insurance for our social structure in the future." Birth control's positive effects would include a reduction in maternal and infant mortality, the decrease in hereditary diseases, the prevention of criminal abortions, the decline in child labor, and a drop in poverty and reliance on charity. A 1935 statement by the president of the MHA further connected family limitation to national economic concerns. "We favor birth control as a new line of defense against publicly supported dependents." The organization unabashedly argued in favor of birth control as "the most practicable means of race betterment." Contending that "among people who practice birth control, the less competent have fewer children than the more competent," the MHA asserted that "when birth control is in general practice, children above the average will out-number those below it, and the quality of the population will gradually rise." Such claims resembled those made by religious figures who campaigned against family limitation practices. Although birth control advocates and opponents reached different conclusions when it came to contraception, both employed elitist and politically conservative arguments to support their position.

The MHA viewed family limitation as one solution to the country's economic crisis and a means to prevent social upheaval, but the women who sought assistance perceived birth control in other ways. Contraception created an alternative to the dangers of illegal abortion and to the strain of childbirth and additional children. Reporting the deaths of five women in one week as a result of midwife-induced abortions, a 1934 article in the *Globe-Democrat* noted the risks many local women took to prevent enlarging their families during difficult economic times. An anonymous letter, written shortly after the MHA opened its clinics in St. Louis, articulated at least one woman's concerns. The unnamed forty-one-year-old mother of seven expressed her "hope it will soon be a time that all women with enough children can find such a place to go for help." She described the dire circumstances that led her to seek contraceptive information: "I have been sick almost all my life.

Have to do all my work including washing. At times I don't see how I can live and work without any pleasure or friends for of course I have to give up all that to keep the house going. I love my husband and children but if this keeps up it will cause a separation I am sure or cause my death and I hate to leave the children. . . . I would love to be happy and smile and enjoy life like other women who are more fortunate than I. As I said I love the children I have, but what good is a sick mother?"

Other women who supported the existence of birth control clinics protested the MHA's arguments. Bette Naysmith Norman of Marion, Illinois, suggested that families on relief voluntarily limit their children, as public relief failed to cover medical and household expenses. However, Norman, a member of the Women's Committee of Local 84, Illinois Workers' Alliance, challenged the notion that the poor should use birth control to save taxpayer money. "We thought that the children of coal miners and other laborers should have as good a chance as those of professional people and the so-called 'leisure class' to whom birth control has always been available because they had the price. Now to have birth control thrust upon us merely to keep the bills down can only be regarded as a gross insult. . . . We are still human beings, and we will not take orders to stop having babies just because someone is afraid of getting a cramp in their pocketbook."

As the depression dragged on, the MHA aided a growing numbers of clients, despite persistent protests against the distribution of contraception. In 1937 Catholic doctors who belonged to the St. Louis Gynecological Society organized against the MHA. In 1941 the MHA faced an even more formidable opponent, U.S. postal authorities who prohibited mailing contraceptive prescriptions to patients. For six weeks, postal authorities held up the MHA's work; finally the federal government ruled that the mailings were legal, as long as the name of the doctor who ordered the contraception appeared on the outside of the package. United States involvement in World War II, with large-scale separation of families and nationwide economic recovery, led fewer women to seek the MHA's services. In response to changing demands, in 1943 the MHA shifted its focus from maternal health to family planning, a result of the organization's decision to become an affiliate of the national Planned Parenthood Association.

The postwar period brought both change and continuity to the work of the Planned Parenthood Association. Members of the Catholic Church, the Missouri Synod of the Lutheran Church, and the Knights of Columbus, as well as individual Catholics who sat on city agencies, led the Board of Public Services to withdraw Planned Parenthood's permit to operate its main clinic on Delmar. In addition, opposition threw into question Planned Parenthood's right to receive public funds and its ability to legally distribute contraceptives. This opposition resulted in two main consequences for the association. For short periods, Planned Parenthood was forced to close the Delmar clinic. However, board members participated in public hearings that eventually reopened it. A second consequence, perhaps more significant in the long-term, was the Board of Public Service's ruling that the clinic could reopen provided that only doctors or pharmacists distribute contraceptive materials at the clinics. This ruling, along with the 1941 decision of U.S. postal authorities, diminished the role of female volunteers and Planned Parenthood board members in the operations of the clinics. It also reduced their role in the effort to provide health care for mothers, as the role of physicians and pharmacists increased.

The events of the 1940s and early 1950s regarding Planned Parenthood illustrated the continual decline of churches as a political and social force in the city, and the concomitant swell of public support for family planning and access to contraception. It would take another feminist movement in the late 1960s and an emphasis on women-centered health care to again expand the role of women in maternal health and family planning.

–Anne Valk

Sources: For information on the protest at the Chase Hotel conference, see the *Post-Dispatch*, 3 December 1935; Norman letter to editor, *Post-Dispatch*, 9 February 1935. For additional information, see anonymous letter from Planned Parenthood Association of St. Louis Papers, WHMC–UMSL; 1935 speeches from 1935 Annual Report for American Birth Control League, Planned Parenthood Papers; and 1935 statement by MHA president in letter to editor, *Post-Dispatch*, 14 February 1935.

Linda White Nattier, "The History of the Planned Parenthood Association of St. Louis" (master's thesis, Southern Illinois University–Edwardsville, 1982).

The best overall study of the birth control movement in the United States is Linda Gordon, *Woman's Body, Woman's Right: A Social History of Birth Control in America* (New York: Grossman, 1976). See also the *Post-Dispatch*, 22 May 1916, 16 June 1932, 9 February 1935, 14 February 1935, 2 December 1935, and 13 December 1935; and the *Globe-Democrat*, 17 June 1932, 20 January 1934, and 3 December 1935.

People's Art Center

In April 1941, nearly thirty people attended a meeting at the Pine Street YMCA to consider the creation of a community center for underprivileged St. Louisans. More than ten years into the depression, advisors of the St. Louis Art Project sought to develop a new community-centered program to employ artists and educate children. Underlying the new initiative was a view that art could be used as a vehicle for social change. In particular, they hoped to address the exclusion of African American artists from the New Deal's Federal Art Project, as well as to compensate for inadequate fine arts programs in the segregated schools for black children. Edna Gellhorn, who attended the April meeting, voiced her opposition to the establishment of a segregated project. Instead, Gellhorn saw an opportunity to attack the historic problem of segregation in the city and to use art to advance interracial understanding. Gellhorn proposed that a new center for the arts be open to all without regard to "race, color or creed." At a meeting the following month, more than three hundred people took up Gellhorn's idea and pledged that "a center should be established with the special needs of the Negro population in mind but in which all who desired to take advantage of its offerings would be welcome."

Initiated during the New Deal as a program of the Works Progress Administration (WPA), the center's founders intended to "teach art in all its phases to the entire community, embracing all racial, religious, social, economic and age groups." The People's Art Center (PAC) was first located in the vacant rectory of the Episcopal Church of the Holy Communion at 2811 Washington Avenue. The WPA funds paid workers and bought furnishings for the new facility. The *Post-Dispatch* praised the new endeavor as an effort by "those who are working to improve race relations and to help members of this minority group [African Americans] find the best way to use their talents." Within months, 270 children and 45 adults enrolled in classes; the courses focused on oil painting, ceramics, print making, dress designing and batik, interior design, and introduction to theater. Located next to the Negro USO, servicemen particularly took advantage of PAC's classes and exhibits.

In 1943 the People's Art Center lost WPA funding and struggled to offer programs. Fewer than ten WPA art projects in the country continued to operate after the federal program dissolved: the People's Art Center was one of the survivors. But in

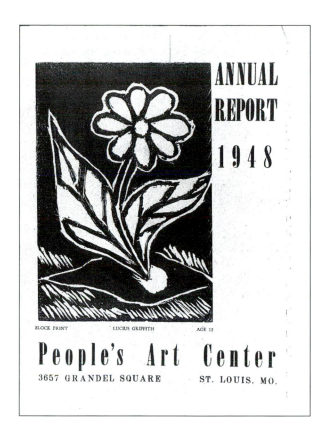

Block Print · Lucius Griffith · Age 12

1943 this future seemed uncertain without federal support. The new director, Elizabeth Green, drew on her connections with wealthy art patrons for volunteers and contributions to underwrite programs. Green was the daughter of Dr. John Green, a pioneering eye specialist in St. Louis. In addition to her involvement with the PAC, Green was active in the St. Louis Training School for Nurses, the City Art Museum, and the Missouri Historical Society. St. Louis women responded to Green's requests to meet the center's needs with characteristic generosity. Irma Rombauer donated two thousand dollars toward the purchase of a permanent building. Aimee Schweig, Alice Bunch, Miriam McKinnie, and Belle Cramer, along with many other artists, instructed students and displayed their work in PAC galleries. Participants in the Inter-racial Committee of the League of Women Voters made personal contributions. And women attended and performed in benefits such as "The Oratorio Chorus of 200 Negro Voices," held at the Kiel Opera House in November 1943.

The fortunes of the People's Art Center improved in 1945 when it joined the Greater St. Louis Community Chest and qualified for

Annual Report of the People's Art Center, 1948. MHS Library municipal funds. With a new economic security, the center purchased a house at 3657 Grandel Square, where it operated for nearly twenty years. The move located the center in a predominantly African American area, although its staff and directors remained committed to offering programming for St. Louisans of all races. Fannie Cook, who sat on the board of directors for many years, expressed this commitment when she declared, "Within the doors of the Center color is not pigmentation which makes a man unfit to eat at our lunch counters; it is something which makes interesting models, thoughtful teachers, selfless board members, and happy, vigorous pupils." By 1945, more than 550 children and adults enrolled in classes; in 1954, that number increased to more than 2,000 from the city and county.

In the late 1950s and early 1960s, the PAC faced new, mainly internal, challenges to its mission to merge artistic education and interracial understanding. Elizabeth Green, who had guided the center throughout the 1940s, at times working without pay, stopped her paid employment, although she continued to sit on the board through the 1960s. In 1950, Mabel Curtis took over for Green and ran the center for more than ten years. Curtis formerly worked for the YWCA and held the post of tenant relations adviser at Carr Square Village before she came to the PAC. As an African American woman and an outspoken opponent of segregation and discrimination, Curtis supported direct attacks on practices that kept the races separate and African Americans subservient. Among her targets, Curtis opposed holding PAC board meetings in segregated facilities. Indeed, Curtis's refusal to enter meeting spaces through back doors reflected the increasing impatience with racial segregation of St. Louis's black population. But when she pointed out her opposition to meeting in such venues, Curtis raised the ire of the PAC's board, who considered such issues outside an art center's proper perview. Faced with conflicting visions of the best way to foster interracial understanding, Curtis found it increasingly difficult to do her job and in 1962 resigned under pressure from board members. Along with such personnel issues, the loss of municipal funding in 1960 forced the center to move to Union Boulevard in 1964 and finally to close the next year.

Despite the changes in education and race relations in the decades following World War II, the People's Art Center continued the mission of its founders: "To strive through the media of art to stimulate interest and participation by all who attend and through its democratic actions, give to all who enter its doors a true sense of human dignity." Yet Curtis's challenges, and the center's eventual closing, suggest that the programs to increase interracial understanding could only make limited headway without a willingness to directly attack, and consistently oppose, the practice of racial segregation.

—*Anne Valk*

Sources: For additional information, see Martin G. Towey, "Design for Democracy: The People's Art Center in St. Louis," in *Art in Action: American Art Centers and the New Deal*, ed., John Franklin White (Metuchen, N.J.: Scarecrow Press, Inc., 1987). See also the *Post-Dispatch*, 16 April 1942; Ernest Calloway Papers, UMSL; League of Women Voters Papers, UMSL; Mabel Curtis Papers, MHS; and Dr. John Green Papers, MHS.

Fannie Cook

"**F**ew white people ever thought of it at all. Few even knew it was there. Though several miles long and several wide, the Ville remained obscure and lived secretly." In the opening pages of her 1946 novel, Fannie Cook introduced her white readers to St. Louis's black middle-class enclave and to Honey Hoop, an African American domestic worker whose life changed when she became a war worker. *Mrs. Palmer's Honey* was a fictionalized commentary on the problems of racial segregation and prejudice in St. Louis during World War II. While the book had a strong political agenda, the author adroitly ensured a wide readership with a deceptively light style and a good plot. St. Louisan Fannie Cook knew her subject and audience well. A dedicated social activist, a skilled communicator, and a believer in the power of the written word, *Mrs. Palmer's Honey* reflected her impassioned involvement in the fight for civil rights, especially those of black Americans. The year it was published, *Mrs. Palmer's Honey* won the first George Washington Carver Memorial Award for an outstanding work dealing with black American issues. Her novel of black oppression in St. Louis was evidence of Fannie Cook's determination to help redress social injustice. *Mrs. Palmer's Honey*, however, explored just one aspect of the broad commitment to social activism that consumed her life.

Fannie Frank Cook was born in 1893 in St. Charles, Missouri, one of the three children of Julius and Jennie Frank. Her father was a German Jew who had come to America in 1881. When Fannie was five years old, her father began working for the Rice-Stix Dry Goods Company, and the family moved to St. Louis. Fannie graduated from Soldan High School in 1911. By 1916, she had earned a B.A. in English from the University of Missouri–Columbia and an M.A. from Washington University. While at Washington University, Fannie married Dr. Jerome E. Cook, a well-known St. Louis physician who became director of medicine and chief of staff at Jewish Hospital. Her first son was born in 1917, and two years later, soon after she started teaching part time at the university, her second son was born.

Fannie Cook's social activism and public service career started when she became a teacher and a member of the League for Women Voters (LWV). In the 1920s, she chaired the league's Education Committee and edited publications for the St. Louis branch. She later edited the *Missouri Bulletin,* the LWV state publication. She was actively involved in the LWV's campaign to reform the elective process of the St. Louis school board. Gradually, she began to attract the attention of local politicians. In 1930 Fannie Cook was appointed chairperson of the Mayor's Race Relations Committee of the Community Council of St. Louis and held that position for several years. The knowledge of St. Louis racism she acquired there strengthened her commitment to racial justice and integration. The Race Relations Committee acted as an arbiter in community racial issues, and, as its chairperson, Fannie Cook was involved in many controversies. She was active in the fight to locate Homer G. Phillips Hospital in the Ville. She worked to establish a vocational school for black students at Franklin School, a consolidated high school in the county, and to initiate training courses at Washington University for black social workers. During this period, she also became involved in local labor issues. She took part in the bitter struggle of the garment workers to join the International Ladies Garment Workers Union, supported striking gas workers, and led a mass meeting on support of a fair wage scale for domestic workers.

In 1935 a heart condition forced Fannie Cook to temporarily curtail her organizational responsibilities and resign from her teaching post. Cook redirected her focus and began her writing career from her University City home at 7068 Maryland Avenue. In 1936 she won one of the *Readers' Digest* one thousand-dollar prizes for new writers with a story about a handicapped girl. Her first novel, *The Hill Grows Steeper*, was published in 1938 and dealt with social and economic problems of modern women.

Boot-heel Doctor, published in 1941, drew on her experiences helping displaced sharecroppers in southeast Missouri. Her long-term involvement fighting sharecropper oppression started in 1939, when she heard about the sharecroppers' sit-down strike along side the highways in the Bootheel. Fannie Cook and fellow St. Louis novelist Josephine Johnson formed a committee to secure relief for the homeless families. The St. Louis Committee for the Rehabilitation of the Sharecroppers bought a ninety-acre plot of land near Poplar Bluff, where they helped destitute families establish a community. Fannie Cook and the committee fought to bring the sharecroppers' plight and the inequities of the system to national attention. She was chairperson of the St. Louis group until it was dissolved in 1949.

Fannie Cook's wartime experiences on the St. Louis Mayor's Race Relations Commission inspired her third novel, *Mrs. Palmer's Honey*, published 1946. Mayor Aloys Kaufmann charged the seventy-two black and white civic-minded citizens on the commission with promoting a greater degree of racial equality and harmony in city affairs.

Fannie Cook. Photograph by Nankin, ca. 1935. MHS–PP

Fannie Cook was an active member of the commission from 1943 to 1946. Her goal was to dismantle segregation, especially public accommodations at hotels, theaters, and department store lunch counters. She resigned in 1946 over the issue of full racial integration of theaters. While on the commission, Fannie Cook also became involved in the issue of restrictive residential covenants. She testified at the St. Louis hearing of the case of *Shelley v. Kraemer* at the request of the Shelley's attorney George L. Vaughn. The case eventually made its way to the U.S. Supreme Court, where in 1948 the court ruled that restrictive covenants were unenforceable.

During the 1940s, Fannie Cook's involvement in other social action organizations provided material for books and stories that reveal the wide range of her interests and views. She served on the Board of Directors and on the Political Action Committee of the Liberal Voters League of St. Louis during the 1944 congressional elections. Her knowledge of political campaigning and the liberal Democratic stance that she took is evident in *Mrs. Palmer's Honey*. She later moved further to the left politically, serving on Progressive Party committees and campaigning to elect Henry Wallace for president.

Fannie Cook served on the Board of Directors of the People's Art Center, an interracial facility that stemmed from the 1942 Missouri Works Progress Administration Art Project. She was an artist with the project, not just a supporter. In 1948 the People's Art Center mounted a solo exhibition of twenty of her paintings, some of which incorporated aspects of her social activism. Fannie Cook drew upon her art center involvement to write *The Long Bridge*, a novel about the St. Louis art scene published shortly after her death in 1949.

A 1948 novel, *Storm Against the Wall*, addressed anti-Semitism in St. Louis, a subject she knew from firsthand experience. Between 1937 and 1939, she corresponded with relatives threatened by Hitler's persecution. During the 1940s, she served on committees that tried to aid victims of German fascism and other war displaced people. She died in 1949.

During the war years, Fannie Cook saw firsthand the contradictions between America's fight against fascism abroad and the religious and racial prejudice that Americans practiced at home. She used her considerable organizational and literary talents to expose injustice and foster integration in racially divided St. Louis.

–Joan Cooper

Sources: The best resource for Fannie Cook is in the extensive collection of papers that she deposited at MHS. The inventory prepared by Jean Douglas Streeter, gives a good synopsis of her life and work. The collection includes personal and professional letters, scrapbooks of clippings, and memorabilia that cover her literary, civic, and political activities from 1874 to 1949. Copies of her books are at MHS library: *Boot-heel Doctor: A Novel* (New York: Dodd, Mead & Co., 1941); *The Hill Grows Steeper* (New York: G. P. Putnam's Sons, 1938); *Mrs. Palmer's Honey* (Garden City, N.Y.: Doubleday, 1946); *Storm Against the Wall* (Garden City, N.Y.: Doubleday, 1948); and *The Long Bridge* (Garden City, N.Y.: Doubleday, 1949). Cook's effort on behalf of sharecroppers is the subject of a dramatic work by St. Louisan Lyn Rubright.

Housewives' League

In 1931 middle-class African American women organized a boycott of the St. Louis Dairy Company plant, headquartered at 2000 Pine Street. The women, members of the newly formed Housewives' League, viewed their action as one means to solve the problems of black unemployment. In more than sixty years of operation, the dairy–along with every other dairy in town–had failed to hire African American men to work as milk wagon drivers. The Housewives' League urged black women to exercise the "power of the purse." "Don't Buy Where You Can't Work," it exhorted women who managed family incomes. In response to the housewives' pressure, the St. Louis Dairy added seven black drivers to its payroll; by 1937, the White Baking Company and the Pevely Dairy had also added black drivers to their routes. When a new Woolworth store opened at 2612 Franklin Avenue in 1932, the Housewives' League demonstrated until the store hired two African American salesgirls. The Nafziger Baking Company, retailers of "Taystee Bread," also succumbed to consumer pressure and hired African American women as "Taystee Hostesses" to spend Saturdays giving away samples in grocery stores in black neighborhoods. These boycotts created only a small number of jobs, but the protests showed the economic power of African American women. The boycotts also demonstrated an important strategy in the arsenal that black women used toward racial progress.

As the Great Depression gripped St. Louis, African American organizations struggled to counteract the poverty and unemployment prevalent in their communities. The Housewives' League, along with the Urban League and more militant organizations, worked to expand employment opportunities and stretch family incomes. However, the Housewives' League's approach differed from that of other organizations. The league, founded in the spring of 1931, combined two facets of African American women's organizational work: a focus on women's role in the home, and a drive for African American economic self-determination. Formed by members of the St. Louis College Women's Club, the league's women joined in campaigns to promote black businesses, increase African Americans' employment opportunities, and educate consumers. They emphasized women's traditional roles as homemakers to urge St. Louis women to purchase groceries and household supplies from black businesses, while they pressured white-owned businesses to hire more black workers. It also tried to ameliorate economic insecurity by preparing women to be smarter shoppers.

Although members of the Housewives' League crafted a public role for themselves as political activists, they did not seek to overturn traditional ideas about sex roles. Instead, the Housewives' League emphasized the sexual division of labor in two ways. It primarily secured jobs for men and young women, rather than for married women. In addition, it coordinated educational programs for its members, including seminars by home economists and health practitioners who distributed material regarding diets and budgeting. Thus, even in times of economic crisis, league members perpetuated middle-class ideals of the home.

In 1936, after several years of inactivity, the St. Louis organization revived and affiliated itself with the National Housewives' League of America, Inc., an association that worked closely with the National Negro Business League (NNBL). The Housewives' League embraced many of the principles of the NNBL, organized at the turn of the century by Booker T. Washington, and encouraged financial and commercial development by African Americans. The Housewives' League's first two presidents, Mrs. W. C. Bridges and Ida B. Haskell, were both married to physicians and did not hold paid jobs; in contrast, Kitty Hall, the league's third president from 1936 to 1949, worked as a matron at the Eden Theater on North Grand. The diversity of the larger membership reflected a transition to a less elite leadership. The 1943 roster of members included cafe owners, a hat shop proprietor, maids, secretaries, and beauticians, as well as the wives of shop owners, physicians, and insurance agents. A number of these women and their husbands

belonged to both organizations. For example, Mrs. Beulah Kilgore-Bailey, manager of the Rainbow Tea Room at 4133 Enright Street, Mae Layne, owner of Layne's Hat Shop at 4215 Easton, and Ethel L. Merriweather, proprietor of the Lucky Leaf Restaurant at 1024 N. Vandeventer, belonged to both the NNBL and the Housewives' League. Thus, the St. Louis Housewives' League included women who could directly benefit from campaigns to support African American business establishments.

The Housewives' League remained active into the 1980s, although the depression marked the peak of its effectiveness and use of direct-action protest. After the 1930s, the league focused more on consumer education and charitable work rather than boycotts and actions that required the participation of larger numbers of people. During the depression, Housewives' Leagues across the country had an economic impact that compared favorably with Congress of Industrial Organizations (CIO) organizing efforts and government hirings of black workers. In addition to these concrete outcomes, the Housewives' League represented an important initiative by African American women to draw on their neighborhood and professional contacts and mobilize their female counterparts for mass campaigns for self-determination and economic improvement. As such, the league helped lay the groundwork for civil rights campaigns during and after World War II.

–Anne Valk

Sources: The 1943 membership list of the Housewives' League and the National Negro Business League can be found in the *Metropolitan St. Louis Negro Directory*. To determine occupations, locate members in the 1942 City Directory. The *Negro Directory* also includes advertisements of businesses owned and operated by Housewives' League members. Nathan B. Young, *Your St. Louis and Mine* (St. Louis, 1937), 54, 79, describes the new fields of employment open to black workers as a result of the 1930s demonstrations, although the author never identifies the Housewives' League by name. WHMC–UMSL contains the history of the St. Louis Housewives' League and the program of the 1980 convention. Little has been written about the National Housewives' League of America, Inc. See Darlene Clark Hine, et al., eds., *Black Women in America: An Historical Encyclopedia* (Bloomington: Indiana University Press, 1996), 584–86, for a description of the Housewives' League of Detroit, and an article by Hine in Nancy A. Hewitt and Suzanne Lebsock, eds., *Visible Women: New Essays on American Activism*

(Urbana: University of Illinois Press, 1993); Jacqueline Jones, *Labor of Love, Labor of Sorrow: Black Women, Work, and the Family from Slavery to the Present* (New York: Vintage Books, 1985), 215. See also *St. Louis Argus*, 1 May 1931, 8 May 1931, and 4 March 1932.

Garment Workers Unite

Bertha Lichtenberg's mother taught her to make a gingham dress when she was eleven years old. Four years later she made three dollars a week at a summer job running a hemstitching machine in the Ely-Walker handkerchief factory on North Florissant Avenue. Supported by her older working brothers, she did not look for work again until she married in 1929. Then Bertha went down to the Washington Avenue garment district, convinced the floor lady at the Epstein and Pearline Clothing Company that she was an experienced dressmaker, and went to work for $3.50 a week sewing dresses. Laid off six months later, she went to the Deluxe Company where she earned 12.5 cents a piece, making dresses that sold for a dollar. In a few months, she moved on again.

Garment District. These buildings on Washington Avenue housed the St. Louis garment industry until the 1960s. Photograph by George Rothenbuescher, 1999.

In the early years of the depression, experienced garment workers like Bertha Lichtenberg could usually find temporary piece work, but the pay was low and working conditions bad. Sometimes manufacturers with large rush orders locked the doors and coat rooms to keep the workers at their machines. Bertha's father, a union man, "almost threw a fit when it happened," she recalled years later. "The girls got to rolling up their coat and putting it in their workbox, and then we'd sneak down the fire escape and get out." When the International Ladies Garment Workers Union (ILGWU) came to Washington Avenue in 1933 seeking union recognition from the clothing manufacturers, Bertha Lichtenberg was ready. "I knew from my dad talking that the only good shop was a union shop, so I joined."

Although the ILGWU had been active in St. Louis early in the century, it met with little success until President Franklin Roosevelt signed the National Industrial Recovery Act (NIRA) in June 1933. Section 7a of the act guaranteed trade unions the right to organize and to bargain collectively. The legislation also empowered the National Recovery Administration to establish a system of minimum wages and maximum hours. The U.S. Supreme Court ruled the NIRA unconstitutional in 1935, but the Wagner Act, enacted the same year, gave organizers from industrial unions like the International Ladies Garment Workers the same protection.

The St. Louis clothing industry was centered along Washington Avenue, between Eighth and Twentieth Streets. Most of the factories were small businesses run by local owners. Six out of ten workers were female. American-born dressmakers worked along side hundreds of immigrants, primarily Eastern European Jews and Italians. African Americans could not find skilled work in the garment industry until unions admitted them during World War II. The typical prewar garment worker came from an immigrant family that had arrived in St. Louis between 1904 and 1910. The male head of household earned about a thousand dollars a year; a female garment worker received about half that amount doing piece work twelve to fourteen hours a day. Women worked on the sewing machines and as finishers; men held the higher paying jobs of pressers, cutters, and pattern makers.

In 1933 the New York–based ILGWU issued a strike call to regional union leaders, instructing them to demand recognition by employers in the women's clothing industry. Meyer Perlstein, an organizer from

Cleveland, called on St. Louis workers to stop work at 10 A.M. on August 10 and march to a mass meeting at the Gaiety Theater, at the corner of Fourteenth and Locust Streets. "I was twenty years old then," recalled Jessie Sulkowski, one of the nearly two thousand workers who walked off the job that morning. "We walked out because some were making five dollars a week, working from about seven o'clock until–some of them–ten o'clock in the evening. . . . I was out seven months."

Dressmakers struck the Ely-Walker, Forest City Manufacturing, Rice-Stix, and H. Lowenbaum Companies first. Within the week workers from other factories joined them in seeking union recognition and hiring preference for union members. Hundreds of striking women from forty-eight shops walked the garment district picket lines, tangling with police and strikebreakers who tried to enter the buildings. Like Jessie Sulkowski, Bertha Lichtenberg participated fully in the strike, reporting for picket duty each day at the Union Hall at Eleventh and Franklin Streets. She later recalled confrontations with strikebreakers, or "scabs." "Six of us would get around her, and she couldn't go nowhere with us pushing her. And we'd get her around the corner of the building. And we'd get her against the wall and tell her she should join the union." Strike violence escalated in late August, when two women from the Ely-Walker dress factory reported that picketers ripped their clothes off as they left work. Police arrested the alleged attackers and held the torn clothing as evidence, but on September 2 the factory closed down.

From the windows of a nearby factory, Sara Macaluso witnessed violence at Forest City Manufacturing Company on the corner of Sixteenth Street and Washington Avenue. She recalled that she did not want to get involved despite her low wages and poor working conditions because she feared losing her job. Clothing shop work was usually available in the depression-ridden city, and a dressmaker often bore the whole burden of family support. Myrtle Kappesser went out the first day but returned to work before the strike ended because "there was nobody hardly working on both sides of my family. . . . And I figured I had a job and I just tried to keep it."

Wages and union representation were the two issues keeping the owners and the workers from settling the strike. Despite sixteen warrants issued against them for wage violations, manufacturers insisted they were meeting NIRA guidelines. The core dispute, however, centered on the issue of what union representation entailed. Manufacturers wanted an open shop where workers would not be required to join the union; the union argued that an open shop would be open to everyone but union members. On September 4, Mayor Bernard Dickman appointed six men and one woman, Edna Gellhorn, to a labor mediation board to help settle the strike.

Before the board could meet, however, the union and the owners of four silk dress factories reached a settlement. Workers secured a minimum wage 10 percent over NIRA codes. The contract called for a "preferential shop" where anyone could work but union members could not be refused, nor could workers be fired for union membership. Manufacturers recognized the ILGWU as the official bargaining agent for their workers; shop committees would be elected by the membership. Negotiations dragged on much longer with owners of factories that produced cotton dresses. Some dressmakers remained on picket lines until 1935.

From the time of the first depression-era ILGWU contracts until the garment industry left the city thirty years later, in part to escape unionism, women took active grass-roots roles in union activities. Not all embraced union membership at the time of the strikes, but they understood the issues and the relationship between labor and capital. Eula Carson, who joined the union in 1939, was elected shop chairlady at Curlee Manufacturing shortly afterward. "When I was shop chairlady, I guess they thought all I wanted to do was fight," she said, "but you've also got to manage. That's one thing I learned about. You go in there bullheaded you know, you're not going to get very far. You've got to sit down and talk things over, bring out your points, and then you begin to put the two points together . . . then we'd see who wins." In spite of their rank-and-file prominence, women rarely rose to positions of national union leadership.

When retired garment workers reminisced in the late 1970s, most placed their work experiences at the center of their lives. Many had made lifelong friends on Washington Avenue; some still sewed regularly. Union workers often earned good money and benefits. However, even when the industry paid low wages for long hours at the sewing machine, it usually offered creative and satisfying work, relatively steady employment, and the companionship of other women.

Sources: Katharine Corbett and Jeanne Mongold conducted interviews with retired garment workers in 1977 for an exhibit on the ILGWU organizing strikes. Tapes, transcripts, and photographs assembled for the exhibit are preserved at WHMC–UMSL. The interviews were not a representative sample because no Jewish women were included, even though many garment workers were Jewish immigrants. Paul Preisler Collection, WHMC–UMSL, contains photographs of strike activity and some union information. See also Katharine T. Corbett, "St. Louis Garment Workers: Photographs and Memories," *GH* 2, no. 1 (spring 1983) for a description of the interview process and the use of historical phonographs to elicit memories. Information on ILGWU and organizing strikes are from the *Post-Dispatch*, August to December 1933, February to May 1935. See also Leon Stein, *Out of the Sweatshop: The Struggle for Industrial Democracy* (New York: Quadrangle, 1977), and Wendy Gamber, *The Female Economy: The Millinery and Dressmaking Trades, 1860–1930* (Urbana: University of Illinois Press, 1997).

The papers of Doris Preisler Wheeler, WHMC–UMSL, contain information on ILGWU activities in St. Louis and the Missouri Socialist Party during the Great Depression. Wheeler's first husband, Paul Preisler, took the photographs documenting the ILGWU organizing strikes. In 1935 she became educational director for the ILGWU and for the next fifteen years was active in St. Louis union and social welfare organizations, often with her second husband, Morice Wheeler, who was also a socialist and union activist. Like earlier socialist women, Doris Wheeler worked with both radical and liberal organizations in St. Louis. A study of her life and work would reveal much about social activism in the interwar years.

Funsten Nut Pickers Strike

On May 15, 1933, more than half of the African American women who worked in the Funsten Nut Company's four St. Louis factories walked off the job. They were being paid three cents a pound to pick nuts from 6:45 A.M. to 4:45 P.M. Monday through Friday and until noon on Saturday. At that rate, it required patience, manual dexterity, caution, and speed to pick enough pecan meat from the shells to earn $1.80 a week. Funsten's few white nut pickers worked shorter hours and earned four cents a pound for the same work. The five hundred black women who struck for equal pay and higher wages won their demands in eight days with the support of the Communist Party and a mayor's arbitration committee of civic leaders.

At the time of the settlement, company president Eugene Funsten insisted that he had not made a profit in two years. Decades later, the Funsten Nut Company, which had cut wages steadily between 1929 and 1933, admitted to making an annual profit of 10 percent throughout the depression years.

With more than twelve hundred employees in 1933, the Funsten Nut Company may have been the city's largest employer of black women. The majority were middle-aged women with families. African Americans worked at plants at 3404 Walnut Street, 233 Chestnut Street, 4241 Easton Avenue, and in the basement of the main factory at Sixteenth Street and Delmar Boulevard. In 1929 their average wages had been close to ten dollars a week, but in the first three years of the depression wages had dropped to less than two dollars. Many of the workers were on the relief rolls of the Provident Association.

In the spring of 1933, members of the Communist Party who had friends employed at Funsten began organizing workers into a local of the Food Workers Industrial Union. On April 9, 1934, twelve women at the Easton Avenue plant demanded higher wages: ten cents for halves and four cents for pieces. When they received no response from the company, the nut pickers called a strike for May 15.

Holding a brick in one hand and a Bible in the other, Carrie Smith, who had worked eighteen years for Funsten, rallied strikers with the slogan, "We demand ten and four." Within a week twelve hundred workers had walked off the job. Nearly all the Funsten black workers and some of the white women joined the union. Every morning at 5 A.M. strikers and their families picketed the main plant on Delmar along with supporters organized by the Communist Party. Workers from the smaller Central Pecan Company and Liberty Nut Company also walked out. Strikers organized a central committee, a negotiating committee, and a relief committee which fed about twelve hundred women daily.

Strike committees solicited support from community groups. Two white and two black women, accompanied by a lawyer from the American Civil Liberties Union, met with the mayor's Social Justice Commission at Temple Israel. The women brought with them eight unopened pay envelopes containing four days wages. Two held just over two dollars, the other six about $1.50. Rabbi Ferdinand M. Isserman commended the Communist Party for taking up the cause of the nut pickers when everyone else had ignored a wage scale which he considered "un-American, and which did not make possible even the barest subsistence." The *Post-Dispatch* cited the Funsten strike as reason enough for a uniform code of minimum wage laws that would prevent excessive wage slashing and sweatshop conditions.

Although the *Post-Dispatch* and the city's white liberals denounced Funsten for its appalling wage scale, they did not protest the company's policy of racial discrimination. Only the *Argus*, a St. Louis black weekly, decried Funsten's practice of paying white workers more than African Americans for the same work. On the third day of the strike, the workers rejected Funsten's offer of a one-third pay raise. Prepared to accept a guaranteed $4.50 a week, two white and three black women called on Mayor Bernard Dickman to arbitrate the dispute. When the mayor offered his sympathy but insisted that the strike was not a municipal concern, the women reminded him that some of the relief funds distributed by the Provident Association came from the city treasury.

Dickman appointed an interracial committee of civic leaders to investigate the nut pickers' grievances. Only then did John T. Clark, head of the Urban League, take up the cause of the plight of the communist-supported nut pickers. Meanwhile, the strikers kept up the pressure on the streets, throwing stones and food at policemen bringing strikebreakers to work in the plants.

On May 23, the striking women voted unanimously to accept a settlement with Funsten negotiated by the union and the mayor's committee. Under the agreement they would earn eight cents for halves and four cents for pieces. Black and white workers would receive the same rate of pay. Six days after the settlement, the now-recognized union prevented Funsten from laying off one-third of the returning workers.

Union organizers established eleven interracial locals of the Food Workers Industrial Union during the nut pickers strike, the first major St. Louis strike of the depression. Later in 1933, after President Franklin Roosevelt signed the National Industrial Recovery Act affirming the right of unions to organize, women in the garment industry who struck the factories along Washington Avenue rallied supporters with the slogan, "Do as the nut pickers did!"

The Funsten nut pickers had struck to raise their pay and to end a discriminatory wage system. By working together in their negotiations with the company, the civic commission, and the communist-supported organizers, black and white women kept the issue of racial injustice at the center of their protest. While their fierce determination to organize inspired other workers, in terms of racial cooperation, very few actually "did what the nut pickers did."

Lucas Park Fountain. Hahn's sculpture is the centerpiece of Lucas Park. Photograph by George Rothenbuescher, 1999.

Nancy Coonsman Hahn created the Margaret Kincaid fountain that stands in Lucas Park behind the St. Louis Public Library at Fourteenth and Locust Streets. Hahn set off a local controversy in 1929 when she revealed her first design for the fountain. The scantily dressed dancing maidens encircling the model prompted the observation that the city could get along very well without "this young upstart of an artist." Hahn modified her design to depict very small children, which proved to be acceptable to a conservative public.

Hahn's ambition had always been to portray "the innocence of childhood, the joy of living." Born in St. Louis in 1888, she began working with clay as a student of Frederick Oakes Sylvester at Central High School. She studied at the St. Louis School of Fine Arts and George Julian Zolnay's Master School of Sculpture.

Hahn, whose major works were cast in bronze, worked on clay throughout her career. In 1922 Daughters of the American Colonists selected her design *Memorial to Pioneer Women* for a public monument. Presented to the city in 1929, the thirty-two-inch bronze statue depicting a mother and two children stood on a granite base in front of the Jefferson Memorial Building in Forest Park. In 1969 vandals removed the statue, but it was recovered a few days later and eventually joined the collections of the Missouri Historical Society.

Nancy Coonsman Hahn also sculpted a female figure of victory for a war memorial commissioned by the Missouri legislature. Erected on a country road near Varennes, France, the statue honored Missourians who fought in World War I. A plaster replica of the statue stood in the city hall rotunda in St. Louis until it was destroyed when the bronze plate bearing the names of the men who had been killed in action fell on it.

The city of Memphis also awarded Hahn a commission for a war memorial, and her statue *The Doughboy* is considered one of her most significant public works. The St. Louis Art Museum bought two of Hahn's works, a bust of a young girl titled *Maidenhood* and a bust of William Marion Reedy, the pioneering newspaper editor, which is now in the Missouri Historical Society collections. A popular, gifted artist, she was able to reproduce a likeness so faithfully that a critic insisted "one almost sees life glowing through the inanimate figures."

–Kathleen Butterly Nigro

Sources: The most extensive study of the strike is Myrna Fichtenbaum, *The Funsten Nut Pickers Strike* (New York: International Publishers, 1992). Dowden, "Over This We Are Determined to Fight," deals with the attitude of the Urban League toward the nut pickers. The local press published articles and editorials during the strike. See the *Post-Dispatch, Globe-Democrat, St. Louis Star-Times,* and the *Argus,* 15–30 May 1933. The script for a slide show produced by Patricia Adams and Nancy Brown on striking women in the 1930s is available at WHMC–UMSL.

See also Rose Feurer, "The Nutpickers' Union, 1933–34: Crossing the Boundaries of the Community and Workplace," in *"We Are All Leaders": The Alternate Unionism of the Early 1930s,* ed., Staughton Lynd (Urbana: University of Illinois Press, 1996). Information on the activities of the Communist Party and the Socialist Party in local labor disputes can be found at WHMC–UMSL.

Sitting-in at Stix

The owners of St. Louis department stores designed their facilities to lure female shoppers with attractive tearooms, and later efficient lunch counters for their white customers. But when black women went downtown to shop at Stix, Baer & Fuller, Famous-Barr, or Scruggs, Vandervoot & Barney, they were not permitted to eat in the stores' restaurants. On Saturday July 8, 1944, forty black women and fifteen white women challenged this policy by sitting at the lunch counters of the three department stores and waiting all day to be served. They carried placards declaring, "Practice the democracy you preach" and "Fox holes are democratic, are you?" Hattie Duvall's sign proclaimed that she had invested five sons in the D-Day invasion a month earlier. All three stores

Members of the March on Washington Civil Rights Committee Protest Jim Crow Laws in Downtown Restaurant. Halftone from the *St. Louis Argus,* July 1944. MHS–PP

closed their counters rather than serve the demonstrators.

The lunch counter protest was one of the first civil rights sit-ins in the nation. Organized by Pearl Maddox, the Citizens Civil Rights Committee (CCRC) began sitting-in at Stix lunch counter and negotiating with the department store in May. "We shall sit at the lunch counters, not only of Stix but of all stores in St. Louis," Maddox declared through the local black press, "waiting to be served, keeping faith with our sons, and fathers who die to insure the rights of human beings." The massive but quiet and orderly July demonstrations attracted crowds inside the stores, while outside students from the Eden Seminary and Saint Louis University distributed several thousand CCRC handbills.

The three lunch counters remained segregated, but the demonstrations provoked the first coverage of the sit-ins from the white press and a response from the Mayor's Race Relations Commission. When the commission offered to act as mediators if the CCRC would end the sit-ins, Pearl Maddox acquiesced. The store owners, however, agreed to serve black patrons only at basement lunch counters, a decision CCRC members found unacceptable. In a letter to Stix, Baer & Fuller, Pearl Maddox pointed out the contradiction inherent in upholding the myth of racial superiority while black and white Americans waged a world war against the same beliefs.

Meetings among the race relations commission, the store owners, and CCRC continued into 1945 with little progress. During the negotiations, Fannie Cook considered resigning from the commission due to its opposition to civil rights demonstrations, unwillingness to interfere with how department store owners ran their businesses, and acceptance of the widespread attitude that integrating "social relations" such as eating should not be rushed. In the end, only Scruggs, Vandervoot & Barney integrated a lunch counter, although the store retained its "whites only" policy in the upstairs dining room. Famous-Barr offered to open a separate counter for black shoppers, but the CCRC refused the offer of separate but equal status. By agreeing to end the demonstrations, Maddox and the CCRC surrendered their most powerful weapon against the store owners. The Mayor's Race Relations Committee gave them little in return.

In 1954 the Congress of Racial Equality (CORE) helped bring about integrated dining at drug stores, dime stores, and the basement lunch counter at Famous-Barr, but it took another four years before all department store restaurants served African Americans. St. Louis did not pass a public accommodations law permitting black women access to the same places as white women until 1961.

–Joan Cooper

Sources: This essay is based on the account of the department store sit-ins in Patricia L. Adams, "Fighting For Democracy in St. Louis: Civil Rights During World War II," *MHR* 80, no. 4 (July 1986), an excellent account of civil rights activity in St. Louis during the war years. For local context, see also Betty Burnett, *St. Louis at War: The Story of a City, 1941–1945* (St. Louis: Patrice Press, 1987), and for national context, Hartmann, *The Home Front and Beyond*.

For more on St. Louis civil rights activity in the war years and for the March on Washington movement, see the Theodore D. McNeal Scrapbook, 1941–1944, WHMC–UMSL. See also the Urban League reports for the war years and oral histories of the period, WHMC–UMSL. The *St. Louis Argus* and the *St. Louis American* are useful news and editorial sources, while the *Post-Dispatch* and the *Globe-Democrat* gave scant attention to African American civil rights demonstrations and labor strikes. For an insightful fictional account of a black woman's experiences working with a union in a defense factory, see Cook, *Mrs. Palmer's Honey*. The Fannie Cook Papers at MHS include information on her work with the Mayor's Race Relations Commission. For background to the war years, see Katharine T. Corbett and Mary E. Seematter, "No Crystal Stair: Black St. Louis 1920–1940," *GH* 8, no. 2 (fall 1987).

St. Louis Women in the Military

On May 27, 1943, more than fifty stenographers, waitresses, housewives, and business women appeared at the Federal Building in downtown St. Louis eager to join the army. They were applying for the twenty-nine places allotted Missouri women in the officers' training program for the new Women's Auxiliary Army Corps (WACs). For the first time, the federal government officially permitted women to participate in the military defense of their country—a defining part of citizenship. In all, more than two thousand St. Louis women volunteered for military service in World War II. Several hundred local nurses joined the nurse corps, and at least one women, Adela Riek Scharr, became a member of the Women's Auxiliary Ferrying Squadron (WAFS). Most servicewomen did traditional women's work, but Scharr, a pilot, was an exception. At the end of the war, she learned firsthand that such an exception was only temporary.

Jessie Housley Holliman. Halftone from *Your St. Louis and Mine*, by Nathan Young, ca. 1937. MHS Library

Jessie Housley Holliman, an African American artist, painted The Origins of Freemasonry in 1941. Commissioned by the Grand Lodge of the Masonic Temple Association of St. Louis, the fresco mural is located in the foyer of the York Rite Masonic Temple at 3681 Lindell Boulevard. Holliman, who graduated from the Art Institute of Chicago, produced two other murals for St. Louis public buildings that no longer exist.

Although Jessie Holliman could never remember a time when she did not want to be an artist, she was also a practical woman. Realizing that the opportunities for black female artists were extremely limited, Holliman, a 1925 graduate of Sumner High School, enrolled in Stowe Teachers College after returning home from Chicago. She taught elementary school for many years, but continued to study art in New York and at the Washington University School of Fine Arts. Because Washington University did not admit black art students, however, she could only attend as a model. During the depression she attended free classes that Joe Jones gave for unemployed artists. She also did fashion illustrating for Kline's, a St. Louis clothing store.

During the mid-1930s, Holliman learned the art of fresco mural painting, which, unlike most modern murals that are executed in oil or acrylic paint on a dry wall or canvas, uses color on wet plaster in a slow, painstaking procedure. The Urban League commissioned her first mural, *Racial and Industrial Harmony,* for their building at 3017 Delmar Boulevard, which has since been demolished. In September 1941, then-Senator Harry S Truman, a Free Mason, dedicated her thirty-eight-foot mural, *The Origin of Free Masonry*. Holliman's only other St. Louis mural, *Christ's Fellowship,* in the Central Baptist Church at Ewing and Washington Avenues, was destroyed by fire in 1971.

–Kathleen Butterly Nigro

Approximately 350,000 women served in the armed services, making up about 2 percent of all military personnel. The majority entered the WACs and the Women Accepted for Volunteer Emergency Service (WAVES), the women's naval corps. Smaller numbers went into the Marine Corps Women's Reserve, the Coast Guard Reserve Corps (SPAR), and the Women's Airforce Service Pilots (WASPs). In addition, about 74,000 qualified nurses served in the Army Nurse Corps (ANC) and the Navy Nurse Corps (NNC). Apart from the ANC and the NNC, which the Army and Navy had established in the early part of the century, the other women's corps were formed as temporary wartime expediencies. Most of them became permanent branches of the services in 1948. Although the women's corps were temporary, servicewomen received the same benefits and veteran status as the men. The WASPs, who battled for their benefits until 1977, were the one exception.

The majority of servicewomen were single high school graduates in their twenties. With the exception of nurses, most women stayed in the United States. They were clerical and secretarial

workers, storekeepers, and radio and telephone operators. Although some worked with highly secret planning or decoding units and others drove and maintained military cars and trucks, most women worked at jobs similar to those they had in civilian life.

As in civilian life, African American servicewomen faced both racial and gender discrimination. The WAC accepted black women as enlisted personnel and as officers but put them in segregated units and never fully utilized their job skills and training. Many black servicewomen resisted, and some even protested after being assigned only unskilled menial work. Only pressure from the black press and civil rights organizations convinced the military to send one black women's unit, a central postal directory unit, overseas in 1945. Despite the acute shortage of nurses, the ANC accepted only a few black nurses, and they were generally limited to nursing black patients and prisoners-of-war in the States. Although the WAVES did not accept black women until late 1944, it immediately integrated them into existing units.

A substantial number of military women served in the St. Louis area. The first women stationed at Jefferson Barracks since its founding in 1826 arrived in March 1943. The sixty-two WACs lived in the barracks but worked six-day weeks at the Army Air Force aeronautical chart plant in St. Louis.

Nurses from the 21st General Hospital Unit Arriving at Camp Benning. Photograph (rotogravure) by Art Witman, from the *St. Louis Post-Dispatch Pictures Magazine*, 22 February 1942.

WAVES were assigned to duty at the Naval Air Station at Lambert Airfield, and WASPs and Airforce WACs served at Scott Field. Two hundred and twenty-six SPARs lived and worked downtown at the Coast Guard headquarters.

Nurses from all the local hospitals were among the few women from the city who served overseas. In 1940 the 21st General Hospital Unit, organized by Washington University and Barnes Hospital during the First World War, was reconstituted and called to duty. Early in 1942, sixty members of the medical, nursing, and dental faculties went to Fort Benning, Georgia, for training before going abroad in two units. The 21st General Hospital went to Sidi Ben Hanifa, North Africa, at the end of 1942, where they nursed the wounded from the Tunis-Bizerte battles. In 1943 the unit was then sent to Naples, Italy. The other, renamed the 21st Station Hospital, served in East Africa, Persia, and Palestine. Early in 1943, another unit from St. Louis, the 70th General Hospital, sponsored by Saint Louis University, arrived in North Africa. The unit included faculty members from the medical school and 113 locally trained nurses. The 70th General Hospital served in Assi Bou Nif, North Africa, and then moved in early 1944 to Pistoia, Italy, to nurse the wounded from the Italian Campaign.

Unlike other military women, nurses were expected to work in or near combat zones. They were with the troops in every theater of war. At least fifteen American nurses were killed in action, twenty-six wounded, and a few reported missing in action. Nurses with army units in the Philippines when the Japanese attacked Bataan and Corregidor cared for the sick under combat conditions. When General Jonathan Wainwright surrendered to the Japanese in May 1943, three nurses from the St. Louis area were among the fifty-four American and twenty-nine Filipino nurses with the eleven thousand troops. They were interred in civilian prison camps for the duration of the war.

The nurses, in a traditionally feminine role, posed no threat to the status of military men. However, one group of women directly challenged gender roles and discovered how powerful cultural norms could be. The civilian Women Airforce Service Pilots were organized in 1943, but they disbanded in 1944 when returning male combat veterans took over their duties.

Adela Riek Scharr, born and raised in St. Louis, became one of the first women to serve in the Women's Auxiliary Ferrying Squadron, which later became the WASPs. Trained as a teacher, she began taking flying lessons in 1935 at Lambert Field. By

1940, Scharr had become the first female commercial pilot, the first female ground instructor, and the first female flight instructor in St. Louis. In September 1942, the Ferrying Division of Air Transport Command invited her to join a civilian group of female pilots being organized to deliver military planes to bases in the United States. The Air Transport Command recruited qualified women pilots because increased aircraft production and the demand for pilots overseas had used up the pool of available civilian male pilots. At about the same time, it began training less experienced women pilots. By the end of 1944, 1,074 women had graduated from the training program.

Scharr and the other women pilots ferried almost every type of military aircraft around the country, from bombers and fighter planes to huge transport carriers. They also served as instructors and test pilots and towed targets for firing practice, often with live ammunition. The women were civilians, paid by the Civil Service Commission, but they were subject to military procedures and regulations.

Since the female pilots were ineligible for military pay, security, or benefits, plans were made early on to militarize the division in the same fashion as the other women's service branches. In late 1943, Congress introduced a bill to expand the WASPs and make them a division of the Army Air Force. The proposal did not come to a vote until June 1944. By then, combat pilots were returning from tours of duty overseas and wanted the women's jobs and the accompanying flight pay. Also, many flying cadets, civilian pilots, and trainers were being drafted or returned to the Army for overseas infantry duty. Safe domestic flying was an appealing alternative to combat. A powerful lobby that included the civilian pilots, aviation industries and associations, and veterans groups organized to defeat the 1943 bill. Congressmen and the media opposed the women for taking jobs from civilian male pilots, declaring them less qualified than the men. The WASPs and their supporters lacked the power to counter this emotional, exaggerated attack. The bill was defeated, and by the end of 1944 the WASPs disbanded.

Adela Scharr returned to St. Louis and went back to teaching. In the 1970s she was part of a group organized to fight for military status for former WASPs. Despite the changes in social attitudes, five years lapsed before President Carter signed the bill making WASPs veterans of the Air Force. Women who served in the other female branches of the military and performed duties that did not challenge the gender status quo saw their branches permanently incorporated in the armed forces in 1948.

–Joan Cooper

Sources: For general information and background on women in the armed services, see Hartmann, *The Home Front and Beyond,* and Olga Gruhzit-Hoyt, *They Also Served: American Women in World War II* (Secaucus, N.J.: Carol Pub. Group, 1995). For St. Louis women in the services, see Burnett, *St. Louis at War;* Juliet M. Gross, "Missouri and the War," *MHR* 37, no. 4 (July 1943), 38, no. 1 (October 1943); and the *Post-Dispatch,* WAC enrollment, 27 May 1942, WAC at Jefferson Barracks, 21 March 1943. An excellent book on the WAC, which also includes good information on the treatment of black women and lesbians in the army, is Leisa D. Meyer, *Creating GI Jane: Sexuality and Power in the Women's Army Corps During World War II* (New York: Columbia University Press, 1996). See also Major General Jeanne Holm, *In Defense of a Nation: Servicewomen in World War II* (Arlington, Va.: Vandermere, 1997). For the role of wartime nurses, see Philip A. Kalisch and Margaret Scobey, "Female Nurses in American Wars: Helplessness Suspended for the Duration," *Armed Forces and Society* 9, no. 2 (winter 1983): 215–44. For St. Louis's university units, see Ralph E. Morrow, *Washington University in St. Louis: A History* (St. Louis: MHS Press, 1996), and the *Globe-Democrat,* 29 December 1942 for the Saint Louis University unit. The fascinating history of the WASPs can be found in Molly Merryman, *Clipped Wings: The Rise and Fall of the Women Airforce Service Pilots (WASPs) of World War II* (New York: New York University Press, 1998). See also St. Louisan Adela Scharr, *Sisters in the Sky* (Gerald Mo.: Patrice Press, 1986), and Dains and Sadler, eds., *Show Me Missouri Women.* For local comments and arguments over WASPs, see the *Globe-Democrat,* 3, 8–11 May 1944.

The Home Front

Few St. Louis women served in the armed forces or the nursing corps during World War II. Most played a less glamorous role in the war effort, but their patriotic service as volunteers and war workers, combined with their ability to adapt domestic life to meet new challenges, kept the home front functioning.

Once mobilization began, it was not long before St. Louisans felt the full impact of war. In 1941 defense and war production plants expanded, creating thousands of new jobs that drew workers to St. Louis. In the northwest part of the city, where many of the largest plants were located, areas like

Wellston experienced severe housing shortages, school overcrowding, and extra demands on recreational facilities. These factors added to the increasing strains that war placed on women. Although some of the women who came to St. Louis were young and single, many were wives of servicemen, some stationed at Jefferson Barracks. Military wives had to cope with loneliness, anxiety, and loss of income. Many servicemen's wives received the minimum allotment of fifty dollars a month. Half of all servicemen's wives were in the labor force.

St. Louis also became the temporary, and not wholly welcoming, home and workplace for 150 Japanese-Americans sent here from the West Coast by the War Relocation Authority. Some resident Asian, German, and Italian families underwent police interrogation and had assets frozen and property seized. Many St. Louis women lost husbands and close relatives; 522 St. Louis servicemen were killed in action, 159 died from other causes, and 67 died of disease. All women, however, experienced the stresses wartime placed on marital and familial life, as marriage, birth, and divorce rates rose dramatically. Despite a booming economy, wartime shortages of consumer goods made women's domestic work harder.

Shortages of consumer goods began soon after Pearl Harbor. The federal government imposed a rationing system to conserve essential war production materials and to ensure fair distribution of scarce commodities. Tires, cars, and gasoline were among the first items restricted, which put pressure on the city's transportation system and on thousands of working women. Shoes were rationed to three pairs a year. Sugar was restricted in May 1942, and ration books were issued to everyone. By the end of March 1943, almost all processed food, dried, frozen, or canned, and meat, cheese, and fat were rationed. Housewives became adept at juggling menus, coping with sudden shortages, and taking advantage of sudden gluts. This was particularly burdensome for the working housewife and mother who had to cope with these domestic duties and a forty-eight-hour workweek, which might include shift work. Few stores stayed open late, and scarce items frequently sold out by early afternoon. Shortages of household equipment like refrigerators, stoves, vacuum cleaners, and even pots and pans added to the problem.

Young people found opportunities in wartime St. Louis to challenge traditional expectations of teenage behavior. Juvenile delinquency became a nationwide concern in response to a rising crime rate in young people. When increasing numbers of middle-class offenders appeared, the public demanded action from local authorities. In St. Louis, Mayor William Dee Becker created a juvenile crime commission. Local agencies were most concerned, however, with the increase in sexual activity among teenage girls.

In September 1942, juvenile court officers, concerned about a 20 percent rise in the juvenile delinquency rate among young girls, led a squad of military police in a raid on Downs Amusement Park at 8600 South Broadway, close to Jefferson Barracks. After questioning thirty girls between the ages of thirteen and sixteen, they ordered twelve to appear in juvenile court the next day to determine whether they were delinquent. Juvenile officials and the press chastised parents for not controlling their daughters and for permitting them to socialize with servicemen. The raid set off a series of surprise visits to amusement parks, dance halls, and taverns to control the behavior of women and girls. City health officials and the military blamed women for the increase in venereal disease, but the police who raided and closed brothels and arrested women suspected of prostitution also targeted other young women as well. A squad of policewomen picked up girls found late at night on the streets or in bars. No such measures were used to curb similar male behavior.

The wartime economy created more job opportunities for teenagers, which resulted in a drop in school attendance. Mayor Becker launched a "Back-to-school" campaign aimed at getting teenagers back in the classroom while providing them with practical work experience. Most school children, however, did not become delinquents or dropouts. They participated in voluntary programs, particularly in the scrap metal collections, in the increasingly youth-oriented popular culture of a country at war.

Thousands of women in St. Louis answered the call for volunteers; many for patriotic reasons, others because they were lonely or thought it fashionable. After Pearl Harbor, city authorities quickly organized a civil defense program and recruited women volunteers to train and act as air raid wardens. Women volunteered their time to explain the intricacies of the rationing system to St. Louis families. More than fifty-two thousand St. Louis women took Red Cross first-aid classes or trained as nurse's aids, and many others packed surgical dressings. A few local women volunteered for the Red Cross overseas. Mary Metcalfe Rexford served in a clubmobile (a mobile canteen) near battle areas in Europe. Virginia Irwin, a *Post-Dispatch* reporter,

worked for the Red Cross in Europe prior to becoming an accredited war correspondent. She would be one of the first Americans and the only woman to enter Berlin during the Russian attack.

Women served on the boards of government and local wartime agencies. St. Louisan Margaret Hickey was chairwoman of the Women's Advisory Committee of the War Manpower Commission from 1942 to 1945. The success of the war bond drives owed much to the efforts of the many women involved. Even the women who did not volunteer helped the war effort by saving cans, scrap metal, rubber, and kitchen fats, tending victory gardens, and donating thousands of units of blood.

Almost every established organization in the city expanded or created programs to help the war effort, from collecting scrap metal and rubber to helping care and entertain the thousands of servicemen and women passing through St. Louis. The YWCA trained many young women to be hostesses at the segregated United Service Organization (USO) recreational facilities in the city. The YWCA established a storefront, drop-in recreational center for women defense workers in Wellston. It proved only marginally successful because many women in defense work were married with home responsibilities, and most single young working women were local girls with their own social connections.

A Woman Inspects Rationed Bologna at a Meat Counter in Webster Groves. Rotogravure by Jack Gould from the *St. Louis Post-Dispatch Pictures Magazine,* 8 April 1945.

During the war, St. Louis women benefited from better jobs and more money, but they had to struggle, often alone, with the social and economic upheaval war created on the home front. As women had during the Civil War and World War I, they kept house and home together during disruptive times.

–Joan Cooper

Sources: Information on the home front in St. Louis is the focus of Burnett, *St. Louis at War.* See the *Globe-Democrat*, 14 September 1941, and 15 September 1942, for information on the raid at the Downs Amusement Park. Newspapers are an excellent source for uncovering community attitudes about youth and popular culture in the war years. See also David March, *History of Missouri,* vol. 2 (Missouri, 1967), and Gross, "Missouri and War"; Dorothy Dysart Flynn, "Missouri at War," *MHR* 38, no. 1 (October 1943), briefly mentions the rise in juvenile delinquency in St. Louis, an area where more research is needed. The YWCA Collection, WHMC–UMSL, provides information on USO and recreational activities provided for military personnel and defense workers. For the story of two St. Louis overseas volunteers with the Red Cross, see Anne R. Kenney, "She Got to Berlin: Virginia Irwin, *St. Louis Post-Dispatch* War Correspondent," *MHR* 79, no. 4 (July 1985): 456–79. See also Oscar Whitelaw Rexford, *Battlestars and Doughnuts: World War II Clubmobile Experiences of Mary Metcalf Rexford* (St. Louis: Patrice Press, 1989), and Mary Metcalfe Rexford Collection, WHMC–UMSL. Two useful studies of American women during the war are Karen Anderson, *Wartime Women: Sex Roles, Family Relations, and the Status of Women During World War II* (Westport, Conn.: Greenwood Press, 1981), and Hartmann, *The Home Front and Beyond.*

"Rosie the Riveter" at the Small Arms Plant

A visitor to the shop floors of the U.S. Cartridge Small Arms Plant in 1943 may have been jarred at the sight of so many women wearing pants and filling bullets with gunpowder. Most jobs in defense work were unlike traditional female occupations in St. Louis's schools, food processing plants, and garment industries. When the United States entered the war after Pearl Harbor, defense contractors turned to black men and white women to replace white men leaving for armed services. While the entrance of women into defense jobs was controversial, many St. Louisans felt that the exigencies of war justified a break with tradition.

During World War II, St. Louis was home to "the woman behind the man behind the gun"– literally. Women at the Small Arms Plant in St. Louis had helped manufacture more than two billion rounds of ammunition by mid-1943. One third of new wartime jobs for women in St. Louis were at Small Arms, where nearly half of the plant's forty-two thousand employees were women by mid-1943.

The Small Arms Plant, on 291 acres at Goodfellow and Bircher in the Wellston suburb northwest of the city, was near several other war materials plants and a host of new residences and entertainment venues serving defense workers. Throughout the war, women manufactured bullets, fuses, and other types of ammunition. After the war, however, most women lost their defense jobs and could only find work in female-dominated manufacturing fields and other low-paying, traditionally female positions: teaching, clerical and sales work, and domestic service.

Prewar St. Louis had a relatively high proportion of working women, so the wartime rise in women's employment was less noticeable, and less controversial, than in other cities. But it did raise some eyebrows, and some protest. Because they lay outside the traditionally female-dominated service and helping professions, most St. Louisans saw defense jobs as characteristically masculine. They were dirty and dangerous, involved heavy machinery, and required wearing pants–still considered too revealing for women in the 1940s. Third-shift jobs were often most convenient for working mothers who wanted to be home after school or shop for groceries during the day. Yet, many feared for the safety, and morality, of women going to work at midnight. While the sight of women performing heavy industrial tasks defied what many believed to be properly feminine work, many others felt that the desperate need for war materials justified dramatic action.

Federal employment agencies responded to the controversy by assuring the public that women could do many defense jobs without losing their femininity or endangering their virtue, even if they had to wear pants and tie back their hair. The agencies pointed out that women in defense work supported the men–husbands, fathers, and brothers–on the battlefield, portraying the jobs as extensions of their family responsibilities and expressions of their patriotism.

A government pamphlet distributed to defense employers around the nation by the Personnel Division of the Secretary of State assured them that

"women are pliant–adaptable. Women are dexterous–finger-nimble. Women are accurate–precision workers. Women are good at repetitive tasks." The federal government thus advised employers to hire women for semi-skilled jobs involving "light" repetitive processes. However, semi-skilled jobs paid less than skilled ones, and by labeling jobs as "men's" or "women's," some employers took advantage of gender perceptions to reduce or maintain low wages for certain positions.

The personnel division also expressed the widely held sentiment that women should hold these jobs for the duration of the war only: "Women can be trained to do almost any job you've got, but remember 'a woman is not a man.' A woman is a substitute–like plastic instead of a metal." Cultural attitudes reinforced by expert advice limited women's opportunities in defense plants during the war and all but assured they would be fired afterwards.

While women worked at several defense plants in St. Louis, including Curtiss-Wright Airplane Corporation and the Amertorp Torpedo Factory, the largest number worked at Small Arms. This was no coincidence. The work they performed at Small Arms was generally light, very repetitive, and relatively safe and clean, not so different from food processing, sewing, or tobacco manufacturing. Thousands of women inspected munitions for safety and quality-control, filled bullets with gunpowder, and cleaned bullet sleeves at various stages of production. Men usually operated the heavy machinery and tested the ammunition at the plant's firing range.

These concepts of "natural" gender characteristics directly limited women's economic opportunities. The additional burden of racism kept black women from faring as well in the wartime expansion of high-paying factory jobs. As with most other companies, Small Arms, when they hired African Americans at all, hired black men first. Many defense contractors cited a lack of separate toilet and locker-room facilities as reasons for not hiring black women. Others feared that racial conflicts on the shop floor would hurt production levels.

Backed by the Fair Employment Practices Commission and Roosevelt's executive order barring racial discrimination in war hiring practices, in 1942 the local chapter of the March on Washington Movement held protest marches at Small Arms, demanding more and better jobs for African Americans. Demonstrators carried signs reading, "We Are Helping to Stop Hitler in Europe. We Demand That You Stop His Practices Here," and "We Fight for the Right to Work as Well as Die for Victory for the United States."

The march proved more successful for black men than for black women, but the following year Small Arms employed nearly six thousand African Americans, one thousand of them women who

Back of C.S. Assembly Line, 26 January 1943, Curtiss-Wright. Photograph by F. Dale Smith, 1943. MHS–PP worked as operators and inspectors. Yet, segregation tainted concrete gains. Until 1945, black employees worked in a separate building on the Small Arms grounds. If no jobs were open in that building, no black women were hired. The last hired, black women were also the first fired as defense production wound down.

Despite a no-strike pledge by national union leadership, wildcat strikes (work stoppages by rank-and-file members unauthorized by union leadership) were common during the war, at times surpassing the levels of union activism of the militant 1930s. Racism motivated some such strikes, as when thirty white women at Small Arms struck in May 1943. They protested the hiring of black men to handle materials and equipment in white-staffed areas of the plant. The women returned to work when Small Arms decided to fire the black men and not rehire them until it could arrange segregated facilities.

The United Electrical Workers circulated a pamphlet disputing the company's account of the strike and asserted that the company had hired black men because it could pay them lower wages than those demanded by white workers. The union claimed that they struck to protect high union wages and were not motivated by racial prejudice. Employers who wanted to reduce wages for jobs held by women also met resistance from unions. The unions wanted to maintain the high levels of pay for the men who would fill those jobs after the war.

As the war ended and defense plants began converting to peacetime production, thousands of employees of both sexes were laid off. While many women sought new jobs, they found it difficult to match the high wages and skill levels of defense work. Three times as many women as men collected unemployment benefits from the United States Employment Service one month after V-J Day. At the same time, 70 percent of job listings specified that only men need apply. After the war, most national unions did not support women who felt it was their right to keep jobs in defense plants. From the unions' point of view, women simply held jobs for veterans, many of whom were also union men.

War work indirectly benefited black women, as many left low-paying domestic work for sales and service positions vacated by white female defense workers. Black women kept many of these positions after the war.

While the women at Small Arms pushed gender boundaries by taking men's jobs during the war and earned more in defense jobs than in previous ones, such gains were temporary and did not truly change the gender structure of the work force. While women kept working after the war, the vast majority of jobs available to them were in traditionally female, and low-paying, occupations such as clerical and sales positions. In St. Louis, perhaps the most lasting effect of women's defense work was that it enabled some African American women to move from domestic work into better jobs.

–Katherine Douglass

Sources: Much of the information in this piece comes from the unpublished paper, "St. Louis Women in World War II," prepared by Katharine Corbett for the 1984 St. Louis Women Historians Conference. The quotations by the Personnel Division of the Secretary of State comes from Chester W. Gregory, *Women in Defense Work During World War II: An Analysis of the Labor Problem and Women's Rights* (New York: Exposition Press, 1974), 12. See also "The Life History of a Cartridge"; St. Louis Ordinance Plant, "Bullets by the Billions," MHS vertical file.

Information on a racially motivated strike at Small Arms from the *St. Louis Star Times*, 11 May 1943; the *Post-Dispatch*, 10 May 1943; and the *Globe-Democrat*, 11 May 1943. See also the *Chicago Defender*, 6 May 1944. Description of protest march on Small Arms in 1942 and contents of protesters' signs from *St. Louis American*, 25 June 1942. Information on activities of FEPC in St. Louis from *St. Louis Argus*, 3 August 1944, and "Summary Sent to FEPC by March on Washington Movement in 1944," WHMC–UMSL. Information on March on Washington Movement, racial conflict at defense factories, and union fights for increasing pay for "women's jobs" are from *St. Louis Labor History Tour* (1994). Numbers of women facing layoffs from the *Globe-Democrat*, 21 September 1945.

More information on union activity at Small Arms can be found in "Failure of Unions to Register for Defense Employment Aids Anti-Union Employers," *St. Louis Labor Tribune*, 14 January 1942; "Small Arms Organization Still Under Way Says Clark," *St. Louis Labor Tribune*, 22 April 1942; and "AFL Small Arms Organizing Committee Needs Full Assistance of the Entire Labor Movement," *St. Louis Labor Tribune*, 24 June 1942.

More information on how gender characteristics made women more appropriate for munitions manufacture can be found in "Over 13,000 Women Gainfully Employed in Nation at Present," *St. Louis Labor Tribune*, 27 July 1942, and "Close to 2,000,000 Women Are Now Workers in War Plants," *St. Louis Labor Tribune*, 28 October 1942.

Margaret Hickey

When Margaret Hickey opened the Miss Hickey's Training School for Secretaries in 1933, many businesses were failing and economic prospects looked grim. Nevertheless, the school located at Delmar and Skinker Boulevards attracted its first class, mostly Washington University graduates, who paid about fifty dollars a month to learn secretarial and accounting skills. Miss Hickey's School flourished and remained in her hands until she sold it to a national firm in 1969. The school was only the first in a series of ventures that brought Margaret Hickey positions of influence in volunteer organizations, government, and business, where she tirelessly promoted equal economic opportunity for women.

The second daughter of a foreign service officer, Margaret Hickey was born in Kansas City, Missouri, in 1902. She spent her childhood at her father's various diplomatic posts in Europe and the Ottoman Empire. The family moved back to Kansas City in 1914, where, after years of home schooling, Margaret went to a local high school. She later attended Vassar College, but after three years she returned to Kansas City and took a job as a typist-researcher for the *Kansas City Star*.

The job changed the course of her life. Hickey's research for courthouse reporters opened her eyes to the legal inequalities facing women. She also became a social reformer in the peace movement. Hickey's job and interests led her to join the local chapter of the National Federation of Business and Professional Women. Other members encouraged her to study law. In 1923 Hickey enrolled in the University of Kansas City Law School and supported herself by working part-time at the newspaper. She graduated in 1928, passed the Missouri bar, and opened her own practice in St. Louis just at the start of the Great Depression.

Hard times soon hit Hickey's practice. She decided to help herself and her potential clients by organizing a career counseling and re-training program at the YWCA. She ran the course from 1931 to 1933, when a New Deal government agency took it over. Hickey's success with business education led some businessmen to suggest that she start her own school. She borrowed money from her mother and immediately opened her own business school. Miss Hickey's Training School for Secretaries was so successful that Margaret Hickey gave up her law practice to become a full-time businesswoman. In 1934 she married Joseph T. Strubinger, a lawyer fourteen years her senior, but her public name remained Miss Margaret Hickey.

Hickey's reputation spread beyond St. Louis. She served on the advisory committee of the Social Security Board, lectured nationwide on employment issues, and addressed women's problems on a committee of the federal Office of Emergency

Planning, a New Deal agency. There, she met Frances Perkins, Roosevelt's Secretary of Labor who later recommended her for a wartime government position. She served as chair of the Women's Advisory Committee (WAC) of the War Manpower Commission (WMC) from 1942 to 1945.

As chair of the WAC, Hickey soon discovered she had little influence with the powerful male War Manpower Commission. The WAC studied the problems of women war workers and made recommendations to the WMC; however, Hickey complained that the WMC ignored the advisory committee's proposals. Later invited to serve on the Labor Management Committee (LMC), she discovered that she had no vote on it. She learned she was not even expected to sit with the men when they deliberated issues or made policy. Hickey protested, but the LMC still refused her a vote, claiming that no special representation was given to minority groups. This attitude was indicative of the position held by the main policy-making bodies who made wartime decisions that affected women.

Despite its problems, Margaret Hickey's position on the WAC brought her national recognition. She became president of the National

Margaret Hickey, President, National Council on Social Work.
WHMC–UMSL

Federation of Business and Professional Women in 1944 and served until 1946. Aware that government and industry had recruited women as a temporary wartime measure, she urged women workers when the war ended not to allow themselves to be forced out of their jobs or to give up their advances. Her appointment as public affairs editor of the *Ladies Home Journal* in 1946 gave Margaret Hickey a platform for her views on women's employment rights until the 1970s. In her monthly "Public Affairs Department," Hickey encouraged women to make politics their business. Voting and holding office were as important to a woman's family, she wrote, as cooking and cleaning. The *Ladies Home Journal*, while promoting domesticity, also reflected Hickey's views by featuring articles on women in business, politics, and the professions.

From the 1950s to the late 1970s, Hickey continued to press for equality in the workplace. She was in great demand as a consultant and lecturer, served on many boards and advisory committees, and was a deputy to the chairman of the American Red Cross. Hickey chaired the Federal Employment Policies and Practices Committee, served on President Kennedy's Commission on the Status of Women, and was appointed by President Lyndon Johnson to chair the Advisory Council on the Status of Women. In these positions she worked for passage of 1960s civil rights legislation and the removal of barriers to women's professional advancement.

Margaret Hickey died in 1994 at her home in Tucson, Arizona. Although she spent much of her time in Washington and in the Philadelphia office of the *Ladies Home Journal*, she had lived in University City until her husband's death in 1973. And despite her national career, she is best remembered by St. Louisans for Miss Hickey's, the secretarial school that prepared thousands of young women for jobs in St. Louis offices.

–Joan Cooper

Sources: There is no comprehensive study on Margaret Hickey that evaluates her work locally or nationally. The best source for information is the large collection of papers she deposited at WHMC–UMSL in 1974, the records of the Business and Professional Women's Club, and the records of the government agencies she worked with located in the National Archives, Washington, D.C. For background on efforts for women's rights, especially during World War II, see William H. Chafe, *The Paradox of Change: American Women in the 20th Century* (New York: Oxford University Press, 1991), and Hartmann, *The Home Front and Beyond*. For an analysis of Hickey's influence on the *Ladies Home Journal*, see Joanne Meyerowitz, "Beyond the Feminine Mystique: A Reassessment of Post-War Mass Culture, 1946–1958," *Journal of American History* 79, no. 4 (March 1993).

Child Care for Wartime Working Mothers

Edna Knop and Daisy Meyer dropped their sons Bobby and Harry David at the Irving School Center every morning on their way to their wartime jobs. Like a thousand other St. Louis children in 1944, the boys were enrolled in a federally funded day-care facility. Their mothers, who paid three dollars a week for six days of care, were in the small group of working mothers who could leave their children at a day-care center. Most found their own child-care solutions, just as women had before the war and would continue to do after it was over.

During the depression, the federal government and employers had discouraged married women, especially mothers of young children, from seeking work, but the demands of war and a serious labor shortage gradually changed this position. Patriotic fervor, media expectations, and the need for wages drew a significant number of mothers into the work force. Widespread female employment provoked both positive and negative reactions, but few issues were as potentially contentious as those involving the working mother. When a mother went out to work, she challenged deeply entrenched social assumptions that her only proper job was to be a housewife and mother. Consequently, until high job turnover and absenteeism in the female work force affected war production, employers and the government ignored the needs of working mothers. But once studies showed that lack of provisions for child care affected production, employers put pressure on federal authorities to fund day-care centers.

The government had supported some day nurseries during the depression through the Works Progress Administration (WPA). In 1943 the WPA was abolished and the Federal Works Agency took over the nurseries, expanding the program with funds granted by the Lanham Act, legislation enacted to help fund construction of wartime child-care centers.

From the beginning the wartime day-care program had problems. Traditional attitudes about women's proper place hampered federal, state, and local efforts. Even those who recognized the need for public day-care centers argued for them to be temporary emergency measures essential to the war effort, not measures to help working mothers. Bureaucratic delays and political infighting between federal agencies did little to facilitate rapid expansion of the centers. At the peak of the program, the centers cared for fewer than 10 percent of children who needed them. Working mothers, too, were ambivalent about public day care. Many did not want to entrust their children to strangers, others thought using public nurseries was accepting charity, still others could not afford even the small weekly fees. The majority of women made their own informal arrangements. For working mothers without family or community connections, however, public day care was essential.

St. Louis women had long recognized the need for day care. Middle-class women established the South Side Day Nursery in 1886 specifically to care for the children of poor working women. In 1927, eleven day nurseries served 520 St. Louis children. Apart from the nonsectarian South Side Day Nursery, four were run by Protestant Churches, four by Roman Catholic groups, one by the Neighborhood House Association, and one by the Urban League, which had a facility for sixteen black children. During the depression the WPA supplied some workers for existing centers and operated four additional centers for white children and two for African Americans.

In 1943 the first of the few new centers supported by Lanham Act funds opened in St. Louis, but the facilities were able to care for only a small number of eligible children. By late 1945, there were fifteen centers in the city and four in the county serving approximately one thousand children. Black children attended three centers. Including the existing sectarian and nonsectarian centers, there were probably about two thousand children of working mothers in day care during the war. Even with the increase in centers, demand exceeded supply, and all had long waiting lists. The South Side Day Nursery, which limited enrollment to fifty, had forty children on the waiting list. Long hours and the lure of more lucrative war work created staff shortages that also affected enrollment. Since there were two hundred thousand women in the work force at the peak of war production in late 1943, obviously most working mothers relied on informal child-care arrangements.

Prior to the war many of the agencies that ran day-care centers received funding from the Community Chest—an annual public campaign to

raise money for local charities and welfare organizations. They did not receive government funds. But when the Lanham Act went into effect in 1943, these child-care centers began receiving federal money along with the centers established as a wartime measure. The government provided about 44 percent of their funding, which made them less dependent on Community Chest support and parent fees. When the war ended, however, Lanham Act funds stopped, and the wartime facilities closed. Working mothers suddenly found they had only half as many places to leave their children, and they were more expensive.

The end of the war signaled a return to many prewar norms and practices. Employers expected women to give up their jobs and go back home. Those who wanted or needed to work were expected to return to lower paying women's jobs. Federal, state, and local authorities did little to assist working mothers, and organized day care remained dependent on charitable donations and parent fees. The Social Planning Council of St. Louis City and County made social attitudes about organized day care clear in a 1947 report. Their survey revealed that St. Louisans spent five times more on skin creams ($910,000) than they did on day-care services ($171,161). Although women's job opportunities expanded during World War II, the

Edna Knop and Daisy Meyer Walk Their Children to the Irving School Center Before Going to Their Jobs. Photograph by Jack Gould from the *St. Louis Post-Dispatch Pictures Magazine*, 18 June 1944.

conflict over publicly funded child care revealed that most Americans still believed that a mother's place was in the home and that day care was not a community priority.

–Joan Cooper

Sources: Two excellent books that discuss wartime child-care issues are Chafe, *The Paradox of Change,* and Hartmann, *The Home Front and Beyond.* See also Howard Dratch, "The Politics of Child Care in the 1940s," *Science and Society* 38, no. 1 (spring 1974). For information on St. Louis child-care facilities, see *South Side Day Nursery History, 1886–1986*, MHS. See also Health and Welfare Council Collection of Metropolitan St. Louis, 1911–1975, and the Family and Children's Services of Greater St. Louis Collection, WHMC–UMSL. See also the *Post-Dispatch,* 18 June 1944, and the *St. Louis Argus,* 9 July 1943, and 30 June 1944.

The Joy of Cooking

In 1930 Irma Rombauer, a fifty-four-year-old widow from a prosperous south St. Louis family, asked her daughter, Marion, to design a cover for the little book of recipes she was compiling. Marion drew a slender woman in medieval dress, encircled by a hungry dragon. The woman held the beast at bay with a mop held high above her haloed head, while a lady's purse dangled delicately on her other arm. The figure was St. Martha of Bethany, the author explained on the flyleaf of the privately printed cookbook, a mythical, versatile French woman famous for taming the dragon, Tarasque, and for lending "her benign influence to the wielders of pot and pans" as the patron saint of cooking.

Rombauer cheerfully declared versatility to be the hallmark of the modern woman. She hoped *The Joy of Cooking* would help busy, inexperienced housewives prepare meals as right for the 1930s as those their mothers had produced for turn-of-the-century guests. Irma, who had dipped her cooking spoon in both eras, was prepared to be their guide. If some modern women saw irony in the image of a joyful, embattled cook, they were quite willing to follow her into the kitchen. Beginning with this amateur edition, Irma Rombauer enlarged, revised, and promoted her little St. Louis cookbook until she reached millions of American women who tamed their own culinary dragons with practical instructions delivered in her witty, friendly style.

In 1930 a middle-class St. Louis housewife confronted a kitchen different from her mother's.

Not only was the space likely to be smaller and much of the cooking equipment new, but also the work itself required different skills. The kerosene lamp and the coal-fueled cookstove were only memories for many St. Louis households, but most modern technology arrived slowly and piecemeal. This was particularly true in the kitchen. Prewar kitchens in middle-class homes were large, busy spaces. Usually several people toiled together making three elaborate meals a day from "scratch," relying on traditional techniques learned at the side of experienced older women. The coal stove glowed with heat; the cook kept perishable foods in the icebox, as far from the beast as possible.

Traditional housekeeping changed profoundly in a single generation. Because the mechanical refrigerator, or even the well-insulated icebox, could stand next to an insulated gas stove, architects reduced the size of the kitchen. The young housewife usually prepared meals alone, without the assistance of an experienced cook or helpful daughters, now busy with their own after-school activities. Canned soups, all-purpose flours, and other mass-marketed convenience foods filled the cabinets of her more efficient kitchen. She kept an electric mixer and a waffle iron on the counter. Her produce bin held out-of-season and exotic vegetables. A modern woman, she loved to delight her family and friends with attractive, interesting new dishes, but she preferred they not take too much time or expertise to prepare. For special occasions, however, she wanted to know how to fix a rich traditional dessert like her mother used to serve. Her cookbook needed to be as up-to-date as her busy life.

Irma von Starkloff Rombauer was an unlikely cookbook author, let alone one whose handbook would become a kitchen bible for generations. Her German parents, Max von Starkloff, a successful physician, and his wife Clara Kulman, a kindergarten teacher trained by Susan Blow, had immigrated to St. Louis before the Civil War. The Starkloffs' social circle of prospering German families enveloped their two daughters. Irma, born in 1877, spoke little English before age five. Bewildered by "American" neighbors, as she characterized the families who lived near her Carondelet home, she was ten when her parents moved to a large home in a German neighborhood on Chouteau Avenue. Surrounded by family and friends, they enjoyed music, talking liberal politics, storytelling, and good German food prepared by servants. Although she attended public schools in St. Louis until she was twelve, Irma spent the next five years in Swiss boarding schools while her father served as United States consul to Bremen, Germany. After the family returned to St. Louis in 1894, she enrolled briefly at the Washington University School of Fine Arts. A charming, socially accomplished, upper middle-class young woman, she lived in the family's fashionable new home in Compton Heights.

In 1899 Irma married Edgar Rombauer, a young liberal lawyer from an equally prominent St. Louis German family. An avid camper, Edgar was the more experienced cook, but Irma quickly learned enough to be a successful hostess, while putting most of her energy into the women's alliance of the Unitarian Church and other literary and musical women's clubs. In 1903 she had a daughter, Marion, and in 1907 a son, Edgar. Irma joined The Wednesday Club in 1911, throwing herself into its many varied study groups and civic projects. Like other women of her generation who regretted not having attended college, Irma educated herself through her club work. She also found an outlet in The Wednesday Club for her growing competitiveness and ambition, working her way through the ranks to the presidency. The lifelong friendships Irma made in the club sustained her through every crisis until her death in St. Louis in 1962.

In February 1930 Edgar Rombauer killed himself. Although he had a successful law practice and served as president of the Urban League and briefly in city government, he had suffered periods of depression throughout his married life. Irma, whose children were grown and educated, was not left destitute, despite the faltering economy. She moved with Marion to an apartment at 5712 Cabanne Avenue in the West End and began looking for something interesting and creative to do that would bring in some income.

Irma's decision to publish a cookbook may have seemed foolish to friends who appreciated her creative energy and ability to "whip something up" but doubted her actual prowess in the kitchen. With the exception of the German baking learned as a child, she had always assigned most of the actual cooking to servants. But it was just this combination of experience and talent that enabled Irma Rombauer to reach a younger generation of housewives. Because she considered meal preparation only one aspect of a woman's busy life, she did not make her young readers feel guilty for abandoning their mothers' traditions for short cuts and convenience foods. At the same time, she recognized that they needed clear, written instructions for the basic procedures they had not learned through culinary apprenticeship. In 1931 Irma paid a Clayton printing company three thousand dollars to produce the first edition of *The Joy of Cooking,* an informal selection of recipes solicited from women in her family, church, and clubs, compiled with the assistance of Marion and Mazie Whyte, Edgar's former secretary.

Irma personally marketed the three-dollar cookbook to bookstores and by direct mail, but she was not content with local exposure and immediately started seeking a commercial publisher. Her lifelong relationship with Bobbs-Merrill, the firm that published all subsequent editions of *The Joy of Cooking,* was stormy and exploitive, but the partnership produced the most successful cookbook in American publishing. The 1936 Bobbs-Merrill edition established a distinctive recipe format that Irma insisted women would appreciate: a step-by-step method of preparation that introduced each ingredient as it was needed. Not only did this make cooking less intimidating, but it also added to the personal tone that distinguished her book from other more institutional competitors like *The Settlement Cookbook* and Fannie Farmer's *Boston Cooking-School Cookbook*. With each new edition, Irma, with Marion's assistance, reconceptualized and revised the book so that it continued to stay in tune with new trends in cooking and changing middle-class priorities. Irma's emphasis on mass-marketed foods like Jell-O and canned soups coincided with the American shift away from ethnic cooking to a more standard cuisine. At the same time, she responded to the growing popularity of ersatz Chinese and Mexican dishes. When Marion Rombauer Becker began revising the book without her mother, *The Joy of Cooking* reflected the daughter's greater interest in nutrition and enthusiasm for health foods.

Irma sold the three thousand copies of the original 1931 edition. Bobbs-Merrill sold 52,151 copies of their first edition published in 1936. Irma's revised 1943 edition of *The Joy of Cooking* enjoyed huge sales in the immediate postwar years. Marion took a larger role in revising the 1951 edition, which sold 732,114 copies before 1958. Marion prepared the hugely successful 1963 edition at her home in Cincinnati while her mother lay dying in St. Louis. Sales increased yearly until preparations began for the 1974 edition. By 1996, sales of the 1974 hardback and paper editions had reached 8.3 million. Irma Rombauer made a costly mistake when she gave Bobbs-Merrill the copyright to the 1931 edition, but the Rombauer family prospered

Co., 1951). See also entry for Irma Rombauer by James Beard in *NAW*.

For the impact of technology and advertising on American housekeeping, see Strasser, *Satisfaction Guaranteed*; Strasser, *Never Done*; and Ruth Cowan *More Work for Mother: The Ironies of Household Technology from Open Hearth to the Microwave* (New York: Basic Books, 1983); and Jessica H. Fox and Thomas J. Schlereth, *American Homelife, 1880–1930: A Social History of Spaces and Services* (Knoxville: University of Tennessee Press, 1992). For history of American foodways, see Laura Shapiro, *Perfection Salad: Women and Cooking at the Turn of the Century* (New York: Farrar, Straus and Giroux, 1986); Waverley Root and Richard de Rochemont, *Eating in America: A History* (New York: Ecco Press, 1981); and Kathryn Grover, ed., *Dining in America, 1860–1900* (Amherst: University of Massachussetts Press, 1987).

from the steady sales of the publishing company's best-selling title.

If *The Joy of Cooking* became known as the cookbook for women who didn't know much about cooking and didn't care to know more than was necessary to set a good table, then it reflected not only the views of its author, but also millions of other American women. With the cooking "beast" under control at home, they could pick up their purses and follow other perhaps more satisfying pursuits.

Sources: Much of the information for this essay was drawn from Anne Mendelson, *Stand Facing the Stove: The Story of the Women Who Gave America* The Joy of Cooking (New York: Henry Holt & Co., 1996). Mendelson not only relates the history of Irma and Marion Rombauer's cookbook, placing it within the context of changes in American cooking culture, but also analyzes their relationship to each other and to their publisher. Information on Rombauer's activities in The Wednesday Club can be found at the club archives. Additional information on St. Martha can be found in Omer Englebert, *The Lives of Saints*, trans., Christopher and Anne Fremantle (New York: D. McKay

Dust Cover of the First Edition of The Joy of Cooking, *by Irma Rombauer, 1931.* Photograph by Allied Photocolor, 1999. MHS Library

Sara Teasdale

Literary critics praised Sara Teasdale for the purity of her emotion, calling her "a true lyric poet, master of a fresh and unforced melody." But as she matured as an artist and her work grew stronger, she became less able to cope with life. When she committed suicide in 1933, the *Post-Dispatch* praised her poetry, particularly her "beautiful verses about marriage," but attributed her death to the failure of her fifteen-year union to a St. Louis businessman. Declaring that "women poets should not marry if they desire to remain poets," the newspaper posthumously chastised Teasdale for trying to be both wife and poet and for choosing poetry and death over marriage and life. Sara Teasdale struggled for years to be both a creative free spirit of the 1920s and a conventional married woman.

Born in 1884, Sara Teasdale was the youngest child of John W. Teasdale, a successful St. Louis wholesale grocer, and his wife Mary E. Willard. Sara was a shy and dreamy child, who, as she grew older, retreated into a private world of classical literature and romantic poetry. By the time she graduated from Hosmer Hall High School in 1903, Sara had impressed her friends and teachers with her talent for writing lyric verse.

Sara Teasdale joined a supportive group of young women, who, like herself, pledged to devote their lives to art and individual creative expression. Known as the Potters, the eight recent high school graduates produced a single copy of a magazine, *The Potter's Wheel*, each month from 1903 to 1907. They considered themselves to be serious artists and encouraged each other professionally and emotionally. William Marion Reedy, impressed by Sara's contributions to *The Potter's Wheel*, began publishing her work in his St. Louis literary weekly, *Reedy's Mirror.*

Always reclusive and in poor health, Sara Teasdale had much in common with nineteenth-century poets like Emily Dickenson, Christina Rossetti, and Emily Bronte who never married. Sara might have worked in the seclusion of her indulgent parents' comfortable West End home at 3668 Lindell Boulevard or their later residence at 38 Kingbury Place, but she chose instead to leave St. Louis to pursue her writing career. She did not attend college. In 1905 she toured Europe and the Holy Land with her mother and in 1911 made the first of many long annual visits to New York. There, she met men and women as committed to art and literature as she was. By age twenty-five, she had published many verses in national magazines and two books of poetry. However, she found herself torn between conflicting desires–seclusion in St. Louis and participation in the modern artists' culture centered in New York. From her parents' home she corresponded with other writers, including poet Vachel Lindsay who came to St. Louis in 1914 to court her.

That same year Sara Teasdale married Ernst Filsinger, a St. Louis manufacturer and expert in foreign trade. They moved to New York and began married life in the first of a series of hotel apartments. Ernst became vice president of the Royal Baking Powder Company. In 1917 Sara dedicated a volume of romantic verses, *Love Poems,* to her husband. It won a prize from the Poetry Society of America and included the following poem, "Wisdom."

> When I have ceased to break my wings
> Against the faultiness of things,
> And learn that compromises wait
> Behind each hardly opened gate,
> When I can look Life in the eyes,
> Grow calm and very coldly wise,
> Life will have given me the Truth
> And taken in exchange–my youth.

Ernst Filsinger was considered by others to be a devoted husband who respected his wife's need for privacy and release from domestic chores. But he traveled a great deal on business, and Sara did not accompany him. Although she was frequently ill, she continued to write prodigiously, publishing her own well-received work and editing other volumes of poetry. As the years passed, she

gradually found that simply being married restricted her freedom to be a person in her own right. Her work took on the tone evident in the last stanza of "The Solitary."

> Let them think I love them more than I do,
> Let them think I care, though I go alone,
> If it lifts their pride, what is it to me,
> Who am self-complete as a flower or a stone?

In 1929 Sara divorced Ernst Filsinger. She traveled abroad to do research for a biography of Christina Rossetti. But her growing unhappiness, created in part by the conflict between her St. Louis heritage, with its emphasis on convention and marriage, and her artistic desire to be free to create and suffer on her own terms, proved too much for Sara Teasdale to bear. On January 28, 1933, she took her own life. She requested that her body be cremated and her ashes scattered in the sea "that there remain neither trace or remembrance." Her family, however, interred them in St. Louis's Bellefontaine Cemetery.

Sources: Sara Teasdale's best-known work included *Flame and Shadow* (1920), *Dark of the Moon* (New York: The Macmillan Co., 1926), and the posthumous *Strange Victory* (1933). The many factors that contributed to Sara Teasdale's creative success and personal despair are discussed in Carol B. Schoen, *Sara Teasdale* (Boston: Twain Publishing, 1986) and William Drake, *Sara Teasdale, Woman and Poet* (New York: Harper & Row, 1979). For biographical information see John Hall Wheelock, "Sara Teasdale," *NAW.* The poem "Wisdom" is from William Drake, ed., *Mirror of the Heart: Poems of Sara Teasdale* (New York: The Macmillan Co., 1984). "The Solitary" poem is from *Dark of the Moon.* See the *Post-Dispatch,* January 29–February 5, 1933 for local reaction to her suicide.

*Aerial View of St. Louis from East Side Showing the Cleared Riverfront
Site of the Jefferson National Expansion Memorial.* Newly constructed
interstates sped suburbanization and transformed the places where
women shopped, worked, attended school, and lived. But urban
renewal projects that facilitated the region's growth generally
bypassed poor St. Louisans who were left in substandard housing.
Photograph, 1948. MHS–PP

8

Women and Postwar St. Louis, 1945–1965

In 1951 the *St. Louis Labor Tribune* defined women's role in postwar America for readers of its "For Women Only" column. To aid the fight against communism by melding their private responsibilities to family with participation in their community, women should provide "morale, public opinion, civil defense, shopping, caring for children, running the schools, serving hot meals, cleaning and patching clothing, collecting and paying taxes, [and] taking up the garbage."

Ten years later, novelist Fannie Hurst returned to St. Louis to deliver the Founders' Day address at Washington University. Using the occasion to lecture her middle-class audience on the topic of postwar society and family life, Hurst railed against newspaper and magazine articles that emphasized

women's domestic role. "It is essential for the woman to get out of the home and find out what this world is about," Hurst urged, and she warned her audience that limited roles for women wasted their intellect and infected marital relations with discontent. Instead, Hurst encouraged women to keep up-to-date on current affairs through reading and television and to maintain their interest in the larger world of work and political affairs even after marriage. Familial "togetherness" is not enough, Hurst admonished, to satisfy women.

Family in Living Room of Suburban Home, 1961. Posed Shot for Parent's Magazine. Photograph by Mac Mizuki, 1961. Mizuki Collection, MHS–PP

Hurst's speech and the *Labor Tribune*'s column show St. Louisans' efforts to define women's role in the period following World War II. As they struggled to reconcile customary definitions of femininity, familial demands, a gradual expansion in opportunities outside the home, and their own expectations, St. Louis women, like those across the nation, faced the competing forces of change and continuity in this era, perhaps more than at any time. The dawn of the atomic age, the beginning of the Cold War, and the consequent need for a sense of security and stability shaped ideologies about family and community life. At the same time, a vibrant consumer economy helped create the era's ideal—a well-equipped suburban home, its occupants and appliances carefully tended by a full-time homemaker.

Domesticity lay at the heart of the era's tension between tradition and transformation. Many women welcomed the stability of marriage and motherhood after the disruptions of economic depression and war. More Americans married at younger ages, raised more children, and divorced less frequently, sharply reversing a century of demographic trends. Large families bonded by "togetherness" could provide a defense against Cold War fears and the communist menace. But the role of the suburban housewife remained an ideal for some, an impossibility for others. As women strove to find happiness through home, family, and relationships, they inadvertently expanded society's expectations of their sex. The domestic ideal that placed women within the confines of their homes and at the center of their families was also used by women to expand their public presence throughout the city. Even as popular opinion and the practices of government and industry remanded Rosie the Riveter to the household after the war's end, the economic demands of her family propelled ever more women like her back into the work force. While not directly challenging sex roles, women used their greater numbers and their education to expand their employment opportunities, to improve their working conditions, and to increase their political voice as voters, activists, and elected officials. Some women directly confronted barriers that limited their opportunities. African American women pursued court cases and civil rights legislation to desegregate schools, workplaces, neighborhoods, and public accommodations. Teenagers and lesbians gained new visibility in public life and constructed new models of womanhood. As consumers, workers, family members, and political actors, women contributed to a social and economic transformation that shaped the modern city.

The era's most visible changes placed women within the confines of suburban homes in the clusters of ranch houses that went up in the Mandalay subdivision in Manchester, and in Florissant's Lang-Royce neighborhood and Paddock Hills subdivision. The dream of suburban life motivated families of all races, and some black families relocated to the older northern suburbs of Pagedale, Wellston, and Pine Lawn. In the new suburban developments that encircled the city, home builders created and captured an interest in larger and improved living spaces to accommodate bigger families. Three- and four-bedroom homes outfitted with multiple bathrooms, a family room for television viewing, a backyard for barbecues, and a driveway and two-car garage replaced the standard two-bedroom home or multifamily dwelling of the prewar era. Bowing to Cold War fears, some new homes even included backyard or basement bomb shelters.

Suburban developments largely owed their existence to federal programs that encouraged home ownership, housing construction, and the expansion of the metropolitan area's infrastructure. Before the war, the Home Owners' Loan Corporation helped citizens refinance their home mortgages. The Federal Housing Administration and the Veterans Administration stimulated home sales after the war by offering low-interest loans. The best-known program, the 1946 Servicemen's Readjustment Act, also called the G.I. Bill of Rights, extended low-interest mortgages to veterans and their families, putting private home ownership within reach of thousands. St. Louis mirrored a national rise in home ownership: in 1940, approximately 40 percent of families owned their homes, but by the 1960s, this rate had increased to 60 percent. Easy access to credit, along with postwar prosperity and the expanding size of families, helped fuel a boom in residential construction. Builders constructed an estimated one hundred thousand new private dwellings in the metropolitan area between 1945 and 1957, housing more than sixty thousand families. Developers pitched the new suburban enclaves to families by promoting an image of wholesome domestic life within the confines of welcoming, homogeneous communities.

Although most new residential construction took place outside the city borders, women who resided in the city nonetheless felt its effects. Regardless of their race or religion, virtually all but the wealthiest city residents experienced a decline in the quality of life in St. Louis's urban neighborhoods as the balance of economic power shifted with the upwardly mobile population to surrounding suburbs. Urban renewal projects moved people out of declining neighborhoods, and the construction of highways reconfigured the physical contours of St. Louis. Although intended to reverse the trend of residential and commercial movement to the suburbs, the new highways encouraged retail businesses and manufacturers to relocate outside the city lines. Suburbanization in the St. Louis area dated back to the nineteenth century, but it accelerated with the mass production of automobiles and federal spending on highways. As newly developed subdivisions located away from public transportation and growing numbers of city workers lived in the suburbs, the demand for a more extensive highway system increased. Road construction prioritized private travel over public transportation, encouraging automobile use and precipitating the eventual demise of the streetcar in 1966. Existing roads, incapable of accommodating the increased traffic, gave way to interstates that also served the interests of civil defense planners who sought escape routes in case of atomic attack. Two of the first three contracts awarded under the Federal Highway Act came to St. Louis, Interstate 70 being one of the first sections of the new national highway system. Eventually, $250 million in federal funds was spent on St. Louis interstates.

For city residents the new highways created inconveniences and disruptions that primarily benefitted suburbanites and helped depopulate their neighborhoods. Interstates, access ramps, and large-scale construction projects also damaged women's businesses and institutions. Madame Touhy's, a lesbian bar, was demolished for the construction of Busch Stadium. In 1951, highway construction forced the South Side Day Nursery to vacate its building at 1621 South Tenth Street, its home for sixty-six years. Lacking sufficient funds to relocate, the center placed its children in other nurseries. Women's charitable organizations came to the rescue, donating funds to open a new facility in 1954 at Iowa Avenue and Crittenden Street.

The whirlwind of residential building did not completely overlook the city, however. Modern high-rise accommodations, such as the Plaza Square complex located near Union Station, offered apartment housing for middle-class city residents. For others, low-income housing projects provided relief from the dilapidated residences that predominated in many areas of the city. According to the 1950 U.S. Census, St. Louis contained the worst slum housing of the ten largest cities in the country. Albeit most homes now were equipped with electricity, central heating, and a refrigerator,

one in four still lacked hot running water, private flush toilets, and private baths or showers. These conditions jeopardized the health of residents and challenged women to keep their homes clean and safe. The city's poorest neighborhoods suffered the highest rates of infant mortality, and working mothers who resided here relied on child care more than women in other parts of the city.

Black residents especially suffered from the effects of old, dilapidated housing in crowded urban neighborhoods. In the areas with the worst housing conditions, nearly 60 percent of the occupants were African American. Mill Creek Valley exemplified these problems. A 465-acre area that stretched from Twentieth Street west to Grand Boulevard, and from Olive Street south to the railroad tracks, Mill Creek Valley was home to many of the city's African American migrants. By 1954, 95 percent of the area's twenty thousand residents were African American. City planners responded to derelict housing with slum clearance. Under the rubric of urban renewal, the city made a massive effort to redevelop areas within the city. But this strategy actually displaced residents as already limited housing was torn down to make room for new highways and business districts. In 1959, with the approval of city voters, the demolition of Mill Creek Valley began, and the loss of homes and neighborhoods forced thousands of black St. Louisans to relocate. Similar development projects upset other city neighborhoods and set residents in motion to find new homes.

Clinton-Peabody Terrace Public Housing. Constructed in 1942, this low-rise housing project for white families provided new housing units for poor St. Louisans. Photograph by CDA Collection, 1954. MHS–PP

The *Shelley v. Kraemer* decision ended the legal practice, if not always the custom, of restricting black home ownership in particular areas, and it contributed to major social geographic transformations, especially in north St. Louis. Still, St. Louis newspapers advertised real estate under separate headings for "colored" into the 1950s, and banks denied mortgages to many potential homeowners. Restrictive covenants and racist lending practices also limited the movement of single women, the poor, and Jewish families into some new suburban homes and older urban neighborhoods. Nonetheless, the *Shelley* ruling cleared the way for other African American families to move onto blocks that were previously off-limits to them. The Penrose neighborhood, constructed in the 1920s near Kingshighway and Natural Bridge Road, underwent a transition in the early 1960s when middle-class African American families, mostly professionals, relocated there. Simultaneously, out-of-state migration, especially from the South, increased St. Louis's black population. Population shifts often sparked fear among white residents for their safety and the general condition of the area, thus precipitating further out-migration of these older inhabitants and contributing to an increased proportion of black city residents. Between 1950 and 1960, the city gained 61,000 nonwhite residents (virtually all African American) and lost 168,000 white residents. In the area west of Kingshighway, the African American population increased by fifty times, from 1,150 in 1950 to 57,300 people in 1960, and the white population in that area decreased by seventy percent, falling from 81,500 to 24,400 residents.

Geographically confined to some of the most derelict areas in the city, many African Americans struggled economically, as the scarcity of housing and increased demand inflated prices of residences and rents. In addition, they had to endure insults to their dignity and dangers to their health, safety, and well-being. In this context, the new public housing complexes offered improved living conditions for families. In 1954, Mrs. Etta McCowan, along with her children and grandchildren, moved to the newly built Pruitt Apartments, located at the intersection of Jefferson and Cass Avenues. The low rent for her subsidized four-bedroom apartment freed four of McCowan's children to pursue higher education rather than take unskilled jobs. McCowan's granddaughters participated in the many recreational activities available in the housing project, including Girl Scouts and a junior choir. Along with housework and child care, McCowan kept busy as both her building's elected officer in the Pruitt

Established city neighborhoods offered one possible solution for people displaced by urban renewal, but St. Louis real estate agents and property owners had maintained restrictive covenants since the 1910s, a practice established to prevent white homeowners in specific neighborhoods from selling their property to nonwhite buyers. And for nearly as long, black families had sought to eliminate the practices that restricted their mobility. In 1939, Ethel and J. D. Shelley and their six children attempted to move into a home at 4600 Labadie Avenue. Citing the restrictive covenant agreement among white property owners in the neighborhood, Louis W. and Ethel Lee Kraemer, who lived at 4532 Labadie, sued on behalf of the Marcus Avenue Improvement Association to prevent the Shelleys' occupancy. Driven by the necessity to pursue their rights, the Shelleys challenged the discriminatory laws in the courts with legal representation from the National Association for the Advancement of Colored People (NAACP) and the Real Estate Brokers' Association. With the assistance of local attorney Margaret Bush Wilson, they took their case to the U.S. Supreme Court, where Thurgood Marshall argued it. In 1948, the Court issued the *Shelley v. Kraemer* decision, ruling that racial restrictive covenants were unenforceable.

Children Play as Others Look on from Benches, Pruitt-Igoe, 1956. The city's neglect combined with a lack of recreation, commerce, and public transportation to deteriorate this massive complex. Mizuki Collection, MHS–PP

Tenant Council and treasurer of the Pruitt Credit Union. These activities gave McCowan a way to join with her neighbors to address community issues.

As the largest of the new public housing complexes, Pruitt-Igoe became the new home of many of the city's displaced residents. Other housing projects included Cochran Gardens, which opened downtown in 1953; Vaughn in 1957 in the central corridor; and Darst-Webbe on the near south side in 1957. Like suburban subdivisions, the new public housing attracted residents by promoting an image of homogeneous community life and convenient, affordable living. But unlike private subdivisions, which used informal practices to maintain homogeneity, the public housing projects adhered to racial quotas. The Pruitt-Igoe project originally consisted of two separate complexes. The Pruitt Apartments, completed in 1954, comprised twenty eleven-story buildings initially intended for black residents. The Igoe Apartments, a complex of thirteen eleven-story buildings for white tenants, was completed one year later. In its drive to dismantle legal segregation and erase economic barriers that confined black St. Louisans, the St. Louis NAACP's housing division sued the housing authority, ending segregation in low-rent public housing. Frankie Freeman, the NAACP lawyer who argued this case, considered it her most significant civil rights victory. After the December 1954 decision, some complexes, such as the Darst-Webbe housing project in south St. Louis, included both black and white tenants. However, most of Pruitt-Igoe's 11,500 residents, like the McCowans, were black.

The income guidelines were set low so that public housing units held mostly families headed by women, many of them recipients of Aid to Dependent Children (ADC) or Social Security. For these residents, the public housing complexes initially provided facilities that compared favorably to their old dwellings. The apartments were new, and the buildings included amenities like elevators, laundry facilities, and limited tenant governance. Thus, although they did not fulfill the dream of private home ownership, public housing represented an improvement for residents. Like suburbanites, residents created a neighborly and cooperative environment. Garden plots and window boxes, shared responsibility for watching children, recreational and social organizations formed by residents, and tenant management helped improve daily life.

Over time, poorly conceived architecture and neglect by the city led the massive Pruitt-Igoe complex to deteriorate. External factors, such as the lack of recreation, commerce, or public transportation in the area, deprived residents of many conveniences. The preponderance of poor black women and children no doubt made it easy for housing authorities to disregard residents' complaints about poor maintenance in buildings where water, electricity, and elevators frequently malfunctioned and where they worried about their children's safety. St. Louis women's organizations attempted to ameliorate conditions for families who lived in the complexes according to their own views of residents' concerns and needs. In the mid-1950s, Planned Parenthood volunteers held afternoon "tea parties" in private apartments in the complex to inform women about their services. While Planned Parenthood worked to support women who sought to limit the size of their families, other organizations focused on child and family issues. Social workers who belonged to the Gamma Omega Chapter of Alpha Kappa Alpha (AKA), a black women's sorority, initiated the Youth Life Project. In collaboration with the St. Louis Welfare Office, sorority sisters worked with ADC recipient families over a period of several years to offer advice and assistance ranging from diet and health care to information about recreation facilities and planning field trips for children. Girl Scouts and Boy Scouts provided recreation for Pruitt-Igoe children.

Yet Pruitt-Igoe residents perceived their problems differently and accordingly took a different tack to address their problems. The tenant council, on which Etta McCowan served, included elected representatives from each separate building who joined to address day-to-day problems and to improve conditions at the complex. In the late 1960s, when orderly procedures failed to yield drastic improvements, the tenant council at Pruitt-Igoe and other complexes called for rent strikes organized by residents to protest the poor maintenance of low-income housing facilities. These strikes would galvanize thousands of St. Louis public housing residents to use their collective economic power to press for improved conditions and a voice in governance in their communities.

As the region's geography transformed with the razing of established neighborhoods and new construction, women traveled new routes to work and new directions to furnish their homes, stock their cupboards, and clothe their families. Even as workplaces and businesses slowly vanished from downtown areas, St. Louis developers and business people tried to entice city shoppers with new suburban-style shopping centers. Hampton Village, the first such shopping center in the city, opened in

1946 at the intersection of Hampton and Chippewa. To women who did the family's shopping, it offered abundant parking and a large supermarket at the center. Hampton Village soon expanded to include a Walgreen's drug store, a J.C. Penney's department store, and smaller stores. In 1951, a Famous-Barr opened at the intersection of Kingshighway and Chippewa in the southern part of the city, employing approximately one thousand people.

Although these new construction projects brought convenient shopping into south side neighborhoods, retail stores, like homes and workplaces, shifted to the suburbs. Stix, Baer & Fuller launched a new branch store in the Westroads Mall in August 1955. That same month, another Famous-Barr store opened as the first unit in the Northland Shopping Center, featuring 150 departments, along with an exhibition hall that was available for public use. With a 41-acre, 5,099-car parking lot surrounded the 8-acre, fully air-conditioned store, Northland offered the convenience of one-stop shopping. River Roads, built in 1963, was the first local development to follow the national trend of enclosed malls. At the same time, in the core retail area downtown—bordered by Fourth, Thirteenth, Lucas, and Walnut Streets—virtually no new construction occurred after 1940. Other areas within the city lacked the space required for shopping malls that merged commercial and public space. Unable to compete, the old commercial districts shrank as businesses fled for new developments outside the city.

Hampton Village Shopping Center and Bettendorf's, 1949. Businesses tried to entice women to shop for their families in suburban-style shopping centers. Photograph by Dorrill Studios, 1949. Allied Photocolor Collection

Whether in the new suburban-style malls or remaining downtown businesses, shopping became a prominent activity for housewives and women of all ages. After more than a decade of depression and wartime deprivation, Americans sought domestic fulfillment through consumerism. As the targets of advertising campaigns that sought to sell everything from televisions, automobiles, and refrigerators to homes, postwar women marveled at the array of new appliances and features available for their homes. *St. Louis Argus* columnist Priscilla verbalized women's fantasies in 1945 when she dreamed about the "do-itself" house of the postwar world. Walls, drapes, rugs, and upholstery "impregnated with phosphorus" would obviate the need for lamps. Homes could be easily constructed and rearranged by use of "pre-fabricated sections to suit your family. The walls will be movable and easy to handle and easy to change." Thousands of visitors to annual displays organized by the Home Builders Association of Greater St. Louis viewed model homes furnished with automatic dishwashers, garbage disposals, blenders, baseboard heaters, additional closets, picture windows, and remote-controlled television sets. "The labor saving devices make our hearts beat faster," Priscilla remarked to her female readers.

By 1960, the U.S. Census defined the incomes of 60 percent of American families as "middle class." Greater financial resources stimulated consumer spending on goods that increasingly came to be considered "necessities." That year, 87 percent of American families owned a television, and 75 percent owned a car. Sales of household appliances and furniture had increased by 241 percent since 1945. Teenagers accounted for much consumer spending. By 1958, young women spent some $20 million annually on lipstick, $25 million on deodorant, and $9 million on home perms. Yet even with, or perhaps because of, increased access to consumer goods, women struggled to balance their changing roles as mother, wife, and public citizen. Labor-saving appliances did not ease the domestic burden of women; rather, new household technology simply replaced one set of tasks with another, creating "more work for mother." Larger families and larger incomes spurred middle-class families to move to bigger homes, increasing the amount of space to be cleaned, dusted, and vacuumed.

As in virtually every other area, the postwar domestic ideal affected women of different races and economic classes in distinct ways. As Priscilla's statements suggest, middle-class women's dreams of graceful and easy homemaking transcended race, but most African American and low-income women were denied the means to acquire a home full of consumer goods as they struggled to provide safe and suitable home environments for their families. Increasingly, women looked toward paid employment to ease their families' economic burdens and to bring consumer items within reach.

Some women found employment in industries that adapted to the demographic shifts of the postwar era. The era's increased marriage rates had been a boon for St. Louis, making the city a leading producer of wedding gowns, led by Bridal Originals, Inc., the largest plant in the country devoted to ready-to-wear bridal gowns. Bridal Originals was one of more than forty manufacturers in the city's thriving ready-to-wear clothing industry. Making lingerie, junior dresses, sportswear, and wedding gowns, manufacturers tried to stay ahead of the twin forces of competition and fashion trends. Fearing insufficient profits or obsolence, manufacturers and the International Ladies Garment Workers Union (ILGWU), which represented women workers, agreed to speed up production with assembly lines and stop watches. Such concessions undercut the economic position of women factory workers, but, nonetheless, kept them employed. Consumer demand, moreover, helped the company grow. When Bridal Originals opened in 1948 at 1871 Cass Avenue, it hired thirty people; by 1960, the factory, located on three floors of a building at Washington Avenue and Tenth Street, employed nearly four hundred women in the manufacture of ready-made gowns. Far removed from the excitement and glamour of weddings, women workers operated assembly line sewing machines, while a smaller number hand-sewed to finish the gowns. Thanks to their labor, Bridal Originals outfitted brides across the country; on a single day in February 1960, the company shipped out twenty thousand bridal gowns and attendants' dresses.

Bridal Originals and other St. Louis manufacturers sought to appeal to and shape the tastes of postwar shoppers. Paradoxically, the production of bridal gowns and other such goods required an expanded female work force, and the acquisition of such products increasingly required an expanded family income. At the same time, expanded production of bridal gowns also reflected society's demand that women cede to their appropriate role: wife. Thus, while advertisers and manufacturers emphasized women's role in the home, the consumer economy pushed and pulled more women into the work force. Older married women represented the largest increase in the labor force. Among working-class and low-income families, the need for women's

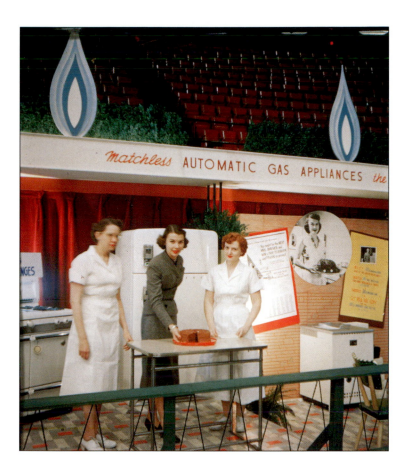

income remained as important as in previous eras. Women's ability to buy what they wanted varied according to the type of job they held and their family's income. Race and sex segregation continued to hinder women's employment and, consequently, the lifestyle of their families.

Industry, like domesticity, showed little change in women's roles before and after the Second World War. Participating in wartime industry, women proved their value as workers and established their ability to operate independently of men at home and in the workplace. But even before the war ended, St. Louis and the nation converted away from wartime production and integrated servicemen back into Rosie the Riveter's jobs. The expectation of postwar domesticity for women indicated the temporary nature of wartime changes. Wartime propaganda emphasized women's femininity even as it exhorted them to take nontraditional roles in industry. Although no one disputed their contributions during World War II, industry

Gas Appliance Display at Home Show. Advertisements and annual displays of domestic labor-saving devices awed postwar women. Color stereo slide by Eugene Taylor, 1954. MHS–PP

continued to view women as a reserve labor force, reliable in times of national emergencies but inappropriate when men could fill jobs in factories and as white-collar professionals. After the war's end, traditional ideas about sex roles actually hardened. Rosie the Riveter had stepped into traditionally male occupations to mitigate the labor shortage, but after 1945 she found herself searching for employment in "pink-collar women's jobs" and predominantly female areas of industry.

Within a month after the Japanese surrender, women faced an altered employment situation. In September 1945, the *Globe-Democrat* reported that women filed three times as many claims for unemployment compensation as men did. At the same time, the St. Louis branch of the U.S. Employment Service reported that only one-third of the industrial jobs available through the center were open to women. Moreover, employers who would hire women offered them lower pay than men. Although a typical female industrial worker during the war averaged seventy-five cents an hour for forty-eight hours of work, with time-and-a-half for overtime, women's wages had declined by September 1945 to forty-five cents an hour for a forty-hour week. In addition to the loss of jobs for some working women, government-sponsored child care ended with industrial reconversion. The Board of Education, which ran St. Louis's fifteen federally funded child-care centers, ordered facilities shut down once women were no longer needed for wartime production. Although the child-care centers never took in large numbers of children, they had provided a valuable resource for those women able to use their services.

African American women, last hired and first fired from jobs in industry, found themselves with little choice but to return to domestic work at the war's end. Yet the experience of public work changed African American women's expectations and self-images. Priscilla, the *St. Louis Argus* columnist, reminded her readers in 1945 that women forced back into domestic service after wartime industrial jobs would, and should, expect to be "treated as women engaged in industry [and] not as pseudo members of the family who are there to be imposed upon." Priscilla's warning applied to fewer women as the postwar era progressed: suburbanization, the emphasis on domesticity, and access to modern appliances decreased homemakers' reliance on household employees and led to a subsequent decline in jobs in this field.

Even as jobs diminished in some fields, the U.S. Census reveals that the percentage of St. Louis women who worked rose steadily between 1940 and 1960, from a low of 33.4 percent of women in 1940 to 35.6 percent in 1950 and approximately 40 percent in 1960. As in earlier decades, and despite continued racial discrimination that limited the types of jobs open to them, African American women participated in the paid labor force at slightly higher rates than white women. Their growing presence aside, women's employment options remained limited and their work continued to be viewed as supplemental, not essential, to the nation's economy, even if it was important to their own families' income. St. Louis industries' reliance on defense contracts during the Korean War reinforced this trend. Cartoons in the *Post-Dispatch* depicted a 1950s Rosie as girlish, feminine, and eager to return to wartime work. Most women clustered in clerical and office work, service work, and in jobs as factory operatives, producing clothing and canning food. Some of the largest local Department of Defense contracts went to corporations—McDonnell Aircraft, Monsanto, Emerson Electric—that were located outside the city limits and hired relatively few women. But as manufacturers of nondurable goods such as shoes, boots, and canned food received government contracts that figured in the millions of dollars in the late 1940s and early 1950s, women employees reaped some of the economic benefits of the country's defense efforts. In December 1950, for example, the federal government contracted with Pet Milk to produce 31,000 cases of evaporated milk and the International Shoe Company to manufacture 240,000 pairs of boots. Even when defense contracts raised employment levels in the city to an all-time high in the first months of 1951, sex-based job discrimination persisted. According to the head of the local office of the Division of Employment Security, the war created "an increasing demand for skilled male workers in many occupations, and there is a heavy demand for women in office and service jobs."

When the Korean War ended, the work force remained solidly sex-segregated, but observers despaired as more married women gradually found employment. In 1955, the *Post-Dispatch* warned that "Men are Losing Grip on the Labor Market" as about one-third of U.S. workers "now powder their noses on the job." Though many women worked to meet their family's basic needs, popular opinion nonetheless attributed women's interest in paid employment to a desire to acquire "bright new gadgets that modern couples now feel are necessary for a rich full life—a new car, television set, automatic dishwasher." Media and manufacturers emphasized working women's fashion and office relationships, ignoring the dilemmas of married women who struggled to balance their paid work with their domestic responsibilities and glossing over reality for the many women whose mundane work provided little in the way of romance or glamour. These beliefs about women's work reinforced workplace policies that promoted women's short-term employment at relatively low wages.

As women's presence in the work force increased in the postwar years, they challenged the barriers—both legal and customary—that limited their families' economic status or their own personal fulfillment. Older women prompted attention to retirement and pensions, issues taken up by the ILGWU and teachers' unions. Married women pressured companies to establish child-care facilities. Most prominently, African American women challenged racial discrimination that constrained their employment opportunities and family incomes. In 1950, Priscilla asked *St. Louis Argus* readers to boycott shops that failed to hire black workers. "Can we enjoy the American way of life if we are not able to earn a wage that affords a decent standard of living? Let us try hard to convince employers that we can work as well as fight."

Women such as Priscilla and Marian O'Fallon Oldham built on the successes of the Housewives' League during the depression and the NAACP and March on Washington movement during World War II to try to overturn racial barriers to employment. While Priscilla used the power of the pen to stir black shoppers, Oldham took to the streets to break down racial discrimination in hiring. For fifteen years, Marian regularly spent late afternoons on picket lines pressing businesses to open up restaurants and jobs to African Americans. As in desegregation efforts before and during the war, women like Oldham played a central role as participants in and leaders of grassroots movements for social change. By these actions, they influenced the goals and activities of organizations that successfully fought discrimination. As in earlier periods, too, African American women felt the effects of both race *and* sex oppression, even as they played central economic and political roles in their communities. In the process of pressing for societal transformation, African American women transformed their own lives as they developed political skills and self-confidence and prepared to gain formal political power.

Marian O'Fallon Oldham graduated from Stowe Teachers College and taught and counseled black students at Washington Elementary School. Professional women like O'Fallon gradually experienced expanded employment opportunities after the war, but racial discrimination created barriers to achievement and prosperity that women tackled head-on. As a high school student, O'Fallon had participated in civil rights activities. In 1948, she became a founding member of the local chapter of the Congress on Racial Equality (CORE). Three years later, Marian married Charles Oldham, a white lawyer and St. Louis CORE founding member. Avoiding Missouri's anti-miscegenation laws, the couple traveled to Michigan to marry.

CORE members formed interracial chapters where they challenged discrimination directly and uncompromisingly by use of nonviolent, direct-action techniques including boycotts, picket lines, and sit-ins. Women members of CORE, including Marion Oldham, were recognized as leaders in the mixed-sex chapter. Between 1948 and 1954, a small group of twenty-five CORE members gathered after work to protest prohibitions that kept African Americans from eating at the YMCA, YWCA, department stores, and drugstores. CORE members attempted to eat together in lunchrooms; when refused service, they tried to negotiate with management and, failing that, organized picket lines to persuade other patrons to boycott that business. Like the Housewives' League in the 1930s, CORE appealed to women shoppers to use economic pressure for political change. The group included teachers, lawyers, and university students. Already employed or headed for professional careers, most CORE members were more concerned with the treatment they received when they shopped than with increasing their own work options.

In 1953, after five years of effort, Oldham and members of St. Louis CORE had desegregated the two Sears outlets, the Greyhound terminal, and all but one of the downtown dimestores' restaurants. They turned next to employment discrimination. Targeting Woolworths, McCrory's, Krogers, and downtown banks, CORE urged businesses to hire black workers, especially in supervisory and sales positions. By December 1960, the group could boast that more than twenty African Americans had been hired in white-collar jobs in downtown businesses, including the Bank of St. Louis and a furniture store.

During the summer of 1963, St. Louis CORE reached new levels of visibility when it staged demonstrations at the Jefferson Bank. Based on a survey conducted the previous year, CORE determined that only six black workers held non-menial positions at all of the financial institutions downtown. Jefferson Bank, with a large proportion of black customers, refused to hire black tellers and thus became a main target of picketers. For seven months, CORE picketed in front of the bank; other

organizations, including the NAACP and AKA sorority, joined the demonstrations. Oldham's actions led to her arrest for violation of a restraining order taken out by the bank to keep CORE demonstrators from blocking customers' entry to the bank. She spent eleven days in jail, while hundreds of activists continued to block the bank's entrance. Once released from jail, Oldham returned to the sidewalk in front of the bank. The demonstrations finally ended in March 1964, when the bank agreed to hire five black clerical employees.

Through her CORE activities, Oldham participated in an expansion of opportunities available to black St. Louisans. At the same time, her own work environment changed, as schools were transformed by the era's baby boom, economic prosperity, and desegregation efforts. After World War II, high school education became the standard for most St. Louisans. Rising expectations along with a population explosion meant increased numbers of students, even as the number of available teachers declined and technology transformed education. At the same time, schools became an arena of political confrontation, and relatedly, sites for young people to develop their own styles and mores.

The system of racial segregation that prevailed in both public and private schools began to crack

CORE (Congress on Racial Equality) Demonstrators Demanding Equal Opportunity Employment in Front of Jefferson Bank, 16 January 1964. Photograph by Jack January, 1964. MHS–PP

during World War II. Julia Davis, a teacher at Simmons Elementary School from 1926 until she retired in 1961, participated in many educational transformations during her career. She began with small but bold steps to challenge legally mandated segregation: in 1943, Davis and her Simmons students joined with white students from Jackson School for a performance of patriotic songs. While Miss Hanks, the white teacher, played the piano and Miss Davis conducted, the interracial group of students sang "The Star Spangled Banner" and "America the Beautiful." Davis, who continued to teach at Simmons until her retirement, focused on integrating her curriculum, if not her classroom. She pioneered in teaching African American history and, in 1961, used her own savings to establish the Julia Davis Fund at the St. Louis Public Library for the purchase of books and materials by and about African Americans. In 1974, the St. Louis Public Library opened a branch on Natural Bridge Road, named in her honor, to house the materials she collected.

During the World War II era, as earlier in the century, few organizations called for an end to the system of segregated schools; rather, civil rights and teachers' groups urged that St. Louis ameliorate conditions in the black schools by improving school buildings, eliminating overcrowding, and equalizing black and white teachers' salaries. White residents, however, opposed even these small gains. In 1945, when the Board of Education proposed to convert the previously white Cote Brilliante school, it faced opposition from the Marcus Avenue Improvement Association. That association, which had previously participated in the *Shelley v. Kraemer* case, filed a suit to prevent the changes to the school on behalf of twenty-one hundred white families in north St. Louis. A Board of Education survey showed that a predominantly black population lived in the area surrounding the school, but the white petitioners asked that the school reopen for white children. The NAACP, the St. Louis March on Washington Committee, the Urban League, and a number of black churches urged that the school enroll black students. After public hearings to consider the issue, the Board of Education ruled in favor of the civil rights groups, and Cote Brilliante opened to black students in September 1945, despite the continued opposition of some white residents.

Two years later, the city's Catholic grade schools, high schools, and Saint Louis University desegregated, albeit with some opposition from north St. Louis residents. But persistent and strong leadership from the city's new Archbishop Joseph

Ritter, who threatened resisters with excommunication, pushed through the change. The public schools took longer to follow. In response to the Supreme Court's 1954 *Brown v. Board of Education of Topeka* decision, the school board instituted a three-part plan for gradual desegregation. Over the course of a year, the city schools desegregated, beginning with the colleges and special schools, followed by the general high schools, and finally ending with the technical and elementary schools.

Due to the high level of residential segregation throughout the city, the school board's plan to draw new school districts according to neighborhood lines failed to integrate students. Teacher assignments and clauses that let children elect to remain at their current schools, rather than attend the one closest to their home, also prevented a smooth or complete transition. Josephine Turner, a math teacher at the all-black Sumner High School, was transferred against her will to Central High School in 1956. As one of the few black teachers in previously all-white Central, Turner faced white colleagues "who wouldn't speak up until the day I left four years later." In the face of such hostility, Turner transferred to nearly all-black Soldan.

Black residents and civil rights advocates repeatedly urged the Board of Education to address the inadequacies of its integration plan, at times taking to the streets to demand attention. As in the case of segregated public facilities and employment discrimination, ending segregation in the schools required direct action. In June 1963, CORE, along with churches and civil rights organizations, demonstrated in front of the school board office to demand more complete integration, the assignment of teachers without regard to race, and newly drawn school boundaries. Although the protesters won the ear of the school board and support for their demands from a citizens' advisory committee, the problems of devising a truly integrated school system in a residentially segregated region remain a concern to this day.

Other alterations in teachers' work lives coincided with the end of racially separate school systems. After 1954, school boards hired more African American teachers and administrators. But as schools faced the challenge of educating larger numbers of pupils now in school until the twelfth grade, they needed more teachers. Married women made up one pool of potential workers, but they had been excluded from employment since 1897. In 1941, St. Louis teachers Mildred Holmes and Anita Weis contested the Missouri statute that forced women

teachers to resign upon marriage. Like the two thousand women employed by the St. Louis public schools, Holmes and Weis had trained at the white Harris Teachers College. After graduation, both women taught in south St. Louis schools for more than six years before marriage. Firing married women teachers wasted the money spent to train them and denied the importance of their classroom experience to the education they provided for young people. With the support of the League of Women Voters (LWV) and the local teachers' unions, Holmes and Weis pursued their case to the state supreme court before winning the right to reinstatement. The reform affected Stowe graduates, as well, and permitted Marian Oldham to combine her work in the city schools with her growing family and her civil rights activities.

At the same time that a high school education became the norm for St. Louis young people, popular culture and peers increasingly influenced their behavior and aspirations. Radio and television shaped and were shaped by the tastes of consumers, especially teenagers. Through advertising and programs, women performers and media stars stimulated consumer trends and defined women's role. For thirteen years in the 1940s and 1950s, Louise Munsch hosted *Just for Women* on WEW Radio. Munsch, born in St. Louis in 1915, taught speech and drama and offered the first courses in television and radio for academic credit in the area. She also became the first person in the St. Louis region to present a women's show on FM radio. *Just for Women* featured interviews with celebrities, human interest stories, and reports from local social service and cultural agencies as well as commentary by Munsch. The show provided a model for other radio programs: Gloria Pritchard's show *World of Women*, which broadcast from 1957 to 1965 on KATZ, focused on African American women's concerns and used biographical scripts of historical figures written by Julia Davis. After KSLH, the radio station sponsored by the St. Louis Board of Education, began broadcasts in 1950, women teachers created, produced, and starred in programs primarily intended for classroom use. Lucille Sutherland, principal of the Ashland School, wrote and produced *Your United Nations. Let's Find Out*, a series written and narrated by Gertrude B. Hoffsten, encouraged young students to conduct simple science experiments. A highly successful show, by 1957 this program broadcast on more than fifty stations nationwide.

Like radio, television provided a means for women to convey their ideas and talents to broader audiences. In 1947, KSD broadcast the first television program in St. Louis, and it continued as the city's only station until 1953. By 1955, more than half of American homes owned a television, and four television stations served St. Louis viewers, broadcasting network shows, current affairs programs, game shows, soap operas, and other daytime programs aimed at women. The locally produced *Charlotte Peters Show* offered a daytime variety program that aired at noon on KSD, Channel 5, beginning in 1956. The show mixed audience participation and appearances by St. Louisans and celebrity guests with her own song and dance performances. Peters built a female audience with her fast-paced show and her ability to depict herself as an ordinary housewife, not a star. Her family called her "Big Mom," and Peters described herself as a Webster Groves housewife who loved her family, food, and show business. By talking about her domestic role on her show, Peters became a commercial force whose product recommendations spurred consumer trends and attracted advertisers. St. Louis broadcasters, dubbing her the "Queen of Local Television," competed to hire Peters and to woo her audience. When Peters moved her show to KTVI, Channel 2, in 1964, she commanded an unheard-of salary of forty thousand dollars. The *Charlotte Peters Show* finally went off the air in 1970, one of the country's last locally produced daytime variety programs.

As the case of television demonstrates so well, at the same time that postwar domestic ideology ensnared many women within the bounds of home and family, women also experienced new degrees of liberation. In the 1950s and early 1960s, television viewing placed recreation within the private confines of homes, even as television performers like Peters became public figures. Other groups of women, especially teenagers and lesbians, gained new visibility, creating and enjoying public forms of recreation and constructing new definitions of femininity. Like middle-class housewives and working women, postwar consumerism and economic prosperity enhanced the visibility of and opportunities for unmarried and young women by creating jobs that provided money for recreational spending. Peers, popular culture, and the marketplace influenced teens' and lesbians' activity. Although teens and lesbians absorbed the message that marriage was the only acceptable goal for women in the 1950s, their responses to this imperative differed.

Employment opportunities and independence through new apartment housing drew unmarried women to the city and helped foster a culture of recreation and dating. For lesbians, better jobs freed them from economic dependence on men, while communities of women created opportunities for social lives and fulfilling personal relationships. Despite persecution, gay women created a subculture that bonded them on the basis of a shared identity. In St. Louis, lesbian communities centered around bars and coffeehouses such as Madame Touhy's. The clusters of bars located near the intersection of Olive and Grand attracted a mixed crowd that included lesbians, gay men, and prostitutes. On the south side, the California Bar at Shenandoah and California drew women athletes who avidly participated in bowling and softball. On Sundays, barbecues and buffets at Burke's Bar on Jefferson near Gravois brought together women from throughout the city. Participating in activities at these gathering places developed a sense of community that helped lesbians endure harassment and police raids, nurture relationships, and socialize.

Similarly, baby boom children who were teenagers by the late 1950s and early 1960s participated in a youth culture that reflected the nation's newfound affluence, embraced consumerism, and generated new forms of cultural expression. Teenagers comprised a growing youth market with its own distinct tastes and trends in clothing, music, and entertainment. St. Louis's own *Prom* magazine, produced throughout the era, publicized activities at the local high schools and self-consciously sought to "serve as a constructive influence" on teens' behavior and aspirations through its advertisements, columns on municipal government, monthly updates of school activities, articles detailing career opportunities, profiles of area prom queens, and coverage of the local music scene. The *St. Louis Argus* launched the "Teens 'nd Tweens" column to report news from the schools and about parties, social clubs, and youth church groups.

Former St. Louisan Chuck Berry touched on the double lives of young women when he sang:

> Sweet Little Sixteen, she's got the grown-up blues
> Tight dresses and lipstick, she's sportin' high-heeled shoes.
> Oh but tomorrow morning she'll have to change her trend
> And be sweet sixteen and back in class again.

As the song illustrates, the rock 'n roll music that young people listened to was charged with sexual meaning. Popular culture commercialized and glamorized sex and women's sexuality, yet traditional norms continued to emphasize marriage as a prerequisite for sex and a goal for women. Movies, advertisements, and teen magazines focused on women's sexuality and linked sex and glamour to promote consumerism among girls. White buck shoes and junior dresses were two fashion trends started in St. Louis. They were fashionably up-to-date and attractive but not sexual, indicating that their wearer was a "good" woman. They also, along with other accouterments, determined one's reputation and opportunities to "go steady" or go on dates to the bowling alley, movie theater, drive-in, or school dance. Despite popular culture's sexualized images of women and the emphasis on dating, tradition dictated that "good" women put off sex until marriage. Not surprisingly, or perhaps as a way to resolve the conflict between tradition and the messages of postwar culture, women married at a younger age during the 1950s. But early marriage eclipsed college and careers for young women, and many baby boom teenagers later ushered in a mid-1960s transition away from traditional gender values of earlier generations as they took advantage of new liberating options for work, college, and relationships.

Teenagers and lesbians, along with civil rights activists and media stars, were among the groups whose activities expanded popular notions of women's place, even as they felt pressure to conform to traditional roles. Civic-minded women also gradually–and sometimes inadvertently–challenged restrictive norms as they sought new opportunities in electoral politics. The introduction of women onto juries in 1946 signaled one such expansion of women's civic role. In September of that year, the first three women were sworn onto a circuit court grand jury. But when Judge Waldo C. Mayfield remarked, "It's the best-looking grand jury I ever impaneled," he indicated that there was little progress toward equality.

Women politicians after World War II built on and extended the work of earlier Progressive Era reformers. Leonor K. Sullivan, a member of the U.S. House of Representatives from 1953 to 1976, began her political career by assisting her husband, Congressman John B. Sullivan. Born Leonor Alice Kretzer in 1903, Sullivan attended school in St. Louis, worked in a factory, and directed the St. Louis Business School. After her marriage in 1941, she became her husband's campaign manager and administrative assistant. Following John's death in 1952, Leonor ran for his congressional seat despite the opposition of St. Louis's Democratic fathers, who wanted a man to fill the position. As a representative,

Sullivan believed she could offer a woman's view of politics: "Women naturally think in terms of how legislation will affect the family and home life, their primary interests," she said in 1956.

Throughout her career, Sullivan focused on many issues taken up by earlier women reformers, including consumer protection laws and welfare assistance for needy families. The first woman from Missouri to serve in the U.S. House of Representatives, Sullivan cosponsored the 1963 Equal Pay Act and introduced bills to provide full social security benefits for women who retired at age sixty-two and income tax deductions for their educational expenses. Despite her commitment to the equality of working women, she opposed the Equal Rights Amendment, because it contradicted her ideas about women's roles. As she told a reporter in 1977 shortly before she retired:

> Women are needed in Congress because they think differently from men, especially on issues about the family. The woman is really the one that the whole family life revolves around. I've fought to do away with discrimination against women who work—equal pay for equal

Leonor Sullivan Votes in Mason School at Southwest and Sulpher Avenues, Election Day, 1960. Photograph by Ed Burckhardt, 1960. MHS–PP

work—and to break down bars that kept women out of some trades and professions. But those are now laws. We don't need the Equal Rights Amendment.

Sullivan's movement into public office—initially running for her deceased husband's seat before being re-elected on her own merit—exemplified a typical trajectory for women who held elective office before World War II. But after the war, St. Louis women gradually forged other paths to civic service. When Virginia Brungard climbed the stairs of city hall to start her new job as St. Louis's Director of Public Welfare in July 1953, she became the first woman to serve in any St. Louis mayor's cabinet. At the time, Brungard was also one of only two women in the mayoral cabinet of any major U.S. city. As Director of Public Welfare, a position she held from 1953 until the department was reorganized in 1959, Brungard administered a $16 million annual budget, managed a department of forty-three hundred employees, and oversaw four hospitals, five health centers, thousands of acres of parks, eleven recreation centers, two corrective institutions, five public bath houses, and the Bureau of Public Defenders and Legal Aid. As this "lady in a man-sized job" put it, her position encompassed "everything from ice skating to rat catching." Like Charlotte Rumbold, who had seen the social value of recreational spaces for St. Louisans early in the century, Brungard took a special interest in parks and playgrounds. While thousands of St. Louisans traded life in the city for residence in newly built suburban communities complete with lawns and playgrounds, Brungard hoped that revitalized city parks would help to "prevent crime and to brighten lives" of city dwellers. When the Department of Public Welfare split into three separate divisions in 1959, Mayor Raymond Tucker named Brungard to direct the newly established Department of Parks, Recreation, and Forestry.

In many ways, Brungard seemed an unlikely person to break barriers for women and enter municipal politics. A third-generation St. Louisan whose father, William H. O'Connell, was an architect and builder, Brungard grew up on Castleman Avenue and attended McKinley High School and Harris Teachers College. She abandoned an earlier teaching career to dedicate twenty years to the comfort of her family and the responsibilities of her three-story, ten-room house in Compton Heights. After World War II, Brungard found herself relieved from many domestic responsibilities. Her grown children had earned college degrees and established careers, and although she entertained frequently, a maid shouldered many household tasks.

With this greater freedom, Brungard became active in the League of Women Voters (LWV), where she organized candidate forums, supported state legislation to allow the employment of married women teachers and put women on juries, and lobbied for city ordinances to end segregation in movie houses, exterminate rats, and open Cote Brilliante School to black children. The league also educated the public through its Citizens' Committee on Atomic Energy. Brungard's work with the LWV integrated her into a network of civic-minded women, educated her in city government, and provided her with political skills that she transferred to other arenas.

Like many other women of the era, civic activism in women's organizations served as a springboard for Brungard's move into electoral politics. At the end of World War II, women held few elective offices throughout the country, but during the 1950s they increased their presence in municipal government. By 1960, some ten thousand women occupied city posts. When Brungard ran for a position on the new Board of Freeholders in 1949 in an unprecedented move—and one that conflicted with the practices of the national LWV—the St. Louis chapter formally backed her candidacy and helped her win election. Her service on the board "was the most rewarding experience I ever had," Brungard stated. Similar to her Progressive Era counterparts and her contemporary, Leonor Sullivan, Brungard concluded that women's domestic role was of primary importance, but "as the family reaches maturity, a woman can go into civic affairs as an elected or appointed officer, thus giving her a chance to accomplish something for her community."

After three years on the volunteer board, Raymond Tucker asked Brungard to head a Women's Committee to campaign on behalf of his nomination as mayor. Tucker's desire to generate women's support for his campaign reflected male politicians' awareness of women's power in electoral politics. Long after campaigns for woman suffrage had resulted in passage of the Nineteenth Amendment, women and men both feared and welcomed the possibility of a women's voting bloc. But election results failed to reveal any significant difference in male and female voting patterns until the 1952 presidential campaign, when women's support for Dwight D. Eisenhower surpassed that of men.

Volunteering her time to Tucker's campaign, Brungard hosted coffees at homes throughout the city, telephoned voters at home, and distributed literature on election day. When Tucker won the primary election by fewer than two thousand votes in the spring of 1953, he credited the unprecedented involvement of women–as voters and volunteers–as the key to his victory.

In her years in civic service, Brungard won St. Louisans' respect for the way she tackled her job. But Brungard's success also provided a lesson for other women who contemplated the pursuit of public office. No matter how far she rose in municipal politics, St. Louis media reinforced that Brungard was a "woman politician," not simply a politician. Brungard's own statements emphasized that civic service, even in the form of paid employment, did not override, and in fact converged with, a woman's domestic role. "Women are willing to go in politics if they are encouraged," Brungard told readers of the *Globe-Democrat*'s Everyday section. Politics "can be a stage in life for the middle-aged woman who wants to accomplish something after the children are grown. When the children are young her place is at home, but she can learn what's going on, find out what makes good government and how to vote to get it."

Even as she continued to emphasize domesticity, women like Brungard forged a public life and achieved a new prominence for women in city politics. In the postwar period, women accelerated their involvement in electoral politics and continued their participation, albeit in altered forms. Grassroots organizations and the major political parties bestowed increased recognition of the importance of women's electoral participation. In Missouri, the major parties began to woo women voters in 1960, and the *Globe-Democrat* predicted that women held the power to decide the upcoming fall elections: "If one single group can be said to hold the power of absolute decision, it is this group. There are now 3,250,000 more eligible women voters than men voters." The predictions rang true. Although women previously had lagged behind men in the rate of the turnout for elections, by 1964 more women than men went to the polls. With the power of numbers, St. Louis women voters exercised their civic responsibility and assured that candidates for political office would have to pay attention to their interests.

In their distinct ways, women such as Brungard, Oldham, McCowan, Sullivan, Davis, Munsch, and Peters challenged the image of the suburban housewife who came to typify the era. Each also demonstrates how women's lives in St. Louis changed during the two decades following World War II, as a result of both demographic pressures and the pressures that women themselves brought to

bear on conditions they considered discriminatory or limiting. By emphasizing women's traditional roles in the home and as caretakers, these women inadvertently and gradually changed society's expectations. Women broke some barriers of sexism and racism to increase their education and employment options, to strengthen their public presence, to gain greater political influence, and to demand their rights. Yet despite their increasingly visible presence in public life, women's domestic roles were slower to change. And despite Leonor Sullivan's optimism about the effect of the legislation she passed to assure the equality of working women, inequities between women and men, as well as among women, abounded throughout the period and beyond. Plenty of unfinished business remained on the road to racial and sexual equality, and in the late 1960s, new generations of St. Louis women would take up the challenge of making new opportunities for themselves.

–*Anne Valk*

Sources: The story of the postwar period is the story of the entire region, not of St. Louis City or one community. Researchers need a different view of "local" history for the last half of the twentieth century, one that incorporates the metropolitan region and the connections between the city and the suburbs. For background information about changes in the region after World War II, see Cornelia F. Sexauer, "The Development of a St. Louis County Suburb Post World War II: St. Ann, MO 1942–1953," unpublished paper, 1994, and Cornelia Sexauer, "St. Louis in the 1940s–1950s: Historical Overview and Annotated Bibliography" (St. Louis: MHS, 1993). The "Progress or Decay" series in the *Post-Dispatch*, March, April, and May 1950, delineates some of the major concerns for the region. For information about the development of modern shopping malls, see Lizabeth Cohen, "From Town Center to Shopping Center: The Reconfiguration of Community Marketplaces in Postwar America," *American Historical Review* (October 1996): 1050–81. John A. Wright, *Discovering African-American St. Louis: A Guide to Historic Sites* (St. Louis: MHS Press, 1994), and Tim Fox, ed., *Where We Live: A Guide to St. Louis Communities* (St. Louis: MHS Press, 1995) provide information about specific sites connected with women in St. Louis and provide information about the changing geography of the postwar period. Material about Marian O'Fallon Oldham comes from the MHS vertical file and August Meier and Elliott Rudwick, *CORE: A Study in the Civil Rights Movement 1942–1968* (Urbana: University of Illinois Press, 1975). Information about lesbian bars and culture comes from Nan Sweet, "Herstory: Finding the Lesbian Heritage," *The Lesbian and Gay News-Telegraph* (November 1988). A semi-autobiographical novel by

Frankie Hucklenbroich, *A Crystal Diary* (Ithaca, N.Y.: Firebrand Books, 1997) describes attitudes toward lesbians, as well as lesbian culture, in St. Louis in the late 1940s and 1950s. Mary K. Dains and Sue Sadler, eds., *Show Me Missouri Women: Selected Biographies* (Kirksville, Mo.: Thomas Jefferson University Press, 1989) contains profiles of many St. Louis women who exerted an influence on the city after World War II, including Leonor Sullivan and Louise Munsch Dopking. See also a collection of interviews at UMSL, including Frankie Freeman and other prominent activists and professional women.

Information on Virginia Brungard is from Marjorie Louise Purvis, "St. Louis Women of Achievement and Community" (Ph.D. dissertation, Saint Louis University, 1973); Dickson Terry, "First Woman in the Mayor's Cabinet," *Post-Dispatch,* 7 July 1953; and "Lady in a Man-Sized Job," *Globe-Democrat,* 20 February 1955. For information about women and electoral politics, see William S. White, "The Women Voters," *Globe-Democrat,* 21 September 1960; Susan M. Hartmann, *From Margin to Mainstream: American Women and Politics Since 1960* (New York: Knopf, 1989); and Marilyn Gittell and Teresa Shtob, "Changing Women's Roles in Political Volunteerism and Reform of the City," *Signs* 5, no. 3: S67–S78. See Susan M. Hartmann, The Other Feminists: Activists in the Liberal Establishment (New Haven: Yale University Press, 1998), which argues that women working in male-dominated liberal associations such as the American Civil Liberties Union and the International Union of Electrical Workers promoted a feminist agenda in the 1960s and 1970s.

Charlotte Peters Papers, including scripts and videotapes, are archived at WHMC–UMSL. Other information comes from Mary Kimbrough, ed., *Outstanding Women in Media: Trailblazers in St. Louis* (St. Louis: Press Club of Metropolitan St. Louis, 1992), and the MHS vertical file. For general information about the significance of television to postwar families, see Lynn Spigel, *Make Room for TV: Television and the Family Ideal in Postwar America* (Chicago: University of Chicago Press, 1992). KETC and educational television information is drawn from "Reassessing Educational TV in St. Louis," *St. Louis Commerce* (November 1955): 46–53. Information about local programming is available in the Radio and TV Industry in St. Louis Pamphlet Collection, MHS.

For information about Pruitt-Igoe and other public housing projects, see Alpha Kappa Alpha, Gamma Omega Chapter, St. Louis, Scrapbook, 1920–1980, WHMC–UMSL; "The McCowan Clan of Wendell Pruitt Homes Shows Value of Public Housing," *St. Louis Argus,* 2 September 1960; and Lee Rainwater, *Behind Ghetto Walls: Black Families in a Federal Slum* (Chicago: Aldine Atherton Inc., 1970). Population information comes from the U.S. Census and reports compiled by local research organizations, including Urban League, "The Negro Population in St. Louis," excerpted in the *Post-Dispatch*, 5 June 1961. For information about school desegregation, see Employees Loan Company, *Negroes: Their Gift to St. Louis*, 1964; *Commemorative History of the St. Louis Public Schools, 1838–1988*; profile of Josephine Turner in *Proud* (March/April 1975); Julia Davis vertical file, MHS; *Negroes: Their Contribution to St. Louis*; and *Post-Dispatch*, 20–21 June 1963. Carpenter, *St. Louis: The Social Life of a Modern Metropolis* (St. Louis: Washington University Department of Sociology and Anthropology, 1954) summarizes studies of St. Louis, primarily those completed as Washington University Ph.D. dissertations, and includes long summaries of studies of Carr Square Village, race relations, and high school student behavior.

For general overviews of women and the post–World War II period, especially the relationship between work and domesticity, see William H. Chafe, *The Paradox of Change: American Women in the 20th Century* (New York: Oxford University Press, 1991); Susan M. Hartmann, *The Home Front and Beyond: American Women in the 1940s* (Boston: Twayne Publishers, 1982); Elaine Tyler May, *Homeward Bound: American Families in the Cold War Era* (New York: Basic Books, 1988); Elaine Tyler May, "Rosie the Riveter Gets Married," in *The War in American Culture: Society and Consciousness During World War II*, eds., Lewis A. Erenberg and Susan E. Hirsch (Chicago: University of Chicago Press, 1996). A collection of some of the newest scholarship on women in the 1950s that challenges traditional stereotypes about the era is contained in Joanne Meyerowitz, ed., *Not June Cleaver: Women and Gender in Postwar America, 1945–1960* (Philadelphia: Temple University Press, 1994).

For information about industrial work after World War II, reconversion, and the demands of women workers, see the *Post-Dispatch,* 15 March 1959; Ruth Milkman, "Rosie the Riveter Revisited: Management's Postwar Purge of Women Automobile Workers," in *On the Line: Essays in the History of Auto Work,* eds., Nelson Lichtenstein and Stephen Meyer (Urbana: University of Illinois Press, 1989); and Dorothy Sue Cobble, "Recapturing Working Class Feminism: Union Women in the Postwar Era," in Meyerowitz, *Not June Cleaver.* Sharon Pedersen, "Married Women and the Right to Teach in St. Louis, 1941–1948," *MHR* 81, no. 2 (January 1987): 141–158, recounts the effort to end restrictions on married women teaching in the public schools.

Information about teens and youth culture comes from *Prom* magazine, MHS. See also Wini Breines, *Young, White, and Miserable: Growing Up Female in the Fifties* (Boston: Beacon Press, 1992). Chuck Berry's lyrics, "Sweet Little Sixteen" (1958), copyright Jewell Music Publishing Co., Ltd., London.

Abbreviations

MHS	Missouri Historical Society
WHMC–UMSL	Western Historical Manuscripts Collection at the University of Missouri–St. Louis
MHS–PP	Missouri Historical Society Photograph and Print Collection
GH	*Gateway Heritage*
BMHS	*Bulletin of the Missouri Historical Society*
MHR	*Missouri Historical Review*
SLAH	Katharine T. Corbett, Howard S. Miller, Mary E. Seematter, and Alex Yard, *St. Louis in American History*, 4 units (St. Louis: Missouri Historical Society, 1992–1994)
NAW	Edward T. James, ed., *Notable American Women: 1607–1950: A Biographical Dictionary*, 2 vols. (Cambridge, Mass.: Belknap Press of Harvard University Press, 1971)

About the Authors

SUSAN BEATTIE is a student at the University of Missouri–St. Louis in the Museum Studies master's program. She holds a graduate fellowship at the Missouri Historical Society, helping to develop the new Community Partners program.

JOAN COOPER gained an M.A. in history at the University of Missouri–St. Louis. She lives in St. Louis and is a freelance historian.

KATHERINE DOUGLASS is the Editor of *Gateway Heritage*, the quarterly magazine of the Missouri Historical Society.

KATHLEEN BUTTERLY NIGRO teaches English and women's studies in the St. Louis area and coordinates community events to foster appreciation of women in the literary arts.

ANNE VALK teaches in the Department of Historical Studies at Southern Illinois University–Edwardsville, where she offers courses in women's history, oral history, and public history. She is currently writing a book on the women's movement in the 1960s and 1970s.

KATHARINE T. CORBETT is the former Director of Interpretation at the Missouri Historical Society. She teaches St. Louis history and women's studies at University College at Washington University and University of Missouri–St. Louis. She has published widely on St. Louis history.

Katharine Thomas Corbett. Photograph by Sarah T. Turner, 1999.